Destinies

Canadian History Since Confederation

D1368704

FOURTH EDITION

Destinies

Canadian History Since Confederation

R. Douglas Francis
University of Calgary

Richard Jones
Université Laval

Donald B. Smith
University of Calgary

NELSON

✦ ™

THOMSON LEARNING

Australia • Canada • Mexico • Singapore • Spain • United Kingdom • United States

Canadian Cataloguing in Publication Data

Francis, R.D. (R. Douglas), 1944–
   Destinies: Canadian history since Confederation

4th ed.
Includes bibliographical references and index.
ISBN 0-7747-3665-8

1. Canada — History—1867–　.　I. Jones, Richard, 1943–　.
II. Smith, Donald B., 1946–　.　III. Title.

FC164.F73 1999　　　71.05　　　C99-930892-0
F1033.F73 1999

Senior Acquisitions Editor: Heather McWhinney
Senior Developmental Editor: Martina van de Velde
Production Editor: Shana Hayes
Production Coordinator: Cheryl Tiongson
Copy Editor: John Eerkes
Permissions Editor: Cindy Howard
Cover and Interior Design: Sonya V. Thursby, Opus House Incorporated
Cover Illustration: Eric Colquhoun
Typesetting and Assembly: IBEX Graphic Communications Inc.
Map Illustrations: Deborah Crowle
Printing and Binding: Webcom Limited

For more information contact
Nelson Thomson Learning,
1120 Birchmount Road,
Scarborough, Ontario, M1K 5G4.
Or you can visit our internet site at
http://www.nelson.com

This book was printed in Canada.

3 4 5　　04 03

We dedicate this fourth edition to our parents:
Vera Pauline Francis and Robert George Francis
Richard Ditzel Jones, and in memory of Evelyn Allen Jones
Jean Boyd Smith, and in memory of John Caulfield Smith

Preface

Origins and *Destinies* are designed with the introductory student of Canadian history in mind. We have made a conscious attempt to provide readable and enjoyable texts for students embarking on a study of Canada's past. A rich array of photographs and charts supplement the prose. Because we believe it is essential that students know the social and cultural as well as the political and economic history of Canada, all four aspects are emphasized throughout the two volumes. We have also included the historical development and contribution of the Native peoples, French-speaking and English-speaking Canadians, recent immigrants, women, and minority groups. As well, we have been conscious of the need to include the history of each of the country's regions, while keeping Canada as the focal point. Our texts incorporate the most recent historical research, and we have provided students with extensive and up-to-date annotated bibliographies at the end of each chapter to identify the major historical writings on the events covered. We also include a comprehensive index to each volume that provides, in particular, reference to subjects and topics in the text that are of value in identifying material of use for student essays.

Origins and *Destinies* are divided into thematic sections. At the beginning of each section is a brief introductory overview of themes highlighted in the chapters, followed by a "Time Line" listing the key events discussed. Each chapter treats a major topic or period, and we essentially follow a chronology to help students understand how events developed through time. As well, headings and subheadings throughout the chapters will assist students in understanding the material. At the end of each chapter is a section entitled "Linking to the Past" that directs students to additional information for selected topics on the World Wide Web, and "Related Readings" that identify useful articles in the fifth edition of R. Douglas Francis and Donald B. Smith, eds., *Readings in Canadian History*, volume 1, *Pre-Confederation*, and volume 2, *Post-Confederation*.

Because historians are partial observers and participants in the world around them, their work mirrors their own time. Current concerns, conventions, and perceptions are reflected in the very issues that historians select for study. We have, therefore, included a series of boxed inserts that highlight the debate and difference of opinion among historians on controversial topics in the past. As well, since history is the action of individuals, we have added to this fourth edition of *Origins* and *Destinies* new "Historical Portraits" that highlight the life of some well-known, and some not well-known, individuals who shaped and were shaped by the times in which they lived. We hope these portraits will help students to appreciate the personal side of Canada's historical development.

Origins, the first volume, tells the story of pre-Confederation Canada—of the Native peoples and of the coming of the Norse, the Portuguese, the Spanish, the Basques, and particularly the French and the British who eventually established permanent European settlements. Anyone seeking to understand our diversity must first examine the era when our present regional personalities were first formed in Atlantic Canada, in the St. Lawrence River valley, on the Great Lakes, on the Red River, and on the Pacific coast.

Destinies, the second volume, takes Canada's story from 1867 to the present day. Unlike the United States, our country did not experience a uniform wave of expansion westward from the Atlantic seaboard. In many cases, the European communities in Canada began as pockets of settlement, independent of one another, founded at different times, and with people of various European backgrounds. In *Destinies*, we show how Canada came to take the transcontinental form it did, and how the various groups within its boundaries united together. We point out the various regional, ethnic, and social tensions as well as our more harmonious moments.

Students seeking more extensive bibliographical information are directed to the following works. Important annotated bibliographical guides to the study of Canadian history include M. Brook Taylor, ed., *Canadian History: A Reader's Guide*, vol. 1, *Beginnings to Confederation* (Toronto: University of Toronto Press, 1994); Doug Owram, ed., *Canadian History: A Reader's Guide*, vol. 2, *Confederation to the Present* (Toronto: University of Toronto Press, 1994); Carl Berger, ed., *Contemporary Approaches to Canadian History* (Toronto: Copp Clark Pitman, 1987); and John Schultz, ed., *Writing about Canada: A Handbook for Modern Canadian History* (Scarborough, ON: Prentice-Hall, 1990). An invaluable bibliography (without annotation) is Paul Aubin and Louis-Marie Côté's *Bibliographie de l'histoire du Québec et du Canada/Bibliography of the History of Quebec and Canada*, published (in several volumes) by the Institut québécois de recherche sur la culture in Quebec City. Easy to use, it contains more than 100 000 titles, all published between 1946 and 1985. Current bibliographies of the most recent publications are published in every issue of the *Canadian Historical Review* and the *Revue d'histoire de l'Amérique française*.

ACKNOWLEDGEMENTS

In preparing the first edition of *Origins*, we benefited enormously from the advice and suggestions of many Canadian historians. We would like to thank Gratien Allaire of the Faculté Saint-Jean, University of Alberta; Phillip Buckner of the University of New Brunswick; Jean Daigle of the Université de Moncton; Olive Dickason of the University of Alberta; John Dickinson of the Université de Montréal; Robin Fisher of Simon Fraser University; Gerald Friesen of the University of Manitoba; James Hiller of Memorial University of Newfoundland; Douglas Leighton of the University of Western Ontario; Ken Munro of the University of Alberta; Colin Read of the University of Western Ontario; and Phyllis Senese of the University of Victoria, who each read and provided us with criticisms of individual chapters within their respective research areas. On several specific issues we benefited from the comments of Michel Granger of Brooks, Alberta (on the Acadians); James Helmer of the University of Calgary (on recent archaeological findings); Ingeborg Marshall of Portugal Cove, Newfoundland (on the Beothuk); Bea Medicine of the University of Calgary (on the Native peoples' views of their origins); Dale Miquelon of the University of Saskatchewan (on recent historical writing on the economic impact of the conquest of New France); Keith Regular of Elkford, B.C. (on Newfoundland); and Daniel Richter of Dickinson College, Carlisle, Pennsylvania (on the Iroquois Confederacy).

With regard to the first edition of *Destinies*, we thank the following people, who read chapters of the manuscript and offered valuable criticism and advice: Douglas Baldwin of Acadia University; Gail Cuthbert-Brandt of Glendon College, York University; John English of the University of Waterloo; Gerald Friesen of the University of Manitoba; Jim Miller of the University of Saskatchewan; William Morrison of Brandon University; Howard Palmer of the University of Calgary; Margaret Prang of the University of British Columbia; John Thompson of McGill University; Keith Walden of Trent University; and William Westfall of York University.

The following historians read the manuscripts in their entirety for Holt, Rinehart and Winston. Although they did not always agree with our approach and interpretation, they offered very valuable suggestions for improving the final manuscripts. For *Origins*, we wish to thank Joseph Cherwinski of Memorial University of Newfoundland, Douglas Leighton of the University of Western Ontario, Olive Dickason of the University of Alberta, and Phyllis Senese of the University of Victoria. For *Destinies*, we thank William Acheson of the University of New Brunswick, Thomas Socknat of the University of Toronto, Donald Swainson of Queen's University, and Eric Sager of the University of Victoria.

With regard to the preparation of the second edition of *Origins* and *Destinies*, we thank Elizabeth Abbott and Laurel Sherrer of Chronicle Publications in Montreal for allowing us to look through illustrations collected for the *Chronicle of Canada* project. We thank the following individuals for their remarks on *Origins* and *Destinies*: Doug Baldwin at Acadia University; Sarah Carter at the University of Winnipeg; Olive Dickason at the University of Alberta; A. Ernest Epp at Lakehead University; R.H. Roy and Phyllis Senese at the University of Victoria; and M. Brook Taylor at Mount Saint Vincent University. John David Hamilton of Keswick, Ontario, and Mark Dickerson of the University of Calgary provided help specifically with Chapter 16, "Aboriginal Canada and the North," in *Destinies*. With regard to the preparation of *Origins*, we are very grateful to Jean Barman of the University of British Columbia for allowing us to see her history of British Columbia, *The West Beyond the West* (Toronto: University of Toronto Press, 1991), before publication, and to Olive Dickason for permitting us to read the first draft of her history of Amerindians in Canada, *Canada's First Nations* (Toronto: McClelland & Stewart, 1992).

For the third edition of *Destinies*, we are indebted to Roger Hall, University of Western Ontario; Robert Burkinshaw, Trinity Western University; and Bonnie Huskins, University College of the Fraser Valley.

For the fourth edition, we thank John Belshaw at University College of the Cariboo, Patricia Roome at Mount Royal College, and George A. Davison at College of New Caledonia for their remarks.

At Harcourt, we benefited enormously from a dedicated and enthusiastic editorial staff. We wish to thank Heather McWhinney, senior acquisitions editor, for her assistance in helping us to prepare the fourth edition and for guiding the proposal through the initial editorial process. Martina van de Velde, senior developmental editor, kept us on track and ensured that the books' format was correct. Eliza Marciniak and Tammy Guiler, editorial assistants, helped research World Wide Web information for this edition. Shana Hayes, production editor, was meticulous in seeing the books through the copy-editing and page-proof stages. Sue Mykyjewicz, marketing co-ordinator, assisted in the promotion and marketing of the two volumes, and Sonya Thursby of Opus House created and updated the attractive design. Our thanks to all who have made this fourth edition possible!

We wish to thank our children — Marc, Myla, and Michael Francis; Marie-Noëlle, Stéphanie, Serge-André, and Charles-Denis Jones; and David and Peter Smith and our wives Barbara, Lilianne, and Nancy — for their support throughout this project. We dedicate these volumes to our parents.

A NOTE FROM THE PUBLISHER

Thank you for selecting *Destinies: Canadian History since Confederation*, Fourth Edition, by R. Douglas Francis, Richard Jones, and Donald B. Smith. The authors and publisher have devoted considerable time to the careful development of this book. We appreciate your recognition of this effort and accomplishment.

We want to hear what you think about *Destinies: Canadian History since Confederation*. Please take a few minutes to fill in the stamped reader reply card at the back of the book. Your comments and suggestions will be valuable to us as we prepare new editions and other books.

Contents

PART TWO *Urban and Industrial Canada, 1867–1914*

CHAPTER SIX *Boomtime: Industrialization at the Turn of the Century 136*

CHAPTER SEVEN *The Impact of Urban and Industrial Growth 155*

CHAPTER ELEVEN

The 1920s: A Decade of Adjustment 256

PART FOUR *Modern Canada, 1945–2000*

List of Maps

List of Time Lines

CHAPTER ONE

Canada: Date Line, 1867

Governor General Lord Monck congratulated Canada's first Parliament on laying "the foundation of a new nationality." Brave and hopeful words these were, as four of the British North American colonies — Canada West (Ontario), Canada East (Quebec), Nova Scotia, and New Brunswick — lacking a common identity and even the most elementary sense of a shared experience (beyond being subjects of the British empire) united into Confederation on July 1, 1867. The other British North American colonies at the time — Newfoundland, Prince Edward Island, and British Columbia — chose to continue as separate British colonies, initially feeling there were no benefits to be gained through union. Yet in just one decade, this new Dominion would expand to include British Columbia and Prince Edward Island, as well as the vast majority of Rupert's Land.

POPULATION

The First Nations numbered approximately 30 000, or roughly 1 percent of Canada's total population of 3.5 million. Over the last two centuries European diseases — particularly smallpox, new to the Americas — had decreased their numbers. The three largest groups were the Ojibwa, in Ontario; the Iroquois, in Ontario and Quebec; and the Mi'kmaq (Micmac), in Nova Scotia and New Brunswick.

Section 91 (subsection 24) of the British North America (BNA) Act assigned to the federal government responsibility for "Indians and lands reserved for Indians." Most lived on reserves out of sight of the dominant society, although they were controlled by missionaries and governmental authorities. The non-Aboriginal population had been raised and educated in total ignorance of the First Nations; thus they knew little about their history and culture. They believed that the Native peoples were about to disappear biologically or assimilate culturally into the larger society as modernity advanced and "progress" continued.

People of French descent made up roughly a third of the total population, a percentage that remained constant for almost a century. The great majority — more than 85 percent — resided in Quebec and had roots in North America extending back two centuries. The Acadians in New Brunswick and Nova Scotia numbered nearly 10 percent of the French-speaking population. Only 3 percent of Canada's francophones lived in Ontario, mainly in the area adjacent to Quebec.

Amerindians from Kahnawake, Canadian lacrosse champions, 1869. In the late nineteenth century, Amerindians lived apart from the rest of Canadian society.

Lee Pritzker Collection/National Archives of Canada/C-1959.

People of British descent accounted for 60 percent of Canada's population in 1867. A diverse group, they included descendants of Loyalists who had settled on British territory after the American Revolution. Most, however, were British immigrants (and their descendants) who had emigrated to British North America between 1815 and 1870, some 1.3 million in total. They were of diverse backgrounds, including English, Welsh, Highland and Lowland Scots, and Catholic and Protestant Irish. The English made up 15 percent of the total Canadian population, and the Welsh 5 percent. The Scots constituted nearly 16 percent, while the Irish made up 25 percent.

English-speaking and French-speaking Canadians lived in two separate worlds a century ago. P.-J.-O. Chauveau, the first premier of Quebec after Confederation, compared Canada to the famous staircase of the Château de Chambord in France, built to allow two persons to ascend it without meeting, and even without seeing each other except at intervals. "English and French, we climb by a double flight of stairs toward the destinies reserved for us on this continent, without knowing each other, without meeting each other, except on the landing of politics."

The remaining 8 percent of the Dominion's population consisted of non-British and non-French immigrants and their descendants from Europe and the United States. The majority were from German-speaking states and were welcomed because of the intermarriage of the British monarchy with members of the German principalities. There were, as well, about 65 000 Africans. While some were of American Loyalist descent, most had arrived as fugitive slaves before the American Civil War via the Underground Railroad, a loose network of abolitionists who aided slaves. They established such settlements as Wilberforce and Elgin in Canada West (Ontario). Dawn, now Dresden, in southwestern Ontario was the best known because Josiah Henson — believed to be the model for the character of Uncle Tom in Harriet Beecher

A Historical Portrait

JOSIAH HENSON

Josiah Henson was born into slavery on a Maryland plantation in 1789. His earliest recollection at the age of three or four was the day he saw his father return from a terrible beating. As Josiah later recalled, "His right ear had been cut off close to his head and he had received a hundred lashes on his back." His "crime"? He struck a white man, the farm overseer, for brutally assaulting Josiah's mother.

Soon afterwards, the Hensons' master split the family up. He sold Josiah's father to a plantation in Alabama and auctioned off Josiah's mother, brothers, sisters, and Josiah himself to separate owners. Fortunately, Josiah was later reunited with his mother.

As slaves, Josiah and his mother lived in appalling conditions, eating corn meal and salted herring. "Our lodging," he recalled, "was in log huts, of a single small room, with no other floor than the trodden earth, in which ten or a dozen persons — men, women, and children — might sleep." By his twenties, the conscientious, hard-working man had so gained his master's respect that he appointed him farm superintendent. When it became clear, however, that his owner had no intention of granting him his freedom, Josiah, who had married fifteen or so years earlier and now had a family, escaped with his wife and four children to Canada.

The Hensons spent six difficult weeks following the Underground Railway to Upper Canada. On October 28, 1830, they crossed the Niagara River. Immediately, Josiah fell on his knees and gave thanks. In their new home, the Hensons founded an African community named Dawn, near present-day Dresden, Ontario. With the

(continued)

Queen Victoria receives Josiah Henson at Windsor Castle, March 5, 1877.

The American Museum in Britain, Claverton Manor, Bath, England.

financial assistance of a group of Boston Unitarians they began the British American Institute for Fugitive Slaves, a school to educate ex-slaves and to teach them a trade.

In the late 1840s, Josiah dictated his life story. It was published in Boston as *The Life of Josiah Henson Formerly a Slave Now an Inhabitant of Canada* in 1849. Three years later Harriet Beecher Stowe's novel *Uncle Tom's Cabin* appeared. It proved a sensation, the most popular anti-slavery book published before the outbreak of the American Civil War. The fact that many people identified Josiah Henson as the prototype for the fictional "Uncle Tom" made him famous. Stowe, however, never categorically stated this; people just inferred that it was true. As a result of his fame, Henson made several lecture tours of Britain to raise money for the Dawn settlement.

When the American Civil War ended, many Afro-Americans in Upper Canada returned to the United States, and the community of Dawn died out. In his late eighties, Josiah made his final visit to Britain to meet Queen Victoria at Windsor Castle. He died in Dresden in 1883.

In 1983, Canada Post issued a special stamp to commemorate the one-hundredth anniversary of Henson's death. Josiah Henson was the first African-Canadian to be so honoured. The stamp depicts Henson in the foreground and a line of slaves walking the Underground Railway, following the North Star to Canada, in the background.

Stowe's *Uncle Tom's Cabin* (1852) — lived there. Although slavery had not existed in British North America since the early nineteenth century, racial prejudice existed. Blacks faced discrimination in land grants, schooling, employment, and voting rights.

POPULATION DISTRIBUTION

Ontario and Quebec had nearly four-fifths of the Dominion's population, with more than 1.5 million people in Ontario and about one million in Quebec. The other fifth of Canada's population resided in the Maritime provinces, with 400 000 people in Nova Scotia and roughly 300 000 in New Brunswick. By the mid-1860s, the arrival of immigrants from the British Isles had diminished. There would not be another wave of immigrants until the turn of the century. Indeed, many Canadians left in the late nineteenth century for factory jobs in the rapidly industrializing northeastern American states. The disappearance of good farmland in Ontario forced many Ontarians to emigrate to the American midwest to farm.

In all three areas of the country — Ontario, Quebec, and the Maritimes — different ethnic groups lived in separate settlements. Acadians, for example, resided on New Brunswick's northeastern shore, Scots on Cape Breton, Irish in the Ottawa valley, German-speaking Mennonites in Ontario's Waterloo county, around Berlin (as Kitchener was then known), and ethnic Germans in Lunenburg County, Nova Scotia.

The other British American colonies later incorporated into Canada had small populations. Newfoundland had only 150 000 inhabitants, the majority being Irish Catholics, and Prince Edward Island a mere 94 000 — approximately the population of Montreal in 1867 — of which a significant number were Scottish and Acadian French. In British Columbia some 10 000 white settlers lived among an estimated 30 000 Native people. The Northwest — the Mackenzie River and Hudson Bay

Sir John A. Macdonald, around 1871. The fact that he served as the Dominion's prime minister from 1867 to 1873 and again from 1878 to 1891 established the late nineteenth century as the Macdonald era in Canadian politics.

Notman Studio of Ottawa/National Archives of Canada/C-10144.

watershed — had perhaps 50 000 inhabitants, mostly Native people. The Arctic islands were home to several thousand Inuit.

POLITICS

WEB LINKS

John A. Macdonald, the Dominion's first prime minister, had by 1867 already served in politics for nearly a quarter of a century. A man with warm personal charm and a sense of humour, he preferred practical politics to philosophical debate. A masterful politician, he would remain in the prime minister's office, with the exception of a five-year Liberal interlude in the mid-1870s, from 1867 until his death in 1891. Quite rightly, the late nineteenth century is often referred to politically as the Macdonald era.

To win support in Quebec, Macdonald relied on George-Étienne Cartier, particularly as he himself spoke no French. From 1854 onward, Cartier served as Macdonald's principal lieutenant. After 1867, he often replaced him as prime minister and as leader of the government in the House of Commons. Macdonald once referred to Cartier as "my second self," and in many respects he was.

Cartier and Macdonald both believed in the possession of property as a necessary condition for public office. They admired the British parliamentary system, particularly the monarchy, and distrusted American republican values such as the secret ballot and universal suffrage. In his mid-twenties, Cartier had taken up arms against England in the Rebellion of 1837, but as an older man he made his peace with the status quo. In many respects he became more British than many English-speaking Canadians. The successful Montreal businessman had large investments in the Grand Trunk Railway and served as director of several banking, insurance, and transportation companies. From 1867 until his death in 1873, Cartier came second only to Macdonald in the Conservative party, which they, in effect, had both founded in 1854.

Cartier's support of Confederation had probably been the decisive factor in Quebec's acceptance of the scheme. Even so, among the French-speaking members of the assembly of the United Canadas the decision had been close, only 27 to 21 in one key vote. Cartier won over a sufficient number of his fellow French-Canadian politicians by pointing out that through Confederation they gained their own legislature with power over their own education system, civil law, and local institutions. As well, the French language became one of the federal Parliament's official languages.

Macdonald and Cartier began a political convention that has continued, more or less, since Confederation: the co-operation within the governing party of a generally English-speaking prime minister and a generally French-speaking lieutenant. Such an alliance has ensured the French-Canadian minority a voice in federal politics.

THE NEW POLITICAL REALITY

British North American union meant a new beginning in politics. The various political factions and parties that existed before Confederation — the Tories and the Clear Grits (or Reformers) in Canada West, the parti bleu and the parti rouge in Canada East, the conservative and reform factions in New Brunswick and Nova Scotia — coalesced into two major parties: the Conservatives and the Liberals (Reformers), with representation and, eventually, a party machinery throughout the Dominion. Initially, these two national parties had genuine ideological differences. For the first 30 years after Confederation, the Conservatives generally favoured the establishment of a strong central government and a policy of tariff protection. In contrast, the Liberals championed provincial autonomy and free trade.

In the first federal election, in November 1867, only a limited number of Canadians — males who owned property, being only 20 percent of the total population — could vote. They also had to declare their party preference openly, since there was no secret ballot. This system of open voting led to abuse. Street brawls occurred at election time. Candidates openly bribed voters. Employers coerced employees to vote "the right way." Elections were also held at different times in different areas of the country, greatly influencing electoral results. These abuses would be corrected in the mid-1870s, when the Liberals came to power and brought in electoral reforms.

Macdonald chose his first cabinet carefully. Anxious for his party to appear truly national, he selected individuals from the various regions and interest groups — Maritimers, Quebeckers, and Ontarians; Protestants and Roman Catholics; Irish, Scottish, English, and French Canadians; businessmen, farmers, fishermen, and, occasionally, even working people. The Conservatives also created the first federal bureaucracy to carry out the responsibilities assigned to the federal government under section 91 of the BNA Act, which concerned national or interprovincial affairs. This meant jobs, or rather rewards, for the party faithful. Most of the approximately 500 civil-service positions went to former bureaucrats from the United Canadas, with only a few token positions going to Maritimers.

THE NATURE OF CONFEDERATION

Unity in diversity became the goal of the Fathers of Confederation. They sought to establish domestic peace between English- and French-speaking Canadians, and between Protestants and Roman Catholics, through the creation of a political nationality that recognized and protected ethnic and religious differences.

Sir John A. Macdonald addressing a meeting in Toronto. From the Canadian Illustrated News, *April 31, 1878. "One thinks of those audiences, dead and gone now, the noise, the whisky, the laughter the tobacco, the smell of unwashed humanity: political meetings were entertainment, the translation of newspapers into life" (P.B. Waite, "Reflections on an Un-Victorian Society," in D. Swainson, ed.,* Oliver Mowat's Ontario *[Toronto: Macmillan, 1972], p. 26).*

National Archives of Canada/C-68193.

Despite their laudable intentions, Canada's founders built disunity into the political structure. The new Canadian system, by combining aspects of the American federal and the British parliamentary forms of government, resembled a carriage pulled by two horses moving in different directions. Some Canadian politicians had wanted a Canadian equivalent of the British unitary state — a state with a strong central government and weak municipal governments, a legislative union. Having seen the United States rent by civil war in the early 1860s, John A. Macdonald favoured such a union to prevent a similar occurrence in Canada.

French-speaking Canadians and many Maritimers opposed this. French Canadians refused to accept a highly centralized government in Ottawa. Furthermore, many areas of the Maritimes lacked municipal governments, a fact that made the centralization of all powers with Ottawa totally impractical from an administrative point of view. The Fathers of Confederation therefore agreed on a compromise: a federal union in which the central government controlled matters of general and common interest, and the provincial governments had authority over local concerns.

For more than a century, historians, political scientists, and legal experts have debated the Fathers of Confederation's true intentions. Those who believe they sought to build a strong central government point out that the BNA Act delegated only precise and very circumscribed powers to the provincial governments. In contrast, the federal government gained the important economic and taxation powers, including the right to grant subsidies to the individual provinces. Ottawa also received the right to make laws for the "peace, order and good government of Canada" in relation to all matters not exclusively assigned to the provincial legislatures. Centralists also contend that the phrase "peace, order and good government of Canada" and the phrase "regulation of trade and commerce" incorporated all powers not exclusively given to the provinces; hence the residuum of powers lay with the federal government. Furthermore, they point out that the lieutenant governors of the provinces, appointees of the Dominion government, could reserve and disallow provincial legislation.

In contrast, provincial-rights advocates argue that since the colonies established the union, Confederation constituted a compact made among themselves. Furthermore, they point to the general phrase "property and civil rights in the province" in section 92 of the BNA Act, which deals with the constitutional rights of the provinces, as proof of the provinces' broad powers. They also note that the provinces received a structure of government parallel to that of the federal government, implying that the provinces' association with the Crown was similar, not subordinate, to the Dominion's. Finally, they direct attention to legal tradition: in the late nineteenth and early twentieth centuries, the Judicial Committee of the Privy Council, the highest court of appeal in the British empire, consistently interpreted the Constitution in favour of the provinces.

CANADIAN-BRITISH-AMERICAN RELATIONS

Nationhood did not mean independence in 1867. By law and by desire, Canada remained a British colony, with the British Parliament controlling Canada's external affairs. In 1867, Canadians, particularly English-speaking Canadians, considered the imperial connection as the best means for Canada to fulfil its destiny.

At the time of Confederation, most Canadians believed themselves to be British North Americans, a people different from, and superior to, the Americans. They regarded the American form of government as inferior to the British. Yet, as historian Frank H. Underhill has pointed out, by 1867, with Confederation, Canadians had actually become more American than British.[1] Federalism was an American, not a British, form of government. In adopting an egalitarian model, Canadian society became closer in its composition to American than to British society.

THE ECONOMY

More than 80 percent of the Canadian labour force in 1867 worked in the primary industries — farming, fishing, and lumbering — to produce the staple products of wheat, fish, and timber. Fishing was the main occupation of the majority of Nova Scotians in the small fishing villages that dotted the coastline. Neighbouring New Brunswick seemed an immense forest broken by the numerous streams that carried the logs to sea, and by pockets of agricultural settlement. Only the Ottawa valley, with its massive red and white pines, truly rivalled New Brunswick for the timber trade. The abundant softwood trees, such as pine, spruce, and tamarack, were ideal for shipbuilding and for construction in Britain and the northeastern United States.

Where Historians Disagree

THE MEANING OF THE BNA ACT

WEB LINKS

Since the passage of the British North America Act in 1867, historians have disagreed as to its meaning. Some commentators view it as an act of the British Parliament; others, as a political contract among four British North American colonies to establish a new country. Still other observers see Confederation as a cultural compact between English- and French-speaking Canadians.

A.R.M. Lower, writing in the nation-building tradition of the 1940s in his *Colony to Nation* (Toronto: Longmans, Green, 1946), saw the BNA Act as an act of the British Parliament, imposed from above and with authority emanating from the Crown. "What happened in 1867," he writes, "was that the Crown, in the fullness of its wisdom, decided to rearrange its administrative areas in British North America.... All were cast into the crucible of Imperial omnicompetence and came out remelted, shining, new, and fused" (p. 328). This interpretation implies that the central government — the new Canadian equivalent of the old imperial authority — alone inherited the wide-sweeping powers of the central authority, including the sole right to change the Constitution. Historian Donald Creighton supports this view.

Those who oppose this interpretation of the events of 1867 dispute the centralizing nature of the BNA Act. They claim that the Constitution was the end result of a pact. But these historians disagree among themselves as to the nature of that pact. Some claim it was an agreement among the provinces; others, a compact between the two founding cultural groups — English-speaking and French-speaking Canadians.

Historians who support the idea of a provincial pact point out that the colonies, provinces after 1867, had met together to decide on the nature of the new nation and on the powers that they would relinquish to the central government. The historical perspective behind the Tremblay Report of 1956 (Province of Quebec, *Report of the Royal Commission of Inquiry on Constitutional Problems*, vol. I, 1956, p. 22) was based on this interpretation. It stated that "the Union of 1867 met the common needs of the provinces," implying that what powers the provinces had given away could be taken back if they felt the federal government was using its delegated powers unwisely or unconstitutionally.

A few historians have argued that the BNA Act constituted a compact between the two founding linguistic groups — English- and French-speaking Canadians. This compact was not a legal or even a political commitment so much as it was a moral one, an unwritten understanding that underlay the negotiations of the BNA Act and indeed grew out of the historical circumstances of the time. Historian George F.G. Stanley argued this position in "Act or Pact: Another Look at Confederation" (in the *Canadian Historical Association Report*, 1956). Writing on the eve of the Quiet Revolution in Quebec, he noted that "the idea of a compact between races was not a new one in 1865; it had already become a vital thing in our history. It influenced both the political thinking and the political vocabulary of the day; and it was already on the way to becoming a tradition and a convention of our constitution" (p. 13). The implication was that the compact remained only so long as it served the needs of both parties involved.

Since our current understanding of the nature of Canada rests to such a great extent on our view of the BNA Act, this debate remains central in any discussion of the nature of Canada.

Breaking a log jam in the Miramichi region of New Brunswick, 1890. Lumbering and shipbuilding were major occupations in the Maritimes in the late nineteenth century.

Provincial Archives of New Brunswick/ P6-185.

In 1878 Canada could claim the fourth-largest merchant marine in the world, behind only the fleets of Britain, the United States, and Norway. In 1865, for example, the Maritimes built more than 600 vessels. The ports of Saint John, Halifax, Yarmouth, Quebec, and Montreal were major shipowning centres. But as steel ships replaced wooden ones, and as steam replaced sails as the source of energy, the era of wood, wind, and sails would soon decline. Some Maritimers equated the close of their "golden age" with Confederation, and they resented union. Stephen Leacock, Canada's famous humorist, best expressed this feeling: "The shades of night were falling, and the night was called Confederation."[2]

FARMING

The vast majority of Canadians in 1867 lived on farms. Agriculture was important in Nova Scotia, especially in the Annapolis valley; in New Brunswick, farmers made up more than half the labour force. In southern Quebec, dairy farming predominated. Some Quebec French-speaking farmers, with the encouragement of the Roman Catholic church and the Quebec government, colonized the Saguenay–Lake St. Jean region, the Laurentians, and Témiscamingue in the upper Ottawa valley. These "colonist farmers" had to clear the land of forests before breaking ground. Even then, farming in most northern areas was marginal because of poor soil, short frost-free periods, and long distances from market centres. As the joke went, the northern farmers raised two crops: one stone, the other snow.

Probably for every migrant who went north, ten more left for the United States, a movement known as "the Great Haemorrhage." French-Canadian leaders, seeing hundreds of thousands of French Canadians leave for jobs in neighbouring New England, feared that the sizable anglophone population — roughly 25 percent of Quebec's population — might become the majority in the province one day.

Wheat farming served as "the engine of economic growth"[3] in Ontario, according to the economic historian John McCallum. At the time of Confederation the best agricultural land lay in the province, where 60 percent of the working population farmed. Coarse grain or flour made up half of all exports at mid-century. By the time of Confederation, the peak of wheat production had been reached, with most of the good farmland occupied and some of the older districts becoming exhausted. Fortunately for Ontarians, just as they faced an agricultural crisis, the Canadian government acquired the vast prairie land to the west, which served as an outlet.

TRANSPORTATION AND COMMUNICATION

In 1867, Canada's roads left much to be desired. Some widely used wagon trails had been upgraded to "macadamized" roads — built by putting down layers of successively smaller stones and gravel — but these roads were costly. To help pay for them, road builders placed tollgates every eight kilometres or so to extract payment from users. By the 1840s and 1850s, plank roads (planks of white pine, ten centimetres thick, covered with fine gravel or pitch, and laid across and spiked to two logs placed parallel to each other in the roadbed) began replacing macadamized roads. Plank roads were less costly and provided, according to the reports of seasoned stagecoach travellers at the time, a comfortable, smooth ride.

Boats and trains made transportation more efficient. Steamboats plied the Atlantic coast, the St. Lawrence River, and the Great Lakes. A network of canals enabled small vessels to reach the Great Lakes via the St. Lawrence River. Water travel proved the most efficient mode of transportation in the 1860s, but it had disadvantages: the shipping season was short; the risk of damage due to storms great; and the cost of building and maintaining canals remained high.

Railways revolutionized transportation. They opened up inland areas previously inaccessible to settlement. The British North American colonies had embarked in the 1850s on an ambitious building scheme. By the time of Confederation, 3330 km of track had already been laid, including the 1600 km of track for the Grand Trunk Railway that stretched from Sarnia to Lévis, making it the longest railway in British North America at the time. Railway building had been one of the chief reasons behind Confederation. To win Maritime support for Confederation, the Canadian politicians promised an intercolonial railway to link the Maritimes with Ontario and Quebec.

Most trains ran only about as fast as a horse and carriage. But on good track, like that between Toronto and Montreal, they reached a speed of 50 km per hour. In summer, sparks from the wood-burning engines often caused forest fires. In winter, the iron rails occasionally split, derailing the train. During snowstorms, passengers had to shovel snow from the tracks. Then, too, railway building was costly, more likely to end in debt than in profit. Still, railways were felt to be indispensable for trade and for industrial capital. They also stimulated "progress." For these reasons, and because they had a vested interest as shareholders, Canadian politicians generously subsidized railways with public money.

TRADE AND INDUSTRIALIZATION

Until the mid-nineteenth century, British North America traded almost exclusively with Britain. During the 1840s, however, the mother country abandoned its long-established system of preferential trade with its colonies in favour of free trade.

The British North American colonies sought an alternative and found it in the Reciprocity Treaty of 1854 with the United States. But a protectionist American Senate rescinded the free-trade treaty in 1866. Now the British North American colonies needed increased internal (domestic) trade. Confederation was intended to promote trade between the four new provinces.

In 1867, Canadians produced raw materials and imported manufactured goods: textiles, textile fibres, agricultural products, consumer goods, and iron products. Canada was, however, on the eve of its industrial revolution, an era of large-scale production of manufactured goods by means of machinery located in factories. Economic historian O.J. Firestone considered the 1860s as the turning point toward a modern industrial society, pointing to the fact that 20 percent of Canada's gross national product (GNP) came from manufacturing — a dramatic increase from the preceding decade. Manufacturing employed nearly 200 000 Canadians in roughly 40 000 establishments. Most of these were small family businesses attached to the owner's residence and employing only a few people doing jobs by hand, such as blacksmith shops, sawmills, gristmills, and distilleries. Until mid-century, they generally supplied only local needs on a custom or repair basis.

Increasingly, however, factories and machinery replaced home workers and artisans. Mechanization, for example, came to the agricultural-implements industry. Daniel Massey, a farmer at Newcastle, east of Toronto, had been manufacturing ploughs, harrows, reapers, and other simple horse-drawn instruments since 1849.

Canadian shops and factories in the large urban centres of Montreal, Toronto, Quebec, Hamilton, Saint John, and Halifax had begun to specialize. Shipbuilding in Quebec used new British industrial techniques, as did the boot and shoe industry of Toronto. In Hamilton, iron smelting and steel production had begun. By 1867, manufacturing was concentrated in the Montreal area and in the vicinity of Toronto, as well as at the western end of Lake Ontario, from Hamilton westward to Brantford. Such mechanization and specialization centralized production in factories, broke down traditional self-sufficient households, and divided labour into repetitive tasks, but it also expanded production and made consumer goods available at cheaper prices.

The nation's financial institutions continued to be small and inexperienced. Some chartered banks existed, along with a host of unincorporated "private banks." Most of their business consisted of providing capital for new industries. Evidence shows that, early on, many of these industries made handsome profits that enabled the owner to repay his loans and invest the rest in the expansion of the business. Also evident in the Canada of 1867 were "building societies," the forerunners of today's trust and loan companies. They concentrated on mortgage lending. Life and fire insurance existed, most of their policies underwritten by British and American firms. The only Canadian life insurance company at the time was Canadian Life, with its head office in Hamilton.

URBANIZATION

In 1867, only one in five Canadians lived in urban centres, communities with a population over 1000. The streets and lanes smelled of horses. Streets were unpaved. Public places carried the odour of tobacco from both smoking and spitting. Canada had three large cities. More than 105 000 people lived in Montreal, 60 000 in Quebec City, and 50 000 in Toronto. Six other cities had populations greater than 10 000:

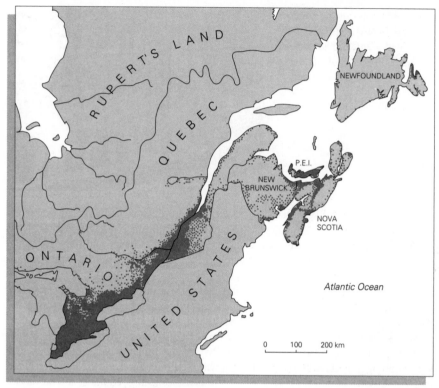

Chief areas of settlement in Canada, 1867.

Source: Based on John Warkentin, *Canada: A Geographical Interpretation* (Toronto: Methuen, 1968), p. 45.

two were in the Maritimes (Saint John and Halifax), and four in Ontario (Hamilton, Ottawa, Kingston, and London). A host of smaller towns in the range of 1000–5000 dotted the Canadian landscape. Only the larger cities, thanks to their extensive rail connections, could service a region that went beyond the adjacent rural area. Montreal's hinterland, for example, included the rural areas of southwestern Quebec as well as eastern Ontario.

Saint John and Halifax grew slowly, compared with cities in central Canada. Many of the manufacturers in these two port cities faced hard times because they lacked a large local market and faced competition from wealthier entrepreneurs in central Canada. Industrialists in the Maritimes looked forward to the completion of the Intercolonial Railway, which would, they hoped, make Ontario and Quebec economic hinterlands of Halifax and Saint John.

SOCIAL LIFE

In 1867, most Canadians lived and worked on their own farms, as close to neighbours, kin, and their own ethnic group as possible. In Quebec, only thirteen years

An evening with friends in Quebec in days gone by. Family and friends provided social cohesion in rural Canada in the nineteenth century.

....

National Archives of Canada/C-1125

earlier, the seigneurial system had been abolished; individual farmers had acquired title to their lands. Limited financial means made consumer goods a luxury. The village elite generally consisted of the curé, the doctor, the notary, and the local merchants. In Quebec City and Montreal, French Canadians lived amidst a substantial English-speaking population.

In the 1860s, English-speaking Canadians were a third of Quebec City's population and half of Montreal's. This English-speaking population contained the great majority of the province's commercial and business elite, which included many of the most powerful business figures in British North America, including individuals such as the Scottish-born John Redpath, a stonemason who had accumulated capital through large-scale building projects, with the profits from which he built Canada's first sugar refinery, and the Molsons, Montreal brewers with interests in steamships, banking, and railways.

Next door in Ontario, most of the population consisted of recent immigrants or children of immigrants. The majority were freehold farmers who had acquired their land within the last generation. Ontario farmers tended to be better off economically than their Quebec counterparts. They owned larger farms that were newly cultivated and subsequently more productive. People lived farther apart, however, and were divided by their different Christian denominational ties.

In these pioneer communities, taverns served as a source of news. More sober talk occurred at the workplace, the gristmill, the general store, and the blacksmith shop in the local village or hamlet. Local agricultural societies also brought people together. As in the United States, many males joined fraternal organizations such as the Oddfellows and the Independent Order of Foresters. Protestants belonged to the Orange Lodge and the Masons. A number of organizations sponsored picnics and parades. The most important centre for social life, however, remained the church.

Ontarians moved frequently in the 1860s. A study of several townships along Lake Ontario near Port Hope revealed that within a five-year span more than half the people were recent occupants or had moved from one place to another within the region. David Gagan's study of Peel County at mid-century confirms this, as does Michael Katz's study of mid-century Hamilton.[4] An increasing number were leaving the country for the cities and towns. Physical mobility, however, did not always mean social mobility, although the incentive for moving was often to better one's life.

In the Maritimes, people lived either in rural areas or in small towns. With sparse populations, poor roads, and a topography that encouraged settlement along the coast, communities often lay many kilometres from one another. In 1867, no major railways yet existed to link communities. In addition, the diversified economy of the Maritimes — fishing, lumbering, mining, and farming — separated people according to interests and livelihood. Maritimers in 1867 identified with their particular locale and lacked a provincial consciousness.

THE INDUSTRIAL CITY

Canadian cities in 1867 were, with the exception of Montreal, pre-industrial. Rich and poor lived in close proximity, with social distinctions marked by the location of a person's home on a street or by the location of a particular street in a district. In Montreal, however, predominantly working-class districts were already evident in the city core and along the St. Lawrence River and Lachine Canal. Well-to-do families were leaving the inner city to live in the spacious, clean, and airy districts of the west end, with its numerous parks and good public services. The modern industrial segregated city had, in Montreal at least, made an appearance in 1867. By 1914, it would be commonplace throughout the country.

In the urban centres of Ontario, Quebec, and the Maritimes, the upper classes lived well, in houses with high-ceilinged rooms, wide verandas, big front lawns, hot running water, and inside toilets. These houses still carried the dank smell of the gas used for lighting at night; since furnaces did not come into general use until the 1880s, each room was heated by a fireplace. Bathtubs had just been introduced. In many cases servants cleaned the house, cared for the children, and cooked the meals. A middle class was emerging, made up chiefly of merchants and artisans, who were replacing professionals as an elite. Their power and prestige, measured more in wealth than in education, were displayed in prestigious homes crammed full of knick-knacks and bric-a-brac.

Working-class families in the city lived an entirely different existence. A typical family had one or two rooms in a tenement house (a place shared with five or more other families) that was poorly ventilated, lacked lighting and running water, and had no yard or indoor toilet. Their daily diet contained no fresh vegetables and only small quantities of meat and dairy products. Disease, poverty, and death were ever present. Newborn children of the poor were almost as likely to die as to live. In Montreal in 1867, for example, one out of four children died before reaching the age of one, most often from impure water or from intestinal diseases caused by unpasteurized milk. (Pasteurization only became common in North America in the early twentieth century.) Children fortunate enough to survive the first year had to avoid smallpox, the major cause of infant death. Among adults, especially women, tuberculosis was the leading killer.

WOMEN

Women made up almost 50 percent of the population in 1867, yet they did not have the right to vote; they had almost no access to higher education or professional training; and they had few legal rights. They were defined by their role in the "domestic sphere," as wives and mothers at the service of husbands and children. In the days

"Work," a drawing that appeared in the journal L'Opinion Publique, *November 2, 1871. In the late nineteenth century, gender inequality was as common as class inequality.*

National Archives of Canada/C-108134.

before modern conveniences, their duties lay in the arduous work of keeping a good home. Their daily tasks consisted of cleaning house, cooking, sewing, weaving, and making butter, the rhythm being broken only by church services on Sundays. The change of seasons varied the pattern only slightly, and added garden and field work at harvest time.

A satirical cartoon in *L'Opinion Publique*, an illustrated journal of the day, reveals what many working-class women's sentiments must have been. The gruff-looking husband sits at the table heaped with food, while his wife, on her knees, scrubs the floor. In the background one sees laundry hanging. She comments to him: "You complain about your 10 hours of labour; I have just worked for 14 hours, and my day is not finished yet."

Marriage was more a communal than private affair. Courting occurred in supervised settings, and marriage was a public event. The average ages at marriage in 1867 were 24 for females and 27.5 for males, higher than those of their counterparts in European society. The few surviving women's diaries of this period speak little of love and romance and emphasize instead economic conditions. Economic security rather than romance seemed to influence most marriage decisions, especially among the lower class. Women also relinquished their personal property and any wages earned upon marriage. Under British common law, in effect everywhere except Quebec, husband and wife were legally one. A wife could not sign a contract, be sued in her own name, take her husband to court, or initiate divorce proceedings. Despite such

In May 1872, about 1500 workers paraded through Hamilton in support of the movement to institute a nine-hour working day. From the Canadian Illustrated News, *June 8, 1872. Increasingly, strikes and parades became in the late nineteenth century a recognizable form of protest as well as a means to enhance working-class solidarity and identity.*

National Archives of Canada/C-58640.

restrictions, over 95 percent of women married. They also bore large families, 7.8 children on average by mid-century.

Jobs existed for women in the cities, mainly as domestics or as factory workers. By 1871, 42 percent of the industrial work force in Montreal consisted of women and children. Female employees were sought after, particularly as unskilled workers in such industries as clothing, tobacco, and footwear, because they were reliable and cheap labour. In the factories, a woman received half the wages of a man doing a similar job. No unions existed to represent them.

Children, in many ways, became the forgotten group in society, a group without legal rights. Often those from poorer families had to leave school to help support their families. Most working-class children had little hope of rising above their parents' level and social status.

TRADE UNIONS

The federal government did not legally recognize unions until 1872. In the 1860s, the unions that did exist represented skilled workers in a particular locale or a special trade, such as typesetting, shoemaking, and moulding. The first unions for non-skilled workers had appeared in shops that had introduced modern technology, a development that was beginning to undermine jobs. Increasingly, employers saw workers as employees rather than as apprentices. They brought workers under one roof and paid them according to the quantity, rather than quality, of their work.

Some workers responded to these changed conditions in the workplace by rioting. By 1867, however, strikes and parades were replacing riots as more acceptable forms of protest. They were also used to demand better wages and working conditions. On June 10, 1867, for example, 10 000 workers paraded in the streets of Montreal as a show of worker solidarity and as an appeal for improved wages and working conditions.

Nuns of the Hôtel-Dieu Hospital, Quebec City, around 1870. Nunneries provided single Quebec women with an opportunity to serve others. The sisters taught in the schools and administered the hospitals in Quebec.

Louis-Prudent Valle/National Archives of Canada/PA-139146.

RELIGION AND EDUCATION

In 1867, churches gave spiritual and moral guidance and, often, social assistance. Almost all Canadians in 1867 belonged to one of the major denominations. The Roman Catholic church, the largest in Canada, claimed as members 40 percent of the country's population (in Quebec, 85 percent). Quebec had a dual school system that consisted of a majority Catholic system and a minority Protestant system, both protected by law. The church controlled the Catholic education system by supplying its teachers and its curriculum.

The female religious orders taught in the schools and administered the hospitals. They cared for the sick, the abandoned, and the poor. Between 1850 and 1920 the number of nuns in Quebec increased tenfold, from 600 to more than 6500. Clearly for a small number of Quebec women the religious life provided an alternative to marriage, spinsterhood, factory work, or emigration. Female religious communities gave many of their members the opportunity to obtain an excellent education, to occupy responsible administrative positions, and to use their training as teachers, nurses, and social-assistance workers.

In Protestant Canada, Anglicans slightly outnumbered Presbyterians, who outnumbered Methodists. Even within these denominations, divisions and distinct groups existed. These Protestant religious groups favoured voluntarism, the legal separation of church and state. They believed that religious instruction should be provided by the church only, in Sunday schools. The Roman Catholic church, in contrast, maintained that the school system should provide religious, as well as regular, instruction. It therefore opposed the abolition of denominational schools. Protestant groups denounced separate Catholic schools, seeing them as evidence of undue religious influence in education. In Ontario (Canada West), the "voluntarists," under Egerton Ryerson, the first superintendent of education in the province, had succeeded in creating a non-denominational public school system in the 1840s that would later become the model for education in the western provinces.

Schooling had little priority in Canada in the 1860s, although most provinces moved to a form of taxation on property holders to finance state-operated schools.

Children fortunate enough to receive formal education, however, might have their classes in the corners of warehouses, blacksmith shops, stores, tanneries, or private homes. Their schooling rarely went beyond the basic "3 Rs" — "reading, 'riting, and 'rithmetic." Sometimes teachers had little more education than their students. The most important requisite to teach was simply a willingness to work for low pay and to enforce discipline. Some teachers had to be satisfied with no salary; only board and lodging were provided. Local school boards often expected male teachers to help their landlords with outdoor chores, and female teachers to mind the children, help prepare meals, and sew and darn when not teaching.

In Ontario, the middle and upper classes paid for their children to attend grammar schools (renamed "high schools" in 1871 by Ryerson) and collegiate institutes. In high school, the students learned English, commercial subjects, and natural science, especially agriculture; and in collegiate institutes they also studied the classics in preparation for university. In Quebec, the Roman Catholic church operated classical colleges, which trained the province's future lawyers, doctors, and priests. Most of the seventeen universities were affiliated with a religious denomination, but by 1867 three exceptions already existed: the University of Toronto, Dalhousie College in Halifax, and the University of New Brunswick in Fredericton. They served an elite of only 1500 students in total, mostly sons of the well-to-do (women were not admitted) or a few aspiring members of the upper middle class. Within the university curriculum, the faculties of arts and theology dominated, as teaching and the clergy were the dominant career options after graduation. The arts course was traditional, with an emphasis on classical languages, mathematics, and philosophy. Natural science was assuming greater importance. Engineering courses had not yet been introduced.

At the moment of Lord Monck's address in November 1867, Canada was a rural, predominantly farming, society. Social distinctions divided the rural population, and great physical distances isolated communities. In the few towns and cities, social classes existed, but segregation by social districts was only beginning. The Canadian economy remained largely pre-industrial, but manufacturing had started in a few large urban centres. Exports included mainly wheat, timber, and fish. Politically, the new nation experimented with a new two-party system and with a new Constitution that left much to be resolved. The new Dominion also lacked a sense of nationalism. As Prime Minister John A. Macdonald put it: Confederation, "now in the gristle," needed to "harden into bone."

NOTES

1. Frank H. Underhill, *The Image of Confederation* (Toronto: Canadian Broadcasting Corporation, 1964), pp. 11–12.
2. Quoted in Underhill, *Image of Confederation*, p. 6.
3. John McCallum, *Unequal Beginnings: Agriculture and Economic Development in Quebec and Ontario until 1870* (Toronto: University of Toronto Press, 1980), p. 5.
4. David Gagan, *Hopeful Travellers: Families, Land, and Social Change in Mid-Victorian Peel County, Canada West* (Toronto: University of Toronto Press, 1981); and Michael Katz, *The People of Hamilton, Canada West: Family and Class in a Mid-Nineteenth Century City* (Cambridge, MA: Harvard University Press, 1975).

LINKING TO THE PAST

WEB LINKS

The BNA Act
http://www.canadahistory.com/bna1867.htm
The full text of the 1867 British North America Act, which marked the beginnings of Canada as a nation.

The Fathers of Confederation
http://www.nlc-bnc.ca/confed/foc.htm
A closer look at the Fathers of Confederation, including photographs and period biographies for members such as John A. Macdonald and George Etienne Cartier.

John A. Macdonald on the Federal System
http://www.nlc-bnc.ca/confed/speeches/sph0003.htm
Excerpts from a speech made by John A. Macdonald during the Confederation debates.

Canadian Confederation Celebrations
http://www.nlc-bnc.ca/confed/celebrat.htm
This site features the celebrations of Confederation, including newspaper articles, poems, and music.

BIBLIOGRAPHY

For overviews of Canada in the 1860s and interpretative essays on Confederation see Donald G. Creighton's "The 1860s," in J.M.S. Careless and R.C. Brown, eds., *The Canadians: 1867–1967* (Toronto: Macmillan, 1967), pp. 3–36, and Creighton's introductory chapter in his *Canada's First Century, 1867–1967* (Toronto: Macmillan, 1970). Other accounts include F.H. Underhill, *The Image of Confederation* (Toronto: Canadian Broadcasting Corporation, 1964); and W.L. Morton, *The Critical Years* (Toronto: McClelland & Stewart, 1964). On federal–provincial relations see Ramsay Cook, *Provincial Autonomy, Minority Rights and the Compact Theory* (Ottawa: Queen's Printer, 1969). A French-Canadian historian's view of Quebec and Confederation is Marcel Hamelin's *Les premières années du parlementarisme québécois (1867–1878)* (Québec: Presses de l'Université Laval, 1974). On the Maritimes and Confederation see D.A. Muise, "The 1860s: Forging the Bonds of Union," in E.R. Forbes and D.A. Muise, eds., *The Atlantic Provinces in Confederation* (Toronto: University of Toronto Press, 1993), pp. 13–47; and for British Columbia, George Shelton, ed., *British Columbia and Confederation* (Victoria: Morriss Printing, 1967).

George M. Grant's *Picturesque Canada*, 2 vols. (Toronto: Belden Bros., 1882), provides a contemporary view of Canada at the end of the nineteenth century. Superb illustrations from the period appear in Mary Fallis Jones, *The Confederation Generation* (Toronto: Royal Ontario Museum, 1978). Jacques Hébert's *Ah! Mes Aïeux* (Montréal: Éditions Radio-Canada, 1968) reviews the social and political life of French Canadians in 1867, using selections from contemporary newspapers.

Portraits of Canada's first prime minister are available in Donald G. Creighton, *John A. Macdonald: The Old Chieftain* (Toronto: Macmillan, 1955); P.B. Waite, *Macdonald: His Life and World* (Toronto: McGraw-Hill Ryerson, 1975); Donald Swainson, *Sir John A. Macdonald: The Man and the Politician* (Kingston: Quarry Press, 1989); and Michael Bliss, "Macdonald: The Prince of Canada," in his *Right Honourable Men: The Descent of Canadian Politics from Macdonald to Mulroney* (Toronto: HarperCollins, 1995), pp. 3–29. On Macdonald's political philosophy see P.B. Waite, "The Political Ideas of John A. Macdonald," in Marcel

Hamelin, ed., *The Political Ideas of the Prime Ministers of Canada* (Ottawa: Éditions de l'Université d'Ottawa, 1969), pp. 51–67; and Cynthia M. Smith and Jack McLeod, eds., *John A.: An Anecdotal Life of John A. Macdonald* (Toronto: Oxford University Press, 1989). A popular account of Canada's first prime minister is Lena Newman, *The John A. Macdonald Album* (Montreal: Tundra Books, 1974). For studies of George-Étienne Cartier see Jean-Charles Bonenfant's sketch in the *Dictionary of Canadian Biography*, vol. 10, *1861 to 1870* (Toronto: University of Toronto Press, 1972), pp. 142–52; Alastair Sweeney, *George-Étienne Cartier: A Biography* (Toronto: McClelland & Stewart, 1976); and Brian Young, *George-Étienne Cartier: Montreal Bourgeois* (Montreal/Kingston: McGill-Queen's University Press, 1981).

For a review of the Canadian economy at the time of Confederation consult Michael Bliss, *Northern Enterprise: Five Centuries of Canadian Business* (Toronto: McClelland & Stewart, 1987); Kenneth Norrie and Douglas Owram, *A History of the Canadian Economy*, 2nd ed. (Toronto: Harcourt Brace, 1996); and Graham Taylor and Peter A. Baskerville, *A Concise History of Business in Canada* (Toronto: Oxford University Press, 1994). On industrial development see O.J. Firestone, *Canada's Economic Development 1867–1953* (London: Bowes & Bowes, 1958). For an overview of the economic history of post-Confederation Quebec useful studies include P.-A. Linteau, R. Durocher, and J.-C. Robert, *Quebec: A History, 1867–1929* (Toronto: James Lorimer, 1983); and for the earlier period John McCallum, *Unequal Beginnings: Agriculture and Economic Development in Quebec and Ontario until 1870* (Toronto: University of Toronto Press, 1980).

John Warkentin and R.C. Harris, *Canada Before Confederation* (Toronto: Oxford University Press, 1974), provides an overview of regional societies in Canada to the mid-nineteenth century. Quantitative studies of class and social structure of two areas of Ontario are available in Michael Katz, *The People of Hamilton, Canada West: Family and Class in a Mid-Nineteenth Century City* (Cambridge, MA: Harvard University Press, 1975); and David Gagan, *Hopeful Travellers: Families, Land, and Social Change in Mid-Victorian Peel County, Canada West* (Toronto: University of Toronto Press, 1981). For a study of Montreal see Bettina Bradbury, *Working Families: Age, Gender, and Daily Survival in Industrializing Montreal* (Toronto: McClelland & Stewart, 1993). On family life see Bettina Bradbury, ed., *Canadian Family History: Selected Readings* (Toronto: Copp Clark Pitman, 1992). For a view of Canada's governing society in Ottawa from 1867 to 1914 see Sandra Gwyn, *The Private Capital: Ambition and Love in the Age of Macdonald and Laurier* (Toronto: McClelland & Stewart, 1984).

Alison Prentice et al., *Canadian Women: A History*, 2nd ed. (Toronto: Harcourt Brace, 1996); and Marta Danylewycz, *Taking the Veil: An Alternative to Marriage, Motherhood, and Spinsterhood in Quebec, 1840–1920* (Toronto: McClelland & Stewart, 1987) review the status of women in the mid-nineteenth century. Peter Ward's *Courtship, Love, and Marriage in Nineteenth-Century English Canada* (Montreal/Kingston: McGill-Queen's University Press, 1990) is a pioneering study of this social-history topic. Ellen M. Thomas Gee provides a statistical study of the same subject in "Marriage in Nineteenth-Century Canada," *Canadian Review of Sociology and Anthropology* 19(3) (August 1982): 311–25. On women in the Maritimes see Janet Guildford and Suzanne Morton, *Separate Spheres: Women's Worlds in the 19th-Century Maritimes* (Fredericton: Acadiensis Press, 1994). Collections of articles in Canadian women's history include Alison Prentice and Susan Mann Trofimenkoff, eds., *The Neglected Majority: Essays in Canadian Women's History*, vol. 2 (Toronto: McClelland & Stewart, 1985); and Veronica Strong-Boag and Anita Clair Fellman, eds., *Rethinking Canada: The Promise of Women's History*, 2nd ed. (Toronto: Copp Clark Pitman, 1991). On women and the law see Constance Backhouse, *Petticoats and Prejudice: Women and Law in Nineteenth Century Canada* (Toronto: The Osgoode Society, 1991). D. Owen Carrigan,

Crime and Punishment in Canada: A History (Toronto: McClelland & Stewart, 1991), and Jim Phillips, Tina Loo, and Suzan Lewthwaite, *Crime and Criminal Justice in Canadian History: Essays in the History of Canadian Law*, vol. 5 (Toronto: University of Toronto Press, 1994), deal with this important subject.

Craig Heron's *The Canadian Labour Movement: A Short History* (Toronto: James Lorimer, 1989) surveys Canadian labour history. See, as well, Bryan D. Palmer, *Working-Class Experience: Rethinking the History of Canadian Labour, 1800–1991* (Toronto: McClelland & Stewart, 1992). Quebec developments are reviewed in the early pages of Jacques Rouillard's *Histoire du syndicalisme québécois* (Montréal: Boréal Express, 1989).

For further discussion of religion see W.L. Morton, "Victorian Canada," in his edited collection *The Shield of Achilles* (Toronto: McClelland & Stewart, 1968), pp. 311–34; John S. Moir, "Religion," in *The Canadians: 1867–1967* (cited earlier), pp. 586–605; and John W. Grant, *A Profusion of Spires: Religion in Nineteenth-Century Ontario* (Toronto: University of Toronto Press, 1988). On education consult Susan E. Houston and Alison Prentice, *Schooling and Scholars in Nineteenth-Century Ontario* (Toronto: University of Toronto Press, 1988); Bruce Curtis, *Building the Educational State: Canada West, 1836–1871* (London: Althouse Press, 1988); and J. Donald Wilson, Robert M. Stamp, and Louis-Philippe Audet, eds., *Canadian Education: A History* (Toronto: Prentice-Hall, 1970).

Political parties at the time of Confederation are discussed in Gordon T. Stewart, *The Origins of Canadian Politics: A Comparative Approach* (Vancouver: University of British Columbia Press, 1986). For a discussion of Canadian–British–American relations around the time of Confederation, see C.P. Stacey, *Canada and the Age of Conflict: A History of Canadian External Relations*, vol. 1, *1867–1921* (Toronto: Macmillan, 1977). On Canadian–American relations see J.L. Granatstein and Norman Hillmer, *For Better or For Worse: Canada and the United States to the 1990s* (Toronto: Copp Clark Pitman, 1991). For the story of the Native peoples see Olive P. Dickason, *Canada's First Nations* (Toronto: McClelland & Stewart, 1992); and E.S. Rogers and Donald B. Smith, eds., *Aboriginal Ontario* (Toronto: Dundurn Press, 1994). The best overview of African-Canadians remains Robin Winks, *The Blacks in Canada: A History*, 2nd ed. (Montreal/Kingston: McGill-Queen's University Press, 1997).

Excellent maps and charts are available in L.R. Gentilcore et al., eds., *Historical Atlas of Canada*, vol. 2: *The Land Transformed, 1800–1891* (Toronto: University of Toronto Press, 1993).

PART ONE

Building the New Dominion, 1867–1914

Time Line: 1867–1914

1867 ~ Nova Scotia, New Brunswick, Quebec, and Ontario join Confederation
1868 ~ Founding of the Canada First movement
1869 ~ Purchase of Rupert's Land from the Hudson's Bay Company
     ~ Outbreak of Red River Resistance
1870 ~ Manitoba becomes a province
1871 ~ British Columbia joins Confederation
     ~ Treaty of Washington signed
     ~ Joseph Guibord affair continues
1872 ~ Homestead Act passed
1873 ~ Prince Edward Island joins Confederation
     ~ North-West Mounted Police (NWMP) established
     ~ Pacific Scandal
     ~ Liberal party comes to power under Alexander Mackenzie
1875 ~ Supreme Court of Canada established
1876 ~ Treaty Six signed
     ~ Indian Act passed
1877 ~ Treaty Seven signed
1878 ~ Conservatives re-elected under John A. Macdonald
1879 ~ National Policy of high tariff established
1880 ~ Britain transfers jurisdiction over the Arctic islands to Canada
1885 ~ Outbreak of North-West Rebellion
     ~ Execution of Louis Riel
     ~ Completion of the Canadian Pacific Railway

1887 ~ First interprovincial premiers' conference held
1889 ~ Manitoba Schools Question controversy begins
1896 ~ Liberal party comes to power under Wilfrid Laurier
     ~ Beginning of major wave of immigration
1897 ~ British preferential tariff established as part of the Liberals' national policy
1899 ~ Outbreak of South African War
1903 ~ Founding of the Ligue nationaliste
     ~ Alaska Boundary Dispute settled
1905 ~ Alberta and Saskatchewan become provinces
1910 ~ Naval Service Bill introduced
     ~ Combines Investigation Act passed
1911 ~ Conservatives win federal election under Robert Borden

Introduction

The mid- to late nineteenth century saw the formation of European nation states, including Germany in 1866 and Italy in 1871; of national consolidation — as occurred in the United States after the Civil War; and imperial expansion, in the case of Britain, France, Germany, and the United States. Canada witnessed all three developments in a phenomenally short period of time: the three British North American colonies of Nova Scotia, New Brunswick, and the United Canadas came together in 1867 to create the new nation state of Canada; within ten years, the country had expanded to include all of the existing British North American colonies with the exception of Newfoundland. The new nation had also undertaken imperial expansion to the Pacific and the Arctic Oceans. It subjected the indigenous population of Native peoples and Métis through military might, first in 1869–70 in the Red River, and then in 1885 in the North-West Territories.

Creating the physical boundaries of a new nation state proved easier than fostering a sense of nationalism. Since the traditional components of cultural nationalism — a common language, a common cultural tradition, or a common religion — were not present, national enthusiasts looked to geography and especially to an economic policy of railway building, protective tariffs, and large-scale immigration to promote a feeling of nationalism.

This national policy, as well as the decision of the Fathers of Confederation to create a federal union with political power divided between Ottawa and provincial governments, necessitated the working out of Dominion–provincial relations. This proved acrimonious. Also to be resolved were relations between French-speaking and English-speaking Canadians. A century of bitterness and suspicion preceded Confederation, yet a *modus vivendi* had existed in the union itself. Tension and compromise prevailed from 1867 to 1914. Finally, the new country needed to work out relations with Britain and the United States. Most Canadians favoured continued affiliation with the British empire; Dominion status did not mean independence. Equally, Canadians sought trade with the United States, while clearly rejecting any form of political union.

For most Canadians, Confederation did not change their daily lives. They continued to identify more with their colonial (now provincial) and local area than with the country as a whole, and they pursued their livelihood as they had prior to Confederation. The year 1867 and the event of Confederation were not momentous. Still, the very act of union of the three British North American colonies put into place a new structure and a new dynamic for economic, political, and social change.

CHAPTER TWO

Three Oceans, One Country: 1867–1880

In his first administration, from 1867 to 1872, John A. Macdonald worked to keep the fragile creation called Canada together and to round it out by purchasing Rupert's Land from the Hudson's Bay Company. He would bring in Manitoba and British Columbia as provinces and prepare for Prince Edward Island's entry in 1873. By 1880, Canada would acquire the Arctic region from Britain. The Conservatives had to persuade Nova Scotia, a reluctant partner in Confederation, to remain in Canada. Other challenges included American threats of taking control of the North-West Territories and even, on occasion, talk of annexing all of Canada, a result of some Americans' belief in their "manifest destiny" to control the entire North American continent. On the Atlantic coast, Newfoundland and Prince Edward Island wanted better terms before consenting to join Confederation, while on the Pacific, British Columbia remained isolated from the other British North Americans by the vast, undeveloped North-West Territories.

THE NOVA SCOTIA REPEAL MOVEMENT

Nova Scotia opposed union with the Canadas from the beginning. Charles Tupper, the province's pro-Confederation premier since 1863 and the leader responsible for bringing Nova Scotia into Confederation, refused to hold a referendum or even to debate the question in the legislative assembly because he knew his government would lose on the issue. A report in the anti-Confederation newspaper, the *Novascotian*, made no secret of Tupper's unpopularity for supporting union: "Dr. Tupper was burned in effigy here on Monday night last. We are only sorry it was not in person." The Halifax *Morning Chronicle* included an obituary notice for the province of Nova Scotia in its issue of July 1, 1867.

When Nova Scotians did have a chance to vote, in September 1867, they elected anti-confederates to 18 of the 19 federal seats. Tupper was the only confederate to win his seat, and then by less than a hundred votes. In a provincial election the same year, Nova Scotians elected 36 anti-confederates and only 2 pro-confederates. In the first meeting of the provincial legislature, the anti-confederates presented repeal resolutions to end the "bondage" of Confederation.

The Anti-Confederation League, later patriotically renamed the Nova Scotia Party, was formed in 1866 and led by Joseph Howe. The popular and seasoned politician, the "Father of Responsible Government in Nova Scotia" and premier from 1860 to 1863, represented a generation of Nova Scotians who remembered Nova Scotia's once-flourishing triangular trade with Britain and the West Indies. A dedicated British imperialist, he wanted to strengthen the colony's ties with Britain, not weaken them through British North American union. After the repealers' stunning victories over the Unionists in the elections of 1867, Howe headed a committee to London in early 1868 to obtain the Colonial Office's sanction for Nova Scotia's release from Confederation. But Britain wanted to lessen, not increase, its obligations to its British North American colonies. The colonial secretary refused to meet Howe.

Other anti-confederates, particularly the business interests in the province, favoured annexation to the United States. After Britain adopted free trade in the 1840s, Nova Scotians developed a lucrative trade with the United States through the Reciprocity Treaty of 1854, until a protectionist American Senate rescinded it in 1866. In 1867, many Nova Scotians preferred a renewal of reciprocity, even annexation to the United States, to union with Canada.

John A. Macdonald saw Canada's opportunity. He knew Howe opposed union with the United States. The prime minister now promised him a cabinet position, control over provincial patronage, and better terms for Nova Scotia — an increased debt allowance and a 25 percent increase in the federal subsidy to the province. Although his opponents accused him of betraying Nova Scotia, Howe ran for federal office in a by-election. Assisted by a very generous campaign donation, estimated at $30 000, supplied jointly by the federal Conservative government and central Canadian business interests, Howe won and subsequently joined the federal cabinet.

Howe's "conversion" to Canadian federalism undermined the repeal movement. Only the annexationists remained. In June 1869, the Anti-Confederation League formally changed its name to the Annexation League. The timing could not have been worse: their manifesto, advocating closer relations with the United States, coincided with a brief period of prosperity that undermined their economic grievances. Furthermore, the United States did not appear particularly interested at this time in annexing Nova Scotia.

The final offer of better terms won over the moderate anti-confederates. But Confederation would remain the central issue facing Nova Scotians for generations to come. In order to weaken opposition to Confederation, Tupper, Howe, and New Brunswick's Charles Tilley successfully pressured Macdonald to give utmost priority to the construction of the Intercolonial Railway. The new 800-kilometre publicly funded railway line, completed in 1876, ran from Rivière-du-Loup in Quebec, along New Brunswick's north shore, to link up with existing lines to Halifax and Saint John.

THE CANADIAN ACQUISITION OF RUPERT'S LAND

Macdonald's Conservative government also faced serious trouble in the Northwest. American senators and congressmen talked openly of annexing the region. In 1864, the United States Congress granted a charter for the construction of the Northern Pacific Railway from St. Paul, Minnesota, to Seattle, Washington. It would be built close to the international border with the intention of capturing more of the trade of the British territory.

In 1868, the Canadian government began negotiations in London with the British government and representatives of the Hudson's Bay Company (HBC) to acquire Rupert's Land, roughly defined as all territory whose rivers flowed into Hudson Bay. The agreement reached in 1869–70 constituted one of the largest real-estate deals in history. For an area ten times the size of what was then Canada, the Dominion government agreed to pay the HBC a cash sum of £300 000 (approximately $1.5 million) and to allow the company to retain one-twentieth (roughly 2.8 million ha) of the land of the "fertile belt" (the area along the North Saskatchewan River), as well as the land immediately surrounding its trading posts. (Over time, the company would receive over $120 million from the sale of its land.) The company agreed to transfer the land to the British government, which then turned the territory over to Canada. Historian Chester Martin maintained that the land deal "transformed the original Dominion from a federation of equal provinces ... into a veritable empire in its own right."[1]

ADMINISTERING THE NORTHWEST

While the negotiations were underway, the Canadian government made preparations to administer the new territory. In June 1869, Parliament passed the "Act for the Temporary Government of Rupert's Land and the North-West Territory." It proposed a colonial system of government with an appointed governor and council only — a political structure similar to the ones that had existed in the British North American colonies prior to the granting of elected assemblies. Representative and responsible government, and provincehood, would have to await a larger population. The Canadian government made immediate plans to build a road from the Lake of the Woods to Fort Garry in the Red River colony and dispatched a survey crew to the Red River for an eventual railway to link the Northwest to the rest of Canada. As well, it appointed William McDougall as the first lieutenant governor. McDougall set off by way of St. Paul, Minnesota, to take up his administrative duties in the Red River colony. But he never reached his destination. A group of Métis in the Red River colony, under their leader, Louis Riel, a 25-year-old Métis from a well-established Red River family and educated in Montreal, forbade McDougall and his entourage to enter Rupert's Land. The Métis also drove out the survey crew. Since the HBC had not yet officially transferred Rupert's Land to Canada, Ottawa had no legal authority in late 1869 to deal with the Red River uprising.

The mixed-blood population in the Red River area consisted in 1869 of three groups. About half were French Métis, offspring of the intermarriage of French fur traders and Amerindian women. About another third were the "country born," descendants of Scottish and Amerindian parents. The remainder were the descendants of Selkirk's original Scottish settlers and newly arrived immigrants from the Canadas, who together numbered only about 1000 people, less than 10 percent of the total Red River colony's population.

THE MÉTIS RESISTANCE OF 1869–1870

The French Métis resented that they had not been consulted over the sale of their homeland. They also disliked the aggressive action and haughty attitude of the small group of Canadian expansionists in the Red River colony who were working to bring the region into Confederation. In their local newspaper, *The Nor'Wester*, these men ridiculed the Métis and proclaimed Canada's right to take control of the Northwest as part of the country's "manifest destiny." The Métis reacted by occupying Upper Fort Garry, the seat of government, on November 2, thus gaining effective control of the Red River colony. They then established their own provisional government.

Not waiting for the announcement of the official transfer of the Red River colony to Canada on December 1 as planned, William McDougall forged his own royal proclamation, to which he attached Queen Victoria's name. On the night of November 30, he crossed the border to proclaim Canada's sovereignty over the Red River colony. He did not know that the Canadian government had decided to delay taking over the territory until the dispute was resolved.

Prime Minister Macdonald opened negotiations with the Métis. He intended to send out an armed expedition to the Red River colony to secure Canada's control of the region, but knew he could not do so until summertime. He feared that by then the United States, which only two years earlier had purchased Alaska from the Russians and had clearly expressed an interest in the Northwest, might annex the territory. He dismissed William McDougall and asked the influential Bishop Alexandre Taché of the Red River colony to return from Rome, where he had been attending the Vatican Council, to assist in reaching a settlement. The prime minister also appointed Donald A. Smith of the Hudson's Bay Company to negotiate on behalf of the Canadian government.

Riel's provisional government drew up a bill of rights in November 1869, outlining its grievances and demands. That bill became the basis for negotiations. At two very well-attended public meetings in the Red River colony held in freezing weather in mid-January, Smith promised the Red River colony a better deal, to be decided by a committee of Métis and the Canadian government.

Meanwhile, the Canadian expansionist party in the Red River colony took action into its own hands. It used the general store owned by John Schultz, a sometime medical doctor and merchant and the leader of the Canada party, as its headquarters to agitate the Métis and oppose Riel's provisional government. The Métis raided the store and imprisoned the Canadians. They agreed to release prisoners who promised either to leave the colony or to obey the provisional government. A few, like Schultz, refused to comply. He managed to escape, however, by using a knife, hidden in a pudding by his wife, to cut the ropes on the windows and to lower himself out. He then gathered together supporters for an ill-fated attack on Fort Garry. The Métis captured members of the raiding party, including Thomas Scott, a 28-year-old Protestant Irishman and member of the Orange Lodge.

Scott proved to be a difficult prisoner. He insulted and provoked his Métis guards. Riel decided to hold a Métis court to try Scott for contempt of the Métis provisional government. The court voted to execute the troublemaker. Riel agreed, in order, he claimed, "to make Canada respect us." (Some historians have since argued that Riel complied with the court order so as to maintain his control of the Métis.) On March 4, 1870, a firing squad executed Scott.

Scott's execution turned the Métis resistance from a distant western struggle into a national crisis. Protestant Ontario now had a martyr. When a group of Scott's Red River associates arrived in Toronto to drum up support for their cause, a huge crowd came out to hear their version of the uprising in the West:

Louis Riel (seated directly in the centre) with his council, 1870. Riel and his council's resistance to Canada's attempted seizure of the Red River led to the Manitoba Act of 1870, which brought Manitoba into Confederation as the first new province.

National Archives of Canada/PA-12854; Manitoba Museum of Man and Nature/3661.

It would be a gross injustice to the loyal inhabitants of Red River, humiliating to our national honour, and contrary to all British traditions for our Government to receive, negotiate or meet with the emissaries of those who have robbed, imprisoned and murdered loyal Canadians, whose only fault was zeal for British institutions, whose only crime was devotion to the old flag.

A different perception prevailed in Roman Catholic Quebec. French Canadians viewed Riel as the protector of the French-speaking Métis against an aggressive group of Canadianists from Ontario, backed by the Orange Order.

John A. Macdonald proposed a compromise. To appease the Métis and the French Canadians of Quebec, his government passed the Manitoba Act in May 1870, based on the negotiations between the Red River's three-person delegation and the Canadian government. The Red River colony could enter Confederation as a province. To satisfy Canadianists in the colony and Ontario, the prime minister agreed to send an armed force to secure the Northwest.

THE MANITOBA ACT

The new province of Manitoba, as defined in the Manitoba Act, included geographically only the 35 000 km² around the Red River settlement and Portage la Prairie to the west. The rest of the area became the North-West Territories. Manitoba obtained its own legislative assembly, four federal members of Parliament, and two senators.

But, unlike the other provinces in Confederation, Ottawa denied Manitoba control over its own public lands and natural resources. These remained under the federal government's control, to be used "for the purposes of the Dominion."

The Manitoba Act also addressed the linguistic and educational rights of the French-speaking population. In 1867 the Fathers of Confederation had not discussed the rights of French Canadians outside the province of Quebec. In particular, they had made no provision in the BNA Act for constitutional rights for French-speaking Canadians in new provinces joining Confederation. Thus, Manitoba became the test case. Should French be recognized as an official language? Should separate schools be permitted in provinces with a sizable Roman Catholic population at the time of union with Canada? The Manitoba Act recognized both French and English as official languages. It also established a confessional school system on the Quebec model, with separate Protestant and Catholic divisions.

Basing their opinion on the Manitoba Act, some historians have argued that the Fathers of Confederation intended to create a bilingual and bicultural country in which French-speaking Canadians would have linguistic and educational rights equal to those of English-speaking Canadians. Other historians disagree. Donald Creighton, for example, has argued that no evidence exists that the Fathers of Confederation, particularly Macdonald, intended to create a bilingual and bicultural nation. Macdonald agreed to French-language rights and separate schools only because he was being pressured by a "dictatorial Riel"[2] to act quickly; otherwise Canada might lose the Northwest to American expansionists. Creighton maintains that the "Act for the Temporary Government of Rupert's Land and the North-West Territory," drawn up in the spring of 1869, rather than the Manitoba Act, more accurately reflected Macdonald's and the Canadian government's views. This earlier act, he points out, contained no reference to separate schools.

In a rebuttal to Creighton, historian Ralph Heintzman points out that this earlier act was only temporary and therefore not expected to spell out in detail the nature of the new province.[3] He considers the Manitoba Act to be more representative of the Canadian government's views. He also goes on to argue that in its agreement on language and educational rights for French-speaking Manitobans, the Manitoba Act reflected the ongoing "spirit of Confederation" that was evident between English-speaking and French-speaking Canadians at the time of Confederation.

THE WOLSELEY EXPEDITION

Manitoba's entry into Confederation did not end the tensions in the region. In the spring of 1870, Macdonald sent out the promised military force under Lieutenant Colonel Garnet Wolseley. As the troops approached, Riel got word of their arrival and fled. Upon finding Fort Garry abandoned, Wolseley reported in his diary: "Personally, I was glad that Riel did not come out and surrender, as he at one time said he would, for I could not then have hanged him as I might have done had I taken him prisoner when in arms against his sovereign." Riel had left, convinced that he had achieved a great victory for his people. He had won them provincial status, as well as land and cultural rights. Among those land rights was the agreement to set aside a reserve of 600 000 ha for the Métis and their children.

Riel's victory proved transitory, however. Migrants from the rest of Canada, particularly Ontario, quickly moved into Manitoba and took over land once occupied by the Métis. One group of Ontarians seized Métis land on the Rivière aux Ilets de Bois and, in a symbolic gesture of defiance, renamed the river "the Boyne," after William of Orange's decisive victory over the Roman Catholics in Ireland on July 12, 1690. Ontarians soon dominated the political, economic, and social life of the new province. They also worked to eliminate the land and cultural rights of the Métis population. They introduced amendments to the Manitoba Act that made it difficult for the Métis to prove that they owned the land. Discouraged, many Métis left the province and went farther west into either the North-West Territories or the Dakotas and Montana.

BRITISH COLUMBIA ENTERS CONFEDERATION

WEB LINKS

With the Northwest secured, the Canadian government now considered negotiating with the colony of British Columbia. Although First Nations constituted the majority of the population in this Pacific coast colony, no one thought to consult them about Confederation. Over the years, two separate colonies had evolved, one on Vancouver Island and the other on the mainland. In 1866, the two united into the single colony of British Columbia. The united colony now had three options: remain a separate British colony, join the United States, or unite with Canada.

Economically, British Columbia was tied closely to the United States. Many of its business firms were branches of American establishments. Much of the colony's trade of its raw materials was to the south. In addition, the colony communicated with the outside world via the United States. American vessels, for example, provided the only regular steamship service. Mail required both local and American stamps on letters abroad because it travelled by way of San Francisco. When railways made transcontinental travel feasible, an American line, the Union Pacific, completed in 1869, provided British Columbia with connections to the Atlantic seaboard.

Despite the strong American influence, British loyalties remained firm. Indeed, according to historian Hugh Johnston, the non-Native population saw British Columbia as "a British outpost on the edge of an American frontier."[4] The Royal Navy provided protection. The colonial government followed British parliamentary tradition. It also had a predominance of British politicians, from the governor to the majority of representatives in the legislative council. By contrast the Americans, although large in numbers, had relatively few representatives in government.

British Columbia had only limited ties to Canada. Few Canadians resided in the colony. Nor did any overland route exist to link this West Coast colony to the rest of British North America. Nevertheless, those Canadians who did reside in the colony constituted an influential and vocal minority: Amor de Cosmos ("Lover of the Universe," alias William Smith) would become premier in 1872, while John Robson headed the Confederation movement in the colonial assembly. Prime Minister Macdonald corresponded with these pro-Confederation politicians. As well, Macdonald had the British government appoint Anthony Musgrave, the governor of Newfoundland and a known supporter of Canadian Confederation, as the new governor of British Columbia when Governor Seymour, who had opposed union, died in 1869. The Colonial Office agreed, since the British government wanted to lessen its commitment to its West Coast colony without losing it to the United States.

British Columbia's settler population was very small in the 1870s. This photo, taken outside the legislative buildings in Victoria, shows the entire British Columbia civil service in 1878.

British Columbia Archives/HP-17826.

Britain valued British Columbia as a link in its "all red route to the Orient" — an imperial trading network tying Britain to India and China through British territory. In convincing British Columbia to join its other British North American colonies, Britain could achieve both objectives. William Gladstone, Britain's prime minister at the time, argued that Victoria, as "the San Francisco of British North America," could achieve greater commercial and political power as part of Canada than as "the capital of the isolated colony of British Columbia."

THE CANADIAN GOVERNMENT NEGOTIATES

Soon after taking office, Governor Musgrave appointed a three-member delegation to open up negotiations with the Canadian government. The committee drew up its list of demands. British Columbia would consider joining Confederation if the Canadian government agreed to: assume the colony's $1 million debt; implement responsible government in the province; undertake a public-works program; and complete a road to link British Columbia with the rest of the country.

The British Columbia delegation found a receptive audience in Ottawa. A committee headed by George-Étienne Cartier agreed to all the demands. Ottawa would assume the provincial debt and would request Britain to implement responsible government. It would undertake a public-works program that would include underwriting a loan to build a dry dock and maintaining a naval station at Esquimalt. In addition, the Canadian government promised not just a road but a railway, to be begun within two years of British Columbia's entry into Confederation and completed within ten years. It was a most ambitious promise. The United States, with ten times Canada's population, had only recently, and with great difficulty, built its first transcontinental railway.

1867

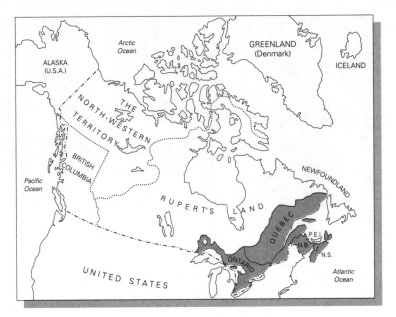

1870

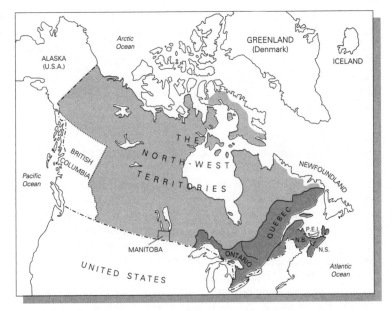

*Canada's territorial evolution from a nation of four provinces (1867),
to five (1870), to seven (1873), and to nine (1905).*

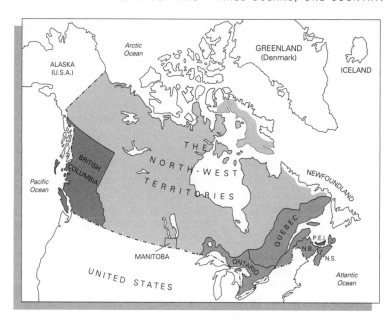

1873

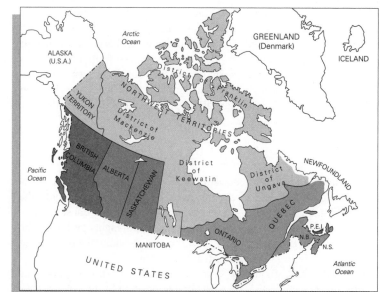

1905

Source: These maps are based on information taken from National Topographic System map sheet number MCR 2306. © 1969, Her Majesty the Queen in Right of Canada with permission of Energy, Mines and Resources Canada.

On July 20, 1871, British Columbia joined Confederation. Canada now stretched from the Atlantic Ocean to the Pacific Ocean. In the same year, by the Treaty of Washington, Britain and the United States confirmed the borders between Canada and the United States, ending the threat of an American seizure of lands above the 49th parallel.

The agreement with British Columbia left one important issue unresolved, that of Aboriginal lands. At the time of British Columbia's entry into Confederation, land treaties had been concluded for only a tiny portion of Vancouver Island. In 1873, the federal government requested British Columbia to acknowledge Aboriginal land title and to increase the allotment of reserve land for a family of five from 10 to 80 acres (4 to 32 ha). Premier George Walkem objected, claiming that the Native peoples already had enough land. His government reflected the prevailing attitude of the time that the Native peoples never owned the land, that ownership was a right reserved for non-Native settlers only.

AN UNWILLING NEWFOUNDLAND AND A RELUCTANT PRINCE EDWARD ISLAND

Only Newfoundland and Prince Edward Island remained as potential new provinces. Of the two, Newfoundland seemed more likely to join Confederation. Although the colony had not sent representatives to the Charlottetown Conference in September 1864, it did send two representatives — Frederick B.T. Carter, leader of the opposition, and Ambrose Shea, Speaker of the House of Assembly — to the Quebec Conference a month later. Both men became converts to Confederation, especially after hearing the generous financial terms that Macdonald and the other representatives from the Canadas promised Newfoundland in Confederation. But neither they nor the governor of Newfoundland, H.W Hoyes, could persuade a dubious public, especially the merchants in St. John's and the Roman Catholic population, about the benefits of Confederation.

OPPOSITION TO CONFEDERATION IN NEWFOUNDLAND

WEB LINKS

In the 1860s, Newfoundland had little association with the other British North American colonies. Many Newfoundlanders believed that their island's destiny lay to the east — the Atlantic Ocean and Britain — rather than to the west in a transcontinental nation. Their economy was based on cod fishing and sealing. Eighty percent of the island's working population earned its living from the sea. Newfoundlanders traded with Britain and the West Indies, not with British North America.

Newfoundland Roman Catholics opposed joining Confederation because they feared that a wider union would offset their favourable position in the colony. They had their own government-funded schools, which many believed a union with "Protestant Ontario" might threaten. Also, Irish Catholics saw Confederation as comparable to the unfavourable union of Ireland and England.

Union with Canada became the chief campaign issue in the election of 1869. Charles Fox Bennett, a St. John's merchant, headed the anti-Confederation faction. He pointed out the negative economic consequences of Confederation: Canadian taxes on boats and fishing gear, and exploitive competition from the mainland. He reminded Newfoundlanders of Nova Scotia's opposition to Confederation, while

St. John's, around 1890. Its harbour and the heavily settled part of the island faced the Atlantic Ocean and Britain, not the North American continent and Canada.

Provincial Archives of Newfoundland and Labrador/B4-25.

injecting his own strong dose of local Newfoundland nationalism. As one contemporary folk song ran:

> Would you barter the rights that your fathers have won?
> No! Let them descend from father to son,
> For a few thousand dollars Canadian gold,
> Don't let it be said that our birthright was sold.
> Newfoundland's face turns to Britain
> Her back to the Gulf.
> Come near at your peril
> Canadian wolf!

Pro-Confederationists appeared on the defensive. They could only present union with Canada as an uncertain alternative to the current depressed economy of Newfoundland rather than as a bold positive move. Furthermore, an improved sealing and fishing season in 1869 worked against their cause. In the end, Newfoundlanders rejected Confederation, with nineteen seats in the colonial assembly going to anti-confederates and only eight to confederates. According to one account, as soon as the election results became known,

> the fishermen and mechanics of St. John's ... put together a large coffin labelled "Confederation," which was placed on a vehicle draped in black, and this was drawn by scores of willing hands through the town, headed by a band playing the Dead March, and escorted by an immense crowd, to the head of the harbour, where a grave was dug below highwater mark and the coffin solemnly interred.

That defeat effectively ended the Confederation debate in Newfoundland for the next 25 years.

OPPOSITION TO CONFEDERATION IN PRINCE EDWARD ISLAND

Initially, Prince Edward Island opposed Confederation more strongly than did Newfoundland. Its representatives at the Charlottetown and Quebec conferences had pressed the Canadian delegates the furthest on the possible negative effects of Confederation for the Maritime region. Furthermore, only recently had some islanders succeeded in freeing themselves from absentee landlords who had extracted onerous rents from them. They had no desire to substitute a new set of landlords — Canadian proprietors — for the ones they had just lost. Even pressure through the Colonial Office failed to persuade the islanders to join Confederation. If anything, economic union with the United States had more appeal to many islanders, who saw it as a possible return to the prosperity the island had enjoyed during the period of the Reciprocity Treaty (1854–66). In 1868, American congressman Benjamin Butler visited Charlottetown to negotiate a reciprocal trade agreement.

Fear of an American annexation of Prince Edward Island led Prime Minister Macdonald to reopen negotiations. Late in 1869 he extended another invitation to the islanders to join Confederation. He agreed to more generous financial terms than in 1864; guaranteed communication and transportation links with the mainland; and promised islanders assistance in buying off the remaining British absentee landlords who still owned large tracts. At the same time, the Canadian prime minister convinced Britain to block a reciprocal trade agreement between Prince Edward Island and the United States. Yet the islanders still resisted.

By the early 1870s, however, financial problems on Prince Edward Island made Confederation more appealing. A coalition government headed by J.C. Pope had embarked in 1871 on an ambitious railway-building scheme that threatened to push the island into bankruptcy In 1872, work on the railway ceased for lack of funds. The Union Bank of Prince Edward Island, which held large numbers of the railway debentures, feared a financial collapse and appealed for assistance. The London financiers replied that the island would be in a better negotiating position if it joined Canada.

This time Charlottetown approached Ottawa. In early 1873, the Canadian government renewed its earlier offer: to assume the island's debt; to pay the annual interest on an $800 000 imperial loan; to provide a special subsidy of $45 000 to buy out the absentee landowners and thus bring all land under provincial control; and to take over the railway guarantee. As well, it promised to establish and maintain an efficient all-year steamer service between the island and the mainland.

In the election of April 1873, the choice became Confederation or the imposition of increased taxes to pay off the debt. In the end, provincial debt and railways were the real "Fathers of Confederation" in Prince Edward Island.

On July 1, 1873, Prince Edward Island joined the Dominion of Canada as its seventh province. The Charlottetown newspaper, the *Patriot*, recorded the public's response:

> On Tuesday, July 1st, whether for weal or woe, Prince Edward Island became a province of the Dominion of Canada. At 12 o'clock noon, the Dominion flag was run up on the flag staffs at Government House and the Colonial Building, and a salute of 21 guns was fired from St. George's battery and from HMS *Spartan* now in port. The church and city bells rang out a lively peal, and the volunteers under

review at the city park fired a *feu de joie*. So far as powder and metal could do it, there was for a short time a terrible din. But among the people who thronged the streets there was no enthusiasm.

With the exception of Newfoundland and the Arctic archipelago, Macdonald had now completed the consolidation of British North America.

Initially, Canada had no interest in the Arctic archipelago, seeing it only as a frozen wasteland. Britain had secured a prior claim to the region as a result of the sixteenth- and seventeenth-century journeys of Martin Frobisher, John Davis, and William Baffin, as well as the mid-nineteenth-century British naval expeditions in search of Sir John Franklin, whose party of more than 100 had disappeared in the mid-1840s in an attempt to find the Northwest Passage. In July 1880, the British government transferred title to its Arctic "possessions" to Canada, once again without bothering to consult the Native peoples in the region.

Three oceans, one country — in just thirteen years, Canada had become Britain's largest colony. In the first decade after Confederation, the Dominion of Canada acquired three new provinces and an enormous geographical area. Fear of American encroachment was a factor in its rapid expansion, but internal economic pressures such as the need for more land for agricultural development, the necessity of east–west trade, and a growing railway-building program also contributed. By 1880, Canada had become a transcontinental nation. Now came the challenge of working out new Dominion–provincial relations, reconciling regional differences, and creating a Dominion-wide economic policy.

NOTES

1. Chester Martin, *Dominion Lands Policy* (Toronto: McClelland & Stewart, 1973), p. 9.
2. Donald G. Creighton, "Macdonald, Confederation, and the West," in *Towards the Discovery of Canada: Selected Essays* (Toronto: Macmillan, 1972), p. 234.
3. Ralph Heintzman, "The Spirit of Confederation: Professor Creighton, Biculturalism, and the Use of History," *Canadian Historical Review* 52 (1971): 267–68.
4. Hugh Johnston, "Native People, Settlers and Sojourners, 1871–1916," in H.J.M. Johnston, ed., *The Pacific Province: A History of British Columbia* (Vancouver: Douglas & McIntyre, 1996), p. 177.

LINKING TO THE PAST

The Rupert's Land Act, 1869
http://www.miredespa.com/wmaton/Other/Legal/Constitutions/Canada/English/rpl_1868.html
The full text of the Rupert's Land Act of 1869, which expanded Canada to include parts of the Northwest formerly controlled by the Hudson's Bay Company.

Louis Riel
http://library.usask.ca/northwest/background/riel.htm
A detailed biography of Louis Riel, who led the 1869 Métis resistance to the sale of Rupert's Land.

The Manitoba Act, 1870

http://insight.mcmaster.ca/org/efc/pages/law/cons/Constitutions/Canada/English/ma_1870.html

The full text of the Manitoba Act of 1870. A compromise between the Canadian government and the Métis on Rupert's Land, this act brought Manitoba into Confederation as the first new province.

British Columbia Terms of Union

http://www.miredespa.com/wmaton/Other/Legal/Constitutions/Canada/English/bctu.html

The original document detailing the terms of union under which British Columbia was admitted into Confederation.

Proposed Terms of Union, 1869

http://www.geocities.com/Yosemite/Rapids/3330/constitution/1869prop.htm

A document showing the proposed terms of union between Canada and Newfoundland in 1869. The agreement was defeated, however, and Newfoundland did not raise the issue for another 25 years.

BIBLIOGRAPHY

Students interested in the Atlantic region's resistance to Confederation should consult Ged Martin, *Britain and the Origins of Canadian Confederation, 1837–67* (London: Macmillan, 1995); and his edited collection, *The Causes of Canadian Confederation* (Fredericton: Acadiensis, 1990). For Nova Scotia also see R.H. Campbell, "The Repeal Agitation in Nova Scotia, 1867–1869," *Nova Scotia Historical Society Collections* 25 (1942): 95–130; George Rawlyk, ed., *The Atlantic Provinces and the Problems of Confederation* (St. John's: Breakwater, 1979); and Colin D. Howell, "Nova Scotia's Protest Tradition and the Search for a Meaningful Federalism," in David J. Bercuson, ed., *Canada and the Burden of Unity* (Toronto: Macmillan, 1977), pp. 169–91. Joseph Howe's views are presented in J. Murray Beck, *Joseph Howe*, vol. 2, *The Briton Becomes Canadian, 1848–1873* (Montreal/Kingston: McGill-Queen's University Press, 1983), and in Beck's booklet *Joseph Howe: Anti-Confederate* (Ottawa: Canadian Historical Association, 1965). A very good summary of historical developments in the Atlantic region since 1867 is E.R. Forbes and D.A. Muise, eds., *The Atlantic Provinces in Confederation* (Toronto: University of Toronto Press, 1993). On Newfoundland's resistance to Confederation see James Hiller, "Confederation Defeated: The Newfoundland Election of 1869," in *Newfoundland in the Nineteenth and Twentieth Centuries: Essays in Interpretation* (Toronto: University of Toronto Press, 1980), pp. 67–94; and the relevant section in Frederick W. Rowe, *A History of Newfoundland and Labrador* (Toronto: McGraw-Hill Ryerson, 1980). Francis Bolger reviews Prince Edward Island's decision to join Canada in *Prince Edward Island and Confederation* (Charlottetown: St. Dunstan's University Press, 1964). Popular studies are Donald Weale and Harry Baglole, *The Island and Confederation: The End of an Era* (Charlottetown: Williams & Crue, 1973); and the chapter entitled "Confederation" in D.O. Baldwin, *Land of the Red Soil: A Popular History of Prince Edward Island* (Charlottetown: Ragweed Press, 1990). Ronald Tallman, "Annexation in the Maritimes? The Butler Mission to Charlottetown," *Dalhousie Review* 53 (1973): 97–112, shows the American influence, which almost caused Prince Edward Island to reject Confederation.

Alvin C. Gluek, *Minnesota and the Manifest Destiny of the Canadian Northwest: A Study in Canadian–American Relations* (Toronto: University of Toronto Press, 1965), examines American annexationist sentiments toward the Canadian Northwest. On the Riel resistance, see W.L. Morton's introduction to *Alexander Begg's Red River Journal* (Toronto: Champlain Society, 1956); see also George F.G. Stanley, *The Birth of Western Canada* (London: Longmans, Green, 1936; rep. Toronto: University of Toronto Press, 1960), and Stanley's *Louis Riel* (Toronto: Ryerson Press, 1963); and J.M. Bumsted, *The Red River Rebellion* (Winnipeg: Watson & Dwyer, 1996). On the military expedition see George F.G. Stanley, *Toil and Trouble: Military Expeditions to Red River* (Toronto: Dundurn Press, 1989). Hartwell Bowsfield's *Louis Riel: The Rebel and the Hero* (Toronto: Oxford University Press, 1971) is a short popular biography. Bowsfield has also edited a collection of articles on Riel entitled *Louis Riel: Selected Readings* (Toronto: Copp Clark Pitman, 1988). All of Riel's writings have been edited by George F.G. Stanley et al., *The Collected Writings of Louis Riel*, 5 vols. (Edmonton: University of Alberta Press, 1985). On Manitoba's entry into Confederation see W.L. Morton, *Manitoba: A History* (Toronto: University of Toronto Press, 1957); Donald G. Creighton, "John A. Macdonald, Confederation and the Canadian West," *Historical and Scientific Society of Manitoba*, 3rd series, no. 23 (1966–67), reprinted in Donald G. Creighton, *Towards the Discovery of Canada: Selected Essays* (Toronto: Macmillan, 1972), pp. 229–37; and Ralph Heintzman, "The Spirit of Confederation: Professor Creighton, Biculturalism, and the Use of History," *Canadian Historical Review* 52 (1971): 245–75. Three studies on the Métis in the Red River and Manitoba in the late nineteenth century are Thomas Flanagan, *Métis Lands in Manitoba* (Calgary: University of Calgary Press, 1991); Frits Pannekoek, *A Snug Little Flock: The Social Origins of the Riel Resistance 1869–70* (Winnipeg: Watson & Dwyer, 1991); and Gerhard Ens, *Homeland to Hinterland: The Changing Worlds of the Red River Métis in the Nineteenth Century* (Toronto: University of Toronto Press, 1996).

On British Columbia and Confederation see Margaret Ormsby, *British Columbia: A History* (Toronto: Macmillan, 1958), and Ormsby's "Canada and the New British Columbia," *Canadian Historical Association Report* (1948): 74–85. W. George Shelton's *British Columbia and Confederation* (Victoria: Morriss Printing [for the University of Victoria], 1967) is a worthwhile collection of essays. See also Jean Barman, *The West Beyond the West: A History of British Columbia* (Toronto: University of Toronto Press, 1991) and Hugh J.M. Johnston, ed., *The Pacific Province: A History of British Columbia* (Vancouver: Douglas & McIntyre, 1996).

For maps and charts see L.R. Gentilcore et al., eds., *Historical Atlas of Canada*, vol. 2, *The Land Transformed, 1800–1891* (Toronto: University of Toronto Press, 1993).

CHAPTER THREE

A "National Policy"?

"The future of Canada depends very much upon the cultivation of a national spirit." So spoke Edward Blake, the premier of Ontario and future leader of the Liberal party, in 1874. Over a century later, the challenge of creating a national spirit in such a large and diverse country remains the one constant in Canadian life. Both the rise of the Canada First Movement in English-speaking Canada and the presence of the Ultra-montanes in Quebec revealed the new Dominion's deep ethnic and religious divisions in the 1870s.

In the late nineteenth century no agreement existed on the definition of a Canadian. When French-speakers referred in French to "Canadians," it was to themselves alone. They called English-speakers *les Anglais*. English-speakers, in turn, considered themselves to be the only Canadians and termed those speaking French as French Canadians. The Native peoples did not use the term "Canadians" to describe themselves because they had their own designations for their own nations, such as Dene, Anishinabe (Ojibwa), or Innu (Montagnais), names which meant "people" or "human beings" in their languages.

Could common economic goals and interests unite Canadians? John A. Macdonald's Conservative government believed so. In 1879, his party set out to create a Dominion-wide economic policy of nation building based on a "National Policy" or national tariff to protect Canada's infant industries. Once in place, the Conservatives argued, the tariff would provide the capital to help pay the expenses of building the transcontinental railway. The railway, in turn, would foster east–west trade by linking an industrialized East with the soon-to-be-developed agricultural West. The growth of central Canadian industry, the settlement of the West, and the building of the transcontinental railway would create a nation. After 1896, the Liberals under Wilfrid Laurier accepted the Conservatives' policy.

EMERGING ENGLISH-CANADIAN AND FRENCH-CANADIAN EXPRESSIONS OF NATIONALISM

In the spring of 1868, five young English-speaking Canadian nationalists met in Ottawa to launch the Canada First Movement. Concerned about the lack of myths, symbols, and national spirit surrounding Confederation, they sought to identify and promote a nationalism for the new Dominion of Canada. They believed that Canada's greatness lay in its northern climate and rugged landscape, which combined to create a superior Anglo-Saxon race. They saw English-speaking Canadians as the "Northmen of the New World."

Neither French Canadians nor the Native peoples belonged in the Canada First Movement's vision of the new Dominion. In reality, "Canada First" meant "English Canada First." The members showed their true colours through their support of Dr. John Schultz and his group of Canadian expansionists in the Northwest who wanted to bring the Red River colony into Confederation as a "new Ontario." Their divisive brand of nationalism or Canadian-ness placed French Canadians against English Canadians, and the Native peoples against non-Natives. Canada Firsters refused to concede that several "nationalisms," not one, existed in Canada.

While Canada First sought a British and Protestant Canada, many French Canadians wanted a French-speaking, Roman Catholic nation. In the late nineteenth century, Quebec became more French and Catholic than it had been since the time of New France. The provincial government cultivated closer ties with France under Napoleon III, especially after the French helped to protect the papal lands in central Italy against Giuseppe Garibaldi's army, which was fighting for the unification of Italy. Five hundred volunteer soldiers, the *Zouaves*, or "mercenaries of the Lord," left Quebec between 1868 and 1870 to serve in the papal army.

Ignace Bourget, the influential bishop of Montreal, and his disciple, Louis-François Laflèche, later named the second bishop of Trois-Rivières, led the ultramontane movement within the Roman Catholic church. Laflèche set down the basic principles of its nationalism in 1866:

> A nation is constituted by unity of speech, unity of faith, uniformity of morals, customs, and institutions. The French Canadians possess all these, and constitute a true nation. Each nation has received from Providence a mission to fulfill. The mission of the French Canadian people is to constitute a centre of Catholicism in the New World.

Ultramontanes believed in the subordination of the state to the church. In their view, the pope constituted the supreme authority over religious and civil matters. Bourget reminded his followers in a circular in 1876: "Let us each say in his heart, 'I hear my *curé*, my *curé* hears the bishop, and the bishop hears the Pope, and the Pope hears our Lord Jesus Christ.'"

Resistance to the ultramontanes arose in the Institut canadien, begun in 1844 in Montreal. Later, other centres founded branches of the Institut canadien throughout Lower Canada. French-Canadian professionals initially organized the branches to serve as literary societies and debating clubs. They encouraged free thought and sponsored their own libraries free of church censorship. Many of the Institut's members had been influenced by the writings of such French liberal thinkers as Voltaire, Rousseau, and Montesquieu, as well as by British writers such as Bentham and Mill. They believed in the separation of church and state. Many members of the Institut canadien supported the parti rouge in the 1850s and, after the demise of the parti rouge, became Liberals.

Recruits for the Zouaves needed a letter of recommendation from their parish priest. They had to be unmarried, or widowers without young children, and between the ages of 15 and 40. The photo shows nine Quebec papal Zouaves in Italy in 1868.

Archives de la chancellerie de l'Archevêché de Montréal/ACAM-FP-Zouaves pontificaux.

THE GUIBORD AFFAIR

Bishop Bourget attempted to silence the opposition. He denied the sacraments to members of the Institut, including the right of burial in consecrated ground. When Joseph Guibord, a former vice-president of Montreal's Institut canadien, died in November 1869, the Roman Catholic church refused to give him a Christian burial. Since the case addressed the larger issue of civil versus ecclesiastical supremacy, the Institut supported Henriette Brown Guibord, his widow, when she took her local *curé* to court. As the case proceeded through the various appeal courts, Guibord's coffin rested for six years in a vault in Montreal's Mount Royal cemetery. Finally the Judicial Committee of the Privy Council, the supreme law court in the British empire, ruled in 1874 that burial was a civil right.

The controversy over Guibord's burial continued, however. During one attempt to bury him in September 1875, a thousand protesters met the funeral procession at the cemetery gates and tried to force it back by throwing stones and brandishing clubs. The *Times* of London reported that these events had created "a state of something like a civil war" in Montreal. Guibord's widow had died in 1873 and has been peacefully buried in the family plot in the Catholic cemetery. Friends of her late husband now demanded that he be allowed to join her in their final resting place. This time, with an escort of more than 1200 militiamen and regular soldiers, they succeeded. They placed Guibord's coffin on top of his wife's grave in poured cement to prevent vandalism. Immediately, Bourget deconsecrated Guibord's plot, although he left his wife's, only centimetres beneath his body, in a state of grace. Guibord's body still lies in unconsecrated soil in Montreal's Côte des Neiges cemetery, near today's Université de Montréal.

The ultramontanes began a political movement in 1871. They issued a *Programme catholique*, which proclaimed the church's right to advise Roman Catholics on how to vote. Catholics were expected to vote for the *bleus* (Conservatives), blessed with the colour of heaven, and not for the *rouges* (Liberals), damned by the colour of the fires of hell. In all cases, the ultramontanes favoured candidates who endorsed the church's views on marriage, education, and social order. A number of French-Canadian politicians, including such Conservatives as George-Étienne Cartier and Joseph-Adolphe Chapleau, opposed this mixing of religion and politics.

By 1870, extreme and conflicting nationalisms had surfaced in both English- and French-speaking Canada. These movements reflected an attempt on the part of extremists in both linguistic groups to define a nation in cultural, rather than political, terms.

LIBERAL RULE: 1873–1878

The Conservatives won the federal election of 1872, but just one year later a political scandal broke. It was revealed that Macdonald and Cartier had accepted more than $300 000 in campaign funds from Sir Hugh Allan, president of a large shipping concern, whose newly created Canada Pacific Company was a major contender for the government charter to build the transcontinental railway promised to British Columbia. The major financial backing for Allan's group came from the United States.

An American railway tycoon, angry at having been left out of the consortium, supplied the Liberal opposition with the incriminating evidence of a financial kickback to the Conservatives from Allan and his American backers. While donations of this sort were part of the political customs of the day, one of this magnitude was not. The Liberals accused the Conservatives of immorality and corruption. Macdonald denied involvement: "These hands are clean," he assured the House of Commons in one of the best speeches of his political career. But fearing a want-of-confidence vote, he announced his cabinet's resignation on November 5. The governor general asked the Liberals to form a government, which they did without an election being held. Then, in January 1874, the new prime minister, Alexander Mackenzie, dissolved Parliament and called an election, which the Liberals won.

LIBERAL LEADERSHIP

WEB LINKS

Alexander Mackenzie, a poor farmer's son, was born in Scotland, not far from Macdonald's birthplace in Glasgow. He came to Canada at the age of 20 and worked as a stonemason. The acerbic political critic Goldwin Smith once remarked that if Mackenzie's strong point as prime minister consisted in his having been a stonemason, his weak point consisted in his being one still: cold, hard, and colourless.

Mackenzie inherited numerous political problems. For one thing, the Liberal party had little internal unity. Rather than being a party, it was more a free-wheeling coalition of factions — *rouges*, Clear Grits, and Liberal Reformers — who had come together less out of a sense of common philosophy or a unified party platform than out of a common dislike for the Conservatives and their program. The Liberals deeply distrusted "big business interests," while idealizing rural life. Endorsing the farmers' viewpoint on the tariff, they favoured free trade over protection. They also argued for provincial rights.

The Liberal party needed a strong leader to pull its divergent groups together and to provide direction. George Brown had been such a leader — at least for English-speaking Liberals — but he had resigned after his defeat in the 1867 election; Alexander Mackenzie was not. The fact that a number of influential party members challenged Mackenzie's leadership compounded the problem. Brown lurked in the background; Richard Cartwright, a Conservative defector who left after Macdonald denied him the post of minister of finance, wanted a senior post; Antoine Dorion led the party's *rouge* faction and sought the role of Mackenzie's Quebec lieutenant. Finally, Mackenzie faced the enigmatic Edward Blake, former premier of Ontario (1871–72) and a brilliant parliamentary debater, but indecisive about whether or not to stay in the party.

THE LIBERALS' POLITICAL PROBLEMS

Mackenzie took office just as Canada entered an economic depression. Two months earlier, the North American and European financial boom of the 1860s and early 1870s broke. As trade declined, the federal debt increased sharply. Mackenzie responded by slowing down the railway-building scheme the government had inherited from the Conservatives, despite British Columbia's threat to leave the union over the government's broken promises. One of the major expenditures the Liberals incurred came from the establishment of the Royal Military College at Kingston, which opened its doors on June 1, 1876.

Due to the Dominion's economic depression, the Liberals concentrated on constitutional and political questions. In 1875, they established the Supreme Court of Canada as a national appeal court. While final appeal still rested with the Judicial Committee of the Privy Council in Britain and would continue to do so on civil matters until 1949, the Supreme Court became the first Canadian court to review Canadian laws. The Liberals also restricted the powers of the governor general, Britain's representative in Canada, by withdrawing his right to disallow legislation without consulting the Canadian Parliament.

Among political reforms, the Liberals introduced the secret ballot and the practice of holding the entire general election on the same day in each constituency across the country. They also closed the taverns on election day to reduce the possibility of buying votes for drinks. Controverted elections were transferred out of the hands of parliamentarians and into the courts. Mackenzie and his cabinet extended the federal franchise effectively to all non-Native males, whether they held property or not. The Liberals also ended the system of dual representation that allowed an individual to hold a federal and a provincial seat simultaneously.

THE NATIONAL POLICY OF JOHN A. MACDONALD

WEB LINKS

The Mackenzie administration lacked an economic agenda. It had wanted a reciprocity treaty with the United States similar to the one signed in 1854, and had in 1874 successfully drafted such a treaty. But the American Senate defeated the bill, leaving the Liberals without a viable commercial policy.

The Conservatives found an alternative. On the eve of the 1878 election, a lobbying group of the Canadian Manufacturers' Association convinced John A. Macdonald and the Conservative party to accept a protective system of higher tariffs. Increased import duties, they argued, would promote manufacturing in Canada, thus diversifying the Canadian economy. As Macdonald argued at the time, "We must by every reasonable means, employ our people, not in one branch of industry, not merely as farmers, as tillers of the soil, but we must bring out every kind of industry, we must

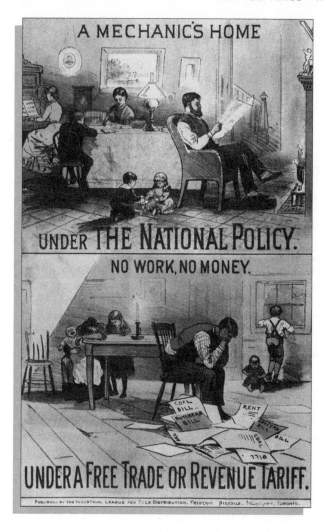

According to the National Policy's supporters, a high tariff meant prosperity (top); free trade meant unemployment and poverty.

....

National Archives of Canada/C-95466.

develop the minds of the people and their energies." They pointed out how import duties in Britain and the United States had enabled these countries to advance industrially and that, with a transcontinental railway, the same could happen in Canada. Western Canadian farmers could help their Ontario counterparts to feed the growing number of industrial workers in central Canada, who in turn could supply the farmers throughout Canada with agricultural equipment and other manufactured goods. Macdonald in turn convinced the electorate that the creation of an east–west economy provided the answer to the depression. In 1878 the Conservatives returned to power with a majority government.

This policy of nation building — the "national policy," as Macdonald called it — rested on three essentials: the National (capital N) Policy, or high protective tariff; the completion of a transcontinental railway; and the settlement of the West through immigration. In 1879, the Conservatives raised the tariff on textiles, iron and steel products, coal, and petroleum products by 10 to 30 percent, thus achieving their first objective of a high protective tariff. In their budget speech, the Conservatives referred to the tariff as the National Policy, an integral part of the larger "national policy" of nation building. By calling the protective tariff the National Policy, the Conservatives were suggesting that all Canadians would benefit and that Canada would become a nation in more than name only.

DEBATE OVER THE NATIONAL POLICY

Advocates of the National Policy argued at the time that a protective tariff was necessary to shift trade from a north–south to an east–west axis. The tariff would, in Macdonald's words, "make this union a union in interest, a union in trade, and a union in feeling." It would provide Canadians with their own national market, thus reducing their dependency on the United States. Furthermore, manufacturers — both Canadian and foreigners building plants in Canada — would ensure more jobs for Canadian workers, technicians, and managers.

In contrast, the Liberals argued that the tariff would erect a fiscal barrier around the country. Furthermore, they maintained that, while the tariff or National Policy was "National" in name, it was regional in interest. It served the needs of central Canadians alone, and more specifically, the needs of the manufacturers and industrialists of the urban centres of Ontario and Quebec, who could live off the bounty of the government. The tariff would serve only to heighten divisions between the various regions of the Dominion, placing the Maritimes and the West against Ontario and Quebec. Furthermore, it would put the burden of national unity on the hinterland regions, which would become the suppliers of raw materials for the prosperous metropolitan centres of central Canada. In social terms, a corresponding inequality would develop, since workers, farmers, and fishermen would have to pay a higher price for consumer goods, whether imported (as a result of the higher tariff) or produced in Canada (as a result of higher production costs). The Liberals drove home the point in a pamphlet they published in 1882:

> The farmer starting to his work has a shoe put on his horse with nails taxed 41 percent; with a hammer taxed 40 percent; cuts a stick with a knife taxed 27-1/2 percent; hitches his horse to a plough taxed 30 percent; with chains taxed 27-1/2 percent. He returns to his home at night and lays his wearied limbs on a sheet taxed 30 percent, and covers himself with a blanket on which he has paid 70 percent tax. He rises in the morning, puts on his humble flannel shirt taxed 60 percent, shoes taxed 30 percent, hat taxed 30 percent, reads a chapter from his Bible taxed 7 percent, and kneels to his God on a cheap carpet taxed 30 percent ... and then he is expected to thank John A. that he lives under the freest Government under heaven.

THE LIBERALS' NATIONAL POLICY

Despite Liberal opposition at the time of the implementation of the National Policy in 1879, the Liberal party under Wilfrid Laurier would adopt its own version of the National Policy in their first budget after coming to power in 1896. In 1897,

W.S. Fielding, the Liberal finance minister, introduced a tariff that maintained high duties on imported goods, such as textiles and iron and steel products coming from the United States, and goods from other countries that restricted the entry of Canadian goods. At the same time, the new policy lowered tariffs to any country admitting Canadian goods at a rate equal to the minimum Canadian tariff. As Britain already adhered to such a policy, it became known as the "British tariff."

BUILDING THE CANADIAN PACIFIC RAILWAY

A transcontinental railway, an indispensable part of nation building, was the second component of the national policy. Settlers wishing to go from Toronto to Manitoba via British territory in the 1870s, for example, had to travel by steamboat across the Great Lakes and over eastern Manitoba's lakes and rivers, with wagon journeys at the portages, then by wagon on the newly completed Dawson Road to Winnipeg, and finally by wagon on rough roads to their destination. The alternative was to go through the United States, where American immigration agents often succeeded in persuading Canadian travellers to settle in the American West. Furthermore, British Columbia's entry into Confederation depended on the "trail of iron" as the only means to link this isolated colony to central Canada. Finally, a transcontinental railway, it was felt, would permit Canada to compete with the United States as a great North American nation. Railways meant power in the nineteenth century, and power meant influence.

GOVERNMENT INVOLVEMENT IN RAILWAY BUILDING

The Canadian government had a history of involvement in railway building prior to the construction of the Canadian Pacific Railway (CPR). In the 1840s and 1850s, the government of the Canadas had gone into heavy debt to help finance the Grand Trunk Railway and other colonial lines. As part of the Confederation agreement, the Canadian government itself financed the extension of the Grand Trunk line, known as the Intercolonial Railway, from Rivière-du-Loup, the eastern terminus, to Halifax, adding substantially to the Dominion's debt.

Yet, despite the expense of the Intercolonial Railway, the Conservative government embarked on the even more ambitious and riskier railway to the Pacific Ocean. This line, which, when completed, would be two-thirds longer than any other single railway line then existing in the world, was projected to run through 5000 km of forest, prairies, and mountains to link together 3.5 million people scattered over vast distances. "An act of insane recklessness," protested Alexander Mackenzie in 1872, although his administration would be pressured into continuing the project. The building of the CPR took on the dimensions of a national dream — and, at times, the qualities of a political nightmare.

Why did the Conservative government agree to undertake this mammoth project? Several compelling reasons explain its decision. The United States in the past had threatened to annex the Northwest and was in a position to do so, especially after the completion of its first transcontinental, the Union Pacific Railway, in 1869. Only with a Canadian railway could the Dominion secure effective control over the region of the North-West Territories that it had acquired in 1869–70. Such a railway allowed Canada

Where Historians Disagree

THE NATIONAL POLICY

The national policy of high tariffs, railway building, and development of the West, first established by the Conservative government in the late nineteenth century, generated considerable debate at the time and much debate since among historians and economists. Donald Creighton spoke for many in the central Canadian national-ist tradition in arguing that the national policy, especially the protective tariff of 1879, was an essential component of Canada's growth as an independent nation. In *The Dominion of the North* (Toronto: Macmillan, 1957), Creighton writes: "In international affairs, the tariff asserted the principle of independence as against both Britain and the United States. In domestic matters, it expressed the hope for a new varied and self sufficient national life" (p. 346). In "The Nationalism of the National Policy" (*Readings in Canadian History: Post-Confederation*, 5th ed. [Toronto: Harcourt Brace, 1998]), Craig Brown notes the success of the national policy in instilling a feeling of nation-alism in Canada when traditional national symbols, such as a common language, a common cultural tradition, or a common religion, were absent.

Historian Ben Forster has noted how other factors — besides, or possibly instead of, nationalism — were important in shaping Canada's national policy. In *A Conjunction of Interests: Business, Politics, and Tariffs, 1825–1879* (Toronto: University of Toronto Press, 1986), he points to a wide range of political and economic factors and interests — including business, industry, agriculture, and government — as all having made a contribution from 1825 to 1879 in shaping the policy.

Economist John Dales has questioned the success of the national policy as a policy of nation building. In "Canada's National Policies" (*Readings in Canadian History: Post-Confederation*, 5th ed. [Toronto: Harcourt Brace, 1998]), Dales argues that the national policy was from the beginning a "dismal failure." Railway building became an expensive undertaking for the Canadian taxpayer through heavy govern-ment subsidies to the Canadian Pacific Railway Company, established in 1880 to build the transcontinental line. Second, immigration and the settlement of the West did not occur until well after the national policy was in place and then for reasons independent of the national policy itself. Third, the high tariff placed region against region. It also created an artificial climate for industrial growth that ironically made Canada more, not less, dependent on the United States through a branch-plant economy.

Historian Michael Bliss agrees that the protective tariff fostered the "American-ization of the Canadian economy," but points out that that was exactly what it was intended to do. "By 1911," he writes in "Canadianizing American Business: The Roots of the Branch Plant," in I. Lumsden, ed., *Close the 49th Parallel etc.: The Americaniza-tion of Canada* (Toronto: University of Toronto Press, 1970), the "concern ... was not to limit what had already been called an American 'invasion' of Canada, but rather to sustain and encourage the branch-plant phenomena" (p. 29).

Some historians in western Canada and the Maritimes have presented the negative impact of the National Policy of tariff protection, especially on their regions. In *Canada and the Burden of Unity* (Toronto: Macmillan, 1977), David Bercuson writes, "The ill effects [of the National Policy] abound: high prices for the manufactured

(continued)

products of Central Canada (added to by shipping costs) and the loss to East and West of significant commercial intercourse with New England and the northwestern areas of the United States" (pp. 3–4). It resulted in the growth of industry in central Canada at the expense of the hinterlands.

Economist Kenneth Norrie has countered this viewpoint in reference to western Canada. In "The National Policy and Prairie Economic Discrimination, 1870–1930" (in Donald Akenson, ed., *Canadian Papers in Rural History*, vol. 1 [Gananoque, ON: Langdale, 1978]), he argues that the lack of industrial development in the West had nothing to do with the National Policy and everything to do with the West's location — away from the heart of North American development — and its lack of a sufficient population base to make industrialization viable.

The debate on the National Policy received renewed vigour during the national debate over both the Canada–United States and the North American free-trade agreements in the late 1980s and early 1990s. Central to any discussion of the future of Canada, the National Policy will long be a subject of debate.

to compete with the United States as a great North American nation. It would also enable Canada to be a worthy member of the British empire by being part of a westerly "all red route to the Orient." Canadian politicians, moreover, believed in the resource potential of this vast territory. Two scientific expeditions into the Northwest, the British Palliser and the Canadian Hind expeditions in the late 1850s, reported that the Northwest contained millions of hectares of fertile land. Moreover, the promise to British Columbia of a transcontinental railway within ten years of the province's entry into Confederation obliged even the Liberal government to build it. Finally, the Red River Métis's resistance in 1869–70 (see Chapter Two) had made the Canadian government conscious of the need for quick military access to the region, which only a railway could provide.

THE SEARCH FOR A PRIVATE COMPANY

Macdonald's Conservative government initially favoured a private company to undertake the project. Before the depression of the mid-1870s, two companies competed for the contract: the Interoceanic Company of Toronto, headed by Senator David Macpherson and backed by British financiers; and the Canada Pacific Company, a Montreal consortium under Sir Hugh Allan, president of the Merchants' Bank, with American financial backing. Macdonald favoured a merger of the two companies, but neither Macpherson nor Allan would agree. The government awarded the contract to the Canada Pacific Company in return for generous financial contributions on Allan's part to the Conservative campaign fund in the election of 1872. The resulting Pacific Scandal forced the Macdonald Conservative government to resign and ended the short-lived Canada Pacific Company.

The new Liberal government continued the railway, but only on those sections where settlement warranted construction and only as public money became available, relying on waterways and even American lines to fill the gaps. To move slowly, however, meant reneging on the Conservatives' promise of completing the railway to

British Columbia in ten years. Edgar Dewdney, the surveyor and MP, responded: "The Terms, the Whole Terms and Nothing but the Terms." Already, British Columbia and railways had become inseparable.

When the Conservatives resumed office in 1878, an upturn in the economy enabled them to find a new private company, the Canadian Pacific Railway Company (CPR), made up of a group associated with the Bank of Montreal, headed by George Stephen, R.B. Angus, and Donald Smith. The syndicate agreed to build the railway across northern Ontario from Callander (near North Bay) to Port Arthur and from Winnipeg to Kamloops by May 1, 1891. In return, the government offered the new company $25 million in financing and 25 million acres (10 million ha) of land consisting of alternate sections not already sold in a belt nearly 40 km wide on both sides of the track across the Prairies. Land not "fit for settlement" could be exchanged for better land elsewhere. The company also obtained free of charge the 1200 km of track already completed or under construction, which had an estimated worth of $31 million. The government promised that construction materials would be exempt from duty. As well, CPR property and its capital stock would be free from taxation. Its grant of 10 million ha of land was also tax exempt for 20 years or until it was sold. Finally, the government agreed to a monopoly clause: no competing line could be built south of the main CPR line until 1900.

In Parliament, Liberals, and even some Conservative backbenchers, questioned the need for such generous terms. The two-month debate that followed proved one of the longest and most bitter in the history of Parliament. As popular historian Pierre Berton has pointed out, more than a million words were spoken, more than in the Bible's Old and New Testaments combined.[1] Yet Macdonald held his party together, and the Conservatives voted down the 25 amendments proposed by the Liberal opposition.

THE CPR ROUTE

The new CPR Company decided to alter the route of the railway from that proposed by Sandford Fleming's survey team in the early 1870s along the North Saskatchewan River and through the Yellowhead Pass to a southerly prairie route through Pile O' Bones Creek (Regina), Swift Current, Fort Calgary, and the Kicking Horse Pass. A number of reasons account for this sudden shift. First, the company feared that the Northern Pacific Railway would siphon off the trade of the southern prairies, bringing the region within the American sphere of influence. Second, Elliott Galt, the son of Alexander Galt, a Father of Confederation, had discovered coal deposits near Lethbridge that could be exploited as a source of fuel for the locomotives on the southern route. Third, John Macoun, a botanist and recent leader of a scientific expedition in the West who had visited the area during the wettest decade in more than a century, reported that the southern prairies were not the desert that John Palliser had earlier described. (Palliser had seen it in the 1850s, one of the driest periods.) Most important, the company hoped through the sudden switch to bypass speculators, who had bought up land along the proposed northern route. When speculators attempted to do the same along the southern route — guessing where divisional points and stations might be — the company arbitrarily changed its plans and placed stations and divisional points at spots not originally intended. In this way, the CPR retained control over the land profits to be made from Brandon to Revelstoke.

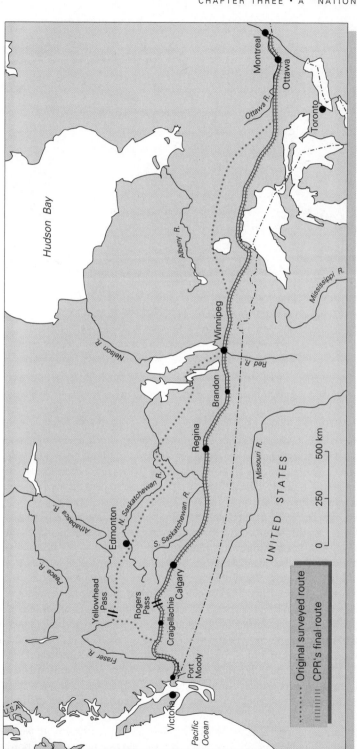

The original surveyed route and the final route of the CPR.

The CPR's Mountain Creek Bridge under construction in the Selkirks. Building the rail line through the mountain ranges proved one of the most challenging tasks facing the Canadian Pacific Railway Company, and cost the lives of hundreds of Chinese navvies.

Glenbow Archives, Calgary, Canada/NA-782-13.

Once the government confirmed the route, construction began. In 1881 the syndicate hired William Cornelius Van Horne, a robust, impetuous, and experienced American engineer, as general manager to oversee construction. Van Horne drove his men without mercy. He boasted that his construction gang, which at one time had 5000 workers and 1700 teams of horses, could lay 800 km of prairie track in a year. The line reached Calgary in August 1883. When asked the secret of his success, the hard-boiled Van Horne replied, "I eat all I can; I drink all I can; I smoke all I can and I don't give a damn for anything."

Still ahead lay the difficult mountain terrain. Surveyors had already chosen the Kicking Horse Pass through the Bow River valley, despite its steep incline, as the best route through the Rocky Mountains. Only late in the summer of 1882, however, did Major A.B. Rogers, an experienced railway surveyor, locate a pass that would allow the CPR to cross the more westerly Selkirk Mountains. He insisted that the pass bear his name. Difficulties abounded: laying track along the sides of mountains, blasting tunnels through rock, bridging swift mountain rivers. The construction of the British Columbia section, particularly that built by Andrew Onderdonk from Port Moody on the coast nearly 400 km into the interior, cost enormous amounts of time and money and took the lives of hundreds of the estimated 15 000 Chinese workers who had been hired as cheap labour. Chinese-Canadians had a saying that "for every foot of railway through the Fraser Canyon, a Chinese worker died." Onderdonk himself estimated that three Chinese died for every kilometre of track that was laid.

Construction costs rose because Van Horne insisted on the best materials to ensure long-term use. On Macdonald's insistence, he also had to build along the north

WEB LINKS

Chinese railway camp at Kamloops, British Columbia, 1886.

British Columbia Archives/67609.

shore of Lake Superior instead of relying on the inefficient waterway system or on competing American lines. This meant blasting through hundreds of kilometres of what Van Horne called "engineering impossibilities" — Precambrian rock. In addition, the company had to buy up eastern lines to connect the Pacific railway with Toronto and Montreal. When the CPR's construction boss was asked about the prospect of not having sufficient funds to complete the project, he replied, "If we haven't got enough, we'll get more, that's all about it." The money did come — from investors, from the sale of stock, and from bank loans. When these sources proved inadequate, the company turned to the only remaining source, the government.

In the summer of 1883, the syndicate needed an estimated $22.5 million — an enormous sum, almost an entire year's revenue for the federal government. Pressed by opposition within his own party against further concessions, Macdonald replied that the CPR might as well ask for the planet Jupiter. But J.H. Pope, Macdonald's secretary, reminded his leader: "The day the Canadian Pacific bursts, the Conservative party bursts the day after." Macdonald convinced his party to agree to another loan, but only after the CPR agreed to mortgage the entire main line, all the rolling stock, and everything else connected with the railway. The CPR also promised to make the railway even more political. It would provide more political appointments to jobs; secretly it would back several Conservative newspapers; and it would construct a terminus at Quebec City to please French-Canadian voters. The money kept construction going through 1884, but by the end of that year, the company once again plunged toward bankruptcy.

On the evening of March 26, 1885, George Stephen met with Macdonald to appeal for more government money. The prime minister turned him down. He knew his party would never agree to another loan. Stephen returned home convinced the railway would, after all, go under. Then, in the morning, came the extraordinary

The driving of the last spike, November 7, 1885, 9:30 A.M., at Craigellachie, British Columbia. The important CPR financial backer Donald A. Smith (later Lord Strathcona) holds the heavy spike hammer. Behind Smith stands white-bearded Sandford Fleming, former engineer-in-chief, to the left is the burly figure of W.C. Van Horne, CPR general manager.

Glenbow Archives, Calgary, Canada/NA-218-3.

news: the Métis had rebelled under Louis Riel, defeating the North-West Mounted Police in a battle near Duck Lake in the North-West Territories (see Chapter Four). Macdonald's luck had saved him once again. The uprising justified the railway. That day in Parliament, the government voted to send troops out on the railway to fight Riel and the Métis. It also introduced a bill to finance the remaining mountain section of the railway.

On November 7, 1885, Donald Smith drove in the last spike at Craigellachie, named for a rocky crag in Scotland where Smith grew up — a proud moment for all who had been involved in the project. The American-born Van Horne remarked that "to have built that road would have made a Canadian out of the German Emperor." He also boasted that a train could now make the trip from Montreal to Vancouver in a mere 85 hours, with a first-class ticket costing $123.35 (a railway labourer then earned $2 a day). In 1886, daily mail service was inaugurated across the nation. But the cost of such national pride was high. The Pacific railway cost the Canadian government 10.4 million ha of the best prairie land, an estimated $63.5 million in public funds, and government loans of $35 million. Yet as a private company it did very well, and it would by 1905 have capital of $228 million. While a technological wonder, it also became economically, in the words of its critics, a "crushing burden" or a "strangling octopus." Was the project worth the effort and the extra expense at the time? The North-West Rebellion of 1885 saved Macdonald from the necessity of answering that question. The CPR allowed for the immediate dispatch of over 3000 troops westward.

Most Canadians have seen the famous "Last Spike" photograph, but how many have viewed the workers' version? After the "big shots" departed, the construction crew, with the help of a friendly photographer, staged their own "Last Spike" ceremony.

Canadian Pacific Railway Company Collection/National Archives of Canada/C-14115.

TWO NEW TRANSCONTINENTAL RAILWAYS

During the economic boom of the Laurier era (1896–1911), Canada added two new transcontinental railways. The first was the Canadian Northern Railway. Begun by Donald Mann and William Mackenzie, two Ontario-born entrepreneurs, the company had built up sufficient financial strength by 1901 (through the building of branch lines and the incorporation of rival companies' near-defunct charters, which often included substantial land grants — a policy discontinued during the Laurier era) to expand transcontinentally. It applied for federal financial assistance to build from Port Arthur (now Thunder Bay) to Montreal. The second new transcontinental, the Grand Trunk Railway, an eastern-based company, wanted to build a line westward to profit from prairie grain traffic. The logical solution would have been for the two companies to co-operate, but both feared that the other would dominate in any joint venture. Laurier refused to force a merger, as he believed that the country could support three transcontinental railways. He assured Parliament: "This is a time for action. The flood tide is upon us that leads on to fortune; if we let it pass it may never recur again."

The Liberals backed the Grand Trunk. They even offered to build the difficult 2880-km-long eastern section of the railway, at government expense, through Ontario and Quebec to Moncton, New Brunswick. This section, known as the National Transcontinental, would be leased to the Grand Trunk for 50 years at a modest annual rate of 3 percent on construction costs. The first seven years of operation would be rent free. A new company, the Grand Trunk Pacific, a subsidiary of the Grand Trunk, would build the western section from Winnipeg to the Pacific. The federal government agreed to guarantee 75 percent of the bond money for its construction. Despite such financial support, the line was a failure, especially the British Columbia section — "the most expensive and least remunerative portion of the railway," according to historian Frank Leonard, due to "many actions, 'a thousand blunders,' which senior and junior GTP managers carried out."[2]

Meanwhile, Mann and Mackenzie went ahead with their transcontinental line, convinced that Ottawa would, if they encountered difficulties, assist them as well. As a result, in many areas of the West, these competing lines ran parallel to each other and sometimes within sight of one another. As historian T.D. Regehr notes, "a short distance west of Portage la Prairie, a traveller going north could cross eight parallel east–west lines within the space of 55 km."[3]

The Conservative opposition denounced the Liberals' railway-building scheme as a "$200 million vote catcher, designed to carry elections rather than passengers." Ultimately, both lines ended in bankruptcy. But in the meantime, the two companies added 18 000 km of prairie railway — six times more line than the CPR had when completed in 1885. It gave Canada the dubious distinction of having by 1914 more kilometres of rail line per capita than any other country in the world.

The new lines also opened up lucrative mining areas in northern Ontario and Quebec, and they provided employment for thousands during the construction and operational phases. It remains debatable, however, whether the tremendous cost to the Canadian taxpayer was justified. This is also true, of course, of the cost of public financing of the CPR from 1881 to 1885.

THE DOMINION'S STRATEGY FOR THE NORTHWEST

Development of the West constituted the third component of Macdonald's national policy. Without a populated West, no justification existed for a transcontinental railway; without a railway, east–west trade could not occur. And without internal trade, the National Policy of tariff protection was meaningless.

In preparation for settlement, the Canadian government surveyed the land into townships similar in size to those in the American West because this pattern was familiar to American immigrants. Each township was 36 square miles (92 km²) and consisted of 36 sections that were one square mile (2.6 km²) and contained 640 acres (259 ha) each. Sections were subdivided into more manageable quarter-sections of 160 acres (65 ha).

Not all land was available for settlement. The HBC had received "one twentieth of the land of the fertile belt" as part of the agreement of 1869–70. In Manitoba, the Canadian government appropriated, as part of the Manitoba Act of 1870, 1.5 million acres (600 000 ha), or one-seventh of the new province, for the benefit of the Métis. The CPR received 25 million acres (10 million ha), and other railway companies also

A Survey of a Standard Prairie Township

Source: D.G. Kerr, ed., *Historical Atlas of Canada* (Don Mills, ON: Nelson, 1981), p. 62.

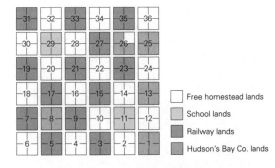

☐ Free homestead lands
▨ School lands
▧ Railway lands
▨ Hudson's Bay Co. lands

received land as part of their contracts until the practice ended in 1894. Additional land was set aside for schools and to compensate the HBC for its surrender of its charter to Rupert's Land in 1870. The remaining land belonged to the federal government to sell or to turn over to private land companies to sell.

To encourage settlement, the government passed the Dominion Lands Act in 1872. It provided 160 acres (65 ha) free to each head of family or 21-year-old male if he paid a $10 registration fee, resided on the land for three years, cultivated 30 acres (12 ha), and built a permanent dwelling. The government believed that free land would pay for itself by bringing in immigrants who would need consumer goods. This, in turn, would generate manufacturing and trade.

Women's rights in the West with regard to property were seriously curtailed. Married women did not qualify for free land under the Dominion Lands Act, and only a few widowed women succeeded in receiving the 160-acre land grant. In 1886, the North-West Territories government abolished a woman's right to the dower — a one-third interest in her husband's property upon widowhood. Western Canadian women protested this legislation for over thirty years before it was rescinded in 1917.

ESTABLISHING CANADIAN LAW IN THE NORTHWEST

To ensure peaceful settlement, the federal government established territorial courts and organized the North-West Mounted Police (NWMP). The 300 "Mounties" began their work in the Northwest in 1874 after a long and difficult march across the southern prairies. They established posts throughout the region. The most important were Fort Walsh in the Cypress Hills, Fort Macleod on the Old Man River, and Fort Calgary at the junction of the Bow and Elbow rivers. The NWMP administered Canadian law to the Native peoples, the whisky traders, and the early settlers in an area larger than western Europe. Their success lay in what they represented: their red tunics and white helmets symbolized British law and tradition, a collective as opposed to an individual authority. As the writer Wallace Stegner pointed out, "One of the most visible aspects of the international border [in the West] was that it was a colour line: blue below, red above, blue for treachery and unkept promises, red for protection and straight tongue."[4]

TREATIES WITH THE FIRST NATIONS

WEB
LINKS

Before settlement could proceed, the federal government had to negotiate treaties and place the Native peoples on reserves. The government adhered to the Royal Proclamation of 1763, which prohibited settlers from occupying territory that the First Nations had not first surrendered to the Crown. The Canadian government also made treaties to avoid the "Indian wars" that had occurred in the United States. Between 1871 and 1875, the government negotiated Treaties Number One to Five, affecting the Native peoples in what is now northwestern Ontario, Manitoba, and southern Saskatchewan. In 1876, Treaty Number Six was signed with the Cree of present-day central Saskatchewan and Alberta. The last of the treaties on the plains, Treaty Number Seven, followed in 1877 with the Blackfoot-speaking nations and the Sarcee (T'suu Tina) and Stoneys.

NWMP Commissioner James Macleod, standing second from right, with his men at Fort Walsh in the Cypress Hills, in what is now southwestern Saskatchewan, in the late 1870s. Macleod treated the Native peoples with dignity and respect. The Blackfoot called him "Stamixotokan," or "Bull's Head," and welcomed his promise of a new order.

Glenbow Archives, Calgary, Canada/NA-52-1.

According to the government's interpretation of the treaties, the First Nations agreed to "cede, release, surrender, and yield up to the Government ... all their rights, titles, and privileges whatsoever" to the lands in question forever in return for certain reserve lands, amenities, and the right to fish and hunt on Crown lands. In the case of Treaty Six, the government also promised federal government assistance in the event of "any pestilence" or "general famine," along with a "medicine chest" to be kept by every Indian agent. The Cree insisted on these additional rights because they could foresee the negative impact of disease and declining buffalo herds on their traditional way of life. The First Nations in the Treaty Seven area, in particular, envisioned the treaty as a pact of friendship, peace, and mutual support between the two parties. They did not intend on giving up their sovereignty. Among the Cree, who had a better idea of the meaning of the agreements than their Métis relatives, some believed the agreements allowed the newcomers only the use, not the ownership, of their land.

The federal government used the Indian Act of 1876, as amended in 1880, to oversee Native affairs. It legally viewed the First Nations peoples as minors or special wards of the Crown, without the privileges of citizenship. In this way, the government controlled all aspects of the Aboriginal peoples' lives. This became the task of the newly created Department of Indian Affairs and its Indian agents. As John A. Macdonald, its first minister, pointed out, "The great aim of our legislature has been to do away with the tribal system and assimilate the Indian people in all aspects with

Before and after: Propaganda photos used to promote the benefits of Native residential schools. From Thompson Ferrier, Indian Education in the North West *(Toronto: Department of Missionary Literature of the Methodist Church, 1906), pp. 4–5.*

National Archives of Canada/C-104585 and C-104586.

the inhabitants of the Dominion, as speedily as they are fit for the change." Both Conservative and Liberal governments pursued the same goal.

One way to achieve this objective was to promote "enfranchisement," or the relinquishment of Indian status by granting full citizenship privileges. Adult First Nations males, deemed of good character, free of debt, and fluent in English or French, could, after a probationary period of three years, apply to relinquish their treaty and statutory rights under the Indian Act, as well as their right to live in the reserve community. In return, they gained British citizenship with all legal privileges including the right to vote, as well as private ownership of their share of band reserve lands and funds. Initially, the Aboriginal peoples of western Canada were excluded from this procedure because the government considered them still too "uncivilized." Few of Canada's First Nations people, however, agreed to enfranchisement because it meant abandoning their reserves and relinquishing their traditional culture. Status Indian women who married non-Indians (whites, Métis, or Native people not governed by the Indian Act) had no choice in the matter. Under the Indian Act, they lost their Indian status automatically when they married.

Another way in which the government attempted to assimilate the Native people was by outlawing their cultural practices. Particularly offensive from the government's perspective was the potlatch, because it reinforced traditional Native beliefs and practices. The government used various tactics, including making it an offence in the amended Indian Act of 1884 "to encourage or participate in the potlatch." It instructed Indian agents to collect evidence to use in court cases, played off religiously

Frank Tried to Fly and George Left Hand, Blackfoot (Siksika) Indians, sowing seed by hand in the 1880s, North Camp, Blackfoot Reserve. Many Plains Indians made a determined effort to adjust to farming shortly after the demise of the buffalo.

Glenbow Archives, Calgary, Canada/NA-127-1.

converted Native people who opposed the potlatch against traditionalists, and used extortion to pry ceremonial regalia from West Coast Native people. In the end, however, the potlatch survived and even flourished. The same held true for the Sun (Thirst) dances. The government objected in particular to the custom of young Aboriginal people "mutilating" their bodies during the bloody "making a brave" parts of the celebration. While some bands did alter certain practices to prevent a total ban on the dances, they prevented the government from eliminating such customs.

Schools became the third, and most draconian, of the assimilation schemes. Ottawa gave Christian missionaries control of the reserves and residential schools. Among residential schools were industrial schools that taught skills in agriculture and trades for boys and household skills for girls between the ages of 14 and 18. Three were established in western Canada in 1883–84, at Qu'Appelle, Dunbow (just east of High River), and Battleford. By the turn of the century, 20 such schools operated in the West.

Historian J.R. Miller has characterized these schools at the turn of the century as "ineffective, harsh, unsafe."[5] There the church workers taught the Native children in English or, in many parts of southern Quebec, in French, to become Christians, to denounce their own cultural traditions, and to assimilate into "white" society, especially to become farmers. Yet First Nations farms consisted of a small parcel of land, not always of good quality, and a few rudimentary implements — what historian Sarah Carter has described as "two acres and a cow."[6]

RANCHING

Ranching became the first major occupation in the newly surrendered western lands, with beef the major export. The foothills region and the southern grasslands, with their short grass, numerous coulees and streams to provide water for livestock, and the winter "chinook" winds that regularly melted the snow and exposed the grass for winter pasture, proved suitable for cattle ranching.

Initially, ranching existed as a small-scale operation. A few Mounties bought small ranches after their three-year enlistment terms expired. They knew the terrain, were used to western living, and had already established contact with the First Nations. They supplied the beef for the local police force and for the status Indians' rations in the early 1880s, after the extermination of the prairie buffalo herds.

This era of small-scale ranching proved short-lived, however. During the 1880s, "the golden age of ranching," a few wealthy gentlemen ranchers from Ontario, Quebec, France, and Britain established large ranches — the Cochrane Ranch, the North West Cattle Company, the Walrond Ranch, and the Oxley Ranch Company — which monopolized the business. The coming of the CPR in 1883, the federal government's embargo on live cattle imports from the United States, and a generous land-lease system that allowed ranchers to lease up to 100 000 acres (40 000 ha) for 21 years at the modest rate of two cents a hectare all benefited the big ranchers.

IMMIGRATION AND THE SETTLEMENT OF WESTERN CANADA

Successful settlement of the West necessitated large-scale immigration. Up until the turn of the century, however, only a limited number of immigrants entered the Northwest from outside Canada. Instead, most new settlers were migrants from Ontario, English-speaking Quebec (French-speaking Quebeckers did not move out West in great numbers), and the Maritimes, who, being the first to arrive, became the established elite, ensuring that the region became integrated with the rest of the country. Then, at the turn of the century, the last great continental land rush occurred in the Canadian West. By 1911, one Canadian in every four lived in the West.

First came the Mennonites, descendants of the radical Anabaptists of the Reformation era and followers of Menno Simons (1496–1561), a religious leader in the Netherlands. They left their homes in southern Russia, now Ukraine, in response to the fear of the intense Russification policy of the Tsarist government and its introduction of universal conscription. The sect's religious beliefs centred on pacifism, non-involvement with government, and a strict interpretation of the Bible. The Canadian government provided travel assistance and a promise that the Mennonites could settle in communal villages, or *strassendorffs*, and enjoy religious freedom as well as exemption from military service. The 7000 Mennonites who arrived in the 1870s settled on two reserves, one southeast and the other southwest of Winnipeg.

In the mid-1870s, 2000 Icelanders left their homeland, with its limited supply of fertile land and declining fishing industry, to settle on the shores of Lake Winnipeg, a number of them coming by way of Kinmount, Ontario, where they helped build the Victoria Railway from Lindsay to Haliburton. They named their new western settlement Gimli, meaning paradise. Floods in 1879 and 1880 forced many to resettle elsewhere in Manitoba or move into the Dakotas. Despite these setbacks, the original settlement prevailed and had even begun to prosper by the turn of the century.

Selected groups of Jewish immigrants came to western Canada in the 1880s. Sir Alexander Galt, Canada's high commissioner in London, joined the archbishop of Canterbury and several titled English gentlemen in aiding victims of Russia's pogroms

SHARE OF POPULATION BY PROVINCE, CENSUS YEARS 1871–1911

	1871	1881	1891	1901	1911
			(percentage of total)		
Maritimes	20.7	20.1	18.2	16.7	13.0
Prince Edward Island	2.5	2.5	2.3	1.9	1.3
Nova Scotia	10.5	10.2	9.3	8.6	6.8
New Brunswick	7.7	7.4	6.6	6.2	4.9
Quebec	32.3	31.4	30.8	30.7	27.8
Ontario	43.9	44.6	43.7	40.6	35.1
Prairie Provinces	0.7	1.4	3.2	7.9	18.4
Manitoba	0.7	1.4	3.2	4.8	6.4
Saskatchewan	—	—	—*	1.7	6.8
Alberta	—	—	—*	1.4	5.2
British Columbia	1.0	1.1	2.0	3.3	5.4
Yukon	—	—	—	0.5	0.1
North-West Territories	1.3	1.3	2.0	0.4	0.1

*INCLUDED WITH NORTH-WEST TERRITORIES

Source: Calculated from M.C. Urquhart and K.A.H. Buckley, eds., *Historical Statistics of Canada* (Toronto: Macmillan, 1965), Series A2-14. Reproduced in Kenneth Norrie and Douglas Owram, *A History of the Canadian Economy*, 2nd ed. (Toronto: Harcourt Brace, 1996), Chapter 16.

(massacres of Jews) and offered the Canadian prairies as a refuge. The Canadian government encouraged the new settlers to farm, and they established rural farming communities, but few remained in these communities. Most chose instead to become small shopowners, merchants, or labourers in urban centres, particularly Winnipeg, Canada's major western city at the turn of the century.

The Mormons were the largest single American group to arrive in western Canada before 1896. Charles Ora Card, a religious leader, entrepreneur, and colonizer from Utah, first led them northward in 1887 to establish farms at Lee's Creek (later renamed Cardston in honour of their leader), Sterling, and Magrath in present-day southern Alberta. The Canadian government encouraged them to settle in the Palliser Triangle area because of their experience in dryland farming in Utah. By 1912, some 7000 Mormons lived in Alberta, sufficient numbers to warrant the building of a temple at Cardston, which when completed in 1923 was the only Mormon temple outside of the United States.

AN IMMIGRATION BOOM

Between 1896 and 1914, more than 1 million people came to western Canada, thus ensuring the success of the third component of the "national policy" — settlement of the West. What had changed by 1896 to account for this tremendous influx of immigrants? Both "push" and "pull" factors played a role in the decision of so many to leave their native lands for Canada. The push factors varied as widely as did the migrants themselves. Many left because of limited prospects in their homeland. The industrial revolution in Europe had raised the number of births and lowered the death rate. In the countryside, particularly in eastern Europe, farmers had to divide their relatively poor agricultural land into smaller parcels to provide for their off-spring. In Galicia, the northeastern province of the Austro-Hungarian empire, each peasant family needed about 7 ha for subsistence, yet most farms were only half that size and some families had to get by on less than a hectare. A new class of landless peasants emerged.

In the European cities, working-class people lived in cramped slum quarters. The Canadian government's promise of 160 acres (65 ha) of good farmland offered an escape. For the Americans who moved north and the prosperous British immigrants who came on the advice of friends or relatives already in Canada, the move was an adventure, a chance to strike out on their own and to become self-sufficient.

Others, like the Mennonites, Hutterites, and Doukhobors, sought religious freedom. Both Galician Slavs and Jews faced ethnic persecution in the Austro-Hungarian empire. A large number of Asians came to work on the railroads in British Columbia as contract labourers or simply in search of a better way of life. Many immigrants were single men who hoped to make enough money either to return home prosperous or, if they were married, to bring their families to Canada.

The pull factors were equally varied and related to world conditions in general and the Canadian West's attractions in particular. The rapid growth of international trade after 1896 meant jobs. Prosperity also increased demand for raw materials, especially for food for the growing urban population. Western farmers could benefit from a ready market and a high price for Canadian wheat. Increased prosperity also meant declining interest rates and lower freight rates, which in turn resulted in higher profits for exports of Canada's bulky natural resources. Most important of all, Canada benefited from the closing of the American frontier after 1890. After the best land — especially well-watered land — in the American West ceased to be available, the Canadian prairies became the "last best West."

Improved farming conditions also made the Canadian West attractive. Better strains of wheat, such as Marquis, discovered by the Canadian plant breeder Charles Saunders in 1909, matured earlier than Red Fife. Wheat could now be grown in northern areas of Alberta and Saskatchewan without risk of frost damage. The price of wheat quadrupled between 1901 and 1921. Better machinery such as the chilled-steel plough (introduced from the United States), improved harrows and seed drills, and tractors and threshers aided western farmers.

SIFTON PROMOTES THE WEST

WEB LINKS

Credit also goes to Clifford Sifton, an energetic Manitoba politician with a business background, who became the minister of the interior in the Laurier government. As his predecessors had, he first completely reorganized his department on political lines, bringing it directly under his control. Out went the incumbent Conservative appointees, including the deputy minister, and in came Liberal supporters and loyal personal friends. Then he pressured the HBC and the CPR to sell their reserved lands at reasonable rates to prospective settlers. He discontinued the practice of using land grants as incentives to railway promoters. Sifton also simplified the procedure for obtaining a homestead and encouraged settlers to buy up an adjacent section, if available, by allowing them the right to pre-empt such land — that is, to make an interim claim on it and to purchase it at a reduced rate from the government later on.

His department produced numerous pamphlets — *The Wondrous West*; *Canada: Land of Opportunity*; *Prosperity Follows Settlement*; and *The Last Best West* — which contained glorified descriptions of conditions in the Canadian West. In 1896 alone, his department printed 65 000 pamphlets; four years later, the figure reached 1 million. Millions of brochures were sent out to prospective immigrants in the United States and Europe, in over a dozen languages. As well, he advertised in thousands of newspapers, arranged for lecture tours and promotional trips for potential settlers (particularly Americans), and offered bonuses to steamship agents based on the number of immigrants they brought to Canada.

IMMIGRANT GROUPS

British immigrants came mostly on their own at their own expense. There were exceptions. The Barr colonists, a group of Londoners who came together under the aegis of Reverend Isaac Barr at the turn of the century, settled in the Lloydminster area on the border between Saskatchewan and Alberta. Also, some 80 000 "Home Children" came to Canada between 1867 and 1924 to work as agricultural and domestic servants. They were organized and sent by child-care organizations in England, the largest being the Barnardo Home. Most British immigrants adjusted relatively easily to Canadian life. They did not have to learn a new language or radically different customs, and many were relatively well off. Those who lacked farming experience, however, had a more difficult time adjusting. Some drifted into the booming prairie towns in search of work; others first learned how to farm as hired hands.

Sifton placed American immigrants high on his list of desirable settlers. Although not British, the majority were of Anglo-Saxon extraction. As they already spoke English, they mixed easily with their Canadian neighbours and participated fully in their new communities. As well, many were experienced farmers. They sold their farms at home at a high price and bought new ones in Canada at a low price. One Iowa farmer, for example, sold his old homestead for $250 per hectare and bought good land in Manitoba for $18 per hectare. Many ex-Canadians returned. About a third were newcomers from Europe, such as Germans and Scandinavians who had initially settled in the American West but now wanted better land for their children.

In this age of racial-superiority theories, African-Americans were not welcomed. While Canadian agents were telling white Americans that the climate of the Northwest was mild and healthy, they informed black Americans of the region's rigorous and severe climate. When a group of well-to-do African-Americans from Oklahoma crossed into Canada in 1910, local newspapers, especially the Edmonton *Journal* (Edmonton was reported to be their destination), warned of an "invasion of Negroes." In the end, the effort to restrict black immigrants succeeded. Between 1901 and 1911, fewer than 1500 African-Americans came to Canada, compared with hundreds of thousands of other Americans.

A Historical Portrait

ROBERT: A BARNARDO BOY

Robert* was a "Home Child," one of some 80 000 British boys and girls sent to Canada between 1868 and 1925 to work as agricultural and domestic servants. He belonged to the Barnardo Homes, the largest of the child-care organizations in England, begun by Dr. Thomas Barnardo in 1870 in London's East End, to assist waifs, strays, orphans, and street urchins by providing them with a "home." The original Barnardo Home had a sign out in front that read: "No destitute child ever refused admission." While in operation, the Barnardo Homes took in over 30 000 destitute children.

Robert was one of them. He was admitted into the home on November 23, 1921, at the age of 9, along with an older brother, Alfred, and a younger brother, Harold. Another brother, Sidney, was old enough to be on his own. Their mother, Emily, had died from pregnancy complications in 1920, and their father, Edward, a brewer's labourer, died a year later from pneumonia. A maiden aunt, Annie, took them in for a brief time, but when she was unable to care for them any longer, they were admitted to the home. They were given the familiar Barnardo uniform of a tunic, a pair of red-striped trousers, and a hat like that of a Salvation Army officer.

From the beginning, Dr. Barnardo had arranged to send "his" children overseas to "the colonies," where he believed they had a better chance at a new life than in the slums of London. Robert had a choice of going to either Canada or Australia, and chose Canada. He and his brother Harold left England on the ss *Melita* on September 18, 1924, with the customary "Barnardo trunk" that contained all of their earthly possessions; Alfred stayed in England with Sidney. It was the last time the four brothers would see each other.

Upon arrival in Canada Robert and Harold were sent to the Barnardo's Canadian Office and Distributing Home for Boys in Toronto. From here, they were sent north to Bracebridge, where a widow requested two boys to help on her farm. Like so many Home Children, the boys did not have a good initial experience in Canada. She saw them as indentured labourers. They ate separately from the family and slept in an unheated section of the house. They were underfed, and Robert recalled drinking the cow's milk from the bucket before taking it into the house. They attended school but missed many days when needed around the farm. Robert wrote to the officials in Toronto to complain about the harsh conditions, and an inspector came out, but only after informing the lady of his impending visit. Robert recalled that day as the only time he ate with the family and had a scrumptious meal. When the official left, conditions became even more intolerable.

It was customary for employers of Home Children to pay them a wage when they reached the age of 15. When Robert became 15, the lady let the boys go. They were then sent down to the Niagara Peninsula, where a large number of Barnardo boys were located, to assist on the fruit and vegetable farms. Robert's new "home" was a wonderful contrast to his first; the farm owner, Sidney Wright, had been a Barnardo boy himself. Robert got to be part of the family, enjoying the privileges of regular family members. Unfortunately, he was let go when, during the depression, the family could no longer afford him. He moved to another farm in the area, where

(continued)

Robert Francis, as a young boy.

R. Douglas Francis.

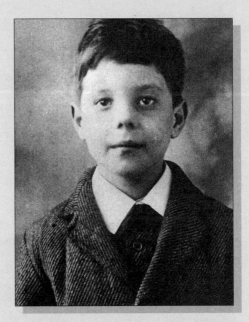

once again he was treated as "just a Barnardo boy." He stuck it out until he married a local girl whose parents owned a farm, at which time he took over the family farm. The couple had three children and lived in the community for the remainder of their lives.

*Robert is Robert Francis, the father of one of the textbook authors.

EUROPEAN IMMIGRANTS

The Canadian government had little success in attracting large numbers of western Europeans. France, for example, had a low birth rate and a well-balanced economy that provided ample work for its population. It also had its own colonies to populate, such as Algeria. Moreover, the French government openly discouraged Canadian immigration agents because it feared a future war with Germany, whose population was almost double that of France.

The Scandinavian countries also restricted emigration, fearing the negative result of such migration, especially of skilled workers, on their own economies. Germany prohibited immigration agents within its borders and fined steamship lines for carrying emigrants. Still, between 1901 and 1911, the German population in the three Prairie provinces increased from 46 844 to 147 638. Many of these immigrants came from German-speaking settlements in eastern Europe rather than directly from Germany, and were sponsored by German Roman Catholic organizations.

To get around these emigration restrictions, Clifford Sifton allowed W.T.R. Preston, Canada's immigration inspector in London, to set up in 1899 a clandestine

Canada promised free land to all settlers, in thirteen languages.

National Archives of Canada/C-6196, C-89536, and C-89542.

organization, the North Atlantic Trading Company, to work with European shipping agents to bring western Europeans to Canada. Each agent received a $5 bonus for every healthy man, woman, or child over twelve who was a bona fide farmer. This illegal scheme ended in 1905 after public outcry against undue profiteering, but not before the company had succeeded in bringing in thousands of emigrants from western Europe.

IMMIGRANTS IN "SHEEPSKIN COATS"

Sifton encouraged the immigration of eastern Europeans, particularly Ukrainians, seeing them as ideal settlers. By World War I, 170 000 Ukrainians had come to Canada from the Austro-Hungarian empire. They left for a variety of reasons but were attracted to Canada for one main reason — *vilni zemli*, or free land. The first group of 4000 Ukrainians — or Galicians, as the immigration agents called them because they came from the province of Galicia — settled at Star and Josefberg, 65 km east of Edmonton. This forested area assured them an abundant supply of wood, a scarce commodity back home. Soon the tightly knit farming communities grew into villages of timber and whitewashed-clay houses with thatched roofs, and distinctive churches with onion-shaped domes.

THE DOUKHOBORS

Some 7000 Doukhobors (meaning "spirit wrestlers") came from Russia in the late 1890s because of persecution for their pacifist and anti-tsarist beliefs. Leo Tolstoy, the great Russian novelist, and Peter Kropotkin, a leading Russian anarchist, admired their simple, communal lifestyle and agreed to arrange for their emigration from Russia. James Mavor, a professor of political economy at the University of Toronto and a friend of Kropotkin's, arranged for them to settle in Canada. They founded three colonies, two near Yorkton, Saskatchewan, and another near Saskatoon. They held land collectively, in a special arrangement agreed upon by the Canadian government, and lived in communal villages.

All was peaceful until a radical wing calling itself the Sons of Freedom marched toward Winnipeg in search of Christ and a new earthly paradise, and in expectation of the arrival of their leader, Peter Veregin, recently released from captivity in Russia. The group walked naked through the Doukhobor villages in a quest for a state of purity akin to that of Adam and Eve before the Fall. Public outcry provided an excuse for Frank Oliver, Clifford Sifton's successor as minister of the interior (1905–11), to confiscate half of their Saskatchewan land on the grounds that the Doukhobors had refused to cultivate quarter-sections, to swear allegiance to the Crown, or to register births and deaths. (The federal government had exempted them from these conditions in 1898.) In protest, 5000 Doukhobors trekked to the Kootenay district near Grand Forks, British Columbia, where Peter Veregin had purchased private land.

Although he tolerated eastern European immigrants as potentially good farmers, Sifton disdained southern Europeans. He believed them to be migratory labourers who would only settle in the urban centres. "I don't want anything done to facilitate Italian immigration," the minister of the interior warned his assistants, as he did not think they would succeed. As a result, those Italian immigrants who did arrive mostly came illegally, through the help of *padros*, or employment agents, who worked with the railway companies and business interests to find work for these unskilled labourers.

ASIAN IMMIGRANTS

Asian immigration occurred mainly on the West Coast. In the 1850s, at the time of the Fraser River gold rush, the first Chinese, Chang Tsoo and Ah Hong, arrived. They were followed about 20 years later by a small number of Japanese. By 1911, nearly 10 percent of British Columbia's population was Asian. To restrict further immigration, the federal government imposed a head tax on all Chinese immigrants, first of $50 in 1885, which rose to $100 in 1900 and then to $500 by 1903. Still, many paid the tax, enabling Ottawa to collect $4 381 550 in head taxes from Chinese between 1885 and 1908. The government was prevented from doing the same with the Japanese because Japan was a military ally of Britain and a major trading partner of Britain and Canada. Instead, the Canadian and Japanese governments mutually agreed to restrict Japanese immigrants to Canada to 400 a year.

The head tax succeeded in reducing overall Chinese immigration, particularly female immigrants, since many married men could not afford to bring their wives, and few single men could pay the tax for single women who might become their wives. Some companies, such as the railways, paid the head tax, or simply brought in Chinese males illegally because they worked hard and for low wages. The estimated 15 000 Chinese who laboured on the construction of the CPR between 1880 and 1885 saved the company approximately $3.5 million. Asians also worked in mining, land clearing, public works, lumbering, salmon canning, and market gardening.

A few immigrants also came from India. As British subjects, they had a special claim for entry into another country of the British empire. Dr. Sundar Singh spoke for his Sikh community when he reminded the Empire Club in 1912: "We are subjects of the same Empire." But West Coast citizens opposed their entry. In May 1914, the ship the *Komagata Maru* brought nearly 400 Punjabis, mostly Sikhs, to Vancouver. For two months, port authorities refused them entry. Finally the Punjabis were forced back to India, amid cries of "White Canada forever" and refrains of "Rule Britannia."

NATIVIST ATTITUDES

With the arrival of various ethnic groups in significant numbers at the turn of the century, concern arose as to their place in Canadian society. Few English Canadians were as tolerant as the western Canadian reformer and author Nellie McClung. In her book, *In Times Like These*, she wrote:

> Among the people of the world in the years to come, we will ask no greater heritage for our country than to be known as the land of the Fair Deal, where every race, colour and creed will be given exactly the same chance — for immigrants "the Land of the Second Chance."

A theory of the proper ethnic hierarchy developed among English Canadians. As ethnic historian Howard Palmer notes, the hierarchy was based on each group's "physical and cultural distance from London (England) and the degree to which [its] skin pigmentation conformed to Anglo-Saxon white."[7] Not surprisingly, the British and Americans, for the most part Anglo-Saxon Protestants, stood at the top of the list of desirable immigrants. But not all British received a warm welcome; some employment ads read, "No English Need Apply." Canadians resented the haughty attitude of upper-class Englishmen in particular, many of whom refused to fit into Canadian society. Most northern and western Europeans, particularly Scandinavians, Germans, and Dutch, were considered by many English Canadians to have the best qualities of Anglo-Saxons and were welcomed. After the "chosen races" came the central and eastern Europeans, generally respected as industrious people and good farmers. Ukrainians and Doukhobors were least tolerated because of their exclusiveness. Lowest in the hierarchy of European immigrants came Jews and southern Europeans, both considered difficult to assimilate and poor farmers. Ranked well below Europeans came those of African background and Asians (Japanese, Chinese, and South Asians) — all believed to be unassimilable.

Asians faced overt discrimination. While many were kept out by the head tax on Chinese immigrants and quotas on Japanese immigrants, those who did enter the country remained marginalized, being denied the franchise in the western provinces, barred from the professions, and subjected to discrimination in housing and access to public places. They also faced physical persecution. In 1907, for example, the Asiatic Exclusion League of Vancouver led a march of 10 000 people through Chinatown, brandishing sticks, stones, bricks, and bottles, and damaging buildings and assaulting residents. They entered the Japanese quarters, too, but were pushed out. It took the police four hours to control the crowd. The government responded by restricting Asian immigration even more.

The tax certificate for Lau Shong (or Shing), 1912, for $500, the amount required to bring in Chinese immigrants.

....

National Archives of Canada/C-96443.

The First Nations people also continued to face discrimination. Frank Oliver, as minister of Indian affairs and minister of the interior, passed a law in 1908 that allowed the government to remove Native people from reserves near towns of more than 8000 residents. Then in 1911, he amended the Indian Act to allow companies and municipalities to expropriate reserve land for roads, railroads, or other public purposes. If the First Nations resisted, the government held back necessary funds. Aboriginal people attempted to secure jobs in the industrial economy, but often faced worse discrimination than immigrants. At the same time that the Canadian government was encouraging the assimilation of Aboriginal people into white society through farming on reserves and through residential and industrial schools, it was denying them the means to succeed in the emerging industrialized society.

Underlying these racist attitudes, so blatantly expressed at all levels of Canadian society at the turn of the century, were different views of the ideal Canadian society. Few English Canadians thought in terms of a culturally pluralistic society. Most English-speaking Canadians could not even believe that a nation of two languages was viable. "Anglo-Saxons" were at the pinnacle of human "civilization." They sought to create a homogeneous culture based on British-Canadian customs and the English language. They looked to the churches and especially the schools to inculcate these values and one language. They had no easy interchange with the new immigrants, who spoke little or no English. Most believed that "foreign" immigrants could only become Canadians by abandoning their own customs and language so as to assimilate.

By 1914, the era of nation building was complete. A national economic policy was in place, established by the Conservatives in the period up to 1896 and continued by the Liberals after 1896. It consisted of a National Policy, or high tariff; the completion of the transcontinental Canadian Pacific Railway; and settlement of the West through large-scale immigration. But certain groups, classes, and regions of the country felt alienated or neglected. Their discontent contributed to a new era of protest and a resurgence of regionalism.

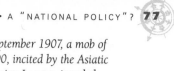

In September 1907, a mob of 10 000, incited by the Asiatic Exclusion League, invaded Vancouver's Chinatown, and then moved into the Japanese quarter of the city. The photo shows the damage to a Japanese-Canadian grocery store.

William Lyon Mackenzie King Collection/ National Archives of Canada/C-14118.

NOTES

1. Pierre Berton, *The National Dream* (Toronto: McClelland & Stewart, 1970), p. 363.
2. Frank Leonard, *A Thousand Blunders: The Grand Trunk Pacific Railway and Northern British Columbia* (Vancouver: University of British Columbia Press, 1996), pp. 4–5.
3. T.D. Regehr, "Triple Tracking," *Horizon Canada* 7 (1986), p. 1878.
4. Wallace Stegner, *Wolf Willow: A History, a Story, and a Memory of the Lost Plains Frontier* (New York: Viking, 1966), p. 101.
5. J.R. Miller, *Skyscrapers Hide the Heavens: A History of Indian–White Relations in Canada* (Toronto: University of Toronto Press, 1989), p. 198.
6. Sarah Carter, "Two Acres and a Cow: 'Peasant' Farming for the Indians of the Northwest, 1889–97," *Canadian Historical Review* 70(1) (March 1989): 27.
7. Howard Palmer, "Reluctant Hosts: Anglo-Canadian Views of Multiculturalism in the Twentieth Century," in R. Douglas Francis and Donald B. Smith, eds., *Readings in Canadian History: Post-Confederation*, 5th ed. (Toronto: Harcourt Brace, 1998), p. 127.

LINKING TO THE PAST

WEB LINKS

Alexander Mackenzie
http://www.axionet.com/vantech/departments/ssproj/alex.htm
A short biography of Alexander Mackenzie, the second prime minister (and the first Liberal prime minister) to hold office following Macdonald's resignation in 1872.

National Policy
http://www.canadahistory.com/newpage34.htm
Excerpts from John A. Macdonald's speech regarding his "National Policy," the economic platform that brought the Conservatives back to power in 1878.

Treaties

http://www.inac.gc.ca/treatdoc/index.html

This site from Indian and Northern Affairs Canada provides the full text to a number of treaties, including Treaties One to Seven, which covered the period 1871 to 1877 and dealt with the division of the Northwest.

The Chinese Immigration Act, 1885

http://www.asian.ca/law/cia1885.htm

Selections from the 1885 Chinese Immigration Act, which restricted Asian immigration to Canada.

Clifford Sifton

http://timelinks.merlin.mb.ca/referenc/db0053.htm

A biography of Clifford Sifton, who helped to increase immigration to the West during his time as minister of the interior.

RELATED READINGS

The relevant articles from R. Douglas Francis and Donald B. Smith, eds., *Readings in Canadian History: Post-Confederation*, 5th ed. (Toronto: Harcourt Brace, 1998), for this chapter are Craig Brown, "The Nationalism of the National Policy" pp. 3–8; John Dales, "Canada's National Policies," pp. 9–18; John Marlyn, "Under the Ribs of Death," pp. 112–24; Howard Palmer, "Reluctant Hosts: Anglo-Canadian Views of Multiculturalism in the Twentieth Century," pp. 125–40; and J.R. Miller, "Owen Glendower, Hotspur, and Canadian Indian Policy," pp. 140–62.

BIBLIOGRAPHY

The nationalism of the Canada First movement is discussed in the chapter "The First Fine Careless Rapture," in F.H. Underhill, *The Image of Confederation* (Toronto: Canadian Broadcasting Corporation, 1964); and in David Gagan, "The Relevance of 'Canada First,'" *Journal of Canadian Studies* 5 (November 1970): 36–44. On the rising French-Canadian nationalism of the 1870s see Jean-Paul Bernard, *Les Rouges: libéralisme, nationalisme et anticléricalisme au milieu du XIXe siècle* (Montréal: Presses de l'Université du Québec, 1971); Nive Voisine and Jean Hamelin, eds., *Les ultramontains canadiens-français* (Montréal: Boréal Express, 1985); Arthur Silver, *The French-Canadian Idea of Confederation, 1864–1900*, 2nd ed. (Toronto: University of Toronto Press, 1997); Mason Wade, "Growing Pains: 1867–96," in his *The French Canadians: 1760–1945* (London: Macmillan, 1955), pp. 331–92; "The Clerical Offensive" in Susan Mann Trofimenkoff, *The Dream of Nation: A Social and Intellectual History of Quebec* (Toronto: Gage, 1983), pp. 115–31; and Louis Lemire, "'The Guibord Unpleasantness,'" *The Beaver* (August/September 1992): 36–44.

Dale Thomson's *Alexander Mackenzie: Clear Grit* (Toronto: Macmillan, 1960) gives a good portrait of Canada's second prime minister. On Edward Blake see F.H. Underhill, "Edward Blake," in C.T. Bissell, ed., *Our Living Traditions* (Toronto: University of Toronto Press, 1957), pp. 3–28; and Joseph Schull's two-volume biography, *Edward Blake: The Man of the Other Way* (Toronto: Macmillan, 1975) and *Edward Blake: Leader in Exile* (Toronto: Macmillan, 1976). The ideas underlying Canadian liberalism in the 1870s are examined by F.H. Underhill in "The Political Ideas of the Upper Canadian Reformers, 1867–1878," in his *In Search of Canadian Liberalism* (Toronto: Macmillan, 1960), pp. 68–84; and by W.R.

Graham in "Liberal Nationalism in the 1870's," *Canadian Historical Association Report* (1946): 101–19. On the politics of the Laurier era see R.C. Brown and R. Cook, *Canada, 1896–1921: A Nation Transformed* (Toronto: McClelland & Stewart, 1974); and three biographies of Laurier: Joseph Schull, *Laurier: The First Canadian* (Toronto: Macmillan, 1965); Richard Clippendale, *Laurier: His Life and World* (Toronto: McGraw-Hill Ryerson, 1979); and Réal Bélanger, *Wilfrid Laurier: quand la politique devient passion* (Québec: Presses de l'Université Laval, 1986).

On the national policy see Ben Forster, *A Conjunction of Interests: Business, Politics, and Tariffs, 1825–1879* (Toronto: University of Toronto Press, 1986); Donald G. Creighton, *British North America at Confederation* (Ottawa: J.O. Patenaude, Printer to the King, 1939); R.C. Brown, *Canada's National Policy, 1883–1900: A Study in Canadian–American Relations* (Princeton, NJ: Princeton University Press, 1964); and John Dales, *The Protective Tariff in Canada's Development* (Toronto: University of Toronto Press, 1966). The *Journal of Canadian Studies* 14 (Autumn 1979) is devoted to "The National Policy, 1879–1979." Pierre Berton's two-volume popular study, *The National Dream: The Great Railway, 1871–1881* (Toronto: McClelland & Stewart, 1970) and *The Last Spike: The Great Railway, 1881–1885* (Toronto: McClelland & Stewart, 1974), describes the building of the Canadian Pacific Railway. For a less nationalistic view of the railway see A.A. den Otter, "Nationalism and the Pacific Scandal," *Canadian Historical Review* 69(3) (September 1986): 315–39; and David Cruise and Alison Griffiths, *Lords of the Line: The Men Who Built the CPR* (New York: Viking, 1988). Andy den Otter discusses the ideology of technological nationalism in the context of the CPR in *The Philosophy of Railways: The Transcontinental Railway Idea in British North America* (Toronto: University of Toronto Press, 1997). See as well R.A.J. Phillips, *Canada's Railways* (Toronto: McGraw-Hill, 1968). On railway building during the Laurier era consult T.D. Regehr, *The Canadian Northern Railway: Pioneer Road of the Northern Prairies, 1895–1918* (Toronto: Macmillan, 1976); and G.R. Stevens, *Canadian National Railways*, 2 vols. (Toronto: Clarke Irwin, 1960). On the Grand Trunk Pacific see Frank Leonard, *A Thousand Blunders: The Grand Trunk Pacific Railway and Northern British Columbia* (Vancouver: University of British Columbia Press, 1996). R.B. Fleming has published *The Railway King of Canada: Sir William Mackenzie, 1849–1923* (Vancouver: University of British Columbia Press, 1991). In *The Canadian Pacific Railway and the Development of Western Canada* (Montreal/Kingston: McGill-Queen's University Press, 1989), John A. Eagle examines the CPR's contributions to western Canadian economic growth between 1896 and 1914. On the relationship of railways and government see Ken Cruikshank, *Close Ties: Railway, Government, and the Board of Railway Commissioners, 1851–1933* (Montreal/Kingston: McGill-Queen's University Press, 1991). Suzanne Zeller's *Inventing Canada: Early Victorian Science and the Idea of a Transcontinental Nation* (Toronto: University of Toronto Press, 1987) and her *Land of Promise, Promised Land: The Culture of Victorian Science in Canada* (Ottawa: Canadian Historical Association, 1996), examine the role of scientists in shaping the idea of a transcontinental nation.

On the development of the Canadian West in the 1870s and 1880s see Gerald Friesen, *The Canadian Prairies: A History* (Toronto: University of Toronto Press, 1984). Also useful is L.G. Thomas, ed., *The Prairie West to 1905: A Canadian Source Book* (Toronto: Oxford University Press, 1975), for an introduction to such topics as government and politics, law and order, the ranching frontier, and the development of transportation and communication. On settlement patterns in the West see Chester Martin, *"Dominion Lands" Policy*, published in an abridged form (Toronto: Macmillan, 1973). For an account of homesteading see the essays in David C. Jones and Ian Macpherson, eds., *Building Beyond the Homestead: Rural History on the Prairies* (Calgary: University of Calgary Press, 1985). A detailed study of settlement in one prairie town is Paul Voisey, *Vulcan: The Making of a*

Prairie Community (Toronto: University of Toronto Press, 1988). For a discussion of the North-West Mounted Police see R.C. Macleod, *The North-West Mounted Police and Law Enforcement, 1873–1905* (Toronto: University of Toronto Press, 1976). For a review of the image of the NWMP consult Keith Walden, *Visions of Order: The Canadian Mounties in Symbol and Myth* (Toronto: Butterworths, 1982). On ranching see David Breen, *The Canadian Prairie West and the Ranching Frontier, 1874–1924* (Toronto: University of Toronto Press, 1982).

Useful surveys of Amerindian–non-Native relations that cover this period are J.R. Miller, *Skyscrapers Hide the Heavens: A History of Indian–White Relations in Canada* (Toronto: University of Toronto Press, 1991); Olive P. Dickason, *Canada's First Nations* (Toronto: McClelland & Stewart, 1992); A.J. Ray, *I Have Lived Here Since the World Began* (Toronto: Key Porter, 1996); and his *The Canadian Fur Trade in the Industrial Age* (Toronto: University of Toronto Press, 1990). See as well J.R. Miller, *Canada and the Aboriginal Peoples 1867–1927.* CHA Historical Booklet No. 57 (Ottawa, 1997). The essays in F. Laurie Barron and James B. Waldram, eds., *1885 and After: Native Society in Transition* (Regina: Canadian Plains Research Centre, University of Regina, 1986) are also helpful. Indian policy is reviewed by Brian Titley in the early chapters of his *A Narrow Vision: Duncan Campbell Scott and the Administration of Indian Affairs in Canada* (Vancouver: University of British Columbia Press, 1987). The government's farming policy for the Native peoples is outlined in Sarah Carter, *Lost Harvests: Prairie Indian Reserve Farmers and Government Policy* (Montreal/Kingston: McGill-Queen's University Press, 1990). Richard Price, ed., *The Spirit of the Alberta Indian Treaties* (Montreal: Institute for Research on Public Policy, 1979) contains valuable essays and transcripts of interviews made in the mid-1970s with Native elders. Jean Friesen provides a modern view of the treaties in "Magnificent Gifts: The Treaties of the Indians of the Northwest, 1869–70," *Transactions of the Royal Society of Canada,* series 5, vol. 1 (1986): 41–51. Several good biographies of prairie chiefs have been published by Hugh A. Dempsey: *Crowfoot* (Edmonton: Hurtig, 1972), *Red Crow* (Saskatoon: Western Producer Prairie Books, 1980), and *Big Bear* (Vancouver: Douglas & McIntyre, 1984). For Big Bear see as well J.R. Miller, *Big Bear (Mistahimusqua)* (Toronto: ECW Press, 1996). Edward Ahenakew's *Voice of the Plains Cree* (Toronto: McClelland & Stewart, 1973) provides a valuable Native assessment of conditions for the First Nations of the Canadian prairies in the early twentieth century. Shorter treatments of these and other Amerindian leaders appear in the *Dictionary of Canadian Biography,* vols. 11, *1881 to 1890* (1982), 12, *1891 to 1900* (1990), 13, *1901 to 1910* (1994), and 14, *1911 to 1920* (1998) (Toronto: University of Toronto Press). A good case study of an eastern Canadian Indian reserve in the late nineteenth century is Hélène Bédard's *Les Montagnais et la réserve de Betsiamites: 1850–1900* (Quebec: Institut québécois de recherche sur la culture, 1988).

Overviews of immigration to western Canada are available in R.C. Brown and R. Cook's chapter "Opening Up the Land of Opportunity," in *Canada, 1896–1921: A Nation Transformed* (Toronto: McClelland & Stewart, 1974); Pierre Berton's *The Promised Land: Settling the West, 1896–1914* (Toronto: McClelland & Stewart, 1984); Gerald Friesen's *The Canadian Prairies: A History* (Toronto: University of Toronto Press, 1984); and Valerie Knowles, *Strangers at Our Gates: Canadian Immigration and Immigration Policy, 1540–1990* (Toronto: Dundurn Press, 1992). See as well, Paul Robert Magocsi, ed., *Encyclopedia of Canada's Peoples* (Toronto: University of Toronto Press for the Multicultural Society of Ontario, 1999).

On immigration to western Canada in the pre-1896 era see Norman Macdonald, *Canada: Immigration and Colonization, 1841–1903* (Toronto: Macmillan, 1966). Robert Painchaud reviews early French-speaking settlement in *Un rêve français dans le peuplement de la Prairie* (Saint-Boniface, MB: Éditions des Plaines, 1987). Royden K. Loewen, *Family, Church, and Market: A Mennonite Community in the Old and the New Worlds, 1850–1930*

(Toronto: University of Toronto Press, 1993) describes the Mennonite community in western Canada in the late nineteenth century. Clifford Sifton's role in promoting immigration to the West is examined in D.J. Hall, "Clifford Sifton: Immigration and Settlement Policy, 1896–1905," in Howard Palmer, ed., *The Settlement of the West* (Calgary: University of Calgary Press, 1977), pp. 60–85, and in D.J. Hall's two-volume biography, *Clifford Sifton*, vol. 1, *The Young Napoleon, 1861–1900* (Vancouver: University of British Columbia Press, 1981), and vol. 2, *The Lonely Eminence, 1901–1929* (Vancouver: University of British Columbia Press, 1985).

The immigration of British home children is the subject of Joy Parr's *Labouring Children: British Immigrant Apprentices to Canada, 1869–1924* (Montreal/Kingston: McGill-Queens University Press, 1980); and Kenneth Bagnell's *The Little Immigrants* (Toronto: Macmillan, 1980). On British images of Canada, see R.G. Moyles and D. Owram, *Imperial Dreams and Colonial Realities* (Toronto: University of Toronto Press, 1988). On American farmers' immigration to western Canada see Carl Bicha, *The American Farmer and the Canadian West, 1896–1914* (Lawrence, KS: Coronado Press, 1968); and Harold Troper, *Only Farmers Need Apply* (Toronto: Griffin House, 1972). European immigration is discussed in Donald Avery, *"Dangerous Foreigners": European Immigrant Workers and Labour Radicalism in Canada, 1896–1932* (Toronto: McClelland & Stewart, 1979). George Woodcock and Ivan Avakumovic's *The Doukhobors* (Toronto: McClelland & Stewart, rep. 1977) deals with this important group. The story of Jewish immigration to Canada is told in Irving Abella, *A Coat of Many Colours: Two Centuries of Jewish Life in Canada* (Toronto: Lester & Orpen Dennys, 1990); and Gerald Tulchinsky, *Taking Root: The Origins of the Canadian Jewish Community* (Toronto: Stoddart, 1992). The European immigrants' perspective can be gleaned from John Marlyn's novel, *Under the Ribs of Death* (Toronto: McClelland & Stewart, 1957); and from R.F. Harney and H. Troper's *Immigrants: A Portrait of the Urban Experience, 1890–1930* (Toronto: Van Nostrand Reinhold, 1975).

Black immigration to western Canada is covered in Robin Winks, *The Blacks in Canada: A History*, 2nd ed. (Montreal/Kingston: McGill-Queen's University Press, 1997). On Asian immigration to British Columbia in the pre-World War I era see Jin Tan and Patricia E. Roy, *The Chinese in Canada* (Ottawa: Canadian Historical Association, 1985); Peter Ward, *White Canada Forever: Popular Attitudes and Public Policy toward Orientals in British Columbia* (Montreal/Kingston: McGill-Queen's University Press, 1978); Patricia Roy, *A White Man's Province: British Columbia Politicians and Chinese and Japanese Immigrants, 1885–1914* (Vancouver: University of British Columbia Press, 1989); and Hugh Johnston, *The Voyage of the Komagata Maru: The Sikh Challenge to Canada's Colour Bar* (Delhi: Oxford University Press, 1979). On nativist attitudes see Howard Palmer, *Patterns of Prejudice: A History of Nativism in Alberta* (Toronto: McClelland & Stewart, 1982).

CHAPTER FOUR

The Fragile Union: The Resurgence of Regionalism

"We have come to a period in the history of this country when premature dissolution seems to be at hand." So wrote Wilfrid Laurier, the official leader of the opposition, in the early 1890s. Canada appeared to have failed. Bickering between Ottawa and the Dominion's seven provinces had become endemic. A provincial-rights movement flourished in Ontario; secessionist sentiments resurfaced in Nova Scotia; and regional protest arose in the Northwest. In Quebec, French-Canadian nationalist feeling strengthened in reaction to the execution of Louis Riel, the Jesuits' Estates Act, and the Manitoba Schools Question. As well, a deep economic depression resulted in 1 million people leaving for the United States in the 1880s. No one seemed to know the solution to Canada's problems; some, like Laurier, questioned whether a solution existed.

THE PROVINCIAL-RIGHTS MOVEMENT IN ONTARIO

Oliver Mowat, Liberal premier of Ontario from 1872 to 1896, can rightfully be considered the "father of provincial rights." He endorsed the concept known as the provincial-compact theory — a belief that Confederation was a compact entered into by the provinces of their own volition, and one that could be altered only with their consent. As premier of Ontario, Mowat continued the policy of Edward Blake, his predecessor, of making the province dominant within the federation. One opportunity to do so arose over the question of the boundary line between Ontario and Manitoba.

THE ONTARIO BOUNDARY DISPUTE

WEB LINKS

The origins of the Ontario–Manitoba boundary dispute dated back to pre-Confederation days. No precise boundary line had ever been established between Rupert's Land and the colony of Upper Canada (Ontario).

Mowat argued that Ontario's western boundary should run due north from the source of the Mississippi River, which was slightly west of Lake of the Woods at a place called Rat Portage (present-day Kenora). He referred to western explorations

82

during the French regime to justify his claim. (Some of his supporters went even further and claimed that Ontario should extend as far as the forks of the Saskatchewan River!) In contrast, Macdonald and the federal Conservatives argued that the boundary between Ontario and Manitoba should be drawn near Port Arthur on Lake Superior. Macdonald wanted to restrict Ontario's size so as to lessen its influence in Confederation.

The issue remained unresolved when the federal Liberals came to power in 1873. The following year, the two Liberal governments agreed to establish an arbitration board, which ruled in favour of Ontario. But before the board's decision became law, the federal Liberals were defeated in 1878 and the newly elected Conservatives refused to ratify the arbitrators' award. Instead, in 1881 Macdonald unilaterally awarded the disputed territory — from Lake of the Woods eastward to Thunder Bay — to Manitoba, thereby introducing that province into the controversy. Since the federal government owned Manitoba's natural resources, this arrangement allowed Ottawa to control the land and the mineral rights. The prime minister also granted land and timber rights to logging companies in the disputed area.

After two years of legal chaos, both governments agreed to submit the issue to the Judicial Committee of the Privy Council in London, the supreme legal authority in the British empire. Mowat himself pleaded Ontario's case, and won. In 1884 the Judicial Committee fixed the western limits of Ontario at the northwest angle of Lake of the Woods (the present boundary). Still John A. Macdonald delayed. Not until 1889 did the federal government confirm Ontario's boundaries and the province's rights to the natural resources within the disputed territory.

POWERS OF THE LIEUTENANT GOVERNOR AND FEDERAL DISALLOWANCE

Subsequently Mowat won a series of victories in other disputes with the federal government, notably over the powers of the lieutenant governor, and the federal power of disallowance (the right granted to the federal government in the BNA Act to disallow any provincial law considered to be in conflict with federal law). According to the BNA Act, the federal government appointed lieutenant governors, paid their salaries, and had the right to dismiss them at any time. At the time of Confederation, Macdonald had believed this would serve to keep provincial policies in harmony with national objectives.

Mowat argued instead that the lieutenant governor had the same position in the province as the governor general in the federal government, thus making the provinces co-ordinate sovereignties on a par with the federal government on constitutional matters. Once again the Judicial Committee of the Privy Council upheld Mowat's position. In its ruling of 1892, it declared that a lieutenant governor "is as much the representative of Her Majesty, for all purposes of provincial government, as the Governor-General himself for all purposes of the Dominion Government."

The Ontario premier advanced provincial interests on yet another front. He argued that the provinces had certain legal powers before Confederation that they retained after 1867; one was the right to issue liquor licences. In 1884 the Ontario government passed the Act Respecting Licensing Duties, which the federal

For years, the Canadian, Ontario, and Manitoba governments fought over the boundary line between Ontario and Manitoba. This map of Canada in 1882 shows the contested area.

Source: Based on information taken from National Topographic System map sheet number MCR 2306. © 1969, Her Majesty the Queen in Right of Canada with permission of Energy, Mines and Resources Canada.

government immediately disallowed. Ontario took the dispute to court in the case of *Hodge v. the Queen*. The Judicial Committee upheld Ontario's position, arguing that the provinces had full authority in their own realm of legal jurisdiction.

PROTEST IN ATLANTIC CANADA

Mowat had provincial rights allies in Atlantic Canada. The anti-confederate sentiments of the mid-1860s re-emerged in the 1880s as Maritimers became increasingly dissatisfied with their perceived inferior position in the new Dominion. The custom, for example, of flying flags at half-mast on July 1, which first began in 1867, continued in many Atlantic communities.

Difficult economic conditions contributed to regional dissatisfaction. For one thing, the Americans had countered the Conservatives' high tariff of 1879 with their own high import duty on Maritime fish. As a result, fish and lobster exports dropped a staggering 75 percent in the early 1880s. Shipbuilding also declined, as iron steamers replaced wooden sailing ships. Yarmouth, for example, once a thriving centre of Nova

Scotia's shipbuilding industry, built only six vessels in 1880, four in 1884, and none in 1887. Many Nova Scotians left in search of jobs elsewhere.

SECESSION THREATS IN NOVA SCOTIA

From 1878 to 1884, Nova Scotia's Conservative government appealed to Ottawa for financial assistance. But Macdonald's top priority remained the CPR and the development of the West. The unwillingness of Ottawa to help contributed to the Liberals' victory in 1884 on a wave of anti-confederate sentiment.

W.S. Fielding, the new premier, also attempted to extract larger subsidies from Ottawa. When he proved no more successful than his Conservative predecessor, he introduced a secessionist resolution in the Nova Scotia legislature in 1886. The premier appealed to the other Maritime provinces also to secede and to create an independent Maritime nation.

New Brunswick, however, declined Nova Scotia's offer of Maritime union, seeing it as a ploy to benefit Halifax. New Brunswick had also just received federal financial support for a rail line to Saint John. Prince Edward Island also resisted Maritime union, believing it would result in the loss of control over the island to a "distant" mainland. Fielding himself retreated, despite a stunning victory of 29 of the 39 seats in the provincial election of 1886. He sensed insufficient support within the province. At the same time, his pressure tactics worked: the federal Conservative government lowered freight rates and offered generous financial assistance for railway building in the province.

NEWFOUNDLAND CONSIDERS JOINING CONFEDERATION

In Newfoundland, major economic changes in the late nineteenth century raised the prospects of union with Canada once again. The fishing industry, which by 1885 employed nine out of ten of the island's work force and accounted for nearly all of its exports, experienced a serious slump. Between the early 1880s and the late 1890s, industry earnings fell by 36 percent as a result of decreased exports to the United States and increased competition from other fishing nations, such as Norway.

The Newfoundland government successfully negotiated a reciprocity agreement with the United States in 1890, only to have the Colonial Office veto it. The Canadian government had protested that the agreement, if ratified, would hurt the fishing industry within the Maritimes.

At the same time, Newfoundland witnessed a bank crash in 1894. When the newly elected Whiteway government in 1895 faced default on interest payments on its loans, the Newfoundland premier approached the Canadian government about union. Although only a few years earlier Ottawa had offered Newfoundlanders generous terms of union, by 1895 the political climate had changed. Prime Minister Mackenzie Bowell feared that better terms for Newfoundland would reopen appeals from other provinces. Whiteway also found little enthusiasm on the island for union. Had not Canada scuttled Newfoundland's reciprocity negotiations with the United States? The talks broke down, and Newfoundland would wait another half-century before joining Confederation.

DISCONTENT IN THE NORTHWEST

Macdonald's political horizons extended little beyond the Ottawa–Toronto–Montreal triangle. He soon faced problems in the Northwest as well as in the Maritimes. In Manitoba, settlers complained that the lack of transportation competition in the West kept rates high. They paid more to ship their goods than did central or eastern Canadians, as the monopoly clause, by which no competitive lines could be built in the region for 20 years after the completion of the CPR, gave the railway free rein to charge exorbitant prices.

Manitoba responded by chartering competitive lines to the American border. The federal government disallowed these provincial charters on the grounds that they went against the "national interest." The new Liberal premier, Thomas Greenway, then began building a railway from Winnipeg to Emerson. He warned the federal government that, if it were opposed, he would solicit American financial — and, if need be, military — support. The federal government gave in, abandoned its policy of disallowance, and bought out the CPR monopoly.

The most serious challenge arose farther west. The First Nations, particularly the Crees in the Treaty Number Six area, in what is now central Alberta and Saskatchewan, felt betrayed by the federal government's failure to keep its treaty promises of providing food rations in time of scarcity. The government had not anticipated that the buffalo would disappear so quickly and had willingly inserted the "famine clause" in Treaty Number Six in 1876. Despite its promise, however, the debt-ridden federal government did little, aside from supplying insufficient amounts of second- or third-rate food. The Native peoples also resented the government's refusal to allow them to choose their own reserve lands, as promised in the treaty. Ottawa prevented the establishment of large concentrations of reserves first in the Cypress Hills area and then around Battleford.

The Métis in the region resented Ottawa's failure to act on their land claims. After the Red River resistance of 1869–70, many of the Métis moved to the South Saskatchewan River valley, around the village that became known as Batoche. Once again, their livelihoods appeared threatened as settlers moved in. They appealed to the federal government to recognize their land claims and to allow them to keep their river-lot system instead of making them conform to the rectangular plan imposed elsewhere in the territories. By the end of 1884, Ottawa had still not responded to their petitions.

Many of the settlers at Prince Albert, northeast of Batoche, were also discontented. The CPR's decision to reroute the railway through the southern region left them hundreds of kilometres away from a rail link to eastern markets. As well, the more politically active settlers demanded an elected assembly for the North-West Territories and representation in the federal Parliament.

THE RETURN OF LOUIS RIEL

The Métis, with the support of the "country-born" (English-speaking mixed-bloods) in the Prince Albert area, brought back Louis Riel to lead their protest against the federal government. They believed that Riel could obtain for the Northwest what he had for Manitoba fifteen years earlier. But the Riel who returned in 1885 was not the Riel of 1869. During the intervening years, he had been hospitalized in two mental asylums in Quebec and had then spent years in exile in the United States. He became

The last great buffalo herds had vanished from the Canadian plains by the end of 1879. The photo shows buffalo bones ready for loading on a CPR boxcar in the late 1880s. Most of the buffalo bones went to the United States, to be used for bleaching sugar and manufacturing fertilizer.

Glenbow Archives, Calgary, Canada/NA-448-3.

convinced that God had chosen him to be "prophet of the New World," responsible for creating a reformed Roman Catholic state on the prairies. He saw his return to western Canada as part of God's plan.

THE NORTH-WEST REBELLION OF 1885

Initially, Riel and his followers avoided violent action. They petitioned Ottawa on December 16, 1884, to ask for more liberal treatment for the Native peoples, a land grant for the mixed-bloods, responsible government for the North-West Territories, western representation at Ottawa, a reduction of the tariff, and the construction of a railway to Hudson Bay as an alternative to the CPR. The federal government acknowledged receipt of the petition and promised to appoint a commission to investigate problems in the Northwest. But apart from making a list of mixed-bloods, it promised no specific action. Moreover, it failed even to mention the Métis grievances.

Subsequently, in mid-March, Riel established a provisional government with himself as president and Gabriel Dumont as adjutant general. By this point the non-Native settlers in Prince Albert had broken their informal alliance with him, and only a small number of First Nations people followed the Métis in taking up arms. Riel then armed his supporters at Batoche and attempted to duplicate the successful resistance in the Red River colony in 1869–70. The Métis leader underestimated, however, how much the situation had changed in fifteen years. A federal police force existed in the North-West Territories; thousands of settlers had located there; and a newly completed railway linked the region to central Canada. Moreover, this time the Roman

Where Historians Disagree

THE CAUSES OF THE NORTH-WEST REBELLION OF 1885

Earlier generations of English-speaking Canadian historians blamed the North-West Rebellion of 1885 on one man: Louis Riel. The rebel leader incited violence; his actions were those of a madman. R.G. MacBeth wrote in *The Making of the Canadian West* (Toronto: W. Briggs, 1905) that "rebellion was rampant with a madman at its head" (p. 144). In contrast, French-Canadian historians saw Riel as a misguided leader acting out of concern for his Métis people amid troubles brought about by the federal government's mismanagement of the Northwest. Both groups of historians saw Riel and the rebellion largely in terms of the continuing controversy of English Canadians versus French Canadians, Protestants versus Catholics.

Canadian historiography took a new turn in the 1930s. Influenced in part by the "frontier" school of thought, already well established in American historiography, several Canadian historians saw the Métis as frontier hunters and nomads who opposed the advancing frontier of a different cultural group. In *The Birth of Western Canada* (London: Longmans, Green, 1936), George F.G. Stanley saw the rebellion of 1885 as a clash between "primitive and civilized peoples" (p. vii). French ethnologist Marcel Giraud also subscribed to this cultural-conflict thesis, while American writer Joseph Kinsey Howard depicted Riel in *Strange Empire: The Story of Louis Riel* (Toronto: James Lewis & Samuel, 1952) as the symbolic leader of all North American Aboriginal people struggling to free themselves from white domination.

Historian W.L. Morton denied that the Métis were "primitive": they were an advanced society, one whose interests and values simply differed from those of other Canadians. Moreover, by 1885, the Métis formed part of a larger western Canadian society that felt aggrieved by the indifference of Ottawa to western concerns. The rebellion of 1885 was therefore more than a Métis uprising incited by one man; it was a resistance by the people of the Northwest, including, at least initially, the First Nations, the Roman Catholic clergy, and settlers in addition to the Métis. It was the first of a series of western protest movements against central Canada in general, and the federal government in particular, for their failure to address western complaints.

Thomas Flanagan questions whether the Métis had to rebel to force the Conservative government to act. In *Riel and the Rebellion: 1885 Reconsidered* (Saskatoon: Western Producer Prairie Books, 1983), Flanagan argues that "the Métis grievances were at least partly of their own making; that the government was on the verge of resolving them when the Rebellion broke out; that Riel's resort to arms could not be explained by the failure of constitutional agitation" (p. 146). Flanagan does not exonerate Ottawa, but claims that the government's mistakes were "in judgment, not part of a calculated campaign to destroy the Métis or deprive them of their rights" (p. 147). Flanagan argues that Riel acted as much out of self-interest or, at least, private motives, as for his Métis followers.

Historian D.N. Sprague has challenged Flanagan's assertion that the government was playing fair. In *Canada and the Métis, 1869–1885* (Waterloo, ON: Wilfrid Laurier University Press, 1988), he argues that Métis grievances over land claims in Manitoba during and after the resistance of 1869–70 continued to poison Métis–Ottawa relations in Saskatchewan, where so many Métis had fled when the situation

(continued)

in Manitoba became intolerable. Sprague implies that the federal government deliberately provoked Riel into forming a second provisional government so as to accuse him of treason.

Recently, the debate has shifted away from Riel to the Métis themselves. Why did they follow Riel? The shift in perspective has led to the study of Métis society in an effort to explain what conditions prevailed within the community that would have caused its members to follow Riel into rebellion. A recent examination of Métis society in the South Saskatchewan River valley is Diane Payment's *"The Free People — Otipemisiwak": Batoche, Saskatchewan, 1870–1930* (Ottawa: National Historic Parks and Sites, Parks Canada, 1990).

In *Homeland to Hinterland: The Changing Worlds of the Red River Metis in the Nineteenth Century* (Toronto: University of Toronto Press, 1996), Gerhard Ens argues that the economy and society of the Red River Métis underwent dramatic change between 1840 and 1890 from being pre-capitalist and "subsistence" to a dynamic capitalist market economy, based on the buffalo-robe trade, and that the Métis were active agents in this transformation. By mid-century, however, this "cottage industry" of buffalo-robe trade was occurring beyond the Red River colony in the North-West Territories, thus resulting in a sizable out-migration of Red River Métis well before 1870 and the colony's incorporation into Confederation. Ens maintains that migration after 1870 was part of this earlier trend as economic opportunities for the Métis in Manitoba continued to decline, along with the added economic difficulties the Métis experienced as a result of the "intolerant actions and behaviour of the incoming Protestant settlers from Ontario" (p. 170), rather than as a result of any action by the Canadian government. Furthermore, he argues that the split between the Métis who supported Riel in the uprising of 1869–70 and those who opposed him occurred not along racial lines — French versus English Métis — but along class lines. Those who followed Riel believed Manitoba could still be their economic "homeland." Those who did not simply moved further West in search of better economic opportunities, but only to re-enact, unfortunately, the same scenario 15 years later in the North-West Rebellion of 1885. By this time, however, the West as a whole had become an economic "hinterland" to central Canada.

Catholic church opposed him, denouncing him as a heretic for his unorthodox religious views.

THE MILITARY CAMPAIGN

On March 26, 1885, Dumont and his Métis followers successfully routed a group of about 100 settler-volunteers and the North-West Mounted Police at Duck Lake, near Batoche. Then a band of Crees surrounded Battleford, while militant Cree warriors killed nine people near Frog Lake, northwest of Battleford.

The federal government dispatched troops to the Northwest on its almost-completed railway. Within a month, more than 3000 troops, under the command of Major General Frederick Middleton, arrived, joining the 2000 volunteers and

A Historical Portrait

WILL JACKSON (HONORÉ JAXON)

Will Jackson, secretary to Louis Riel in 1884–85, was one of the most interesting individuals to emerge from the North-West Rebellion. The former University of Toronto student, labour radical, convert to Baha'i, English-Canadian-turned Métis, spent a lifetime helping others, but died in poverty at the age of 90 in New York City in 1952.

Jackson was born into a Methodist family in Toronto on May 13, 1861. Several years later they moved to Wingham, about 150 kilometres northwest of Toronto, where his father opened a store. A good student, Will completed high school, and then studied classics for three years at the University of Toronto. His father's sudden bankruptcy, however, prevented Will from completing his final year. In 1881, he followed his family to Prince Albert in the North-West Territories, where his father began a farm implement business.

Will was elected secretary of the local farmers' union. The short man with the loud, booming voice soon became a familiar sight, riding on horseback to meetings throughout the Prince Albert district. Vigorously, Will attacked the federal government's harsh land regulations and its maladministration of the Northwest. He advocated a settlers' alliance with the Métis at neighbouring Batoche, who, concerned about their land claims, had just invited Louis Riel back from the United States. Thus fate brought the two men together. Jackson would support Riel to the end, long after the Prince Albert settlers broke away from him.

On May 12, 1885, Canadian troops took Will into custody as Riel's secretary and sent him to Regina to be tried. The Regina court committed the prisoner, who was long-haired with a full beard and wore a Métis headband, to the lunatic asylum at Lower Fort Garry. There he wrote his assessment of Riel: "The oppression of the aboriginal has been the crying sin of the white race in America and they have at last found a voice...."

On November 2, 1885, Will escaped and crossed the border into the United States. He now identified himself as a Métis and changed his name to the French-sounding Honoré Jaxon. In Chicago, he became a labour organizer and helped the carpenters fight for an eight-hour working day. In 1894 he joined Coxey's Army of unemployed as they marched on Washington, D.C. Three years later he converted to Baha'i, the new world religion from Persia, which stressed the simplicity of living and service to suffering human beings.

Honoré returned to Canada for two years from 1907 to 1909 but was disillusioned by the old injustices that remained. He went back to the United States and ended up in New York City in the 1920s. He loved the city, with its museums and libraries. His life mission became the establishment of a library for the Aboriginal people of Saskatchewan. Throughout the 1930s and 1940s he bought old books and pamphlets and saved newspapers, whatever he considered of value, and stored them in his apartment.

His dream died on December 13, 1951: on that icy-cold morning, he was evicted by his landlord. His library went first to the street, then to the New York City dump. In poor health and broken in spirit, Honoré Jaxon died in New York one month later, on January 10, 1952.

(continued)

Honoré Jaxon, sitting by his library, which is about to be transported to the New York City dump, December 13, 1951.

New York Daily News.

Mounties already in the Northwest. Middleton organized the troops in three columns, at Qu'Appelle, Swift Current, and Calgary.

The Métis ambushed Middleton at Fish Creek, south of Batoche, on April 24. The battle ended in a stalemate; the Métis and Native peoples, although poorly equipped, proved to be superb fighters. Lieutenant Colonel William Otter successfully relieved Battleford, but on May 2, Poundmaker defeated his force at Cut Knife Hill. Major General Thomas Bland Strange led the Alberta Field Force from Calgary, by way of Edmonton and the North Saskatchewan River, against Big Bear's band at Frenchman's Butte in late May. As at Fish Creek, the encounter was a draw, with both sides retreating at the same time.

The main battle took place at Batoche, Riel's headquarters, beginning on May 9. The three-day standoff ended when, out of frustration, Middleton's troops charged the Métis. The defenders, now out of ammunition, retreated. Riel surrendered on May 15, while Dumont and others fled to the United States.

Poundmaker gave himself up on May 26 and Big Bear did the same on July 2. The federal government's decision to send large quantities of rations to the starving Native peoples undermined their resistance. Fortunately for the federal government, most of the Native peoples were committed to a political solution. They kept their promise not to take up arms against the Crown, and only about 4 percent of them joined Riel. If they and the other Métis communities had joined the uprising, the

Gabriel Dumont, military leader of the Métis in 1885, and previously, in the "buffalo days," their leader in the hunt.

Glenbow Archives, Calgary, Canada/ NA-1177-1.

settlement of the West would probably have been postponed for at least a decade by continuing warfare.

In the trials that followed, the Canadian government prosecuted more than 125 Native people. The First Nations received harsher treatment than the Métis. The government convicted 44 First Nations people, eight of whom were hanged publicly. This mass hanging, the largest in Canadian history, demonstrated Ottawa's determination to punish any challenge to its authority. Big Bear and Poundmaker each received prison sentences of three years, although both leaders had spoken against participation. Poundmaker had joined only when attacked by the Canadians; Big Bear participated to moderate the actions of the militants in his band. They were released before their terms ended, because of poor health; both died within a year of their release.

RIEL'S TRIAL

A jury of six men, all of British background, tried Louis Riel for treason in a Regina courtroom. Riel pleaded not guilty. His lawyers wanted to fight for acquittal on the grounds of insanity, but he refused to comply. Riel maintained that the federal government was insane. "The federal government," he claimed, "besides doing nothing to satisfy the people of this great land, has even hardly been able to answer once or give a single response. That fact indicates an absolute lack of responsibility, and therefore

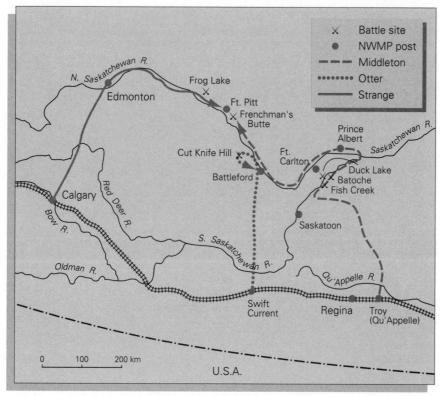

Military operations in the North-West Rebellion, 1885. This map shows the routes of the three military columns: to Batoche, under Major General Middleton; to Battleford, under Lieutenant Colonel Otter; and to the Ft. Pitt area, under Major General Strange.

insanity complicated by paralysis." Two doctors — James Wallace of Hamilton and Daniel Clark of Toronto — examined Riel during the trial. Both concluded that Riel was sane, that he could distinguish right from wrong. Dr. François Roy, who had treated Riel at the Beauport asylum in Quebec, testified that Riel was insane and in no condition "to be master of his acts."

Riel's speech in English to the jury eloquently summarized his role in the rebellion:

> No one can say that the Northwest was not suffering last year ... but what I have done, and risked, and to which I have exposed myself, rested certainly on the conviction I had to do, was called upon to do something for my country.... I know that through the grace of God I am the founder of Manitoba.... Even if I was going to be sentenced by you, gentlemen of the jury, I have the satisfaction if I die — that if I die I will not be reputed by all men as insane, as a lunatic.... Gentlemen of the jury, my reputation, my liberty, my life are at your discretion.

The jury deliberated for an hour before reaching its verdict: Riel was guilty of treason.

Big Bear (front row, second from the left) and Poundmaker (front row, far right), shown at their trials, 1885. Father André (back row, second from the right) spent the night before Riel's execution in prayer with him. He walked with him to the scaffold.

Glenbow Archives, Calgary, Canada/NA-3205-11.

THE EXECUTION OF RIEL

Only the federal cabinet could commute the court's decision. Appeals for clemency came from Canada, the United States, Britain, and France. Many members of the Orange Order, however, remembered Thomas Scott's execution fifteen years earlier. In contrast, many in Quebec demanded that the French-speaking Riel be exonerated. Once again, the country was divided.

Prime Minister John A. Macdonald twice postponed the execution. The second time, he appointed a medical commission to re-examine the question of Riel's sanity. The commissioners concluded that Riel was sane. November 16, 1885, became the new execution date. On that clear and chilly morning, Riel mounted the gibbet at Regina. The executioner, who had been imprisoned by Riel in Fort Garry in 1869, placed the rope around Riel's neck, the priest performed the last rites, and the trap door was sprung. A Métis, a French-Canadian, and later a western-Canadian, martyr was born.

It has been argued that Macdonald decided, in words attributed to him, that "Riel must swing" to keep Ontario loyal to the Conservative party. He gambled that Quebec would continue to give its support. His French-Canadian lieutenants, Hector Langevin, Adolphe Caron, and Adolphe Chapleau, were denounced as traitors for standing by their leader. Sir John A. Macdonald was burnt in effigy in the streets of Montreal. Clearly Riel's execution contributed to the demise of the Conservatives in Quebec in the 1890s and to the rise of the Liberals. The Sunday following the hanging of Riel for treason, Wilfrid Laurier, a young Liberal politician, declared at a huge Montreal rally: "If I had been on the banks of the Saskatchewan, I too, would have shouldered a musket."

Louis Riel's address to the jury during his trial at Regina, July 1885.

Glenbow Archives, Calgary, Canada/NA-1081-3.

The North-West Rebellion of 1885 marked a transition; henceforth on the Prairies, the settler society would dominate. Many events symbolized the transition: the execution of Riel and the imprisonment of Big Bear and Poundmaker; the use of the newly completed CPR to transport troops West to suppress the insurgents; and the establishment of an elected territorial assembly a year later, in 1886, in which no Métis were present. Possibly the most poignant, however, was the animus generated over the capture of two white women — Theresa Delaney and Theresa Gowanlock — by a group of Cree during the rebellion. In accounts of the capture, confinement, and ultimate release of these two white women, they came to embody the virtues of the "civilizers" from the East and, by contrast, the "barbaric" nature of the indigenous Native population, especially Native women. The liberation of these captives at the hands of the supposedly cruel, treacherous "savages" marked the triumph of the forces of "good" over "evil" and provided a rationale for the "necessary" suppression of the minority by the dominant society.

RISING FRENCH-CANADIAN NATIONALISM

The aftermath of 1885 contributed to the growing rift between English- and French-speaking Canadians. The Riel controversy intensified the nationalist sentiment of some French-Canadian leaders. They equated French-Canadian nationalism with provincial autonomy. Honoré Mercier, leader of the Quebec wing of the Liberal party after 1883, expressed this nationalist position in the mid-1880s. At the same rally in Montreal at which Wilfrid Laurier declared his support for the Métis, Mercier denounced the federal Conservative politicians who had been responsible for Riel's execution: "Riel, our brother, is dead, victim of fanaticism and treason — of the fanaticism of Sir John and some of his friends, of the treason of three of our people who sold their brother to keep their portfolios."

The Quebec Liberal leader appealed to his fellow Quebeckers to form an exclusive French-Canadian party, a Parti national, that would put French-Canadian interests first: "We felt that the murder of Riel was a declaration of war against Quebec; and that, therefore, French Canadians had a duty to cease their fratricidal quarrels and unite in a crusade to preserve the nation in Quebec from encroaching federal power." Mercier won the provincial election of 1886.

A French-Canadian response to Riel's execution. In English translation, the caption reads, "Louis Riel, Métis leader, executed November 16, 1885, political martyr! Guilty of having loved his oppressed compatriots! Victim of Orangist fanaticism, to which politicians without soul and without heart have sacrificed him. May true patriots remember this!!"

Archives Deschâtelets, Ottawa.

LOUIS RIEL,

CHEF METIS,

Exécuté le 16 Novembre 1885,

MARTYR POLITIQUE !

Coupable d'avoir aimé ses compatriotes opprimés !

Victime du fanatisme orangiste, auquel l'ont sacrifié des politiciens sans âme et sans cœur.

Que les vrais patriotes s'en souviennent !!

As premier, Mercier endorsed a theory of provincial rights that complemented Oliver Mowat's. T.J.J. Loranger, a Quebec court judge, best expressed Mercier's position in his *Letters upon the Interpretation of the Federal Constitution Known as the British North America Act* (1884). Loranger argued that each level of government, federal and provincial, was sovereign in its own area of jurisdiction and that the federal government had only limited power to deal with transprovincial concerns.

THE FIRST INTERPROVINCIAL CONFERENCE

To assist him in his challenge to Ottawa, Mercier called an interprovincial conference in 1887, the first of its kind. Two provinces declined the invitation — British Columbia and Prince Edward Island, which both had Conservative governments — while the other five provincial Liberal governments accepted. The federal Conservative government ignored the conference, dismissing it as a partisan session of provincial Liberal governments.

The premiers summed up the provincial-rights position. They argued that Confederation was a contract among several British colonies that had sought to establish a new country. Therefore, the provinces should control the federal government. Among their demands they called for larger federal subsidies, abolition of the federal power of disallowance, and Senate reform to strengthen provincial power.

A photo of the first interprovincial conference, called by Honoré Mercier in 1887, to challenge the authority of the federal government. The Quebec premier appears seated second from the left. Ontario's Oliver Mowat, the "Father of Provincial Rights," is seated in the centre. W.S. Fielding, who tried during his premiership to take Nova Scotia out of Confederation, is beside Mowat on the right.

National Archives of Canada/C-11583.

Macdonald refused to meet the premiers to discuss their complaints, but their protest did have an effect. From this time onward, the prime minister became cautious about using the federal power of disallowance. In 1888, he capitulated on the issue of the Manitoba railway legislation, which allowed Manitoba to build provincial rail lines, and a year later he gave in on the Ontario boundary question.

In 1887, Wilfrid Laurier became the federal Liberal leader. He proposed a French-Canadian nationalism that was an alternative to Mercier's, one that included French Canadians across the country. Initially, this was not so. In the 1860s, for example, he opposed Confederation. But Laurier became reconciled to union in the early 1870s, when elected to the House of Commons, and he began the brilliant career that led him to become prime minister. While he blamed the federal government for neglecting the Métis grievances, he appealed for moderation on both sides.

WEB
LINKS

CULTURAL AND RELIGIOUS FEUDS

Laurier's appeal for unity between English and French Canadians and Protestants and Roman Catholics went unheeded in the racially and religiously intolerant atmosphere of the late nineteenth century. Two issues — the Jesuits' Estates Act and the Manitoba Schools Question — revealed just how bitter ethnic relations and religious differences had become.

THE JESUITS' ESTATES CONTROVERSY

The dispute over the Jesuits' Estates began in 1888. During the French regime, the Jesuit order obtained large grants of land. After the conquest and the disbanding of the order by the pope in the early 1770s, ownership of these properties passed first to the British government and then to the province of Lower Canada. In the early 1840s, however, Bishop Ignace Bourget brought back the newly established Jesuits to Quebec. The Jesuits now appealed to the provincial government either to have their property returned or to receive financial compensation. Disputes arose within the Roman Catholic hierarchy in Quebec. Some argued that funds from the estates should go to the Catholic schools. Premier Mercier sought the aid of the pope as arbiter. In his proposed Jesuits' estates bill, Mercier agreed, on the basis of the pope's recommendation, to distribute $400 000 (a sum well below the actual value of the land) among the Jesuits, Université Laval in Quebec City, and the Catholic dioceses of the province. He awarded a further $60 000 to Protestant postsecondary educational institutions in Quebec.

Many in Ontario reacted vehemently to the idea of consulting the pope. D'Alton McCarthy, a fiery anti-Catholic and a Conservative MP from Ontario, insisted that the pope had no right to meddle in Canadian affairs. He moved a resolution in the House of Commons to have the federal government disallow the Jesuits' Estates Act. He and twelve supporters became known as "the noble thirteen" or "the devil's dozen," depending on one's perspective. They considered the act to be the latest in a series of attempts by the Jesuits and French-speaking Roman Catholics to rule Canada. McCarthy insisted on one common Canadian nationality based on the English language and preferably British Protestant culture. Since, however, Prime Minister John A. Macdonald refused to intervene in this provincial matter, McCarthy and his followers lost. Still, the battle was far from over. Ethnic and religious tensions now centred on the school question.

THE NEW BRUNSWICK SCHOOL QUESTION

The first dispute over denominational schools since Confederation occurred in New Brunswick. The BNA Act recognized denominational schools that existed *by law* before the union in the four original provinces. Denominational schools existed by custom in New Brunswick before the union, but not by law. In 1871 the New Brunswick government proposed legislation to amend the Schools Act to introduce a non-sectarian school system, which would deny public support to "separate" parish schools teaching French and providing religious instruction. To New Brunswick's Roman Catholics, both Acadians and Irish, this legislation meant depriving them of a right that they had enjoyed in fact, if not by law, at the time of Confederation. They requested the federal government to disallow the act under section 93 of the BNA Act, which included the right to intervene to protect the educational rights of a minority.

The federal Conservative government refused to intervene. Macdonald argued that the act lay within the province's jurisdiction. Roman Catholics did not lose any rights that they had had *by law* at the union or that they had acquired since. Hence the prime minister refused disallowance, or federal remedial action under section 93. Furthermore, he was reluctant to interfere in education — an area that was clearly, by the

BNA Act, under provincial jurisdiction. The federal government did make a strong appeal to the New Brunswick legislature to consider minority rights, but stopped at that.

The New Brunswick School Question provided the only precedent for the courts and the politicians when the Manitoba Schools Question arose in the late 1880s and early 1890s; but because it dealt with educational rights in a founding province of Confederation whose rights had been written into the original BNA Act, it was not really applicable. On the matter of linguistic and educational rights of the French-Canadian and Roman Catholic minorities in new provinces entering Confederation, the Fathers of Confederation said nothing.

THE MANITOBA SCHOOLS QUESTION

Manitoba became a significant test case because in 1870 it had an almost equal number of French- and English-speaking, Roman Catholic and Protestant inhabitants. The Manitoba Act of 1870 conferred language and school rights on French and English, Roman Catholics and Protestants.

By 1890, however, the situation had changed in Manitoba. The English-speaking Protestant population in Manitoba had increased tenfold by 1890, greatly outnumbering the French-speaking Canadians. Many French-speaking Métis had left the province. Moreover, French-speaking Canadians from Quebec did not join their English-speaking compatriots to the same extent in moving West in the late nineteenth century, despite a concerted effort by the French-speaking clergy of the Roman Catholic church in the West. Distance was a major factor. For French-speaking settlers contemplating leaving Quebec, New England was closer and more convenient, and almost everyone in Quebec had relatives or friends living there. Quebeckers could also be assured jobs as factory workers or labourers in New England. Should they wish to farm, opportunities existed in the American West with much easier access than in the Canadian West before the completion of the CPR in 1885. Thus the Northwest held little appeal.

Interference in Manitoba's separate school question came from the outside. In August 1889, D'Alton McCarthy delivered an emotional speech at Portage la Prairie against denominational schools in Manitoba as undermining the future greatness of Canada. A few months earlier, he had supported the formation of an Equal Rights Association, which claimed in its platform to stand for "equal rights of all religious denominations before the law, special privileges for none," by which was meant a single language — English — and a single system of public schools. According to McCarthy and his followers, Canada's minorities, especially the French-Canadian and Métis Roman Catholics in the West, should not have "special concessions." On the same platform as McCarthy at Portage la Prairie sat Joseph Martin, attorney general for the Manitoba government. He pledged his government's support in abolishing the dual school system, as well as French as an official language, in Manitoba.

In 1890, the Manitoba government passed a Schools Act that established a provincial department of education and a system of non-sectarian public schools that alone would receive the provincial grant for education. Denominational schools could still exist, but without government funding. Those contributing to such schools would have to do so in addition to their public-school taxes. The same session of the legislature abolished French as an official language, contrary to section 23 of the Manitoba Act of 1870.

MANITOBA CATHOLICS FIGHT SCHOOL LEGISLATION

Discontented Roman Catholics had three options open to them: appeal to the federal government to use its right of disallowance of provincial legislation; take the issue to the courts to have the legislation declared *ultra vires*, or unconstitutional; or appeal to Ottawa to intervene on behalf of the minority through remedial legislation as set out in section 93 of the BNA Act. Eventually, they pursued all three possibilities.

Macdonald resisted using the federal government's right of disallowance, fearing that the Manitoba electorate's disapproval of such an action would strengthen the provincial government's power. He favoured court action and even agreed that the federal government would pay the legal costs of the appellant. The case, known as *Barrett v. the City of Winnipeg*, went through the provincial court, which upheld the Manitoba government's position, to the Supreme Court of Canada, which upheld the right of the Roman Catholic minority to have state-supported separate schools. Then, the Judicial Committee of the Privy Council reversed this decision in favour of the Manitoba government's position. During the same period, the territorial assembly of the North-West Territories in 1892 followed Manitoba's lead in denying the French language official status in the legislature, the courts, and schools — all rights granted in the North-West Territories Act of 1875 (and amended in 1877).

One final option remained. The Manitoba Roman Catholics appealed to the federal government for remedial action under section 93 of the BNA Act. The Judicial Committee of the Privy Council eventually ruled that, yes, the federal government had the constitutional right to intervene on behalf of the minority even though the Manitoba law had been judged valid. The Conservatives introduced the remedial legislation bill in Parliament in January 1896. The government established a nine-member board to run the separate-school system, to be supported by the Roman Catholics' own tax monies; the schools in this system would share a portion of the provincial educational grant; and, to ensure proper standards, the separate schools would be inspected regularly and funds would be withheld if they were judged inefficient. Clearly, remedial legislation favoured the Roman Catholic position. But Parliament dissolved on April 23, with the bill still not passed into law. Four days later, MacKenzie Bowell resigned as Conservative leader under pressure from the Orange wing of his party, angered over his handling of the schools question.

THE ELECTION OF 1896

The Conservatives entered the federal election of 1896 with a new leader, Charles Tupper — the party's fifth leader in five years. After Macdonald's death in 1891, no one seemed capable of holding the party together. The Manitoba Schools Question was only one of several contentious issues in the election, although an important one. In Quebec, the Conservatives stressed during the election campaign that they had introduced remedial legislation on behalf of the Manitoba Roman Catholics. In English-speaking Canada, Conservative candidates emphasized that the bill was not, and might never become, law Some English-speaking Conservatives even spoke openly against the party position on this controversial issue. Outside Quebec, the Conservatives also remained on the defensive over their high tariff policy and were being blamed for the country's continuing economic depression.

The Conservative party had mixed opportunities in the election campaign. In Quebec, the Roman Catholic hierarchy issued a pastoral letter appealing to parishioners to vote for candidates who promised to support remedial legislation. But many of the French-Canadian Conservatives who knew of their party's internal split refused to work during the campaign. Adolphe Chapleau, the party's leading figure and lieutenant governor of Quebec, sat quietly in Quebec City, refusing to intervene. Israël Tarte, a one-time Conservative organizer, had already defected to the Liberals.

The Liberals were in an enviable position. As the opposition, they could denounce the Tories without having to offer concrete alternative policies. On the controversial schools question, for example, Wilfrid Laurier had not taken a strong stand during the stormy parliamentary session of 1896. During the election campaign, the Liberal leader simply promised that his Liberal government, if elected, would end the dispute through compromise with the Manitoba Liberal government in a way that would respect provincial rights. "If it was in my power," he said in 1895, "and if I had the responsibility, I would try the sunny way." To voters weary of the wrangling between the federal government and the provinces, the "sunny way" seemed appealing. In Quebec, the Liberals had the advantage of a French-Canadian Roman Catholic leader. Liberal leaders in the province reminded Quebeckers that if they turned Laurier down as prime minister they would never live to a see a French-Canadian prime minister in Ottawa.

The Liberals narrowly won the election of 1896. Outside Quebec, they tied the Conservatives in the number of seats. But in Quebec they obtained two-thirds of the seats.

THE LAURIER-GREENWAY COMPROMISE

Laurier opened negotiations. He and Manitoba's Premier Greenway struck a compromise: there would be no state-supported denominational schools, but religious instruction would be allowed in the public schools for half an hour at the end of each day. Roman Catholic teachers could be employed in urban schools with 40 Roman Catholic pupils or in rural districts with 25. On the language question it was agreed that, when ten of the pupils in any school system spoke the French language or any language other than English as their native language, the teaching of such pupils would be conducted in English and French or the other language "upon the bilingual system."

The French-Canadian Roman Catholic minority in Manitoba would have obtained more under the Conservatives' remedial legislation. The compromise allowed religious instruction but led to the abolition of the state-supported separate-school system. French would be retained only when sufficient population warranted it; hence, it lost the status of equality with English that it had had under the Manitoba Act of 1870. It became a language like any other in Manitoba, all of which were unofficial except English. (In 1916, at the height of World War I, even the bilingual clause of the Laurier–Greenway compromise was abolished, making English the only language of instruction in the province's schools.)

The Roman Catholic hierarchy in Canada accused Laurier of capitulating to the English-Canadian Protestants. Laurier argued that the agreement was the best that could be hoped for, given the Roman Catholics' minority position. Some Canadian bishops appealed to the pope to intervene on behalf of the Manitoba Roman Catholics. The pope sent Monsignor Merry del Val to investigate the issue. The papal adviser reported that while the compromise was unsatisfactory, these terms were the best that the Roman Catholics could, under the circumstances, obtain.

THE AUTONOMY BILLS

The schools question in the West arose again in 1905, with the creation of the two new provinces of Saskatchewan and Alberta. The original ordinances of the North-West Territories Act of 1875, as amended in 1877, had provided for both Protestant and Roman Catholic schools to receive public funding. As well, both French and English could be used as languages of instruction. In the early 1890s, however, the territorial government made English the official language of instruction in the Roman Catholic school system, restricting French to the primary grades only for French-speaking children. Then, in 1901, the territorial government restricted religious instruction to the last half hour of the school day, as was the case in Manitoba.

When the time came to draw up the autonomy bills to bring Saskatchewan and Alberta into existence, Charles Fitzpatrick, the federal minister of justice and a Quebec Roman Catholic, and Henri Bourassa drafted the educational clause to restore the original system of 1877. The clause permitted the free establishment of Roman Catholic and Protestant schools as well as the use of French in the school system. Clifford Sifton, who drafted the rest of the autonomy bills, opposed the educational clause, claiming it went against the wishes of the government of the North-West Territories. He resigned from the cabinet in protest.

Laurier intervened and allowed Sifton to redraft the educational clause, although he did not invite him back into the cabinet. Sifton's revised clause restricted the rights of the French-Canadian Roman Catholic minorities to the limited concessions granted in the ordinance of 1901. Laurier accepted the "honourable compromise," as he described the Sifton amendment. But Bourassa denounced it as infringing on the rights of French Canadians as set out in the original North-West Territories Act. He maintained that French-Canadian Roman Catholics in the West should enjoy the same rights that English-Canadian Protestants enjoyed in Quebec. In the end, however, the Sifton amendment became law.

The period from 1880 to 1914 saw a resurgence of regionalism. Provincial-rightists successfully challenged the power of the central government on a number of constitutional issues, thus making Canada in practice a federal state with a more even division of power between the central and provincial governments. Regional protests arose in the Maritimes with the attempt by Nova Scotia once again to secede from Confederation and in the West over the North-West Rebellion of 1885. As well, English- and French-speaking Canadians feuded over Riel's execution, over the Jesuits' Estates Act in Quebec, and over linguistic and religious rights in schools, first in Manitoba and then in Saskatchewan and Alberta. These disputes contributed to the defeat of the Conservatives in the 1896 election and of the Liberals in the 1911 election.

Interior of a school near Vulcan, Alberta, at the turn of the century. Teachers insisted that children from non–English-speaking countries speak English in the classroom. Legally, even French-Canadian students were obliged to do so in Alberta after their first two years of elementary school as a result of ordinances passed by the territorial government in the 1890s.

Glenbow Archives, Calgary, Canada/NA-748-41.

LINKING TO THE PAST

The Ontario Boundary Act, 1889
http://www.miredespa.com/wmaton/Other/Legal/Constitutions/Canada/English/coba_1889.html
The full text of the 1889 Ontario Boundary Act, which settled the dispute between Ontario and Manitoba and fixed the western limits of Ontario.

The North-West Rebellion of 1885
http://www.schoolnet.ca/collections/E/
Scroll down to "History" under the subject listing, and then choose "Northwest Rebellion of 1885," which features a wide range of information about the rebellion. By following the table of contents link to "The 1885 Resistance," you will also find a detailed chronology of events, including biographies of key participants.

Sir Wilfrid Laurier
http://cnet.unb.ca/achn/pme/wlcb.htm
A brief biography of Prime Minister Wilfrid Laurier, including details about his background and career. A more descriptive biography, as well as an anecdote about Laurier's time as prime minister, can be accessed at the bottom of the page.

The Laurier–Greenway Compromise
http://www.nelson.com/nelson/school/discovery/cantext/western/1896mani.htm
The Laurier–Greenway Compromise, also known as the Manitoba School Act of 1896, attempted to resolve the issue of religion and language in education.

RELATED READINGS

The topics in this chapter can be examined in greater depth in the following articles from R. Douglas Francis and Donald B. Smith, *Readings in Canadian History: Post-Confederation*, 5th ed. (Toronto: Harcourt Brace, 1998): Christopher Armstrong, "Remoulding the Constitution," pp. 21–44; J.R. Miller, "Unity/Diversity: The Canadian Experience; From Confederation to the First World War," pp. 44–53; David Lee, "The Métis Militant Rebels of 1885," pp. 57–74; and A. Blair Stonechild, "The Indian View of the 1885 Uprising," pp. 75–91.

BIBLIOGRAPHY

For an overview of Dominion–provincial relations in the late nineteenth century see P.B. Waite, *Canada, 1874–1896: Arduous Destiny* (Toronto: McClelland & Stewart, 1971), and the *Report of the Royal Commission on Dominion–Provincial Relations*, Book 1 (Ottawa: J.O. Patenaude, Printer to the King, 1940).

The provincial-rights movements in Ontario is discussed in J.C. Morrison, "Oliver Mowat and the Development of Provincial Rights in Ontario: A Study in Dominion–Provincial Relations, 1867–1896," in *Three History Theses* (Toronto: Ontario Department of Public Records and Archives, 1961); and Christopher Armstrong, *The Politics of Federalism: Ontario's Relations with the Federal Government, 1867–1942* (Toronto: University of Toronto Press, 1981). See, as well, Margaret Evans's biography *Sir Oliver Mowat* (Toronto: University of Toronto Press, 1992). On political protest in Atlantic Canada in the 1880s see Judith Fingard, "The 1880s: Paradoxes of Progress," in E.R. Forbes and D.A. Muise, eds., *The Atlantic Provinces in Confederation* (Toronto: University of Toronto Press, 1993); T.W. Acheson, "The Maritimes and 'Empire Canada,'" in D.J. Bercuson, ed., *Canada and the Burden of Unity* (Toronto: Macmillan, 1977), pp. 87–114; E.R. Forbes, *Aspects of Maritime Regionalism, 1867–1927* (Ottawa: Canadian Historical Association, 1983); and George Rawlyk, ed., *The Atlantic Provinces and the Problem of Confederation* (St. John's: Breakwater Books, 1979). Rawlyk also deals with developments in Newfoundland in the 1880s and 1890s, as does Frederick W. Rowe in *A History of Newfoundland and Labrador* (Toronto: McGraw-Hill Ryerson, 1980). On western Canada see T.D. Regehr, "Western Canada and the Burden of National Transportation Policies," in D.J. Bercuson ed., *Canada and the Burden of Unity* (Toronto: Macmillan, 1977), pp. 115–41. David Cruise and Alison Griffiths discuss the impact of the CPR rates in *Lords of the Line* (Toronto: Viking, 1988).

The most authoritative account of the North-West Rebellion is Bob Beal and Rob Macleod, *Prairie Fire: The 1885 North-West Rebellion* (Edmonton: Hurtig, 1984). For the Native perspective on the 1885 Rebellion see Blair Stonechild and Bill Waiser, *Loyal Till Death: Indians and the North-West Rebellion* (Calgary: Fifth House, 1997); and J.R. Miller, *Big Bear (Mistahimusqua)* (Toronto: ECW Press, 1996). On aspects of the conflict between the Natives and the Anglo-Canadians on the Prairies see Walter Hildebrandt, *Views from Fort Battleford: Constructed Visions of an Anglo-Canadian West* (Regina: Canadian Plains Research Centre, University of Regina, 1994). For a historical perspective on the

Delaney–Gowanlock captivity see Sarah Carter, *Capturing Women: The Manipulation of Cultural Imagery in Canada's Prairie West* (Montreal/Kingston: McGill-Queen's University Press, 1997). Hugh A. Dempsey explains the participation of Big Bear's band in *Big Bear* (Vancouver: Douglas & McIntyre, 1984), as does J.R. Miller in *Big Bear (Mistahimusqua)* (Toronto: ECW Press, 1996). George Woodcock discusses Gabriel Dumont's role in *Gabriel Dumont* (Edmonton: Hurtig, 1975). On Louis Riel see the readings cited for Chapter Two of this book, as well as Thomas Flanagan, *Louis "David" Riel: "Prophet of the New World"* (Toronto: University of Toronto Press, 1979), and his *Riel and the Rebellion: 1885 Reconsidered* (Saskatoon: Western Producer Prairie Books, 1983). For a critical view of the government's handling of the Riel affair consult D.N. Sprague, *Canada and the Métis, 1869–1885* (Waterloo, ON: Wilfrid Laurier University Press, 1988). An alternative explanation for the uprising is available in Gerhard Ens, *Homeland to Hinterland: The Changing Worlds of the Red River Metis in the Nineteenth Century* (Toronto: University of Toronto Press, 1996). A historiographical article is J.R. Miller, "From Riel to the Métis," *Canadian Historical Review* 69(1) (March 1988): 1–20. Diane Payment's *"The Free People — Otipemisiwak": Batoche, Saskatchewan, 1870–1930* (Ottawa: National Historic Parks and Sites, Parks Canada, 1990) provides an in-depth study of the important Métis community of Batoche. For the reaction of Ontarians to Riel see A.I. Silver, "Ontario's Alleged Fanaticism in the Riel Affair," *Canadian Historical Review* 69(1) (March 1988): 21–50. All of Riel's writings have been edited by George F.G. Stanley et al., *The Collected Writings of Louis Riel*, 5 vols. (Edmonton: University of Alberta Press, 1985). A number of excellent articles on the events of 1885 are contained in *NeWest Review* 10(9) (May 1985), a special "1885" issue. For a discussion of the military engagement at Batoche see Walter Hildebrandt, *The Battle of Batoche: British Small Warfare and the Entrenched Métis* (Ottawa: National Historic Parks and Sites, Parks Canada, 1985).

George F.G. Stanley reviews the various interpretations of Riel in "The Last Word on Louis Riel — The Man of Several Faces," in F. Laurie Barron and James B. Waldram, eds., *1885 and After: Native Society in Transition* (Regina: Canadian Plains Research Centre, University of Regina, 1986), as does Doug Owram in "The Myth of Louis Riel," *Canadian Historical Review* 63(3) (September 1982): 315–36. George Melnyk's *Radical Regionalism* (Edmonton: NeWest, 1982) and his edited collection *Riel to Reform: A History of Protest in Western Canada* (Saskatoon: Fifth House, 1992) examine the roots of western protest and its relationship to regional identity.

Quebec's views on federal–provincial relations are analyzed in R. Cook, *Provincial Autonomy: Minority Rights and the Compact Theory, 1867–1921* (Ottawa: Queen's Printer, 1969); and Arthur Silver, *The French-Canadian Idea of Confederation, 1864–1900* (Toronto: University of Toronto Press, 1982). See also Mason Wade, *The French Canadians: 1760–1945* (Toronto: Macmillan, 1955), pp. 331–446; and Susan Mann Trofimenkoff, *The Dream of Nation: A Social and Intellectual History of Quebec* (Toronto: Gage, 1983), pp. 150–66. Honoré Mercier's views are presented in Gilles Gallichan, *Honoré Mercier: La politique et la culture* (Sillery, PQ: Septentrion, 1994).

J.R. Miller's *Equal Rights: The Jesuits' Estates Act Controversy* (Montreal: McGill-Queen's University Press, 1979) deals with that subject in depth. On the Manitoba schools question and its impact on the election of 1896 consult Paul Crunican, *Priests and Politicians: Manitoba Schools and the Election of 1896* (Toronto: University of Toronto Press, 1974). On Rome's position in the controversy see Roberto Perin, *Rome in Canada: The Vatican and Canadian Affairs in the Late Victorian Age* (Toronto: University of Toronto Press, 1990). Lovell Clark has compiled a collection of sources in *The Manitoba School Question: Majority Rule or Minority Rights* (Toronto: Copp Clark, 1968). On D'Alton McCarthy's role see J.R. Miller, "D'Alton McCarthy, Equal Rights, and the Origins of the Manitoba Schools

Question," *Canadian Historical Review* 54 (December 1973): 369–92. Gilbert L. Comeault, "La question des écoles du Manitoba — un nouvel éclairage," *Revue d'histoire de l'Amérique française* 33(1) (juin 1979): 3–23, stresses the local origins of the Manitoba schools question. Treatment of the schools question in Alberta and Saskatchewan can be found in Manoly R. Lupul, *The Roman Catholic Church and the North-West School Question: A Study in Church–State Relations in Western Canada* (Toronto: University of Toronto Press, 1974). On Sifton's contribution see D.J. Hall, *Clifford Sifton*, vol. 2, *The Lonely Eminence, 1901–1929* (Vancouver: University of British Columbia Press, 1985).

The politics of the 1890s are discussed in John T. Saywell's introduction to *The Canadian Journal of Lady Aberdeen, 1893–1898* (Toronto: Champlain Society, 1960); Lovell Clark, "Macdonald's Conservative Successors, 1891–1896," in John Moir, ed., *Character and Circumstance: Essays in Honour of Donald Grant Creighton* (Toronto: Macmillan, 1970), pp. 43–62; H.B. Neatby and J.T. Saywell, "Chapleau and the Conservative Party in Quebec," *Canadian Historical Review* 37 (March 1956): 1–22; P.B. Waite, *The Man from Halifax* (Toronto: University of Toronto Press, 1985); and H. Blair Neatby, *Laurier and a Liberal Quebec: A Study in Political Management* (Toronto: McClelland & Stewart, 1973). A recent biography is that by Réal Bélanger, *Wilfrid Laurier: quand la politique devient passion* (Québec: Presses de l'Université Laval, 1986).

CHAPTER FIVE

Imperialism, Continentalism, and Nationalism

A century ago, no one really believed that Canada could thrive politically, economically, and culturally as a fully independent country. George Ross, Ontario's minister of education and later premier (1899–1905), proposed one option: an increased role in the British empire. "As Canadians," he stated in 1896, "we should teach more of Canada and in teaching Canada we should teach it as only one colony of the vast British empire on whose dominion the sun never sets." Another group of English Canadians favoured instead closer economic or even political association with the United States. Goldwin Smith, a historian-cum-journalist and long-time critic, became the continentalists' most articulate spokesman. A third option, presented by Henri Bourassa of Quebec, was most popular among French-speaking Canadians. The Quebec nationalists argued that Canada should formulate its own foreign policy as an autonomous nation within the British empire. Eventually Canadians blended the three approaches. They evolved a close relationship with both Britain and the United States, while maintaining a degree of autonomy.

THE NORTH ATLANTIC TRIANGLE AND THE TREATY OF WASHINGTON

The triangular relationship among Britain, the United States, and Canada broke down in the 1860s. After the North won the U.S. Civil War in 1865, it immediately demanded compensation from Britain and Canada for "supporting" the South. Britain had allowed Confederate agents to purchase ships and ammunition in Britain. One such ship, the *Alabama*, inflicted heavy losses on American merchant shipping. Other British vessels, such as the *Trent*, carried Confederate envoys to England to raise financial assistance for the southern cause. As a final irritant, the British North American colonies had been used, on at least one occasion, as a base for Confederate soldiers to attack the North.

The Americans had contributed to the tensions too. The American Congress cancelled the Reciprocity Treaty in 1866, and some Congressmen assumed that economic collapse north of the border would follow, causing the British North American colonies to seek union with the United States. As well, the American government did nothing to prevent the Fenian Brotherhood, a radical group of Irish-Americans who hoped to capture Canada for use as a bargaining tool for the independence of Ireland, from making raids across the border. The Fenians continued their attacks until 1871. Prominent American leaders also talked openly of annexing Canada as part of their "manifest destiny" to control the North American continent.

Both English Canadians and many French Canadians saw Britain as their protection from the United States. Thus Canada welcomed the 15 000 British troops stationed in the new Dominion in 1867. It was the British government, wanting to reduce expenses, that insisted on their withdrawal by 1871. At the same time, however, Canadian leaders wanted greater control over their internal affairs. They also insisted on a stronger voice within the British empire, especially as they became aware of Britain's willingness to sacrifice Canada in the interests of British–American harmony.

British and American leaders agreed to call a conference in Washington to settle outstanding disputes between the two countries resulting chiefly from the Civil War, in particular the *Alabama* claims. The United States also wanted to bargain for the right to fish in the territorial waters of the Maritime provinces and to use those provinces' ports — privileges denied since 1818, except during the term of the Reciprocity Treaty from 1854 to 1866. Canada hoped to use the fisheries question as leverage to force the Americans to renew the Reciprocity Treaty. In addition, it wanted compensation for damages caused by Fenian raids. On the Pacific Ocean, a clear boundary line between Vancouver Island and the American mainland had not yet been determined.

For the first time, a Canadian, Prime Minister John A. Macdonald, attended an international conference as a participant. Although he spoke for Canada, he was officially part of the three-member British delegation and was therefore expected to represent Britain as well. This dual role placed Macdonald in an awkward position; he realized, "If things go well my share of the kudos will be but small, and if anything goes wrong I will be made the scapegoat at all events so far as Canada is concerned." From Macdonald's perspective in the negotiations, the British proved all too willing to bargain away Canadian interests for a lasting Anglo–American peace.

The Americans did well by the Treaty of Washington. They succeeded in keeping the question of compensation to Canadians for the Fenian raids off the conference agenda, yet obtained $15.5 million as a settlement for their own *Alabama* claims. They won the right to fish in British North American territorial waters in return for a cash payment, subsequently agreed upon by an arbitration committee to be $5.5 million. As well, they obtained free navigation in perpetuity on the St. Lawrence River. Through an arbitration process by which the German kaiser decided the merits of the San Juan Islands boundary dispute, the Americans acquired these islands, east of Victoria, too.

The Canadians received very little of a concrete nature: the right to free navigation on three remote Alaskan rivers, and the removal of duties on Canadian fish exported into American markets. Yet, in one respect, Canada did well: through the Treaty of Washington, the United States recognized Canada as a separate nation in North America. Canada no longer needed the British military garrison, as the United States confirmed and recognized Canada's borders.

Macdonald returned from Washington determined to obtain a greater Canadian voice in deciding imperial policy. The prime minister later appointed Alexander Tilloch Galt, who had briefly served as the Dominion's first finance minister in 1867,

The Treaty of Washington commissioners in 1871. Prime Minister John A. Macdonald is third from the left. This was the first international conference in which a Canadian leader participated.

M.B. Brady/National Archives of Canada/ C-2422.

as high commissioner for Canada in London. Only reluctantly did the British government approve the new quasi-diplomatic post, and then only on the condition that Canada would not use the term "minister." The delegate became a "high commissioner," a title the Canadian diplomatic representatives in the United Kingdom and other Commonwealth countries retain today. Galt's tasks included the promotion of Canada's exports to Britain and of British investment in Canada, as well as the encouragement of British emigration to the Canadian Northwest.

CONTINENTALISM

Generally speaking, the Liberals — more so than the Conservatives — favoured stronger continental ties in the 1880s and 1890s. Closer links between the two countries could take many forms. Freer trade, for example, appealed particularly to the exporters of fish, farm products, and timber. Some Liberals simply wanted a return to the Reciprocity Treaty of 1854 or a restricted reciprocity agreement, which would apply to natural products only. Others favoured unrestricted reciprocity, or free trade, in some manufactured goods as well as in natural resources. Still others proposed commercial union — an integrated economic union with a free interchange of all products, a sharing of internal revenue taxes, and a common tariff policy against other countries. At the extreme end of this spectrum came political union.

All of these positions naturally depended on the Americans' openness to some kind of association. In the 1870s, however, protectionists dominated the Senate, and the Republican administrations turned down Canadian offers to renegotiate a reciprocity treaty.

THE TRADE QUESTION AND THE 1891 ELECTION

The trade issue came to a head in the election of 1891. The Liberals declared their support for closer Canadian–American ties, although they differed on what form they should take. Goldwin Smith, the outspoken historian-cum-journalist, wrote a tract for the election, *Canada and the Canadian Question*, in which he made the case for political union with the United States. He argued that Canada was an unnatural country economically, geographically, and culturally. Political expediency alone held it together. Canada's natural destiny lay in a larger North American nation. Smith looked toward continental union as the means to assimilate the French Canadians, whom he regarded as a most backward people. He also wanted to open up the natural north–south trade axis of the continent and to achieve a federation of North America's English-speaking people. Richard Cartwright, former minister of finance in the Mackenzie government, saw commercial union between the two countries, with a common tariff against outsiders, as being in Canada's best interest. By contrast, Edward Blake, former leader of the federal Liberal party (1881–87), opposed unrestricted reciprocity, seeing it as a threat to national interests. Laurier, as party leader, pressured Blake into silence on his opposition until after the election, at which time Blake publicly denounced the policy in an open letter to his constituency. In the middle stood Wilfrid Laurier. Commercial union appealed to him in principle but was too extreme for a party platform, so he committed the party to unrestricted reciprocity instead.

Canadian manufacturers opposed any form of reciprocity. In 1887, they published a manifesto warning that reciprocity would adversely affect the infant industries of Canada that were still struggling under the National Policy to survive a recession. Macdonald claimed that unrestricted reciprocity threatened Canada's independence because it would ultimately lead to political union with the United States. He maintained that protectionism was the means to uphold the British connection. He declared his loyalty to Britain in his popular campaign slogan, "A British subject I was born, and a British subject I will die," and proceeded to drape himself in the British flag.

THE 1891 ELECTION RESULTS

The Conservatives won the election of 1891, but only by a narrow majority of 27 seats. They lost seats to the Liberals in close votes in the rural areas, which tended to support free trade, but won most of the urban vote in Ontario and Quebec, where protectionism was strong. They made their real gains, however, in the outlying provinces — "the shreds and patches of Confederation," as the disgruntled Liberal Richard Cartwright called them. The Conservatives won in all three Maritime provinces on the loyalty issue and returned fourteen out of a possible fifteen members in the West. With the open backing of the CPR, they won every seat but one (in Manitoba) along the railway's main line from Vancouver to Montreal. When asked about that one loss, Cornelius Van Horne, president of the CPR, replied that it must have been a case of pure oversight on the CPR's part.

The election of 1891 ended unrestricted reciprocity as a Liberal policy. Nearly two decades would pass before the Liberals would champion "continentalism" once again.

IMPERIALISM

Many English-speaking Canadians favoured stronger British ties through imperial federation. After 1875, British attitudes to empire changed. Benjamin Disraeli's statement in the 1850s that colonies were "millstones around the neck of the British" had

THE OLD FLAG.
THE OLD POLICY.
THE OLD LEADER.

The Conservatives' election poster for the 1891 campaign, showing Sir John A. Macdonald being carried forth with the flag by the farmer and the factory worker. Macdonald campaigned on a platform of loyalty to "the old [British] flag, the old [National] policy," and himself as "the old leader" of the Conservative Party.

McCord Museum of Canadian History, Montreal/M965.34.8.

given way to a new imperialism in the late nineteenth century. Indeed, Disraeli himself, as Conservative prime minister, became one of its most ardent supporters, having come to appreciate the importance of colonies in maintaining Britain's military and economic supremacy in the world. In particular, they proved important for British hegemony as Germany and Italy became major European powers and as the United States threatened to supplant Britain as the leading English-speaking country in the world.

Rivalry between imperial countries meant competition for colonial markets and for world trade, thus giving an economic emphasis to the new imperialism. The cry from imperialists that "trade follows the flag" led British manufacturers and many in the working class to support imperialism in the late nineteenth century. Depressed economic conditions in England during the 1880s and 1890s strengthened the new movement.

Imperialism, however, represented for many of its followers much more than trade, tariffs, and guns. It was an intellectual and spiritual force. Imperialists believed implicitly in the superiority of the Anglo-Saxon "race." Applying Charles Darwin's theory of evolution in the animal kingdom to society, race theorists argued that some races were born "superior" — were better fit to survive — than others, and that, in Britain and in colonies settled by whites, the Anglo-Saxons constituted the elite.

Imperialists argued that their "race's" superior position made it imperative for "Anglo-Saxons" to spread their "virtues" — their values and Christian beliefs, the two being considered synonymous — to the less fortunate "infidels" of Asia, Africa, and the Pacific islands. They believed they must take up this "white man's burden," as the British author Rudyard Kipling expressed it.

Women played an ambiguous role in the imperialist movement. Through such organizations as the Imperial Order Daughters of the Empire (IODE), founded by Margaret Polson Murray during the South African War, women were strong advocates of imperial sentiment. The novelist Sara Jeannette Duncan, in her fine novel *The Imperialist* (1904), presented an Ontario community loyal and attached to Britain, but that rejected substantial imperial commitments. British women, however, were much more than advocates of imperialism; they were also symbols, or icons, of imperialism, as representatives of the moral, religious, and spiritual components of its ideology. They were the bearers of the finest British civilization and thus the true "empire builders." Their children were the offspring of the dominant race, and thus the means to ensure its survival. English-Canadian imperial literature extolled the virtues of the fairer sex of the empire builders, by contrasting the noble attributes of British women with the degenerate qualities of "coloured women" in the subservient colonial society. As well, protecting this "fairer sex" became a pretext for suppressing and controlling the indigenous population. Once again, then, racism and imperialism were fused to accentuate the superiority of the conqueror by emphasizing the inferiority of the conquered, the "others" in the imperial--colonial relationship.

IMPERIALISM AS NATIONALISM

English-Canadian imperialists believed that Canada could offer the British empire much, economically, militarily, and spiritually. In turn, the empire could advance Canada's national interests. In this sense, as historian Carl Berger has written, "imperialism was one form of Canadian nationalism."[1] These imperialists thought that Canada would soon become the heart of the British empire. Throughout history, they pointed out, all great races had come out of northern climates. English-speaking Canadians were the last group of Anglo-Saxons to struggle in a cold, rugged, northern climate, and this struggle "in the true north, strong and free" had strengthened their will to survive. It prepared them to assume the mantle of imperial grandeur as it passed from British hands. While Canadians aided the empire, they would also be helping themselves. English-Canadian imperialists envisioned imperial federation as a means to free Canada from economic depression, ethnic tension, provincialism, and threatened American annexation, enabling it to reach greater heights — "a sense of power" — in the world.

Imperialism drew its greatest support in Canada from a small English-speaking social and political elite, mainly Protestant ministers, lawyers, teachers, and politicians. In 1887 they formed a Canadian branch of the Imperial Federation League, an organization begun in Britain three years earlier. Descendants of United Empire Loyalists joined in large numbers, seeing imperialism as the fulfilment of their long-time dream of a "United Empire," which gave the league its greatest support in Ontario and the Maritimes.

A Historical Portrait

SARA JEANNETTE DUNCAN

Sara Jeannette Duncan symbolized the "new woman" of the late nineteenth century. She was the first Canadian woman to become a journalist and counted among her friends two other "exceptional" women: Pauline Johnson, the Mohawk poet; and Augusta Stowe, the daughter of Emily Stowe, the first woman to graduate from a Canadian medical school.

Sara was born in Brantford, Ontario, in 1861. Her parents encouraged her to enjoy "romping and fresh air" and even to play hockey with her brothers. But in terms of career choice for their oldest child, they were quite traditional, encouraging Sara to become a teacher. She attended Normal School but loathed teaching, and decided instead to pursue a career in journalism. Her first breakthrough came in 1882, when a Boston magazine, *Outing*, accepted her account of a trip she and her brother made to Quebec. Two years later, she travelled to the New Orleans Cotton Centennial and sold her account of that journey to a series of Canadian and American newspapers. Her success enabled her to obtain a job as a columnist for the Toronto *Globe*, the first woman to do so.

In 1886, she and a female friend embarked on a world tour — unchaperoned — by going "the wrong way" via Asia rather than Europe. They visited Japan, Ceylon, and India before arriving in England. Sara participated in what were considered "unladylike activities" for the time: riding a locomotive cowcatcher through the Rockies; travelling by donkey, camel, and elephant in India, and taking a catamaran to Ceylon. Her account of her tour came out in serial form in a popular British magazine as "A Social Departure," and then appeared in book form under the same title.

Upon marriage to an English official she met in India, she settled there. Her finest novel was *The Imperialist*, published in 1904. It combined her intimate knowledge of Canada from growing up in Brantford (the novel was set in "Elgin," the county where Brantford was located) with her wider knowledge of the British empire, acquired through her world travels. She would have agreed with her fellow Canadian nationalist, J.S. Ewart, when he questioned at the time: "How can Canadians love the British empire which they have not seen, when they do not love their own country which they have seen?" Her novel was designed to do both: familiarize Canadians with the British empire and instill in them a love for their own country.

Duncan viewed imperialism along the lines of the Canadian imperialists of her day. She too admired Britain as the Mecca of the race, but was repulsed by the materialism and militarism of the British imperialists. What imperialism needed was a new seat of power, and Duncan saw Canada as the logical new location. "In the scrolls of the future it is already written that the centre of the Empire must shift — and where, if not to Canada?" she has her protagonist, Lorne Murchison, ask rhetorically. The proper imperial tie would boost Canadian nationalism and hence ward off the danger of absorption into the United States. As an ardent nationalist, she held Canada in the highest esteem.

(continued)

During World War I, Sara Jeannette Duncan moved from India to England. In 1919, she and her husband, who by this time had become a reporter, had an opportunity to accompany the Prince of Wales on his Canadian tour. It was her last visit to her homeland. On July 22, 1922, she died of pneumonia. She was buried in England under a gravestone with the simple inscription: "This leaf has blown far."

LEADERS OF THE CANADIAN IMPERIAL FEDERATION LEAGUE

The Imperial Federation League attracted some colourful individuals. In Toronto, Colonel George Taylor Denison was the most dynamic member. A descendant of a long line of enthusiasts of the British military tradition, Denison wanted to follow an army career, although he was educated as a lawyer. His connections secured him the post of police magistrate in Toronto, where speed, not justice, was apparently his main concern. Denison prided himself on once trying 180 cases in three hours — an average of one case a minute. By the 1880s he was ready to commit himself to a new cause, and he found it in the Imperial Federation League. His 1892 book, *The Struggle for Imperial Unity*, might have been entitled, in the words of one reviewer, "How I Saved the Empire." For 30 years, from 1880 to 1910, the fiery magistrate would be Canada's most outspoken exponent for imperial unity.

Two other "Georges" — George Munro Grant and George Parkin — became leaders in the Imperial Federation League. Unlike Denison, they were concerned with the intellectual and spiritual aspects of imperialism. Grant was a Presbyterian minister. After his schooling at Pictou Academy in his native Nova Scotia, he attended Glasgow University in the 1850s, a time when Scottish clerics debated the social function of Christianity. In 1877 he became principal of Queen's University, a position he held for a quarter-century, until his death in 1902. Grant's imperialism grew out of his religious fervour. He saw imperial unity and Christian unity as one and the same thing, for British imperialism embodied Protestant Christian values. He admonished Anglo-Saxons to sacrifice themselves to save the empire in distant corners of the globe, so as to allow others to benefit from the virtues of the "Anglo-Saxon race."

George Parkin argued for the humanitarian side of imperialism. John S. Ewart once described Parkin as "the prince of Imperialists and their first missionary." Parkin never became a minister, but he found an outlet for his missionary zeal in education. The youngest of thirteen children from a poor New Brunswick family, he began teaching high school in his native province. In 1885, he joined the Imperial Federation League. He soon became one of the movement's greatest leaders, writing three books on the subject of imperialism. As well, he became principal of Upper Canada College in Toronto from 1895 to 1902, at which time he was invited to become organizing secretary for the Rhodes Scholarship Trust, an educational fund honouring Cecil Rhodes, the British South African arch-imperialist and mining magnate. The scholarships enabled gifted students from the British empire to attend Oxford University. Parkin used the position to tour the empire to spread the gospel of imperial federation. A bust of Parkin still stands in Rhodes House at Oxford as a reminder of his contribution to the imperialist cause.

Parkin's *Imperial Federation: The Problem of National Unity* (1892) set out a vision of a single British imperial nation that would unite all Anglo-Saxons in the world as a common cultural group. What made Anglo-Saxons a great people, in Parkin's estimation, was their moral sense of mission — their willingness "to assume vast responsibilities in the government of weak and alien races." He viewed the empire as an instrument for the betterment of mankind, providing freedom from ignorance and advancement for the non-white races.

WEB LINKS

Stephen Leacock was a younger member of the Imperial Federation League, and later of the British Empire League, as the organization came to be known after 1896. Born in England in 1869, he grew up on a farm near Lake Simcoe in Ontario. After schooling at Upper Canada College and the University of Toronto, he became the modern-language master at Upper Canada College in 1891. He never enjoyed secondary-school teaching, which he described as "the only trade I could find that needed neither experience nor intellect," and so left in 1899 to study economics and political science at the University of Chicago. In 1903, with his Ph.D. in hand, he joined the staff of McGill University, where he taught economics and political science for 35 years.

Best remembered as one of Canada's finest humorists, Leacock expressed his serious side in his writings on imperialism. He saw imperial unity as a means by which Canadians could transcend their parochial and narrow provincial concerns to achieve a "Greater Canada," to use the title of one of his writings on imperialism. To him, imperialism was much more than trade and military exploits; it was buying citizenship in the greatest empire the world had ever known — one upon which the sun never set.

These men — Denison, Grant, Parkin, and Leacock — led the imperial movement in Canada in the pre–World War I era. Their writings and public speeches emphasized Canada's interest in distant imperialist wars and in British affairs. They advocated, as well, closer links with the mother country through a transatlantic cable and through the penny post. Large numbers of middle-class English Canadians identified with their message, but French Canadians, Métis, the Native peoples, and the growing number of non–Anglo-Saxon immigrants did not. Thus, ironically, in their enthusiasm to use imperialism as a means to unite Canadians, they divided them.

IMPERIALISM AND QUEEN VICTORIA'S DIAMOND JUBILEE

British imperialism peaked in the 1890s. Joseph Chamberlain, appointed to the Colonial Office in 1895, personified the imperial spirit and spearheaded the movement. Two years later, Queen Victoria celebrated her Diamond Jubilee — her 60 years as the ruling monarch — in a spectacular celebration to show the world the splendour and the might of the British empire. Representatives from all the colonies, including Canada's new prime minister, Wilfrid Laurier, joined in the military parades and reviews, assemblies of school children, patriotic speeches, unveiling of monuments, and numerous banquets. Special commemorative stamps were issued, among them a Canadian stamp showing a map of the world splashed with red for all the British possessions. The inscription read: "We hold a vaster empire than has been." A year after Queen Victoria's Diamond Jubilee, several provinces established Empire Day on May 23 — the day before Queen Victoria's birthday. Ontario, Nova Scotia, and the Protestant schools of Quebec celebrated the occasion in 1898, and other provinces followed suit. The day was designed to use the public schools for promoting patriotic sentiments.

Where Historians Disagree

THE NATURE OF IMPERIALISM

Historians have disagreed as to the nature and impact of imperialism in Canada's past. Inspired by William Lyon Mackenzie King's efforts to achieve Canadian independence, liberal nationalist historians of the interwar years viewed imperialism as an obstacle in the way of Canada's evolution from colony to nation. Oscar Skelton, author of *The Life and Letters of Sir Wilfrid Laurier* (Toronto: Oxford University Press, 1921) and later undersecretary of state for external affairs (1925–41), argued that imperialism hindered the growth of Canadian independence. It also caused disunity, as French Canadians could not identify with the imperial vision.

In his writings in the 1930s, liberal-nationalist historian Frank H. Underhill equated imperialism with colonialism. The British connection embroiled Canadians in imperial wars of no direct interest to them. Only later did Underhill see the British empire in positive terms, as a liberal association that had granted self-government to its colonial dependencies and that had been the foundation for the modern British Commonwealth of Nations. Such a positive view became possible only after imperialism had ceased to be an active and pervasive force in the world and in Canadian thought.

In the post–World War II era, Donald G. Creighton and other conservative-nationalist historians looked to the imperial connection as the counterforce to the menacing pull of continentalism, and thus Canada's means of maintaining independence in North America. Creighton depicted John A. Macdonald as the great Canadian statesman who had understood the importance of British imperialism in safeguarding Canada against American continentalism. "The diplomatic and military support of Great Britain," Creighton wrote in "Macdonald and the Anglo-Canadian Alliance" in *Towards the Discovery of Canada: Selected Essays* (Toronto: Macmillan, 1972), "could alone offset the political preponderance of the United States; and Macdonald proposed therefore to bring in the old world to redress the balance of the new" (p. 223). In *Canada and Imperialism, 1896–1899* (Toronto: University of Toronto Press, 1965), historian Norman Penlington argued that English-Canadian imperialists in general had seen the empire as Canada's means to strengthen its position vis-à-vis the United States.

Historian Carl Berger shifted the focus of the debate in *The Sense of Power: Studies in the Ideas of Canadian Imperialism, 1867–1914* (Toronto: University of Toronto Press, 1970). He showed that imperialism was more an intellectual than a political, economic, or military phenomenon, that it was primarily a concept in the mind of those who endorsed it. In reality, Berger argued, imperialism was "one variety of Canadian nationalism" (p. 9). Canadian imperialists believed that Canada could achieve a "sense of power" and thus fulfil its destiny as a great nation through the imperial connection.

Berger's argument that imperialism was an indigenous phenomenon promoted largely by an elite of English-Canadian thinkers has been challenged by historian Robert Page. In a review of Berger's book, entitled "Carl Berger and the Intellectual Origins of Canadian Imperialist Thought, 1867–1914," *Journal of Canadian Studies* 5 (August 1970), Page wrote that "external events and a very strong international climate of opinion" (p. 40), including such phenomena as the popular enthusiasm

(continued)

surrounding Queen Victoria's Diamond Jubilee and the patriotism that came forth during the Boer War, also contributed. Furthermore, Page questions Berger's strictly nationalist perspective on imperialism, arguing that a study of the attitudes toward imperialism among businesspeople, for example, would undoubtedly yield a different, more economic, perspective.

WEB LINKS

THE SOUTH AFRICAN WAR

In 1899, the British empire extended over a quarter of the earth's land surface and contained nearly a quarter of its people. Britain's navy, the largest in the world, made it the greatest maritime power. When British imperial expansion in southern Africa brought the island kingdom into conflict with the Boers — the descendants of European settlement, mainly Protestants from the Netherlands — the result seemed a foregone conclusion. The British assumed they would immediately defeat the two tiny Boer, or Afrikaner, republics, the Transvaal and the Orange Free State. Yet the struggle of the British empire against the two small African states turned out quite differently. Initially, in fact, the Afrikaners inflicted a series of defeats on the British. They knew the country, and effectively practised guerrilla warfare techniques. Britain turned to its dominions, including Canada, for help.

Canadian imperialists saw their chance to prove their unquestioned loyalty. The English-language newspapers, especially those in Montreal and Toronto, demanded immediate Canadian participation. Lord Minto, the governor general, and Major General Edward Hutton, commander of the Canadian militia, worked out plans for a Canadian contingent, without informing Prime Minister Laurier. A cable from Joseph Chamberlain, the British colonial secretary, thanked Canada for its "offer to serve in South Africa." His thanks were premature, however, since the Canadian government had not yet made an official statement of support.

Prime Minister Laurier tried to temper this enthusiasm. While he admired the British empire as the world's leading protector of the liberal values of liberty and justice, he opposed imperial federation. The Canadian cabinet, not the British colonial secretary, should decide Canada's participation.

The South African War aroused strong anti-imperialistic sentiments in Quebec. If French Canadians sympathized with anyone in the struggle, it was with the Boers, whom they regarded as a kindred oppressed minority. Henri Bourassa, a young politician and brilliant orator like his grandfather, the legendary Louis-Joseph Papineau, opposed Canadian involvement in this distant imperialist war. Bourassa equated imperialism with militarism and commercialism, and thus condemned the British empire "not because it is British, but because it is Imperial. All empires are hateful. They stand in the way of human liberty, and true progress, intellectual and moral. They serve nothing but brutal instincts and material objects." He was not, however, prepared to advocate Canadian independence, believing that internal divisions between English- and French-speaking Canadians within an independent Canada might lead to annexation to the United States, which he opposed even more. He favoured an eventual independent Canada within the British empire, a country in which the two linguistic groups respected each other.

Before World War I, many English Canadians considered themselves Britons overseas, but few exceeded this western Canadian woman's zeal for the empire.

Glenbow Archives, Calgary, Canada/ NA-1643-4.

THE CANADIAN COMPROMISE ON THE SOUTH AFRICAN WAR

For two days, Laurier's cabinet met to find a solution. On October 13, 1899, Laurier devised a compromise solution. He proposed that "in view of the well-known desire of a great many Canadians who are ready to take service under such conditions," the government would equip and transport a volunteer force of 1000 men for service on the British side. Once in South Africa, however, the troops would become the British government's responsibility and would fight as British soldiers. Laurier reminded imperialists and French Canadians alike that this decision to send troops should not be "construed as a precedent for future action." (Eventually Canada sent 7300 men to South Africa, of whom 245 died overseas, more than half from disease.)

English-Canadian imperialists were unhappy with Laurier's compromise. John Willison, editor of the Toronto *Globe*, wanted Canada to assume full responsibility for Canadian troops in South Africa. Margaret Polson Murray, a native of Scotland and long-time resident of Canada, founded the Imperial Order Daughters of the Empire (IODE), an organization whose motto — "One Flag, One Throne, One Country" — made its wishes known. This new patriotic organization, with its first chapters in Fredericton and Montreal, sought to promote Britain and British institutions in the schools and publicly supported a united empire. By World War I, it would become one of the largest English-Canadian women's voluntary associations. In Montreal, a group of McGill students attacked the offices of the anti-war French-language newspapers in the city and fought street battles with French-Canadian university students.

Henri Bourassa denounced Laurier as *un vendu*, a sellout to the English-Canadian imperialists. He warned that the mere fact of sending troops established a dangerous precedent, since Britain would expect support every time the empire got entangled in future wars. He resigned his seat in protest on October 18, 1899, only to be re-elected as an independent by acclamation six months later.

The members of the Prince Edward Island Transvaal contingent before their departure for South Africa. In total, some 7300 Canadian volunteers fought in the South African War (1899–1902).

Patent and Copyright Office Collection/National Archives of Canada/C-7983.

Joseph Chamberlain, hoping to capitalize on the imperial sentiment generated by the South African War, called a colonial conference in 1902. Laurier resisted closer imperial unity. On the eve of the colonial conference, he assured Parliament that he would not "bring Canada into the vortex of militarism which is the curse and blight of Europe." At the conference itself, he steadfastly opposed having Canada become part of a consolidated imperial defence force. He would only agree that Canadians must contribute to their own defence.

Canada assumed responsibility for the British-controlled ports of Halifax and Esquimalt, British Columbia, in 1904. Then in 1909 Joseph Pope, former private secretary to Sir John A. Macdonald and secretary of state after 1896, established the Department of External Affairs to deal with aspects of the Dominion's foreign affairs. Laurier believed the department would allow Canada to become more autonomous in its external relations without offending British or English-Canadian imperialists.

GROWING FRENCH-CANADIAN NATIONALISM

Imperialist sentiments in English-speaking Canada contributed to a parallel French-Canadian nationalism in Quebec. In 1903, a group of young French-Canadian nationalists, inspired by Henri Bourassa, founded the Ligue nationaliste and their own newspaper, *Le Nationaliste*, in 1904. The organization had a three-point program: Canadian autonomy within the British empire; provincial autonomy within a federal state; and the rational development of Canada's resources. Other French-Canadian nationalists founded the Association catholique de la jeunesse canadienne-française (ACJC), or "Catholic Action of French-Canadian Youth," in 1904. This group, under the leadership of Abbé Lionel Groulx of Valleyfield, Quebec, recruited members for their youth group from the classical colleges in the Montreal region. They saw the Roman Catholic church as playing an important role in shaping Quebec nationalism.

Their thinking was in line with that of Jules-Paul Tardivel, a Franco-American born in Kentucky, who came to Quebec in 1868 to study French and then took up the causes of ultramontanism and French-Canadian nationalism. In his newspaper, *La Vérité*, and in *Pour la Patrie* (1895), a futuristic novel, Tardivel proposed Quebec's separation from Canada to create a Roman Catholic state on the banks of the St. Lawrence River. In an exchange published in 1904, Tardivel and Bourassa outlined their differing conceptions of French Canada. Tardivel distinguished between his exclusive French-Canadian form of nationalism and Bourassa's broader Canadian nationalism. Tardivel wrote: "Our own nationalism is French-Canadian national-ism. . . . For us our fatherland is — we do not say precisely the Province of Quebec — but French Canada; the nation we wish to see founded at the hour marked by Divine Providence is the French-Canadian nation." Bourassa replied:

> For us the fatherland is all Canada, that is, a federation of distinct races and autonomous provinces. The nation that we wish to see develop is the Canadian nation, composed of French Canadians and English Canadians, that is of two elements separated by language and religion, and by the legal dispositions necessary to the preservation of their respective traditions, but united in a feeling of brotherhood, in a common attachment to the common fatherland.

In this interchange lay the essence of two currents of twentieth-century French-Canadian nationalism: one leading to separatism, the other to a bilingual and bicultural nation.

THE ALASKA BOUNDARY DISPUTE

WEB

LINKS

At the turn of the century a new dispute arose between Canada and the United States, this time over the boundary between Alaska and the Yukon Territory. The dispute had its origin in the Anglo–Russian Treaty of 1825, which had established an ambiguous boundary line, "to follow the summit of the mountains situated parallel to the coast," between British and Russian territory running north from Portland Channel. Unfortunately, the territory encompassed many mountain chains and an uneven coast.

The Americans adopted the Russian stance on the border after they purchased Alaska in 1867. They sought a continuous border along the Pacific coast, and after British Columbia joined Confederation in 1871, they denied Canada's claim to several fiords with access to the Yukon. The news that gold had been discovered in the Yukon in 1897 suddenly made the boundary question of utmost importance. Prospectors crossed the mountain passes into the Yukon, and by the summer of 1898, Dawson City had a population of more than 20 000 people, making it temporarily the largest

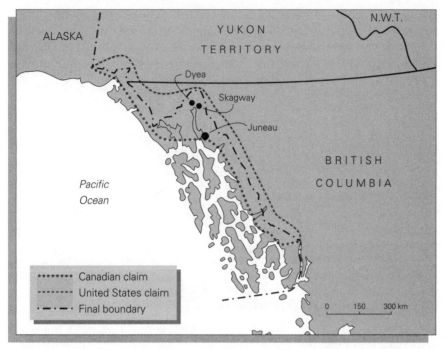

The Alaska boundary dispute, 1903, showing the Canadian and American claims, and the final settlement.

Canadian city west of Winnipeg. In June 1898, the federal government made the Yukon a separate territory with its own commissioner, to help prevent the area from becoming a *de facto* part of Alaska.

Both the Canadians and the Americans, along with the British, agreed to settle the issue through a joint commission. Britain, which continued to have sovereign control over Canada's foreign policy, made the appointments and named five Canadians to the six-member Anglo–Canadian commission. It appeared at first as though a quick settlement could be reached, but negotiations broke down as each side refused to compromise.

To break the deadlock, the three countries agreed in 1902 to appoint a six-member tribunal, three from each side, to review the disputed border. Britain appointed a British judge and two Canadian lawyers for its side. The United States government appointed three members who came to the bargaining table determined to secure the full acceptance of the American claim. Furthermore, Theodore Roosevelt confidentially informed the British that if the Americans failed to win the case, he would "run the line" on their claim.

In the end, Lord Alverstone, the lone British member of the tribunal, sided with the Americans. He agreed that the boundary line should be around the heads of the inlets, giving the United States territorial control of them. He also agreed to the equal division of the four islands at the mouth of Portland Channel. Thus, in a vote of four to two, the commission voted in favour of this settlement. Both

Miners packing their equipment and supplies up the Chilkoot Pass, 1897–98, on their way to the Klondike gold fields. On reaching the summit, they had to return to get another load. It took many ascents, because the NWMP required each miner to have a year's supply (about 500 kg) of provisions upon entering Canada.

E.A. Hegg/National Archives of Canada/C-5142.

Canadian commissioners voted against, and refused to affix their signatures to, the award of the tribunal.

Canadian historians have since debated whether or not Alverstone made his decision strictly for diplomatic reasons. Recent writers tend to argue that the Canadian position was actually the weaker of the two, while at the same time agreeing that the American threats weakened their case.

Regardless of the merits in hindsight of Alverstone's decision, many Canadians at the time, including the prime minister, considered it "one of those concessions which have made British diplomacy odious to Canadian people." A growing number of English Canadians came away from the incident convinced that Canada needed greater control over its own foreign affairs, since Britain could not be relied upon to safeguard Canadian interests.

RENEWED PROSPECTS OF RECIPROCITY WITH THE UNITED STATES

After the contentious Alaska boundary dispute was resolved, Canadian–American relations improved. By 1910, closer trade seemed imminent. Surprisingly, this time the Americans took the initiative. President William Howard Taft, who came to office in 1909, favoured lower tariffs, arguing that expanding American industries badly needed Canadian raw materials. On January 26, the Liberals announced that a reciprocal trade agreement had been reached with the Americans that, in essence, renewed the popular Reciprocity Treaty of 1854. The proposal allowed Canadian natural products free entry into American markets in exchange for letting American manufactured goods into Canada at a lower tariff rate.

Contrary to the Reciprocity Treaty of 1854, however, this agreement was to come into effect through concurrent legislation passed by the two governments rather than by treaty. This arrangement would enable Canada to avoid seeking British approval. The American Congress passed the legislation in July 1911. It remained only for the Canadian Parliament to give its approval.

Then, opposition to the reciprocity agreement arose in central Canada. Clifford Sifton, no longer a westerner but rather a well-established Torontonian, led a group of Ontario entrepreneurs who opposed the agreement because they believed it threatened Canada's economic future and its close ties with the British empire. "These resolutions," Sifton warned, "spell retrogression, commercial subordination, the destruction of our national ideals and displacement from our proud position as the rising hope of the British empire." He organized a group of eighteen prominent Toronto manufacturers, industrialists, and financiers to petition the government against the agreement. The group went on to become the core of a newly created Canadian National League. The league published a pamphlet, *The Road to Washington*, which warned that the United States intended to annex Canada.

Inopportune statements by imprudent American politicians aided the league's campaign. Champ Clark, speaker-designate of the House of Representatives, said of the agreement: "I am for it, because I hope to see the day when the American flag will float over every square foot of the British North American possessions clear to the North Pole." President Taft himself noted that "Canada stands at the parting of the ways." By this he meant that Canada had to choose between remaining an isolated protectionist country or trading with the Americans. But anti-American proponents in Canada interpreted the statement to mean that Canada had to choose between Britain and the United States. Emotional arguments about loyalty and nationalism replaced economic ones.

THE NAVAL CRISIS

The controversy over reciprocity coincided with the contentious naval question. Tension between Germany and Britain increased at the turn of the century. In 1908, the British press warned of the threat to Britain's control of the high seas from Germany's growing naval strength. The British Conservative opposition demanded that the government immediately build eight super-battleships, or dreadnoughts. Many English Canadians insisted that Canada contribute. But French-Canadian nationalists like Henri Bourassa opposed such a move, claiming it would only lead to greater Canadian involvement in imperial and European wars of no interest to Canada.

The Liberals and the Conservatives agreed that Canada should eventually establish a Canadian navy, rather than contribute funds regularly to the British admiralty. But the two parties differed on the best *short-term* policy: Conservatives favoured an emergency direct cash contribution to Britain in the present crisis, while Liberals

WEB LINKS

wanted the immediate establishment of a Canadian navy under Canadian command, to be used by Britain, if the Canadian Parliament approved, in the event of war.

In January 1910, Laurier introduced the Naval Service Bill. He proposed that Canada construct five cruisers and six destroyers and establish a naval college to train Canadian officers. Although the force would be under the control of the Canadian government, it could, "in case of war," be placed under imperial control with the Canadian Parliament's approval.

OPPOSITION TO THE NAVAL SERVICE BILL

Although Laurier saw the Naval Service Bill as a suitable compromise, his opponents disagreed. On the one hand, imperialistically minded conservatives, both federal members of Parliament and provincial premiers, denounced this "tin-pot navy," as they described it, as a disgrace to Canada's role in the empire. The *Montreal Daily Star* stated on November 2: "Now if the empire — including Canada — were at war, and the Canadian navy were to refuse to go into action, how would that action differ from cowardice on the field of battle — from betrayal of a brother people — from treason to the king?"

On the other hand, Bourassa and the *nationalistes* opposed the Naval Service Bill because it went too far; this navy could be used to fight imperial wars of no interest to Canada. "It is the most complete backward step Canada has made in half a century," Bourassa declared. Bourassa favoured a navy for home defence but not one that would involve Canada in the "whirlpool of militarism." He questioned whether Canada needed a navy at all, since the only threat to the country could come from the United States, with whom Canadians had enjoyed a century of peace.

Since 1905, Bourassa's attacks against Laurier had become more strident. By 1907, he had left federal for provincial politics; and in 1910, he established a daily newspaper, *Le Devoir*, in which he championed his vision of Canada as an independent member of the British empire, one that placed Canadian interests first. In that year, the *nationalistes* ran a candidate against the Liberals in a by-election in the "safe" seat of Drummond–Arthabaska. Laurier, who had represented the district in the Quebec legislature, campaigned personally on behalf of the Liberal candidate, only to see the *nationalistes* win.

THE 1911 ELECTION

During the 1911 election campaign, Laurier faced vigorous attacks from both imperialists in Ontario, who branded him a continentalist on the reciprocity issue, and French-Canadian nationalists, who accused him of being an imperialist on the naval issue. "I am neither," an exasperated Laurier protested during an election rally in St. Jean, Quebec, in August. "I am a *Canadian*." His policy, he claimed, was one of "true Canadianism, of moderation, or conciliation." The Liberals, however, tarnished by corruption and inefficient government after fifteen years in office, lost the election. The combined opposition of Ontario imperialists and Quebec nationalists over the issues of reciprocity with the United States and imperial defence helped to deprive Laurier of victory.

BORDEN'S CONSERVATIVE GOVERNMENT

Robert L. Borden's cabinet reflected the practical and uninspiring nature of his government. No single minister stood out as dynamic or memorable, with the possible exceptions of the irascible Sam Hughes, minister of militia and defence, or George Foster, minister of trade and commerce. Yet, collectively, the Borden cabinet ran an efficient government. Limited French-Canadian representation, however, crippled his cabinet in reference to any political issues bearing on Quebec.

Despite strong Quebec opposition, the prime minister, as his own secretary of state for external affairs, introduced the Naval Aid Bill in December 1912. It provided a direct cash contribution of $35 million to Britain to build three dreadnoughts. One of Borden's French-Canadian cabinet ministers resigned in protest, but the prime minister persevered. The Liberals attacked the Naval Aid Bill as a sham and as an inadequate alternative to Laurier's naval program. Eventually, the Conservatives imposed closure — for the first time in Canadian legislative history — to cut off the debate. The Liberals countered by using their strong majority in the Senate to defeat the bill. Ultimately, the issue died when military experts questioned the efficiency of dreadnoughts against submarines. Thus, on the eve of World War I, Canada had neither made a contribution to the British navy nor built up a navy of its own.

For half a century after Confederation, Canadians debated the nation's destiny. Many politicians and critics felt that Canada was incapable of being a great nation; they sought to enhance its national status through some form of association with either Britain, in an imperial federation, or the United States, in a continental association. But English Canadians and French Canadians could not agree on the nature and extent of imperial union, while entrepreneurs and farmers disagreed over the nature and extent of a continental connection. Few thought in terms of Canadian independence; most felt that the country was not yet strong enough, or sufficiently united, to be independent.

NOTES

1. Carl Berger, *The Sense of Power: Studies in the Ideas of Canadian Imperialism, 1867–1914* (Toronto: University of Toronto Press, 1970), p. 259.

LINKING TO THE PAST

The Reciprocity Treaty of 1854
http://www.nlc-bnc.ca/confed/docs/doc00008.htm
The full text of the 1854 Reciprocity Treaty between the United States and Canada, which, although it was cancelled in 1866, continued to have considerable influence on the economic relations between the two countries.

Stephen Leacock
http://www.nlc-bnc.ca/leacock/bio2.htm
A detailed biography of Stephen Leacock.

Canada's Military Legacy: The Boer War

http://www.dnd.ca/menu/legacy/boer_e.htm

This site from the Department of National Defence offers a short history of Canada's involvement in the South African War of 1899. It looks at Canada's military role, events on the homefront, and the people and places involved.

The Alaska Boundary Dispute

http://www.ac.wwu.edu/~jay/pages/dan.html

An overview of the Alaska Boundary Dispute between Canada and the United States, with information on causes and reactions, as well as selected articles from period newspapers.

Wilfrid Laurier on the Naval Bill

http://www.nelson.com/nelson/school/discovery/cantext/speech/1910lana.htm

The full text of Laurier's speech to the House of Commons in regard to the 1910 Naval Service Bill, which helped to establish the Canadian navy.

Robert L. Borden

http://cnet.unb.ca/achn/pme/rlbcb.htm

A brief biography of Prime Minister Robert L. Borden, with additional links to a descriptive biography and an anecdote about his time in office.

RELATED READINGS

The following articles in R. Douglas Francis and Donald B. Smith, eds., *Readings in Canadian History: Post-Confederation*, 5th ed. (Toronto: Harcourt Brace, 1998), relate to this topic: Carl Berger, "Imperialism and Nationalism, 1884–1914: A Conflict in Canadian Thought," pp. 91–95; and J. Levitt, "Henri Bourassa on Imperialism and Bi-culturalism, 1900–1918," pp. 96–107.

BIBLIOGRAPHY

The most comprehensive survey of Canada's relations with Britain and the United States is C.P. Stacey, *Canada and the Age of Conflict: A History of Canadian External Relations*, vol. 1, *1867–1921* (Toronto: Macmillan, 1977). See also John Bartlet Brebner, *The North Atlantic Triangle: The Interplay of Canada, The United States and Great Britain* (New Haven, CT: Yale University Press, 1945). W.L. Morton discusses the Treaty of Washington in *The Critical Years: The Union of British North America, 1857–1873* (Toronto: McClelland & Stewart, 1964). For a quick review of the state of the British empire in the late nineteenth century see James Morris's *Heaven's Command* (London: Faber and Faber, 1973), and his *Farewell the Trumpets* (London: Faber and Faber, 1978).

Canadian–American relations in the late nineteenth century are dealt with in J.L. Granatstein and Norman Hillmer, *For Better or For Worse: Canada and the United States to the 1990s* (Toronto: Copp Clark Pitman, 1991); and C.C. Tansill, *Canadian–American Relations, 1875–1911* (Toronto: The Ryerson Press, 1943). Goldwin Smith's *Canada and the Canadian Question* (Toronto: Hunter, Rose, 1891; rep.: University of Toronto Press, 1971) is an interesting contemporary statement. Also of importance are W.R. Graham, "Sir Richard Cartwright, Wilfrid Laurier and the Liberal Party Trade Policy, 1887," *Canadian Historical Review* 33 (March 1952): 1–18; F.H. Underhill, "Edward Blake, the Liberal Party and Unrestricted Reciprocity," *Canadian Historical Association, Report* (1939), 133–41; and

P.B. Waite, *The Man from Halifax: Sir John Thompson, Prime Minister* (Toronto: University of Toronto Press, 1985). A collection of interpretative essays is Allan Smith, *Canada — An American Nation?: Essays on Continentalism, Identity, and the Canadian Frame of Mind* (Montreal/Kingston: McGill-Queen's University Press, 1994).

Norman Penlington's *The Alaska Boundary Dispute: A Critical Appraisal* (Toronto: McGraw-Hill Ryerson, 1972); and John Munro's *The Alaska Boundary Dispute* (Toronto: Copp Clark, 1970) cover this issue in Canadian–American relations; the latter is a collection of primary and secondary sources. A third study that touches on the question of Canada's sovereignty in the Yukon dispute is W.R. Morrison's *Showing the Flag: The Mounted Police and Canadian Sovereignty in the North, 1894–1925* (Vancouver: University of British Columbia Press, 1985). In *Land of the Midnight Sun: A History of the Yukon* (Edmonton: Hurtig, 1988), Ken S. Coates and William R. Morrison provide an overview of the territory. For the impact of the Great Rush see Charlene Porsild, *Gamblers and Dreamers: Women, Men, and Community in the Klondike* (Vancouver: University of British Columbia Press, 1998).

Carl Berger's *The Sense of Power: Studies in the Ideas of Canadian Imperialism, 1867–1914* (Toronto: University of Toronto Press, 1970), analyzes the beliefs of English-Canadian imperialists. On the negative side of imperialism see Sarah Carter, *Capturing Women: The Manipulation of Cultural Imagery in Canada's Prairie West* (Montreal/Kingston: McGill-Queen's University Press, 1997). Norman Penlington's *Canada and Imperialism, 1896–1899* (Toronto: University of Toronto Press, 1965), discusses Canadian imperialism in the context of the South African War. A more recent study is Carman Miller, *Painting the Map Red: Canada and the South African War 1899–1902* (Montreal/Kingston: Canadian War Museum, McGill-Queen's University Press, 1992). See also Robert Page, *The Boer War and Canadian Imperialism* (Ottawa: Canadian Historical Association, 1987), and his book on the subject, *Imperialism and Canada, 1895–1903* (Toronto: Holt, Rinehart and Winston, 1972). Useful collections of essays are: Colin M. Coates, ed., *Imperial Canada 1867–1917* (Edinburgh: Centre of Canadian Studies, University of Edinburgh, 1997); *Imperial Relations in the Age of Laurier* (Toronto: University of Toronto Press, 1969), edited by Carl Berger, and Frank H. Underhill's collection of interpretative lectures, *The Image of Confederation* (Toronto: Canadian Broadcasting Corporation, 1964), also edited by Carl Berger. On the Boy Scout movement and imperialism see Robert H. MacDonald, *Sons of the Empire: The Frontier and the Boy Scout Movement, 1890–1918* (Toronto: University of Toronto Press, 1993). On literature and the empire see Barrie Davies, "'We Hold a Vaster Empire Than Has Been': Canadian Literature and the Canadian Empire," *Studies in Canadian Literature* 14(1) (1989): 18–29; and Sara Jeannette Duncan, *The Imperialist* (1904), reprint (Toronto: McClelland & Stewart, 1990). On Duncan's life see Marian Fowler, *Redney: A Life of Sara Jeannette Duncan* (Toronto: Anansi, 1983); and Thomas E. Tausky, *Sara Jeannette Duncan: Novelist of the Empire* (Port Credit, ON: P.D. Meaney, 1980). For a discussion of Duncan's ideas as presented in her writings, see Misao Dean, *A Different Point of View: Sara Jeannette Duncan* (Montreal/Kingston: McGill-Queen's University Press, 1991).

French-Canadian views on imperialism and nationalism during this era can be found in M. Wade, *The French Canadians, 1760–1945* (Toronto: Macmillan, 1955), pp. 447–535; and in Susan Mann Trofimenkoff, *The Dream of Nation: A Social and Intellectual History of Quebec* (Toronto: Gage, 1983), pp. 167–83. Joseph Levitt's *Henri Bourassa on Imperialism and Bi-culturalism* (Toronto: Copp Clark, 1970) and his pamphlet, *Henri Bourassa, Catholic Critic* (Toronto: Canadian Historical Association, 1976), summarize the ideas of this French-Canadian thinker.

The debate over naval defence is discussed in C.P. Stacey, *Canada and the Age of Conflict: A History of Canadian External Relations*, vol. 1, *1867–1921* (Toronto: Macmillan, 1977). For the conflicting views in Quebec see the chapter entitled "Nationalism vs.

Imperialism: 1905–11," in Mason Wade's *The French Canadians: 1760–1945* (Toronto: Macmillan, 1955), pp. 536–607. The issue of reciprocity in the 1911 election is analyzed in L.E. Ellis, *Reciprocity, 1911: A Study in Canadian–American Relations* (Toronto: The Ryerson Press, 1939). Paul Stevens, ed., *The 1911 General Election: A Study in Canadian Politics* (Toronto: Copp Clark, 1970) is a compilation of primary and secondary sources. On the formation of the Department of External Affairs see John Hilliker, *Canada's Department of External Affairs*, vol. 1, *The Early Years, 1909–1946* (Montreal/Kingston: McGill-Queen's University Press, 1990).

The fortunes of the Conservative party are discussed in R.C. Brown, *Robert Laird Borden: A Biography*, vol. 1, *1854–1914* (Toronto: Macmillan, 1975); and in John English, *The Decline of Politics: The Conservatives and the Party System, 1901–20* (Toronto: University of Toronto Press, 1977).

For maps and charts on the period see the *Historical Atlas of Canada*, vol. 2, *The Land Transformed, 1800–1891*, edited by L.R. Gentilcore et al. (Toronto: University of Toronto Press, 1993); and vol. 3, *Addressing the Twentieth Century, 1891–1961*, edited by Donald Kerr and Deryk W. Holdsworth (Toronto: University of Toronto Press, 1990).

PART TWO

Urban and Industrial Canada, 1867–1914

Time Line: 1867-1914

1867 ~ Beginning of the Society of Canadian Artists
~ Founding of the National Lacrosse Association

1869 ~ Timothy Eaton opens his first dry-goods store at Queen and Yonge streets in Toronto—the beginning of the T. Eaton Company

1872 ~ Trade Union Act passed

1874 ~ Alexander Graham Bell conceives of the telephone in Brantford, Ontario
~ Founding of the Women's Christian Temperance Union (WCTU)

1875 ~ New Brunswick's Mount Allison University is the first university in the British empire to grant a degree to a woman, Grace Annie Lockhart

1877 ~ Toronto Women's Literary Club becomes first Canadian women's suffrage organization

1878 ~ Passage of the Canadian Temperance Act, popularly known as Scott's Act, allows each municipality or county to decide whether it will be "wet" or "dry"

1879 ~ Beginning of the Provincial Workmen's Association for coal miners in Nova Scotia

1880 ~ Calixa Lavallée composes "O Canada" for a St. Jean Baptiste Day celebration
~ Beginning of the Canadian Academy of the Arts
~ Ned Hanlan wins the world rowing championship

1883 ~ Founding of the Trades and Labour Congress of Canada (TLC)

1885 ~ Establishment of Banff National Park

1886 ~ Founding of the Amateur Hockey Association of Canada, the first national hockey association

1887 ~ Establishment of the first bird sanctuary in North America at Last Mountain Lake, North-West Territories

1889 ~ Royal Commission on the Relations of Labour and Capital issues report

1891 ~ James Naismith of Almonte, Ontario, invents the game of basketball

1893 ~ Lord Stanley donates Stanley Cup to amateur hockey championships
~ Beginning of the National Council of Women, the first official voice of the Canadian women's movement
~ Algonquin Provincial Park created in Ontario

1894 ~ Labour Day becomes a national holiday
~ Founding of the Toronto Mendelssohn Choir

1895 ~ Founding of the École littéraire de Montréal
~ Alfred Fitzpatrick begins the Reading Camp Association, the forerunner of Frontier College
1897 ~ Beginning of the first Women's Institute near Stoney Creek, south of Hamilton, Ontario
1899 ~ Ralph Connor's novel *The Sky Pilot* published
1900 ~ Department of Labour established
~ Alphonse Desjardins begins his *caisses populaires*, or credit unions, in Quebec
1903 ~ Beginning of the Ligue nationaliste, a French-Canadian nationalist group in Quebec
1904 ~ Founding of the Association catholique de la jeunesse canadienne-française (ACJC)
1905 ~ Founding of the Industrial Workers of the World (IWW), or "Wobblies," as the trade union became known
1907 ~ The Arts and Letters Club formed in Toronto as a meeting place for artists and literary figures
1908 ~ Henry Ford introduces the Model T
1909 ~ Governor General Earl Grey donates Grey Cup for the Canadian football championship
~ Jack Miner begins a study of migratory bird habits at his farm at Kingsville, Ontario
1910 ~ The Royal Commission on Industrial Training and Technical Education established by the federal government
1911 ~ Founding of the École Sociale Populaire (ESP), a Jesuit-based social-reform movement
1914 ~ Workmen's Compensation Act passed in Ontario

Introduction

At the turn of the century, Canada underwent as rapid and substantial a change to urbanization and industrialization as any other country in the Western world, but in absolute terms, it lagged behind developments in both Britain and the United States. Canada lacked the financial and economic infrastructure, the expertise, and the technology to enable it to keep pace with these vastly more populated countries. What Canada did possess, however, was an abundance of natural resources that were in demand for industrialization: timber, minerals, water power, and land fit for large-scale agricultural production. The exploitation of natural resources, along with manufacturing, were behind the economic expansion that occurred in Canada from 1867 to 1914.

The change was evident by comparing Canada in 1867 with Canada in 1914. In 1867, 80 percent of the population lived on farms or in hamlets or small villages, and worked in primary industries such as farming, fishing, and lumbering. By 1914, nearly 50 percent lived in towns or cities, and worked in secondary or service industries. Such growth fostered optimism in Canada's future, which in turn led to further growth, making the two decades spanning the century, 1890 to 1910, a period of "economic takeoff."

While virtually all Canadians were affected to some degree by the change occurring around them, not all benefited to the same extent from industrialization. Regionally, central Canada — Ontario and Quebec — advanced the most, followed by the West and then the Maritimes. Ethnically, Anglo-Celtic Protestants were more prosperous than other ethnic and cultural groups. In gender terms, males benefited more than females, consistently receiving jobs with higher wages or salaries. Socially, the upper and middle classes enjoyed greater advantages over the lower working class. Indeed, a new class of poor appeared — the urban poor — who were in some respects worse off than their rural counterparts, since they depended on others for the basic necessities of life and lived in slum or run-down areas of towns and cities. They worked in factories or shops that were hazardous to their health, had monotonous jobs, and faced extended periods without work and thus wages. It was often necessary for both parents and even older children to work in order to survive. Fraternal societies, unions, and even taverns attempted to help the working poor, but with limited success.

Middle-class social reformers worried about the negative impact of urbanization and industrialization on Canadian moral values, ethical standards, and social mores. Believing that their values and attitudes were the right ones for the survival of civilization, they attempted to impose them upon the working class. There arose as well in the late nineteenth century a belief in environmental determinism: the conviction that individuals were shaped as much, if not more, by society as by hereditary traits. Thus, social reformers believed that if they could create the perfect society, they could produce perfect individuals who were morally upright, responsible citizens. As a result, a host of social reform movements arose in conjunction with urbanization and industrialization premised on an optimistic faith in being able to create the perfect society. Each group of reformers had their own vision of what constituted the perfect society and how best to achieve it, but together they attempted to mould the new urban and industrial society to desirable ends. As well, some Canadians wanted to cultivate the arts so as to make Canada a more cultured and civilized society, while others favoured popular culture as a means of enjoyment and relaxation from the drudgery and burdens of work.

As a result, Canada in 1914 had become a more sophisticated, prosperous, modern, and complex society than it had been 50 years earlier. Canadian leaders ranked their country as being among the most civilized in the Western world. They were proud of their achievements in such a short time and confident in their future.

CHAPTER SIX

Boomtime: Industrialization at the Turn of the Century

"To visit Canada just now is a bracing experience.... For Canada is conscious, vocally, uproariously conscious, that her day has come.... A single decade has swept her diffidence, and has replaced it by a spirit of boundless confidence and booming enterprise." So wrote J.A. Hobson, the well-known English economist and journalist, in his *Canada Today*, published in 1906. At last, a number of factors combined — worldwide prosperity, the success of the national policy, better world prices for raw materials, a decline in freight rates, and a new attitude toward business — to enable Canada to undergo its industrial revolution. Not all regions experienced uniform and sustained growth. The Maritimes languished, while the West developed as a great agricultural area, and central Canada became the heart of industrial growth. Overall, however, Canada entered an age of prosperity through industrialization and resource extraction, although its industrial growth was modest compared with that of Britain and the United States.

CANADA'S ECONOMIC EXPANSION

At the turn of the century, the national policy finally worked as intended. Growth in farming, fishing, lumbering, and mining increased the demand for road construction, rail transportation, and shipbuilding. Stimulated by additional foreign investment, industry and manufacturing expanded to meet the increased demand for consumer goods. The CPR and the two new transcontinental railways — the Canadian Northern and Grand Trunk Pacific/National Transcontinental — brought hundreds of thousands of immigrants westward and took away to market the West's natural resources. Railways were also major employers. By World War I, Canada prided itself on having 55 000 kilometres of track, spanning from coast to coast. Equally, a growing rural population in the West required eastern manufactured goods, from agricultural implements to common household items. Employers needed workers in iron and steel foundries, agricultural-implements works, machine shops, textile and shoe factories, and a host of other manufacturing plants that supplied consumer goods. Service industries, as well as governments (national, provincial, and municipal), became major employers.

This photo shows the head office (the building with columns in the centre) of one of the most powerful financial institutions in Canada in the late nineteenth century, the Bank of Montreal, St. James Street, Montreal, 1887.

McCord Museum of Canadian History, Montreal/Notman Photographic Archives

FINANCIAL INVESTMENT

Canada's abundant natural resources and increasing population now made it an attractive country for investment. The federal government provided direct, as well as indirect, financial assistance to private companies. The governments of Quebec and especially Ontario also invested heavily in development. They offered bonuses, subsidies, and guarantees to industrialists to locate new plants within their borders. Banks provided another source of internal revenue. They too, like business corporations, underwent consolidation, declining in number from 48 to 18 between 1880 and 1920, although the number of branches increased from 300 to 4676. The three largest — the Bank of Montreal, the Royal Bank (also with its headquarters in Montreal), and the Toronto-based Bank of Commerce — centralized their operations, invested in new industries, and provided capital for entrepreneurs.

Foreign investment increased as well. British financiers invested in railways, construction, and business, chiefly in the form of indirect portfolio investments (loans in the form of bonds). In contrast, American interests, who preferred ownership to indirect investment, continued to build branch plants in Canada to avoid tariff restrictions. By 1913, some 450 American-owned branch plants existed in Canada, with assets of over $400 million. Many Americans invested heavily in mining and in the growing pulp and paper industry. Most politicians and Canadians in general looked favourably on American direct investment as a source of investment, as an assurance of more jobs in Canadian industries, and as a means to stem the emigration of Canadians to the United States.

Large-scale industrial production required substantial amounts of capital. To encourage large-scale investment, Canadian businesses adopted the concept of limited liability. Individual investors contributed only a portion of the necessary sum and, if the company failed, they lost only their own contribution and no more.

Limited liability opened up the investment field. Large corporations — "immortal beings" in terms of commercial law — predominated. In 1902, a handful of consolidated companies existed; by 1912, there were nearly 60. These mergers involved nearly 250 smaller companies. Especially noteworthy were Dominion Canner Limited, which in 1910 amalgamated 34 smaller canning factories; Canada Cement, a consolidation of eleven cement companies in 1909; and Stelco (the Steel Company of Canada), formed in 1910 out of several small Ontario and Quebec iron and steel mills. The young New Brunswick financier Max Aitken, the son of a Presbyterian minister, who was later to become Sir Max and eventually Lord Beaverbrook and who created Canada Cement and Stelco, became the "merger king" by buying and combining companies to form trusts and larger companies. (Aitken was so skilled at mergers that one friend commented at the time of his death that now he could "set about merging heaven and hell.")

ROLE OF GOVERNMENT IN THE ECONOMY

As the age-old saying went, the government that governed best, governed least. Ottawa did nothing to regulate the monopolies, apart from passing the Combines Investigation Act of 1910. This act allowed government to investigate monopoly price-fixing. But during its nine-year life span, the investigation board dealt with only one case. Clearly business had a free hand in the boom years before World War I.

State involvement in the economy did occur, however. Fear of American absorption of Canadian industries encouraged government involvement to help fledgling Canadian businesses and to provide an overall national strategic plan. In the case of Ontario Hydro, public ownership came about because of the need for cheap energy on the part of businesses in Toronto and other southern Ontario towns and cities. When it seemed likely that a small privileged business group alone might harness the tremendous energy power of Niagara Falls, business interests rallied behind Adam Beck, a manufacturer of cigar boxes and the Conservative member for London in the Ontario legislature, to urge Ontario's nationalization of the hydroelectric power industry. Beck's movement succeeded. "From the outset," notes historian H.V. Nelles, "the crusade for public power was a businessmen's movement; they initiated it, formed its devoted, hard-core membership, and, most importantly, they provided it with brilliant leadership. By the phrase 'the people's power,' the businessmen meant cheap electricity for the manufacturer, and it was assumed that the entire community would benefit as a result."[1]

Beck, the aggressive founder and promoter of the Hydro-Electric Power Commission of Ontario, built it up until, by the time of his death in 1925, it had become the largest publicly owned power authority in the world. Today, a larger-than-life-sized statue of Beck stands near the Ontario Hydro building on Toronto's University Avenue with the provincial legislature in the background.

A NEW ATTITUDE TOWARD BUSINESS

The new economy necessitated a new managerial class and a skilled industrial labour force. In many ways, primary schools became training grounds for the workplace. In factory-like institutions, teachers taught young people the values of punctuality, obedience, thrift, and self-discipline — values essential for an industrial society.

*Cooking class at a
Canadian ladies'
college, 1906.*

William James Topley/
National Archives of Canada/
PA-42227.

As historian Michael Cross notes: "Children learned to obey clocks."[2] Girls studied domestic science, while boys learned mechanical skills or how to prepare for business. In 1903, Ontario granted money to schools for shop and domestic-science courses. Under the Industrial Education Act, Ontario established trade schools. The Quebec government also built secondary technical-education schools in Montreal and Quebec City. Nova Scotia opened the Technical University of Nova Scotia in 1907, a postsecondary trades college.

Since education was outside of federal jurisdiction, Ottawa could not intervene directly in the provincial area of technical education. It did, however, establish in 1910 the Royal Commission on Industrial Training and Technical Education, which investigated the current state of Canadian education. Four years of war intervened before the federal government could act on the report. Then, in 1919, the federal Technical Education Act established a fund of $10 million for technical education over the next decade.

At the turn of the century, Canadians honoured business successes. In a poll taken in 1908 by the *Canadian Courier*, nine out of ten of those named "Canada's Top Ten Biggest Men" were captains of industry and railway magnates. The philosophy of social Darwinism prevailed: the best naturally succeeded, for survival belonged to the fittest. Successful businessmen believed that they prospered because they were virtuous and moral and that their wealth proved their virtue. Many young English-speaking Canadians accepted the theory of the popular American writer Horatio Alger that anyone could rise from rags to riches through hard work, thrift, and self-discipline.

English-speaking Canadians had numerous role models for success: Herbert Holt, the billion-dollar recluse who founded the Montreal Light, Heat and Power Company in 1902 and became president of the Royal Bank; Henry Pellatt, active in the formation of Canadian General Electric and owner of Toronto's Casa Loma, one of the most palatial residences in North America; Joseph W. Flavelle, president of the William Davies Meat Packaging Plant in Toronto and chairman of the Bank of Commerce and the National Trust Company; Francis H. Clergue, founder of the Algoma Steel Company of Sault Ste. Marie, Ontario; Patrick Burns, owner of the Burns Meat Packing Company of Calgary; and Max Aitken, Canada's "merger king," a millionaire by the age of 30.

WEB LINKS

Few Canadian merchants eclipsed the success of Timothy Eaton, who opened his Toronto dry-goods store at Yonge and Queen streets in 1869. The young immigrant from Ballymena, Northern Ireland, introduced two new revolutionary practices to Canadian merchandising. First, he accepted cash only. Second, he promised "money refunded if goods not satisfactory." Eaton also knew the value of advertising and took out full-page ads in the Toronto papers. By 1882, business had grown to such an extent that he transformed his operation with a department store that eventually would have three floors, 35 departments, electric lights (the first in a Canadian store), the first elevator, and the first store restaurant-café. In the late 1880s, he introduced evening closings at 6 p.m., and, in the summer months, a Saturday afternoon holiday. Next he started an Eaton's mail-order catalogue, a volume soon to be termed "the Prairie Bible" in western Canada. The "governor," as his employees dubbed him, by the time he died in 1907 at age 72, employed over 9000 people ("associates," Eaton preferred to call them) in his stores in Toronto and Winnipeg, in his Toronto and Oshawa factories, and in his overseas offices in London and Paris.

Some Canadian entrepreneurs built up industrial empires beyond Canadian shores, especially in the Caribbean, Mexico, Brazil, and Spain. Brazilian Traction (later Brascan, but always best known to Brazilians simply as "The Light") became a Canadian business success story. "The Light" combined Canadian entrepreneurship, American engineering power, and European capital. As its underwriters, the company had such prominent Toronto capitalists as William Mackenzie, George Cox, Joseph Flavelle, E.R. Wood, Henry Pellatt, and A.E. Ames. Other Canadian-owned companies in foreign lands included the Mexican Light and Power Company in Mexico City; the West Indies Electric Company in Kingston, Jamaica; the Havana Electric Railway Company in Cuba; and the Demerara Electric Company in Georgetown, British Guiana. These industrial empires on domestic and foreign soil were worth millions of dollars and employed tens of thousands of workers.

RISE OF A MANAGERIAL CLASS

These entrepreneurs and other corporate leaders relied on a new, skilled managerial class to run the complex, day-to-day operations of their expanded business: increased production data, costs, personnel, and internal communications. These managers were often trained in "scientific management," a term coined by the American Frederick W. Taylor. "Scientific managers" used workers to complete simple and routine jobs at a proficient speed for a minimum wage. Concerned only with growth and profit, they gave little thought to the aesthetics of the workplace, the needs of workers, or the possibility of profit sharing. Offices, as they became automated with the introduction of such devices as typewriters and Hollerith punch-card machines, resembled factories in terms of routine production. Work was judged in terms of efficiency.

Beneath this managerial class and closely supervised by it were the clerical workers who carried out the daily routine office jobs. Increasingly, women performed the mechanized and highly specialized jobs. Women clerks did not replace male clerks, but rather ended up doing inferior clerical work under them. This "feminization of clerical work" occurred at a rapid rate in the decade from 1910 to 1920, when clerical positions in general more than doubled. Women acquired most of the new

Stenographer pool, land department, CPR Department of National Resources, Calgary, 1915. Women did clerical work at the turn of the century, but became ghettoized at the lowest levels of office work.

Glenbow Archives, Calgary, Canada/NA-5055-1.

typewriting jobs. During the war years (1914–1918), in particular, female clerks replaced male clerks who went off to war. By 1920, male managers and female secretaries had become the norm.

URBANIZATION

Industrialization accelerated urbanization. Industrial growth required factories, workers, large banks, commercial institutions, and transportation services. During the period 1890–1920, Montreal and Toronto, the two largest and most advanced industrial cities, almost tripled their population, each surpassing the half-million mark. But the most rapid urban growth occurred in the West, thanks mainly to large-scale immigration. Winnipeg's population increased to seven times its former size; Vancouver's, twelve times (growing at a rate of 1000 new residents per month in the peak year of 1910); and Calgary's, sixteen times. Of all the major western cities, though, Saskatoon eclipsed the rest in rate of growth, rising from several hundred to nearly 10 000 people in the first decade of the new century. From 1901 to 1911, the Canadian urban population increased 63 percent. In 1901, Canada had only 58 urban centres with a population greater than 5000. By 1911, that number had grown to 90.

Urban centres became heartlands that controlled the surrounding hinterland region, providing the rural inhabitants with manufactured goods and services; but these centres themselves became hinterlands dependent on larger cities beyond. This dependency created a link with Montreal and Toronto, the only two Canadian metropolises not themselves hinterlands of other Canadian cities — although they were dependent on metropolitan centres outside Canada such as London, New York, and Chicago.

The dominance of Montreal and Toronto dated back to the mid-nineteenth century and the railway boom. After 1885 and the completion of the CPR, Montreal's and Toronto's influence reached to the Pacific. Their real growth, however, occurred in the 1890s and early 1900s, due to rapid industrialization.

ECONOMIC DEVELOPMENT IN THE EAST AND WEST

The nature and extent of industrial and urban growth varied across the country. In the Maritimes, the resource-based economy lost some of its momentum. The West Indies sugar trade fell dramatically in the 1870s, when a world glut of sugar caused prices to collapse, resulting in a decline in trade between Nova Scotia and the West Indies. In the same decade Britain's demand for Maritime lumber and wooden ships fell, seriously weakening Nova Scotia's and New Brunswick's economies. An industrial economy developed to supplement the region's resource economy. Businesspeople in Nova Scotia, for instance, invested in steel products, such as steel rails and locomotives, to take advantage of the Cape Breton coal fields. At one point in the early 1880s, thanks in large part to the Intercolonial Railway and the National Policy, Nova Scotia's industrial growth on a per capita basis had actually outstripped that of Ontario and Quebec.

In the long run, however, the Maritimes' industrial expansion faltered. Some historians have pointed out that the region lacked resources as extensive or diverse as, for example, Ontario's. Although Cape Breton had coal, timber, iron ore, and fish, its agriculture could not compete. Distance from the large markets of central Canada and the small regional population in Atlantic Canada combined to create a significant obstacle to expansion for factories in the region. As well, Maritime investors, like their Canadian counterparts elsewhere, saw western and central Canadian development as potentially more lucrative. Local banks, for example, themselves swallowed up by central-Canadian-owned banks, invested outside the region.

As industrialization declined, Maritime cities grew at a slower rate than did cities elsewhere. Halifax's population increased by only 16 000 people between 1871 and 1911 to a total of 46 619, while that of Saint John, New Brunswick, actually declined, then regained a modest number, to bring its population to 42 500 by 1911. These cities remained small, with modest hinterlands of their own. In time, however, they became dependants of Montreal and, to a lesser extent, of Toronto.

GROWTH IN THE WEST

British Columbia's economy shifted from its Pacific orientation (southward to California) toward central Canada, thanks to the completion of the CPR. The provincial economy was still predominantly resource-based: mining, forestry, fisheries, and agriculture. Mining speculation ran at a fever pitch by the turn of the century — so much so, a local journalist noted, that British Columbia was cursed with a "class of

A view of Victoria harbour in 1886. During the 1890s, a new building code limited downtown construction to brick or stone buildings, resulting in the pulling down of the city's deteriorating wooden structures, like the ones shown here.

William Molson Macpherson Collection/ National Archives of Canada/PA-62200.

crooks who prefer to mine the public instead of the ground." Lode gold and silver were mined in the Slocan and Boundary districts in the 1890s, but precious metals were superseded by copper, lead, and zinc after 1900. The smelting, or refining, of these base metals required large-scale smelters. The first successful smelter opened near the Rossland mines at Trail Creek in 1895, and a second, Cominco, in the Kootenays. Coal mining, especially in and around Nanaimo on Vancouver Island, also contributed to the province's economy.

Forestry, however, outdistanced mining in terms of both wealth and employment. Logging increased by an astonishing 400 percent between 1900 and 1910, and wood-product manufacturing provided numerous jobs. Until 1912, and the passage of the Forestry Act, trees were cut without concern for reforestation or the preservation of Crown land.

Fisheries, especially the salmon fisheries, expanded and consolidated in a highly competitive business that pitted Natives, whites, and Japanese-Canadians against each other. British Columbia Packers Association emerged as the most powerful salmon packing company after 1902 and used the most modern technology, including the "Iron Chink" — a racist term applied to the butchering machine for processed fish that replaced work previously done by Chinese- and Japanese-Canadian workers.

Agriculture was slow to get established in British Columbia, but by World War I it ranked second to forestry in terms of output. Fruit farming was the most commercially viable, especially after the introduction of refrigerated rail cars at the turn of the century, since much of the fruit was exported. Even manufacturing grew in the late nineteenth century, outdistancing that of the Prairie provinces and almost reaching Ontario standards. In 1880, British Columbians contributed over 1 percent of the net value of Canadian manufactures; by 1890, the figure was close to 5 percent, more than equal to the growth of its share of the national population. Still, the province's distance from the centre of the industrial development in central Canada, combined with the high freight rates and the small regional market, prevented the province from becoming a substantial and ongoing secondary-manufacturing base. Rather, British Columbia, like the Maritimes, became another hinterland region.

On the Prairies, wheat was king. The world demand for wheat after 1896 opened up areas on the northern fringe and in the arid Palliser Triangle to production, thus increasing substantially both the wheat lands and yields. In 1901, there were 55 000 prairie farms occupying 15.4 million acres (6.2 million ha), of which 70 percent was in wheat; by 1911, those numbers were 200 000 farms and 58 million acres (9 million ha), of which 59 percent was in wheat. In terms of yields, that amounted to a record 208 million bushels in 1911. Such growth justified and necessitated new rail lines, especially to service the new areas of settlement. Rail lines in the region doubled from 1885 to 1900, to 6000 km, and then tripled again to 18 000 by 1913. But the Prairies faced the same problem that British Columbia and the Maritimes faced: too small a regional market and too limited resource endowments to foster substantial secondary manufacturing. Thus, the Prairies became subservient to central Canada in terms of economic growth and dominance.

RISE OF CITIES IN THE WEST

Victoria and Vancouver vied for dominance in West Coast trade. Vancouver won out by 1914 because of the excellent dock and terminal facilities on Burrard Inlet and its role as the western terminus of the CPR. This new status fostered the growth of transportation, wholesaling, and resource companies in the city. By 1914, its population reached 155 000, while that of Victoria, the provincial capital, stood at only 35 000. Again, such growth necessitated a variety of retail, manufacturing, and professional services. The completion of the Panama Canal in 1914 enabled Vancouver to surpass Winnipeg as Canada's major western city. Prairie farmers could now ship wheat to European markets through Vancouver and the Panama Canal. On the eve of World War I, Vancouver stood between two worlds. As its historian, Robert McDonald, notes: "At one level Vancouver functioned as a metropolitan city, managing resource industries, directing transportation and commerce, and providing a growing range of business and professional services for the region. At another it continued to be a city on the frontier, a new society different from Burrard Inlet's nineteenth-century lumber communities yet still subject to the vicissitudes of a regional economy narrowly based on resource extraction and promotion."[3]

Urbanization occurred at a rapid rate on the Prairies. In 1870, at the time of the region's incorporation into Confederation, no urban centres existed in it; by 1911, there were seventeen incorporated cities and 150 incorporated towns. Five dominant cities emerged by 1914: Winnipeg, Saskatoon, Regina, Edmonton, and Calgary. Each serviced a surrounding agricultural hinterland: Calgary, the ranching and farming country of southern Alberta; Edmonton, central Alberta; Regina and Saskatoon, the wheatlands of Saskatchewan; and Winnipeg, southern Manitoba.

Winnipeg's location as the "gateway to the West" with rail links to the East enabled it to make the entire West its hinterland. Thanks to this strategic location, it became the third-largest manufacturing city in pre–World War I Canada. Nicknamed the "Hub City," it stood at the junction of three transcontinental railways. It processed rural agricultural products and, in return, sold construction materials to settlers — lumber, bricks, finished steel, and cement, as well as some manufactured goods. The city employed thousands in its rail yards, the largest in the world by 1904, with as many as 1800 freight cars passing through in a single day. But the eastern cities dominated even Winnipeg. Ultimately, all western rail lines led to Montreal and Toronto.

A view of Victoria harbour 35 years later, in 1910. Construction on the impressive new legislative buildings shown in the background began in 1893.

....

William H. Gibson/National Archives of Canada/PA-59895.

INDUSTRIALIZATION AND URBANIZATION IN CENTRAL CANADA

At the turn of the century, industrialization occurred largely in Ontario and Quebec. In 1900, both provinces together produced over four-fifths (82 percent) of the total value of Canadian manufacturing. In Quebec, much of the new industry was small-scale and labour-intensive textiles, boot and shoe production, saw and flour mills, and cigarette and cigar manufacturing. Two new industries emerged: hydro-electricity and pulp and paper.

Ontario's growth initially was based on industries in a series of towns and cities throughout southern Ontario that "fed" the demands of a booming agricultural hinterland economy, and that depended chiefly on coal as a source of energy and on iron production. In both cases, Ontario had an advantage over Quebec because of the province's proximity to the Pennsylvania coal fields and the Minnesota iron ranges. Also, a network of rail lines crisscrossed Ontario, linking the numerous towns and cities to the rural countryside and to other urban centres. By the turn of the century, Ontario already had many manufacturing centres scattered from Windsor to Cornwall — London, Berlin (later Kitchener), Guelph, and Peterborough, with the largest concentration at the western end of Lake Ontario, including Toronto, Hamilton, Brantford, St. Catharines, and Niagara Falls. These centres produced tariff-protected goods such as engines, farm implements, stoves, furniture, and canned goods. Hamilton, a steel-producing town, became as well the home of large rail-car shops. Most of Ontario's largest head offices, financial institutions, factories, and warehouses located in Toronto.

By comparison, only two major industrial cities dominated Quebec: Montreal and Quebec City. A few small textile towns grew up in the Eastern Townships, but most did not develop into manufacturing centres comparable to the smaller towns and cities of Ontario. The province instead concentrated on the small-scale manufacturing of shoes, textiles, lumber, and foodstuffs (flour, sugar, dairy products) — light industries utilizing cheap and abundant labour for a limited domestic market. These industries were concentrated near the rail facilities of the two main cities. Montreal had the advantage here over Quebec City, the latter becoming more

"Gateway to the West," Winnipeg, 1905. A million immigrants passed through the Canadian prairies' largest urban centre between 1896 and 1914; 100 000 stayed in the city.

Provincial Archives of Manitoba/N-7968.

isolated from the major canals and rail networks without a bridge over the St. Lawrence. Montreal also had the majority of financial institutions to provide capital for businesses in the city. Quebec City, by comparison, had depended on the square-timber trade and shipbuilding, both of which declined in the late nineteenth century.

The second industrial revolution, according to Albert Faucher and Maurice Lamontagne, began in 1911, when hydro-electric power replaced steam as the main source of industrial energy. Pulp and paper, and later minerals, became the new resource products. Ontario continued to expand during this "second industrial revolution" thanks to mineral production and the pulp and paper mills in the north, and hydro-electric power, especially in and around Niagara Falls.

In the Laurentian Shield to the north, Quebec had vast spruce forests for the pulp and paper industry, and an abundance of water power for electricity. Between 1900 and 1910, power production in the province increased by more than 300 percent. The pulp and paper industry experienced similar phenomenal growth in the same period due to American demand for newsprint. Initially, the pulp produced by Canadian-based companies went for processing in the United States. But at the turn of the century the Quebec government, at the urging of Quebec nationalists, placed an embargo on exports of pulp from Crown lands. Subsequently, Quebec pulp mills began producing their own newsprint for export. The Laurentide Company, established in 1877, became Canada's first and largest newsprint maker at the time. By 1914, Quebec had become a leading industrial province. More than two-thirds of its population worked in non-agricultural activities, and roughly one-half of its population lived in urban centres.

THE UNIQUENESS OF QUEBEC'S INDUSTRIAL DEVELOPMENT

For French Canadians, Quebec's industrialization had a unique and disturbing aspect: they had almost no control over it. In 1910, of Canada's entrepreneurs, only one out of 40 were French speaking. French Canadians were the labourers, not the owners of industry. Exceptions existed — Senator Louis Forget and his nephew Sir Rodolphe Forget, powerful financiers and investors in Quebec industries; Senator Frédéric-Liguori Béique, director of the Banque d'Hochelaga and later president of the Banque Canadienne Nationale; Alfred Dubuc, owner of the Chicoutimi Pulp Company in the Saguenay valley; and Georges Amyot, an influential textile magnate — but these men stood out, precisely because they were the exceptions.

Was this imbalance due to French Canadians' limited pool of capital? Perhaps in part, but French-speaking Canadians in the Dominion faced a language obstacle. The language of business was English. Historian Michel Brunet has argued that in the early twentieth century "the Quebec English-speaking business community constituted a select private club into which only a few assimilated former French Canadians were admitted."[4]

Some historians blamed the Roman Catholic church, which promoted an out-dated humanistic education, particularly at the classical college level. The provincial government tried to correct this by offering financial support for the establishment of technical schools. In 1907 it created the École des Hautes Études Commerciales (HEC), a university-level business school. The difficulty of finding corporations in which French was the working language, however, remained. Recent studies show that the Roman Catholic church did not always oppose industrialization. Sometimes it encouraged it, especially in many urban and one-industry-town parishes, as a means to stem emigration and the loss of parishioners.

THE FRENCH-CANADIAN RESPONSE TO INDUSTRIALISM

French Canadians divided into two camps on the question of "foreign" ownership. Jules-Paul Tardivel, the ultramontane nationalist and editor of the newspaper *La Vérité*, best expressed the viewpoint of those wanting to avoid involvement in industry: "It is not necessary for us to possess industry and money.... We would no longer be French Canadians but Americans like the others.... To cling to the soil, to raise large families, to maintain the hearths of spiritual and intellectual life, that must be our role in America."

Others, like Errol Bouchette, a French-Canadian economist, urged Quebeckers to accept industrialization as the best means to survive in North America. Not even agriculture could survive, he argued, if outsiders controlled the rest of Quebec's economy. "Emparons-nous de l'industrie" (Let us take over industry!) was his rallying cry.

"NEW ONTARIO"

Industrialization advanced fastest and farthest in southern Ontario, especially in the period from 1890 to 1914, which economic historian Ian Drummond calls the province's "heroic age."[5] As noted earlier, the province's proximity to the Pennsylvania coal fields

Where Historians Disagree

INDUSTRIAL GROWTH IN QUEBEC

Two questions relating to the industrialization of Quebec have led to much discussion. First, why did Quebec lag behind neighbouring Ontario in its industrialization? Second, why were French Canadians excluded from the control of industry in their province when industrialization finally occurred?

In the early 1950s two Quebec economists, Albert Faucher and Maurice Lamontagne, argued that Canadian industrialization occurred in two stages, or two "industrial revolutions" — one from 1866 to 1911, the other after 1911. In the first, industrial growth depended chiefly on the ability to produce iron and steel, resources that Quebec had in short supply and that were unavailable nearby. Ontario, by contrast, benefited from its proximity to the Pennsylvania coal fields and the Minnesota iron ranges. In the second stage, growth depended on the availability of hydro-electric power, which by 1911 had become the new source of industrial energy. Here Quebec was well blessed, but by this time Ontario had already developed an industrial infrastructure, and Quebec could not catch up.

Other economic historians have questioned Faucher and Lamontagne's identification of the "industrial takeoff" period in Quebec. John Dales contends in *Hydroelectricity and Industrial Development in Quebec, 1898–1940* (Cambridge, MA: Harvard University Press, 1957) that that industry experienced its greatest growth — 310 percent — in the first decade of the twentieth century. In *Croissance et structure économique de la Province de Québec* (Québec: Ministère de l'industrie et du commerce, 1961), André Raynauld argues that in some decades, such as the period 1910–20, Ontario accelerated faster than Quebec, but that over the extended period 1870–1957, the two provincial economies grew at almost parallel rates, each one taking its turn as the leader in industrial growth. Thus, overall, Quebec did not lag behind.

Historians H.V Nelles and C. Armstrong agree. In "Contrasting Development of the Hydro-Electric Industry in the Montreal and Toronto Regions, 1900–1930," in Douglas McCalla, ed., *The Development of Canadian Capitalism: Essays in Business History* (Toronto: Copp Clark Pitman, 1990), pp. 167–90, they argue that by 1920, both Ontario and Quebec produced the same quantity of hydro-electric power. But the two provinces differed in the nature of control of this key energy source. In Ontario it was publicly owned through Ontario Hydro, thus making it available to a larger industrial base, whereas in Quebec two very large privately owned companies controlled profits and alone benefited.

Economic historian John Isbister looks to the differing agricultural economies of the two provinces for his explanation. Quebec produced insufficient surplus food to serve its urban centres. Agriculture was "a subsistence sector, economically isolated, not integrated into the wider market system," compared with Ontario. Cultural explanations, according to Isbister, explain this; Quebec had "a different attitude toward the farming life. The Quebec habitant was a peasant, poor and self-sufficient, not a man of business." Only in the twentieth century would this attitude change, and by then Ontario farmers had surged ahead.

(continued)

Recently, Quebec historians Paul-André Linteau, René Durocher, and Jean-Claude Robert have questioned whether Quebec industrialized at a slower pace than Ontario even at the turn of the century. In *Quebec: A History, 1867–1929* (Toronto: James Lorimer, 1983), they argue that by dwelling on the resource-oriented industries, historians and economists have overlooked the sustained growth in manufacturing in Quebec at the turn of the century, which shows the period to be one of industrial takeoff.

The second question — why French-speaking Quebeckers have failed to become the leaders of industry in their own province — has also proven to be contentious. Historians Maurice Séguin ("The Conquest and French-Canadian Economic Life," translated from, "La Conquête et la vie économique des Canadiens," *Action nationale* 28 [1947]: 308–26, in Dale Miquelon, ed., *Society and Conquest: The Debate on the Bourgeoisie and Social Change in French Canada, 1700–1850* [Toronto: Copp Clark Publishing, 1977], pp. 67–80) and Michel Brunet ("The British Conquest and the Decline of the French-Canadian Bourgeoisie," translated from "La Conquête anglaise et la déchéance de la bourgeoisie canadienne [1760–1793]," in *La Présence anglaise et les Canadiens* [Montréal: Beauchemin, 1958], pp. 49–109; in Miquelon, *Society and Conquest*, pp. 143–61) contend that New France had a dynamic business class, but that its members returned to France after the conquest because of poor business opportunities under the British conquerors. With the departure of the French bourgeoisie, British interests stepped in, causing French Canadians to lose their economic role completely.

Another interpretation denies the existence of a viable business class in New France. It contends that the French Canadians' non-progressive business mentality led to British commercial superiority. Historian Fernand Ouellet has championed this interpretation. In any event, both sides agree that anglophone business interests controlled the economy of Quebec in the nineteenth century. Current debate has revolved around the question of how this small minority was able to maintain its favoured position.

Some anglophone historians blame the church-dominated educational system, with its emphasis on a classical education rather than on training in science and commerce, for the failure of French-speaking Canadians to go into business. But recent research does not entirely bear this out. Some science and commerce courses were in fact part of the school curriculum in Quebec. Historians Craig Brown and Ramsay Cook argue that where the church and the schools did err was in putting nationalism ahead of practical economic considerations: "Education ... had a moral and patriotic function, to which practical training for economic life was secondary" (*Canada, 1896–1921: A Nation Transformed* [Toronto: McClelland & Stewart, 1974], p. 132). Historians Paul-André Linteau, René Durocher, and Jean-Claude Robert explain the gap in industrial leadership of French-Canadian businesspeople in terms of limited technological know-how. Unlike English-speaking immigrants in Quebec, whose contact with their place of origin provided them with important business links and an international perspective, French Canadians lacked an "information network." Their contacts and know-how never extended beyond the confines of Quebec.

and the Minnesota iron deposits helped, as did the high protective tariff. Furthermore, the extensive railway system that tied the industrial core at the western end of Lake Ontario to the rest of the province, and to all of Canada, proved of major importance. But another decisive factor was the wealth of timber and minerals in northern Ontario. Suddenly this area — "New Ontario" — ceased to be perceived as an unproductive wasteland of rocks, lakes, and muskeg. In the period from 1890 to 1914, several northern Ontario towns and minerals became synonymous: Sudbury — nickel; Cobalt — silver; Timmins — gold. By 1914, the mineral-resource base of northern Ontario became accessible through rail transport to major urban centres outside the region.

The environmental cost of development was high. Unlike the placer mining in California and the Klondike, where prospectors readily retrieved ore through panning, most mining strikes in northern Ontario required large-scale, sophisticated equipment. In nickel production, for example, the ore had to be mined from the rock and then burned in the open air to concentrate the metal and reduce the sulphur content. The government had no regulations for environmental protection. The miners cleared the land of trees to fuel the roasting process, while sulphur and arsenic fumes escaped from the smokestacks into the atmosphere and poisoned the surrounding vegetation.

The great deal of investment capital and technical skill required led to rapid consolidation of the existing companies. In 1902, the Canadian Copper Company at Sudbury consolidated with several other smaller American companies to form the International Nickel Company of Canada (Inco). In the Porcupine district, three large companies — Hollinger (Canadian-owned), Dome (American-owned), and McIntyre (Canadian-owned after 1915) — soon controlled 90 percent of the gold production. In Sault Ste. Marie, F.H. Clergue, an American-born entrepreneur, built an industrial empire, the Consolidated Lake Superior Company, by using largely American capital.

The Ontario government assisted promoters. In 1891, in response to the recommendations of a royal commission on Ontario's mineral resources, the government established the Bureau of Mines "to collect and publish information and statistics on the mineral resources and mining industry." It also established the School of Mining at Queen's University in the early 1890s (later merged into the university's Faculty of Applied Sciences). As well, the provincial government handed out loans, railway land grants, timber leases, and mineral rights. Only when production began did the province demand royalty payments. By 1904, one-quarter of the province's revenue came from forestry. Mining equally contributed large sums to the provincial treasury.

MINING TOWNS IN NORTHERN ONTARIO

A host of mining towns developed. Some, such as Golden City, Elk Lake, and South Porcupine, were little more than camps made up of shacks and log cabins; others became company towns, built and owned by the town's only employer. Only a few, such as Sudbury and Timmins, became main service or distribution centres for the entire region. All of these northern Ontario mining communities depended on the capricious rise and fall of world metal prices. In time they came under the dominance of Toronto, the provincial capital, their main supply base, the focus of their rail transport, and the source of money for many of the mining and forestry companies.

The building of two new transcontinental railways across northern Ontario in the early twentieth century opened up vast areas of the Native peoples' hunting and trapping grounds to settlement and resource development. It also eliminated the Native peoples' jobs as freighters. The photo shows HBC Native voyageurs on their way to Flying Post with supplies from Biscotasing on the CPR, northwest of Sudbury, around 1900.

Archives of Ontario/Acc. #10144.

From 1880 to 1914, Canada underwent its industrial revolution as a result of the success of the national policy, the large-scale financial investment from within the country and abroad, and a new, more positive attitude towards business. Manufacturing and large-scale industrial production, and accompanying urban growth, meant increased prosperity and an overall higher standard of living. But not all regions of the country, nor all social classes, benefited equally from the economic expansion. The social costs of rapid change were high.

NOTES

1. H.V. Nelles, *The Politics of Development: Forests, Mines and Hydro-Electric Power in Ontario, 1849–1941* (Toronto: Macmillan, 1974), pp. 248–49.
2. Michael Cross, "The Canadian Worker in the Early Industrial Age," in Gregory S. Kealey and W.J.C. Cherwinski, eds., *Lectures in Canadian Labour and Working-Class History* (St. John's: Canadian Committee on Labour History and New Hogtown Press, 1985), p. 49.
3. Robert A.J. McDonald, *Making Vancouver: Class, Status, and Social Boundaries, 1863–1913* (Vancouver: University of British Columbia Press, 1996), p. 148.
4. Michel Brunet, "The French Canadians' Search for a Fatherland," in Peter Russell, ed., *Nationalism in Canada* (Toronto: McGraw-Hill, 1966), p. 55.
5. Ian Drummond, *Progress without Planning: The Economic History of Ontario from Confederation to the Second World War* (Toronto: University of Toronto Press, 1987), p. 104.

LINKING TO THE PAST

WEB LINKS

Timothy Eaton
http://www.schoolnet.ca/collections/wayfarers/eaton.htm
A biography of Timothy Eaton that details his beginnings and his rise to success as a department-store magnate.

The Substance of Development, 1871–1928
http://www.upei.ca/~rneill/topic_18.html
A detailed account of Canada's economic development during the period 1871–1928.

British Columbia's Resource Development
http://www.bcarchives.gov.bc/exhibits/timemach/gallery09/frames/index.htm
A detailed look at the economic development of British Columbia and its dependence on natural resources. Through description and photographs, this site examines the historical growth of industries such as forestry, mining, and fishing in the province.

RELATED READINGS

The following articles in R. Douglas Francis and Donald B. Smith, eds., *Readings in Canadian History: Post-Confederation*, 5th ed. (Toronto: Harcourt Brace, 1998), deal with topics relevant to this chapter: P-A. Linteau, R. Durocher, J.-C. Robert, "Urbanization in Quebec," pp. 165–73; and Stephen Davies, "'Reckless Walking Must Be Discouraged': The Automobile Revolution and the Shaping of Modern Urban Canada to 1930," pp. 173–84.

BIBLIOGRAPHY

Michael Bliss's *Northern Enterprise: Five Centuries of Canadian Business* (Toronto: McClelland & Stewart, 1987) provides a comprehensive history of Canadian business. See, as well, Graham Taylor and Peter Baskerville, *A Concise History of Business in Canada* (Toronto: Oxford University Press, 1994). On economic developments consult Kenneth Norrie and Douglas Owram, *A History of the Canadian Economy*, 2nd ed. (Toronto: Harcourt Brace, 1996). Two chapters — "The Triumph of Enterprise" and "French Canada and the New Industrial Order" — in R.C. Brown and R. Cook, *Canada, 1896–1921: A Nation Transformed* (Toronto: McClelland & Stewart, 1974) deal with industrialization and urbanization in English and French Canada, respectively. On Quebec consult also Paul-André Linteau, René Durocher, and Jean-Claude Robert, *Quebec: A History, 1867–1929* (Toronto: James Lorimer, 1983); and Susan Mann Trofimenkoff, *The Dream of Nation: A Social and Intellectual History of Quebec* (Toronto: Gage, 1983), pp. 132–49 and 167–83.

Michael Bliss deals with Canadian business's attitudes in *A Living Profit: Studies in the Social History of Canadian Businessmen, 1883–1914* (Toronto: McClelland & Stewart, 1974). Fernande Roy has studied the economic outlook of francophones in Montreal in *Progrès, harmonie, liberté: le libéralisme des milieux d'affaires francophones à Montréal au tournant du siècle* (Montréal: Boréal Express, 1988). Joy L. Santink's *Timothy Eaton and the Rise of His Department Store* (Toronto: University of Toronto Press, 1990) is an important study of this prominent Canadian merchant. For a general debate on industrialism in Ontario consult Ian Drummond, Louis P. Cain, and Majorie Cohen, "CHR Dialogue: Ontario's Industrial Revolution," *Canadian Historical Review* 69(3) (September 1988): 283–314.

On industrialization in the Maritimes see T.W. Acheson, D. Frank, and J. Frost, *Industrialization and the Underdevelopment in the Maritimes, 1880 to 1930* (Toronto: Gara-mond Press, 1985); Kris Inwood, *Farm, Factory and Fortune: New Studies in the Economic History of the Maritime Provinces* (Fredericton: Acadiensis Press, 1993); the relevant chapters in E.R. Forbes and D.A. Muise, eds., *The Atlantic Provinces in Confederation* (Toronto: University of Toronto Press, 1993); and W. Acheson, "The National Policy and the Industrialization of the Maritimes, 1880–1910," in G. Stelter and A.F.J. Artibise, eds., *The Canadian City: Essays in Urban and Social History* (Toronto: McClelland & Stewart, 1977; rev. ed., Ottawa: Carleton University Press, 1984), pp. 93–124. For Newfoundland see David Alexander, "Economic Growth in the Atlantic Region, 1880–1940," in E. Seager, L. Fisher, and S. Pierson, comp., *Atlantic Canada and Confederation: Essays in Canadian Political Economy* (Toronto: University of Toronto Press, 1983), pp. 51–78.

On British Columbia see Allen Saeger, "The Resource Economy, 1871–1921," in Hugh J.M. Johnston, ed., *The Pacific Province: A History of British Columbia* (Vancouver: Douglas & McIntyre, 1996), pp. 205–52; Frank Leonard, *A Thousand Blunders* (Vancouver: University of British Columbia Press, 1996); Jeremy Mouat, *Roaring Days: Rossland's Mines and the History of British Columbia* (Vancouver: University of British Columbia Press, 1995); and Martin Robin, *The Rush for Spoils: The Company Province, 1871–1913* (Toronto: McClelland & Stewart, 1972).

Major studies in English of industrialization in Quebec include A. Faucher and M. Lamontagne, "History of Industrial Development," in M. Rioux and Y. Martin, eds., *French-Canadian Society* (Toronto: McClelland & Stewart, 1964), pp. 257–71; J.H. Dales, *Hydroelectricity and Industrial Development in Quebec, 1898–1940* (Cambridge, MA: Harvard University Press, 1957); and W.J. Ryan, *The Clergy and Economic Growth in Quebec, 1896–1914* (Québec: Presses de l'Université Laval, 1966). For information on Quebec's banks consult Ronald Rudin, *Banking en français* (Toronto: University of Toronto Press, 1985); and, for background on its credit unions, Ronald Rudin, *In Whose Interest? Quebec's Caisses populaires, 1900–1945* (Montreal/Kingston: McGill-Queen's University Press, 1990).

For Ontario's resource development see H.V. Nelles, *The Politics of Development: Forests, Mines and Hydro-Electric Power in Ontario, 1849–1941* (Toronto: Macmillan, 1974); Duncan McDowall, *Steel at the Sault: Francis H. Clergue, Sir James Dunn, and Algoma Steel Corporation, 1901–1956* (Toronto: University of Toronto Press, 1984); and Jean L. Manore, *Cross-Currents: Hydroelectricity and the Engineering of Northern Ontario* (Waterloo, ON: Wilfrid Laurier University Press, 1999).

For the impact of industrialization and urbanization on the Native peoples consult Edward S. Rogers and Donald B. Smith, eds., *Aboriginal Ontario* (Toronto: Dundurn Press, 1994). Also of importance for Canada as a whole is Christopher Armstrong and H.V. Nelles, *Monopoly's Moment: The Organization and Regulation of Canadian Utilities, 1830–1930* (Philadelphia: Temple University Press, 1986). On Canadian investment abroad the following studies are important: C. Armstrong and H.V. Nelles, *Southern Exposure: Canadian Promoters in Latin America and the Caribbean, 1896–1930* (Toronto: University of Toronto Press, 1988); and Duncan McDowall, *The Light: Brazilian Traction, Light and Power Company Limited, 1899–1945* (Toronto: University of Toronto Press, 1988).

On urbanization see J.M.S. Careless's booklet *The Rise of Cities in Canada before 1914* (Ottawa: Canadian Historical Association, 1978), and his *Frontier and Metropolis: Regions, Cities and Identities in Canada before 1914* (Toronto: University of Toronto Press, 1989). Consult as well Richard Preston, "The Evolution of Urban Canada: The Post-1867 Period," in R.M. Irving, ed., *Readings in Canadian Geography*, 3rd ed. (Toronto: Holt, Rinehart and Winston, 1978), pp. 19–46; and the collection of articles in Stelter and Artibise, eds., *The Canadian City* (cited earlier). The Canadian Museum of Civilization has sponsored eight volumes in its series of histories of major Canadian cities: *Regina* (1989) by J. William Brennan, *Ottawa* (1986) by John H. Taylor, *Winnipeg* (1977) by Alan Artibise, *Calgary* (1978) by Max Foran, *Vancouver* (1980) by Patricia Roy, *Hamilton* (1982) by John C. Weaver, *Toronto to 1918* (1983) by J.M.S. Careless, and *Toronto since 1918* (1985) by James Lemon.

For a detailed study of urbanization in the Maritimes see J.M.S. Careless, "Aspects of Metropolitanism in Atlantic Canada," in M. Wade, ed., *Regionalism in the Canadian Community, 1867–1967* (Toronto: University of Toronto Press, 1969), pp. 117–29. On British Columbia see Robert A.J. McDonald, *Making Vancouver: Class, Status, and Social Boundaries, 1863–1913* (Vancouver: University of British Columbia Press, 1996); and Norbert McDonald, *Distant Neighbors: A Comparative History of Seattle and Vancouver* (Lincoln, NE: University of Nebraska Press, 1987). On the Prairies consult Paul Voisey, "The Urbanization of the Canadian Prairies, 1871–1916," *Histoire Sociale/Social History* 8 (1975): 77–101; A.F.J. Artibise, "The Urban West: The Evolution of Prairie Towns and Cities in 1930," *Prairie Forum* 4 (1979): 237–62; and A.F.J. Arbitise, ed., *Town and City: Aspects of Western Canadian Urban Development* (Regina: Canadian Plains Research Centre, University of Regina, 1981).

CHAPTER SEVEN

The Impact of Urban and Industrial Growth

Industrialization and urbanization changed the lifestyles of Canadians. In rural areas, they contributed to the migration of family members into the towns and cities in search of work. Farming, too, became more a business enterprise. Machinery replaced people, and tasks became more routine. Since machinery was expensive, farmers purchased larger farms to pay for it. In the cities, rural migration, along with immigration, led to the rise of large working-class districts in the congested and polluted city centre and middle-class areas in the clean, spacious suburbs. In the inner city, many worked outside the home in large factories or in offices at specialized and routine jobs for long hours. Women and some working-class children worked outside the home for wages much lower than those paid to men for doing the same job. Workers began to identify as a social class through clubs, fraternal organizations, and, for purposes of better wages and working conditions, unions.

THE IMPACT ON RURAL SOCIETY

WEB LINKS

On the eve of Canada's urban and industrial revolution, farming was a fairly stable occupation. The family farm in many parts of Canada still remained a relatively self-sufficient unit. Farm families produced a substantial amount of the food they consumed and sold the surplus. Farmers tried still to pass their farms down from generation to generation, usually to the eldest son. Younger sons tried to save money to purchase their own farms. Farmers' daughters could expect to help on the family farm in preparation for marriage — preferably, their parents hoped, to a young farmer in the district.

Industrialization altered this lifestyle. The introduction of labour-saving machines — hay mowers, reapers, threshers, and tractors — enabled a farmer to bring more land under cultivation. A mechanical haymower, for example, allowed a farmer to cut 10 acres (4 ha) a day, or 40 times as much as had been the case previously. By 1900, farmers, using labour-saving machinery, produced a bushel of wheat in one-hundredth of the time required only 30 years earlier. Now a farmer required greater revenue from the farm to pay for the expensive equipment he used. Large-scale farms became common. Dairy and fruit farming also became agribusiness. As well, improved and increased rail and steamship service that included cold-storage facilities and lower freight rates made it possible for Canadian farmers to sell their produce abroad — in Britain, for example.

The nature of work changed. It became more routine and specialized. Farmers also began to take over what had previously been considered women's work. The production of butter and cheese or the canning of fruit, for example, now occurred in factories. By 1901, cheese factories produced 40 percent of Canadian cheese. Large-scale dairy farms produced the milk to supply these cheese factories. Economist Marjorie Cohen notes, "As large dairy herds developed, dairying ceased to be a part-time occupation for farm women and more and more became the major work of males on the farms."[1]

Mechanization also reduced the number of older children needed to work the farm. This encouraged some to seek jobs in the cities. Better-paying jobs and better working conditions also lured the younger generation from the land. Rural depopulation became a concern. Many social commentators, such as John MacDougall, a minister from Spencerville, Ontario, whose lectures on rural life were incorporated in *Rural Life in Canada: Its Trends and Tasks* (1913), warned of the dire consequences of a declining rural population. Society at large continued to associate rural living with good moral values.

THE IMPACT ON NATIVE PEOPLE

On the West Coast, salmon processing came under the control of the British Columbia Packers Association after 1902, which replaced Aboriginal people with Japanese as fishers, boat builders, and processors, since they would work for lower wages, could be relied on for year-round fishing, and were less prone to strike. Asians also replaced Native people in the canneries, although both groups were subordinate to Euro-Canadians as managers. The introduction of modern assembly line and processing equipment eliminated jobs in general in fish-processing plants.

Commercialization in the northern fur trade also affected the Native peoples adversely. Initially, at the turn of the century, this was not the case. Rising fur prices and increased demand in Europe created a lucrative market. New companies, such as the Revillon Frères of Paris and the Northern Trading Company, challenged the Hudson's Bay Company's monopoly, resulting in increased demand, higher prices, and cash fur buying. Prosperity had its downside, however. The influx of non-Native hunters and trappers led to increased competition. Fur resources were quickly depleted. As well, the federal and provincial governments introduced conservation methods and laws that provided some protection for wildlife, but failed to fully consider the Aboriginal peoples' commercial, ceremonial, and subsistence needs and treaty rights.

The loss of these trading and employment opportunities within the fur industry would not have been so dramatic if the northern Aboriginal people and Métis had had viable alternative means of livelihood, but they did not. Even such alternatives as working on the railroads, supplying the railway ties, or working in mining areas as above-ground workers erecting buildings, clearing sites, and constructing roads were increasingly given to new immigrants. "By mid-century," Arthur Ray notes, "many northern Native groups were probably more dependent on hunting and trapping than they had been at anytime since the late eighteenth century."[2]

LIFE IN THE INDUSTRIAL CITY

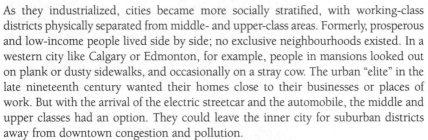

WEB
LINKS

As they industrialized, cities became more socially stratified, with working-class districts physically separated from middle- and upper-class areas. Formerly, prosperous and low-income people lived side by side; no exclusive neighbourhoods existed. In a western city like Calgary or Edmonton, for example, people in mansions looked out on plank or dusty sidewalks, and occasionally on a stray cow. The urban "elite" in the late nineteenth century wanted their homes close to their businesses or places of work. But with the arrival of the electric streetcar and the automobile, the middle and upper classes had an option. They could leave the inner city for suburban districts away from downtown congestion and pollution.

The city centres became both business and industrial districts, around which the majority of the working class lived. A number of long-established cultural institutions, such as churches and social clubs, were removed from the city centre and relocated in more luxurious and pleasant suburban areas. Many city centres became ghettoized and undesirable places to live. The Commission of Conservation, established by the federal government in 1909, noted in its *Annual Report* in 1914:

> Industrial smoke disfigures buildings, impairs the health of the population, renders the city filthy, destroys any beauty with which it may naturally be endowed and tends, therefore, to make it a squalid and undesirable place of residence, and this at a time when economic influences are forcing into cities an ever increasing proportion of our population.

In Montreal and Toronto, the two largest and most industrialized Canadian cities, most working-class people rented rooms in either boarding or tenement houses — old wooden cottages or two-storey buildings with little or no yard area. Rent could be as high as $10 or $12 a month for basement rooms, roughly 25 percent of an unskilled worker's wages. Some philanthropists, such as Toronto's Sir Joseph Flavelle and Hart Massey, subsidized workers' houses near their factories. In 1913, Ontario passed the Ontario Housing Act to provide municipal support for upgraded working-class districts. But before World War I, most working-class families had to face intractable landlords on their own. Few families owned their own houses, since house prices remained well beyond the means of the ordinary worker.

An average family of five typically lived in a one-or-two-room flat: damp, unventilated, inadequately lighted, and poorly heated. Overcrowding remained a constant problem. In Toronto, for example, rapid growth led to a housing shortage. Some families lived in hastily constructed shacks, in backyard tents, or even on the street. In summer, a stench rose from the cesspools and outdoor privies.

Wife beating and the sexual abuse of children were common. Very often such violence in working-class districts was associated with drinking, unemployment, and destitution. Wives had little legal recourse because male-dominated courts rarely challenged the husband's proprietary right over his wife's person and her sexuality. If anything, judges questioned the woman's character. Because of high legal costs, divorce also remained out of the question for most abused women.

Children, particularly those of the working class, enjoyed fewer rights and privileges than did women at the turn of the century. Family responsibilities began early, and children had to grow up and mature quickly. In Montreal, a grade three

On May 16, 1913, the Toronto department of health photographed this scene of slum housing in full view of City Hall.

....

City of Toronto Archives/
RG-8-32-187.

education was the norm for working-class children. They had to enter the work force as soon as possible (age 11 or 12 being the norm) to supplement the family income. The census of 1871 revealed that 25 percent of boys and 10 percent of girls between the ages of 11 and 15 held jobs outside the home; this did not include boys hired to do odd jobs or girls working as domestics. Ontario and Quebec passed Factory Acts prohibiting the hiring of boys under 12 and girls under 14, but they had little impact due to poor enforcement and the difficulty of taking recalcitrant factory owners to court. Those unfortunate enough to end up in court had a greater chance of being penalized than protected and of being sent to harsh probationary institutions such as the Toronto Mercer Reformatory or Vancouver's Boys' Industrial School.

Recent research enables us to make some generalizations about those children most likely to work outside the home and those who stayed home. Young daughters were less likely than young sons to be employed outside the home, since girls, by the age of 15 or 16, made only half to two-thirds of the wages paid to boys of the same age for doing a similar job. Patriarchal attitudes also opposed daughters working in factories. As well, girls up to the age of 16 were required at home to help run the household. Generally, poorer working-class families sent their daughters out to work because of economic necessity.

WORKING CONDITIONS IN CANADA'S CITIES
....

Industrialization created difficult working conditions. During the peak season the average labourer spent at least six days a week, ten to twelve hours a day, and upward of 60 to 70 hours a week in poorly ventilated, noisy, and dirty factories. Foremen organized the factory operations for maximum efficiency and often levied fines for tardiness or talking to fellow workers on the job. Industrial accidents and deaths occurred frequently. One manufacturer advertised his product in the *Montreal Star* (April 4, 1903) with this enticement: "Remember you are insured for $100 if accidentally killed while wearing these overalls."

Job security did not exist. Victims of industrial accidents had no workers' compensation. Furthermore layoffs, especially during the slower winter months, occurred

Sir William Van Horne, president of the CPR (1888–99). The Sudbury Journal *reported on May 10, 1894, that he earned $50 000 annually. This was 100 times what a butcher, carpenter, machinist, or millwright earned.*

National Archives of Canada/C-8549.

regularly. Even in good times, unemployment was common. Before the federal government introduced unemployment insurance in 1940, layoffs meant months of subsistence without wages.

    Urban life, however, had its attractions. Young people, both men and women, left the farm in increasing numbers to find work in the congested, noisy cities. Generally, factory wages were better. Although the working hours were long, they still were shorter than those on the farm, with at least one day a week off and, often, Saturday afternoon as well. Cities had taverns, sports events, music halls, and, soon, the cinema.

THE STANDARD OF LIVING

The cost of living in urban centres rose quickly at the turn of the century, continuing to outpace wages. The federal Department of Labour issued "typical weekly expenditure" budgets listing those items necessary for a family of five to enjoy a minimum standard of living. Though it allowed for only 0.6 kg of fresh meat per week per person, less than a litre of milk a day for a family of five, and no fresh vegetables or fruit, this minimum was well beyond the reach of most individual bread-winners. In 1901, the estimated cost of living was $13.38 a week. But, at best, the average male worker could, without layoffs, make $425 a year in 1901, an average of $8.25 a week. (The modern definition of poverty is any individual or family having to spend more than 70 percent of total income on basic needs such as food, fuel, and shelter.) Thus, many working-class families needed at least two incomes to survive.

This store at the turn of the century shows the diversity of items available to those who had money to purchase them, including Jello, which had just come on the market in 1897.

Provincial Archives of New Brunswick/P18-163.

WOMEN IN THE WORKPLACE

At the turn of the century, women made up only about one-seventh of the paid work force. Usually they worked outside the home only between the ages of 14 and 24. After marriage, they rarely returned to paid work, unless widowhood, desertion, or illness in the family forced them to do so. The routine of housework — rearing children, cleaning, cooking, washing, mending, and shopping — meant full and exhausting days in an era before labour-saving devices. Marriage, motherhood, and domesticity remained intertwined in the minds of most women, no matter to which class they belonged. This was considered women's "proper sphere." Men dominated the "public sphere." Nevertheless, many women supplemented the family income by taking in boarders, doing part-time sewing, or doing laundry.

The most economically pressed mothers had no choice but to work outside the home in female-related jobs in textile factories, as waitresses, or as domestics. Women without familial support had to find work. In these cases, they had to rely on friends, neighbours, relatives, or on working-class associations. Sometimes immigrant women could count on the support of ethnic groups to provide mutual aid and, occasionally, employment agencies. Increasingly, however, there arose a large number of working women who were single, non-immigrant girls, popularly known as "working girls," who performed non-domestic waged work outside the home. Being single, young, independent and alone, they became the concern of moral reformers who saw them as a threat to the ideal Canadian society as made up of morally upright, married, and motherly women.

Middle-class women depended on domestic help at the turn of the century. Families were larger then, homes harder to keep clean, and food preparation much more time-consuming. Domestics tended to be young girls from rural areas or immigrant women. In 1891, 40 percent of all women working outside the home were employed as domestics.

Domestic servants, if working away from the protection of family or friends, were vulnerable to sexual exploitation. The most typical response of those victimized was simply to leave. Not in one case, however. Carrie Davies, an 18-year-old servant of Charles Albert Massey, a member of the farm machinery family founded by Hart Massey, opposed his sexual advances and finally shot and killed him. About a thousand sympathetic supporters in Ontario contributed to her trial-defence fund in 1915. The jury acquitted her for murdering her employer.

Women preferred factory work's higher wages and shorter hours to domestic service. In 1900, they still worked up to 60 hours a week. Textile and shoe factories hired women because they could pay them lower wages (approximately half of what men earned) and because they were better workers for the type of work to be done. Women made up about two-thirds of the work force in the textile industry in 1880 and almost half by 1900. Most female workers were between the ages of 14 (the youngest age permissible for girls to work after 1885) and 24 (the normal marrying age). Historian Jacques Rouillard describes the typical working conditions in a textile factory:

> It was not so much the physical effort required by the machines, as the tremendous speeds at which they functioned and the attention they demanded, which taxed the nervous system of the worker. The noise caused by the hundreds of weaving machines as well as the high degree of humidity in the spinning and weaving rooms were especially irritating. This damp atmosphere, maintained to keep the thread from breaking, resulted in fatigue among the workers and often led to loss of appetite and anemia. Many of the young women had to quit their jobs, unable to overcome the tension they suffered in this atmosphere.[3]

Most of all, women sought office jobs away from the noise and pressure of the factory. By the turn of the century, women had taken most of the clerical jobs. Conventional wisdom held that women's "natural" feminine characteristics — sympathy, adaptability, courtesy, and even nimble fingers — made them particularly suitable for clerical work. Male clerks, however, retained the senior managerial positions. Other women worked as department-store clerks or telephone operators, two of the most "feminized" occupations at the turn of the century.

After domestic, factory, and office work, teaching was the most important female occupation. The public schools had greatly expanded in the late nineteenth century. At the turn of the century, women constituted three-quarters of the teaching profession. Teaching was considered an acceptable occupation for women, and one that allowed for the possibility of some upward mobility, although it provided little financial security. Women received low salaries and had little chance of advancing to become department heads or principals. Increasingly, female teachers lost their jobs if they married.

A small number of women worked as nurses. Thanks to Florence Nightingale's campaign, nursing had become respectable at the turn of the century although not

A Historical Portrait

EMILY JENNINGS STOWE

Emily Jennings became the first female public-school principal in Upper Canada, and, immediately after Confederation, the first Canadian woman to practise medicine openly. She was also one of the country's first suffragists.

Born near Norwich, Upper Canada, on May 1, 1831, Emily Jennings came from a Quaker background. Since the Society of Friends (Quakers) gave women the same status as men, she grew up in an atmosphere of complete gender equality. Her struggle to achieve equality for women began in 1852 when she applied for admission to Victoria College in Cobourg. Refused on the grounds that she was female, she then applied successfully to the Toronto Normal School. She graduated with first-class honours in 1854. She taught until her marriage in 1856 to John Stowe, owner of a carriage business in neighbouring Mount Pleasant.

Shortly after the birth of their third child in 1863, John Stowe contracted tuberculosis and had to leave the family for treatment. With the financial help of the Jennings family, and the support of her sister, Cornelia, who agreed to care for Emily's children, Emily prepared for a medical career.

Barred from medical school in Canada because she was female, Emily enrolled at the New York Medical College for Women, a homeopathic (or natural medicine) institution in New York City. She graduated in 1867. But when she returned to Canada, the College of Physicians and Surgeons refused to certify her. So for over a decade she practised medicine in Toronto without a licence. She was not prosecuted for doing so, but was charged in 1879 with having performed an abortion. In the lengthy trial that followed, she successfully defended her qualifications, skill, and professional conduct. After her acquittal, the College of Physicians and Surgeons granted her a medical licence.

Dr. Stowe helped to organize the Women's Medical College in Toronto (the forerunner of Women's College Hospital) in 1883. That same year, her daughter Augusta achieved her mother's own goal of 20 years earlier — she obtained a medical degree from the University of Toronto. Augusta Stowe became the first woman to receive a Canadian medical degree.

Emily Stowe treated her husband on terms of perfect equality. When John Stowe regained his health, she supported him while he retrained as a dentist. After his graduation, the Stowes practised side by side at 111 Church Street in Toronto, until Emily retired in 1893.

While in New York City as a medical student, Emily became interested in feminist causes. Upon her return to Canada she launched the Toronto Women's Literary Club, a pseudonym for a suffrage group, the first in Canada. It issued a magazine, the *Citizen*, that championed women's education and enfranchisement. In 1883, the group reconstituted itself as the Canadian Woman's Suffrage Association. Six years later, the group helped to form the Dominion Women's Enfranchisement Association. Dr. Stowe became its first president, a position she held until her death in 1903.

In a note she wrote in 1896, Emily Stowe provided her own best epitaph: "My career has been one of much struggle characterised by the usual persecution which attends everyone who pioneers a new movement or steps out of line with established custom."

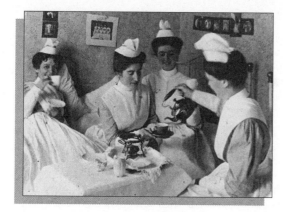

Tea-time for nurses, Calgary General Hospital, 1904. Nurses put in long hours at low wages.

Glenbow Archives, Calgary, Canada/ NA-2600-3.

yet recognized as a profession. Many saw the Victorian Order of Nurses (VON), formed in 1897, as a model public-health nursing service. Women, however, could only with great difficulty enter existing Canadian medical schools. After graduation, few hospitals provided them with hospital privileges. Unable to attract enough patients, a number of Canada's early female doctors became instead medical missionaries overseas.

HEALTH

Frequent illness complicated the normal daily problems of living and working. Montreal in particular remained a most unhealthy city in which to live, especially for children. At the turn of the century, approximately one out of every four infants died before the age of one. City inhabitants suffered from impure water, unpasteurized milk, and the limited use of vaccines for smallpox, diphtheria, and tuberculosis. Families had no sick benefits or hospital or life insurance to protect them. Women were expected to provide essential health care at home.

Society denounced attempts to limit family size. A country seeking to increase its population size had a stake in encouraging women to have large families. Limitation of family size, especially among those of British stock, was considered "race suicide." Section 179 of the Criminal Code of Canada, prepared in 1892, read: "Everyone is guilty of an indictable offence and liable to two years' imprisonment who knowingly, without lawful excuse or justification, offers to sell, advertise, publish an advertisement of or has for sale or disposal any medicine, drug or article intended or represented as a means of preventing conception or causing abortion." Despite such threats, many married women, anxious to limit their family size, sought birth-control information. Many lacked even the basic information taught to children today in elementary school. But as historian Angus McLaren has written: "Doctors would not discuss the merits of the most reliable forms of contraception — the condom, douche, and pessary — because they associated them with the libertine, the prostitute, and the midwife."[4] A few doctors, and a greater number of hacks, performed abortions, but since abortions were illegal it is difficult to know how many occurred. As well, some women had self-induced abortions. Statistics of women who died from improper abortions are available for a later period, however: an estimated 4000 women died from abortions between 1926 and 1946.

CHARITABLE AND SOCIAL INSTITUTIONS FOR THE WORKING CLASS

At the turn of the century, churches and private philanthropic organizations administered limited charitable help. Early in the century, Toronto had more than 50 charitable organizations and 20 churches providing relief to the poor. Montreal had nearly 30 shelters and outdoor-relief agencies for the poor, as well as about a dozen old-age homes and a dozen orphanages. Between 1900 and 1911, these institutions provided relief for 2000–3000 families in their respective cities each year — usually a meal of soup, bread, and tea, and a bath and a bed. Generally society held that, with the exception of the handicapped and the aged, individuals alone were responsible for their plight. Thus charities provided only temporary relief as a stop-gap measure.

Skilled workers looked to fraternal organizations for financial and emotional support. Associations and lodges such as the Orange Lodge, the Masons, the Oddfellows, and the Independent Order of Foresters, along with sporting clubs for baseball, snowshoeing, rowing, and lacrosse, gave their members (female workers could not belong) a sense of importance and self-worth and a feeling of camaraderie. Some associations had mutual-aid plans to care for sick members and to assist widows and orphans in the event of a member's death. They also gave workers a means to express publicly and collectively their discontent with industrial capitalism. Parades through the streets of towns and cities to show both solidarity and defiance became a popular form of protest. Association life was, as labour historian Bryan Palmer notes, "a realm apart from the troubled conflicts of the workplace"[5] and an important phase on the road to a working-class consciousness.

UNIONS

Between 1850 and 1890, labour unions took root in Canada. At first, most unions were local, dispersed across the country, and specialized. Initially, the government refused to grant them legal recognition or to accept workers' right to collective bargaining. The first victory came in 1872, after more than 100 Toronto printers stayed off the job for almost two months. They went on strike for a nine-hour day, protesting that "nine hours a day, six days a week is enough for any man to work." George Brown, in 1864 a Father of Confederation, and Liberal editor of the Toronto *Globe*, opposed the strikers. But his arch-rival, Prime Minister John A. Macdonald, enacted the Trade Union Act, which recognized the right of unions to exist and to organize without fear of prosecution as illegal associations, so long as they registered with the government. Helped by the act, the Toronto printers eventually won better wages and a 54-hour work week. The implementation, at the same time, of the Criminal Law Amendment Act, however, constituted a step backward. This act imposed severe penalties, including a prison sentence, for most forms of picketing and union pressure. Picketing remained illegal in Canada until 1934.

Knights of Labor procession, King Street, Hamilton, 1885. Parades were an expression of workers' solidarity and a means to achieve public recognition.

W. Farmer/National Archives of Canada/PA-103086.

In the late nineteenth century, skill, religion, ethnicity, and gender divided the Canadian working class. Only a minority of Canadian workers belonged to unions, and those who did affiliated with a variety of groups, among which two stand out: the Knights of Labor and the American Federation of Labor.

The Knights of Labor, an American organization founded in 1869, enjoyed its greatest success among workers in Ontario and Quebec, although it had branches across the country. Its secret rituals enjoyed great popularity among its followers. At its moment of greatest expansion, it had more than 450 assemblies and over 20 000 members across Canada. The Knights believed in developing a working-class consciousness through the organization of workers by industry rather than by craft. The organization used its newspapers, the *Pallidium of Labour* and the *Labour Advocate*, to educate the working class to its ideals. The Knights' platform urged, wherever possible, arbitration instead of strikes, an eight-hour day, an end to child labour, the passage of health and safety legislation, and equal pay for equal work. As an industrial, rather than a craft union, the Knights took in semi-skilled and unskilled workers as well as women and blacks, although not Asians.

Most unions refused to support women, arguing that by improving women's wages they encouraged women to remain at work, where they took jobs away from men. Despite such a general negative attitude, some unions, such as the Knights of Labor and others, attempted to organize female telephone operators, retail clerks, laundry workers, waitresses, and even domestics. In some industries, women formed their own unions. In the garment industry, for example, a number of women joined locals of the International Ladies' Garment Workers Union. Their success in this

Young Cape Breton miners at the pit head, 1903. Canada's industrial revolution depended on coal, and Cape Breton Island contained the richest coal deposits in eastern Canada. By 1901, it produced half of Canada's coal.

Beaton Institute, University College of Cape Breton.

WEB

LINKS

particular industry might have come partially from the support of male trade unionists who needed their female counterparts to mount effective strikes. Still, unionized women workers remained more the exception than the rule.

The Provincial Workmen's Association, founded in 1879 by the coal miners of Springfield, Nova Scotia, became the Maritime equivalent of the Knights of Labor. After a slow beginning, it became recognized as the voice of the coal miners, and later represented other Maritime workers. In 1909, however, the Scottish immigrant James Bryson McLachlan helped introduce to Cape Breton a more militant union, a branch of the American-based United Mine Workers of America. Ten years later, the miners at last gained the eight-hour day and made important gains in their standard of living.

Initially, the Knights of Labor controlled the Trades and Labor Congress of Canada (TLC), the central labour organization founded in 1883 by the Toronto Trades and Labor Council as a successor to the Canadian Labor Union (1873–77). Originally it brought together trade unionists from Ontario only. By 1900, however, it had become a Dominion-wide organization.

The TLC moved away from the Knights' approach to reform and organization by industry when it established strong ties with the American Federation of Labor (AFL), a strictly craft-union organization. The conservative leadership of the AFL believed that the primary purpose of unions should be simply to improve the material benefits of its workers — better wages and hours and safer working conditions — rather than to radically reform the capitalist system. It expelled industrial unions such as the Knights from its membership. Internal divisions within the Canadian labour movement greatly undermined the overall effectiveness and clout of trade unions at the turn of the century.

With the decline of the Knights of Labor in the early twentieth century, unskilled workers looked increasingly to politics or radical unions to achieve their objectives. Some worked to create an independent socialist party, while others, who had given up hope that the AFL would become more militant, supported radical unions, such as the Industrial Workers of the World (IWW), founded in 1905. The "Wobblies," as they became known, attempted to organize all workers, regardless of their trade, skill, or sex, into one large union for the purpose of calling a general strike to bring down the capitalist system. The first sentence of their constitution revealed their view of North

American society: "The working class and the employing class have nothing in common." The IWW had little impact in eastern Canada but greater success in western Canada.

In the West, the philosophy of individualism remained entrenched, resulting in a lack of sympathy for any form of collective action. Yet generally conditions remained poor for western workers. Wages were exceptionally low, inflation high, employment sporadic, especially in the primary industries, and working conditions, especially in the mines and railway camps, atrocious. Large-scale immigration into the region proved both the strength and weakness of unions in the region. On the one hand, immigration provided a large pool of unskilled workers who hindered the growth of unions by their willingness to work as "scabs" for low wages. On the other hand, many European, and especially British, immigrants were well versed in socialist ideas and experienced in union organizations.

In Quebec, Roman Catholic unions challenged the Knights and the AFL for the support of French-Canadian workers. The Roman Catholic church assisted in providing church-affiliated unions as an alternative to what it considered to be social-ist and anti-clerical international unions that undermined the church's position among the working class. The clergy first intervened directly in a labour dispute in the Quebec shoe-workers' strike of 1906. One year later, the church founded a union. Its successor would be the Confédération des Travailleurs Catholiques du Canada (CTCC), an exclusively Roman Catholic organization founded in 1921, with a priest, as chaplain, effectively in charge of each local.

LIMITATIONS OF UNIONS IN THE PREWAR ERA

In general, unions had limited success prior to World War I. As late as 1911, less than one-tenth of the national work force belonged to unions. Most unskilled workers and virtually all women remained non-unionized. Unions were also divided, and their leaders suspicious of one another. Furthermore, unions had few rights. Employers could still fire union workers at will or demand that workers sign contracts in which they promised not to join a union. As well, employers brought in immigrant labour-ers on the condition that they work as strike breakers or for extremely low wages. Workers fought back by pressuring the Laurier government to pass the Alien Labour Act in 1908, which prohibited "any person, company, partnership, or corporation, in any manner to pre-pay the transportation of, or in any other way to assist or solicit the importation of immigration of any alien or foreigner into Canada under control or agreement." But the act was rarely enforced and had no impact on controlling companies wanting cheap labour.

Nevertheless, unions did organize strikes — 1000 disputes were recorded between 1900 and 1911, mainly in the manufacturing, construction, transportation, and mining industries. Workers protested against low wages, inadequate working conditions, and managerial tyranny. The views of one Montreal mill manager, as reported in *La Presse* in 1908, characterized the general attitude of managers to workers: "It was not at all his concern whether his employees could live on the wages he paid them. If they don't like it, they can go work somewhere else." Most strikes, however, ended without workers gaining any significant concessions. Many of them erupted into physical violence, with the government calling out the militia to end them. This happened on more than 30 occasions before 1914.

View of the Hillcrest mine in the Crow's Nest Pass. On June 19, 1914, Canada's worst coal-mining disaster occurred here. One hundred and eighty-nine men were killed by an explosion from the methane gas that seeped from the coal face combined with the combustible coal dust. The mine closed in 1949.

Glenbow Archives, Calgary, Canada/NA-629-1.

Governments favoured business interests. The laissez-faire philosophy prevailed, at least with respect to labour. The same governments saw no contradiction in supporting employers by means of tariffs or other economic incentives. The federal Conservative government did, however, establish the Royal Commission on the Relations of Labour and Capital, which in its report in 1889 documented the negative impact of the industrial revolution. Few reforms resulted, although in 1894, the Conservatives officially established Labour Day, the first Monday of September, as a national holiday for working people.

The Laurier Liberal government created the Department of Labour in 1900 to prevent and settle strikes as well as to enforce a fair wage policy. In 1907 it also passed the Industrial Disputes Investigation Act, which prohibited strikes and lockouts in mines or public utilities until a three-member board had investigated the dispute. The Ontario government under James Whitney introduced the Workmen's Compensation Act in 1914, but only after the act met with the approval of employers, who realized that they would also benefit from government compensation to injured workers.

Skilled workers tried to gain influence through politics. They set out their own agenda, such as the sixteen-point program of the Trades and Labor Congress passed at its meeting in 1898, in which they demanded free compulsory education, an eight-hour day, a minimum wage, tax reform, public ownership of railways and telegraphs, extension of the franchise, abolition of the Senate, prohibition of prison and contract labour, legislative elimination of child labour, and opposition to Chinese immigration — the Chinese being perceived as a threat to labour's employment opportunities and wages.

Then they tried to pressure the two traditional parties to adopt some or all of their recommendations. When this approach failed, they fielded their own labour candidates in federal, provincial, and municipal elections. While a few were elected, most labour politicians had limited success and impact, particularly at the federal and provincial levels. Greater success did occur at the municipal level. By 1920, fully 271 working-class candidates ran for political office in 44 municipalities. One hundred and eleven were elected, including labour mayors in Fort William, Port Arthur, Sault Ste. Marie, and Moncton. But overall, workers had a weak political voice in the pre–World War I era.

At the turn of the century, Canadians lived well by world standards, but social injustice and inequalities persisted. Farming had undergone significant change. The family farm had to adjust to mechanization, higher costs, fewer workers, and routine and specialized jobs. Many left the land for the growing urban centres. Cities became socially and physically stratified, with working-class districts in the city centre and middle-class areas in the surrounding suburbs. Both male and female workers lived in cramped quarters and worked long hours, under poor conditions, in factories and offices. In times of need, they looked to charitable and social institutions, and ultimately to unions, for assistance. By the early twentieth century the injustices had become so noticeable that they gained public attention, especially among a rising group of middle-class social reformers.

NOTES

1. Marjorie Griffin Cohen, *Women's Work, Markets, and Economic Development in Nineteenth-Century Ontario* (Toronto: University of Toronto Press, 1988), p. 106.
2. Arthur J. Ray, *I Have Lived Here Since the World Began* (Toronto: Key Porter, 1996), p. 291.
3. Jacques Rouillard, "A Life So Threadbare," *Horizon Canada* 25 (1985): 594.
4. Angus McLaren, "A Motherhood Issue," *Horizon Canada* 87 (1986): 2074.
5. Bryan Palmer, *Working-Class Experience: The Rise and Reconstitution of Canadian Labour, 1800–1980* (Toronto: Butterworths, 1983), p. 80.

LINKING TO THE PAST

WEB
LINKS

The Peopling of Canada, 1891–1921

http://www.ucalgary.ca/HIST/tutor/canada1891/

This site features information on Canadian population and society at the turn of the century, including immigration and migration patterns, settlement of the West, and descriptions of urban and rural life.

The History of Mining in Cape Breton

http://www.schoolnet.ca/collections/coal/minegrap.html

A detailed account of the history of coal mining in Cape Breton, Nova Scotia, with information on early mining methods, on unions such as the Provincial Workmen's Association, and a virtual tour through the Miner's Museum.

Ontario Town Life

http://www.civilization.ca/cmc/cmceng/ca19eng.html

A short description, with photographs, of life in a typical Ontario town at the turn of the century.

RELATED READINGS

....

The following article in R. Douglas Francis and Donald B. Smith, eds., *Readings in Canadian History: Post-Confederation*, 5th ed. (Toronto: Harcourt Brace, 1998), is relevant to this chapter: Bettina Bradbury, "Gender at Work at Home: Family Decisions, the Labour Market, and Girls' Contributions to the Family Economy," pp. 187–206.

BIBLIOGRAPHY

....

On the impact of industrialization and commercialization on Aboriginal people see Arthur Ray, *I Have Lived Here Since the World Began* (Toronto: Key Porter, 1996); Diane Newell, *Tangled Webs of History: Indians and the Law in Canada's Pacific Coast Fisheries* (Toronto: University of Toronto Press, 1993); Bruce Hodgins and Jamie Benidickson, *The Temagami Experience: Recreation, Resources, and Aboriginal Rights in the Northern Ontario Wilderness* (Toronto: University of Toronto Press, 1989); and Kerry Abel, *Drum Songs: Glimpses of Dene History* (Montreal/Kingston: McGill-Queen's University Press, 1993).

Working-class life in the major industrial city of Montreal at the turn of the century is discussed in T.J. Copp, *The Anatomy of Poverty: The Condition of the Working Class in Montreal, 1897–1929* (Toronto: McClelland & Stewart, 1974); and in J. Rouillard, *Les syndicats nationaux au Québec de 1900 à 1930* (Québec: Presses de l'Université Laval, 1979); as well as in his *Histoire du syndicalisme québécois* (Montréal: Boréal Express, 1989). For family life in Montreal see Bettina Bradbury, *Working Families: Age, Gender and Daily Survival in Industrializing Montreal* (Toronto: McClelland & Stewart, 1993). For Toronto see Gregory Kealey, *Toronto Workers Respond to Industrial Capitalism, 1867–1892* (Toronto: University of Toronto Press, 1980); and Michael Piva, *The Conditions of the Working Class in Toronto, 1900–1921* (Ottawa: University of Ottawa Press, 1979). On Atlantic Canada see Daniel Samson, *Contested Countryside: Rural Workers and Modern Society in Atlantic Canada, 1800–1950* (Fredericton: Acadiensis Press, 1994). On epidemics see Michael Bliss, *Plague: A Story of Smallpox in Montreal* (Toronto: HarperCollins, 1991).

On women workers see the relevant sections in Alison Prentice et al., *Canadian Women: A History*, 2nd ed. (Toronto: Harcourt Brace, 1996); Marjorie Griffin Cohen, *Women's Work: Markets and Economic Development in Nineteenth-Century Ontario* (Toronto: University of Toronto Press, 1988); and Graham S. Lowe, *Women in the Administrative Revolution: The Feminization of Clerical Work* (Toronto: University of Toronto Press, 1987). Mary Kinnear, ed., *First Days, Fighting Days: Women in Manitoba History* (Regina: Canadian Plains Research Centre, University of Regina, 1987), contains several essays on women workers. See also J. Acton et al., eds., *Women at Work: Ontario, 1850–1930* (Toronto: Canadian Women's Educational Press, 1974); and Wayne Roberts, *Honest Womanhood: Feminism, Femininity and Class Consciousness Among Toronto Working Women, 1893 to 1914* (Toronto: New Hogtown Press, 1976). A comparative study of men and women workers in the two Ontario towns of Paris and Hanover is provided in Joy Parr, *The Gender of Breadwinners: Women, Men, and Change in Two Industrial Towns, 1880–1950* (Toronto: University of Toronto Press, 1990). For the Maritimes see Janet Guildford and Suzanne Morton, *Separate Spheres: Women's Worlds in the 19th-Century Maritimes* (Fredericton: Acadiensis Press, 1994). Gender conflict is reviewed in Franca Iacovetta and Mariana Valverde, eds., *Gender Conflicts: New Essays in Women's History* (Toronto: University of Toronto Press, 1992).

On working families see Bettina Bradbury, ed., *Canadian Family History: Selected Readings* (Toronto: Copp Clark Pitman, 1992); and R. Marvin McInnis, "Women, Work and Childbearing: Ontario in the Second Half of the Nineteenth Century," *Histoire sociale/Social History* 24(48) (November 1991): 237–62. Women's dealings with the law are the subject of Constance Backhouse's *Petticoats and Prejudice: Women and Law in Nineteenth Century Canada* (Toronto: The Osgoode Society, 1991). On changing notions of sexuality see Gary Kinsmen, *The Regulation of Desire: Sexuality in Canada* (Montreal: Black Rose Books, 1987); Sharon Dale, *Lesbians in Canada* (Toronto: Between the Lines, 1990); and Angus McLaren and Arlene Tigar McLaren, *The Bedroom and the State: The Changing Practices and Politics of Contraception and Abortion in Canada, 1880–1980* (Toronto: McClelland & Stewart, 1986). McLaren has also written a short popular article, "A Motherhood Issue," *Horizon Canada* 87 (1986): 2072–77, on birth control in Canada in the late nineteenth and early twentieth centuries.

The labour movement is discussed in Craig Heron, *The Canadian Labour Movement: A Short History* (Toronto: James Lorimer, 1989); Bryan Palmer, *Working-Class Experience: Rethinking the History of Canadian Labour, 1800–1991* (Toronto: McClelland & Stewart, 1992); and Desmond Morton with Terry Copp, *Working People: An Illustrated History of the Canadian Labour Movement* (Toronto: Summerhill Press, 1990). Also useful is Laurel Sefton MacDowell and Ian Radforth, eds., *Canadian Working Class History: Selected Readings* (Toronto: Canadian Scholars' Press, 1992); and G. Kealey and P. Warrian, eds., *Essays in Canadian Working-Class History* (Toronto: McClelland & Stewart, 1976). On the Provincial Workmen's Association see Ian McKay, "'By Wisdom, Wile or War': The Provincial Workmen's Association and the Struggle for Working-Class Independence in Nova Scotia, 1879–97," *Labour/Le Travail* 18 (Fall 1986): 13–62. David Franks has written a short popular summary of coal mining on Cape Breton Island, "Coal Wars," *Horizon Canada* 44 (1986): 1046–51. Women and unions are discussed in Julie White, *Sisters and Solidarity: Women and Unions in Canada* (Toronto: Thompson Educational, 1993). D. Owen Carrigan, *Crime and Punishment in Canada: A History* (Toronto: McClelland & Stewart, 1991) deals with this important subject.

CHAPTER EIGHT

An Era of Social Reform: 1890–1914

Various social-reform movements arose at the turn of the century. They worked to correct injustices brought about by massive industrialization and rapid urbanization. Each movement offered its own solution. In English-speaking Canada, social gospellers looked to a new religion of social reform; in Quebec, would-be reformers turned to the Roman Catholic church and the family, pillars of French-Canadian society, to initiate social change. Educational reformers proposed a new curriculum, one that would prepare children for the workplace while also providing moral training. Conservationists campaigned to save wildlife and the wilderness. Urban reformers devised the perfect city, with a pleasing architecture and proper social services. Women reformers fought for political equality through female suffrage; they also organized the prohibition movement, to eliminate "demon drink," which they believed was the root of all social ills. Together, these reformers transformed Canadian society on the eve of World War I.

THE SOCIAL GOSPEL MOVEMENT IN ENGLISH CANADA

The social gospel movement was part of a larger movement of religious revival in Britain and the United States that aimed at directly applying Christianity to the collective ills of society to create a perfect "Kingdom of God on Earth." It developed partially in response to a crisis in religious beliefs brought about as a result of the Darwinian concept of evolution. In *The Origin of Species* (1859) and *The Descent of Man* (1871), Charles Darwin, an English naturalist, advanced his theory that humans had evolved, over millions of years, from animals. Darwin's arguments challenged the orthodox Christian belief that God created humans in his own likeness and as special beings during the six days of creation. From their reading of the Book of Genesis, some Christians even provided a precise date for the creation, 4004 B.C.

At the same time that science challenged contemporary Christian theology, a new philosophy of "higher criticism" presented the Bible as literature — a document written by humans, and therefore not the divine and absolute word of God. The Bible thus contained moral and religious truths but not historical and scientific truths. These new ideas undermined many traditional Christian theological teachings and led to new definitions of faith. In response, a number of church leaders directed their attention away from theological questions to social issues. Raw, harsh, industrialized Canada had a host of social problems that needed reforming.

Social gospellers regarded people as inherently good. If individuals erred, they did so not because of any basic weakness or maliciousness of character, but because of their environment. Social gospellers believed in environmental determinism and hoped, therefore, to improve social conditions so as to alter people's character for the good and to create, eventually, an ideal Christian society.

Social gospellers wanted the church to concern itself with social problems, including prostitution, alcoholism, intolerable living and working conditions, and the plight of immigrants, rather than with such "personal sins" as drunkenness, sex, and slovenliness. The Reverend S.D. Chown of the Methodist church summed up the new attitude in a lecture in 1905: "The first duty of a Christian is to be a citizen, or a man amongst men. We are under no obligation to get into heaven, that is a matter entirely of our own option; but we are under obligation to quit sin and to bring heaven down to this earth." Social gospellers strove to create in this world a humane society based on the Christian principles of love, charity, humanity, brotherhood, and democracy.

British and American developments influenced the Canadian social reformers. In Britain, for example, the Fabian Society, a group of social thinkers, labour leaders, and university professors committed to improving society, helped to create the British Labour party. In the United States the Progressives, a middle-class reform movement, exposed social ills in American urban and industrial society. Social gospellers often combined British and American models to design their own reform program.

United in their aspiration to improve the quality of life, social gospellers were often divided on the means to do so. There were as many ways to regenerate and reform society as there were regenerators and reformers.

What one might call the "direct action group" of regenerators worked to give immediate assistance to society's destitute through the establishment of missions and settlement houses. In 1890, the Reverend D.J. Macdonnell, a liberal Presbyterian minister, founded St. Andrews Institute in Toronto to bring his church closer to the working people. Four years later, with financial assistance from the wealthy Massey family of Toronto, a group of Methodists founded the Fred Victor Mission in Toronto, named in memory of Fred Victor Massey (1867–90).

Sara Libby Carson started the first settlement house in 1902 and helped found the Toronto and McGill University settlements. Similar settlement houses in Britain and, especially, Jane Addams's Hull House in Chicago, which offered classes in music and art and provided a gymnasium and day nursery, inspired McGill's and the University of Toronto's programs. By 1920, at least thirteen settlement houses existed in Canada, offering the basic necessities of food and shelter and, often, a night school and a library. Many provided medical care. Others included gymnasiums, clubrooms, savings banks, and nurseries.

The Army of Salvation, better known as the Salvation Army, started by William Booth in England, also established centres in Canada at the turn of the century to help the poor. They modelled themselves after the regular army. Their members wore military-style uniforms and insignia. The ministers were called "officers," and the converts were "soldiers." At their peak, their "field force" enlisted nearly 150 000 in Canada to fight sin and poverty. Among their "field force" were a number of women

A Salvation Army meeting in Calgary, late August 1887. Meetings featured testimony, prayer, music, and song. The Salvation Army, begun by General William Booth in England, came to Canada in 1882.

National Archives of Canada/C-14426.

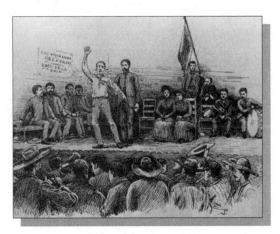

— "Hallelujah lasses" — who preached on street corners and worked in shelters and homes to alleviate the misery of their "sisters."

Some reformers, labelled social purists, concerned themselves with issues of morality (which invariably meant sex), especially prostitution (often referred to as "the white slave trade") along with homosexuality, venereal disease, "feeblemindedness" (masturbation), and abortion. Their aim was to regulate and legislate sexual relations as a means to ensure racial purity and social control. English-Canadian social purists feared that with the influx of large numbers of "foreigners," non-regulated sex would dilute the dominant and superior Anglo-Celtic race. The Reverend S.D. Chown linked the two when he commented, "The immigration question is the most vital one in Canada today, as it has to do with the purity of our national life-blood."

Social control took many forms. Churches hired "morality experts" to address, or had ministers preach on, moral concerns such as extramarital sex, masturbation, homosexuality, prostitution, and abortion. The Reverend W.J. Hunter reportedly lectured to as many as 1500 men a night at St. James Methodist Church in Montreal on such topics. The Reverend C. Sharp told his Toronto congregation in 1908: "God abhors the spirit as prevalent nowadays which condemns motherhood," in reference to the feminist and women's suffrage movement. "How it must grieve Him when He sees what we call race suicide; when He sees the problems of married life approached lightly and wantonly, based on nothing higher and nobler than mere luxury, and gratification of passion." The Methodist and Presbyterian churches established social reform agencies under the umbrella of the Moral and Social Reform Council of Canada, established in 1907, which later changed its name to the Social Service Council of Canada. The Methodist church also recommended and distributed sex manuals, especially the popular eight-volume "Self and Sex" series. The Women's Christian Temperance Union (WCTU) hired purity reformers such as William Lund Clark, Arthur Beall, and Beatrice Brigden to tour schools to warn young people against self-abuse and promiscuity. Clark recommended that "they drink neither tea nor coffee and refrain from dancing and that they seek improved ventilation and take frequent baths." The WCTU also built homes for "fallen women."

Increasingly, however, regulation of sex moved from the church, the family, and the local community to the state. Cities hired social workers, experts on prisons, and psychiatrists to present the latest "scientific" theories, to educate the public on proper moral standards, and to work with the "sexual deviants" in the jails and mental institutions. Some social theorists, known as eugenicists, argued for selective breeding by preventing people deemed to have undesirable mental and physical traits from reproducing. All too often the "unfit" and "inferior" were also foreigners, thus adding an ethnic component to the eugenics movement. Some cities, such as Toronto, under its reform mayor William Howland, established morality departments to arrest and prosecute anyone involved in prostitution or in same-sex relationships. The department targeted in particular single young women — "working girls" — who frequented amusement parks and dancehalls, where they became easy prey for lusty young men, or pimps.

The courts assisted the state in regulating morality. In 1892, the Criminal Code was formulated to include a comprehensive system of offences to "protect" young girls and women by imposing stiff penalties of up to 14 years on brothel operators and those who enticed women into prostitution. It also legislated against "gross indecency," which referred to homosexual acts. Punishment was set at a minimum of 5 years, with provisions for whipping. In Toronto, both children's and women's courts were established to deal with issues of promiscuity and "vagrancy." The aim of the courts, like that of the morality squad and the sexual purists, was to regulate sex for the "good of society" and for the "purity of the race." Children's courts actually worked to the detriment of children, since accused children lost many of the rights of due process and faced more indiscriminate sentencing than accused in adult courts. They were also often sentenced to penal institutions, like Toronto's Mercer Reformatory, where they were lectured on morality while receiving agricultural, manual, or domestic training.

A second group of social gospellers worked to change people's attitudes. They believed that attitudes of greed, competition, and materialism caused society's problems. Through education, however, people could learn of the greater benefits of living in a society governed by Christian principles of love, charity, brotherhood, and democracy. In 1918, William Lyon Mackenzie King, then a young Canadian labour conciliator but in one year to become the leader of the federal Liberal party, published *Industry and Humanity*. He sought to impel Canadians to moral regeneration through Christian principles. Social salvation, he argued, would come to a society that practised the ethical laws of Christianity.

The third group believed in state intervention. They argued that the concept of laissez-faire — the belief that governments should not upset the natural laws of the marketplace — had been used by the wealthy in society to exploit the poor. They advocated, instead, state intervention. An activist government operating on Christian principles of co-operation, democracy, and brotherhood would ensure that all people — not just an elite — benefited from the well-being of society. Government involvement was needed to provide essential social services and welfare assistance for the unemployed and the disabled, and to regulate industry and nationalize key industries to ensure that they served the public good.

For a few social gospellers, such as J.S. Woodsworth — then a Methodist minister, later the founder of the Co-operative Commonwealth Federation (CCF) — these innovative reforms served only as a prelude to a more fundamental restructuring of society. Woodsworth believed that the "Ideal Kingdom of Jesus" was a socialist paradise where everyone worked for the well-being of the whole rather than for its individual parts. True social reform meant replacing the profit motive of capitalism with Christian charity.

WEB

LINKS

IMPACT OF THE SOCIAL GOSPEL MOVEMENT

The social gospel movement raised public awareness of urban and industrial injustices. Social gospellers also, in their outlook, affected, and often directed, other social-reform movements, such as prohibition, women's suffrage, urban reform, and labour movements. The social gospel gave reformers a religious zeal, a sense of purpose that they were working for God's kingdom here on earth. Their efforts contributed to the passing of Ontario's Workmen's Compensation Act in 1914, which established financial benefits for individuals injured in the workplace. Later expanded, the legislation served as a model for similar measures in Nova Scotia (1915), British Columbia (1916), Alberta (1918), and New Brunswick (1918). Social reformers also played a role in the passage in 1916 of the Manitoba Pensions Act, which provided a basic allowance to widowed, divorced, or deserted wives with children. Ultimately, the social gospel movement contributed to the rise of the CCF in the 1930s. Social gospellers prepared the way for the establishment of our modern social-welfare system.

Religious and social historians have debated whether the social gospel movement gave religion a new beginning, or hastened its decline. Religion, according to these theorists, has always re-evaluated and renewed itself in changing times. The social gospel movement was one of those eras of renewal. Another group, the secularists, argue instead that social gospellers, in attempting to make religion more relevant to everyday concerns and thus to move it away from abstract, theological issues, ironically denied religion its distinctive spiritual function. As a result, religious leaders became indistinguishable from social scientists. In essence, the clergy became lay sociologists; the sacred became secular.

ROMAN CATHOLIC SOCIAL ACTION IN QUEBEC

The origins of social reform in Quebec lay in the Roman Catholic church's emphasis on personal humanity and on its principles of social justice and Christian charity. In his encyclical *Rerum Novarum* (1891), Pope Leo XIII urged that "some opportune remedy be found quickly for the misery and wretchedness pressing so unjustly on the majority of the working class." Catholic social reformers in Quebec believed that religion constituted the "remedy." They felt that the family and the church, rather than the state, could best deal with social problems. The ideal Christian social order, church leaders argued, rested on the family and the French-Canadian nation. Thus in Quebec, Roman Catholic values and French-Canadian nationalism became intertwined with social reform.

ROLE OF THE CHURCH IN SOCIAL REFORM IN QUEBEC

The Roman Catholic church initiated and supported various social-reform movements in Quebec. In 1911, for example, the Jesuits founded the Montreal-based École Sociale Populaire (ESP) to develop a social doctrine for the church. The ESP published pamphlets, organized study groups and retreats, and worked to sensitize the clergy to the social needs of their parishioners. In 1902, priests at Université Laval established the Société du parler français to increase French Canadians' awareness of French vocabulary in a largely English-language-oriented urban and industrial society and to eliminate anglicisms in business and industry.

In the classical colleges, religious instructors created the Association catholique de la jeunesse canadienne-française (ACJC) in 1904. It sought to encourage among Quebec's youth a unique French-Canadian and Catholic response to the province's social problems. The popular young Abbé Lionel Groulx of Valleyfield became the chief leader of the ACJC. In 1907, the Quebec diocese started a newspaper in Quebec City, *L'Action sociale*, later renamed *L'Action catholique*, that addressed social problems. It campaigned for the prohibition of alcohol or at least strict government control of the manufacturing and sale of alcoholic beverages. It also called for film censorship to protect Catholics from possible "corruption."

Many priests supported the *caisses populaires*, the credit unions founded in 1900 by Alphonse Desjardins, the French-language recorder for *Hansard* in the House of Commons, as their way of improving Quebec society. Desjardins believed that lack of capital was the reason for French Canadians' handicap in business. He established his savings and lending co-operatives to assist French-Canadian enterprises to get started in the hopes of improving the living standards of the working class and of bringing economic liberation to the Quebec people.

By 1907, the *caisses* had assets of more than $48 000, certainly not enough to pose a serious threat to the established banks and credit institutions in Quebec, but sufficient to establish new co-operative ventures. By the time of Desjardins's death in 1920, more than 200 *caisses populaires* existed, mainly in Quebec but also among French-speaking Canadians in Ontario, Manitoba, and Saskatchewan, as well as among Franco-Americans in New England.

French-Canadian priests also promoted Catholic unions for Quebec workers (see Chapter Seven). Church leaders feared that workers in secular unions, especially American-controlled ones, would become too materialistic and too socialistic in their outlook. The church rejected the idea of organizing workers along class lines, favouring instead Roman Catholic unions based on a spirit of Christian charity and employer–employee co-operation.

The church also lent its moral support to the Ligue nationaliste, a middle-class group of reformers founded in 1903. Besides concerning themselves with Canada's position in the British empire and Quebec's status within Canada, they formulated a French-Canadian and largely Catholic response to problems arising out of Quebec's urbanization and industrialization on the assumption that French Canadians needed to retain their identity in an increasingly secularized society. They believed in the family as the fundamental social unit of society and in Christian values as the bulwark of society. Thus they viewed individual or family businesses as compatible with Roman Catholic teachings, while opposing large-scale capitalism, which, they felt, was guided by mercenary concerns. The state, they argued, should curtail the excessive monopolization of big business by preventing private control of utilities. Ultimately, they favoured a society based on Christian values of co-operation and a concern for the public good.

EDUCATIONAL REFORMERS

Perceptions of education, like religion, changed during the reform era. Earlier, educators had concerned themselves with preparing children for the workplace as quickly as possible by teaching good work habits. They viewed children as miniature adults, to be placed into adult society as quickly as possible. By the turn of the century, however, a new generation of educators, strongly influenced by Friedrich Froebel, a European philosopher, advocated a child-oriented education that treated children as children, not miniature adults, by providing them with love and by protecting them from the harsh realities of adult life.

To some educational reformers, kindergartens provided the answer. James L. Hughes, a Toronto school inspector, and his future wife, Ada Marean, established the first Canadian public-school kindergarten in 1883 to provide, in Froebel's words, "reverent love for the child, profound respect for his individuality ... and freedom and self-activity as the condition of most perfect growth physically, intellectually, and spiritually." Four years later, in 1887, Ontario formally incorporated kindergartens into the public-school system. The Free Kindergarten Association in Winnipeg advocated the same for Manitoba, arguing that "the proper education of children during the first seven years of their lives" did "much to reduce poverty and crime in any community."

In Montreal and Quebec City, nuns ran *salles d'asile* or day-care centres for children of working parents. Between 1898 and 1902, more than 10 000 children attended. In addition to these centres, which offered care on a daily basis, orphanages, provincial asylums, and homes for the poor also provided care for children of destitute families.

Other educational reformers worked for different objectives. Some called for temperance education to warn children of the evils of alcohol, while others asked for social programs in public health and in physical and mental hygiene. Reformers also advocated practical or "manual training" in farming and industrial work to prepare children for future jobs. They were successful in getting a number of provinces to introduce technical courses in domestic science, gardening, and shop or industrial arts.

All educational reformers appreciated the importance of extended and free schooling. They succeeded by 1905 in getting all provinces except Quebec to legislate free schooling and compulsory attendance for youngsters up to the age of 12. School attendance, especially in elementary school and increasingly in secondary schools too, soared, doubling from 1891 to 1921.

Two exceptional educational reformers were John Kelso and Alfred Fitzpatrick. Kelso, a young police reporter for the Toronto *World*, was concerned about the street urchins who could not be reached through the regular educational system. He quit his job to begin the Humane Society. When its members seemed only marginally interested in the plight of children, he began yet another organization, the Children's Aid Society. In 1899, Alfred Fitzpatrick, a Presbyterian minister from Nova Scotia, created the Reading Camp Association, later called Frontier College, to bring education to immigrant workers in the lumber shanties and railway bunkhouses across northern Canada. Fitzgerald recruited university-student volunteers to give night classes in the "three Rs" and in basic civics. One of the young men whose social conscience was aroused by his work in the camps was Norman Bethune, later renowned for his medical work in Spain and China in the 1930s.

WEB LINKS

THE URBAN REFORM MOVEMENT

Urban reformers formed an important part of the social-reform movement. Inspired by the "City Beautiful" movement in the United States and Europe, they believed that reform must include the urban environment — the physical structure of the city, its

The Children's Aid Society, founded by John Kelso, opened its first shelter in Toronto in 1892. This photo of the shelter was taken in the mid-1890s.

....

City of Toronto Archives/SCI-3.

aesthetic nature, and the quality of its municipal government. According to historian Paul Rutherford, what united urban reformers was "less a single creed and more a common approach to a wide variety of urban problems."[1] They worked to transform the existing urban environment into a humane and beautiful one.

The earliest urban reformers included newspaper editors who concentrated on the sordid side of urban life. Through their popular, sensational, and inexpensive newspapers (the penny press), among them Montreal's *Daily Star* and *La Presse* and Toronto's *Telegram* and *World*, the editors appealed to their readers' emotions both to sell newspapers and to raise public concern over child abuse, slums, prostitution, and political corruption. Seldom, however, did they have concrete solutions to offer.

Reform-minded businesspeople and concerned citizens also helped raise public consciousness. Herbert Ames financed a sociological study of a working-class ward in Montreal, entitled *The City Below the Hill* (1897). G.A. Nantel wrote *La métropole de demain*, a grandiose scheme for the better governance of Montreal. Samuel Wickett spoke and wrote in Toronto regularly on the importance of efficient and expert municipal governments as the first step to urban reform. In Winnipeg, J.S. Woodsworth wrote the highly acclaimed *My Neighbour* (1911), about the problems of living in the modern city.

A host of professionals — engineers, architects, surveyors, medical people, and urban planners — offered advice on how to create the perfect city, each group naturally emphasizing the importance of its particular discipline. Architects, for example, emphasized the need for stately buildings, while urban planners stressed parks, treed

Norman Bethune (third from the left), a labourer–teacher with Frontier College, near Whitefish on the north shore of Georgian Bay, 1911. Bethune would become famous for his medical assistance during the 1930s, first to Spanish civilians during the Spanish Civil War and then to communist Chinese fighting against Japanese invaders.

Frontier College Collection/National Archives of Canada/C-56826.

boulevards, and adequate housing. Medical professionals gave precedence to clean water, air, and pasteurized milk.

These urban reformers had limited success in the pre–World War I era because vested interests strongly opposed their proposals. Developers, for example, saw little profit in expensive urban renewal. Nor were badly funded municipal governments prepared to act, for the reforms suggested often came at a high price, in terms of increased taxes.

WILDERNESS AND WILDLIFE CONSERVATION

The idea of conservation emerged only slowly in Canada. The popular Canadian naturalist Farley Mowat recalls in his book *Sea of Slaughter* a story about his grandfather, Gil Mowat. "One autumn weekend in 1884, he and three companions left on a weekend duck hunting trip. They left armed with double-barrelled 10-gauge shotguns. They returned with 140 canvasbacks, 227 redheads, about 20 scaups, 84 blacks, about five dozen teal, and enough additional assorted kinds to quite literally fill the four-wheeled farm wagon that brought them and their trophies home."[2] Out of pride, the men took photographs of their kill. No one questioned their excessive waste.

In 1885, the federal government reserved to the Crown more than 26 km^2 of land around the mineral springs near the railway station of Banff. It would protect the hot springs and the scenery from private exploitation. Ottawa had taken the first step in the creation of Canada's national parks. Two years later, it extended the area to 675 km^2. It then officially turned the reserve into a national park, Rocky Mountains Park (renamed Banff in 1930).

WEB

LINKS

Banff began as a recreation park rather than a conservation area, although the latter would soon become its chief function. In 1887, the first bird sanctuary in North America opened at Last Mountain Lake, in present-day Saskatchewan. In 1893, the Ontario government established Algonquin Park, south of North Bay, as the province's first wilderness area. Other provinces followed Ontario's example in establishing their own provincial parks.

By the early twentieth century, the overexploitation of the country's wildlife was becoming obvious. Major improvements in firearm technology, combined with the rapidly increasing commercial value of certain types of wildlife, led to the extinction of certain species. The Plains bison herds disappeared on the Canadian side of the border as early as 1879. By 1900, the great prairie herds of pronghorn antelope declined to a tiny fraction of their original number. Hunted thoroughly, the passenger pigeon had vanished from Nova Scotia by 1857, from Manitoba by 1898, and from Ontario by 1902. By 1900, trumpeter swans had disappeared from eastern Canada, as had wild turkeys before them.

Slowly, a conservation mentality developed. It was cultivated by back-to-nature movements, such as the Alpine Club, Field-Naturalists' Clubs, Woodcraft Clubs, and the Boy Scout and Girl Guides movements, that were premised on the importance of a wilderness experience for good health, spiritual rejuvenation, and refuge from hectic city life. Schools in British Columbia, Nova Scotia, Ontario, and Alberta initiated nature study classes in the first decade of the twentieth century through the initiative of naturalists' societies, farm organizations, and experimental farms. The upper-middle and upper classes purchased cottages in the Georgian Bay and Muskoka areas of Ontario, the Lake of the Woods region near the Manitoba–Ontario border, the Lower Lakes and Murray Bay in Quebec, and the Bras d'Or Lakes on Nova Scotia's Cape Breton Island.

The federal government responded slowly and reluctantly to the need for conservation. It did, however, establish the Commission on Conservation (1909–21), which helped to secure the passage in 1916 of the Canada–United States Migratory Birds Convention Treaty, an agreement that ensured international protection for migratory bird populations throughout their ranges. The commission hired James Harkin as national parks branch commissioner in 1911 to oversee Canada's existing national parks and establish new ones. In 1919, the Canadian government convened the first national wildlife conference to discuss with the provinces how best to conserve the country's wildlife.

Later, in the 1930s, the popularity of Grey Owl (born Archie Belaney) assisted the conservation movement. Through his books, films, and lectures, he advocated the protection of Canada's wilderness and wildlife. When the young Belaney first arrived at Lake Temagami in northeastern Ontario from England in 1907, he met the Ojibwa, whose identity he assumed. He came to learn about their view of the universe and its inhabitants, and discovered that one of the fundamental differences between his inherent beliefs and those of his assumed people was their notion of what was "human." To the Native peoples, all animals, fowls, fish, trees, and stones were endowed with immortal spirits and possessed supernatural powers. Humans were a part of this animated world, not its master. Much of what he later wrote as Grey Owl in the 1930s attacked the well-worn and much-abused biblical notion that humans should "have dominion over" all creatures.

WOMEN AND SOCIAL REFORM

By the 1890s a "new woman" had appeared, demanding an active role in society. Local, provincial, and national women's organizations such as the Woman's Christian Temperance Union, the National Council of Women, the Young Women's Christian

A Historical Portrait

GREY OWL

Archie Belaney was born in Hastings, Sussex, England, on September 18, 1888. Abandoned by his parents, he was raised by his two maiden aunts, the Misses Belaney. From early boyhood he was fascinated by Amerindians and dreamt of living among them. His aunts, however, wanted him to take up a profession after leaving grammar school. But finally they gave their consent. Archie left for Canada in 1906. Apart from two years abroad with the Canadian army in World War I, he spent the remainder of his life as a trapper, guide, and later conservationist, in northern Canada.

In 1910, he married Angele Egwuna, an Ojibwa woman from Lake Temagami, Ontario. She taught him how to canoe, trap, and to speak some Ojibwa. But the marriage did not last. Knowing nothing of a stable family relationship, he followed in his father's footsteps and abandoned his wife and their young daughter in 1912. Several other relationships followed over the next quarter of a century, the most important being with Gertrude Bernard, whom he called Anahareo, a beautiful young Iroquois woman whom he married in a traditional Native ceremony in northern Quebec. She convinced him in the late 1920s to abandon trapping and to work and write for the conservation of Canada's wildlife and forests.

In his articles and books, Belaney wrote as Grey Owl. The *Canadian Who's Who* of 1936–37 summarized his romantic stories about his origins: "Born encampment, State of Sonora, Mexico; son of George, a native of Scotland, and Kathrine (Cochise) Belaney; a half-breed Apache Indian ... adopted as blood brother by Ojibway tribe,

(continued)

Grey Owl and a beaver, June 1931.

....

Glenbow Archives, Calgary, Canada/
NA-4868-213.

1920 . . . speaks Ojibway but has forgotten Apache." Impressed by his first articles, the Canadian government invited Grey Owl to join the Canadian Parks Branch as a "caretaker of park animals." His first book, *Men of the Last Frontier*, a collection of his published stories and others, appeared in 1931. Three years later came *Pilgrims of the Wild*, a moving account of his life with Anahareo and their struggle to preserve wildlife and the wilderness. Two other books followed, the children's book *The Adventures of Sajo and Her Beaver People* (1935) and *Tales of an Empty Cabin* (1936).

His books became bestsellers. Films were made with him at Prince Albert National Park in Saskatchewan. The public loved the fact that the beaver built their lodge outside — and partially inside — his cabin. He made two lecture tours of Britain, each of several months' duration. During his last visit, in December 1937, the tall, hawk-faced man dressed in buckskin performed at Buckingham Palace for the royal family. No one discovered his true identity, not even in Hastings, which he visited twice. His aunts knew, but they, intensely proud of him, kept his secret.

Physically the tours were demanding, and the constant threat of exposure was very great. Shortly after Grey Owl's return to Beaver Lodge in early April 1938, totally exhausted and run-down, he was rushed to hospital in Prince Albert, where he died on April 13. Swift detective work in Canada and England in the weeks after his death revealed his true identity. His contributions as a writer and spokesperson for conservation received new recognition in the 1970s, when the preservation of the natural environment became a popular concern.

Association (YWCA), and the Dominion Women's Enfranchisement Association assisted women in reaching out to society. By 1912 an estimated one out of every eight adult women — the majority of them middle-aged, middle-class, English-speaking Protestants — belonged to a women's group, thus making these organizations influential agents of social change.

The bicycle aided the liberation of the new woman. This popular vehicle enabled women to abandon restricting, ankle-length, tight skirts in favour of comfortable, loose-fitting clothes such as bloomers, which were loose trousers gathered at the knees. The clergy voiced their concerns about the impact of the bicycle on morals, since women could now go out without chaperones.

Most women accepted the prevailing "scientific" stereotyping of them as womanly and motherly, and consequently accepted as well the belief that their primary task was to guard the home. A battery of books on proper mothering reinforced this belief. But a few women came to believe that their maternal instincts should be used to reform society. "Rocking the cradle for the world" was how Nellie McClung, an influential reformer, saw women's new role. These reform-minded women argued that men had controlled society for ages without making any appreciable improvements; now it was their turn. As McClung explained it:

> Women must be made to feel their responsibilities. All this protective love, their
> instinctive mother love, must be organized in some way, and made effective.
> There is enough of it in the world to do away with all the evils which war upon
> childhood: undernourishment, slum conditions, child labour, drunkenness.
> Women could abolish all these if they wanted to.

Two women cyclists, Flo and Jessie McLennan, Owen Sound, Ontario. Bicycles liberated women from restrictive clothing — and from chaperones.

Glenbow Archives, Calgary, Canada/ NA-2685-61.

THE WOMEN'S SUFFRAGE MOVEMENT

Women reformers saw the vote as the means by which women could obtain the power to reform society. The women's suffrage movement began in Ontario with leaders such as Dr. Emily (Jennings) Stowe. If Ontario led the way in launching a suffrage movement, the Maritimes were the first to admit a woman to a university. In 1875, Mount Allison University in Sackville, New Brunswick, conferred a bachelor's degree in science and literature to Grace Annie Lockhart. She, in fact, became the first woman in the British empire to receive a university degree.

The University of Toronto followed suit, first opening its doors to women in 1884. Many male professors opposed the decision. Daniel Wilson, a professor of history and English literature, considered that a mixed class posed serious problems in the teaching of Shakespeare — because of the sexual allusions in several of the playwright's works. His objection was overruled.

Adelaide (Hunter) Hoodless helped to further the women's cause in another way. Born in 1858, the twelfth child in the family, she apparently received little education beyond elementary school. She married John Hoodless, a wealthy furniture manufacturer. Their fourth child, a son, died in 1889, at the age of 18 months, from the unpasteurized milk that farmers delivered in open cans, which exposed it to bacterial contamination. Seeing an urgent need to teach women nutrition and proper health measures, she offered domestic science or home-economics classes through the

YWCA. Later the dedicated reformer assisted in having the subject introduced in the schools and, eventually, at the Ontario Agricultural College in Guelph and at McGill University. In 1897, she started the first Women's Institute near Stoney Creek, south of Hamilton, Ontario — an equivalent, for women, of the Farmers' Institutes. The new organization helped women to increase their knowledge of farm and household management.

Thanks to Hoodless's unflagging efforts, the University of Toronto eventually created the School of Household Economics. Hoodless also helped found the Victorian Order of Nurses to offer nursing and housekeeping services to impoverished invalids. Although she worked to improve women's role in society, Adelaide Hoodless parted company with the suffragists on the "vote question." She believed that a woman's primary role was to be a wife and mother and that the vote would not aid them in this task. In fact, she feared that the right to vote might lead to the breakdown of home and family.

Women reform leaders in the Prairie provinces generally favoured the stand on the vote taken by the suffragists and were willing to fight for the cause. In the newer settler society of the West, women had found a greater degree of equality. In establishing a homestead and building a farm, women worked alongside their husbands. Early on, they won the support of western farm organizations that also struggled for national recognition and were, therefore, better able to empathize with women's efforts for equality. The *Grain Growers' Guide*, founded in 1908, added a women's column to its paper in 1911, while the Grain Growers' Association of Manitoba, Saskatchewan, and Alberta endorsed women's suffrage as early as 1912.

The presence of a large immigrant population on the Prairies helped the suffrage cause in a somewhat perverse way. Women suffragists protested against giving recent male immigrants the vote while denying it to long-standing Canadian female citizens. As one suffragist bluntly put it: "What an outrage to deny to the highest-minded, most cultured native-born lady of Canada what is cheerfully granted to the lowest-browed most imbruted foreign hobo that chooses to visit our shores."

The West had several outspoken women actively involved in the struggle for female suffrage, such as Emily Murphy, Louise McKinney, Nellie McClung, Irene Parlby, and Henrietta Edwards. Perhaps Nellie McClung, with her gift for oratory, her energy, and her delightful sense of humour, best epitomized the suffrage movement. Her spirited leadership rallied many others to the cause of women's suffrage.

Nellie (Mooney) McClung was born in Ontario in 1873 but educated in Manitoba, where her family began homesteading in 1880. After attending Winnipeg Normal School and teaching for several years, she married Wes McClung, a pharmacist, in 1896. Her fiancé promised her before marriage that he would not stand in the way of her writing career, a promise he kept. Between 1897 and 1911, she had four sons and a daughter, but still found time to write — first poems, sketches, and editorials for Sunday school publications, and later adult stories in leading North American magazines. Early on, her interest in reform led her to write her best-selling novel, *Sowing Seeds in Danny*. In 1912, she joined the Winnipeg Political Equality League, whose president was Lillian Beynon Thomas, another reformer. Nellie wrote her witty but powerful social commentary on suffrage, *In Times Like These*, for the 1916 election in Manitoba, in which suffrage was the major issue. The suffragists made their first breakthrough in that election when the Liberals came to power. The new government introduced a suffrage bill, making Manitoba the first province in Canada to grant women the vote.

Presentation by the Winnipeg Political Equality League for the Enfranchisement of Women of a petition, December 23, 1915. Mrs. Amelia Burritt, then 93 years old, gave the document to the provincial government. In 1916, Manitoba became Canada's first province to grant women the franchise.

Provincial Archives of Manitoba/Events 173/3 (N9905).

WOMEN REFORMERS IN QUEBEC

Women involved in social reform in Quebec had a more difficult battle than their sisters in English-speaking Canada, since French-Canadian tradition cast women almost exclusively in the role of mothers and domestic guardians. Archbishop Bruchési of Montreal defined *féminisme* as "the zealous pursuit by woman of all the noble causes in the sphere that Providence has assigned to her." He added: "There will be no talk in your meetings of the emancipation of woman, of the neglect of her rights, of her having been relegated to the shadows, of the responsibilities, public offices and professions to which she should be admitted on an equal basis with man."

Despite such stern warnings, several French-Canadian women spoke out for the feminist cause. In 1907, Marie Lacoste Gérin-Lajoie, Caroline Béique, and Josephine Dandurand founded the Fédération nationale Saint-Jean-Baptiste, the first French-speaking organization to consolidate women's activities in charitable associations, in education, and in the work force. Marie Lacoste Gérin-Lajoie directed the federation's activities for the first 20 years. The federation offered a forum for women to fight for a variety of causes, including the pasteurizing of milk to reduce infant mortality, better working conditions for women, and the elimination of alcoholism and "white slavery" or forced prostitution. It also contributed to better women teachers' pensions, improved working conditions for women in factories and stores, more home-economics courses, and the establishment of pure milk depots.

The federation, along with the sisters of the Congrégation Notre-Dame, petitioned Mgr. Bruchési to obtain approval for a classical college for women. The bishop agreed only when the newspaper *La Patrie* announced the opening of a French *lycée*, a lay-administered classical college for women. In 1908, Bruchési granted his permission to the Congrégation Notre-Dame to open the École d'enseignement supérieur pour les filles. But the École had to wait until 1926 before gaining the right to call itself a *collège*; it then became the Collège Marguerite-Bourgeoys. In 1910, Marie Gérin-Lajoie, the daughter of Marie Lacoste Gérin-Lajoie, became the École's first graduate. She had the further distinction of coming first in the provincial university-entrance examinations for the province, much to the consternation of the all-male examiners. However, since women could not attend university, they awarded first prize to the male student who placed second.

Marie Lacoste Gérin-Lajoie led the fight for women's suffrage in Quebec. She obtained her legal education by studying from her father's law books and under his supervision. Shocked to learn that the legal status of a woman was that of an adjunct of her husband, with no personal financial or civil independence, she initially considered refusing her future husband's marriage proposal. Only after her suitor pledged his support for the equality of the sexes did she accept. She spent her early married life writing a legal handbook for women while raising her children.

Then, with an English-speaking colleague, she created the Provincial Franchise Committee in 1921 to put pressure on Quebec politicians to grant women the franchise. The committee had no success, and ironically the strongest opposition often came from other women who saw women's suffrage as a threat to their identity as wives and mothers. The fatal blow came when in 1922 the Archbishop of Montreal expressed his disapproval of women voters. In protest, Marie Lacoste Gérin-Lajoie resigned her post as head of the francophone section of the Provincial Franchise Committee, although she continued to promote women's rights.

THE PROHIBITION MOVEMENT

Throughout Canada, many women reformers worked for prohibition. "Demon drink," they argued, wrecked home life and led to inefficiency at work. Prohibitionists argued that the only way to eradicate drinking was to prohibit it through government legislation. They reminded governments that they had a right and an obligation to pass laws for the good of society.

The division of jurisdiction over alcohol between the federal and provincial governments complicated the question. The federal government had the power to restrict the manufacture of, and interprovincial trade in, alcoholic beverages. Provincial governments controlled retail sales. Thus, prohibitionists had to apply pressure on both levels of government.

They achieved an initial victory in 1878 with the passage of the Canadian Temperance Act, popularly known as the Scott Act, which allowed the residents of each municipality or county to decide by a simple majority vote whether it would be

Where Historians Disagree

WOMEN AND REFORM

Although it is a relatively new field of historical study, Canadian women's history has already generated considerable debate. One contentious issue has been the primary motive behind the women's reform movement. Strongly influenced by political history, which prevailed at the time, the first historians to write on the subject in the 1960s and early 1970s focussed on the women's suffrage movement. They argued that women reformers sought only the right to vote, in the belief that political equality would bring with it an era of societal reform. This narrow focus on the ballot box seemed to explain adequately why the movement for reform died out so rapidly in the 1920s, once women's suffrage had been achieved.

Some historians view women's reform as part of a greater "progressive reform" movement that went well beyond a concern for the enfranchisement of women. In his introduction (1974) to Catharine L. Cleverdon's classic study, *The Woman Suffrage Movement in Canada* (Toronto: University of Toronto Press, 1974 [1950]), Ramsay Cook linked women's reform to the social gospel movement. "The suffragists were a part of a more general, middle-class reform movement that was concerned to remove a wide range of injustices and evils that afflicted the country. The most obvious features of this broad reform movement were its Protestant ethos ... its revulsion at the materialism of 'Canada's Century' [a reference to the optimism and expansion of the Laurier era (1896–1911)], its predominantly Anglo-Saxon nationalism, and its often naive optimism. Combined, these elements made up that amorphous but potent phenomenon, the Social Gospel" (p. xvii).

Other historians have questioned this idealized image of women reformers as being motivated by religious zeal. Veronica Strong-Boag argues that power, fame, and influence motivated them, at least those associated with the influential National Council of Women of Canada. In *The Parliament of Women: The National Council of Women of Canada, 1893–1929* (Ottawa: Canadian Museum of Civilization, 1976), Strong-Boag notes that "the female relatives of Canada's powerful men, energized by a changing external environment and by their own recent access to higher education and the professions, had few formal ways of expressing their complementary desires for national leadership and influence" (p. 410). In short, these middle-class women reformers worried more about their own position of power in society than about the disadvantaged.

In *Liberation Deferred? The Ideas of the English Canadian Suffragists, 1877–1918* (Toronto: University of Toronto Press, 1983), Carol Bacchi applied the feminist theories of the 1980s to the leaders of the suffrage movement in the 1910s. She concluded that class more than gender defined their perspective. They were middle-class reformers more than they were feminists, and as such were more conservative than radical in outlook. They succeeded in getting the vote for women, according to Bacchi, only because men in positions of power at the time realized that the vote would not upset the status quo.

In a review of Bacchi's book, which was based essentially on a study only of women leaders in Montreal, Toronto, and the Prairies, historian Ernest Forbes, relying on his own work on Halifax women, challenged her conclusions. In Halifax, at least, suffrage leaders who were feminists before reformers, used their position to

(continued)

encourage women to get out of the home, and even provided them with opportunities to do so. In this respect, they were "revolutionary" in aspiration. Furthermore, he argued that although Halifax suffragists came predominantly from the middle class, they addressed working-class issues. Forbes appealed for more "local studies" to help draw a definitive conclusion about suffragists on a national level (Ernest Forbes, "The Ideas of Carol Bacchi and the Suffragists of Halifax," *Atlantis* 10[2] [Spring 1985]: 119–26).

Historian Margot Iris Dudley took up Forbes's challenge and examined the women's suffrage movement in Newfoundland (Margot Iris Dudley, "'The Radius of Her Influence for Good': The Rise and Triumph of the Women's Suffrage Movement in Newfoundland, 1909–1925," in Linda Kealey, ed., *Pursuing Equality: Historical Perspectives on Women in Newfoundland and Labrador* [St. John's: Institute of Social and Economic Research, Memorial University, 1993]). She discovered a group of women who crossed class lines and even religious divisions between Catholics and Protestants, and who allied themselves with the International Alliance of Women, based in London, England. Her study questions the assumptions that the women's suffrage movement in Canada was middle-class and Protestant.

Recently, some women historians have concentrated on the 1920s to see whether the women's reform movement died out after political emancipation as previously believed. In *Beyond the Vote: Canadian Women and Politics* (Toronto: University of Toronto Press, 1989), historians Linda Kealey and Joan Sangster have studied a group of "radical women" in the 1920s to show that, for these women, left-wing politics became the means to achieve real change, something that was not possible in the more conservative reform movement. Kealey and Sangster argue that these women had to adopt male tactics and abandon the "private sphere" in order to succeed in the traditionally male-dominated "public sphere."

Veronica Strong-Boag has re-entered the debate to argue that the real struggle for reform did not take place in politics — in the public sphere — but rather in a highly politicized private sphere. "Theirs was the feminism of the workplace, day-to-day life. It was not for the most part an organized movement as the campaign for enfranchisement had been, but it flowed from a similar awareness of women's oppression and a desire to end it" ("Pulling in Double Harness or Hauling a Double Load: Women, Work and Feminism on the Canadian Prairie," *Journal of Canadian Studies* 21 [Fall 1986]: 34). Strong-Boag's study underlines the need to rethink the categories of political/apolitical, public/private, and male/female. "We must re-examine," she writes, "our understanding of what is political, where it occurs and who is involved" (p. 34). This challenge promises to keep the debate alive.

Recently, both Janice Newton and Linda Kealey have studied the intersection of women and/or socialist movements in the context of social reform. In *The Feminist Challenge to the Canadian Left, 1900–1918* (Montreal/Kingston: McGill-Queen's University Press, 1995), Janice Newton shows how Canadian women reformers within the socialist movement rejected the middle-class obsession of the suffragists to get the vote and instead worked for equality of working-class women through such organizations as the Canadian Socialists League, the Socialist Party of Canada, and the Social Democratic Party. They were, however, advocates of "maternal feminism," believing that the home could be "a primary site for radical socialist transformation to enhance the autonomy of women" (p. 10).

(continued)

Linda Kealey appeals for a broader definition of "public" and "political" in dealing with women reformers to include "the home, the neighbourhood, and the community, as well as … the union, the party, or the workplace" (Linda Kealey, *Enlisting Women for the Cause: Women, Labour, and the Left in Canada, 1890–1920* [Toronto: University of Toronto Press, 1998], p. 10). She argues that some socialist women reformers were concerned with women workers as wage earners or working-class wives and mothers, while others advocated a radical transformation of the industrial capitalist system. In either case, they succeeded in bringing working-class women's issues into the public domain, despite opposition from men and even middle-class female reformers.

"wet" or "dry." To prohibitionists, this measure did not go far enough, since it still left open the possibility of wet constituencies. They demanded that governments outlaw the liquor trade completely. The federal Conservative government delayed acting on this contentious issue until the mid-1890s, when it established the Royal Commission on the Liquor Traffic. During the election campaign of 1896, the Liberals promised a plebiscite on the question of prohibition if they gained office. When they won, the prohibitionists held them to their promise.

The results of Canada's first plebiscite were split. Every province except Quebec voted on the dry side. But voter turnout throughout Canada had been low — only 44 percent. Furthermore, of those who did vote, only a small majority of about 13 000 had favoured prohibition. Laurier used these "indecisive" results to avoid enacting legislation that he feared would divide the nation. The Liberals' refusal to follow through on their promise angered the prohibitionists and gave them even greater resolve to banish alcohol.

The Protestant ministry, particularly the more evangelical Protestant churches, provided many of the leaders of the prohibition movement. For many, the struggle became part of a religious battle. They urged drinkers to sign "the pledge" card, by which they promised, "by the help of God, to abstain from the use of all intoxicating drinks as a beverage."

The Woman's Christian Temperance Union (WCTU), formed in Ontario in 1874, identified alcoholism as the greatest single cause of domestic violence and divorce. Initially, the WCTU campaigned for prohibition by issuing petitions, circulating literature, and giving speeches. But WCTU members soon developed a new strategy. If women had the right to vote, they argued, alcohol abuse would end. As Mrs. Jacob Spence, first superintendent of the Ontario WCTU's Franchise Department, noted, "The liquor sellers are not afraid of our conventions but they are afraid of our ballots." Prohibition and women's suffrage became mutually supportive causes.

The vision of a purified Anglo-Saxon society inspired many prohibitionists. Drunkenness became associated with "foreigners," whom reformers saw as too liberal in their drinking. Controlling alcohol offered a means of regulating them and of ensuring their conformity in an otherwise heterogeneous society. The greatest support for prohibition came, therefore, from the majority of British descent, who believed themselves superior to other groups that succumbed to alcohol.

Despite their efforts, however, even in English-speaking Canada no consensus existed. The prohibitionists remained in the minority before World War I. On the eve of the war, only Prince Edward Island had implemented provincial prohibition, while on the national level the federal government had resisted pressure to restrict the production and interprovincial distribution of "demon rum" and all liquor in general.

Between 1880 and 1914, social-reform movements arose to correct the injustices brought about by large-scale industrialization and rapid urbanization. Each group of reformers had a different solution and its own blueprint for creating the ideal Canadian society. On the eve of World War I, they had accomplished much, but they still fell short of their ultimate goal of social regeneration.

NOTES

1. Paul Rutherford, "Tomorrow's Metropolis: The Urban Reform Movement in Canada, 1880–1920," in G.A. Stelter and A.F.J. Artibise, eds., *The Canadian City: Essays in Urban History* (Toronto: McClelland & Stewart, 1977), p. 370.
2. Farley Mowat, *Sea of Slaughter* (Toronto: McClelland & Stewart, 1984), p. 69.

LINKING TO THE PAST

J.S. Woodsworth
http://timelinks.merlin.mb.ca/referenc/db0031.htm
A brief biography of J.S. Woodsworth, a prominent Canadian social reformer of the early twentieth century.

Dr. Henry Norman Bethune: A Canadian Hero
http://www.sd83.bc.ca/stu-9806/mabf1.html
A detailed look at the personal life and accomplishments of Dr. Norman Bethune, whose work as a humanitarian led him to propose the idea of universal health care in Canada.

A History of Banff National Park
http://www.worldweb.com/parkscanada-banff/mueums.html
A historical overview of Banff National Park, Canada's first national conservation area. This site includes old photographs and links to information about other national parks in Canada.

Votes for Women
http://www.niagara.com/~merrwill/vote.html#anchor1855139
A brief description of the main legislative acts relevant to women's suffrage in Canada. This site also provides the dates on which women gained the right to vote and to stand for provincial office in each province. Biographies of key women in Canadian history, such as Emily Jennings Stowe, Adelaide Hoodless, and Nellie McClung, are available at http://niagara.com/~merrwill/.

Nellie McClung
http://timelinks.merlin.mb.ca/referenc/db0003.htm
A detailed biography of Nellie McClung, teacher and suffragette in the Canadian West.

RELATED READINGS
....

The following article in R. Douglas Francis and Donald B. Smith, eds., *Readings in Canadian History: Post-Confederation*, 5th ed. (Toronto: Harcourt Brace, 1998), relates to this chapter: Wendy Mitchinson, "Historical Attitudes Toward Women and Childbirth," pp. 233–50.

BIBLIOGRAPHY
....

Chapters 15 and 16 in R.C. Brown and R. Cook, *Canada, 1896–1921: A Nation Transformed* (Toronto: McClelland & Stewart, 1974) provide an overview of the social-reform movements. The social gospel is studied by Richard Allen, *The Social Passion: Religion and Social Reform in Canada, 1914–28* (Toronto: University of Toronto Press, 1971); and Ramsay Cook, *The Regenerators: Social Criticism in Late Victorian English Canada* (Toronto: University of Toronto Press, 1985). On the social gospeller J.J. Kelso see Andrew Jones and Leonard Rutman, *In the Children's Aid: J.J. Kelso and Child Welfare in Ontario* (Toronto: University of Toronto Press, 1981). Kenneth McNaught's study of J.S. Woodsworth, *A Prophet in Politics* (Toronto: University of Toronto Press, 1959), reviews the life of this important social gospel figure. For background to religious life in Ontario at the turn of the century see John Webster Grant, *A Profusion of Spires: Religion in Nineteenth-Century Ontario* (Toronto: University of Toronto Press, 1988); and William Westfall, *Two Worlds: The Protestant Culture of Nineteenth-Century Ontario* (Montreal/Kingston: McGill-Queen's University Press, 1989).

On religion and moral reform consult Mariana Valverde, *The Age of Light, Soap, and Water: Moral Reform in English Canada, 1885–1925* (Toronto: McClelland & Stewart, 1991); Carolyn Strange, *Toronto's Girl Problem: The Perils and Pleasures of the City, 1880–1930* (Toronto: University of Toronto Press, 1995); Gary Kinsman, *The Regulation of Desire: Sexuality in Canada* (Toronto: Black Rose Books, 1987); and Sharon Dale Stone, *Lesbians in Canada* (Toronto: Between the Lines, 1990). On the question of secularism versus religious renewal see Phyllis D. Airhart, *Serving the Present Age: Revivalism, Progressivism and the Methodist Tradition in Canada* (Montreal/Kingston: McGill-Queen's University Press, 1992); David B. Marshall, *Secularizing the Faith: Canadian Protestant Clergy and the Crisis of Belief, 1850–1940* (Toronto: University of Toronto Press, 1992); and John G. Stackhouse, Jr., *Canadian Evangelicalism in the Twentieth Century* (Toronto: University of Toronto Press, 1993). On Canadian women in foreign missions see Rosemary R. Gagan, *A Sensitive Independence: Canadian Methodist Women Missionaries in Canada and the Orient, 1881–1925* (Montreal/Kingston: McGill-Queen's University Press, 1992); and Ruth Compton Brower, *New Women for God: Canadian Presbyterian Women and India Missions, 1876–1914* (Toronto: University of Toronto Press, 1990). See as well Hamish Ion, *The Cross and the Rising Sun: The Canadian Protestant Missionary Movement in the Japanese Empire, 1872–1931* (Waterloo, ON: Wilfrid Laurier University Press, 1989).

Educational reform in the context of social reform is the subject of Neil Sutherland's *Children in English-Canadian Society* (Toronto: University of Toronto Press, 1976). The public-library movement is discussed in Lorne Bruce, *Free Books for All: The Public Library Movement in Ontario, 1850–1930* (Toronto: Dundurn Press, 1994). On higher education see Paul Axelrod and John Reid, eds., *Youth, University and Canadian Society: Essays in the Social History of Higher Education* (Montreal/Kingston: McGill-Queen's University Press, 1989) and for Ontario, A.B. McKillop, *Matters of Mind: The University in Ontario, 1791–1951* (Toronto: University of Toronto Press, 1994). Paul Rutherford's "Tomorrow's Metropolis:

The Urban Reform Movement in Canada, 1880–1920," *Canadian Historical Association Report* (1971): 203–24, and his edited anthology, *Saving the Canadian City, 1880–1920* (Toronto: University of Toronto Press, 1974), deal with urban reform. See, as well, G. Stelter and A. Artibise, eds., *The Canadian City: Essays in Urban History* (Toronto: McClelland & Stewart, 1977), pp. 337–418.

Janet Foster discusses the early conservation movement in *Working for Wildlife: The Beginning of Preservation in Canada* (Toronto: University of Toronto Press, 1978). On the federal Commission on Conservation see Michel F. Girard, *L'Écologisme Retrouvé: Essor et déclin de la Commission de la conservation du Canada* (Ottawa: Les Presses de l'Université d'Ottawa, 1994). For the history of Ontario's provincial parks see Gerald Killan, *Protected Places: A History of Ontario's Provincial System* (Toronto: Dundurn Press, 1993). Farley Mowat's *Sea of Slaughter* (Toronto: McClelland & Stewart, 1984) recounts the destruction of fish and game in northeastern North America. John Wadland recounts the career of naturalist-writer Ernest Thompson Seton in *Man in Nature and the Progressive Era, 1880–1915* (New York: Arno Press, 1978). Donald Smith's *From the Land of Shadows: The Making of Grey Owl* (Saskatoon: Western Producer Prairie Books, 1990) tells the story of the transformation of trapper Archie Belaney to conservationist Grey Owl. Bruce Hodgins and Jamie Benidickson have written one of the first Canadian environmental histories, a study of the Temagami area in northeastern Ontario: *The Temagami Experience: Recreation, Resources and Aboriginal Rights in the Northern Ontario Wilderness* (Toronto: University of Toronto Press, 1989). Chad and Pam Gaffield, eds., provide a useful collection of articles in *Consuming Canada: Readings in Environmental History* (Toronto: Copp Clark, 1995).

For women and social reform see Chapter 7, "The 'Woman Movement,'" in Alison Prentice et al., *Canadian Women: A History*, 2nd ed. (Toronto: Harcourt Brace, 1996); Linda Kealey, ed., *A Not Unreasonable Claim: Women and Reform in Canada, 1880–1920* (Toronto: Canadian Women's Educational Press, 1979), and Micheline Dumont et al., *Quebec Women: A History* (Toronto: Women's Press, 1987). Biographical sketches of Emily Jennings Stowe and Adelaide Hunter Hoodless appear in vol. 13 of the *Dictionary of Canadian Biography* (Toronto: University of Toronto Press, 1994), written by Gina Feldberg (pp. 506–10) and Terry Crowley (pp. 488–93), respectively. A recent good biography of Nellie McClung is Mary E. Hallett and Marilyn Davis, *Firing the Heather: The Life and Times of Nellie McClung* (Saskatoon: Fifth House, 1993). The story of Madame Gérin-Lajoie and her daughter is told in Hélène Pelletier-Baillargeon, *Marie Gérin-Lajoie* (Montréal: Boréal Express, 1985). On the suffrage movement consult Carol Bacchi, *Liberation Deferred? The Ideas of the English-Canadian Suffragists, 1877–1918* (Toronto: University of Toronto Press, 1983); and Catharine L. Cleverdon, *The Woman Suffrage Movement in Canada: The Start of Liberation, 1900–20* (Toronto: University of Toronto Press, 1974 [1950]). On women socialist reformers see Janice Newton, *The Feminist Challenge to the Canadian Left, 1900–1918* (Montreal/Kingston: McGill-Queen's University Press, 1995); and Linda Kealey, *Enlisting Women for the Cause: Women, Labour, and the Left in Canada, 1890–1920* (Toronto: University of Toronto Press, 1998). On the impact of the medical profession on women and reform see Wendy Mitchinson, *The Nature of Their Bodies* (Toronto: University of Toronto Press, 1991).

Prohibition in the Maritimes is examined in E. Forbes, "Prohibition and the Social Gospel in Nova Scotia," *Acadiensis* 1 (1971): 11–36; in Ontario, in Gerald Hallowell, *Prohibition in Ontario, 1919–1923* (Toronto: Ontario Historical Society, 1972); and on the Prairies, in James Gray, *Booze: The Impact of Whiskey on the Prairie West* (Toronto: Macmillan, 1972). On the Woman's Christian Temperance Union see Wendy Mitchinson, "The WCTU," in *A Not Unreasonable Claim* (cited earlier).

Paul-André Linteau, René Durocher, and Jean-Claude Robert, *Quebec: A History, 1867–1929* (Toronto: James Lorimer, 1983); and Susan Mann Trofimenkoff, *The Dream of*

Nation: A Social and Intellectual History of Quebec (Toronto: Gage, 1983), discuss social reform in Quebec. Jean Hamelin and Nicole Gagnon, *Histoire du catholicisme québécois; le XXᵉ siècle*, tome 1, *1898–1940* (Montréal: Boréal Express, 1984), discuss the role of the Quebec church in social reform. Joseph Levitt's *Henri Bourassa and the Golden Calf* (Ottawa: University of Ottawa Press, 1969) analyzes the views of the Ligue nationaliste on social questions. On the *caisses populaires* see Ronald Rudin, *In Whose Interest? Quebec's Caisses Populaires, 1900–1945* (Montreal/Kingston: McGill-Queen's University Press, 1990); and the short sketch by Yves Roby, "A People's Bank," *Horizon Canada* 65 (1986): 1550–55.

CHAPTER NINE

Culture:
1867–1914

D'Arcy McGee, the prophet of Confederation, stated in 1860: "I see in the not remote distance, one great nationality bound by the blue rim of ocean." In this union, he added two years later, he hoped that "a Canadian nationality, not French-Canadian or British-Canadian nor Irish-Canadian" would result. While McGee's dream became a political reality in 1867 and in the subsequent expansion of the Dominion after his death in 1868, culturally the great orator's vision remained a concept rather than a reality half a century later. About the only issue that united the two major linguistic communities was their agreement on the need to extinguish the cultures of the country's Aboriginal communities.

Between 1867 and 1914, both English-Canadian and French-Canadian cultures grew in depth and became less local in scope. In music, Canada produced first-class composers and musicians, and supported numerous orchestras, choirs, operas, and bands. In the visual arts, more sophisticated artistic communities emerged. Literary works in both English-speaking and French-speaking Canada gained a larger audience. An indigenous Canadian theatre grew slowly, in the face of competition from touring American and British theatre productions. Sports clubs proliferated, and teams took on professional status, with teams of expert players and a regular schedule of games. But the Native peoples, unless they participated in the two dominant cultures, received no support or recognition for their cultural traditions or even the maintenance of their language.

MUSIC

Of all the arts, music was the most widespread in both English-speaking and French-speaking Canada at the turn of the century. Sheet music, and later the phonograph, brought the culture of the outside world to many Canadian communities. Sacred music flourished because the churches played a large role in the musical life of the communities. Choirs and choral singing did not require props or musical instruments and made use of local church talent. The typical musician in late-nineteenth-century Canada had to be innovative to survive. He or she usually played the church organ, led the choir, and taught a handful of students. Most of the choirs and choral singers performed locally. Almost all cities in Canada had singing groups; for example, Halifax had the Orpheus Club, and Saint John, the Saint John Oratorio Society.

A few groups achieved national fame. The James Street Baptist Church Choir in Toronto, consisting of 250 voices and under the leadership of choirmaster Augustus Stephen Vogt, had a national reputation. Out of Vogt's choir came the nucleus of the famous Toronto Mendelssohn Choir, which Vogt himself conducted from its founding in 1894 until 1917.

In Quebec, the Montreal Oratorio Society, formed in 1864, acquired national and international fame by the turn of the century, as did the Societé Musicale des Montagnards Canadiens and Les Orphéonistes de Montréal. The choirs and their listening public favoured masses, oratorios, and cantatas, especially works by Bach, Handel, Haydn, and Beethoven. They became another important link to Europe, considered the centre of world culture.

Calixa Lavallée was considered at the time to be Canada's greatest musician. His father, a blacksmith, who also made stringed instruments and was a local band-master, taught him to play the piano, organ, cornet, and violin. The boy's exceptional musical gifts were soon recognized, but significantly, he had to spend most of his adult life making music in the United States to support himself. For a time he served as the artistic director of the New York Grand Opera House. In 1875, he returned to Quebec for five years.

WEB LINKS

In 1880, the lieutenant governor of Quebec asked Lavallée to write a patriotic song for the national convention of French Canadians, organized for the end of June in Quebec. Reversing normal practice, due to lack of time, Lavallée composed the music before the words were written. These were the work of Adolphe-Basile Routhier, a Quebec Superior Court justice, who in a single night wrote four verses, the first of which is still sung by federalists in Quebec. Ironically, "O Canada" was first played on St. Jean Baptiste Day, a fête now recognized as Quebec's national holiday. It became an instant success in the province. The Quebec press proclaimed, "At last we have a truly French-Canadian National Song." "O Canada" was first performed in English in 1901. In 1980, one century after its composition, the Canadian government officially adopted it as Canada's national anthem.

More popular in English Canada at the turn of the century was "The Maple Leaf Forever." Alexander Muir, a Toronto school principal, wrote the song in 1867. Originally it was written as a patriotic poem for a poetry contest in Montreal, where it won second prize. Only afterwards did Muir look for a melody to fit the words — a common practice. When he failed to find an appropriate tune, he wrote his own music.

Well-known French-Canadian composers included Guillaume Couture, organist and conductor of the Montreal Philharmonic Society, whose compositions were religious in purpose. He performed a number of ambitious orchestral programs that gave the citizens of Montreal an exposure to contemporary European repertory not available anywhere else in Canada in such quantity. William Reed, whose *Grand Choeur in D Major* for organ was considered one of the finest organ works ever written by a Canadian, also achieved international fame, as did Clarence Lucas, a prolific composer of orchestral music. As well, there was Ernest MacMillan (later Sir Ernest), whose real fame would come during the war and postwar eras, and Healey Willan, internationally acclaimed for his sacred choral music, especially his anthem *An Apostrophe to the Heavenly Hosts* (1921).

Bands and orchestras were equally popular. Most brass bands formed around the militia camps. Thus when the British regiments left Canada in the early 1870s, their departure caused a temporary stir in band music. Fortunately, some of the

A photo of the Toronto Mendelssohn Choir taken on February 6, 1911. The choir, founded in Toronto in 1894, still flourishes today.

Pringle and Booth/National Archives of Canada/PA-29790.

bandmasters and players decided to stay in Canada. Brass bands were common throughout the country, including a number in Indian residential schools as a means to impose discipline and order. The Septuour Haydn was one of the most successful chamber ensembles, consisting of a string quintet, flute, and piano. Arthur Lavigne of Quebec City founded the group in 1871, and by 1903 it had grown into the Société symphonique de Québec.

Opera in all forms — comic operas, ballad operas, and grand operas — proved popular in the late nineteenth and early twentieth centuries. Tour companies performed most works in large centres, as part of larger North American tours. It was customary for musicians from Europe to dock at Halifax and start their North American tours there. The major cities of eastern Canada were on the same circuit as Boston, New York, Chicago, and Philadelphia. By the turn of the century, popular local opera companies were established in Montreal, Toronto, and Quebec.

The nineteenth century is often referred to as the "age of the virtuoso" — a time when gifted soloists astounded the public with superb performances. Canada became home to four world-class soloists. Frantz Jehin-Prume of Belgium came to live in Montreal. An outstanding violinist, he composed several virtuoso works for violin and piano, and became concertmaster of the Montreal Philharmonic Society. Another violinist, Luigi von Kunits, had a similarly successful career. Born in Vienna in 1870, he accepted an invitation in 1912 to teach at the Canadian Academy of Music in Toronto. Besides playing the standard repertory, he performed his own compositions, including the challenging *Violin Concerto in E Minor*. In the 1910s and 1920s, Calgary-born Kathleen Parlow, an internationally renowned violinist, toured Europe, Russia, North America, and Asia.

Emma Albani was Canada's first native-born musician to achieve international fame. Born Marie Lajeunesse in Chambly, near Montreal, in 1847, she adopted the stage name Emma Albani while on a European tour in the early 1870s. The French-Canadian diva sang at the best opera houses in Europe. In 1886, the British critic Eduard Hanslick wrote of Albani, "By far the best singer at Covent Garden this season, if not the only important one." She made various visits from her home in England to Canada — in 1883, 1889, and a grand tour from Halifax to Victoria in 1896–97.

Calixa Lavallée, the composer of "O Canada." Ironically, Canada's national anthem since 1980 was originally composed in 1880 for St. Jean Baptiste Day, now recognized as Quebec's national holiday.

....

Heritage Canada 5(2) (May 1979): 13.

THE PROMOTION OF CANADIAN CULTURE

Canada's viceroys played an important role in promoting English-Canadian and French-Canadian culture by hosting important cultural activities, attending functions across the country when possible, and buying and displaying Canadian art. Lord Dufferin, Canada's third governor general (1872–78), laid the groundwork for the establishment of the Royal Canadian Academy of the Arts, patterned after the British Royal Academy. Dufferin's successor, the Marquis of Lorne, brought the academy and its successor, the National Gallery of Canada, into existence in the brief interlude of prosperity in the early 1880s.

For the first 30 years, the National Gallery housed only government purchases, donations, bequests, and commissions. Then, in 1907, the federal government established the three-person Advisory Arts Council to promote "the growth of a true taste and general interest in public arts amongst the people of Canada." Three years later, the gallery's first full-time curator, Eric Brown, arrived from England. In the 1910s, Brown encouraged Canadian artists to develop works "along national lines." He helped begin the Canadian War Memorial Fund, which sponsored Canadian artists to go abroad to paint the carnage of World War I.

The prosperity and expansion at the turn of the century led to new government initiatives. Governor General Earl Grey sponsored the Earl Grey Musical and Dramatic Trophy Competition, which held national competitions in different Canadian cities yearly in an effort to elevate the quality of Canadian talent. Grey, a fervent imperialist, also sponsored lecture tours to promote the British empire both within Canada and abroad. Stephen Leacock, who toured Canada, Great Britain, Australia, New Zealand, and South Africa in 1907, was one of the beneficiaries. Grey purchased an entire printing of Robert Stead's book *The Empire Builders* (1908) because he liked its imperial message. To promote the study of Canadian and British history, Grey founded the Historical Landmark Association of Canada in 1907. It had as its mandate the establishment of national historic sites such as the Plains of Abraham, a difficult site to interpret due to strong and conflicting feelings on the part of anglophones and francophones.

By the turn of the century, Canadian governors general and the public could rely on a growing business community for some financial support of the arts. The CPR

Many art galleries in the late nineteenth century had to rely on a coal stove for "climate control."

William James Topley/National Archives of Canada/PA-136767.

hired artists in the 1880s to create works of art for their hotels, châteaus, railcars, and offices and to design their promotional posters. It also gave Dominion Drama Festival finalists a round-trip ticket to Ottawa for the price of a one-way fare to make it possible for the finalists to participate in the annual competitions. For writers and dramatists it often provided free passes for readers of their works across the country and the staging of their plays.

Private family businesses also supported the arts — the wealthy Massey family of Toronto, in particular. As early as the 1870s, the Massey Manufacturing Company established a company band — the Massey Concert Band — a glee club, an employees' orchestra, and even a literary magazine, *Massey's Illustrated*, published between 1882 and 1895. As well, the Massey family purchased a number of church organs for Methodist churches in Toronto. In 1894, Hart Massey built the magnificent Massey Hall, with a seating capacity of 4000, and underwrote the costs of the Toronto Symphony Orchestra and the Toronto Mendelssohn Choir. The family business would continue its generous patronage under Hart's grandson, Vincent, in the interwar years.

VISUAL ARTS

In 1860, on the occasion of the official opening of the Victoria Bridge, a magnificent structure that spanned the St. Lawrence River from Montreal to Longueuil, the government of the Canadas planned a "Great Exhibition." It built a Crystal Palace, which housed a gallery of fine arts on the top floor. The exhibition contained paintings by Quebec's famed Cornelius Kreighoff, known for his quaint depictions of habitant life, and by a younger artist from England, Charles Jones Way, whose majestic paintings of Canadian scenery caught the eye of the Prince of Wales, who visited on his Royal Tour of British North America. Also present were photographs by William Notman, a Scot who by 1860 had established a thriving photograph studio in downtown Montreal. In the 1860s and 1870s, the Notmans opened over a dozen branches in Ottawa, Saint John, Halifax, and even several eastern American cities. Many of Canada's young and aspiring artists of the day got their start in Notman's Studio.

English-speaking artists in the city formed the Art Association of Montreal after the exhibition. Their French-speaking colleagues did not join. In Montreal, English and French Canadians might come into daily contact — even momentarily collaborate in a "Great Exhibition" together — yet each side kept essentially to itself. The two cultures were still strangers to one another.

The Art Association of Montreal became the nucleus for the Society of Canadian Artists, founded in 1867. John Bell-Smith, an English artist who had arrived in Montreal a year earlier, became its first president. The society held its first exhibition in 1868. It contained works by the elite of Montreal artists: C.J. Way; John A. Fraser, a Scot who had worked for the Notman Studio before striking out on his own artistic career; Otto Jacobi, a Prussian who came to Montreal in 1860, in search of adventure and new opportunities; Adolph Vogt, another German who arrived in 1865 via Philadelphia and quickly acquired the reputation of being "a very promising young artist"; William Raphael, a German Jew, best known for his *Behind Bonsecours Market, Montreal* (1866), a painting depicting life on the Montreal wharfs; Harry Sandham, a native Montrealer and a young employee of Notman's Studio; and Allan Edson, from the Eastern Townships. The society set an ambitious goal: to foster a pan-Canadian artistic tradition so as to make Canadian artists known both within Canada and abroad.

Shortly after the formation of the Montreal society, the Ontario Society of Artists formed in 1872. These Toronto-based artists were caught up in the pan-Canadianism of the Canada First Movement. Seven of them met at the home of John A. Fraser, who had moved from Montreal to Toronto to launch the new society. They promised to do everything in their power to promote Canadian art, including holding annual exhibitions of their works and working toward the building of a permanent public art gallery in Toronto.

Out of these two societies, the one in Montreal and the other in Toronto, came the beginnings of the Canadian Academy of the Arts, founded in 1880 with the help of Governor General Lord Lorne. A year later, Queen Victoria officially prefixed "Royal" to its title. Lucius O'Brien became its first president, a position he held for ten years.

O'Brien and the Royal Canadian Academy of the Arts embodied the new spirit of the age. Born at Shanty Bay near Barrie, Ontario, and educated at Upper Canada College in Toronto, O'Brien first painted scenes of his home region of Lake Simcoe. But he clearly "felt a calling to reflect the majestic beauty of his native land,"[1] according to his biographer, and sought opportunities to paint the diverse Canadian landscape. He was among the first Toronto artists to travel on the Intercolonial Railway in 1877 to paint the areas of southern Quebec and the Baie de Chaleurs region of New Brunswick through which it passed. One of O'Brien's most famous paintings, *Sunrise on the Saguenay* (1880), came out of these trips. He exhibited it at the opening exhibition of the Royal Canadian Academy of the Arts in 1880, and it dominated the exhibition.

When *Picturesque Canada*, the most ambitious publishing project of the day, was launched, O'Brien was the chief Canadian contributor, with almost one-quarter

Lucius R. O'Brien, Sunrise on the Saguenay, *1880. This painting, first exhibited at the opening of the Royal Canadian Academy of the Arts in 1880, won O'Brien much praise and recognition.*

National Gallery of Canada, Ottawa. Royal Canadian Academy of Arts diploma work, deposited by the artist, Toronto, 1880.

of the over 500 illustrations in the two volumes. *Picturesque Canada* was based on the highly successful *Picturesque America*. Two Americans, the Belden brothers of Chicago, launched the project. The investors employed Americans who had worked on the previous book on the United States to complete three-quarters of the Canadian illustrations. O'Brien was, in fact, the token Canadian — the Belden brothers claimed that Canadian artists were not experienced enough in preparing work for the volumes, a viewpoint that caused an uproar in the Canadian art community!

George Munro Grant, principal of Queen's University and a Canadian enthusiast, edited the *Picturesque Canada* text. He overlooked the American visual contributions and instead underscored the importance of the volumes for the growth of a pan-Canadian nationalism. "I believe that a work that would represent its characteristic scenery and the history and life of its people," he wrote, "would not only make us better known to ourselves and to strangers, but would also stimulate national sentiment and contribute to the rightful development of the nation." Grant's text and O'Brien's paintings together reflected the growing national spirit of English-speaking Canadians who looked to the Canadian landscape for the essence and the soul of Canada. Cornelius Van Horne, general manager (and later president) of the CPR, invited artists to go west as guests of the CPR and paint western scenes, especially of the Rocky Mountains, which the railway company could use to promote tourism and in turn boost ticket sales.

By the 1890s, a trend began among English-Canadian artists to return to a European-style art and European-trained artists. Canadian artists discovered through the French Barbizon tradition that the essence of a country could be found not in its landscape but in those who inhabited its countryside. They were taken by Millet's paintings of French peasants in rural open-air settings, such as *Woman With a Lamp*, *The Angelus*, and *The Gleaner*. Wyatt Eaton, who had visited Millet in rural France; Horatio Walker, who painted habitant life in Quebec; and Homer Watson, who painted rural Ontario scenes best expressed this new artistic trend in English-speaking Canada.

Horatio Walker grew up in Listowel, Ontario, the son of a lumberman. On trips with his father to Wolfe's Cove in Quebec City, he saw colourful habitants and Native people in canoes, which even at that late date were piled high with furs. Suddenly, his reading of the historian Francis Parkman came alive. In 1880, he took a six-month walking tour down the St. Lawrence from Montreal to Quebec City. On his pilgrimage he visited country folk in their homes, slept in barns, and observed the daily life of the French-Canadian people. He became so fascinated by French Canadians that he became a complete Quebecophile, continually emphasizing a French branch in his ancestry, refusing to speak English, denouncing his fellow Ontarians as "barbarians," and living the remainder of his life on Île d'Orléans, just east of Quebec City.

Homer Watson grew up in Doon, a hamlet in the Grand River valley of Ontario, and attended art school in Toronto in 1874. He visited the Art Students League and numerous galleries in New York in 1876. The landscape artist achieved national and international fame. But always, he came back to his rural Ontario settings and its people as his subjects.

A real opportunity for Canadian artists to achieve international fame and recognition came with the holding of a Colonial and Indian Exhibition in London in 1886 — the year preceding Queen Victoria's Golden Jubilee. The exhibition was to mirror in art the vast material wealth and "civilization" of the queen's vast empire. Canada, considering itself the proudest as well as the most superior of the queen's dominions, wanted to put on a spectacular show. Unfortunately for the artists, the political and business elite of Canada dictated what should be included. Thus Princess Louise, the wife of the governor general and an aspiring artist, received more attention and prominence than did established and reputable Canadian painters. Nonetheless, the Canadian display did contain works by such established painters as Vogt, Raphael, Fraser, and O'Brien. But it was the paintings by a younger, Paris-trained group — Homer Watson, William Brymner, Paul Peel, Robert Harris, and Percy Woodstock — that really caught the critics' eyes.

This younger generation of English-Canadian artists were trained in Paris. The French capital, with its world-famous artists, bohemian lifestyle, and cultural milieu, was the art capital of the world. Wyatt Eaton and Allan Edson, both of Quebec, initiated the French tour. Their contemporaries from Ontario — William Brymner, Paul Peel, and George Reid — and Robert Harris of Prince Edward Island all subsequently went to the French capital and received French academic training. Peel would become Canada's best-known painter in Europe in the late nineteenth century.

One of the finest Quebec artists of the late nineteenth century was Napoleon Bourassa, who was influenced by Ingres, the French neoclassicist, and by historic painting. His student, Louis-Philippe Hébert, achieved great renown in sculpture. Another talented French-Canadian artist of the period, Ozias Leduc, lived in seclusion, unknown to most of his contemporaries except for a handful of devoted artistic friends. His still-life paintings of simple Quebec subjects show a heightened sensitivity and an appreciation of beauty in the ordinary. Most of his income derived from church decoration. He completed some 150 large paintings for 27 cathedrals, churches, and chapels.

At the turn of the century, painting in English-speaking Canada came of age. James Wilson Morrice and Maurice Cullen, both of Quebec, became the leading Canadian practitioners of Impressionism and Post-Impressionism. Morrice was born into a wealthy, established Montreal family. After a brief schooling in law at the University of Toronto, he discovered art to be his real passion. In 1890 he sailed for Europe, on the advice of Sir William Van Horne, who spoke glowingly of young Morrice's artistic talents to Morrice's father. Morrice won instant acclaim. His works were purchased by a number of the great European galleries as well as by the French government and Parisian art connoisseurs. His pictures of Quebec City, particularly his winter sketches of the Quebec-to-Lévis ferry, represent the Canadian side of his work. In the end, however, this gifted Canadian enjoyed more fame in Europe than in his native Montreal.

Morrice's contemporary, the Newfoundland-born Maurice Cullen, influenced a whole generation of Canadian painters with Impressionism. After an unsuccessful initial career in business in Montreal, he left for Paris in 1888 to practise sculpture. There he met the great French Impressionists, especially Monet. Five Cullen canvases were exhibited in the 1894 Salon. The following year he was elected to the distinguished Société Nationale des Beaux-Arts. Yet, despite such recognition in Europe, he returned to Canada in 1895. His acceptance at home was slow and difficult. His work would inspire A.Y. Jackson, a young Montreal revolutionary of the time and a future member of the Group of Seven. Jackson once said of him, "To us he was a hero."

CANADIAN LITERATURE

Canadian poetry in English became established in the 1880s. The "Confederation Poets" — the name literary critics have given to the four poets Charles G.D. Roberts, Bliss Carman, Archibald Lampman, and Duncan Campbell Scott — gave a spiritual dimension to Confederation. Roberts's first volume of poetry, "Orion and Other Poems," inspired Lampman, who later wrote: "It seemed to me a wonderful thing that such a work could be done by a Canadian, by a young man, one of ourselves." The Confederation Poets sought the essence of Canada in nature — in the world of rocks, streams, and woods, and in the lifestyle of the farmer and lumberjack. They were the literary equivalent of the Canada First Movement, seeking to discover the soul of the new nation. These poets depicted nature in the highly romantic terms favoured by the British Romantic poets, such as William Wordsworth, John Keats, and Percy Shelley, who inspired their poetry.

WEB

LINKS

Isabella Valancy Crawford also drew inspiration from the Canadian landscape. She depicted nature as half-human, as possessing a soul that was very much in tune with the human soul. In her mind, both "souls" struggled with love and death — common themes in her nature poetry.

The most famous female poet who wrote about the Native peoples, however, was Pauline Johnson. Born the daughter of a Mohawk chief and his English wife, Johnson — or Tekahionwake, her Mohawk name — celebrated her Iroquois heritage while at the same time expressing a Canadian, and an imperial, feeling. In her poem, "Canadian Born," she expressed her imperialistic fervour:

> The Dutch may have their Holland, the Spaniard have his Spain,
> The Yankee to the south of us must south of us remain;
> For not a man dare lift a hand against the men who brag
> That they were born in Canada beneath the British flag.

In Quebec, a generation of poets used François-Xavier Garneau's magisterial *Histoire du Canada*, published between 1845 and 1848, along with folklore, patriotic feeling, and religion, as themes for their poetry. Not surprisingly, survival, or *la survivance*, became an overriding concern in their poems. Octave Crémazie, for example, expressed the patriotic sentiment of his fellow citizens for their French-Canadian nation and looked to its past under the French empire for their moments of greatness. In the same way, Louis Fréchette, considered the unofficial poet laureate of nineteenth-century French Canada, wrote a series of patriotic poems, *La Légende d'un Peuple* (1887), inspired by dramatic moments of Canada's past from the arrival of Jacques Cartier to the hanging of Louis Riel.

Quebec's poetry came into its own at the turn of the century with the École littéraire de Montréal. Founded in 1895, it received acclaim for its poetry, which broke free of the patriotic-romantic verse that then dominated. Its most famous member was Émile Nelligan. This poet of genius produced some 170 poems when he was between the ages of 17 and 20. Perhaps his best known is "Le Vaisseau d'or" (Ship of Gold). Unlike other members of the "École," Nelligan found his inspiration for poetry less in romantic nature, historical subjects, or patriotic fervour, and more in what Wordsworth called "the still, sad music of humanity," the poetry of the spirit. Exhausted and ill, Nelligan lost his grip on reason in 1899, at the age of 21, and spent the last 41 years of his life in mental institutions. His poetry is still widely read in Quebec, where he enjoys today almost legendary status.

English-Canadian novelists and short-story writers emerged in the late nineteenth century. The passage of Ontario's Free Libraries Act in 1882 led to the establishment of free public libraries throughout the province. Other provinces followed: British Columbia (1891), Manitoba (1899), Saskatchewan (1906), and Alberta (1907), which greatly helped the circulation of Canadian books.

Both Charles G.D. Roberts and Ernest Thompson Seton had popular reputations for their realistic animal stories. Seton was born in England, was raised in Ontario, and lived in Manitoba in the early 1880s before leaving permanently for the United States in 1896. He published his first collection of animal stories, *Wild Animals I Have Known*, in 1898. Eight years later his classic of children's literature, *Two Little Savages*, based on his boyhood experiences of "playing Indian" in Ontario, was published.

The best Canadian novels had regional settings. Norman Duncan's *The Way of the Sea* (1903) and Theodore Goodridge Roberts's *The Harbour Master* (1913) were set in Newfoundland. Lucy Maud Montgomery's first novel, *Anne of Green Gables* (1908), captured the spirit of her native province of Prince Edward Island through her beloved orphan character, Anne Shirley. An instant success, the novel made her, and the island, world-famous. Gilbert Parker's *The Seats of the Mighty* (1898), a historical novel about New France, became an international bestseller. Popular French-Canadian novels of the Quebec rural countryside include Ernest Choquette's *Claude*

Émile Nelligan (1879–1941), the legendary Quebec poet and member of the École littéraire de Montréal. The intense young man already was confined to a mental asylum at the time this photo was taken in 1904.

National Archives of Canada/C-88566.

Paysan (1899). But Charles Chiniquy outdistanced all of his contemporary Quebec authors in terms of the number of editions and translations of his works. His *The Priest, the Woman and the Confessional* (1875); *Fifty Years in the Church of Rome* (1885); and *Forty Years in the Church of Christ* (1899) were popular among Protestant extremists throughout the world because of their vitriolic attacks on the Roman Catholic church.

Stephen Leacock acquired international recognition as one of the great humorists writing in the English language. *Sunshine Sketches of a Little Town* (1912), an affectionate satire of small-town Ontario life in the fictitious town of Mariposa, and *Arcadian Adventures of the Idle Rich* (1914), a parody of city life, were the best known of about 60 books that earned Leacock a reputation as the "Mark Twain of the British Empire." But there was more to Leacock's novels than humour; he had a message, which was to question the values and virtues of liberal capitalism and advocate instead a more humane and spiritual society, even if it was presented with a strong dose of Tory conservatism.

In the West, the settlement of the prairies provided a rich subject and inspiration for a generation of prairie novelists. Authors such as Ralph Connor (Charles Gordon), Robert Stead, Nellie McClung, and Janey Canuck (Emily Murphy) wrote of the settlement experience of the Canadian prairies with highly utopian depictions of the West. The phenomenally successful novels of Ralph Connor sold in the millions and had a larger audience outside the country than within it. He made his reputation with his first novel, *The Sky Pilot* (1899), the story of a North-West Mounted Police officer. All of his western novels capitalized on the romance, adventure, and physical beauty of the early West. His novels also dealt with the familiar theme of good, simple-hearted Christians challenged by scoffers and non-believers who, in the end, were

Father Chiniquy alleged in this major work that the confessions of female parishioners caused some Roman Catholic priests to end their vows of celibacy. This certainly had been his own experience and led to his excommunication. The Protestants embraced him when he began his furious campaign against the "Church of Rome." He made few converts in French Canada.

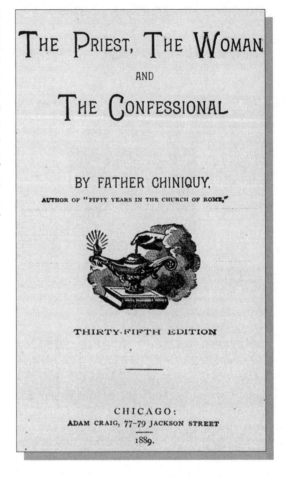

won over to the purer life. They are fine examples of "muscular Christianity" in the late nineteenth century. In British Columbia, Martin Allen Grainger's *Woodsmen of the West* (1908) came to symbolize life in the logging industry on the West Coast. Robert Service's verse, published in his *Songs of a Sourdough* (1907), *The Spell of the Yukon* (1907), and *Ballads of a Cheechako* (1909), established his reputation as a writer of humorous ballads.

These novelists, short-story writers, and poets, along with other less known writers in English, had an outlet for their works in small-circulation Canadian journals: *The Canadian Monthly and National Review* (1872–78), which continued as *Rose-Belford's Canadian Monthly* (1878–82), edited by Graeme Mercer Adam. When the *Monthly* ceased publication, it was followed by *The Week*, edited by Charles G.D. Roberts and with support from Goldwin Smith and other familiar Canadian literary figures. *The Week* went out of existence in 1896, but already *The Canadian Magazine* (1893–1939) had taken up the challenge of expressing English-Canadian nationalism.

Newspapers helped the development of writing in Canada. By the turn of the century, historian David Sutherland notes, "the press had evolved into a truly mass medium. Steam-powered production machinery, cheap newsprint, telegraph communications, a comprehensive rail network, and efficient postal delivery combined to create the penny-a-copy urban daily which made information gleaned worldwide available to more and more Canadians."[2]

The number of daily newspapers doubled in the late nineteenth century to nearly 100 by 1892. Canada's own brand of yellow journalism surfaced — inexpensive newspapers that relied on sensational and often questionable news for their popularity, and on advertisements from large department stores, such as Eaton's, for their financial success. The *Montreal Star*, founded in 1869, later joined by *La Presse*, and the Toronto newspapers — the *Telegram*, the *World*, and the Toronto *News* — all belong to this category. These newspapers had mass circulations. Through satire, they exposed the social snobbery and economic privilege of the Canadian elite. Traditional newspapers — such as the Toronto *Globe* and the Toronto *Mail*, and in Quebec City *Le Canadien*, *Le Journal de Québec*, and *L'Étendard* — continued to exist. However, as earlier in the century, these papers, in their reporting of political events, served as little more than mouthpieces for political parties.

According to cultural historian Paul Rutherford, all the papers, popular or partisan, shared three key ideas: progress, nationalism, and democracy. Newspapers celebrated English-Canadian or French-Canadian achievements, building on past accomplishments and foreseeing future successes.

CANADIAN THEATRE

English-Canadian theatre grew slowly in the period 1867–1914. There existed a theatrical tradition dating back to Loyalist times to build upon, and during certain periods theatre flourished, often under the auspices of an owner and manager (usually one and the same person). One such person was John Nickinson, manager of the Lyceum Theatre in Toronto from 1852 to 1858; he succeeded in bringing in a number of professional performers from England and the United States. But in general, performance halls remained few in number. In their absence, local amateurs and travelling professionals had to perform in the assembly rooms of taverns, which did little to improve the public reputation of theatre. Theatre on the eve of Confederation still remained amateur in nature and limited in scope.

In the late nineteenth century, a few new theatres were established, mainly in the large urban centres. In Montreal, the New Dominion Theatre opened in 1873 to cater to professional drama touring groups. It succumbed, however, to vaudeville or music hall troupes by 1876, a reflection of the type of culture in demand at the time. In Toronto, a new Grand Opera House opened in 1880, which, along with the Princess Theatre and the Academy of Music, housed most of the important cultural events that came to Toronto between 1880 and 1914. From Saint John to Winnipeg, other "Grand Opera Houses," which actually rarely sponsored operas, opened to welcome American and British touring companies.

The prevailing mood in late-nineteenth-century English Canada was, according to the theatre historian Murray Edwards, "essentially anti-theatre."[3] Few Canadians attended productions, fewer still supported their actors, and theatre productions were seldom reported in the local newspapers. One reason for such a low opinion of acting was its association with "immorality and debauchery" in the mind of church leaders. The stage was regarded "as the gate of Hell," according to Edwards. No doubt contributing to this perception were the controversial performances of the flamboyant French actress Sarah Bernhardt. She performed to a full house in Montreal, despite the Roman Catholic church's condemnation of her "heretical" theatre productions. She was also popular in English-speaking Canada during her several visits to Canada.

Theatre developed at the turn of the century with the growth of large cities and the wealth of industrialism. From the beginning, however, it was a foreign phenomenon. American money built most of the new theatres. American touring companies provided nearly all the English-language entertainment. These large companies toured North America, including Canada, and put on the same productions in different cities, regardless of the locale. They made no attempt to use local talent and in fact discouraged the growth of indigenous talent by getting Canadians accustomed to looking beyond Canada's borders for theatrical talent.

Quebec plays often had a political theme to them. In May 1880, Louis Fréchette's *Papineau* appeared at Montreal's Académie de Musique, and his *Retour de l'exilé (The Return of the Exile)* played in June of the same year. Both plays concerned the heroes and events of 1837–38 and advocated a reconciliation of French and English, while still holding out hope of the *Canadiens* one day freeing themselves from British rule. Another play, *Un Bonheur en attire un autre (One Piece of Luck Attracts Another)*, written by Félix-Gabriel Marchand, premier of Quebec between 1897 and 1900, was performed in 1883 at "a benefit for the families of those killed during the 1837/38 Rebellion."

At the same time, the Saint-Jean-Baptiste Society organized *soirées de famille* (family nights) in which young aspiring actors and actresses put on local plays under the guise of "elocution lessons" so as to ward off any interference from the Roman Catholic church. Unfortunately, these *soirées* lasted only three years. Yet another blow to French-Canadian theatre occurred in 1909, when the municipal government of Montreal levied an amusement tax. Attendance dropped, and many reputable and long-established theatres, including the historic Académie de Musique, closed their doors.

Some patrons of the arts became concerned about the "Americanization of English-Canadian theatre." But instead of supporting Canadian actors, they brought in British touring groups. For a while, in the period 1910–1914, a battle existed between these two external groups for the domination of Canadian theatre. With the outbreak of war, however, the British "theatrical invasion" of Canada ended. The Great War also curtailed American productions in Canada. By this time, according to Murray Edwards, the time to cultivate an indigenous theatre had passed. Only in the interwar years would a respectable Canadian theatre develop, in competition with the new moving-picture industry.

POPULAR CULTURE

Canada's first permanent movie house, the Edison Electric Theatre, opened on Cordova Street in Vancouver in 1902. It was followed by Winnipeg's Unique and Dreamland in 1903, Montreal's Nationale and Palais Royale (an impressive 1000-seat cinema) in 1904, and St. John's York in 1906. Each charged its customers a nickel,

An appreciative audience watching a movie at the Innisfail Opera House, Innisfail, Alberta, 1910.

Glenbow Archives, Calgary, Canada/NA-1709-23.

from whence derived the name "nickelodeon." One of the great American stars of the era was Gladys Mary Smith — or, to use her stage name, Mary Pickford — who was born in Toronto in 1893 but moved with her family to New York at the age of five.

SPORTS

Sports clubs gained popularity in the years 1867–1914, particularly in curling, yachting, hunting, golf, and lawn tennis. They provided social meeting places for Canada's political, economic, and commercial elites. Membership was often restricted to people with certain ethnic, religious, and educational backgrounds. But wealth and social position were also becoming criteria for entrance, allowing entry to a new professional and business class, such as lawyers, doctors, entrepreneurs, and bank managers. Women were active in these clubs, although in a clearly defined and subservient role, while racial minorities were barred entirely. They were forced to create their own teams and clubs. In Nova Scotia, blacks in the community of Africville, on the outskirts of Halifax, formed their own baseball and hockey teams, while on the West Coast, Japanese formed a baseball team, called the Asahi. Out of these organizations would come the key figures in the development of amateur sports.

Organized team sports, such as football, baseball, lacrosse, and ice hockey, grew as well in popularity. As people settled in urban centres and worked clearly defined hours in factories or offices, they had more time for sports. Better transportation facilities and communication links also enabled intercity competition. The standardization of rules in sports, in turn, led to the creation of local, provincial, and national associations.

The University of Toronto and McGill University football teams in action during an intercampus match, 1909. Later that fall, the U of T team defeated Toronto Parkdale to win the first Grey Cup.

Canadian Football Hall of Fame and Museum.

Although football made its debut in Canada in the late nineteenth century, it became a recognized national sport only when Governor General Earl Grey donated the cup that bears his name in 1909. At first the sport remained the preserve of an anglophone Canadian elite that was mainly associated with universities in the larger cities of central Canada. Only in the first decade of the twentieth century did football spread to the smaller towns of Ontario and the Prairies. It also became more of a spectator sport. In so doing, it became more "Americanized," except that it retained the oval ball and the rules of rugby — both Canadian contributions to the game. Soccer also was played, particularly by British immigrants. In 1904, the Galt Football Club represented Canada at the Olympic Games in St. Louis, Missouri, and won the soccer gold medal.

Baseball, the most Americanized sport in Canada, became the most Canadian sport in terms of those who either played or watched the game. It required minimal facilities. During the 1870s, baseball clubs emerged in all parts of Canada, and intratown leagues became popular by the 1880s. In rural areas, baseball was played only occasionally, when the farm work allowed it. Very often it was during a picnic or other gathering associated with celebrations, such as May 24th (later Victoria Day), Dominion Day, and Labour Day.

WEB LINKS

Many Canadians considered lacrosse Canada's national sport. The National Lacrosse Association, founded in 1867, and its slogan — "*Our* Country and *Our* Game" — certainly claimed that status. Lacrosse was also closely associated with the game of baggataway, which was played by several First Nations. On the very day of Canada's creation, Kahnawake took the Dominion lacrosse title — at the time, the

Senior baseball, Riverdale, Toronto, May 22, 1915. By the turn of the century, baseball had already become Canada's most popular summer sport.

City of Toronto Archives/Parks 52-515.

equivalent of world championship — by defeating the Montreal Lacrosse Club 3 to 2. The First Nations in eastern North America originated the sport, but non-Natives had altered the game by drawing up new "rules." Even so, the Kahnawake team defeated the Montreal team while playing under the non-Native rules.

Lacrosse had a sporadic history before 1914. After an enthusiastic beginning in the 1860s, it ebbed in the early 1870s as a result of the presence of "rowdy" or undesirable elements at many of the matches. The game revived in the 1880s but also changed from amateur to professional. This change could be seen in the shift from exhibition games, arranged occasionally, to systematized leagues that met and competed on a regular basis for spectators. The game also became a "national" sport, with teams located in urban centres across the country, although the sport lacked a national association until 1912.

Ice hockey had already become *the* Canadian sport by World War I. The first regulated game dates back to 1875 in Montreal, when two nine-man teams from the Montreal Football Club, looking for some winter training, confronted each other. Companies that sponsored the local "amateur" teams hired the first professional players, who were thus paid both to work and to play hockey. Already players earned more money from hockey than from their regular work. Many of the early teams were located in Canada's mining, lumbering, and farming towns, resulting in tough games and ferocious intercommunity rivalry. The sport caught on quickly. By 1880, the number of players per side had been reduced from nine to seven, and a standardized set of rules was also in place. Montreal held the "world championship" in 1883, in which the McGill University team was victorious.

A year later, in 1886, the Amateur Hockey Association of Canada, the first "national" association, was formed. Initially the association was made up of clubs from Montreal, Quebec City, and Ottawa only. Teams from these three cities dominated hockey between 1883 and 1893, the year Lord Stanley, governor general of Canada, donated the coveted Stanley Cup to the champion team, the Montreal Amateur

Association team. The Ottawa Hockey Club, usually referred to as simply "the Ottawas," and later known as "the Silver Seven," and finally renamed "the Senators," won many Stanley Cups. Between 1893 and 1914, three of the original teams won 19 of the 23 competitions.

A group of colleges, universities, and military and athletic clubs founded the Ontario Hockey Association in 1890. Similar associations sprang up in the Maritimes and the West. Montreal had more than 100 hockey clubs in 1895, and by 1905, hockey teams existed in just about every part of Canada. Even a few women's teams existed, in the cities of Saint John, Montreal, Ottawa, Toronto, and Edmonton.

In 1909, the National Hockey Association, the forerunner of today's National Hockey League, launched its inaugural season with seven teams: three from Montreal, one of which was the new French-Canadian team, the Canadiens; and the others from Ottawa, Renfrew, Haileybury, and Cobalt. They employed professional players. By 1912, the three small-town teams had folded, victims of rising costs. The league now consisted of two teams from Montreal, two new ones from Toronto, and a team from both Ottawa and Quebec City. Also by 1912, the first artificial-ice rinks appeared, making playing conditions more stable and also allowing ice hockey to become a West Coast sport. A Pacific Coast Hockey Association formed, which, in 1917, affiliated with the National Hockey Association to create the National Hockey League (NHL).

In four major sports in Canada at the turn of the century — football, baseball, lacrosse, and ice hockey — professionalization had taken over by World War I. Good players could make a living from sports alone because there now existed a group of people, mostly middle class, willing and able to support spectator sports. From this point onward, money and victory overrode gentlemanly conduct and pleasure as the objectives of sports. Sports had become a business. Even the newest sport, basketball, invented only in 1891 by James Naismith, a Canadian physical education instructor at the School of Christian Workers in Springfield, Massachusetts, later became professionalized. These team sports also reflected the dominant cultural values of a competitive urban and industrial society.

NED HANLAN AND ROWING

Toronto's first sport hero, Edward "Ned" Hanlan, "the Boy in Blue," contributed to the professionalization of sports. Known for his long, smooth strokes and sharp clean "catch," he proved to be the best sculler in Ontario in a series of races between 1873 and 1876. His flamboyant personality and good looks made him a popular figure in the newspapers across Canada in the late nineteenth century. He dominated the professional rowing world from 1877 to 1884, winning the Canadian Championship on Toronto Bay in 1877, the Championship of America on the Allegheny River in 1878, the Championship of England on the Tyne River in 1879 (beating the English champions by an astonishing eleven lengths), and ultimately the Championship of the World against Australia's E.A. Trickett in 1880. He continued to row into the 1890s, winning more than 300 races. Crowds greeted him everywhere he went in Canada, and his supporters waited at the telegraph offices to hear reports of his races. A foreign diplomat once said of Canada's first world champion, "His victories have done more than all the advertising and emigration agents combined to make known the position and power of the Dominion of Canada."

MIDDLE-CLASS CULTURE

At the turn of the century, the middle class had more time and money for leisure. Middle-class male leisure activity often crossed class lines to incorporate working-class men as well. What united them was male bonding more than class affiliation. Such willingness to cross class lines was less frequent among women; middle-class women had their own separate and acceptable social organizations, including the church, which they deemed "respectable." They would have nothing to do with working-class associations, including the Salvation Army (which they considered to be working-class religion) or roller-skating rinks, or dance halls. Yet these places gave working-class women a sense of identity and a great deal of enjoyment.

In the larger urban centres, leisure activities arose such as roller-skating rinks, dance halls, amusement parks and theatres, and fairs. The most popular in the Victorian era was the Toronto Industrial Exhibition, the forerunner of the Canadian National Exhibition. Founded in 1879, it entertained a broad segment of the populace of Toronto and its surrounding towns in the last few weeks of summer. Keith Walden points out that in entertaining, the exhibition also educated by helping to "shape understanding in a society being altered profoundly by industrial capitalist production, technological developments, and new ideas and values, including consumerism."[4] Industrial fairs expressed the perspective of the dominant or hegemonic groups in society, usually the industrial and mercantile members of the rising middle class. These fairs and exhibitions in the larger urban centres provided "respectable" leisure to the rising middle class.

WORKING-CLASS CULTURE

A working-class culture fully emerged in both English-speaking and French-speaking Canada in the late nineteenth century. It took shape through a proliferation of associations, societies, clubs, and lodges that had formed earlier but took on a new importance as they replaced institutions of self-help (mechanics' institutes) and community protection (finance companies). They provided a meeting place where male workers (female workers could not belong) of common background and interest could meet and enjoy each other's company. Taverns served the same purpose in larger urban centres. "Joe Beef's Canteen," established in Montreal in the 1860s by Charles McKiernan, an Irish Protestant ex-soldier, was one such place. Because of its rowdy atmosphere, the canteen was the target of reform zealots. But for casual labourers, the unemployed, and transients it provided a haven from the harsh realities of daily life in the slums and factories. Joe Beef's Canteen offered its working-class clientele food, drink, and accommodation — a blanket and access to a tub, a barber, "medical" advice, and "cures" — all for ten cents.

By the 1880s, larger working-class associations such as the Knights of Labor (KOL) assumed the role that Joe Beef's Canteen and other similar establishments, such as Dan Black's Tavern in Hamilton, had played. Through the American-based organization's ritualistic procedure of secret pledges, obedience, and committed charity, working men and women formed a common bond and a sense of pride. Festivals, dinners, picnics, and workers' balls provided social gatherings to "cement the bonds of unity." Until the Knights' decline in the 1890s, workers held labour parades and

Residents of Nelson, British Columbia, celebrated Dominion Day in 1898 with a horse race down the town's main street.

British Columbia Archives/HP-6225.

demonstrations, often drawing thousands to such events from both towns and cities, thus providing visual reminders of labour's strength and solidarity.

The many working-class societies, clubs, lodges, and associations of the pre–World War I era, the taverns like Joe Beef's in Montreal, and the Knights of Labor helped to build a working-class culture.

NATIVE CULTURE

Although many English and French Canadians in the late nineteenth century had a sentimental regard for the Native peoples, it did not extend to a belief that First Nations had a right to keep their ancestral cultures and religions. When, for example, John A. Macdonald proposed the creation of a separate Department of Indian Affairs in 1880, he said: "We must remember that they are the original owners of the soil, of which they have been dispossessed by the covetousness or ambition of our ancestors. Perhaps, if Columbus had not discovered this continent — had left them alone — they would have worked out a tolerable civilization of their own." Yet, in the same speech, Macdonald justified the need for a Department of Indian Affairs "to advance the interests of the Indians, civilizing them and putting them in the condition of white men."

These views were in keeping with the age. Canadians, like the rest of the western world, believed that the Aboriginal peoples were inferior and therefore had

The Six Nations Council, around 1910. After Sir John A. Macdonald gave his speech to the Council on the value of becoming citizens, it was translated into Mohawk. A council speaker then replied that they need not become Canadian citizens because they already constituted a sovereign nation with their own political institutions.

Department of Indian Affairs and Northern Development Collection/National Archives of Canada/C-33643.

to be assimilated into the "superior" Western European culture. Edward Blake, former premier of Ontario and federal leader of the Liberal party prior to Wilfrid Laurier, described the Native peoples in 1888 as "an inferior race, and in an inferior state of civilization." This perspective made it possible to suppress any aspect of Native culture that might get in the way of achieving assimilation. Thus, while English and French Canadians at the turn of the century concerned themselves with cultivating their own cultural traditions, they failed to have the same regard and concern for the Native peoples.

Yet, with a peculiar twist of irony, as Canadians believed that the Native population was about to disappear, they became more fascinated with this "quaint" and disappearing "race." They wanted to include Native ceremonies and customs in their country fairs and stampedes. This worked against the federal government's policy of assimilation, and not surprisingly, the government undermined such popularizing of traditional Native customs and ceremonies. Thus when organizers of the Dominion Exhibition, the forerunner of the Calgary Stampede, invited a number of First Nations people to participate, Frank Pedley, the deputy superintendent-general of Indian affairs, appealed to the minister of agriculture not to give any financial support to the exhibition unless the organizers cancelled the "Indian performance." Unfortunately, for Pedley, he was too late, as the contribution had already been made.

Also to emerge by the turn of the century were cultural traditions of other ethnic groups, as they came in large numbers and brought their customs, ceremonies, and special festivities with them. While many of these customs were frowned upon by the host society, this did not prevent newly arrived ethnic groups from enjoying their own customs in the confines of their communities.

In the years 1867 to 1914, Canadian culture proved to be a delicate but persistent enterprise. Most cultural endeavours began as amateur and local and only slowly evolved into being professional and national. By 1914, both English and French Canada had brought forth a small number of their internationally renowned musicians, visual artists, actors, writers, and sports figures.

NOTES

1. Dennis Reid, "Lucius Richard O'Brien," *Dictionary of Canadian Biography*, vol. 12, *1891–1900* (Toronto: University of Toronto Press, 1990), p. 793.
2. R. Louis Gentilcore et al., eds., *Historical Atlas of Canada*, vol. 2 (Toronto: University of Toronto Press, 1993), p. 133.
3. Murray D. Edwards, *A Stage in Our Past: English-Language Theatre in Eastern Canada from the 1790s to 1914* (Toronto: University of Toronto Press, 1968), p. 28.
4. Keith Walden, *Becoming Modern in Toronto: The Industrial Exhibition and the Shaping of a Late Victorian Culture* (Toronto: University of Toronto Press, 1997), p. xi.

LINKING TO THE PAST

WEB LINKS

The National Anthem of Canada
http://canada.gc.ca/canadiana/anthm_e.html#a3
A short history of Canada's national anthem, complete with sound clips, music sheets, bilingual lyrics, and biographies of the musicians and writers who helped create "O Canada."

The National Gallery of Canada
http://national.gallery.ca/english/art/index.html
The National Gallery of Canada showcases a variety of Canadian art that can be accessed through the collections, exhibitions, or a virtual tour of the gallery.

Selected Poetry of Bliss Carman (1861–1929)
http://www.library.utoronto.ca/utel/rp/authors/carman.html
This site, from the University of Toronto, offers selections from the poetry of Bliss Carman, one of the "Confederation poets," as well as a link to works by Archibald Lampman, another Confederation poet.

A History of Lacrosse in Canada
http://www.bclacrosse.com/info/historyoflaxinCanada.html
A detailed look at the historical development of lacrosse, which is considered to be Canada's national sport.

A Portrait of Edward Hanlan
http://www.schoolnet.ca/collections/portraits/docs/men/ec025318.htm
A photograph and short biography of Edward "Ned" Hanlan, one of Canada's first sports heroes.

RELATED READINGS

In R. Douglas Francis and Donald B. Smith, eds., *Readings in Canadian History: Post-Confederation*, 5th ed. (Toronto: Harcourt Brace, 1998), the following articles relate to material covered in this chapter: Peter DeLottinville, "Joe Beef of Montreal: Working-Class Culture and the Tavern, 1869–1889," pp. 206–29; and Karen Dubinsky, "'The Pleasure Is Exquisite but Violent': The Imaginary Geography of Niagara Falls in the Nineteenth Century," pp. 251–72.

BIBLIOGRAPHY

A synthesis of the arts in Canada has yet to be written. For an overview consult Maria Tippett's *Making Culture: English-Canadian Institutions and the Arts Before the Massey Commission* (Toronto: University of Toronto Press, 1990). For the Laurier era see, as well, Robert J. Lamb, *The Arts in Canada during the Age of Laurier: Papers from a Conference held at the Edmonton Art Gallery* (Edmonton: University of Alberta Press, 1988). The *Dictionary of Canadian Biography*, vols. 9–14, has very good biographical sketches of some of the major cultural figures of this period. For a contemporary commentary on the cultural divisions of French-speaking and English-speaking Canadians at the turn of the century see André Siegfried, *The Race Question in Canada* (Toronto: McClelland & Stewart, 1966 [1907]). On the role of the Canadian Clubs in promoting culture consult Russell R. Merifield, *Speaking of Canada: The Centennial History of the Canadian Clubs* (Toronto: McClelland & Stewart, 1993).

Music is discussed in Helmut Kallmann, *A History of Music in Canada, 1534–1914* (Toronto: University of Toronto Press, 1960); and his edited *Encyclopedia of Music in Canada*, 2nd ed. (Toronto: University of Toronto Press, 1992); Timothy J. McGee's *The Music of Canada* (New York: W.W. Norton, 1985); and, for the early twentieth century, George A. Proctor, *Canadian Music of the Twentieth Century: An Introduction* (Toronto: University of Toronto Press, 1980). For Quebec see, as well, Annette Lasalle-Leduc's *Music in French Canada* (Quebec: Ministry of Cultural Affairs, 1967).

On the history of painting consult J. Russell Harper, *Painting in Canada: A History*, 2nd ed. (Toronto: University of Toronto Press, 1966); and Dennis Reid, *A Concise History of Canadian Painting*, 2nd ed. (Toronto: Oxford University Press, 1988). On landscape painting in the late nineteenth century see Dennis Reid, *"Our Own Country Canada": Being an Account of the National Aspirations of the Principal Landscape Artists in Montreal and Toronto, 1860–1890* (Ottawa: National Gallery of Canada, 1980). For Quebec see, as well, Guy Viau, *Modern Painting in French Canada* (Quebec: Department of Cultural Affairs, 1967). David Karel's *Horatio Walker* (Québec: Musée du Québec, 1987) looks at the life and paintings of this artist. For a review of photography see Roger Hall, Gordon Dobbs, and Stanley Triggs, *The World of William Notman: The Nineteenth Century Through a Master Lens* (Toronto: McClelland & Stewart, 1993). For architecture consult Harold Kalman, *A History of Canadian Architecture* (Toronto: Oxford University Press, 1994).

Literary history is well documented in Carl F. Klinck, ed., *Literary History of Canada*, 2nd ed. (Toronto: University of Toronto Press, 1976); and Eugene Benson and William Toye, eds., *The Oxford Companion to Canadian Literature* 2nd ed., (Toronto: Oxford University Press, 1997). For Quebec see Guy Sylvestre, *Literature in French Canada* (Quebec: Department of Cultural Affairs, 1967). Two biographies of Sara Jeannette Duncan are available: Misao Dean, *A Different Point of View: Sara Jeannette Duncan* (Montreal/Kingston: McGill-Queen's University Press, 1991); and Marian Fowler, *Redney: A Life of Sara Jeannette*

Duncan (Toronto: Anansi, 1983). The life of Father Chiniquy is told by Marcel Trudel in *Chiniquy* (Trois-Rivières: Editions du Bien Public, 1955).

For the history of Canadian theatre in English-speaking Canada see Murray D. Edwards, *A Stage in Our Past: English-Language Theatre in Eastern Canada from the 1790s to 1914* (Toronto: University of Toronto Press, 1968); and Eugene Benson and L.W. Conolly, eds., *The Oxford Companion to Canadian Theatre* (Toronto: Oxford University Press, 1989). For Quebec see Elaine F. Nardocchio, *Theatre and Politics in Modern Québec* (Edmonton: University of Alberta Press, 1986); and Jean Hamelin, *The Theatre in French Canada* (Quebec: Department of Cultural Affairs, 1967). On the colourful performances of Sarah Bernhardt see Ramon Hathorn's lecture to Canada House in London, *Sarah Bernhardt's Canadian Visits* (Leeds: University of Leeds for Canada House, 1992).

Canadian folklore is discussed in Edith Fowke, *Folklore of Canada* (Toronto: McClelland & Stewart, 1990), her *Canadian Folklore* (Toronto: Oxford University Press, 1988), and Paul Rutherford's *A Victorian Authority: The Daily Press in Late Nineteenth-Century Canada* (Toronto: University of Toronto Press, 1982).

For sports in Canada see Alan Metcalfe, *Canada Learns to Play: The Emergence of Organized Sports, 1807–1914* (Toronto: McClelland & Stewart, 1987); and Donald Morrow et al., *A Concise History of Sports in Canada* (Toronto: Oxford University Press, 1989). See, as well, the relevant essays in Morris Mott, ed., *Sports in Canada: Historical Readings* (Mississauga, ON: Copp Clark Pitman, 1989); On hockey see William Houston, *Pride and Glory: 100 Years of the Stanley Cup* (Toronto: McGraw-Hill Ryerson, 1992); and Dan Diamond, ed., *The Official National Hockey League 75th Anniversary Commemorative Book* (Toronto: Firefly Books, 1991).

For a discussion of an emerging middle-class culture in English-speaking Canada see Lynne Marks, *Revivals and Roller Rinks: Religion, Leisure, and Identity in Late Nineteenth Century Small-Town Ontario* (Toronto: University of Toronto Press, 1996); and Keith Walden, *Becoming Modern in Toronto: The Industrial Exhibition and the Shaping of a Late Victorian Culture* (Toronto: University of Toronto Press, 1997).

On working-class culture the best source is Bryan Palmer, *Working-Class Experience: The Rise and Reconstitution of Canadian Labour 1880–1991*, 2nd ed. (Toronto: Butterworths, 1993). An insightful article on taverns and working-class culture is Peter de Lottinville, "Joe Beef of Montreal: Working-Class Culture and the Tavern, 1869–1889," reprinted in R. Douglas Francis and Donald B. Smith, eds., *Readings in Canadian History: Post-Confederation*, 5th ed. (Toronto: Harcourt Brace, 1998), pp. 206–29.

Among the best studies of the impact of the dominant society on the Amerindians are Katherine Pettipas, *Severing the Ties That Bind: Government Repression of Indigenous Religious Ceremonies on the Prairies* (Winnipeg: University of Manitoba Press, 1994); Brian E. Titley, *A Narrow Vision: Duncan Campbell Scott and the Administration of Indian Affairs in Canada* (Vancouver: University of British Columbia Press, 1986); and Edward Ahenakew, *Voices of the Plains Cree* (Toronto: McClelland & Stewart, 1973). For an overview, see Olive P. Dickason, *Canada's First Nations: A History of Founding Peoples from Earliest Times* (Toronto: McClelland & Stewart, 1992); and Arthur J. Ray, *I Have Lived Here Since the World Began* (Toronto: Key Porter, 1996).

PART THREE

The Impact of Two World Wars and the Great Depression, 1914–1945

Time Line: 1914–1945

1914 ~ Canadian participation in World War I begins
~ Parliament passes War Measures Act

1915 ~ Battle at Ypres Salient

1916 ~ Battle of the Somme
~ "Bilingual" schools abolished in Manitoba

1917 ~ Establishment of Canadian National Railways (CNR)
~ Battle of Vimy Ridge
~ Military Service Act (the conscription bill) becomes law
~ Election of Union government under Robert Borden

1918 ~ Armistice signed
~ Outbreak of Spanish flu epidemic
~ All women over the age of 21 (with the exception of status Indians)
gain the right to vote in federal elections

1919 ~ Winnipeg General Strike
~ Canada joins the League of Nations
~ Death of Sir Wilfrid Laurier

1920 ~ Founding of the Group of Seven as an organization of modern artists

1921 ~ Agnes Macphail becomes the first woman elected in a federal election
~ Liberals come to power under William Lyon Mackenzie King
~ Founding of the Progressive movement/party

1922 ~ Founding of the New Symphony Orchestra in Toronto
(now the Toronto Symphony)
~ Insulin made available for the first time for the treatment of diabetes

1923 ~ Halibut Treaty with the United States signed by Canada, not Britain

1925 ~ The United Church of Canada established

1926 ~ Balfour Declaration recognizes the dominions, including Canada, as
autonomous nations in the British Commonwealth of Nations

1927 ~ Emily Carr's work included in an exhibition of West Coast art in Ottawa

1928 ~ Percy Williams wins two gold medals at the Amsterdam Olympics,
making him "the world's fastest runner"

1929 ~ Persons Case recognizes women in Canada as "persons" for legal purposes
~ Stock-market crash and the beginning of the Great Depression

1930 ~ Conservatives under R.B. Bennett elected to office
1931 ~ Statute of Westminster recognizes Canadian independence from Britain
~ Completion of Maple Leaf Gardens in Toronto
1932 ~ Founding of the Co-operative Commonwealth Federation (CCF) party at Calgary
1934 ~ Birth of Dionne quintuplets, the world's first surviving quintuplets, near Callander, Ontario
1935 ~ On-to-Ottawa Trek by unemployed workers; rioting breaks out in Regina
~ Bank of Canada begins operations
~ R.B. Bennett's "New Deal" introduced, but Bennett defeated by Mackenzie King and the Liberals in the general election
1936 ~ Founding of the Canadian Broadcasting Corporation (CBC)
~ Maurice Duplessis and the Union Nationale come to power in Quebec
1937 ~ General Motors Strike in Oshawa
~ Founding of Trans-Canada Air Lines (forerunner of Air Canada)
~ Establishment of the Royal Commission on Dominion–Provincial Relations
1938 ~ Philippe Panneton (Ringuet) completes *Trente Arpents*, translated into English as *Thirty Acres*
1939 ~ King George VI and Queen Elizabeth receive an enthusiastic welcome on their Canadian tour
~ Canada declares war on Germany; beginning of World War II
1940 ~ Signing of Ogdensburg Agreement establishing the Permanent Joint Board on Defence between Canada and the United States
~ Unemployment insurance scheme begun by the federal government
1941 ~ Canadian Women's Army Corps established
1942 ~ Beginning of the expulsion of the Japanese from Canada's Pacific coast
~ Conscription plebiscite held
1943 ~ Canadian servicemen serve in the Italian campaign
1944 ~ Family Allowance Act, Canada's first universal social-welfare program, comes into effect
~ The CCF in Saskatchewan forms the first socialist government in North America
~ Canadian participation in the Normandy invasion
1945 ~ Armistice signed, ending World War II
~ Canada joins the United Nations
~ Hugh MacLennan publishes his novel *Two Solitudes*

Introduction

Like two bookends on a shelf, two world wars enclose the years 1914–1945. The international events of war, economic growth in the 1920s, and depression in the 1930s affected Canada in profound ways. In this 31-year period, Canada became part of the global community.

The country felt the impact of the wars in significant ways. In human terms, Canada sent over 600 000 men out of a population of only 8 million to fight in World War I, and nearly 1 million out of 11.5 million in World War II. Canadian soldiers, sailors, and pilots distinguished themselves in battle, thus contributing greatly to the Allied cause, and advanced Canada's national recognition abroad. But at great cost. Over 60 000 — one tenth of the total number of Canada's soldiers — died in World War I; some 40 000 died in World War II. An even greater number returned home maimed in body and in mind.

World War I transformed the country in other ways. Energy was directed principally toward the production of war-related materials. Since insufficient numbers of men were available to work in the factories and munitions plants, more women were called upon to work outside the home. This did not, however, result in gender equality in the workplace, although it did contribute to women getting the franchise. Women continued to face wage discrimination and were the first to be let go when the economy lagged. War also had a political impact. The state intervened in the lives of Canadian citizens to a greater extent than ever before, regulating and restricting what people could buy; dictating wages and working conditions; introducing new forms of revenue, such as the income tax and the sale of victory bonds; and reallocating resources to maximize war production. Government also took responsibility for the enlistment, equipping, and training of troops. In 1917, the Borden government created a Union party made up of Conservatives and many English-Canadian Liberals as a united war effort. It implemented military conscription. Conscription divided English-speaking and French-speaking Canadians to an unprecedented degree and left a legacy of bitterness that endured long after the war was over.

In the 1920s, economic prosperity eventually returned. A new economy of pulp and paper, mineral production, and the manufacturing of consumer goods replaced the old wheat economy. But the age-old regional, cultural, ethnic, gender, and class divisions remained. Politically, the two traditional parties survived the war, but a new third party, the Progressive party, challenged them. A new political tradition of federal multi-party rule began. Internationally, Canada took control over its foreign relations and achieved independent status.

The Great Depression of the 1930s affected the country profoundly. It occurred at the same time as severe climatic conditions in the Canadian West, making this one of the hardest-hit regions of the country. New political parties, and new radical left- and right-wing movements, emerged, desperate to find a solution to the economic crisis.

World War II might have ended the depression, but it plunged the country into something even more horrific. Although the King government was reluctant to get involved in the war on a major scale, it had no alternative as Hitler's army swept through western Europe. Once again, women were called upon to work outside the home for the war effort. This time they experienced greater gender equality than they did during World War I, but not without a struggle. The war raised the issue of Dominion–provincial relations and of Canada's relationship to Britain and the United States. The King government appointed the Royal Commission on Dominion–Provincial Relations in an attempt to find a solution to the tension between the two levels of government. Internationally, the signing of the Ogdensburg Agreement with the United States in August 1940 saw Canada agree to join in Canadian–American defence of North America. This proved to be the turning point from an era of British alliance to American protection.

The Canada that emerged from World War II in 1945 was as different from the Canada that entered World War I as that of pre-1914 Canada was from the Canada of 1867. While changes had occurred in all areas, perhaps the most significant change domestically occurred in the area of the interventionist state, while internationally the closer military and economic ties with the United States had a profound impact on Canada's foreign policy.

CHAPTER TEN

Canada in the Great War

World War I marked a turning point in Canadian development. Between 1914 and 1918, Canada sent 625 000 men and several thousand women to war — an enormous contribution for a nation of only 8 million people. One in ten of those who fought on the battlefields of Europe died in the service of their country; an even greater number were wounded in the deadly trench warfare. During the war, the government intervened in the affairs of the state to an unprecedented degree, establishing such institutions as the Canadian National Railways, the Canadian Wheat Board, and a federal income tax. The war also initially united, and then divided, Canadians. Conscription set English-speaking against French-speaking Canadians. Workers and capitalists quarrelled bitterly over who contributed the most to the war effort. Social reformers, particularly women suffragists and prohibitionists, used this "war to end wars" to advance their causes. By the war's end, English Canadians sought to gain full control over the Dominion's military and foreign affairs.

CANADA JOINS THE WAR EFFORT

The murder of Archduke Ferdinand, heir to the Austro–Hungarian throne, by a young Serbian nationalist in June 1914 began a chain of events that led to World War I. The European powers' intricate network of alliances and agreements forced them into war. Austria attacked Serbia, an ally of Russia. Germany backed Austria, while France came to the defence of Russia. Britain, the ally of France — which in turn was allied to Russia — had promised to defend Belgium's neutrality. When Germany invaded Belgium, Britain declared war. As a member of the British empire, Canada was automatically at war.

Initially, Canadians united behind the war effort. When Borden summoned Parliament for a special war session on August 18, he told a cheering House of Commons: "As to our duty, we are all agreed, we stand shoulder to shoulder with Britain and the other British Dominions in this quarrel." Throughout the country loyal demonstrations occurred, involving impromptu parades, flag waving, and, in the streets of Montreal, the singing of "La Marseillaise" and "Rule Britannia." Even the anti-imperialist Henri Bourassa initially supported Canadian participation, seeing the survival of France and Britain as vital to Canada. Most English-speaking Canadians viewed the war in black-and-white terms: good versus evil; democracy versus tyranny; the Anglo-Saxons versus the "Huns." Many believed that the Allies would achieve a quick victory — by Christmas.

Canada prepared for war. Unanimously Parliament passed the War Measures Act in 1914, which gave the cabinet the right to suspend the civil liberties of anyone suspected of collaborating with the enemy and to regulate any area of society deemed essential for the conduct of the war. Under the act, Ottawa required all those classified as "enemy aliens" — mostly German and Austro–Hungarian immigrants — to report once a month to the local police or to the Royal North-West Mounted Police. Ottawa interned those who were considered dangerous, as well as anyone who refused to register. It established 24 internment camps, from Halifax to Nanaimo. In very basic camps, such as the one at Castle Mountain in Banff National Park, the internees worked for 25 cents a day. The imprisoned labourers, mainly Ukrainians, helped to build roads, paths, and the Banff golf course. Despite notification from the British Foreign Office in January 1915 that Ukrainians from Galicia (the area of Ukraine under Austro–Hungarian rule) should be given preferential treatment as "friendly aliens," the internment of Ukrainians and some other eastern Europeans continued.

Among those seized in Halifax was a Russian revolutionary who had been taken off a Norwegian ship travelling from New York. After his release, Leon Trotsky joined V.I. Lenin in Petrograd, Russia, to lead the Bolshevik Revolution. During his one-month detainment at Amherst, Nova Scotia, in April 1917, he preached revolution to the 800 internees there. During the war, the Canadian government imprisoned about 8000 individuals. In 1918, a further order in council forbade the printing, publishing, or possession of any publication in an enemy language without a licence from the secretary of state.

THE CANADIAN EXPEDITIONARY FORCE

WEB LINKS

Canada's permanent army in July 1914 numbered only 3000, with an additional 60 000 men in the militia, but their military training was very limited, consisting possibly of one or two nights at the local armoury supplemented by an annual seven- or ten-day training period at summer camp. Its navy consisted of two old British cruisers, the *Nicobe* and the *Rainbow*. As a result of Canadian participation in the South African War, the country had a number of trained officers with actual experience on the battlefield. Cadet training had also been implemented in schools and some universities in most provinces. Sam Hughes, who was of Orange Irish descent, had been a "volunteer" since the age of 12, and had fought in the South African War, was the minister of militia in Robert Borden's government. He had also worked in his own determined way to build up the Canadian militia between 1911 and 1913, much to the consternation of the prime minister. But such preparation had been academic; no one seriously expected war to break out.

At first, tens of thousands of young men answered the call for volunteers. Some came forward convinced of the righteousness of the Allied cause; others looked for adventure, and others for a job during a time of economic depression. Within two months, 30 000 Canadian volunteers were trained at Valcartier, a military camp 25 km

Internees at a prisoner-of-war camp (location unknown), Christmas 1916. By the war's end, the federal government had interned some 8000 individuals in 24 internment camps established across Canada.

Internment Camps Collection/National Archives of Canada/C-14104.

northwest of Quebec City, where they were placed into numbered battalions of about 1000 men, assigned officers, formed into brigades, and then sent overseas as divisions within the Canadian Expeditionary Force. Pleased by the enlistment results and anticipating a short war, Prime Minister Borden promised never to implement conscription.

The First Canadian Expeditionary Force of some 36 000 sailed for England on October 3, 1914, the largest convoy ever to cross the Atlantic until that time. More than 60 percent of the troops, known as "Hughes's Boys" after Sam Hughes, were recent British immigrants, mostly unmarried, frequently unemployed, and emotionally close to Britain. Native-born Canadians of British stock made up 25 percent of the soldiers. The remainder included French Canadians, non-British immigrants, and Native Canadians.

Initially, federal recruiting agents discouraged Canada's "visible" minorities from enlisting, believing them incapable of being good soldiers. As well, "white" soldiers complained of having to fight beside "coloured" men. Nevertheless, a group of some 220 Japanese Canadians signed up and drilled at their own expense, as did over 1000 African Canadians, who made up the entire Number 2 Construction Battalion (CEF). It was formed in Truro, Nova Scotia, where the majority of the 700 who enlisted lived, although it was open to African Canadians from across the country. They went overseas in March 1917 and were stationed in southern France as part of the Canadian Forestry Corps. By the war's end, some 4000 First Nations people had enlisted, a major contribution for a population of only 100 000. Nearly half of the volunteers in the initial Canadian Corps came from the western provinces, another third from Ontario, and the remainder from the Maritimes and Quebec. Individual cities such as Toronto, Montreal, and Winnipeg formed whole battalions from their recruits.

Canadian troops trained on Salisbury Plain in southern England. That first winter of the war was the wettest in years — over a 75-day period, only five days were dry. Heavy mists and occasional snow curtailed training. The troops' inadequate army clothing contributed to illness and poor morale. Then, in February 1915, the 1st Canadian Division, as it became known, joined the British army under the command

A group of soldiers, many of them Ontario Native people, before going overseas in World War I. Photo taken in the North Bay area.

Archives of Ontario/
Acc. 9164 S15159.

of Lieutenant General E.A.H. Alderson for action in Flanders, in northwestern Belgium and adjacent France.

As late as February, many Canadians, including many of English Canada's most respected opinion makers, still regarded the war romantically. In an address on February 23, Maurice Hutton, principal of University College at the University of Toronto, saluted the students and faculty who were going off to fight in France. In his mellifluous Oxford accent he promised, "You will not regret it. When you return your romance will not vanish with your youth. You will have fought in the great war, you will have joined in the liberation of the world." Those already in the killing fields of Flanders knew the Great War's true character.

By the end of October 1914, deadlock had developed on the Western Front. Neither side could make a breakthrough. The two opposing sides faced each other, across a narrow "No Man's Land," in deep trenches stretching from Switzerland to the North Sea. Four years of trench warfare began, all in an area no bigger than southern Ontario.

On the Western Front, all soldiers faced the same intolerable conditions: mud, vermin, rotten food, and the stench of rotting flesh. The soldiers spent hours digging trenches, tunnels, dugouts, and underground shelters, only to have them washed away by the rain and mud or abandoned in haste. Then there was the noise. As Canadian military historian John Swettenham has written, "It has been likened to an infernal orchestra made up of ear-splitting crashes from heavy artillery, the deeper roar of mined charges, the flailing crack of field pieces, the higher-pitched note of rifles, the ghastly staccato rattle of machine-guns, the shriek and wail of shells, and the insect zip and whine of bullets, but no words can ever describe it adequately."[1]

This was a war of attrition, one designed to kill as many of the enemy as possible. The fundamental concept of war remained Napoleonic. Like Napoleon, the belligerent parties tried to destroy the main enemy army. They made no attempt to hit a tactical point, and in fact *blitzkreig* tactics would only develop in the last months of the war.

Amid these horrors came something worse — chemical warfare. The Germans first used chlorine gas, a greenish substance that caused coughing, choking, and

A Historical Portrait

"PRIVATE FRASER"

"I do make Oath that I will be faithful and bear true Allegiance to His Majesty George the Fifth, His Heirs and Successors, and that I will as in duty bound honestly and faithfully defend His Majesty, His Heirs and Successors, in Person, Crown and Dignity, against all enemies, and will observe and obey all orders of His Majesty, His Heirs and Successors, and of all the Generals and officers set over me. So help me God." With those words — repeated in every recruiting station by hundreds of thousands of Canadian volunteers — Donald Fraser, on November 14, 1914, enlisted in the 31st (Alberta) Battalion, Canadian Expeditionary Force. Aged 32, Private Fraser was older than most men in his battalion, but he shared with the majority a common background: they were British immigrants.

Fraser never explained why he decided to enlist. Although well educated in Scotland, he had drifted from job to job since coming to Canada in 1906, first as a farm labourer in Manitoba, then as a bank clerk in Calgary, and finally, on the eve of the war, as a clerk with a Vancouver trust company. He chose to return to Calgary to enlist, possibly because his friends were also enlisting and persuading him to do so. There is no evidence that Fraser had any previous military experience; in this respect, too, he was typical.

Fraser's battalion was equipped, put through elementary military drill and discipline, and sent overseas to England in mid-May 1915. After four more months of "drills and manoeuvres, trench digging . . . courses of special instruction in bayonet fighting, grenade throwing, machine-gunnery, musketry, signalling and map reading," they left on September 16 for France. By the end of the month they huddled in the trenches, "small, damp and cold and overrun with rats." Later he describes the mud: "For want of sunshine and wind, it is impossible for the ground to dry up and after a while we learn that it is useless trying to keep the trenches passable. The rain loosens the earth and the sides cave in. With additional rain the bottom of the trenches become liquid mud which defies all efforts at drainage."

Years later Fraser recalled one close scrape with death. He and four comrades were talking during an enemy shelling. Then,

> a report that sounded like a premature or a short made us bolt out of the way. . . . I rounded the end of the wall and threw myself flat behind it on the side nearest the line. At that moment the shell burst with a tremendous explosion on the other side of the sandbag wall where I was standing a second ago and not more than a yard away from where I lay. The report of the explosion dazed me and I was hit with all sorts of debris as they fell on me in their downward course. The concussion or whatever it is called created a terrific strain on the tissues. I felt as if I was being pulled apart, as if some unseen thing was tearing me asunder, particularly the top part of my body, and especially the head. I know I could not have stood a fraction more without bursting, the outward pull on the tissue was so immense.

Although wounded again at Passchendaele in late 1917, Fraser was one of the lucky ones: he survived, recovered by and large, and received his honourable discharge. Of the 4500 officers and men from Private Fraser's battalion who served in World War I, nearly 1000 were killed.

(continued)

In Calgary in 1919, he married Caroline Mackintosh, a young woman he had known in Scotland, and they had a family. Years later, in the early 1980s, his daughter recalled a comment of her mother's: "He [Donald] lost quite a bit of his strength and vigour, and thus led a quieter life than he ordinarily would have. Also, he was unable to travel any great distance without feeling unwell." Her father died in 1946. Canadian military historian Reginald Roy edited his war diary, *The Journal of Private Fraser, 1914–1918* (Victoria: Sono Nis Press), which was published in 1985. In his preface, Roy describes it as "one of the most vivid personal descriptions of trench life by a Canadian soldier I have ever read."

burning eyes and skin, on April 22, 1915, at the Battle of Ypres. One Canadian officer described it vividly: "A great wall of green gas about 15 or 20 feet high was on top of us. Captain McLaren gave an order to get handkerchiefs, soak them and tie them around our mouths and noses." A British soldier later recalled what he saw when he and his contingent arrived to relieve the Canadians: "We stopped at a ditch at a first-aid clearing station. There were about 200 to 300 men lying in that ditch. Some were clawing their throats. Their brass buttons were green. Their bodies were swelled. Some of them were still alive. Some were still writhing on the ground, their tongues hanging out." Half of the men in surgeon John McCrae's brigade were killed or wounded. While waiting on the rear step of an ambulance for the wounded to arrive, he wrote a poem. "In Flanders Fields" became the most popular poem of the Great War and made the poppy flower the enduring symbol of those who died.

At Ypres, the Canadians made their reputation by preventing a German break-through. But nearly 2000 Canadians lay dead, with another 3410 wounded and 775 taken prisoner, out of a total divisional fighting strength of 10 000. After Ypres, historian Daniel Dancocks explains, "there was no more bravado about an early victory over the Hun, no more fears of missing out on 'the fun.'"[2]

In 1915 and 1916, three more Canadian divisions joined the 1st Canadian Division in France. Lieutenant General Sir Julian Byng, a British regular officer, replaced Alderson as commander of the Canadian Corps. There was also a change of equipment. The Canadian-built Ross rifle, insisted upon by Sam Hughes, jammed in trench warfare. "The least thing would jam it," one soldier wrote, " — a speck of dust, a shower of rain, even a burst of rapid fire. Very often there was difficulty in loading. The Ross Rifle was a standing joke amongst the Imperial troops." In the spring of 1916, the Canadian cabinet overruled Hughes and officially replaced the Ross rifle with the better-built British Lee-Enfield.

The Ross rifle affair highlighted the incompetence of Sam Hughes as minister of militia and defence. He had lost friends in high places. The governor general, the Duke of Connaught, once privately described the controversial and eccentric cabinet minister as a "conceited lunatic." Accused of corruption, of failure to attend to his departmental duties, and of incompetence in handling the administration of the war, Hughes saw his responsibilities reduced. J.W. Flavelle, general manager of the William Davies Packing Company, took over the Imperial Munitions Board, which was responsible for producing munitions in Canada for Britain. By 1917, the board over-saw 60 factories and a quarter of a million workers who produced $2 million a day

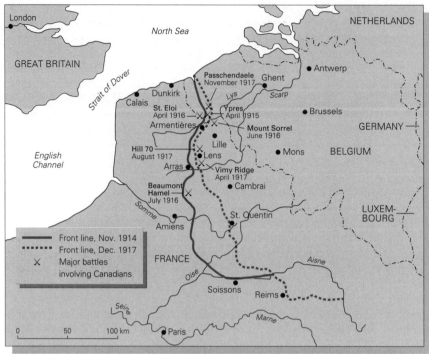

Canada at war, 1914–1917. Minimal advances were made between 1914 and 1917, despite seven major battles involving Canadians.

Source: Based on Elizabeth Abbott, ed., *Chronicle of Canada* (Montreal: Chronicle Publications, 1990), p. 579.

worth of shells, ships, fuses, and even airplanes. R.B. Bennett, a Calgary lawyer and Conservative member of Parliament, chaired the National Service Board, established in the fall of 1916 to increase recruiting. Sir George Perley, the high commissioner to Britain, took charge of the newly created Ministry of Overseas Military Forces to deal with the troops in Britain and at the war front. Finally, in November 1916, Borden sacked Sam Hughes.

THE INTERVENTIONIST STATE

The war forced Ottawa to intervene in Canada's economic, social, and military affairs to an unprecedented degree. Borden's reform of the civil service on the eve of the war helped make the transition easier. His government had implemented regulations that raised the requirements for entry into the civil service. As well, the government in 1912 had passed the Canadian Grain Act, which established the government-controlled Board of Grain Commissioners to supervise, inspect, and regulate grain sales. Thus, in 1917, when the Allied demands for Canadian wheat made it imperative for Canada to step up production and export, the government could intervene further. Through the newly created Board of Grain Supervisors (after 1919 the Canadian Wheat Board), the government regulated all aspects of the production and distribution of wheat. Hectarage in wheat doubled, and the price per bushel increased by more than 50 percent. But the result was that the West was seen only as a wheat-growing area, thus causing it to be overlooked for munition-manufacturing or any form of manufacturing or industrial production. Thus, while towns and cities in other regions, especially central Canada, boomed during the war, western cities barely scraped through and faced high unemployment. The government also regulated the production, distribution, sale, and consumption of coal, wood, and gas fuels. As military historian Desmond Morton notes, "Canadians learned to live with unprecedented government controls and involvement in their daily lives. Food and fuel shortages led to 'Meatless Fridays' and 'Fuelless Sundays.'"[3]

The government also nationalized the Canadian Northern and the Grand Trunk Pacific railways. Both tottered on the edge of bankruptcy by 1915, when a royal commission recommended government takeover to avoid a total collapse. Between 1917 and 1920, the Canadian government incorporated these railways into the publicly owned Canadian National Railways (CNR).

Naturally, such federal government intervention created resentment and accusations of favouritism. Western Canadians accused Flavelle's Imperial Munitions Board of favouring central Canadian firms over those from the West. Maritimers complained of military ships being built in Quebec rather than in Maritime ports. Workers resented the federal government's War Labour Policy, passed in 1918, that prohibited strikes and lockouts. Middle- and working-class Canadians resented the restrictions placed on them by enduring days without meat or fuel when they believed upper-class Canadians were not making the same sacrifices. Farmers and labourers demanded that wealth as well as manpower be conscripted for the war effort.

FINANCING THE WAR

At the outbreak of war, the government depended on revenue from the tariff and the sale of federal bonds to finance the war effort. But as imports declined and as New York replaced London as the main underwriter of Canadian bonds, the government had to look for more money to fund the war. It sold "Victory Bonds," which proved to be immensely popular — more than 1 million Canadians purchased the bonds by war's end, thus generating close to $2 million in revenue. The government also introduced another important innovation: direct taxation. First it imposed a business-profits tax; then, in 1917, it imposed its first federal income tax — 3 percent for a family earning more than $3000 or an individual earning more than $1500. Ottawa promised the new tax would remain only for the duration of the war. While new sources of revenue helped, costs continued to outdistance revenue, which forced the government to borrow vast sums at home and abroad, at high interest rates. The national debt increased fivefold, from $463 million in 1913 to $2.46 billion by 1918.

The increased cost of living hurt people on fixed incomes and cancelled the benefits workers received from increased wages. Workers joined trade unions in an effort to increase their bargaining power. The unions in turn staged strikes.

WOMEN AND THE WAR

Women made major contributions to the war effort. Twenty-five hundred women served as nursing sisters in the Canadian Army Medical Corps, working at station hospitals, on hospital ships, and on ambulance trains. Forty-six died in the service of Canada. Margaret Macdonald, director of the army nursing sisters, received the Royal Red Cross and the Florence Nightingale Medal for her effort.

Women also contributed through their work for voluntary organizations, including the Imperial Order Daughters of the Empire (IODE), Red Cross clubs, the Great Veterans' Association, the Next-of-Kin Association, the YWCA, and the Women's Patriotic Leagues. They rolled bandages and knitted socks, mitts, sweaters, and scarves for the troops; raised money to send cigarettes and candy overseas; and marshalled support for the cause, not least by persuading wives and mothers to allow their men to enlist. They headed the Canadian Patriotic Fund, established in 1914 to assist families of soldiers overseas. They lobbied for mothers' pensions, day nurseries, and health inspection. By 1918, the government established federal agencies, such as the Department of Soldiers' Civil Re-establishment, the Women's Bureau, and the Food Board, to assist them. In this way, the war contributed to a public social-welfare program.

Unmarried women entered the work force in large numbers, as did some married women, to ease the wartime labour shortage. On farms, in factories, and in offices, women filled positions previously occupied by men. In summertime, the YWCA recruited hundreds of female volunteers in the cities and towns to help on farms. The Women's Canadian Club organized a Women's Emergency Corps to recruit women for the munitions-production industries. In its first year of operation, more than 35 000 Ontario and Quebec women signed up.

In wartime industries, however, discrimination remained: lower wages for women, lack of union support, and inadequate day-care facilities. Still, tens of thousands of women filled jobs previously closed to them, even in such male-dominated industries as railways and steel production. A number of women used their new bargaining position to raise social issues such as women's suffrage, child labour, and conditions in jails and asylums.

FIGHTING AT THE FRONT

Canadian soldiers became prized assault troops on the Western Front. In June 1916, they contributed to the battle of Mount Sorrel, in the Ypres Salient, a small triangular area around Ypres. Then, a month later, Canadian soldiers joined French and British soldiers in the massive but ill-conceived Battle of the Somme against heavily fortified German positions. Both sides together suffered over 1 million casualties. Canada's greatest contribution, however, came in the spring of 1917. On Monday, April 9, some 70 000 Canadian soldiers, under the command of Julian Byng, along with British units, made a major attack against the German-held Vimy Ridge. Earlier in the war, both the British and French armies, with heavy losses, had failed to dislodge the Germans. This time, the Canadians took it.

A Paris newspaper described Vimy as "Canada's Easter gift to France." In an editorial headlined "Well Done Canada," the New York *Tribune* wrote that "every

Mud-spattered Canadians return from the trenches, November 1916, Battle of the Somme. During the battle, some 24 000 Canadians and Newfoundlanders died in action, and countless others were maimed.

....

W.I. Castle/National Archives of Canada/PA-1231.

American will feel a thrill of admiration and a touch of honest envy at the achievement of the Canadian troops.... No praise of the Canadian achievement can be excessive." David Lloyd George, the British prime minister, recalled in his memoirs: "The Canadians played a part of such distinction ... that thenceforth they were marked out as storm troops; for the remainder of the war they were brought along to head the assault in one great battle after another." The cost for such praise and national honour was devastating: 3598 killed and 7004 wounded.

Canadians and Newfoundlanders also served with distinction in the air and on the sea. Canada did not have an air force of its own, but some 2500 Canadian flyers, trained in Canada by the Royal Flying Corps after 1917, joined the Royal Air Force (RAF). A number became highscoring "aces," such as British Columbia's Raymond Collishaw, Manitoba's "Billy" Barker, Ontario's Ray Brown (credited with shooting down the notorious Baron von Richthofen — the "Red Baron" — in April 1918), and the legendary Billy Bishop, who shot down 72 German fighters, earning him a Victoria Cross. Canadians wanting to serve at sea joined the Royal Canadian Navy, under the command of the British Royal Navy. Some 8800 Canadians and 200 Newfoundlanders joined. They patrolled Canadian and Newfoundland waters against German U-boats (submarines).

Canadian casualties were high both on land and in the air. Infantrymen burdened down with 30 kg of kit and equipment were no match for German machine guns. Before the British called off the Somme offence, after five months of futile fighting, 24 000 Canadians and Newfoundlanders had died. On the first day of battle alone, the Newfoundland Regiment suffered 720 casualties — three-quarters of the unit and the greatest single disaster in Newfoundland's history. Britain recognized Newfoundland's effort by awarding its regiment the title "Royal." As the British never issued parachutes in World War I, there were no parachute escapes for Canadians from burning or disabled aircraft. The airplanes, too, were very flimsy; more pilots died in crash landings than in the air.

"INVITE US TO YOUR COUNCILS"

After Vimy, Canadian politicians demanded a greater voice in Britain's war policy. At the outset of the war, the British government treated Canada and the other dominions as colonial subordinates, neglecting to consult with them about war strategy or even to keep them informed of developments. When Prime Minister Borden first requested a stronger voice for Canada, Bonar Law, the colonial secretary, who by chance had been born in New Brunswick, replied curtly: "I fully recognize the right of the Canadian government to have some share of the control in a war in which Canada is playing so great a part. I am, however, not able to see any way in which this could be practically done."

When David Lloyd George became prime minister in December 1916, he found a way. He invited the dominion prime ministers to London to meet as an Imperial War Cabinet, a group consisting of the British War Cabinet and dominion representation. There, in March 1917, for the first time, Borden learned about the Allied position, discussed strategy, and, most important, became involved in the decision-making process.

The Imperial War Conference met simultaneously with the Imperial War Cabinet. The representatives passed a host of resolutions, one of which recognized in theory the equality of the dominions with one another and with Britain. It stated that Britain and the dominions agreed that their new constitutional status "should be based upon a full recognition of the dominions as autonomous nations of an Imperial Commonwealth."

RECRUITMENT

With continuous high casualties in Europe, Ottawa stepped up its recruitment drive. In his New Year's Day address of 1916, Borden announced his "sacred promise" that Canada would send a total of 500 000 to the war front. Initially, it appeared that the government could honour its commitment. In January alone, nearly 30 000 volunteers enlisted. By June 1916, the total number of wartime recruitments numbered over 300 000. Then recruitment dropped off dramatically. In summer, the farms needed young men, and year-long munition factories needed more helpers. The government responded by establishing the National Service Board, which had a mandate to "determine whether the services of any man of military age are more valuable to the state in his present occupation than in military duties and either to permit or forbid his enlistment." The government assigned registration cards to every male of military age. It concluded that 475 000 potential recruits existed.

Borden next established the Canadian Defence Force in the spring of 1917. This force was designed to get men who opposed fighting overseas to sign up for home

On June 10, 1916, the 102nd Battalion embarked for overseas from Comox, Vancouver Island. The whole Courtenay–Comox community came to the harbour to see them off.

Courtenay and District Museum and Archives/P215-1141.

defence. They would replace those already in uniform who were willing to serve on the war front. This last desperate attempt to get more troops without conscription failed. In the first month of operation, fewer than 200 signed up.

NATIONAL DISUNITY

As voluntary enlistment dried up, complaints arose about those groups who appeared reluctant to give their full support to the war effort. Once again, the geological fault line that divided French and English Canadians was exposed. Several reasons can be given for the coolness of French Canadians to the war effort. To them, the war was alien and remote. They had few or no emotional ties to Britain or even to France. Few of the officers at the Royal Military College in Kingston, the training school for military officers, were French-speaking, since English was the sole language of instruction. In Quebec, an English-speaking elite with little sympathy for, and even less contact with, French Canadians headed the recruitment effort.

Sam Hughes, the minister of militia and defence, did little to encourage French-Canadian enlistment. He placed French Canadians in English-speaking units and seldom appointed or promoted French Canadians to the rank of officer. Initially, apart from the one French-language battalion, the famed "Vandoos" (the Royal 22nd Regiment of Quebec), English ruled as the language of the army.

An army recruiter makes his pitch near the Toronto City Hall, 1916. Toronto's mayor, Tommy Church, casual in his boater hat, leans against the car.

City of Toronto Archives/SC244-721.

THE ONTARIO SCHOOLS QUESTION

The question of language rights for French Canadians outside Quebec also poisoned relations between French-speaking and English-speaking Canadians during the war years. By 1910, French Canadians, who had been moving into northern and eastern Ontario since the late nineteenth century, made up nearly 10 percent of Ontario's population. These Franco-Ontarians appealed to the Ontario government to protect their bilingual schools (or "English–French schools," as they were called) and to promote French-language interests.

They came under attack from both the Orange Order and Irish Catholics. The Orange Lodge believed that the use of the French language in schools undermined the unity of Canada and of the British empire. Irish Catholics feared that language concessions to French Catholics would give French Canadians control of the separate-school system. The Irish Catholics favoured Roman Catholic — but not bilingual — schools. Bishop Michael Fallon of London, Ontario, led the Irish Catholic opposition. He viewed the bilingual school system as one that "teaches neither English nor French, encourages incompetency, gives a prize to hypocrisy, and breeds ignorance."

James Whitney, the Ontario premier, appointed a commission to investigate. The commissioners pointed out the inadequate training of many teachers in the French–English schools but stopped short of making any recommendations to solve the problem. The Whitney government implemented Instruction 17, or "Regulation 17," which made English the official language of instruction and restricted French to the first two years of elementary school. It also established a commission to enforce its policy. Both the government and opposition, apart from the handful of French-speaking members, agreed with the policy. In 1913, Whitney amended Regulation 17 to permit French as a subject of study for one hour a day. Franco-Ontarians took the government to court on the ruling. While waiting for the Judicial Committee of the Privy Council to deliberate, both sides dug in.

French-speaking Canadians in Ontario and Quebec reacted. At the Guigues school in Ottawa, an "army" of French-speaking mothers, brandishing long hatpins, stood ready to prevent any entry by authorities to remove the bilingual teachers.

On August 22, 1914, vandals stole the bust of Kaiser Wilhelm II from the entrance to Victoria Park in Berlin (now Kitchener), Ontario, and threw it into the lake. After its retrieval (shown here), it was taken to the Concordia Club, a German-Canadian social club, where it became the club's centrepiece. On February 15, 1916, soldiers broke into the clubhouse, carried off "Old Bill," and paraded it up and down King Street. The bust has never been seen since that incident.

Kitchener-Waterloo Record.

Henri Bourassa denounced the Ontario government as more Prussian than the Prussians: French Canadians need not go to Europe to fight the enemy; it resided next door. Bourassa carried his message into Ontario. Everywhere in Ontario, he met hostility from English-speaking Canadians. In Ottawa, for example, an army sergeant climbed up on to the platform during his speech at the Russell Theatre and insisted that Bourassa wave a Union Jack. In the momentary hush, the editor of *Le Devoir* replied, "I am ready to wave the British flag in liberty, but I shall not do so under threats." The curtain fell as the crowd rushed the stage. Bourassa escaped through a back door and calmly finished his speech for friends and newspaper reporters in the lobby of the neighbouring Château Laurier hotel.

The Ontario schools controversy dragged on for years, while Franco-Ontarians were deprived of schooling in their own language. French Canadians considered Canada a bilingual country, while English Canadians in Ontario and the West saw it as an English country with one bilingual province — Quebec — not Ontario or Manitoba. Not until 1927 did the Ontario government find a "satisfactory" solution: each school designated for bilingual education would be considered on its merits by a departmental committee.

The wartime hysteria continued. In Berlin, Ontario, the city government held a plebiscite on whether or not to change the name of this city; over two-thirds of its population was of German descent. In a narrow vote, it was agreed to rename the city "Kitchener," after the British military hero who drowned at sea on June 5, 1916.

THE CONSCRIPTION CRISIS

In the spring of 1917, Prime Minister Borden visited Canadian soldiers in British hospitals and at the front while attending a meeting of the Imperial War Cabinet in London. The desperate situation and the British pressure on Canada to increase its commitment of men convinced him to break the promise he had made at the outset of the war not to introduce conscription for overseas military service. He informed his cabinet of the decision. His French-speaking ministers warned that conscription would "kill them and the party for 25 years" in Quebec but that they would stand behind him in his decision.

The prime minister favoured a coalition government of Conservatives and Liberals as the best means to introduce compulsory service, so he approached Wilfrid Laurier about the possibility. The leader of the opposition faced a major dilemma. While he agreed with the need for a coalition government for the war's duration, he opposed a union government that would introduce conscription, which neither he nor his Quebec followers favoured. "I oppose this bill," he warned when the Military Service Act was introduced in Parliament, "because it has in it the seeds of discord and disunion, because it is an obstacle and bar to that union of heart and soul without which it is impossible to hope that this Confederation will attain the aims and ends that were had in view when Confederation was effected."

OPPOSITION TO CONSCRIPTION

The Military Service Act, the official title of the conscription bill, became law in July 1917. Recruitment, however, did not get underway until January 1918, after the election of a coalition government. Anti-conscriptionist riots broke out in Montreal throughout the summer. Crowds marched through the streets yelling "À bas Borden" (Down with Borden) and "Vive la revolution" (Long live the revolution). Soldiers passing through Quebec in the winter of 1917–18 were pelted with rotten vegetables, ice, and stones when they taunted French-Canadian youth for not being in uniform. More riots followed in the spring of 1918, upon the actual implementation of conscription. The most serious riot, an armed clash in Quebec City on the Easter weekend, left four French-Canadian civilians dead and ten soldiers wounded. Fortunately, the war ended a half-year later, or the violence might have escalated.

Others, besides French Canadians, also opposed conscription. Farmers resented their sons' forced departure from the farm, where they contributed to the war effort through food production. Workers saw military conscription as the first step toward compulsory industrial service, forcing them to remain at one job for the war's duration. Both groups demanded the "conscription of wealth," heavier taxes on the rich and the nationalization of banks and industries, to ensure that financiers and businesspeople made the same sacrifice.

Some pacifist groups, such as the Quakers and the Mennonites, opposed wars as inherently evil and immoral. They upheld their beliefs despite being branded "slackers" by pro-conscriptionists. Others without a religious affiliation opposed war as a wasteful and destructive means of settling world problems. The Canadian Women's Peace Party, forerunner of the Women's International League for Peace and Freedom, championed peace under the leadership, ironically, of Laura Hughes, cousin

Slander!

That man is a slanderer who says that
The Farmers of Ontario
will vote with
Bourassa, Pro-Germans,
Suppressors of Free Speech and Slackers

Never!

They Will Support Union Government

Citizens' Union Committee

An ad placed in The Farmer's Advocate, *December 13, 1917, by the "Citizens' Union Committee." The federal election of December 1917 was one of the most divisive in Canadian history as a result of the implementation of the Military Service Act, or conscription bill, that past summer.*

....

Courtesy University Archives, Killam Memorial Library, Dalhousie University.

of Sam Hughes, and Alice Chown, niece of S.D. Chown, superintendent of the Methodist church and an ardent supporter of the war. They advocated a non-violent struggle at home to reform society in order to root out the inherent causes of violence and war.

UNION GOVERNMENT AND THE ELECTION OF 1917

Despite Laurier's refusal to join Borden in a coalition government, Borden did convince a number of Liberal members of Parliament and provincial Liberal leaders — including Alberta premier Arthur Sifton (Clifford's brother) and Newton W. Rowell, leader of the Liberal opposition in Ontario — to join his Union government. Then he dissolved Parliament and called an election.

Before dissolving Parliament, the Unionists implemented two bills to strengthen their chances at the polls. The Military Voters Act enfranchised all members of the armed forces, no matter how long or short a time they had lived in Canada. The Wartime Elections Act gave the vote to Canadian women who were mothers, wives, sisters, or daughters of servicemen (this did not apply to female relatives of status Indian servicemen), but denied the vote to conscientious objectors and to naturalized Canadians from enemy countries who had settled in Canada after 1902. Arthur Meighen, the solicitor general, reasoned that these aliens had been banned

The view from Halifax's waterfront after the great explosion caused by the collision of a Belgian vessel with a French munitions ship, December 6, 1917. The blast, the subsequent tidal wave, and raging fire killed over 1600 people and injured 9000, including 200 blinded by flying glass.

National Archives of Canada/C-19951.

from enlisting and so should not have the right to vote. He also realized that new Canadians tended to vote Liberal.

Both the Unionists and the Liberals fought the election largely along cultural lines. A Unionist election poster claimed that a vote for Laurier was a vote for Bourassa, the Kaiser, and the Germans. A group of Union supporters issued a map of Canada with Quebec in black, the "foul blot" on the country. On the Sunday before the election, three-quarters of the Protestant ministers across Canada responded to a Unionist circular, appealing for support of the Union party in their sermons.

In Quebec, political leaders painted conscriptionists as a greater danger to the country than the Germans. Bourassa and the *nationalistes* argued that Canada had done enough for the war. "Every Canadian who wishes to combat conscription with an effective logic," Bourassa declared, "must have the courage to say and to repeat everywhere: No Conscription! No Enrolment!"

The outcome of the election was predictable. The Union party won two-thirds of the constituencies outside of Quebec but only three seats, all in English-speaking ridings, in the province. The federal government was now literally an English-Canadian government.

Shortly before the 1917 election, the citizens of Halifax experienced the impact of the war in an immediate and devastating way. Early in the morning of December 6, 1917, a massive explosion occurred in Halifax harbour when the Belgian ship the *Imo* collided with the French munition ship the *Mont Blanc*. In an instant, the city of Halifax was destroyed: over 1600 people were killed, and 9000 — nearly one person in five — were injured. It would take months for the people of Halifax to rebuild their city. Until the explosion of the atom bomb on Hiroshima in 1945, the Halifax explosion was the largest non-natural explosion in history.

The Passchendaele battlefield in Flanders. The photo shows a light railway track ending in a shell hole and a shattered tank lying in a sea of mud. In the background, a shell throws up mud and water.

Archives of Ontario/C224-0-0-10, AO 258.

Meanwhile, the situation in Europe deteriorated. In October 1917, revolution broke out in Russia, and by November, Lenin led the Bolsheviks to power in Russia. They immediately made peace with Germany. Now the Germans could concentrate on the Western Front. The Germans' unrestricted submarine warfare in the North Atlantic had brought the United States into the war against Germany in April 1917, but American troops would not be mobilized in force in Europe until the summer of 1918. In October and November, the Allies suffered hundreds of thousands of casualties in the last phase of Field-Marshal Haig's Flanders offensive, including 16 000 Canadian deaths in the battle of Passchendaele, an attempt to take an insignificant ridge in a sea of mud. Finally, in the spring of 1918, came the all-out German counteroffensive, launched before American troops entered the front lines. Once again the Allies faced defeat. Only with the Germans' "black day" at Amiens in August 1918 did the Allies turn the tide. They pushed the Germans back in the successful "100 Days" campaign. Finally, on November 11, 1918, the Germans surrendered. The war was over.

The war ended too late for Private George Lawrence Price, the last Canadian soldier killed in the Great War. At Mons, France, a sniper fatally wounded him three seconds before the ceasefire came into effect at 11 A.M. Local citizens commemorated his tragic death by including a replica of the Canadian soldier's headstone at the neighbouring St. Symphorien Military Cemetery at the Mons War Museum.

Few Canadian conscripts ever fought on the battlefield in the Great War. While the implementation of conscription had put 100 000 more men into the army by the

Parade in Calgary celebrating the armistice and the end of World War I, November 11, 1918. Because of the influenza epidemic, the Alberta government had two weeks earlier ordered all citizens to wear masks when outside their homes.

Glenbow Archives, Calgary, Canada/NA-431-5.

war's end, only one-quarter of them reached the front before the armistice. In hindsight, one wonders whether conscription was worth the price. Yet, in Borden's defence, no one in late 1917 could have predicted that the long-drawn-out war would finally end one year later. Overall, some 600 000 Canadians fought in the Great War; 60 000 of them died. While this was a huge sacrifice for a country of 8 million, those numbers are dwarfed in the perspective of overall numbers for the Allied cause. Russia lost 1.7 million, France 1.3 million, and the British Commonwealth as a whole close to 1 million. In total, over 5 million Allied soldiers were killed in a war that, in the final analysis, failed to resolve anything.

THE WAR AND SOCIAL REFORM

The war greatly advanced the cause of social reform. English-Canadian reformers argued that just as the troops fought for a noble cause on the battlefront, so should those at home — against materialism, alcoholism, and corruption. Social gospellers saw the war as the final struggle for bringing God's kingdom to earth. As superintendent S.D. Chown of the Methodist church told a church conference on "The Church, the War and Patriotism," "the war is a divine challenge to build the Tabernacle of God amongst men."

THE SUCCESS OF WOMEN'S SUFFRAGE AND PROHIBITION

Women's suffrage and prohibition both gained support during the war. Women reformers argued that men's aggressive nature had caused the worldwide cataclysm. If women only had the right to vote and an opportunity to rule, wars would cease. They also pointed out the inconsistency of fighting for democracy abroad when they were denied the vote at home.

In 1916, the four western provinces granted women the right to vote in provincial elections. Ontario followed in 1917, Nova Scotia in 1918, New Brunswick in 1919, and Prince Edward Island in 1922. In Quebec, where opposition was greatest to the female franchise, women would have to wait until 1940 to gain the right to vote provincially. The influential Roman Catholic church held that only the male heads of families should have this responsibility.

Federally, the franchise came in three stages: the Military Voters Act of 1917 awarded the vote to women serving in the armed forces or as nurses in the war; the Wartime Elections Act extended voting privileges to women, aged 21 years and over, whose fathers, husbands, or sons served overseas; and finally, in 1918, all women, recognized as British citizens in Canada, over the age of 21, gained the right to vote federally. Still excluded from the franchise were status Indians, Asians, and conscientious objectors, including Mennonites and Hutterites.

The war helped the cause of prohibition as well. Prohibitionists equated their struggle with that of the men at the front. The prohibitionists' first victory came in 1915, when the Saskatchewan Liberal government closed all bars, saloons, and liquor stores. Immediately, this move brought liquor under the control of provincially operated outlets. Alberta went further by endorsing outright provincial prohibition later the same year. Manitoba followed in early 1916. By the end of 1917, every provincial government except Quebec had implemented prohibition legislation. In 1918, the newly elected federal Union government imposed prohibition on Quebec. Within a week of his electoral victory in December 1917, Prime Minister Borden moved to prohibit the manufacture, importation, and transportation of any beverage containing more than 2.5 percent alcohol.

FRENCH-CANADIAN REFORMERS DURING THE WAR YEARS

French-Canadian clerics and laypeople pressed for social, not political, reform during the war. In 1917, Father Joseph-Papin Archambault, of the Jesuit-inspired École sociale populaire, issued a tract, *La question sociale et nos devoirs de catholiques*, in which he appealed to Roman Catholics to reach out to the working class. In 1920, he began the Semaines sociales, an annual week-long meeting of clerics and laypeople to discuss social questions.

In Bourassa's view, French-Canadian reform had to remain linked to Canadian Roman Catholic reform in general. At the turn of the century, most French-Canadian nationalists, of whom Bourassa was the most prominent, looked to all of Canada as their homeland. After the conscription crisis of 1917, however, perspectives changed. A small group centred on Abbé Lionel Groulx and the magazine *L'Action française* advanced the idea of an independent, Roman Catholic, and rural French-Canadian nation in the St. Lawrence valley. As historian Mason Wade wrote of Groulx in the early 1920s: "For him the French Canadians possessed most of the essential attributes of a nation, and their attainment of political independence would be a normal part of their coming of age as a people."[4]

ENGLISH-CANADIAN REFORMERS AND THE WAR

English-Canadian reformers regarded the Union government's victory as their own. They wrote a number of books associating the Union government and the war with reform. In *The New Christianity* (1920), Salem Bland, a leading figure in the social gospel movement and a professor at Wesley College in Winnipeg, presented his vision of a socialist Canada operating on the Christian principles of love, equality, brotherhood, and democracy through a new labour church. Stephen Leacock, the political economist-cum-humorist, had doubts about the utopian nature of socialism. In his *Unsolved Riddle of Social Justice* (1920), he favoured instead legislation designed to make the workplace more appealing. In *Wake Up Canada* (1919), C.W. Paterson saw educational reform as the answer to society's ills. Two agrarian reformers, W.G. Good in *Production and Taxation in Canada* (1919) and William Irvine in *The Farmers in Politics* (1920), proposed rural values as the ideal of the future. William Lyon Mackenzie King, soon to become leader of the Liberal party, welcomed the new urban–industrial society in *Industry and Humanity* (1918) — provided that "regenerated men" directed it on Christian principles of co-operation and brotherhood.

POSTWAR UNREST

The Canadian government faced insurrection in 1918 among its soldiers stationed in demobilization camps in Britain and Europe, as rumours spread of favouritism and deliberate delays. To alleviate the tension, army officials began educational classes. When this proved ineffective, the Young Men's Christian Association (YMCA) established the Khaki University in the summer of 1918 under acting president Henry M. Tory, president of the University of Alberta. Its main campus was in Ripon, a medieval cathedral town in Yorkshire, with additional classes held at University College, London, and after the Armistice, at the University of Bonn, Germany. But soldiers simply wanted to get home as quickly as possible and get on with their lives.

To co-ordinate the demobilization effort, the Canadian government created in early 1918 the Department of Soldiers Civil Re-establishment. Even its personnel, however, were unprepared for the difficulties involved in arranging for 300 000 troops to return and be integrated back into society. When they returned to Canada to over-modest appreciation for their sacrifices and few jobs, veterans protested. They used their association, the Great War Veterans' Association (GWVA), the forerunner of the Canadian Legion, to press the government to give preferential treatment to veterans, to provide pensions for those who were disabled, to help financially wives and children of dead soldiers, and to provide proper medical care to veterans. The federal government established the Department of Health in 1919.

The problem of treating disabled soldiers paled in comparison with an even greater domestic crisis in the immediate postwar era: the Spanish influenza epidemic, brought back home almost certainly by returning soldiers. The first major outbreak occurred in September 1918 in Quebec. In some cities, people were ordered to wear gauze masks in public; in others, theatres and schools were closed, public meetings were banned, and church services were cancelled in an effort to check the deadly disease. Since there was no known cure, people tried all kinds of home remedies, from camphorated oil on the chest to Epsom salts and even salted herring around the neck, while volunteers fought the dreaded disease in makeshift hospitals. In the fall of 1919, the federal government established the Department of Health to deal with the epidemic. Eventually an estimated 50 000 Canadians died from this "silent enemy" — almost as many as had died in the war itself.

THE WINNIPEG GENERAL STRIKE

WEB LINKS

Widespread social unrest followed the armistice. Strikes broke out from Halifax to Vancouver as workers tried to make up for the restraints applied in wartime and to protect themselves in an inflationary economy. At the annual meeting of the Trades and Labor Congress in Quebec City in 1918, the western delegates broke rank with the conservative eastern members who controlled the meeting. A month later, the Western Labour Conference called for a single industrial union, the One Big Union (OBU) at its meeting in Calgary. But before its organizers could call the founding convention, new developments broke out in Winnipeg. On May 1, 1919, metalworkers' and builders' unions struck for better wages and improved working conditions. Other Winnipeg union workers, including police officers, fire fighters, and telephone and telegraph operators, joined them on May 15, swelling the numbers of strikers to some 3000, thus enabling them to virtually close down the city. To provide essential services and to regulate the strike, the organizers created a central strike committee. Business and government officials saw this committee, with its power to dictate what went on in the city, as the beginnings of a "Bolshevik uprising." They countered by creating the Citizens' Committee of One Thousand to maintain public utilities.

Fearing that the strike would spread to other centres, the federal government intervened. Arthur Meighen, then the minister of justice and minister of the interior, and Gideon Robertson, acting minister of labour, arrived in Winnipeg to assess the situation. They came convinced that the strike was a conspiracy. Meighen described the strike leaders as "revolutionists of varying degrees and types, from crazy idealists down to ordinary thieves, with the better part, perhaps, of the latter type." Sympathy strikes of varying degrees of success broke out from Prince Rupert, British Columbia, to Sydney, Nova Scotia. Meighen ordered the Royal North-West Mounted Police to arrest ten of the Winnipeg strike leaders, along with labour newspaper editors, including J.S. Woodsworth, and some returned soldiers, on the night of June 16. In protest, the workers organized a silent parade on Saturday, June 21. Violence erupted, and the mayor of Winnipeg called in the Mounties to disperse the crowd. The confrontation saw one man killed and another wounded and many others injured.

"Bloody Saturday," as it became known, ended with the dispersal of the workers and the establishment of military control of the city. The strike collapsed. On June 26, the strike committee called off the strike, without the workers having gained any of their objectives. It did convince them, however, that they must send their own labour

"Bloody Saturday," June 21, 1919, a violent confrontation that occurred between peaceful marchers and the Mounties and special police during the Winnipeg General Strike. Note the burning street car.

David Miller Collection/National Archives of Canada/C-33392.

representatives to Parliament — individuals like the social reformer J.S. Woodsworth, who had edited their strike paper, and would be elected to Parliament as a labour MP for Winnipeg in the federal election of 1921.

ADVANCES TO NATIONHOOD

Four years of fighting had left more than 60 000 Canadians dead, and thousands more returned home maimed and disabled. Prime Minister Borden was determined to ensure that Canada benefited from its major contribution through enhanced national status. First he pressed for dominion recognition in the British empire delegation at the Paris Peace Conference, which met in 1919 to settle the war. The United States questioned why Canada should be involved in the settlement at all, until it was pointed out by the Canadian delegates that Canada had lost more men than the United States in the war. The Big Five (Britain, the United States, France, Italy, and

Where Historians Disagree

THE WINNIPEG GENERAL STRIKE

Canadian labour and working-class historians agree on the importance of the Winnipeg General Strike of 1919, but on very little else. Initially, the historiography reflected the opposing ideological perspectives of the two sides at the time: the strike opponents seeing it as a revolution aimed at creating a Soviet-style regime in Canada; its supporters seeing it as a legitimate tool by which workers could obtain collective bargaining to secure better wages and working conditions.

Historian D.C. Masters wrote the first scholarly study, *The Winnipeg General Strike* (Toronto: University of Toronto Press, 1950). He emphasized the British background of the strike leaders so as to reinforce the legitimacy of the strike within the British democratic tradition and denied any connection between the strike and the One Big Union (OBU) (often seen as an attempt to create a working-class solidarity as a prelude to a Bolshevik-style revolution). He also challenged those who saw the strike as a spontaneous uprising, claiming "it came at the end of a series of controversies which had raged in a crescendo since at least 1917" (p. 127). Thus, he concluded that "there was no seditious conspiracy and that the strike was what it purported to be, an effort to secure the principle of collective bargaining" (p. 134).

In contrast, sociologist S.D. Clark emphasized the importance of the One Big Union in his introduction to D.C. Masters's study, which was part of a series under Clark's general editorship. Clark saw the OBU, along with the Progressive party among western farmers, as "expressions of protest against eastern dominance ... in the tradition of American frontier radicalism" (p. viii). In this respect, Clark concluded, "the movement was revolutionary" — ironically, a direct contradiction to the conclusion that Masters, whose book Clark was introducing, had drawn!

Historian David Bercuson provided the first comprehensive study of the general strike in *Confrontation at Winnipeg* (Montreal/Kingston: McGill-Queen's University Press, 1974). He traced the roots of the strike back to labour unrest in the city in 1906, if not to the turn of the century. The massive influx of immigrants came at a time of major social and industrial changes that turned Winnipeg into a city sharply divided along class lines. Bercuson denied that the strikers were revolutionaries; instead they were striking for legitimate working-class concerns. But, he argued, the fact that they failed to achieve their objectives set back "the cause of labour for at least another generation" (p. 176). Fellow labour historian Irving Abella concurred. "Labour's trauma started at Winnipeg in 1919," he wrote. "With the suppression of the Winnipeg General Strike ... the rapid demise of organized labour in Canada began" (Introduction to Irving Abella, ed., *On Strike: Six Key Labour Struggles in Canada, 1919–1949* [Toronto: James Lewis & Samuel Publishers, 1974], p. xii).

In *Winnipeg 1919: The Strikers' Own History of the Winnipeg General Strike*, 2nd ed. (Toronto: James Lorimer, 1975), historian Norman Penner disagreed with this assessment of the strike's aftermath. To Penner, the strike was above all a political struggle for recognition and rights, and from this perspective, the epic event was "a watershed in the evolution of Canada" (p. xxiii). "[F]or more than a year,"

(continued)

he wrote, "the Winnipeg General Strike and the trials of its leaders kept the labour movement in a constant state of agitation and turmoil which succeeded in translating the economic struggle into a political victory.... Hence the Winnipeg General Strike must be seen as part of the cumulative impact of labour on Canadian life, a constant force which accounts for labour's strength and status in Canada today" (pp. vii–viii).

Bercuson introduced a new issue into the debate in an article ("Labour Radicalism and the Western Industrial Frontier: 1897–1919," *Canadian Historical Review*, LVIII, 2 [June 1977]: 154–75) that examined the strike in the context of the larger issue of western labour radicalism. He argued that western workers were more radical than elsewhere in the country because of unique western frontier conditions, including immigrants who came with utopian dreams of a better lifestyle — only to find themselves up against ruthless and repressive industrialists who thwarted their hopes. Failed expectations, Bercuson argued, were a sure cause for radicalism. He concluded that the Canadian western industrial frontier bred class consciousness and radical working-class attitudes rather than equality and harmony.

Labour historian Greg Kealey vehemently disagreed with Bercuson's theory that the West was more radical than the rest of the country. Also, he questioned his implication that the Winnipeg General Strike could only have occurred in Winnipeg, the most urban of societies. Kealey pointed out in "1919: The Canadian Labour Revolt" (*Labour/Le Travail* 13 [Spring 1984]: 11–44) that the year was punctuated by strikes and labour unrest throughout the country; in fact, labour unrest in Canada in 1919 was really part of an international working-class solidarity. He went on to argue as well that the strike was part of "larger structural changes in capitalist organization on both a national and international scale" (p. 15). Seen from this wider perspective, the strike was not a failure, but only a momentary defeat before labour emerged even stronger in the move toward industrial unionism in the 1940s.

Bercuson replied. In a revised edition of *Confrontation at Winnipeg*, published in 1990, he added a historiographical chapter in which he dismissed Kealey's argument. He claimed that evidence of numerous strikes and/or revolts across the country did not constitute proof of working-class revolt. Few of these strikes were "politically motivated and those that were — the Vancouver general strike, for example — were dismal failures." Nor had Kealey proven that the strikers were consciously trying to overthrow capitalism. Kealey's essay, he claimed, was "little more than pamphleteering. He is rallying the revolutionary troops; he is certainly not advancing scholarship" (p. 202). Then Bercuson criticized Marxist history in general as reading back into the past the present dreams of workers. In the case of the Winnipeg General Strike, there was no evidence of any connection whatever between the strike and the rise of industrial unionism in the 1940s, and "only the most slender thread connecting the strike to the rise of the CCF" (p. 205). As for the significance of the Winnipeg General Strike in Canadian history, it lay in "its unique occurrence that took place for particular reasons and which had specific consequences" and not for some "hidden inner meaning" found only in the mind of historians.

Bryan Palmer entered the debate in his study *Working-Class Experience: Rethinking the History of Canadian Labour, 1880–1991* (Toronto: McClelland & Stewart, 1993),

(continued)

in which he argued that the significance of the strike lay in the fact that it reflected both "the continuity of class struggle *and* the changes that had taken place as a consequence of the twentieth-century conditions of monopoly capital, state intervention, and labour market segmentation."

The debate on what happened in Winnipeg in 1919 and its consequences continues. Clearly, though, the strike remains the best-known example of a general strike in Canadian history.

Japan) wanted to make the important decisions, with the "lesser states" involved only in decisions directly affecting them. Borden found this unacceptable, and he won representation for Canada as a power in its own right, in addition to its collective representation as a member of the British empire delegation. Borden also insisted on Canada's right to membership in the League of Nations' General Assembly as well as eligibility for membership in the governing council of the new international body.

Once in the League of Nations, however, Canada wanted to limit its commitment. It opposed article 10 of the leagues charter, the heart of its collective security system, which bound members to come to the aid of other league members in times of attack. Borden feared that this agreement would commit Canadians to involvement in world disputes that were of no interest to them. (In the end, article 10 remained in place.)

Clearly, by the end of the war and in the immediate postwar period, Canada had taken the first few important steps along the road from colony to nation. Canadians led the way in demanding a new relationship of equality between Britain and its dominions that would, in the 1920s, transform the empire into the British Commonwealth of Nations. As well, the Great War had enabled Canada to gain recognition as a nation in its own right in the international community.

The wartime rhetoric that the war would lead to a better Canada, a glorious nation of peace and prosperity, rang hollow in 1919. The war had strained English- and French-Canadian relations to an unprecedented extent, leading for the first time to the formation of national parties along ethnic rather than political lines. Equally, the war had taxed the nation's capacity in both industrial production and human resources. While Canada had made great strides on the road to nationhood, it had done so at great expense. The total of all Canadian casualties — killed, missing, or prisoners of war — reached a quarter of a million people, more than a third of those who had enlisted.

Canada had also lost its optimism. Fifteen years earlier, Prime Minister Wilfrid Laurier had promised that the twentieth century would be Canada's, just as the nineteenth century had been that of the United States. In 1919, Laurier died. His vision had perished before he did, another casualty of the killing fields of Europe.

NOTES

....

1. John Swettenham, *To Seize the Victory: The Canadian Corps in World War I* (Toronto: Ryerson Press, 1965), p. 106.
2. Daniel Dancocks, *Welcome to Flanders Fields: The First Canadian Battle of the Great War, Ypres, 1915* (Toronto: McClelland & Stewart, 1988), p. 249.
3. Desmond Morton, "World War I," *The Canadian Encyclopedia*, 2nd ed. (Edmonton: Hurtig, 1988), vol. 4, p. 2343.
4. Mason Wade, *The French Canadians, 1760–1967*, 2 vols. (Toronto: Macmillan, 1968), p. 872.

LINKING TO THE PAST

....

WEB LINKS

Canada's Military Legacy: World War I
http://www.dnd.ca/menu/legacy/wwi_e.htm
A closer look at Canada's participation in World War I, with information on Canada's military role, events on the home front, and brief descriptions of people and places.

Canadians in World War I
http://www.civilization.ca/cwm/tour/trww1eng.html
The Canadian War Museum offers an on-line tour of World War I that includes photographs and descriptions of the weapons used in trench warfare.

"What do we owe England?"
http://www.web.net/~peaceweb/cebour.html
An excerpt from the writings of Henri Bourassa, a French Canadian who opposed sending troops to fight for the British empire during World War I.

Robert L. Borden on National Service
http://www.nelson.ca/nelson/school/discovery/cantext/speech/1916bons.htm
A speech by Prime Minister Robert Borden, from 1916, in which he appeals to Canadians to support national service during the latter half of the war.

Citizens' Committee of 1000
http://timelinks.merlin.mb.ca/referenc/db0121.htm
A short description of the Citizens' Committee of 1000, which played a prominent role in Winnipeg's General Strike of 1919, with links to additional information about the strike.

RELATED READINGS

....

The following three articles in R. Douglas Francis and Donald B. Smith, eds., *Readings in Canadian History: Post-Confederation*, 5th ed. (Toronto: Harcourt Brace, 1998) relate to topics in this chapter: "An Open Letter from Capt. Talbot Papineau to Mr. Henri Bourassa" and "Mr. Bourassa's Reply to Capt. Talbot Papineau's Letter," pp. 283–88; and Thomas P. Socknat, "Canada's Liberal Pacifists and the Great War," pp. 289–302.

BIBLIOGRAPHY

For overviews of Canada during World War I see Desmond Morton and J.L. Granatstein, *Marching to Armageddon: Canada and the Great War, 1914–1919* (Toronto: Lester & Orpen Dennys, 1989); Daniel Dancocks, *Spearhead to Victory: Canada and the Great War* (Edmonton: Hurtig, 1987); and R.C. Brown and R. Cook, *Canada, 1896–1921: A Nation Transformed* (Toronto: McClelland & Stewart, 1974), pp. 212–94. A useful collection of essays is Marc Milner, ed., *Canadian Military History: Selected Readings* (Toronto: Copp Clark Pitman, 1993). On Robert Borden see R.C. Brown, *Robert Laird Borden: A Biography*, 2 vols. (Toronto: Macmillan, 1975, 1980); and John English, *Borden: His Life and World* (Toronto: McGraw-Hill Ryerson, 1977). For a study of party and politics during the Borden era consult John English, *The Decline of Politics: The Conservatives and the Party System, 1901–1920* (Toronto: University of Toronto Press, 1977). Joseph Schull's *Laurier: The First Canadian* (Toronto: Macmillan, 1965); and O.D. Skelton's *The Life and Letters of Sir Wilfrid Laurier* (Toronto: Oxford University Press, 1921) deal with the leader of the opposition in the war years.

John Swettenham, *To Seize the Victory* (Toronto: Ryerson Press, 1965) and Robert James Steel, *The Men Who Marched Away: Canada's Infantry in the First World War, 1914–1918* (St. Catharines: Vanwell, 1989) describe Canadian involvement at the front, as does Sandra Gwyn's *Tapestry of War: Politics and Passion: Canada's Coming of Age in the Great War* (Toronto: HarperCollins, 1992). On Canada's involvement in the Ypres Salient see Daniel Dancocks, *Welcome to Flanders Fields: The First Canadian Battle of the Great War, Ypres, 1915* (Toronto: McClelland & Stewart, 1988). Pierre Berton tells the story of Canada's greatest battle in *Vimy* (Toronto: McClelland & Stewart, 1986). G.W.L. Nicholson, *The Fighting Newfoundlander: A History of the Royal Newfoundland Regiment* (Ottawa: Government of Newfoundland, 1964) recounts Newfoundland's contribution to the Allied army. Jean-Pierre Gagnon's *Le 22e bataillon (canadien-français) 1914–1919: Étude sociomilitaire* (Québec: Presses de l'Université Laval, 1987) reviews the story of the famous "Vandoos" in World War I. Information on "Private Fraser" is taken from the "Introduction" and text of Reginald Roy, ed., *The Journal of Private Fraser, 1914–1918 C.E.F.* (Victoria: Sono Nis Press, 1985). On Canada's first military commander consult A.M.J. Hyatt, *General Sir Arthur Currie: A Military Biography* (Toronto: University of Toronto Press, 1987). See also Ronald G. Haycock, *Sam Hughes: The Public Career of a Controversial Canadian, 1885–1916* (Waterloo, ON: Wilfrid Laurier University Press, 1986), and his short sketch "Sam Hughes," *Horizon Canada* 66 (1986): 1580–84. On the Canadian air force see S.F. Wise, *Canadian Airmen and the First World War* (Toronto: University of Toronto Press, 1980).

James W. St. G. Walker looks at race relations in the Canadian army in "Race and Recruitment in World War I: Enlistment of Visible Minorities in the Canadian Expeditionary Force," *Canadian Historical Review* 70(1) (March 1989): 1–26. On the only Canadian black battalion see John G. Armstrong, "The Unwelcome Sacrifice: A Black Unit in the Canadian Expeditionary Force, 1917–19," in N.F. Dreisziger, ed., *Ethnic Armies: Polyethnic Armed Forces from the Time of the Hapsburgs to the Age of the Superpowers* (Waterloo, ON: Wilfrid Laurier University Press, 1990), pp. 178–97. On Canada's Native soldiers see Fred Gaffen, *Forgotten Soldiers* (Penticton, BC: Theytus Books, 1985); and on Canada's black soldiers consult Calvin Ruck, *The Black Battalion, 1916–1920: Canada's Best Kept Military Secret* (Halifax: Nimbus, 1987). The edited work by Bohdan S. Kordan and Peter Melnycky, *In the Shadow of the Rockies: Diary of the Castle Mountain Internment Camp, 1915–1917* (Edmonton: Canadian Institute of Ukrainian Studies Press, 1991) reviews life in one Canadian internment camp. For information about the nearly 4000 Canadians held in German prison camps in World War I see Desmond Morton, *Silent Battle: Canadian Prisoners of War in Germany, 1914–1919* (Toronto: Lester, 1992). Morton has also written *When Your Number's Up: The Canadian Soldier in the First World War* (Toronto: Random House, 1993), a valuable perspective of the war from the vantage point of those who served at the front.

The question of government intervention in the state during the war is discussed in R. Cuff, "Organizing for War: Canada and the United States During World War I," *Canadian Historical Association Report* (1969): 141–56. On the nationalization of the railways see T.D. Regehr, *The Canadian Northern Railway* (Toronto: Macmillan, 1976); and R.B. Fleming, *The Railway King of Canada: Sir William Mackenzie, 1849–1923* (Vancouver: University of British Columbia Press, 1991). Women's contributions to the war effort are discussed in the relevant sections of Alison Prentice et al., *Canadian Women: A History*, 2nd ed. (Toronto: Harcourt Brace, 1996); D. Smyth, "Women at War: The Origins of the Army Nursing Service," *Horizon Canada* 8 (1985): 188–92; and Ceta Ramkhalawonsingh, "Women During the Great War," in J. Acton et al., eds., *Women at Work: Ontario, 1850–1930* (Toronto: Canadian Women's Educational Press, 1974), pp. 261–308. The Halifax explosion is well documented in Alan D. Ruffman and Colin D. Howell, eds., *Ground Zero: A Reassessment of the 1917 Explosion in Halifax Harbour* (Halifax: Nimbus, 1994).

The conscription crisis is covered in J.L. Granatstein and J.M. Hitsman, *Broken Promises: A History of Conscription in Canada* (Toronto: Copp Clark Pitman, 1985 [1977]); and C. Berger, ed., *Conscription 1917* (Toronto: University of Toronto Press, 1969). Mason Wade examines French-Canadian attitudes toward the war in *The French Canadians: 1760–1945* (Toronto: Macmillan, 1955). Students should also consult Elizabeth Armstrong, *The Crisis of Quebec, 1914–1918* (Toronto: McClelland & Stewart, 1974 [1937]). The Canadian peace movement is studied in Thomas Socknat, *Witness against War: Pacifism in Canada, 1900–1945* (Toronto: University of Toronto Press, 1987). Often forgotten are the veterans; consult D. Morton and G. Wright, *Winning the Second Battle: Canadian Veterans and the Return to Civilian Life, 1915–1930* (Toronto: University of Toronto Press, 1987).

For the Ontario schools questions, see Chad Gaffield, *Language, Schooling, and Cultural Conflict: The Origins of the French-Language Controversy in Ontario* (Montreal/ Kingston: McGill-Queen's University Press, 1987); and the articles by Marilyn Barber and Margaret Prang in R.C. Brown, ed., *Minorities, Schools, and Politics* (Toronto: University of Toronto Press, 1969).

For the impact of World War I on social reform, consult John Herd Thompson, "'The Beginning of our Regeneration': The Great War and Western Canadian Reform Movements," *Canadian Historical Association Historical Papers* (1972): 227–45, and his study *The Harvests of War: The Prairie West, 1914–1919* (Toronto: McClelland & Stewart, 1978).

On Canadian imperial and foreign relations during and immediately after the war see R.C. Brown's biography of Borden (cited earlier) and his "Sir Robert Borden, the Great War and Anglo-Canadian Relations," in J.S. Moir, ed., *Character and Circumstance* (Toronto: Macmillan, 1970), pp. 201–24; as well as C.P. Stacey, *Canada and the Age of Conflict*, vol. 1, *1867–1921* (Toronto: Macmillan, 1977). On the flu epidemic of 1918 see Eileen Pettigrew, *The Silent Enemy* (Saskatoon: Western Producer Prairie Books, 1983).

On the Winnipeg General Strike see D.C. Masters, *The Winnipeg General Strike* (Toronto: University of Toronto Press, 1950); Kenneth McNaught and David Bercuson, *The Winnipeg Strike: 1919* (Toronto: Longman, 1974); David Bercuson, *Confrontation at Winnipeg: Labour, Industrial Relations, and the General Strike*, rev. ed. (Montreal/Kingston:

McGill-Queen's University Press, 1990); Norman Penner, ed., *Winnipeg 1919: The Strikers' Own History of the Winnipeg General Strike*, 2nd ed. (Toronto: James Lorimer, 1975); and with regard to the One Big Union, David Bercuson, *Fools and Wisemen: The Rise and Fall of the One Big Union* (Toronto: McGraw-Hill Ryerson, 1978). Sandra Gwyn's *Tapestry of War: Politics and Passion: Canada's Coming of Age in the Great War* (Toronto: HarperCollins, 1992) examines the significance of the war for Canada's advancement.

Donald Kerr and Deryck W. Holdsworth, eds., *Historical Atlas of Canada*, vol. 3, *Addressing the Twentieth Century, 1891–1961* (Toronto: Nelson, 1990), contains a wealth of detail in the form of maps and charts on Canadian society in the early twentieth century.

CHAPTER ELEVEN

The 1920s: A Decade of Adjustment

The 1920s were a decade of adjustment to new postwar conditions. Both major federal political parties chose new leaders, and regional protest movements surfaced in the Maritimes and the West, as these hinterland regions demanded a stronger voice in the "new Canada" of the postwar era. Maritimers formed the Maritime Rights movement to have a greater role in Confederation, while Prairie farmers created the Progressive party to fight for their regional demands. In foreign affairs, Canada continued to move toward autonomy. Economically, a diversification in staple production lessened the country's reliance on the wheat economy. As well, Canadians looked increasingly to the United States rather than to Britain for both financial needs and foreign trade. Major changes occurred in transportation and communications. During this era of general prosperity, and as a result of the aftermath of war, social reform declined. Women still fought for recognition and rights, but in the economic and legal, rather than political, spheres. Labour unions struggled for recognition and increased membership. Cultural developments flourished in both English-speaking and French-speaking Canada, but because of the language differences few points of common contact existed.

NEW POSTWAR POLITICAL LEADERS

WEB
LINKS

As the 1920s began, new men replaced veteran national leaders from the prewar era in the two major parties. William Lyon Mackenzie King succeeded Wilfrid Laurier, who died in February 1919, as Liberal leader, while Arthur Meighen became the Conservative leader and acting prime minister after Robert Borden's resignation in July 1920.

The Liberals chose King at a leadership convention, the first in the country's history, in August 1919. King's loyalty to Laurier during the conscription crisis put him in good favour in the party, especially in Quebec. As well, King appeared to represent change. The grandson of William Lyon Mackenzie, leader of the rebellion of 1837 in Upper Canada, saw himself as a reformer. After graduating from the universities of Toronto, Chicago, and Harvard, with a Ph.D. in political economy from the latter university, he served as deputy minister of labour. In 1908, shortly after his election to the House of Commons, he became Laurier's minister of labour. Defeated in the election of 1911, King returned to the United States to work for the Rockefeller Foundation as a labour conciliator. On the basis of his experiences in the civil service and in industrial relations he wrote *Industry and Humanity* (1918), a discussion of the labour question in Canada. The book, although convoluted and moralistic, did address the pressing problem of the postwar era of the impact of industrialism on society and especially workers. It established King as an authority on contemporary social and economic issues.

The Conservatives met in caucus, rather than in convention, to choose Arthur Meighen as Borden's successor in July 1920. Meighen had attended the University of Toronto at the same time as King. Both men despised each other. Upon graduation, Meighen moved west to Portage la Prairie, Manitoba, to practise law. He entered federal politics in the election of 1908, the same year that his future rival, King, was first elected. Meighen, an outstanding parliamentary debater, became solicitor general in 1913 and minister of the interior in 1917.

Meighen had, by the time he gained leadership of the party, become identified with several of the Conservative and, after 1917, the Union government's controversial policies. He had drafted the conscription bill, which lost him support in Quebec and among farmers in English-speaking Canada. Farmers, who had been exempt from conscription immediately before the election of 1917, were suddenly made eligible after it. Meighen had also introduced the Wartime Elections Act, which denied the vote to Canadians who had emigrated from enemy countries after 1902 — thus losing him part of the ethnic vote. In 1919, he had intervened against the workers in the Winnipeg General Strike. That the Conservative caucus still chose Meighen as their leader attests to his influence in the party, but also reveals the party's loss of touch with political reality.

These two leaders had completely opposite approaches to politics. King sought the road of least resistance and the middle path of compromise. To him, right answers did not exist in politics; there were only answers that seemed better because they offended fewer people. As a result he often spoke in ambiguities and in generalities. Meighen, by contrast, stated his position clearly and unequivocally. He upheld principles over compromise and believed that Canadians should be made to see the truth as he saw it. To him, every problem had a solution, and he clearly articulated solutions without regard for the possible political repercussions.

REGIONAL PROTEST: THE PROGRESSIVES AND THE MARITIME RIGHTS MOVEMENT

In 1920, both new party leaders faced the immediate problem of regional protest movements in both eastern and western Canada. In eastern Canada, the Maritime Rights movement arose in an effort to achieve a greater Maritime regional voice in national politics, while in the West, farmers created their own third party, the Progressive party, to deal with regional complaints.

THE MARITIME RIGHTS MOVEMENT

In the 1920s, Maritimers witnessed a decline in their region's influence in Confederation. Politically, their number of seats in the House of Commons fell by one-quarter (to 31) between 1882 and 1921, partly as a result of the depopulation of the Maritimes, as thousands left the region in search of work. Given that the size of the House of Commons had increased substantially during this period, the percentage drop was even greater. Economically, manufacturing companies in the region re-established themselves in the larger markets of central Canada in order to be more competitive. Both Canadian Car and Foundry of Amherst, Nova Scotia, and the Maritime Nail Company of Saint John, New Brunswick, for example, transferred operations to Montreal in 1921.

A decline in demand for Cape Breton coal and steel hurt that regional industry. The conversion to oil for heating and power had lost markets for Cape Breton's coal. Shipbuilding went into decline as Britain, the United States, and Canada all competed for international sales. The vital Canadian rail market for steel rails collapsed when railway construction ceased in the postwar era. Unemployment became widespread in Cape Breton's heavy-steel industry. The British Empire Steel Company (BESCO), created from a merger of Nova Scotia's coal, steel, and shipbuilding industries, verged on bankruptcy. It responded by attempting to cut miners' and steelworkers' wages. This touched off in 1921 one of the most intense labour disputes in Maritime history. The provincial government had to call in troops to keep order in New Waterford, Cape Breton Island.

The Maritimes also suffered from tariff reductions that had formerly protected its industries. A rise in freight rates, of 200 percent or more, on the Intercolonial Railway equally hurt the region's economy. When the Canadian government nationalized the Intercolonial Railway as part of the Canadian National Railways (CNR), it moved the Intercolonial's head office from Moncton, New Brunswick, to Montreal. The railway thus ceased to promote regional interests and became part of a national system.

Individually the Maritime provinces seemed powerless to stem the economic decline, but collectively their chances were better. A.P. Paterson, a grocer from Saint John, New Brunswick, led a group of influential businessmen and professionals in launching the Maritime Rights movement. He offered a rationale for the movement in a pamphlet, *The True Story of Confederation*, in which he put forward his version of the compact theory of Confederation. He argued that all Canadians should bear the extra economic costs experienced by any region as a result of its disadvantageous geographical location. Convinced that a study of history would reinforce his argument, Paterson helped to fund the establishment of a department of history at the University of New Brunswick.

The Maritime Rights movement demanded increased federal subsidies for the Maritime provinces, more national and international trade through the ports of Halifax and Saint John, and improved tariff protection to strengthen the region's steel and coal industries. The movement's promotion of the tariff separated it completely from discontented Prairie farmers. It also differed from the West in working for change within the traditional two-party system rather than through a third party.

In the election campaign of 1921, the movement pressed Maritime Liberal candidates to swear "to advocate and stand by Maritime rights first, last and all the time." Although taking this pledge helped the federal Liberals to win all but six of the Maritime constituencies, the members of Parliament could not meet their promises. Mackenzie King's Liberal minority government depended too much on Prairie support to be able to raise the tariff.

Disillusioned, Maritime voters switched to the Conservatives in the next election in 1925, giving the party all but three of the 31 seats. Unfortunately for Maritimers, the Liberals returned to power in 1926. King diffused the Maritime Rights

Miners' Houses, Glace Bay. *Lawren Harris, a member of the Group of Seven, painted this scene in one of Cape Breton's mining towns after he visited the coalfields on the island in 1921.*

....

Art Gallery of Ontario, Toronto/
Bequest of Charles S. Band/N-174-1.
By permission of the family of
Lawren S. Harris.

movement by establishing a royal commission to investigate the group's complaints. The Duncan Commission (headed by British jurist Sir Arthur Rae Duncan) recommended major changes for the Maritimes, such as a 20 percent reduction in all rail rates, aid to the steel and coal industries, and increased federal subsidies. The Liberal government, however, agreed only to minor changes. In the meantime, the Maritime Rights movement had disbanded.

THE PROGRESSIVE MOVEMENT

At the turn of the century, western farmers attacked the two traditional parties for neglecting western demands. They wanted reduced freight rates comparable to those in central Canada, an end to the eastern-owned grain-elevator companies' monopoly of the grain trade, an increase in the CPR's boxcar allotment for grain trade, a railway to Hudson Bay to rival the CPR, and most of all, a reduction in the tariff.

During the Liberal era (1896–1911), western farmers had gained some of their demands. The Liberal government passed the Crow's Nest Pass Agreement in 1897, by which the CPR reduced eastbound freight rates on grain and flour and westbound rates on a list of manufactured goods. In return, the company obtained a government subsidy to build a branch line from Lethbridge through the Crow's Nest Pass to Nelson, British Columbia. The new line enabled the CPR to exploit southern Alberta's and British Columbia's mining fields. Ottawa also passed the Manitoba Grain Act in 1900, which improved grain storage at loading platforms and warehouses. Then, in 1902, in the famous Sintaluta case, named after the town in Saskatchewan where the legal challenge arose, the Territorial Grain Growers' Association won its fight against the CPR for failure to provide adequate boxcars for grain shipment at peak periods.

These victories, however, left the western farmers' fundamental problem unresolved. The same economic structure — most notably the tariff, which for western farmers symbolized the inequity of Confederation — remained in place. Farmers resented having to buy their agricultural implements and materials in a closed, protected market and to sell their wheat in an open, competitive market. The tariff, they felt, worked against their best interest, and they demanded that Parliament

Arch Dales's cartoon in the Grain Growers' Guide *in 1915 conveys western farmers' views of Canada's political and economic reality.*

Glenbow Archives, Calgary, Canada/NA 3055-24.

repeal it. After the Liberals' defeat in 1911 on the question of reciprocity with the United States, many farmers talked openly of creating a third party.

Then the war intervened. Out of loyalty, farmers rallied behind the traditional parties. With the election of a "non-partisan" Union government in 1917, farmers hoped that it would remove the tariff. When it failed to do so, Thomas Crerar, a Manitoba farmer, one-time president of the Grain Growers' Grain Company and minister of agriculture in the Union government, resigned from the cabinet in June 1919. Nine other western Unionist MPs followed. They formed the nucleus of a new National Progressive party.

Farmer candidates did well in the provincial elections held immediately after the war. In Ontario, where rural depopulation posed a serious problem, the United Farmers of Ontario won the election of 1919, much to their surprise. Neither the premier, E.C. Drury, a farmer from Simcoe County directly north of Toronto, nor most of his party members had had any previous legislative experience. In Alberta, in the provincial election of 1921, the United Farmers of Alberta (UFA) swept out the incumbent Liberal party, which had been in office since 1905. The UFA won considerable support in southern Alberta, where farmers experienced extreme drought conditions, as bad as they would experience during the Great Depression of the 1930s. In Manitoba, a "Progressive" group of United Farmers formed the government in 1922 under John Bracken. The Progressives also ran farmer candidates in many constituencies across the country in the 1921 election.

The results of that election revealed the political divisions within the country. No party secured a majority, and the three largest parties — the Liberals, Conservatives, and Progressives — each held the majority of its seats in one or two regions of the country only, with a very poor showing elsewhere. Arthur Meighen suffered a humiliating defeat by winning only 50 seats, two-thirds of them in Ontario. Mackenzie King and the Liberals won 116 seats, two short of a majority. They won every Quebec riding and did well in the Maritimes, but west of the Ottawa River held only 26 seats. The Progressives swept the West, winning 39 of the 56 seats, and also gained a significant 24 in Ontario, but the new party had no seats in Quebec and just one in the Maritimes. Five independents were elected, of whom two agreed to work together to represent labour interests. At the opening of the parliamentary session, Alberta's William Irvine informed the House of Commons: "I wish to state that Mr. Woodsworth is the leader of the labour group ... and I am the group." For the first time in Canadian history, the Canadian public had elected a House of Commons divided along regional lines.

THE PROGRESSIVES IN DECLINE

Despite its impressive strength, the Progressive party was split between a Manitoba-based wing under Crerar and an Alberta-based wing under Henry Wise Wood, an American populist farmer who came to Alberta in 1905 and became president of the United Farmers of Alberta in 1916. Crerar wanted the Progressives to act as a pressure group to force the minority Liberal government to implement policies favourable to farmers. He hoped the Progressives would vote in unison, in essence as a party. Wood, in contrast, seeing political parties as inherently evil, wanted to abolish them altogether, in favour of "group government" based on all occupational groups in society. Wood argued that society naturally divided into several economic interest groups, of which the farmers constituted one — the largest on the Prairies. If each group obtained representation in Parliament, then the laws passed would reflect the interests of all rather than those of the particular group that happened to control the party. In this way, group co-operation would replace party competition. The women's section of the UFA — the United Farm Women of Alberta (UFWA) — was particularly enthusiastic about the prospect of co-operation, and was instrumental under President Irene Parlby from 1917 to 1921 in the election of a UFA government.

Unable to resolve their differences, the divided Progressives proved ineffective. They declined the role of official opposition even though, as the second-largest party in the House of Commons, they warranted it. Then, in 1922, Crerar resigned as leader, claiming he could not work with Wood. Robert Forke, Crerar's successor, had no better luck at uniting the party. One of his alleged followers commented that Forke "does not control one Progressive vote other than his own, and he is not always sure about that."

The divisions revealed the Progressives to be little more than a loose federation of regional groups with insubstantial roots in British Columbia, Quebec, and the Maritimes, and with deep divisions within their two regions of strength — the Prairies and Ontario. The party continued to lose political strength throughout the 1920s. By the election of 1930, they had become a spent force.

In many respects, the Progressives attempted the impossible: to base a party solely on farmers at a time of rural depopulation. They wanted to preserve the family farm, to uphold rural values, and to ensure the political dominance of agricultural interests in an increasingly urban and industrial society. Still, the spirit of the Progressives lived on in the philosophy of populism and in the tradition of western protest. Two new western-Canadian-based parties in the 1930s — the Co-operative Commonwealth Federation and the Social Credit movement — would succeed them.

THE ELECTION OF 1925

Meanwhile, from 1921 until 1925, Mackenzie King's minority government ruled precariously, relying on the support of the moderate Progressives. To win over the Progressives, King's Liberal government moderately reduced tariffs and restored the preferential freight rates contained in the Crow's Nest Pass Agreement of 1897, suspended during the war years. In terms of other legislation, however, the Liberals did little. Historians John Thompson and Allen Seager note that "it is impossible to point to a single conspicuous legislative achievement between 1922 and 1925."[1]

In fairness to King on the tariff issue, it must be admitted that he had difficulty trying to reconcile the anti-tariff views of the Progressives and the pro-tariff position of the Maritime Rights movement. The latter wanted tariff protection to strengthen Atlantic Canada's steel and coal industries. It had supported the Liberals in the election of 1921 on this condition. When the Liberals failed to raise the tariff, Maritime voters switched their loyalty to the Conservatives in the 1925 federal election, giving them 28 of their 31 seats.

The Liberals lost heavily in the election of 1925. Their numbers fell from 116 to 99 in a House of Commons with 245 members. The prime minister lost his seat, as did eight other cabinet ministers. Only in Quebec did the Liberals retain their numbers. The Conservatives more than doubled their number of seats, to 116, doing exceptionally well in the Maritimes and in Ontario. The Progressives, divided into moderate and radical wings, saw their strength decline by almost two-thirds, to 24 seats.

THE KING–BYNG AFFAIR

Despite his party's setback, King was determined to stay in office, believing he could win enough support from the moderates among the Progressives to win a loss-of-confidence vote. In the throne speech, King made further concessions to westerners by promising a farm-loan program, the immediate completion of a rail link from the prairies to Hudson Bay, the transfer of the natural resources of the three Prairie provinces to their own control, and tariff revisions. To gain the support of J.S. Woodsworth and his followers, King promised an old-age pension plan.

The situation looked encouraging for the Liberals until a customs department scandal broke. Civil servants had received payoffs for allowing liquor smuggling into the United States, where prohibition remained in force. The Progressives, champions of purity in government, could no longer support the Liberals.

Realizing that his government faced certain defeat, King decided to circumvent normal parliamentary procedure. He asked the governor general, Lord Byng, to

Where Historians Disagree

CAUSES OF REGIONAL PROTEST MOVEMENTS IN EASTERN AND WESTERN CANADA IN THE 1920S

Historians have debated the reasons for the rise of protest movements on the Prairies and in the Maritimes immediately after World War I. Initially, they explained such protests as indigenous to the regions. As a frontier community inhabited by irascible farmers, the prairie West naturally protested against everything from the weather to railways, grain merchants, and the federal government. Political scientist Walter Young, for example, wrote in *Democracy and Discontent: Progressivism, Socialism and Social Credit in the Canadian West*, 2nd ed. (Toronto: McGraw-Hill Ryerson, 1978), "It was thoroughly consistent with the frontier tradition of self-sufficiency and independence that they [the people of the West] should form their own political machines to influence or wrest power from the old and insensitive engines of government in the east" (p. 111). By contrast, commentators viewed Maritimers as innately conservative, in keeping with long residence in this marginal region. Here, protest arose to fight changes that threatened to undermine their way of life. In short, earlier analysts regarded the West as a region that looked to the future and favoured change, while the Maritimes looked to the past and wanted to maintain the status quo.

This view of the regions as having innate qualities, consistent for all time, has given way to a view of regions as dynamic entities, forever changing as a result of the way they function in the larger Canadian context. In the case of the Maritimes and the West, both regions served as hinterlands for the metropolitan centres of central Canada. This metropolitan–hinterland relationship, as historians and regional economists have labelled it, has benefited central Canada at the expense of the outlying regions of the West and the Maritimes. In the "Bias of Prairie Politics," in *Transactions of the Royal Society of Canada*, vol. 49, series 111, sec. 2 (June 1955), W.L. Morton describes how the initial bias of inequality, resulting from the West's weak political representation and its lack of control, until 1930, over its natural resources, set off a series of protests that came to include the Progressive movement. Maritimers also felt cheated in Confederation and linked the beginning of their economic decline with their agreement to unite with the Upper and Lower Canadians. Historian George Rawlyk argues in "Nova Scotia Regional Protest, 1867–1967," in *Queen's Quarterly*, 85 (Spring 1968), that this feeling of persecution in Confederation created a "paranoid style," in which Maritimers "felt that the hostile and almost conspiratorial world of 'Upper Canada' was directed specifically against their beloved Nova Scotia" (p. 107). Such feelings of regional protest tended to erupt in times of economic crises, as happened in the 1920s.

Recent studies of the prairie West and the Maritimes in the interwar years have seen the Progressive and the Maritime Rights movements as part of a wider reform tradition. In "The Social Gospel as the Religion of the Agrarian Revolt," in C. Berger and R. Cook, eds., *The West and the Nation: Essays in Honour of W.L. Morton* (Toronto: McClelland & Stewart, 1976), Richard Allen linked the leadership, ideology, and aspirations of the Progressive movement directly to the social gospel movement. Maritime historian Ernest Forbes, in his book *The Maritime Rights Movement, 1919–1927: A Study in Canadian Regionalism* (Montreal/Kingston: McGill-Queen's University Press,

(continued)

1979), tied the Maritime Rights movement to the "progressive ideology of the period, which increased the pressure upon the small governments for expensive reforms while at the same time suggesting the possibility of limitless achievement through a strategy of unity, organization and agitation. Consequently, regional awareness increased sharply in the three provinces" (p. 38). This broadening of perspective offers a fuller understanding of the complexity and dynamics of regional protest.

dissolve Parliament and call an election before a loss-of-confidence vote could be taken in the House. The prime minister had the constitutional right to make such a request, but the governor general equally had the right to refuse it — and he did. King promptly resigned as prime minister and announced to a surprised House of Commons on Monday, June 28, that the country was without a government.

The governor general asked Meighen, as leader of the opposition, to form a government. He agreed. The new Conservative government lasted only three days before being defeated by a single vote, giving Meighen the dubious honour of presiding over the shortest-lived government since Confederation. Now, the governor general had no choice but to dissolve Parliament and call the election that he had denied King a few days earlier.

In the 1926 election, King maintained that the governor general had acted unconstitutionally. By refusing to take the advice of his elected representative, he had tried to reduce Canada "from the status of a self-governing Dominion to the status of a Crown Colony." King's strategy was brilliant; it enabled him to sidestep the customs scandal, which Meighen claimed was the real issue in the election. The collapse of the Progressives allowed the Liberals to make substantial gains in the West. New promises to Ontario and the Maritimes ensured greater success there too. In this way, King won his first majority government.

FROM COLONY TO NATION

After 1921, King's Liberal government made significant advances in foreign policy. The prime minister wanted greater autonomy for Canada within the British empire, which to him meant avoiding commitments abroad that might force Canada into the arms of Britain. To achieve this objective, King delegated himself minister of external affairs and appointed O.D. Skelton, a Queen's University political economist whose outlook on foreign affairs coincided with his own, as his undersecretary of state for external affairs, a position Skelton held until his death in 1941.

King's government reduced military expenditures and the size of the Canadian armed forces in the early 1920s. Along with the other western democracies, it consistently opposed any attempt to strengthen the military aspects of the League of Nations. Canada, it might be said, was in the league but not of the league. Frequently, Canadian delegates reminded fellow league members of the hundred years of peaceful relations between Canada and the United States. "We think in terms of peace," Senator Dandurand told the league assembly, "while Europe, an armed camp, thinks

"Wooing the West." Cartoonist
Donald McRitchie echoes the
Maritimers' complaints that
the Mackenzie King government
favoured the West's regional
demands over their own.
From the Halifax Herald,
October 3, 1925.

....

Reprinted with permission from
The Halifax Herald Ltd.

in terms of war." Canadians, he went on to say, "live in a fire-proof house, far from
inflammable material. A vast ocean separates us from Europe." The implication was
that Canada could, and should, be isolationist. Prime Minister Mackenzie King
concurred wholeheartedly with this viewpoint.

THE CHANAK CRISIS AND THE HALIBUT TREATY

As an isolationist, King reacted negatively to British attempts to establish a common
imperial foreign policy. The test case became the Chanak crisis. Under the Treaty of
Sèvres, one of the treaties ending World War I, the British government agreed to maintain troops in Chanak, Turkey, to ensure the neutrality of the Dardanelles, the strategic
straits linking the Black Sea to the Mediterranean Sea. In 1922, Turkish nationalists
attempted to oust the British troops in the region.

British leaders appealed for a concerted imperial response. King saw Britain's
appeal as another attempt to embroil the dominions in faraway conflicts of no interest
to them. He replied that only the Canadian Parliament could decide Canadian participation. Parliament happened not to be in session, and he was in no hurry to summon
it. Opposition leader Arthur Meighen, however, did not mince words. "Ready, aye,
ready we stand by you" should have been Canada's answer, he claimed in a statement
that he would later regret. By the time Parliament met, the crisis had passed. The
Liberal government's refusal of automatic support in the Chanak crisis ended the
attempt to define a common imperial policy.

The Halibut Treaty of 1923, a Canadian–American agreement relating to fishing
rights on the Pacific coast, became the next step on the road to greater Canadian
autonomy. By tradition, only agents of the British government signed treaties affecting
the dominions. King resented this "badge of colonialism" and decided to use the treaty
to assert Canada's diplomatic independence. He arranged for Ernest Lapointe, minister of marine and fisheries, to be the sole signatory for Canada. The British reluctantly
consented, fearing that opposition would prompt Canada to establish its own diplomatic relations with Washington, thereby causing even greater disruption.

THE BALFOUR DECLARATION

King and the leaders of other dominions now sought a formal proclamation that would recognize their equality with Britain. That came with the Balfour Declaration, signed at the Imperial Conference of 1926. It recognized the dominions as "autonomous communities within the British empire, equal in status, in no way subordinate to one another in any respect of their domestic or external affairs, though united by a common allegiance to the Crown, and freely associated as members of the British Commonwealth of Nations."

In keeping with its recognized equality, Canada established legations or embassies overseas. In 1927, Ottawa opened a legation in Washington, and the United States opened one in Ottawa. Canada also exchanged representatives with Paris and Tokyo in 1928. Britain posted a high commissioner in Ottawa, who henceforth replaced the governor general as the British government's representative in Canada. Canada had already had a high commissioner in London since 1884.

THE STATUTE OF WESTMINSTER

The final step to securing full Canadian autonomy in foreign affairs occurred in 1931 with the signing of the Statute of Westminster. This act prohibited the British Parliament from declaring any law passed by the Canadian Parliament as being *ultra vires*, or unconstitutional, except for laws amending the British North America Act. Canada insisted on continued British approval for these laws because of the failure of the federal and provincial governments to agree on an amending formula among themselves. Some constitutional authorities have viewed the Statute of Westminster as Canada's equivalent of the American Declaration of Independence because Canada was now constitutionally independent of Britain, except in regard to any laws amending the BNA Act.

THE ECONOMICS OF ADJUSTMENT

Instability marked the Canadian economy in the 1920s. A volatile international situation and, within Canada, a transition from the old staple economy of fish, timber, and wheat to a new resource economy of pulp and paper, mining, and consumer production meant adjustment. In the first two years of the decade Canada faced a serious business depression. This was followed by a couple of years of slow growth before a five-year boom, beginning in 1925.

The postwar world economy faced a dramatic shift. Weakened by war, Britain could no longer continue as the financial and economic world leader; it devalued its pound sterling. In contrast, the buoyant American economy increased the value of the American dollar. For Canada, the transition proved especially difficult because of its traditional dependency on British markets for trade and on British financial institutions for investment money. Within a brief decade, beginning in 1914, British investment fell to less than 46 percent of the total foreign investment in Canada. In contrast, American investment increased to 51 percent. "Never again," economic historians Kenneth Norrie and Douglas Owram write, "would the mother country come close to the United States in its investment in Canada."[2]

Canadians had to adjust to the differing approach of American investors, compared with that of the British. The British preferred indirect investment in the form of bonds and debentures, whereas American investors favoured equity investment (purchasing common shares) and direct control through branch plants. At the time, few Canadians questioned American economic intervention, since they welcomed American investment of any kind. Canadians also increased substantially their exports to the United States. In 1923, for the first time, Canadians exported more to the United States than to Britain. Since, however, the United States tended to be heavily protectionist in the early 1920s, this affected Canadian exports adversely, especially in the manufacturing, construction, and transportation industries.

During this transition and as a result of the postwar depression, a number of Canadian banks and companies closed or underwent restructuring to avoid collapse. The Home Bank, with its 71 branches across the country, folded in 1923. The Merchant Bank, the Bank of Ottawa, and the Bank of Hamilton sought mergers or were taken over by more stable institutions to avoid similar failures. (This instability benefited the larger banks because people looked to them for sound investment.) As well, many companies, nearly 4000 in 1922, went bankrupt. Unemployment in the primary sector rose substantially.

A BRIEF ECONOMIC BOOM

By 1925, the economy experienced a rebound. The booming American economy and an easing of U.S. protectionist policies increased demand for the traditional Canadian staples of wheat and lumber, as well as the newer staples of pulp and paper and base metals. As freight rates and tariffs declined, prices rose. Farmers increased their hectarages of wheat production and established wheat pools to market abundant crops. Annually, western farmers hired more than 50 000 harvesters from eastern Canada. The crop in 1928 proved to be the largest on record — 567 million bushels. Prices also remained high during these years. Vancouver benefited from the wheat boom as prairie farmers increasingly shipped their wheat via Vancouver and the Panama Canal to Europe. By 1925, Vancouver had six storage elevators with a capacity of 6.9 million bushels.

The wheat boom of the mid-1920s did not, however, begin another era of expansion; rather, it signalled the final phase of the long cycle of nation building based on the wheat economy. Canadian farmers now had to compete with other wheat-growing regions of the world, such as Argentina, Australia, and the Soviet Union, for a shrinking world market as wheat consumption declined.

Pulp and paper became Canada's leading new export. At the beginning of the 1920s, paper mills in Canada made more than 795 000 tons of newsprint each day; by the end of the decade, this production increased threefold to 2725 million tons — enough to print 40 billion newspapers a year. Much of the demand came from the United States, where mass-produced daily newspapers needed cheap newsprint. American branch-plant mills in Canada produced most of the newsprint. Several factors contributed to this decision: the availability of inexpensive pulpwood; cheap hydro-electric power; good transportation facilities; and lower American import duties. Politics also played a part; provincial governments either placed an embargo on the export of pulpwood from Crown lands or imposed a stumpage charge on the number of trees cut, an amount that declined if the producers made the pulp in Canada.

Along with increased production came consolidation. By the end of the decade, three giant companies — International, Abitibi, and Canadian Power and Paper — controlled over half of the pulp production, while the next three largest companies controlled another quarter. Americans owned more than one-third of Canada's pulp production.

Mining followed a similar pattern. After a sluggish period in the early 1920s, mining revived as a result of an American demand for Canadian-based metals to produce such consumer goods as automobiles, radios, and electrical appliances. In Quebec, mineral production increased nearly thirtyfold from 1898 to 1929. Whole new areas, such as Noranda (a name combining the words "North" and "Canada"), Rouyn, Malartic, Val d'Or, and Bourlamaque, opened up with the discovery of new lodes of copper, zinc, lead, and precious metals. In British Columbia, Cominco developed new flotation techniques to mill base metals, which revived a dying industry. In Manitoba, a Canadian–American group, incorporated as Hudson Bay Mining and Smelting, refined the ore at Flin Flon, about 100 km north of The Pas, and at Lynn Lake, still farther north. Ontario benefited greatly from the rich mineral deposits in its northland. The nickel companies in the Sudbury area doubled production during the 1920s, thanks in part to the decision of the Canadian government in 1922 to accept nickel coinage. Inco, the International Nickel Company of Canada, controlled more than 90 percent of world production.

Hydro-electric production quadrupled in the mid-1920s, providing power for the pulp and paper industry and for the refineries. This energy source was particularly important for the production of aluminum from bauxite ore, a process that required substantial amounts of electricity. Provincial governments realized the importance of hydro-electric power for industrialization and the high cost involved in building hydro-electric plants. Ontario nationalized private companies and included them in Ontario Hydro. In Quebec, the industry remained in private hands but developed with the provincial government's financial support.

A REVOLUTION IN TRANSPORTATION AND COMMUNICATIONS

Growth in the primary sector — wheat, timber, and minerals — multiplied markets in the secondary sector. The most spectacular secondary growth occurred in the automotive industry. Next to the United States, Canada became "the most motorized country on the globe." The numbers of cars, trucks, buses, and motorcycles on Canadian roads tripled from 408 000 in 1920 to 1.235 million a decade later, while the total capital investment in the industry more than doubled, from $40 million to $98 million.

Initially, Canada produced its own cars. At one time as many as 70 small companies manufactured, assembled, or sold automobiles in Canada. By the 1920s, however, Canadian companies failed to keep pace with their automated American counterparts, which could make mass-produced, less expensive, models. Eventually, the Canadian car manufacturers sold out to the American giants. In 1904, Gordon McGregor of the Walkerville Wagon Works obtained a franchise for Canada and the British empire from the Ford Company of America to establish the Ford Company of

Canada. Sam McLaughlin used American technology, expertise, and money to begin producing McLaughlin cars in Oshawa, Ontario, and then sold his company in 1918 to General Motors of America. From 1923 onward, the Canadian branch of General Motors oversaw the production of the entire line of GM models, including Chevrolets and Cadillacs, and sold them throughout Canada and the Commonwealth. Chrysler, the last of the "big three" manufacturers to appear in Canada, came when the American automobile tycoon Walter P. Chrysler bought out the ailing Maxwell–Chalmers company of Windsor in 1925 to establish the Chrysler Company of Canada. By the end of the decade, the American "big three" manufactured three-quarters of the cars purchased in Canada.

Canadians had already begun, in the words of historian Arthur Lower, to worship "the great god CAR."[3] By the end of the decade, one-quarter of all potential owners had an automobile. The car revolutionized the Canadian landscape as the railway had done 70 years earlier. Roads again became important, and in the cities, paved streets became commonplace. In 1925, Canada had 75 200 km of surfaced roads; by 1930, this had almost doubled (128 000 km). Tire companies and factories emerged to produce tires and spare parts, service stations sprang up, and tourism prospered. The car made it easier to get to vacation areas — where there were roads.

Aviation also expanded greatly in the 1920s. Veteran World War I flying aces, using surplus war planes, opened up the North. They flew geologists and prospectors into remote areas of the Canadian Shield and provided service to isolated northern settlements. These pilots travelled by visual flying; lacking proper maps, they had to stay at low altitudes to spot familiar landmarks. In 1924, Laurentide Air Services began Canada's first regular air-mail service, into the Quebec gold fields at Rouyn–Noranda. Other companies followed, and for several years the Canadian government permitted each company to print and issue its own postage stamps.

Important communications inventions became popular in the 1920s. The telephone, invented about 1875 by Alexander Graham Bell, a Canadian, became a standard household item by the 1920s. With party lines, eavesdropping (rubbernecking, as it was called then) became a national pastime. Radio, the great communications invention of the 1920s, helped to end isolation and loneliness. The first scheduled broadcast in North America took place in Montreal in May 1920, when station XWA (later CFCF) relayed a musical program to a Royal Society of Canada meeting in Ottawa. Others were quick to realize the potential of this new invention. By mid-decade, there were numerous stations (most of them small and low-powered) across the country.

SERVICE INDUSTRIES

Service industries grew to meet the demand of the new consumer age. Retailing, wholesaling, insurance, and banking needs meant more offices and a vast amount of paperwork. The number of managerial and clerical positions grew to keep pace. Mass production, thanks to improved technology, contributed to lower consumer prices. Effective advertising kept consumer goods in the public mind, heightening the demand. Chain stores were popular, accounting for 90 percent of sales by the end of the decade. Their wide array of material goods appealed to every taste. The

Airplanes sharply reduced travel time. In 1934, travellers from Fort McMurray in northern Alberta to Great Bear Lake in the Northwest Territories could choose between 30 days by steamboat or 8 hours by plane.

Canadian Geographical Journal 10(5) (May 1935): 241.

Canadian T. Eaton Company competed effectively with such American chain stores as Kresge's, Woolworth's, and Metropolitan. Large supermarkets, such as Safeway, Dominion, Overwaitea, A & P, Loblaws, and IGA, began replacing the small corner-grocery store and offering a larger variety of food items and cheaper prices. Women dominated as retail clerks in these large grocery and department stores, but not at the managerial level.

DISILLUSIONMENT AND THE DECLINE OF REFORM

The initial euphoria and the hope for world peace following the "war to end wars" died quickly after the armistice. Across the globe many nations, instead of emerging into freedom and liberty, slipped back into tyranny and oppression. The new millennium, embodied in American President Woodrow Wilson's fourteen-point program to ensure world peace forever, never arrived. Canadians' awareness of the failed peace contributed to their disillusionment. On November 12, 1924, the *Varsity*, the student newspaper at the University of Toronto, summarized the Armistice Day address of Professor G.M. Smith, a distinguished soldier and the winner of the Military Cross in the Great War:

> The idealism of youth, and its enthusiasm in fighting for what they considered a good cause, the optimistic spirit which filled the people during the war and reached its climax when the Armistice was signed, all this is shattered by the six years aftermath. The fourteen points became the fourteen disappointments and self-determination has become selfish-determination.

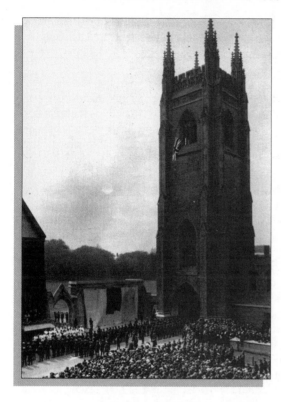

The dedication of the commemorative Soldier's Tower at the University of Toronto, June 5, 1924. The Memorial Wall, in the centre, just about to be unveiled, contains the names of the university's students, graduates, and staff killed in the Great War.

University of Toronto Archives/ A65-0004/006 (2A.16).

After the end of the war, the peace movement gathered strength. League of Nations societies arose across the country in the 1920s, actively supported by the Woman's Christian Temperance Union and the National Council of Women. Other women pacifists joined the Canadian Women's Peace Party and, later, the Women's International League for Peace and Freedom, an organization spearheaded by Violet McNaughton, editor of the women's page of the *Western Producer*. This organization fought to replace cadet training in schools with physical education and to revise curricula and textbooks that glorified war and the military.

Idealism and reform declined. This occurred naturally as each of the reform movements had achieved many of its goals. By 1921, workers had a higher standard of living and had achieved better recognition from employers. Women had the franchise federally and in most provinces. Prohibitionists had succeeded in eliminating legalized drinking. Educational reformers' achievements included better schools, children staying in school longer, and better-qualified teachers. Yet, in a sense, all these groups had failed in their ultimate objective: a new, regenerated, harmonious, and utopian Canada.

PROHIBITION AND WOMEN'S SUFFRAGE

In some instances, a reaction to reform set in. Prohibitionists, for example, saw the provincial temperance acts removed one by one. By the end of the 1920s, government-regulated outlets sold liquor in every province except Prince Edward Island. Ironically, returned soldiers — the very people prohibitionists had used to fight *for* prohibition during the war years — played a large part in ending prohibition, as they demanded legalized drinking.

The women's suffrage movement had obtained the vote, but the electorate returned few women to either federal or provincial governments. Agnes Macphail became the only woman elected in the federal election of 1921 and was Canada's first woman member of Parliament. The teacher from Grey County, Ontario, had not been involved in the women's reform movement, but shared its zeal for absolute equality. She served from 1921 to 1940, when she was defeated. She was then elected to the Ontario legislature from 1943 to 1945 and again from 1948 to 1951 as a CCF candidate. Only one other woman, Martha Black, sat in the House of Commons in the interwar years, representing her husband's Yukon constituency from 1935 to 1940, when he was incapacitated by poor health. Provincially, women did better at entering politics, although the results were a far cry from their expectations. By 1940, only nine women sat in provincial legislatures, all of them in the four western provinces. Mary Ellen Smith of British Columbia held the distinction of being the first woman cabinet minister in the British empire when she was appointed in 1921 as minister without portfolio. However, she held the position for only nine months before resigning. Even the usually optimistic Nellie McClung expressed the disillusionment of the time: "When women were given the vote in 1916–17 . . . we were obsessed with the belief that we could cleanse and purify the world by law. . . . But when all was over, and the smoke of battle cleared away, something happened to us. Our forces, so well organized for the campaign, began to dwindle."

Women faced continued discrimination. Not until 1929, for example, were women considered "persons" in the act stipulating eligibility for the Canadian Senate and a variety of other privileged bodies. In the famous "Persons Case," five Alberta women reformers — Emily Murphy, the first woman police magistrate in the British empire; Irene Parlby, the first woman cabinet minister in Alberta; Nellie McClung, a member of the Alberta legislature; and Henrietta Edwards and Louise McKinney, two suffragists and prohibitionists — succeeded in securing a favourable decision from the Judicial Committee of the Privy Council that they were "persons" and thus eligible for membership in all Canadian legislative bodies.

Urban reform languished in the inter-war years, in part because the middle-class group most involved in reform began to move out of the city centres and into the suburbs. Suburbanization occurred at an astonishing rate with the development of tramlines and the increasing popularity of the automobile.

Social gospellers retreated in the mainstream churches during the prosperous 1920s, as churchgoers became more concerned with personal prosperity and individual salvation than with social regeneration. Church reformers within the Methodist, Presbyterian, and Congregationalist churches did succeed in 1925 in creating the United Church of Canada. They hoped that this new church would rejuvenate the reformers' zeal and challenge the secularization of Canadian society. But when the new church challenged society, it appeared to some as too radical and reform-minded. They left and joined fundamentalist churches that upheld more traditional values and beliefs, or they became members of conservative sects and cults.

Saskatchewan Hall, Campus of the University of Saskatchewan, Saskatoon, about 1910. The University began in 1909, four years after Saskatchewan became a province.

....

Frank Hawkins Underhill Collection/ National Archives of Canada/PA-121376.

L'ACTION FRANÇAISE

In the 1920s, right-wing elements in Quebec's Roman Catholic community reacted to the growing secularization of society. Abbé Lionel Groulx, the editor of *L'Action française*, saw the onslaught of urban and industrial society as anathema to everything French Canadians believed in: the church, the family, and the French-Canadian nation. In his journal, which had only 5000 subscribers at its peak, Groulx launched an all-out attack — *l'action française* — on those forces that he believed were contributing to the anglicization and Americanization of Quebec.

L'Action française called for greater French-Canadian control of the modern industrial economy. While contributors to the magazine deplored the economic weakness of French Canadians, most of them still believed that agriculture should be the cornerstone of the French-Canadian economy. They opposed the growing urban migration, especially to Montreal. To *L'Action française*, the migration threatened the very existence of the French Canadians as traditionally rural, agricultural people.

Historian Susan Mann Trofimenkoff summarized the movement's outlook: "Cities bred standardization, homogeneity, and ultimately, they suspected, assimilation."[4] To counter this urbanization, *L'Action française* stressed the traditional values of the land, the church, and the nation. Groulx placed a special responsibility on women as guardians of the home and the family. In 1922, *L'Action française* flirted with the idea of political independence for Quebec, but it returned by the late 1920s to the position that French Canadians should have more rights within Confederation.

WOMEN IN THE 1920S

Women made only modest gains in the workplace in the 1920s. Not all had the opportunity for a secondary education. In 1929, only a quarter of the national secondary-school student body were women. Of the few who entered the professions, most became teachers or nurses, while only a handful physicians, lawyers, or professors, and a very tiny number, engineers. Nursing took on a new importance in light of the tremendous contribution of nurses during the war and the Spanish influenza epidemic that followed it. In 1919, the University of British Columbia offered the first university-degree program in nursing. Similar programs followed at the University of Toronto and McGill University in the 1920s.

Elsie Hall, class of 1920, first woman graduate of the College of Law, University of Saskatchewan.

....

College of Law, University of Saskatchewan.

Women who worked outside the home in industry or business — 20 percent of the labour force in 1929 — held traditional female jobs as secretaries, sales clerks in department stores, and domestics. Others worked on assembly lines in textile or tobacco factories, canneries, or fish plants. In these jobs, women earned considerably less than men doing the same job. Economic equality, like political equality, remained an elusive goal for women.

Unions did little to organize working women, even in the female-dominated industries. Seldom did they support women on strike. Some union locals included males and females, but even when unions included women, they usually subordinated their interests to men's. Agreements with employers commonly included lower female wage-scales. In some cases, male-dominated unions demanded equal pay for women and men — not to combat discrimination against women but rather to ensure that employers would have no financial reason to replace male employees with females.

In prairie farm homes, women worked as hard as ever. Although many farms were becoming more mechanized in the 1920s, the farmhouses remained very basic. Prairie farm wives were also expected to help outside the house at critical times of the year, while they continued caring for the children, cooking, cleaning, laundering, and sewing. According to historian Veronica Strong-Boag, prairie women were not "pulling in double harness" but "hauling a double load."[5] Rural reform leaders advocated household-science courses, co-operation, and the use of more household appliances as ways of alleviating the burden.

Urban middle-class women enjoyed a higher standard of living than their rural counterparts. Many benefited from modern labour-saving devices such as refrigerators, electric stoves, and vacuum cleaners, and from such luxuries as electricity and running water. Ironically, these "conveniences" increased the amount of time women spent in the home. In many cases this simply raised the standards expected of women in the home.

A battery of "how to parent" books made child rearing more rigorous and scientific. Dr. Helen McMurchy, chief of the newly created Child Welfare Division in 1919, reminded women that "being a mother is the highest of all professions and the most extensive of all undertakings." To prepare them for their new role, girls were encouraged to stay in school longer and to concentrate on domestic-science courses. The few women who dared to "break out" and be unconventional — the "flappers" — dressed more freely, smoked in public, and — most daring of all — drank at parties. The birth-control movement began in Vancouver in 1923 with the formation of the Canadian Birth Control League, the idea inspired by the visit of the American birth-control advocate Margaret Sanger. Women, however, had to wait until the 1930s for any birth-control clinics to open.

THE NATIVE PEOPLES

The experience of the Native peoples in the 1920s varied across Canada. In the northern forested areas, the Amerindians suffered greatly when boom prices for furs led to an influx of non-Native trappers. Intensive trapping resulted in a serious depletion in the numbers of beaver. Wage labour, however, partially compensated for the loss of income from trapping, now necessary to buy trade goods and store food. Some Native people worked as tourist guides, in commercial fishing, as miners, railway workers, and loggers. Reserve farming declined in the south as heavy expenditures became necessary for the new farm machinery. Among the Iroquois, high-steel rigging, although dangerous work, remained popular and lucrative. On the Pacific coast, Native people could obtain jobs in logging and commercial fishing. A number of independent Native operators owned and operated gas-powered gillnetters, trollers, and seine boats.

LABOUR IN THE 1920S

Labour unions faced difficult times in the 1920s, as business attempted to limit trade unions' effectiveness. Wage cuts, industrial consolidation, improved technology, and managerial efficiency weakened the labour movement. Workers retaliated by staging strikes, many of which ended in physical violence. For example, 22 000 coal miners, mainly in Alberta, walked out on strike in August 1922. In 1923, a confrontation occurred in the coal mines of Nova Scotia. James B. McLachlan, the militant Scottish immigrant worker and socialist who had helped found the Amalgamated Mine Workers of Nova Scotia in 1917, led the strike against BESCO, the leading steel company in the region. "War is on us, class war," he proclaimed in one of his fiery speeches. The company's vice-president replied: "Let them stay out two months or six months, it matters not; eventually they will come crawling back." The company eventually mobilized its security force to break up the strike. The workers won some limited concessions, but a legacy of hatred remained. In most other strikes across the country, strikers failed to improve wages or working conditions. As a result, union membership plummeted by more than one-third by mid-decade, reaching a low of 260 000 members.

Unions were also divided. The conservative Trades and Labor Congress (TLC) continued to favour craft unions and advocate advancement only through conciliation and government intervention. Thus the TLC had refused to back the strikers against

A Historical Portrait

ONONDEYOH (FRED LOFT)

Fred Loft, or Onondeyoh ("Beautiful Mountain"), a Mohawk in the Ontario civil service, sought the improvement of the system of education offered to the First Nations. Immediately after World War I the Mohawk veteran established the League of Indians of Canada, the country's first pan-Indian political association.

Fred Loft was born February 3, 1861, on the Six Nations Reserve near Brantford, Ontario. His parents (who spoke English as well as Mohawk) were devoted Anglicans. Fred attended a local school until the age of 12, when he boarded for a year at the Mohawk Institute, an Indian residential school in Brantford. Bitterly, he remembered the horrific experience: "I recall the times when working in the fields, I was actually too hungry to be able to walk, let alone work.... In winter the rooms and beds were so cold that it took half the night before I got warm enough to fall asleep."

Anxious to get the best education possible, he attended high school in the neighbouring non-Native community of Caledonia. After graduation, he won a scholarship to the Ontario Business College in Belleville. After briefly working as a journalist for a Brantford paper, he obtained a job as an accountant in the bursar's office at the Provincial Lunatic Asylum in Toronto, where he stayed for 40 years.

In 1898, the Mohawk civil servant met and married Affa Northcote Geare, a lively, energetic woman of British descent, 11 years younger than he. In Toronto in 1899, Affa gave birth to twins, one of whom died in 1902. Another daughter was born in 1904. For many extras the family depended on Affa, who had a sharp business sense. She bought and sold houses, rented to roomers, and owned stock.

The Lofts had an active life, with season tickets to two Toronto theatres. Fred participated in the Masons and the United Empire Loyalist Association and was active in the militia. Every Sunday he attended church. He also returned regularly to the Six Nations Reserve to visit his family. His daughters spent many summers at the family farm. Unsuccessfully, the Six Nations Council requested the federal government to select him in 1907, and again in 1917, as their superintendent.

As a staunch supporter of Britain, Fred Loft visited Ontario Indian reserves during World War I to encourage Aboriginal recruitment. He was a physically impressive man, standing nearly 6 feet tall and weighing 170 lbs. Anxious to go overseas himself, he served as an officer in France in the Canadian Forestry Corps.

Upon his return from Europe, the Mohawk veteran founded the League of Indians of Canada. The first annual meetings were held in Ontario, then in Manitoba (1920), Saskatchewan (1921), and Alberta (1922). Problems surfaced immediately. Money was short, and correspondence itself proved difficult. As Fred Loft stated, "The sad want of better schooling is evidenced by the fact that scarcely five percent of the adult population on reserves are capable of corresponding intelligently.... This is a most unfortunate admission to be made after 75 years of school work among Indians of Eastern Canada at least." The Department of Indian Affairs' unrelenting opposition to the league, and Loft's poor health in the early 1930s, further weakened it.

At the moment of Fred Loft's death in 1934 the league, apart from its western Canadian branches, had come to a complete stop. But Onondeyoh's attempt to form a pan-Indian political organization in Canada would succeed a generation later: today Canada has the Assembly of First Nations, formerly the National Indian Brotherhood, founded in the 1960s.

BESCO. When Samuel Gompers, the founder of the American Federation of Labor (AFL) and the inspiration behind the TLC, died later that year, McLachlan, invited to the funeral, replied: "Sorry, duties will not permit me to attend, but I heartily approve of the event." In 1927, a new militant All-Canadian Congress of Labour (ACCL) union was established. It favoured industry-wide unions and strike action.

In Quebec, some workers and farmers joined Roman Catholic unions, guided by priests and sanctioned by the church. These unions attempted to isolate their members from the more secular and often socialistic "foreign" — American or English-Canadian — unions. The Confédération des travailleurs catholiques du Canada (CTCC) brought 20 000 workers from a variety of industries and occupations into its organization in 1921. The Union catholique des cultivateurs (UCC) in 1924 had a membership of 13 000 farmers. By the 1930s, the UCC had joined with the clergy to organize farmers' wives and to compete with the state-sponsored Cercles de fermières. Throughout the 1920s, the CTCC and the UCC together never succeeded, however, in attracting much more than one-quarter of the total Quebec union membership.

CULTURAL DEVELOPMENTS

Cultural life flourished in the 1920s in both English-speaking and French-speaking Canada. Arthur Lismer, one of the Group of Seven artists, later recalled: "After 1919, most creative people, whether in painting, writing or music, began to have a guilty feeling that Canada was as yet unwritten, unpainted, unsung.... In 1920 there was a job to be done." French-Canadian artists, writers, and performers shared the same aspiration, although in their case Quebec tended to be their frame of reference.

VISUAL ARTS

WEB LINKS

In English-speaking Canada, the Group of Seven dominated contemporary art. The original members — Frank Carmichael, Lawren Harris, A.Y. Jackson, Franz Johnston, Arthur Lismer, J.E.H. MacDonald, and F.H. Varley — had met before the war. Most had worked for the Grip commercial-art company in Toronto. Artist Tom Thomson was part of this circle of friends, but he drowned in a canoe accident in Algonquin Park in 1917 before the group formed. In the year of his death, he produced *The Jack Pine* and *The West Wind*, two paintings that have become icons of Canadian art, reproduced on stamps, on posters, and in art books. Thomson became an inspiration and patron saint for the Group of Seven, which formed officially in 1920.

The first Group of Seven exhibition was held in May 1920. The exhibition catalogue claimed that art must reflect "the spirit of a nation's growth." The Group of Seven believed that "spirit" could best be found in the land — in the trees, rocks, and lakes of the Ontario northland. They depicted the land in brilliant mosaics of bright colours. For the Group of Seven, the Ontario northland symbolized the nation in the same way that the West did in the American tradition — a mythical land that became a metaphor for the Canadian people. As well, the "North" represented a counterforce to the "South," especially the United States, where urbanization, industrialism, and materialism were undermining the Canadian spirit.

The West Wind, by Tom Thomson, 1917, one of his best-known paintings. Thomson died in a canoe accident in Algonquin Park in 1917, and thus was not a founding member of the Group of Seven when it formed in 1920. He did, however serve as an inspiration for the Group.

....

Art Gallery of Ontario, Toronto. Gift of the Canadian Club of Toronto, 1926.

Some art critics denounced the group's paintings as belonging to the "Hot Mush School" and its members as "paint slingers." The Group of Seven thrived on the criticism. It indicated that their art challenged the establishment and broke new ground. The group found a strong supporter in Eric Brown, director of the National Gallery in Ottawa, who selected their paintings to represent Canadian art at the British Empire Exhibition at Wembley in 1924. By the time the Group of Seven disbanded in 1931, their members were, in the words of historian Douglas Cole, "elevated to the status of Canadian cultural heroes and their work enshrined as national icons,"[6] even though their best-known paintings depicted only one region of Ontario, the Algoma district, a section south of the 49th parallel.

In British Columbia, Emily Carr had begun in 1908 to visit First Nations communities along the Pacific coast and in the interior of the province. She painted scenes of the villages, of the buildings and totem poles. Unable to support herself by her painting alone, she ran a boarding house in Victoria. A trip in 1927 to eastern Canada allowed her to meet Lawren Harris and other members of the Group of Seven. Her contact with the group, particularly Lawren Harris, gave a fresh direction to her work. After first viewing Harris's work, she wrote: "Oh, God, what have I seen? Where have I been? Something has spoken to the very soul of me, wonderful, mighty not of this world."

In 1932, at age 57, she launched into the most productive period of her artistic career. She emphasized nature themes over First Nations subjects in her paintings. When she suffered a heart attack in 1937, she turned to writing. Her first book, *Klee Wyck*, described her early painting trips to First Nations communities. It won her the Governor General's award for general literature in 1941. Klee Wyck, meaning "Laughing One," was the name given Emily Carr by the Nuu-chah-nulth (formerly known as Nootka) people at Ucluelet on the west coast of Vancouver Island.

On the Prairies, Lionel LeMoine FitzGerald, of Winnipeg, and Illingworth Kerr, from Lumsden, Saskatchewan, captured the region's uniqueness on canvas. In the Maritimes, a group of local artists arranged for their own exhibition and issued their own magazine, *Maritime Art*, which by 1940 had become Canada's first full-fledged art magazine. This Maritime group assisted Jack Humphrey and Miller Brittain, both born and raised in Saint John, New Brunswick, where they spent most of their lives, in becoming internationally recognized Maritime artists.

Sculptors Francis Loring and Florence Wyle, together with Elizabeth Wyn Wood and two male sculptors, established the Sculptors Society of Canada in 1928. Sculptors benefited in the 1920s from the postwar enthusiasm for public memorials.

LITERATURE

A new literary culture also emerged in the 1920s. In English-speaking Canada, two new journals appeared to capture and epitomize the cultural renaissance: the *Canadian Forum* and the *Canadian Historical Review*. In the inaugural issue of the *Canadian Forum* in 1920, the editors promised that the journal would "trace and value those developments of arts and letters which are distinctively Canadian." Equally, the *Canadian Historical Review* noted in an article on "The Growth of Canadian National Feeling" in the second issue that the "central fact in Canadian history" has been the evolution of a "national consciousness." The Canadian Authors' Association (CAA), founded in 1921 for the purpose of using literature "to articulate a national identity and to foster a sense of community within the country," aided young English-Canadian writers in publishing their works. The CAA sponsored summer schools and gave literary prizes.

In poetry, E.J. (Ned) Pratt of Newfoundland introduced modernism into Canadian poetry in his *Newfoundland Verse* (1923). A professor of English at Victoria College, University of Toronto, Pratt used familiar Canadian scenes or events, often from his native Newfoundland, as the subjects for his poems and elevated them to mythical proportions. Pratt inspired a younger generation of English-Canadian poets.

At McGill University, a group of young, rebellious poets known as the "Montreal group" — F.R. Scott, A.J.M. Smith, A.M. Klein, and Leo Kennedy — endorsed the modernist movement. They wrote in free verse, discarded the norms of punctuation, and chose their subject material in the modern city. They began two small literary journals, the *McGill Fortnightly Review* (1925–27) and the *Canadian Mercury* (1928–29), as vehicles for their works.

In French-speaking Quebec, a group of young Québécois poets challenged the establishment in the pages of *Le Nigog*. The first arts magazine in Quebec, it was founded by architect Fernand Préfontaine, writer Robert de Roquebrune, and musician Léo-Paul Morin. Ironically, although this group and the "Montreal group" resided in the same city, they worked in isolation from one another.

Most novels of the 1920s continued to be romantic and escapist. Mazo de la Roche's *Jalna* (1927) chronicled the life of the fictional Whiteoaks family. Her romantic depiction of rural Ontario life sold close to 100 000 copies within a few months of publication, resulting in sixteen sequels. Three novels, however, stood out for their realism: Frederick Philip Grove's *Settlers of the Marsh* (1925), in which Grove explored the inner psychic tension of a Norwegian settler on the Prairies; Martha Ostenso's *Wild Geese* (1925), about the tyrannical patriarch Caleb Gare, who aims to dominate both his land and his family and in the process destroys himself; and R.J.C. Stead's *Grain* (1926), which describes the tensions that farm boy Gander Stake faces in having to choose between life on the farm and in the city.

Frederick Philip Grove in the early 1920s, rafting on Lake Winnipeg with his daughter, May. He was actually Felix Paul Greve, a German translator and writer who faked his own suicide in 1909 by appearing to throw himself off a boat. Having successfully escaped his creditors, three years later he surfaced as Frederick Philip Grove in Manitoba. In his lifetime no one in Canada knew his real identity. The true story was only revealed 25 years after his death, when D.O. Spettigue published his biography of Grove, FPG: The European Years *(1973).*

University of Manitoba Archives
and Special Collections,
The Libraries/PC 2, No. 10.

MUSIC

The University of Toronto's Faculty of Music opened in 1919. The university also housed the Hart House String Quartet, founded in 1924 by Vincent Massey, of the influential Massey family. The Masseys also continued to support Massey Hall, the location of many musical performances, including the concerts of the Toronto Symphony Orchestra.

The radio and the phonograph first brought music directly into Canadian homes in the 1920s. Many Canadian musicians got their start on radio. Radio was used effectively to celebrate the Diamond Jubilee of Confederation in 1927. Beginning in 1929, the Toronto Symphony Orchestra performed 25 concerts over the radio, the last of which was devoted entirely to music by Canadian composers. The concerts could be heard throughout the country.

POPULAR CULTURE

English-speaking Canadian popular culture became more Americanized in the 1920s. American-style service clubs such as Rotary, Lions, Kiwanis, and Gyro gained in popularity, although the uniquely Canadian organization the Kinsmen, founded in 1920 in Hamilton, Ontario, held its own. (Half a century later, the Kinsmen would become Canada's largest national service organization.)

Canadians who had never set eyes on the *Canadian Forum* or even the mass-circulation *Maclean's* knew about such American magazines as *Ladies' Home Journal*, *McCall's*, and *Saturday Evening Post*. By 1926, these American magazines had a combined North American circulation of more than 50 million copies of each issue.

Canadian newspapers in the 1920s adopted an "American" style: glossy, plenty of advertising, sensational headlines and stories, comic strips, substantial sports sections, and a heavy reliance on American wire services for international coverage. Circulation of the nationally distributed Toronto *Star Weekly* doubled when it acquired the comic strips *Bringing Up Father*, *Barney Google*, and *Mutt and Jeff*.

Canada's first radio program was transmitted in 1920. By 1930, some 60 stations existed across the country. Offerings were sparse, however; no station transmitted for more than a few hours a day. Programs consisted mainly of news, lectures, or recorded music, compared with the comedies, drama, and live variety of American programs. English-speaking Canadians fortunate enough to be close to the international border listened to American radio stations, which carried popular programs and had stronger transmitters. Rather than compete, Canadian stations bought the right to broadcast these American shows themselves. By 1930, an estimated 80 percent of the programs Canadians listened to came from the United States.

In 1928, the Canadian government established a royal commission — the Aird Commission — to review public broadcasting. The Aird report recommended that broadcasting become a public monopoly, without competitors and with limited commercial content. The Canadian Radio League, founded by English-Canadian nationalists Alan Plaunt, Graham Spry, and Brooke Claxton, concurred. They hoped, as did the members of the Aird Commission, that public broadcasting would help unite Canadians. Out of their efforts would come the Canadian Broadcasting Corporation (CBC) in the 1930s.

Movies also contributed to the Americanization of Canadian culture in the 1920s. Initially, it did not appear that this would be the case; between 1919 and 1923, Canada had a thriving domestic feature film industry that used Canadian settings, casts, and crews. But thereafter, Canadian companies succumbed to the American "Big Five" studios — Paramount, MGM, Warner Brothers, Fox, and RKO. By 1929, these five companies produced 90 percent of all feature films in North America. They continued to make the occasional movie about Canada, but seldom filmed on location.

SPORTS

The professionalization of Canadian sports continued in the 1920s. This meant indoor stadiums, artificial ice, and large payrolls. It also meant greater Americanization. At the beginning of the 1920s, professional hockey was solely Canadian. The Pacific Coast League (formed in 1911), the Western Canadian League (begun in 1921), and the National Hockey League (NHL, inaugurated in 1917) alone competed for the coveted Stanley Cup. Then the NHL expanded into the lucrative urban market of the United States. By 1927, the NHL consisted of five American and five Canadian teams. The Ottawa Senators dominated the NHL in the early years of the decade, winning the Stanley Cup four times.

The NHL, in turn, dominated hockey throughout the 1920s. It paid the average player $900 a year, with a few exceptional players earning upwards of $10 000. Although interest in the amateur trophies — the Allan Cup and the Memorial Cup — continued in the smaller centres, the focus remained on the NHL even after the league shrank to six teams, with only the Toronto Maple Leafs and the Montreal Canadiens in Canada. Almost all the NHL players remained Canadians.

The Bluenose *in full sail —
Canada's most famous ship.
Winner of the International
Fisherman's Trophy for three
successive years (1921, 1922,
1923), the schooner became
immortalized in 1937 with
its reproduction on the
Canadian dime.*

Commercial Photo Service (Halifax)/
National Archives of Canada/PA-41990.

New trophies were donated throughout the decade: the Hart Trophy, for most valuable team player; the Lady Byng Trophy, donated by the governor general's wife, to the player exhibiting the highest sportsmanship and gentlemanly conduct; the Vezina Trophy, to the goaltender allowing the fewest goals against his team; and the Prince of Wales Trophy, awarded to the season's NHL playoff champion team.

In other sports, a number of Canadian amateurs won international recognition. Track and field athletes Percy Williams and Ethel Catherwood won gold medals at the 1928 Olympics. Williams acquired the reputation of being "the world's fastest human." George Young made a name for Canada in swimming by winning the 32 km race from the California mainland to Catalina Island. In the Maritimes, Captain Angus Walters won the International Fisherman's Trophy three years in succession — in 1921, 1922, and 1923. His schooner, the *Bluenose* (the nickname for Nova Scotians), which never lost a race, was immortalized on the Canadian dime. The famous Edmonton Grads women's basketball team, formed from students and graduates of an Edmonton high school, dominated world basketball from 1915 to 1940. They set a world record by winning 502 games and losing only 20 during their entire careers. The Grads were recognized as world champions at international tournaments on four occasions.

Throughout the 1920s, Mackenzie King and his Liberal party dominated politics. King succeeded in diffusing the Maritime Rights movement in the East and under-mining the Progressive movement in the West. He also moved Canada well along the road to independence. Women and labour unions made some gains, but both groups were still far from achieving a position of equality in Canadian society Culturally, English Canadians and French Canadians made important advances, but in terms of popular culture, both groups, especially English Canadians, came increasingly under

American influence. Few Canadians suspected, as the decade came to an end, that it would be followed by the worst depression in world history.

NOTES

1. John Herd Thompson with Allen Seager, *Canada 1922–1939: Decades of Discord* (Toronto: McClelland & Stewart, 1985), p. 112.
2. Kenneth Norrie and Douglas Owram, *A History of the Canadian Economy*, 2nd ed. (Toronto: Harcourt Brace, 1996), p. 322.
3. A.R.M. Lower, *Canadians in the Making: A Social History of Canada* (Toronto: Longmans, Green, 1958), p. 424.
4. Susan Mann Trofimenkoff, *The Dream of Nation: A Social and Intellectual History of Quebec* (Toronto: Gage, 1983), p. 223.
5. Veronica Strong-Boag, "Pulling in Double Harness or Hauling a Double Load: Women, Work and Feminism on the Canadian Prairie," *Journal of Canadian Studies* 21 (Fall 1986): 36.
6. Douglas Cole, "Artists, Patrons and Public: An Enquiry into the Success of the Group of Seven," *Journal of Canadian Studies* 13(2) (1978): 76.

LINKING TO THE PAST

WEB LINKS

William Lyon Mackenzie King
http://cnet.unb.ca/achn/pme/wlmkdb.htm
A brief biography of William Lyon Mackenzie King, with details about his background and career, and a link to a more descriptive biography at the bottom of the page.

Winged Messenger: Airmail in the Heroic Era, 1918–1939
http://www.civilization.ca/membrs/npm/courrier/wm00eng.html
This virtual exhibition from the Canadian Museum of Civilization offers information on early developments in the airplane industry and on the delivery of airmail.

CIQC: A History of Canada's First Radio Station
http://www.ciqc.com/history/fmain.html
These pages from CIQC's web site offer an illustrated history of the station.

Then & Now: Women in Canadian Legislatures
http://www.nlc-bnc.ca/digiproj/women/women97/ewomen97.htm
This site from the National Library of Canada features a number of biographies, including that of Agnes Macphail.

The Persons Case
http://www.swc-cfc.gc.ca/persone.html
A site devoted to Governor General's Awards in Commemoration of the Persons Case. It includes a brief history of the case and biographies of the five women involved in it.

The Group of Seven and Their Contemporaries
http://www.mcmichael.com/group.htm
This site from the McMichael Canadian Art Collection includes biographies of, and reproductions of works by, the members of the Group of Seven and their associates, as well as a brief history of the group.

RELATED READINGS

....

The following articles from R. Douglas Francis and Donald B. Smith, eds., *Readings in Canadian History: Post-Confederation*, 5th ed. (Toronto: Harcourt Brace, 1998), deal with topics pertaining to the 1920s in greater depth: Nelson Wiseman, "The Pattern of Prairie Politics," pp. 305–22, and E.R. Forbes, "The Origins of the Maritime Rights Movement," pp. 322–32.

BIBLIOGRAPHY

....

For an overview of the 1920s consult John Herd Thompson with Allen Seager, *Canada, 1922–1939: Decades of Discord* (Toronto: McClelland & Stewart, 1985). Robert Bothwell, Ian Drummond, and John English supply considerable material on the 1920s in *Canada, 1900–1945* (Toronto: University of Toronto Press, 1987). For the Maritime provinces see David Frank, "The 1920s: Class and Region, Resistance and Accommodation," in E.R. Forbes and D.A. Muise, eds., *The Atlantic Provinces in Confederation* (Toronto: University of Toronto Press, 1993); and Gary Burrill and Ian McKay, eds., *People, Resources and Power: Critical Perspectives on Underdevelopment and Primary Industries in the Atlantic Region* (Fredericton: Acadiensis Press, 1987). Randall White's *Too Good to Be True: Toronto in the 1920s* (Toronto: Dundurn Press, 1993) is an interesting study.

On Mackenzie King's political life in the 1920s see the latter part of R.M. Dawson, *William Lyon Mackenzie King: A Political Biography*, vol. 1, *1874–1923* (Toronto: University of Toronto Press, 1958); and H.B. Neatby, *The Lonely Heights*, vol. 2, *1924–1932* (Toronto: University of Toronto Press, 1980). A popular study is J.L. Granatstein's *Mackenzie King: His Life and World* (Toronto: McGraw-Hill Ryerson, 1977). Roger Graham's *Arthur Meighen: A Biography*, vol. 2, *And Fortune Fled* (Toronto: Clarke Irwin, 1963), and his pamphlet *Arthur Meighen* (Ottawa: Canadian Historical Association, 1965), deal with King's political rival in the 1920s. On political scandal in the 1920s consult T.D. Regehr, *The Beauharnois Scandal: A Story of Canadian Entrepreneurship and Politics* (Toronto: University of Toronto Press, 1989). On the liquor trade of the time see C.W. Hunt, *Booze, Boats and Billions: Liquor Smuggling in the Prohibition Era* (Toronto: McClelland & Stewart, 1988).

Maritime protest in the 1920s is discussed in E.R. Forbes, *The Maritime Rights Movement, 1919–27: A Study in Canadian Regionalism* (Montreal/Kingston: McGill-Queen's University Press, 1979); and David J. Bercuson, ed., *Canada and the Burden of Unity* (Toronto: Macmillan, 1977). David Frank, "Class Conflict in the Coal Industry: Cape Breton 1922," in G.S. Kealey and P. Warrian, eds., *Essays in Canadian Working-Class History* (Toronto: McClelland & Stewart, 1976), pp. 161–84, recounts the story of labour strife on Cape Breton Island. On the Progressive movement see the relevant chapters in Gerald Friesen, *The Canadian Prairies: A History* (Toronto: University of Toronto Press, 1987); John Thompson, *Forging the Prairie West: The Illustrated History of Canada* (Toronto: Oxford, 1998); David Laycock, *Populism and Democratic Thought in the Canadian Prairies, 1910–1945* (Toronto: University of Toronto Press, 1990); Jeffrey Taylor, *Fashioning Farmers: Ideology, Agricultural Knowledge and the Manitoba Farm Movement, 1890–1925* (Regina: Canadian Plains Research Centre, 1994); Walter Young, *Democracy and Discontent* (Toronto: Ryerson Press, 1969); and W.L. Morton, *The Progressive Party in Canada* (Toronto: University of Toronto Press, 1950). On the plight of Prairie farmers in the 1920s see David Jones, *Empire of Dust: Settling and Abandoning the Prairie Dry Belt* (Edmonton: University of Alberta Press, 1987). On the King–Byng affair, consult the King and Meighen biographies cited in the previous paragraph and Roger Graham, *The King–Byng Affair, 1926* (Toronto: Copp Clark, 1967).

On the economics of the 1920s see the chapter "The Stuttering Twenties," in Michael Bliss, *Northern Enterprise: Five Centuries of Canadian Business* (Toronto: McClelland & Stewart, 1987); Kenneth Norrie and Douglas Owram, *A History of the Canadian Economy*, 2nd ed. (Toronto: Harcourt Brace, 1996); W.L. Marr and Donald G. Paterson, *Canada: An Economic History* (Toronto: Macmillan, 1980); and W.T. Easterbrook and H.G.J. Aitken, *Canadian Economic History* (Toronto: Macmillan, 1956). Consult, as well, Tom Traves, *The State and Enterprise: Canadian Manufacturers and the Federal Government, 1917–31* (Toronto: University of Toronto Press, 1979). For Quebec see Paul-André Linteau, René Durocher, and Jean-Claude Robert, *Quebec: A History, 1867–1929* (Toronto: James Lorimer, 1983).

On the decline of social reform in the 1920s see John Herd Thompson with Allen Seager, *Canada, 1922–1939: Decades of Discord* (Toronto: McClelland & Stewart, 1985). Church union is considered in John W. Grant, *The Canadian Experience of Church Union* (London: John Knox Press, 1967); opposition to church union is the subject of N. Keith Clifford, *The Resistance to Church Union, 1904–1939* (Vancouver: University of British Columbia Press, 1985). Susan Mann Trofimenkoff's *Action Française: French-Canadian Nationalism in the Twenties* (Toronto: University of Toronto Press, 1975) analyzes this French-Canadian group. Society in western Canada is discussed in James Gray, *The Roar of the Twenties* (Toronto: Macmillan, 1975).

On women in the 1920s consult Veronica Strong-Boag, *The New Day Recalled: Lives of Girls and Women in English Canada, 1919–1939* (Toronto: Copp Clark Pitman, 1988); Susan Mann Trofimenkoff and Alison Prentice, eds., *The Neglected Majority: Essays in Canadian Women's History*, vol. 1 (Toronto: McClelland & Stewart, 1977), and vol. 2 (1985); Jean Burnet, ed., *Looking Into My Sister's Eyes: An Exploration in Women's History* (Toronto: Multicultural History Society of Ontario, 1986); and Suzanne Morton, *Ideal Surroundings: Domestic Life in a Working-Class Suburb in the 1920s* (Toronto: University of Toronto Press, 1995). Women and politics is discussed in Linda Kealey and Joan Sangster, eds., *Beyond the Vote: Canadian Women and Politics* (Toronto: University of Toronto Press, 1989). On Canada's first woman MP see Terry Crowley, *Agnes Macphail and the Politics of Equality* (Toronto: James Lorimer, 1990). On Quebec women see, as well, Micheline Dumont et al., *Quebec Women: A History* (Toronto: Women's Press, 1987); Susan Mann Trofimenkoff, *The Dream of Nation: A Social and Intellectual History of Quebec* (Toronto: Gage, 1983); and Marta Danylewycz, *Taking the Veil: An Alternative to Marriage, Motherhood, and Spinsterhood in Quebec, 1840–1920* (Toronto: McClelland & Stewart, 1987). For Ontario see Janice Acton et al., eds., *Women at Work: Ontario, 1850–1930* (Toronto: Canadian Women's Educational Press, 1974); and, for the Prairies, Veronica Strong-Boag, "Pulling in Double Harness or Hauling a Double Load: Women, Work and Feminism on the Canadian Prairie," *Journal of Canadian Studies* 21 (Fall 1986): 32–52. On the topic of eugenics see Angus McLaren, *Our Own Master Race* (Toronto: McClelland & Stewart, 1990).

Canadian culture is dealt with in "The Conundrum of Culture," in *Canada, 1922–1939* (as cited earlier), pp. 158–92, and Carl Klinck, ed., *Literary History of Canada: Canadian Literature in English*, 2nd ed. (Toronto: University of Toronto Press, 1976). On cultural nationalism see Mary Vipond, *The Mass Media in Canada* (Toronto: James Lorimer, 1992). For the Maritimes see, as well, Gwendolyn Davies, *Myth and Milieu: Atlantic Literature and Culture, 1918–1939* (Fredericton: Acadiensis Press, 1993); and Ian McKay, *The Quest of the Folk: Antimodernism and Cultural Selection in Twentieth-Century Nova Scotia* (Montreal/Kingston: McGill-Queen's University Press, 1994).

Painting in the interwar years is discussed in J. Russell Harper, *Painting in Canada: A History*, 2nd ed. (Toronto: University of Toronto Press, 1977); Dennis Reid, *A Concise History of Canadian Painting*, 2nd ed. (Toronto: Oxford University Press, 1988); and Ann Davis, *The Logic of Ecstasy: Canadian Mystical Painting, 1920–1940* (Toronto: University of

Toronto Press, 1992). On the Group of Seven consult Peter Mellen, *The Group of Seven* (Toronto: McClelland & Stewart, 1970).

On theatre in Quebec see Elaine F. Nardocchio, *Theatre and Politics in Modern Quebec* (Edmonton: University of Alberta Press, 1986); and Jean Hamelin, *The Theatre in French Canada, 1936–1966* (Quebec: Department of Cultural Affairs, 1968). For music see Timothy J. McGee, *The Music of Canada* (New York: W.W. Norton, 1985); George A. Proctor, *Canadian Music of the Twentieth Century* (Toronto: University of Toronto Press, 1980); Louise G. McCready, *Famous Musicians* (Toronto: Clarke Irwin, 1957); and Ezra Schabas, *Sir Ernest MacMillan: The Importance of Being Canadian* (Toronto: University of Toronto Press, 1994).

On popular entertainment in the West see Don Wetherell and Irene Kmet, *Useful Pleasures: The Shaping of Leisure in Alberta 1896–1945* (Regina: Alberta Culture and Multi-culturalism/Canadian Plains Research Centre, University of Regina, 1990). Radio is discussed in Mary Vipond, *Listening In: The First Decade of Canadian Broadcasting, 1922–1932* (Montreal/Kingston: McGill-Queen's University Press, 1992). William Houston looks at hockey in *Pride and Glory: 100 Years of the Stanley Cup* (Toronto: McGraw-Hill Ryerson, 1992); Dan Diamond, ed., in *The Official National Hockey League 75th Anniversary Commemorative Book* (Toronto: Firefly Books, 1991); and Brian McFarlane in *One Hundred Years of Hockey* (Toronto: Deneau, 1989).

Important reviews of Native history in the interwar years include Arthur Ray, *The Canadian Fur Trade in the Industrial Age* (Toronto: University of Toronto Press, 1990); and his *I Have Lived Here Since the World Began* (Toronto: Key Porter, 1996); Stan Cuthand, "The Native Peoples of the Prairie Provinces in the 1920s and 1930s," in Ian A.L. Getty and Donald B. Smith, eds., *One Century Later: Western Canadian Reserve Indians since Treaty 7* (Vancouver: University of British Columbia Press, 1978), pp. 31–42; John Leonard Taylor, *Canadian Indian Policy during the Inter-War years, 1918–1939* (Ottawa: Indian and Northern Affairs Canada, 1984); Brian Titley, *A Narrow Vision: Duncan Campbell Scott and the Administration of Indian Affairs in Canada* (Vancouver: University of British Columbia Press, 1986); and for Ontario, Sally M. Weaver, "The Iroquois: The Grand River Reserve in the Late Nineteenth Century and Early Twentieth Centuries, 1875–1945," in Edward S. Rogers and Donald B. Smith, eds., *Aboriginal Ontario: Historical Perspectives on the First Nation* (Toronto: University of Toronto Press for the Ontario Historical Studies Series, 1994), pp. 213–57. On Native residential schools during this period see J.R. Miller, *Shingwauk's Vision: A History of Native Residential Schools* (Toronto: University of Toronto Press, 1996). Interesting biographies of Plains Native peoples in these years include Jean Goodwill and Norma Sluman's *John Tootoosis: Biography of a Cree Indian* (Winnipeg: Pemmican Publications, 1984); and Hugh Dempsey's *The Gentle Persuader* (Saskatoon: Western Producer Prairie Books, 1986), about the life of James Gladstone, the twentieth-century Blood leader. For working conditions see Rolf Knight, *Indians at Work: An Informal History of Native Indian Labour in British Columbia, 1853–1930* (Vancouver: New Star Books, 1978); and Stan Cuthand, "The Native Peoples of the Prairie Provinces in the 1920's and 1930's," in *One Century Later: Western Canadian Reserve Indians since Treaty 7* (as cited earlier), pp. 31–42. For developments among the First Nations see Edward Ahenakew, *Voices of the Plains Cree* (Toronto: McClelland & Stewart, 1973); and among the Métis in Western Canada consult Murray Dobbin, *The One-And-A-Half Men: The Story of Jim Brady and Malcolm Norris, Métis Patriots of the 20th Century* (Vancouver: New Star Books, 1981).

Students should consult the excellent maps and charts in Donald Kerr and Deryck W. Holdsworth, eds., *Historical Atlas of Canada*, vol. 3, *Addressing the Twentieth Century, 1891–1961* (Toronto: University of Toronto Press, 1990).

CHAPTER TWELVE

Canada in the Great Depression

The Great Depression dominated the 1930s. The spectacular crash of the New York stock market in October 1929 signalled the crisis. Heavy debt burdens throughout the world created a calamitous economic downturn. Bank failures in both Europe and the United States caused financial instability. International trade declined as nations implemented higher tariff policies to protect their own workers and farmers from foreign competition. Worldwide overproduction caused prices of commodities such as wheat, newsprint, and metals — all important Canadian exports — to fall sharply Unemployment levels increased substantially as industries cut back production in the face of declining demand.

Next to the United States, Canada experienced the western world's most severe decline. Industrial production fell by one-third between 1929 and 1932. During the same years, Canada's gross national product sank by two-fifths, in current dollars. Imports declined in volume by about 55 percent, and exports by 25 percent. The unemployment rate peaked at 20 percent of the *total* civilian labour force in May 1933.

In an age when modern, state-sponsored social-welfare programs did not exist, self-reliance counted most. But it did not suffice. Thousands of Canadians faced, for the first time, the degradation of going on public relief. Single unemployed men were forced into relief camps because of the harsh conditions. Farm organizations, trade unions, and co-operatives attempted to protect the interests of their members. Increasingly, however, people looked to government for answers. Although the Conservatives and the Liberals were voted into office during the Great Depression, many Canadians looked to new third parties, and some even turned to extreme right- and left-wing organizations for hope in their desperate situation. Popular entertainment allowed for an escape from the depressed conditions of everyday life.

THE ADVENT OF THE GREAT DEPRESSION

WEB
LINKS

On October 29, 1929 — "Black Tuesday" — stock markets around the world crashed. The Great Depression that followed lasted a decade and affected the entire western world. The depression hit Canada as severely as it did any other western country, because the nation had expanded so rapidly and so extensively in the first three decades of the twentieth century. In essence, having risen so high, it had farther to fall. Within Canada, the prairie West and British Columbia probably suffered most because of the dependence of these regions on primary industries, especially wheat production, and its overexpansion in the previous decades. Furthermore, Canada was heavily dependent on one market, the United States, which was greatly affected by the economic downturn and resorted to high tariffs in response. Compounding this economic depression, the Prairie West also suffered from a climatic disaster: ten years of exceptional and persistent drought, extreme summer and winter temperatures, unusual weather patterns, and grasshopper infestations. The topsoil turned to dust and blew away. British Columbia had to contend with high numbers of transients, and Vancouver became known as "the Mecca to the unemployed."

Nobody wanted Canada's wheat. Prices fell from $1.29 a bushel in 1928 to 34 cents a bushel by 1932. Even 34 cents a bushel was a deceptively high price. It was for No. 1 Hard, the best wheat on the market, and for wheat delivered to the Lakehead. Most prairie farmers never grew No. 1 Hard, and prices for their No. 3 or No. 4 graded wheat were considerably lower. Also, the farmers paid themselves for the cost of shipping the grain to the Lakehead, eroding profit even further. For some western farmers it was cheaper to burn their crop than to pay the costs of harvesting it.

The wheat pools felt the repercussions. They began in the 1920s advancing (in the fall and winter seasons) a portion of the money expected on next year's crop. This practice was intended to assist farmers in buying seed and getting the wheat crop planted. In the fall and winter of 1928–29, the pools had advanced farmers $1 a bushel. When wheat prices went well below that in the fall of 1929 and continued a downward spiral for five consecutive years, the wheat pools went bankrupt.

Elsewhere, similar dramatic conditions prevailed. Thousands of investors lost everything when mining share prices became worthless. Mines closed down for lack of business. The pulp and paper industry, the other major resource industry, had a similar fate to that of wheat and mining. The industry had overexpanded in the 1920s as a result of an insatiable American demand for pulp and paper. Its expenses could only be recouped if the market continued at record highs. When the depression hit, the newsprint market collapsed and, along with it, the pulp and paper industry. According to one industry analyst, by 1933 the pulp and paper industry was operating at only half of its capacity. Even then the bottomed-out prices kept production costs barely above bankruptcy. Historians Thompson and Seager note that on October 29, "Black Tuesday," "The Toronto *Star*'s index of sixteen key Canadian stocks fell $300 000 000 — a million dollars for every minute that markets were open for trading."[1]

Money markets followed. Banks and other financial institutions generously approved loans in the 1920s, hoping to capitalize on the boom. Foreign capital entered the country to take advantage of good times. With the advent of the depression, financial investors, however, could not retrieve their money or cover their debts. Foreign investment from Canada's two traditional sources ceased; indeed, Britain and the United States recalled their loans to cover demands at home.

Average Canadian investors could not pay the loans now recalled by the banks. Nor could they meet their mortgage payments or pay their property taxes. Farmers' debt levels often exceeded their farms' value. Interest payments alone often exceeded an average farmer's annual income. People abandoned their homes and farms. Banks were saddled with property that no one could afford and that hence had little monetary value.

Dust storm near Lethbridge, Alberta — a familiar sight in Prairie Canada during the "Dirty Thirties."

Glenbow Archives, Calgary, Canada/NA-1831-1.

Companies and factories cut back on wages and employees in an effort to survive. Clerks at Eaton's and Simpson's in Toronto, for example, earned $10 to $13 a week, while those in Montreal earned much less. Weekly pay for male workers in the furniture industry averaged $10, but "boys" of 19 often earned as little as three dollars. In the textile industry, the Royal Commission on Price Spreads, appointed by the Conservative government in 1934, found shocking conditions: a Quebec home worker earning 5 cents an hour; a seamstress paid 9½ cents for sewing a dozen dresses.

Tens of thousands of workers lost their jobs. By 1933, over 20 percent of the entire labour force — one worker out of every five — remained unemployed. In some regions of the country, the figures rose as high as 35 percent and even 50 percent. Since no social-security system existed, the unemployed, the destitute, and the sick had to rely on the charity of others, private groups, or government relief.

R.B. BENNETT'S POLICIES

WEB
LINKS

At the outset of the Great Depression, the Liberals were in office. In the late 1920s, Mackenzie King won over the moderate Progressives to the Liberal party and appeased the Maritime Rights movement with some minor concessions, such as lowering freight rates in Atlantic Canada. Confident of another victory, party organizers remained apathetic and indifferent throughout the election campaign of 1930. The Liberals believed, as did many other politicians in the western world, that this was just another momentary dip in the economy. In the Parliamentary session just before the election, King was pushed into saying he "would not give a single cent, not a five-cent piece" to any provincial Conservative government, a comment that plagued him throughout the election campaign. In contrast, Richard Bedford Bennett, the exuberant Conservative leader, promised that if elected he could, and would, solve the problems of the depression. He won the election.

Once in power, the new prime minister faced the relief problem. Within his first five weeks in office, he introduced the Unemployment Relief Act, which provided $20 million of assistance to the poor — a considerable sum out of a total federal budget of $500 million. But Bennett soon discovered that this was only the beginning of federal relief efforts. Between 1930 and 1938, Ottawa would provide nearly

$350 million in relief for the jobless and for destitute farmers, while municipal and provincial governments added another $650 million. Most of the money went to work-incentive programs, for which municipalities were expected to contribute their share.

The federal government underestimated the destitution of the municipal governments. Already heavily in debt, they, and the provincial governments, had over-extended themselves in the boom years of the 1920s. Furthermore, their tax base eroded as people could no longer pay local property taxes. Indeed, all levels of government faced mounting deficits on a decreased tax base. Toronto's budget for relief increased twenty-fold between 1929 and 1933. By the outbreak of war, Montreal's per capita debt was twice Toronto's. When the province of Quebec, more tight-fisted toward its towns and cities than other provinces, refused to come to Montreal's rescue, the city was forced to declare bankruptcy in 1940.

Municipal, provincial, and federal governments responded by trying to balance their budgets through cutbacks on services. This, in turn, increased unemployment and slowed down the recovery. Realistically, however, governments had few alternatives, given the magnitude of the debt and their low level of revenue. Also, opportunities to borrow abroad did not exist. All countries faced debt and dealt with it the same way — by trying to balance their budgets.

Bennett's high-tariff policy proved the worst possible "solution" to the depression for Canada. He campaigned in 1930 on the promise of "blasting" Canada into world markets. Soon after taking office, he increased tariffs on a number of goods. But this only undermined Canada's competitive edge. As a major exporting nation, Canada greatly depended on the export of key staples — wheat, pulp and paper, and minerals — to foreign markets, especially the American market. Other nations retaliated against Canada's high tariffs with their own protectionist policies. In 1930, the American government imposed the Smoot-Hawley tariff on foreign imports into the United States. Protectionism proved especially damaging to the regions of the West and the Maritimes, which depended heavily on international markets for their primary resources.

As the economic crisis continued, Bennett looked to Britain and the other Commonwealth countries for increased trade. In 1932, Canada hosted an Imperial Economic Conference to explore ways to combat the depression. At the conference, Bennett took an aggressive approach. He refused to make concessions to Britain, yet demanded that the "mother country" open its markets to Canadian goods. The conference failed, although Canada gained a preference in the British market for its wheat, lumber, apples, and bacon. In return, Canada raised the preference for British manufactured goods by simply raising the level of the general tariff.

RELIEF

Thousands faced for the first time the personal degradation of going on relief — the "pogey," as it was called. In a society built on a philosophy of self-help, relief was an admission that one could no longer fend for oneself. Many people lost their sense of self-worth. The jobless had no choice but to fall back on charity, both public and private.

Those on relief faced the further humiliation of having to acknowledge their failure publicly. They lined up in a church basement or firehall waiting for relief. When their turn came, they had to proclaim their destitution, within hearing of every-

Unemployed workers marching through Calgary in the 1930s. In April 1932, the Calgary Trades and Labor Council endorsed two resolutions: first, to protest publicly against the practice of employing married women if their husbands were working; second, to protest against the entry into Canada of immigrants under any circumstances.

Glenbow Archives, Calgary, Canada/NA-4532-1.

one else, and swear that they did not own a car, a radio, or a telephone. Recipients of relief generally had to be in arrears in rent payments and to have received notice of discontinuation of electricity and water service, as well as impending eviction. Then the authorities gave them food vouchers to purchase the minimum necessities at local stores — a further reminder of one's impoverished condition. In Ontario, these relief vouchers averaged $8.07 a week in the winter months. In 1933, North York gave families on relief a maximum of $11.60 a week, although the Toronto Welfare Council estimated that a family of five needed $28.35 a week to maintain an adequate living standard. In Prince Edward Island, relief vouchers amounted to only $1.93, and in New Brunswick they averaged a meagre $1.67.

Used clothing had to be picked up at a private charity centre. Fuel was often wood cut by people on relief themselves as part of their expected tasks to earn relief money. In the prairie West — once the "breadbasket of the nation" — food, along with used clothing and fuel, often came in railcar loads from the rest of Canada. To avoid drifters coming into town for assistance, most municipalities had lengthy residence requirements.

To give those on relief the illusion of working for their relief payments, governments created make-shift jobs known as "boon-doggling." The town of New Toronto, Ontario, for example, required relief workers to haul large stones to vacant lots, where they were smashed and used for road construction. Winnipeg men on relief sawed wood, pulled weeds along city boulevards, and swept the city streets. Rumours abounded of some municipalities that had "relief men" dig holes one day and fill them in the next, simply to keep them occupied.

Recent immigrants faced the added burden of not being welcome. The Immigrant Act allowed for the deportation of immigrants who were on relief. Consequently, some municipalities provided the authorities with lists of immigrants who were receiving government assistance. Between 1930 and 1935, Ottawa returned an unprecedented 30 000 immigrants to Europe.

RELIEF CAMPS

By 1932, the Great Depression had worsened. More than 1.5 million Canadians (15 percent of the nation's population) depended on relief, and the country seemed ripe for rebellion. Of particular concern were unemployed single men, many of whom "rode the rods" across Canada in search of work, begged for food and clothing, camped in shantytowns on the outskirts of cities, and lined up at soup kitchens and hostels for food and shelter. General Andrew McNaughton, chief of the Army General Staff, proposed the establishment of relief camps to offer temporary work and prevent dissidence and violence. Beginning in 1932, the government established numerous camps across the country, usually in isolated areas that were distant from major population centres.

During the four-year period that they existed, an estimated 20 000 single, homeless "volunteers" worked long hours at menial jobs designed simply to keep them busy for a meagre 20 cents a day. Intolerable living conditions in the camps made them ripe for infiltration by communist-led organizations such as the Single Unemployed Workers' Association, an organization funded by the Communist Party of Canada.

THE ON-TO-OTTAWA TREK

In the spring of 1935, men in B.C. work camps jumped the trains en route to Ottawa to protest conditions. They planned to pick up other camp men and unemployed workers along the way. About 2000 trekkers reached Regina before the federal government ordered the RCMP to break up the march. The ensuing confrontation, on Dominion Day, 1935, left one plainclothes policeman dead and numerous strikers and police officers injured. The police arrested 120 of the trekkers and convicted eight of them. Only strike leader Arthur Evans and a few others were permitted to continue to Ottawa, where an unsympathetic prime minister denounced them as "red" agitators and dissidents.

Canada's millionaire prime minister came to represent the callous indifference of the rich to the suffering of the unemployed and destitute, and thus became the butt of numerous jokes. People spoke of "Bennett buggies," engineless cars pulled by horses because the owners could not afford gas; "Bennett boroughs," the shantytowns of makeshift "homes" for homeless men; and "Bennett blankets," the newspapers under which transients slept on park benches. Bennett was ridiculed in a parody of the Lord's Prayer:

> Our Father, who art in Ottawa, Bennett be thy name.
> Give us this day our bowl of soup and forgive us our
> trespasses on the CPR and the CNR as we forgive the

A demonstration of strikers at Market Square on the eve of the Regina Riot on Dominion Day, 1935. During the riot, one plainclothes policeman was killed and numerous strikers and police officers were injured.

Dick and Ada Bird Collection/Saskatchewan Archives Board/R-A27560-1.

bulls from chasing us. Lead us not into the hands of the RCMP, nor yet to the relief camp, for thine is the kingdom the power and glory, until there's an election — Amen.

In fairness to Bennett, beneath his cold exterior existed a warm generosity. Thousands of Canadians wrote personal letters to him expressing their hardships and appealing for help. Very often he sent them money, apparently without any political benefit, since he often insisted on the strictest confidentiality.

Bennett also enacted a number of measures that, over time, strengthened Canada's economy and became permanent structures. He established a central bank, the Bank of Canada, to "promote the economic and financial welfare of the Dominion." His government passed the Natural Products and Marketing Act, which set up a federal marketing board with authority over all "natural products of agriculture and of the forest, sea, lake or river," exported or sold across provincial boundaries. His government also introduced the Canada Grain Board Act, which gave Ottawa control of the marketing of coarse grains, including wheat.

WEB

LINKS

In 1934, Bennett appointed the Royal Commission on Price Spreads to investigate the buying practices of major department stores and labour conditions in certain industries. Out of that commission came legislation to institute unemployment insurance and to regulate wages and working hours. Both bills were struck down by the Judicial Committee of the Privy Council as unconstitutional. In 1940, however, the federal government implemented an unemployment insurance plan after the British North America Act had been amended to allow for Ottawa's intervention into this traditional field of provincial jurisdiction.

BENNETT'S "NEW DEAL"

As the election of 1935 approached, Bennett decided to imitate the example of the popular American president, Franklin D. Roosevelt. In a radio address, he announced his "New Deal" to a surprised audience that included his own cabinet members, who had not been consulted about the reform package. Bennett promised a program of reform that his party would introduce if the Conservatives were re-elected. It included health and unemployment insurance, a maximum work week, financial assistance to farmers to enable them to stay on their farms, and the creation of the Economic Council of Canada to advise the government. (After the election, the Judicial Committee of the Privy Council ruled that many aspects of Bennett's "New Deal" were unconstitutional because they infringed on provincial jurisdiction.) Frank Scott, a McGill law professor and poet, summed up the sceptical response of many Canadians to Bennett's "New Deal" and his "sudden conversion to reform":

> Some glimmering concept of a juster state
> Begins to trouble him — but just too late
> His whole life work had dug the grave too deep
> In which the people's hopes and fortunes sleep.

The voting public expressed its contempt in the election of 1935. It returned Mackenzie King's Liberal party to power with a majority government. Analysts argue that the Liberal victory was more a rejection of Bennett than an affirmation of King. In the popular vote, more than 25 percent of Canadians rejected both of the mainline parties to vote for one of the new parties that entered the election.

THIRD PARTIES

Two of those new parties began on the Prairies. The Co-operative Commonwealth Federation (CCF) had its beginnings at a national convention in Calgary in August 1932. The CCF drew together dissident groups from a broad spectrum of Canadian society, including farmers, labourers, socialists, academics, and disenchanted Liberals. They chose Labour MP J.S. Woodsworth as party leader.

From the beginning, the CCF distanced itself from the two mainline parties by having a clear socialist program to deal with the Great Depression. Woodsworth asked the League for Social Reconstruction (LSR), an organization of left-wing intellectuals who were mostly, although not exclusively, from universities to draft a manifesto for the new party. University of Toronto historian Frank H. Underhill and McGill University jurist Frank Scott did so. Adopted at the party's second annual convention in Regina in 1933, the "Regina Manifesto" set out a ten-point program for the CCF to follow in its effort to "eradicate capitalism" and create a co-operative commonwealth in Canada. The CCF wanted complete control of the economy. It sought the nationalization of the means of production, distribution, and exchange. It worked for a more equitable distribution of wealth, the creation of a welfare state, and the pursuit of international peace through the League of Nations.

The CCF entered its first federal election in 1935 in high hopes. Those expectations were dashed when it won only seven seats, all from the West, although the party did win 8.8 percent of the popular vote. Two of those elected — M.J. Coldwell and T.C. "Tommy" Douglas — later became national party leaders. Although weak in representation, the party did come to acquire the reputation of being "the conscience of the House of Commons." Provincially, the CCF became the official opposition in British Columbia in 1933, in Saskatchewan in 1934, and in Ontario in 1943; but its real breakthrough came in the midst of World War II, when in 1944 Tommy Douglas led the party to victory in Saskatchewan.

SOCIAL CREDIT

WEB
LINKS

In Alberta, a party quite different from the CCF, the Social Credit party, also began in the midst of the depression. Major C.H. Douglas, a Scottish engineer, first enunciated Social Credit theory in the 'teens. Douglas was concerned about the waste and under-utilization of resources in the capitalist system. He did not blame the system, which he admired, but rather blamed the financial institutions that hoarded money, thus preventing consumers from buying the abundant goods that the capitalist system produced. Douglas's solution was for governments to inject more money into the economy and give it to the people to spend.

Douglas's theories awaited a popular leader; Alberta provided one, the charis-matic William "Bible Bill" Aberhart. Born in Ontario, the son of a dairy farmer, Aberhart came west in 1910. The Ontario teacher became principal of a new high school in Calgary. At the same time, he served as a lay preacher in a local Baptist church. In 1925, the radio station CFCN invited him to give Sunday sermons on their "Voice of the Prairie" program. This opportunity enabled him to reach an estimated 350 000 people with his message. With financial contributions from listeners, he built the Prophetic Bible Institute in Calgary, which he later used to distribute Social Credit material.

Aberhart "converted" to Social Credit in the summer of 1932 after the suicide of one of his best students as a result of the depression. Thereafter, he introduced Social Credit economic theory into his weekly sermons. Initially, he hoped one of the established parties would adopt Social Credit. When they failed to do so, he began his own party on the eve of the 1935 provincial election. He promised each citizen a $25-a-month "basic dividend" to purchase necessities. Helping the party on was a sex scandal, in which Premier John Brownlee was sued for seduction by Vivian MacMillan, a junior clerk in the Alberta attorney general's office. The court battle dragged on for seven years before Brownlee was found not guilty, but in the meantime the case ruined his political career. Social Credit swept the province, winning 56 of the 63 seats.

Once in power, the new premier and his party could not implement their elec-tion promises. The federal government challenged the constitutional legality of a province issuing its own currency. The party lacked parliamentary expertise, since the majority of its candidates were political neophytes. Only after the outbreak of war, and especially after the discovery of oil in 1947, did the party become well estab-lished under Aberhart's protégé, Ernest Manning, who took over after Aberhart's death in 1943.

THE RECONSTRUCTION PARTY

H.H. Stevens, a B.C. member of the Bennett government and head of the Select Committee and then of the Royal Commission on Price Spreads, resigned from the cabinet in October 1934 to begin his own party, the Reconstruction party. He promised "to re-establish Canada's industrial, economic and social life for the benefit of the great majority." In the 1935 election, the Reconstruction party won over 8 percent of the popular vote but elected only one candidate, Stevens. The party did, however, make inroads into Conservative support in various constituencies across the country.

COMMUNISTS AND FASCISTS

WEB
LINKS

Extreme left- and right-wing movements, such as the Communist party and Fascist groups, grew during the interwar years. The Communist Party of Canada, founded in 1921 in a barn outside of Guelph, Ontario, thrived in the economic-crisis conditions of the depression, especially among immigrants threatened with deportation. Government repression of the party occurred frequently in the decade by the government invoking section 98 of the Criminal Code, which made it illegal to advocate "governmental, industrial or economic change within Canada by the use of force, violence or physical injury to persons or property, or by threats of such injury" even if the accused did nothing to bring about such changes. In one crackdown in August 1931, party leader Tim Buck and seven others were arrested. As a result of an attempt on Buck's life in Kingston Penitentiary a year later, the "Toronto Eight," as they became known, emerged as the embattled underdogs. They won sympathy from a number of Canadians who believed in the right of left-wing dissident groups to express their views, even if they did not agree with the party's ideology.

Most Canadians who wanted radical change during the depression, however, preferred the peaceful, democratic approach of the CCF to the violent, revolutionary change advocated by the communists. On the eve of World War II, the Communist party supposedly had 16 000 members. But when the Soviet Union signed a non-aggression pact with Adolf Hitler that summer, many communists quit the party in protest. In June 1940, the Canadian government declared the Communist party illegal.

Fascists proved less numerous than communists in Canada. The Deutscher Bund Canada, founded in 1934 and led by German Canadians, never had more than 2000 members, while the Canadian Nationalist party, founded by right-wing militants, and the allied Swastika clubs, added a few thousand more. The latter clubs tried to stop Jews from visiting Kew and Balmy Beaches in east Toronto. At McGill University in Montreal, officials conspired to turn away Jewish applicants. In Quebec, Adrien Arcand patterned his National Social Christian party along Nazi lines. He claimed to represent the last stand of Roman Catholicism against communists and other "atheist" groups. While Arcand remained a marginal and eccentric character, anti-Semitism found support among nationalist movements in the province, such as the Jeune-Canada and the Ligue d'Action nationale.

Not surprisingly, the thousands of persecuted Jews fleeing Nazi Germany found Canada's doors firmly closed. The attitude of the leading member of the immigration department toward Jewish immigrants was that "none was too many." Only a few Canadian leaders, such as Cairine Wilson, Canada's first woman senator and chairperson of the Canadian National Committee on Refugees, denounced Nazi atrocities and urged a liberalization of immigration regulations. Immigration in total reached an all-time low in the 1930s: only 149 000 immigrants were allowed in during the entire decade, and only 5000 of them were Jews.

PROVINCIAL POLITICS AND THE ECONOMIC CRISIS

The depression led to political change in the provinces. In most provinces, voters ousted incumbents, although usually in exchange for governments by well-established, as opposed to new, parties.

Crowd welcoming Tim Buck, national organizer for the Communist Party of Canada, to Nordegg, Alberta, in 1935. The party had a substantial following in the Alberta coalfields in the 1930s.

....

Glenbow Archives, Calgary, Canada/ NA-2635-93.

NEWFOUNDLAND AND THE MARITIMES

Various problems beset Newfoundland, then a British dominion, the most important being the falling price of fish as a result of the depression. In 1932, Sir Richard Squires, the Liberal premier, narrowly escaped being lynched by a mob infuriated by disclosures of scandal, as well as by the government's tough relief policies when almost half of the island's labour force was out of work. Indeed, the British navy had to be called in to assist local police in controlling rioters. A new government, the United Newfoundland party, took power after the election of 1932. It obtained further bank loans only by arguing that the money was needed to ward off "grave threats of insurrection." After a royal commission recommended the dissolution of the legislature, Newfoundland reverted to the status of a British colony, and London was obliged to pay off the colony's debts.

Canadians in the Maritime provinces elected Liberal governments and kept them in office until the 1950s. In Nova Scotia, Angus L. Macdonald, a former law professor, became premier in 1933. Practising an activist style of government, "Angus L." implemented old age pensions and began paving provincial roads. He also appointed a royal commission to investigate Nova Scotia's position in Confederation. Norman Macleod Rogers, who taught political science at Queen's University, drafted the province's submission. It argued for additional compensation for Canada's poorer provinces, since their disadvantageous position resulted from their role in Confederation.

In both New Brunswick and Prince Edward Island, the Liberals came to power on promises of economic and social reform. In New Brunswick, Allison Dysart's government introduced old age pensions, created public works projects, and pressured timber companies into activating their leases or else losing them. In Prince Edward Island, Thane Campbell's government had the distinction of being the first to win every seat in a provincial election. In office, Campbell established a permanent civil service and supported co-operative organizations and marketing boards as its response to the depression.

All three provinces lacked the money to complete the promised reforms. New Brunswick, for example, borrowed heavily to finance its massive public works program. This meant other priorities suffered; spending on education and health services declined to barely half the national average by the end of the 1930s, and illiteracy and infant mortality rates in the province were the highest in the country.

An anti-Semitic poster at Sainte-Agathe, a resort area in the Laurentians north of Montreal, 1939.

······························

National Archives of Canada/PA-107943.
Reprinted with permission of
The Gazette, Montreal.

QUEBEC

In Quebec, the new Union Nationale party defeated the long-standing Liberal government, in power since 1897. Unable to win on his own, Maurice Duplessis, the Quebec Conservative leader, allied his party with a dissident left-wing group within the Liberal party called Action libérale nationale, headed by Paul Gouin, son of former Quebec Liberal premier Lomer Gouin. This "unholy alliance" lasted only long enough to win the provincial election of 1936, at which time the right-wing Duplessis purged his government of the Gouin faction.

Duplessis attacked a number of dissident groups in the province, including socialists, communists, and trade unionists. In 1937 he introduced the "Padlock Law," which made it illegal for any group to use a house or hall "to propagate communism or bolshevism" or to publish or distribute literature "tending to propagate communism." As the bill did not define "communist," it gave the premier a weapon with which to attack any left-wing organization he wished. Duplessis used the law to lock premises suspected of being used for communist activities, to ban publications, and, on a couple of occasions, to arrest dissidents. He attacked union leaders, denouncing them as "dangerous agitators," when unions refused to comply with Quebec's labour laws.

ONTARIO

Next door in Ontario, in 1934, voters ousted the Conservatives, who had been in office since 1923. They elected the Liberals under their flamboyant leader, "Mitch" Hepburn, whose oratorical skills and quick wit served him well on the political hustings. At one country rally, Hepburn gave his speech from the only available stage, a manure spreader. He remarked that it was the first time he had given an address on a "Conservative platform."

Hepburn sided with industrialists against labourers in a bitter sixteen-day strike against General Motors in Oshawa in 1937. He denounced the United Auto Workers union as "communist inspired," and sent in a government-supported police force, dubbed "Hepburn's Hussars" or "the sons of Mitches" to break up the strike. Two of his cabinet ministers, Arthur Roebuck and David Croll, resigned in disgust. Croll proclaimed his "place was marching with the workers rather than riding with General Motors."

BRITISH COLUMBIA

In British Columbia, another flamboyant and self-assured provincial Liberal leader, T.D. "Duff" Pattullo, became premier in the midst of the depression. Pattullo had won and lost fortunes in a business career in the Yukon and northern British Columbia before entering politics. He won the election of 1933 on the promise of "work and wages" for every provincial resident. His program became that of the "little New Deal," which promised a state health-insurance plan, reduced taxes on lower incomes, public works, unemployment insurance, and an economic council with labour representation to study the problem of unemployment. He also believed in injecting money into the economy by spending on major public works projects, such as the Pattullo Bridge and the Alaska Highway. In the words of historian Robin Fisher, his biographer, "The first Pattullo administration offered the most vigorous political response to the depression of any government in Canada."[2] But as in Alberta's case, the government of British Columbia lacked the tax base to make these changes. Pattullo looked to the federal government for loans to help his government fight the "war on poverty." When the Conservative, and then Liberal, administrations in Ottawa refused funding requests, Pattullo fell back on more conservative policies. Nevertheless, he managed to get re-elected in 1937. Pattullo's was the only government in Canada to be re-elected during the depression. It remained in power until 1941, when it was ousted by a Liberal–Conservative coalition party.

LABOUR IN THE GREAT DEPRESSION

Workers became more militant in the desperate conditions of the Great Depression. "Red" trade unions grew, and some affiliated with the Communist Party of Canada. For example, the Workers' Unity League (WUL) was born out of a directive from Moscow that communist-led unions should separate from "reformist" unions, like the All-Canadian Congress of Labour (ACCL), and prepare for the coming world revolution. After signing up workers in mines and shops, the WUL declared strikes to obtain union recognition and better wages and working conditions. At its peak in 1932, the WUL had an estimated 40 000 members. It claimed leadership of most of the strikes across the country in the early 1930s.

Violent confrontation often resulted between police and strikers or between strikebreakers and strikers. The worst occurred in Estevan, Saskatchewan, in 1931, when 600 coal-mine workers walked out of the mines. The owners denounced the strike as "Communist-led," thus ensuring the support of the politicians and the RCMP. The police opened fire during a strikers' parade, killing three unarmed strikers.

The WUL also organized the unemployed by establishing workers' councils in various cities and by circulating a petition, eventually signed by 300 000 people, calling for a national non-contributory unemployment-insurance scheme.

THE CIO IN CANADA

In 1935 a new union, the American-based Congress of Industrial Organization (CIO), began to "organize the unorganized." The Canadian CIO's greatest success occurred in 1937, when the CIO-inspired United Auto Workers led a 16-day strike at the General Motors factory in Oshawa, Ontario. Premier Mitch Hepburn intervened to break the strike because he feared a CIO victory would encourage unionization and strikes elsewhere in the province. The CIO also organized Montreal's female garment workers, as well as coal miners in Nova Scotia.

Despite some successes and much publicity, however, the CIO made little headway elsewhere in Canada in the 1930s. Strong opposition came from business and the craft-dominated Trades and Labor Congress (TLC), which in 1939 expelled the CIO affiliates. The CIO then merged with the weaker All-Canadian Congress of Labour in 1940 to form the Canadian Congress of Labour (CCL).

WOMEN IN THE 1930S

In the 1930s, women's wages fell dramatically and working conditions deteriorated. Initially, the depression benefited women who wanted to work because they could be hired at half a man's wages. Soon, however, came the backlash. Women came under attack for taking jobs away from unemployed men who had wives and families. CCF member Agnes Macphail pointed out that the economic system, not women, was to blame for unemployment and that many women needed to work if they and their families were to survive.

Women faced difficulties getting relief even if they were eligible for it. In addition, many municipalities opposed giving relief to women. Authorities reasoned that single unemployed women posed no threat to society, as did single unemployed men. Furthermore, they assumed that these women would be cared for by their families. A few single women turned to prostitution as a desperate alternative to dire poverty. Some married women assumed the dual responsibilities of "breadwinner" and sole head of the family, as their husbands left home in search of work or simply deserted their families.

Marriage and childbearing remained the norm for women in the 1930s. Over 90 percent of women eventually married. Once married, they were expected to give up their jobs and take up domestic duties. Marriages seldom ended in divorce. Wife abuse did increase, especially during the depression. The police were of little assistance; they usually told victims simply to make the best of matters and to find comfort in their children.

Family size declined in the 1930s. Infant mortality still remained high by today's standards, due to several factors. Babies born in the winter months had to survive the uneven heating of even the best-built residences. Infants also faced a wide range of the "childhood diseases" — measles, mumps, scarlet fever, and whooping cough — illnesses now held in check through public-health programs and by antibiotics.

Birth control was seldom an option women could consider, although by 1937 birth-control clinics existed in Toronto, Hamilton, and Windsor. Also available was A.H. Tyrer's popular book, *Sex, Marriage and Birth Control* (1936). The popular belief of the day was expressed by Dr. Helen McMurchy, director of the Dominion Division of Child Welfare, who described birth control among those of British background as "race suicide." French-Canadian nationalists used the same argument in Quebec. Still, the idea of eugenics — the selective breeding of the fittest and the compulsory sterilization of those considered inferior — gained popularity in the 1930s. Heading the movement were Tyrer and A.R. Kaufman, a wealthy manufacturer, who both believed that the "inferior" working class was producing over half of the nation's children. Among them were the "irresponsible, criminal and mentally deficient" who were the source of "most of our social liabilities." Their solution was to distribute birth-control information and devices and even to perform surgical operations to restrict or prevent reproduction among certain groups.

A few doctors provided birth-control information and devices, but they did so at the risk of losing their medical licence. Dr. Elizabeth Bagshaw, for example, operated a birth-control clinic for working-class women in Hamilton, Ontario. Dorothea Palmer was arrested in a French-Canadian suburb of Ottawa for distributing contraceptive information. At her trial, where both Tyrer and Kaufman lent support, the judge acquitted her because he believed she had acted "for the public good." The poor, he stated, "are a burden to the taxpayer. They crowd the Juvenile Court. They glut the competitive labour market." Still, for some women, self-induced miscarriages seemed to be the only alternative to unwanted children or children they simply could not afford.

Support for birth control tended often to come from socialist groups. Some socialist women believed that the capitalist system encouraged large families so as to have a cheap source of labour for its factories and cannon fodder for its armies. In 1924, British Columbia socialists founded the Canadian Birth Control League to educate working-class women. In 1929, the Saskatchewan section of the United Farmers of Canada recommended the establishment of birth-control clinics staffed by trained doctors.

LIBERAL POLICIES

Once back in power, Mackenzie King's Liberals continued some of the Conservatives' policies to cope with the depression. The Liberals, for instance, supported the Bank of Canada as an essential stabilizing force in a time of financial crisis. After the government purchased a majority of the bank's stock, King made its governor responsible to Parliament for monetary policy.

THE PRAIRIE FARM REHABILITATION PROGRAM

King also continued the Conservatives' policy of aid to the drought-stricken farmers of western Canada. The Liberals even extended assistance by implementing the Prairie Farm Rehabilitation Act (PFRA), which provided money to experiment with new farming methods, especially in the dry-belt area of the Palliser Triangle. The experimental farms in the region applied the latest scientific knowledge to enable the soil to regain its productivity. Two innovations followed: first, the Noble plough, discovered by Charles Noble of Nobleford, Alberta, which cut the roots of weeds without turning over the topsoil to expose it to sun and wind; second, "trash farming" — instead of ploughing and harrowing their fields to make them look neat and clean, farmers were encouraged to leave the dead plants and grain stubble on the field to prevent erosion. The PFRA's program also provided money to build dugouts for spring runoff water for cattle, helped reseed vacant and pasture land, and, in the case of destitute farm families in the Palliser Triangle area, assisted relocation to better farming areas to the north. King did alter the Conservatives' high tariff policy. Charles Dunning, his finance minister and former premier of Saskatchewan, negotiated low tariff agreements with both Britain and the United States.

THE CBC AND TCA

The Liberals created two innovative national institutions and introduced two important social-security measures in the 1930s. In 1936, they established the Canadian Broadcasting Corporation (CBC). According to Graham Spry, whose Canadian Radio League had fought for such an institution, the choice was between "the State or the United States." The government mandated the CBC to regulate private broadcasting and to develop its own network with Canadian content in both official languages. In 1937, the Liberals established the Trans-Canada Air Lines (TCA), the forerunner of Air Canada, as a Crown corporation. Two other federal initiatives proved successful: the Municipal Improvements Assistance Act, which authorized $30 million in federal loans at 2 percent interest for special municipal public-works projects, and the National Housing Act (NHA), which made federally backed mortgages easier to obtain. The NHA provided $30 million worth of mortgages for low-income tenants.

The King government also addressed the relief question. In 1867, relief had been a very minor matter, assigned in the BNA Act to the provinces and municipalities. The King government established the National Employment Commission to re-examine and restructure the administration of direct relief. The commission made two important recommendations: first, that the federal government take over unemployment payments because this was too big and expensive an undertaking for municipal or provincial governments; and second, that the government adopt a policy of deficit financing to provide additional relief and stimulate economic growth. King hesitated in acquiring federal responsibility for unemployment and relief, areas assigned to the provinces in the BNA Act and responsibilities that would increase the federal debt load. He also resisted the Keynesian monetary policy of deficit financing, which went against the traditional liberal policies of laissez-faire and a balanced budget.

THE ROYAL COMMISSION ON DOMINION-PROVINCIAL RELATIONS

Before moving on either issue, King created the Royal Commission on Dominion–Provincial Relations to explore all aspects of relations between these two levels of government in light of the current economic crisis. Heralded by the federal government as the most important royal commission in Canadian history, the Rowell–Sirois Commission, as it became known after its head commissioners, N.W. Rowell of

Ontario and Joseph Sirois of Quebec, recommended a stronger federal-government economic presence. The decision to launch the commission ran into strong provincial opposition from both Hepburn in Ontario and Duplessis in Quebec. Its report did not appear until 1940; Parliament had just a year earlier imposed the War Measures Act, which gave the government licence to impose many aspects of the report's centralist agenda without consulting the provinces, at least for the duration of the war.

RELIGION

Many Canadians turned to religion for solace and direction in the depression. The trend was to move away from radical religion, with its emphasis on social reform, to a more conservative faith, with its emphasis on personal salvation and the importance of tradition. Nevertheless, a few radical groups gained some support during the depression. Some socially minded Protestants looked to the Fellowship for a Christian Social Order, founded by members of the United Church, for answers to the economic crisis. Fellowship insisted that realizing the kingdom of God meant replacing a bankrupt capitalist system with socialism. Critics of the group complained that too many of its members were more committed to the teachings of Karl Marx than those of Jesus Christ.

Student activists could turn to the Student Christian Movement (SCM), an organization begun in 1920 by the YWCA and YMCA. The SCM provided study groups on most Canadian university campuses in the 1930s to discuss social issues and advocate social change. For young girls, the Canadian Girls in Training (CGIT), an organization founded by the YWCA and the Protestant churches in 1917 to train young girls to improve both their lives and those of others, reached its peak of popularity during the depression, when it had an estimated 40 000 members.

Conservative and fundamentalist groups flourished in the decade. Church leaders promised that if people could not find salvation in this world, they could still hope in the afterlife. Disciples of the British Oxford Movement (a predecessor of Moral Rearmament) toured Canada, delivering a message of "revelation, not revolution" to overflow audiences, which on one occasion included R.B. Bennett and his entire cabinet, at Bennett's request.

In Quebec, many in the Roman Catholic church saw the depression as evidence of divine punishment for the sins of humankind — sins that included communism, materialism, urbanization, and even capitalism. They supported a back-to-the-land movement as the best means to combat both unemployment and "moral decrepitude."

THE ANTIGONISH MOVEMENT

Still others, particularly those in the Maritimes, looked to co-operatives as the answer. In 1931, Pope Pius XI issued his encyclical *Quadragesimo anno*, in which he attacked the competitive nature of capitalism as heartless and cruel, and advocated co-operation instead. His appeal found a receptive audience in the co-operative movement in eastern Canada.

Beginning in the late 1920s and throughout the 1930s, Moses Coady, director of the extension department at St. Francis Xavier University in Antigonish, Nova Scotia, and Jimmy Tompkins, a fellow priest, worked to improve the lives of poor farmers,

A Canadian Girls in Training (CGIT) meeting, probably in Toronto, around 1920. The Young Women's Christian Association and the major Protestant denominations established the organization in 1915 to promote the Christian education of girls aged 12 to 17.

Canadian Girls in Training Collection/National Archives of Canada/PA-125872.

miners, fishers, and their families. A representative of this young co-operative move-ment would visit a community and, using local contacts, call a public meeting. A study group would follow to assess the community's economic strengths and weaknesses. After the group's meetings concluded, one or more co-operatives would form to remedy the identifiable weaknesses. The co-operatives might be credit unions, or per-haps co-operatives for selling fish or farm produce. When accused of being too left wing, Father Coady replied: "I'm not a leftist; I'm where the righteous ought to be."

CULTURE IN THE 1930S

During the 1930s, popular culture flourished. New forms of entertainment — radio, for instance — allowed a greater choice of escapes. Owners of radio sets in English-speaking Canada listened to *Amos 'n Andy*, the most popular program of the decade. *Hockey Night in Canada*, with Foster Hewitt, was also a regular favourite. Such record-ing artists as Willie Eckstein, Percy Faith, and Guy Lombardo and his Royal Canadi-ans got their start on Canadian radio, although by 1940 both Percy Faith and Guy Lombardo had left Canada for larger dance floors in the United States. Lombardo's famous "Auld Lang Syne" had its origins in the Scottish communities of Ontario where he played, but it became synonymous with the American New Year's Eve celebration. Don Messer began playing his "old time" fiddle music on radio in the 1930s. Oscar Peterson ran his own radio show, *Fifteen Minutes Piano Rambling*, on Montreal radio station CKAC, beginning in 1940, at the age of 15. French Canadians enjoyed the immensely successful serials written specifically for radio, such as "Le Curé de Village"

Where Historians Disagree

PROTESTANTISM AND REFORM IN THE 1930S

In the late nineteenth and early twentieth centuries, the Protestant churches increasingly advocated and worked for social reform. Essentially, historians have debated whether this move to reform strengthened or weakened the Protestant faith. The decade of the 1930s has been important in this debate, because all churches were called upon to take a more active social role by helping individuals and families who were suffering during the depression.

An earlier generation of religious historians saw a split among the Protestant churches, between conservative and fundamentalist ones that emphasized personal salvation, and liberal and radical ones that stressed social salvation. They also noted a correlation between religious beliefs and political affiliation, at least in regard to new political reform movements and parties on the Prairies in the 1930s. In his study *Sect, Cult and Church in Alberta* (Toronto: University of Toronto Press, 1955), W.E. Mann argued that the greatest support for Social Credit came from the fundamentalist churches and religious sects and cults. Historians David Elliott and Iris Miller disagreed. In their biography *"Bible Bill": A Biography of William Aberhart* (Edmonton: Reidmore Books, 1987), they argue that the mainline Protestant churches, including those adhering to a liberal theology, most strongly supported Aberhart and his Social Credit movement. Analysts of the Co-operative Commonwealth Federation (CCF) have noted an equally strong religious affiliation. In *The Anatomy of a Party: The National CCF* (Toronto: University of Toronto Press, 1969), political scientist Walter Young noted that the party's leadership came largely from the left-wing Methodist church and its offspring, the United Church of Canada. Historian Kenneth McNaught emphasized the importance of Methodism in the life of J.S. Woodsworth, the founding leader of the CCF, in his biography *A Prophet in Politics: A Biography of J.S. Woodsworth* (Toronto: University of Toronto Press, 1959).

More recently, religious historians have examined the social gospel movement in the Protestant churches in the late nineteenth and early twentieth centuries. In *The Social Passion: Religion and Social Reform in Canada, 1914–28* (Toronto: University of Toronto Press, 1971), Richard Allen argued that industrialization and urbanization created new social problems that required the attention of the Protestant churches. The resulting reform impulse inaugurated an era of revivalism that kept Protestantism alive and active well into the twentieth century. In the 1930s, the Fellowship for a Christian Social Order (FCSO), a socialist group consisting largely of ministers and sons of the manse, brought religion to the CCF.

In *The Regenerators: Social Criticism in Late Victorian English Canada* (Toronto: University of Toronto Press, 1985), historian Ramsay Cook disagreed with Allen. He argued that the social gospel movement undermined the Protestant faith by getting churches involved in social issues that were more secular than sacred. As a result, religion went into a decline that has led to the modern secular society.

The anti-secularists replied, led by historian Michael Gauvreau. In *The Evangelical Century: College and Creed in English Canada from the Great Revival to the Great Depression* (Montreal/Kingston: McGill-Queen's University Press, 1991), Gauvreau maintained that the Methodist and Presbyterian churches survived the onslaught of

(continued)

secularism in the late nineteenth century through a reformulation of their tradition of evangelicalism to fit the changing times and emerged with a "persistence and vitality" that served them well in the twentieth century. Far from being a spent force, as the secularists argued, Protestantism was alive and well in the twentieth century, and it played a meaningful role in dealing with social concerns in the 1930s. If Protestantism did decline, it was after the Great Depression, Gauvreau argued.

Historian Neil Semple entered the debate in his study, *The Lord's Domain: The History of Methodism* (Toronto: University of Toronto Press, 1996). Semple pointed out that to the Methodists everything was sacred because "everything belonged to God," and therefore secularism posed no threat. Furthermore, he suggested looking at the sacred–secular issue not as a linear progression but as something that came and went, somewhat like "waves." One such "wave" occurred in the 1930s, when even social gospellers "underwent a traumatic crisis of faith and sought a spiritual revival for themselves and for the entire church" (p. 448).

The debate is certain to continue as religious historians seek to understand the role of religion in the reform impulse of the late nineteenth and twentieth centuries and the impact of that symbiotic relationship on the Protestant faith.

and "La Pension Velder." Radio variety shows were equally popular programs in Quebec. The songs of "La Bolduc," Mary Travers-Bolduc, enjoyed enormous popularity.

Mass magazines, both Canadian and American, featured stories of wealth and glamour, while films from Hollywood portrayed romance and fantasy. Walt Disney's *Snow White and the Seven Dwarfs* became a box-office hit. The birth of the Dionne quintuplets near Callander, Ontario, in May 1934 attracted worldwide attention and brought over 3 million people to see a glimpse of them at a special hospital set up to care for them under the auspices of the Ontario government — a government that quickly appreciated the profit to be made from this "tourist attraction." Even this real-life event was a form of escape for the many who came.

SPORTS

Sports became another form of popular entertainment and a distraction during the depression. In winter, hockey dominated. Hockey stars became household names among sports-minded families: the Toronto Maple Leafs' famous "Kid Line" of Charlie Conacher, Joe Primeau, and Busher Jackson; the legendary Eddie Shore of the Boston Bruins, known for his speed and scoring flair; Francis "King" Clancy of the Toronto Maple Leafs, who once played every position on the ice in a single game; and Howie Morenz of the Montreal Canadiens, with his speed and flashy stickhandling, who was easily the greatest hockey superstar of the 1930s. Shortly after Morenz's tragic death on January 28, 1937, as a result of injuries received in a game, thousands of Montrealers filed past his bier, placed at centre ice in the Montreal Forum.

In summer, baseball continued to be Canada's most popular sport. Every community had a local team, and the larger towns and cities enjoyed franchises in minor professional leagues. As well, Canadians followed American big-league baseball as though it were their own "national" sport and cheered the successes of the legendary Babe Ruth. Canadian baseball fans gathered in front of the newspaper offices to watch the World Series as it was recorded on a scale-modelled baseball diamond, while an announcer described the game as it came in over the wire service.

VISUAL ART

In 1933, the Canadian Group of Painters (CGP) was formed as an expansion of the Group of Seven. It held its first exhibition that year in Atlantic City, New Jersey. During the 1930s, the group focussed its activities in three cities — Toronto, Montreal, and Vancouver. It formed a loose-knit association that provided moral support for artists who were affiliated with it. Younger members included A.J. Casson, Yvonne McKague Housser, Edwin Holgate, Gordon Webber, Isabel McLaughlin, Carl Schaefer, Charles Comfort, Paraskeva Clark, and J.W.G. (Jock) Macdonald. The older members, Arthur Lismer and A.Y. Jackson, the key figures of this new group, linked it directly to the earlier Group of Seven. Art education became an important goal of the CGP. As educational supervisor of the Art Gallery of Toronto, Lismer established the most successful children's art program in North America in the mid-1930s.

Concurrently with the Group of Seven's ascendancy in English-speaking Canada, French-Canadian painters showed a similar fascination with the land. Marc-Aurèle Fortin became a major landscape painter, but his inspiration came from visits to Chicago, Boston, and New York, and later to southern France and northern Italy, where he was especially influenced by the style of the Spanish painter Sorolla y Bastida. His pastoral canvases of the village of Sainte-Rose and of scenes along the north shore of Montreal Island are noted for their subdued colours. After 1935, he began painting in more vibrant, luminous colours. Art critic J. Russell Harper notes: "Fortin accomplished in Quebec what the Group of Seven had accomplished in Ontario: he painted the Quebec landscape as a symbol of the way in which he knew and felt it.... [But] he had one feature which is never found in the work of the Ontario artists: a religious overtone."[3]

Religious subjects also appeared in the early paintings of Jean-Paul Lemieux in the 1930s. He chose colourful Fête-Dieu processions in Quebec streets and other religious events as subjects for his paintings. They too, like Fortin's, were noted for their quiet nostalgia and gentle lyricism. The period also marked the death of a giant from an earlier era, Marc-Aurèle de Foy Suzor-Côté, in 1937. His obituary in the *Montreal Star* recognized him as "French Canada's greatest painter, and one of her greatest sculptors. His large canvases breathe the very atmosphere and colour of the woods of his beloved Quebec."

NOVELS

In the 1930s, Morley Callaghan's three novels — *Such Is My Beloved* (1934), *They Shall Inherit the Earth* (1935), and *More Joy in Heaven* (1937) — stood out as good examples of "critical realism" novels. Irene Baird's *Waste Heritage* (1939) dealt with labour unrest and unemployment in Vancouver during the depression. The most outstanding French-Canadian novel in the 1930s was Ringuet's (Philippe Panneton's) *Trente Arpents*,

Young Canadian (1932), by Charles Comfort. A portrait of fellow-artist Carl Schaefer, whose disillusioned eyes and empty, hanging hands symbolized the Great Depression.

Hart House, Permanent Collection, University of Toronto.

translated into English as *Thirty Acres*, a realistic novel that graphically depicted the transition from rural to urban life in Quebec. It broke with literary tradition in Quebec in describing the French-Canadian farmer as a tragic, rather than heroic, figure. The novel follows the fall of its central character, Euchariste Moisan, from initial prosperity on his farm to an impoverished old age in a New England factory town.

THEATRE

In Quebec, several of the best-known French-Canadian playwrights, such as Gratien Gélinas, learned their trade by writing scripts for radio productions, especially for the Canadian Broadcasting Corporation (CBC), which began broadcasting in French and English in Montreal in 1933.

In 1930, criticism arose once again in Quebec concerning the propriety of the theatre. A Parisian company performed the popular but risqué operetta *Phi-Phi* at Montreal's St.-Denis theatre. A judge declared it indecent, closed it down, and levied $15 fines on each of the actors, their agents, and even the orchestra leader.

Although the Roman Catholic church's opposition to the public performance of theatre had hindered its development in Quebec, the clergy did support amateur theatre for educational purposes. Father Émile Legault founded in 1937 a troupe of young actors at Montreal's Collège de Saint-Laurent that from 1938 to 1952 set the pace for a theatrical renaissance in Quebec. With Legault's encouragement, the group moved from an early emphasis on religious theatre to a concentration on classical and contemporary plays. Félix Leclerc, the famous Quebec singer, songwriter, playwright, and actor, acted with the Compagnons de St. Laurent in the early 1940s.

In English Canada, professional theatre languished in the depressed atmosphere of the 1930s. Most theatre groups, which were barely able to hold on during the good times, folded in the depression. Amateur theatre groups took their place. Governor General Lord Bessborough, a theatre enthusiast, assisted amateur theatre by founding in 1932 the Dominion Drama Festival, an annual competition that included amateur societies at the local, regional, and national levels. The best provincial productions went on to national finals, held each year in a different major city. The first competition was held in Ottawa in April 1933, and included 168 participants. During its nearly 40-year existence, the festival inaugurated the careers of a significant number of later-professional actors and actresses. Unfortunately, it did not have the same success in promoting English-Canadian playwrights.

While professional theatre languished during the 1930s, working-class political theatre emerged. Especially popular was the agitprop troupe (agitprop is a combination of the words "agitation" and "propaganda") theatre used by communist sympathizers to advance class struggle. The conditions of the depression provided both the actors, in the form of unemployed workers and student agitators, and a sympathetic and enthusiastic audience for such theatre.

The Workers' Experimental Theatre became the first agitprop troupe in Canada, and it held its first performance on May 6, 1932, at the Ukrainian Labour Temple. This was followed in the summer of 1933 by three tours through southern Ontario. But their greatest success occurred in December 1933 when the group staged *Eight Men Speak*, a mock trial drama of the arrest two years earlier in 1931 and attempted assassination at the Kingston Penitentiary of Tim Buck, leader of the Communist party. Many of the actors themselves risked arrest (and in some cases deportation) for taking part in the play, while theatre owners were threatened with having their licences revoked should they permit the play to be staged in their theatre. In the end, only one performance of the entire play was performed to a packed audience of 1500 at the Standard Theatre on Spadina Avenue in Toronto.

The depression affected all aspects of Canadian society. Out of desperation, people turned to the government for financial assistance. Governments, in turn, reluctantly accepted new economic and social responsibilities. New political parties appeared, each one offering its own solution to the depression. Women and labourers made only marginal gains. Many turned to religion for guidance. Popular culture flourished as people sought an escape from the harsh reality around them.

NOTES

1. John Herd Thompson with Allen Seager, *Canada, 1922–1939: Decades of Discord* (Toronto: McClelland & Stewart, 1985), p. 194.
2. Robin Fisher and David J. Mitchell, "Patterns of Provincial Politics Since 1916," in Hugh J.M. Johnston, ed., *The Pacific Province: A History of British Columbia* (Vancouver: Douglas & McIntyre, 1996), p. 259.
3. J. Russell Harper, *Painting in Canada: A History*, 2nd ed. (Toronto: University of Toronto Press, 1977), p. 296.

LINKING TO THE PAST

WEB LINKS

The Great Depression
http://www2.excite.sfu.ca/pgm/depress/greatdepress.html#lowcls
This site provides an overview of life during the Great Depression in the Vancouver area, including popular culture, a description of economic and living conditions of different classes, and information on Vancouver's ethnic communities.

Richard B. Bennett
http://cnet.unb.ca/achn/pme/rbbcb.htm
A brief biography of Richard Bedford Bennett, with additional links to a descriptive biography, a photograph, and an anecdote about his time in office.

The Bank of Canada Act
http://canada.justice.gc.ca/FTP/EN/Laws/Chap/B/B-2.txt
The full text of the Bank of Canada Act, which established the Bank of Canada in 1935.

Alberta's Social Credit Party
http://www.freenet.edmonton.ab.ca/socred/history.html
A history of the Social Credit party in Alberta.

A History of the Communist Party of Canada
http://www.communist-party.ca/english/index1.html
From the Communist Party of Canada home page, go to "In Our Archives" to read an official party history and view photographs from the 1920s and 1930s.

Radio Days
http://www.otr.com/new_index.shtml
This site offers information about old North American radio shows (including *Amos 'n Andy*) and audio clips of broadcasts from the 1920s to 1950s.

RELATED READINGS

R. Douglas Francis and Donald B. Smith, eds., *Readings in Canadian History: Post-Confederation*, 5th ed. (Toronto: Harcourt Brace, 1998), contains two articles relevant to this chapter: Nelson Wiseman, "The Pattern of Prairie Politics," pp. 305–22; and James Struthers, "Canadian Unemployment Policy in the 1930s," pp. 333–43.

BIBLIOGRAPHY

A popular account of the 1930s is Pierre Berton, *The Great Depression, 1929–1939* (Toronto: McClelland & Stewart, 1990). For a more scholarly account see John Herd Thompson with Allen Seager, *Canada, 1922–1939: Decades of Discord* (Toronto: McClelland & Stewart, 1985). For a good, brief synthesis see Michiel Horn's booklet *The Great Depression of the 1930s in Canada* (Ottawa: Canadian Historical Association, 1984). The same author has also edited a collection of documents, *The Depression in Canada: Responses to Economic Crisis* (Toronto: Copp Clark Pitman, 1988). A.E. Safarian analyzes economic developments in *The Canadian Economy in the Great Depression* (Toronto: University of Toronto Press, 1959). In *Business and Social Reform in the Thirties* (Toronto: James Lorimer, 1979), Alvin Finkel discusses the reactions of business to Bennett's reform proposals. The stock-market crash of 1929 is discussed in Doug Fetherling, *Gold Diggers of 1929: Canada and the Great Stock Market Crash* (Toronto: Macmillan, 1979).

A wealth of material exists on politics in the 1930s. H. Blair Neatby provides an overview in *The Politics of Chaos: Canada in the Thirties* (Toronto: Macmillan, 1972). On R.B. Bennett consult Larry A. Glassford, *Reaction and Reform: The Politics of the Conservative Party Under R.B. Bennett, 1927–1938* (Toronto: University of Toronto Press, 1992); and Richard Wilbur's booklet, *The Bennett Administration* (Ottawa: Canadian Historical Association, 1969). Two recent biographical sketches on aspects of Bennett's life are P.B. Waite,

The Loner: Three Sketches of the Personal Life and Ideas of R.B. Bennett (Toronto: University of Toronto Press, 1992); and James H. Gray, *R.B. Bennett: The Calgary Years* (Toronto: University of Toronto Press, 1991). Bennett's efforts to stimulate trade with Britain are the subject of an article by Tim Rooth, "Imperial Preference and Anglo-Canadian Trade Relations in the 1930's: The End of an Illusion?" *British Journal of Canadian Studies* 1 (1986): 205–29. See also Ian M. Drummond and Norman Hillmer, *Negotiating Freer Trade: The United Kingdom, the United States, Canada, and the Trade Agreements of 1938* (Waterloo, ON: Wilfrid Laurier University Press, 1989). Federal financial measures are studied in Robert B. Bryce, *Maturing in Hard Times: Canada's Department of Finance through the Great Depression* (Toronto: Institute of Public Administration of Canada, 1986). On the founding of the Bank of Canada and on its first president see Douglas H. Fullerton, *Graham Towers and His Times* (Toronto: McClelland & Stewart, 1986). On the New Deal see Donald Forster and Colin Read, "The Politics of Opportunism: The New Deal Broadcasts," *Canadian Historical Review* 60 (1979): 324–49; and J.R.H. Wilbur, ed., *The Bennett New Deal: Fraud or Portent* (Toronto: Copp Clark, 1968).

How Canada dealt with jobless or "radical" immigrants is discussed in Barbara Roberts, *Whence They Came: Deportation from Canada, 1900–1935* (Ottawa: University of Ottawa Press, 1988). James Struthers has studied the relief question in *No Fault of Their Own: Unemployment and the Canadian Welfare State, 1914–1941* (Toronto: University of Toronto Press, 1983), and, for Ontario, his *The Limits of Affluence: Welfare in Ontario, 1920–1970* (Toronto: University of Toronto Press, 1994). See as well Raymond B. Blake and Jeff Keshen, eds., *Social Welfare Policy in Canada: Historical Readings* (Toronto: Copp Clark, 1995); James G. Snell, *The Citizen's Wage: The State and the Elderly in Canada, 1900–1951* (Toronto: University of Toronto Press, 1995); and Cynthia R. Comacchio, *"Nations Are Built of Babies": Saving Ontario's Mothers and Children, 1900–1940* (Montreal/Kingston: McGill-Queen's University Press, 1993).

On the response of Canadians to the depression see R.D. Francis and H. Ganzevoort, eds., *The Dirty Thirties in Prairie Canada* (Vancouver: Tantalus Research, 1980); Michiel Horn, ed., *The Dirty Thirties: Canadians in the Great Depression* (Toronto: Copp Clark, 1972); James Gray, *The Winter Years* (Toronto: Macmillan, 1990 [1966]), and his *Men Against the Desert* (Saskatoon: Western Producer Prairie Books, 1967); and the poignant L.M. Grayson and Michael Bliss, eds., *The Wretched of Canada: Letters to R.B. Bennett, 1930–1935* (Toronto: University of Toronto Press, 1971). On one memorable episode of the depression see Victor Howard, *"We Were the Salt of the Earth": The On-to-Ottawa Trek and the Regina Riot* (Regina: Canadian Plains Research Centre, University of Regina, 1985). On the relief camps see Laurel Sefton MacDowell, "Relief Camp Workers in Ontario During the Great Depression of the 1930s," *Canadian Historical Review* 76(2) (June 1995): 205–28.

Much material on Canada's socialists is available. Walter Young, *The Anatomy of a Party: The National CCF* (Toronto: University of Toronto Press, 1969), is a good analysis. See also Michiel Horn, *The League for Social Reconstruction: Intellectual Origins of the Democratic Left in Canada, 1931–42* (Toronto: University of Toronto Press, 1980); and J. William Brennan, *"Building the Co-operative Commonwealth": Essays on the Democratic Socialist Tradition in Canada* (Regina: Canadian Plains Research Centre, University of Regina, 1985). Biographical works on J.S. Woodsworth include Grace McInnis, *J.S. Woodsworth* (Toronto: Macmillan, 1953); and Kenneth McNaught, *A Prophet in Politics* (Toronto: University of Toronto Press, 1959). Three studies in intellectual history are David Laycock, *Populism and Democratic Thought in the Canadian Prairies, 1919–1945* (Toronto: University of Toronto Press, 1990); Allen Mills, *Fool for Christ: The Political Thought of J.S. Woodsworth* (Toronto: University of Toronto Press, 1991); and R. Douglas Francis, *Frank H. Underhill: Intellectual*

Provocateur (Toronto: University of Toronto Press, 1986). On Social Credit see David R. Elliott and Iris Miller, *Bible Bill: A Biography of William Aberhart* (Edmonton: Reidmore Books, 1987); and Alvin Finkel, *The Social Credit Phenomenon in Alberta* (Toronto: University of Toronto Press, 1989). On the Communist party see Norman Penner, *Canadian Communism: The Stalin Years and Beyond* (Toronto: Methuen Publications, 1988); Lita-Rose Betcherman, *The Little Band: The Clashes Between the Communists and the Political and Legal Establishments in Canada, 1928–1932* (Ottawa: Deneau, 1982); Ian Angus, *Canadian Bolsheviks* (Montreal: Vanguard, 1981); Ivan Avakumovic, *The Communist Party in Canada: A History* (Toronto: McClelland & Stewart, 1975); and Andrée Lévesque, *Virage à gauche interdit: les communistes, les socialistes et leurs ennemis au Québec, 1929–1939* (Montréal: Boréal Express, 1984). Extreme right-wing movements are examined in Martin Robin, *Shades of Right: Nativist and Fascist Politics in Canada, 1920 to 1940* (Toronto: University of Toronto Press, 1991); Jonathan Wagner, *Brothers Beyond the Sea: National Socialism in Canada* (Waterloo, ON: Wilfrid Laurier University Press, 1982); and Lita-Rose Betcherman, *The Swastika and the Maple Leaf* (Toronto: Fitzhenry & Whiteside, 1975). Pierre Anctil discusses anti-Semitism in Quebec in *Le rendez-vous manqué: Les Juifs de Montréal face au Québec de l'entre-deux-guerres* (Québec: Institut québécois de recherche sur la culture, 1988); as does Esther Delisle, *The Traitor and the Jew: Anti-Semitism and Extreme Right-Wing Nationalism in Quebec from 1929 to 1939* (Montreal: R. Davies, 1993).

On Quebec see Bernard Vigod, *Quebec Before Duplessis: The Political Career of Louis-Alexandre Taschereau* (Montreal/Kingston: McGill-Queen's University Press, 1986); Richard Jones's booklet, *Duplessis and the Union Nationale Administration* (Ottawa: Canadian Historical Association, 1983); and the relevant chapters in Paul-André Linteau et al., *Quebec since 1930* (Toronto: James Lorimer 1991). On the history of the Union Nationale party consult H.F. Quinn, *The Union Nationale*, rev. ed. (Toronto: University of Toronto Press, 1979). For Ontario see John T. Saywell, *"Just Call Me Mitch": The Life of Mitchell F. Hepburn* (Toronto: University of Toronto Press, 1992). Ontario's attempts to secure comprehensive wage legislation are examined in Mark Cox, "The Limits of Reform: Industrial Regulation and Management Rights in Ontario, 1930–7," *Canadian Historical Review* 68 (1987): 552–75. On Duff Pattullo in British Columbia consult Robin Fisher, *Duff Pattullo of British Columbia* (Toronto: University of Toronto Press, 1991); and Allan Irving, "The Development of a Provincial Welfare State: British Columbia 1900–1939," in Allan Moscovitch and Jim Albert, eds., *The Benevolent State: The Growth of Welfare in Canada* (Toronto: Garamond Press, 1987), pp. 155–74.

On the social impact of relief consult L.M. Grayson and Michael Bliss, eds., *The Wretched of Canada: Letters to R.B. Bennett, 1930–1935* (Toronto: University of Toronto Press, 1971); R.D. Francis and Herman Ganzevoort, eds., *The Dirty Thirties in Prairie Canada* (Vancouver: Tantalus Research, 1980); and Dennis Guest, *The Emergence of Social Security in Canada* (Vancouver: University of British Columbia Press, 1980). Personal recollections are available in Barry Broadfoot, *Ten Lost Years, 1929–1939* (Toronto: Doubleday, 1973). For a personal memoir see James Gray, *The Winter Years* (Toronto: Macmillan, 1966). Irving Abella and Harold Troper, *None Is Too Many: Canada and the Jews of Europe, 1933–1948*, 3rd ed. (Toronto: Lester, 1991), is a poignant account of Canada's treatment of Jewish refugees.

Labour in the interwar years is discussed in Bryan D. Palmer, *Working-Class Experience: Rethinking the History of Canadian Labour, 1800–1991* (Toronto: McClelland & Stewart, 1992); Irving M. Abella, *Nationalism, Communism and Canadian Labour: The CIO, the Communist Party and the Canadian Congress of Labour, 1935–1956* (Toronto: University of Toronto Press, 1973); and Paul MacEwan, *Miners and Steelworkers: Labour in Cape Breton* (Toronto: Samuel Stevens Hakkert, 1976). On the 1930s see Evelyn Dumas, *The Bitter*

Thirties in Quebec (Montreal: Black Rose Books, 1975); John Manley, "Communists and Auto Workers: The Struggle for Industrial Unionism in the Canadian Automobile Industry, 1925–36," *Labour/Le Travail* 17 (1986): 105–33; and Michael Earle, "The Coalminers and Their 'Red' Union: The Amalgamated Mine Workers of Nova Scotia, 1932–1936," *Labour/Le Travail* 22 (1988): 99–137.

On women in the 1930s see the relevant chapters in Alison Prentice et al., *Canadian Women: A History*, 2nd ed. (Toronto: Harcourt Brace, 1996); and Veronica Strong-Boag, *The New Day Recalled: Lives of Girls and Women in English Canada, 1919–1939*, rev. ed. (Toronto: Copp Clark Pitman, 1993). The equivalent study for Quebec women is Andrée Lévesque, *Making and Breaking the Rules: Women in Quebec, 1919–1939* (Toronto: McClelland & Stewart, 1994). Consult, as well, articles in Linda Kealey and Joan Sangster, eds., *Beyond the Vote: Canadian Women and Politics* (Toronto: University of Toronto Press, 1989); and Veronica Strong-Boag and Anita Clair Fellman, eds., *Rethinking Canada: The Promise of Women's History*, 2nd ed. (Toronto: Copp Clark Pitman, 1991). Joy Parr's *The Gender of Breadwinners: Women, Men, and Change in Two Industrial Towns, 1880–1950* (Toronto: University of Toronto Press, 1990) covers the period of the depression in her comparison of Hanover and Paris, Ontario.

Birth control is the subject of Angus MacLaren and Arlene Tigar McLaren, *The Bedroom and the State: The Changing Practices and Politics of Contraception and Abortion in Canada, 1890–1980* (Toronto: McClelland & Stewart, 1986); and Mary F. Bishop, "Vivian Dowding: Birth Control Activist," in Veronica Strong-Boag and Anita Clair Fellman, eds., *Rethinking Canada: The Promise of Women's History* (Toronto: Copp Clark Pitman, 1986), pp. 200–07; and Diane Dodd, "The Canadian Birth Control Movement on Trial, 1936–37," *Histoire sociale/Social History* 16 (November 1983): 411–28. On the Dionne quintuplets see the special issue of the *Journal of Canadian Studies* 29(4) (Winter 1995).

University education in the 1930s is the subject of Paul Axelrod's *Making a Middle Class: Student Life in English Canada During the Thirties* (Montreal/Kingston: McGill-Queen's University Press, 1990). On religion see Keith Clifford, "Religion in the Thirties: Some Aspects of the Canadian Experience," in R.D. Francis and H. Ganzevoort, eds., *The Dirty Thirties in Prairie Canada* (Vancouver: Tantalus Research, 1980), pp. 125–40; and J.W. Grant, *The Church in the Canadian Era: The First Century of Confederation* (Burlington, ON: Welch, 1988).

Culture in the 1930s is discussed in John Herd Thompson and Allen Seager, "The Conundrum of Culture," in *Canada, 1922–1939* (as cited earlier), pp. 158–92. On cultural nationalism in the period see Mary Vipond, *The Mass Media in Canada*, rev. ed. (Toronto: James Lorimer, 1992). For the Maritimes see, as well, Gwendolyn Davies, *Myth and Milieu: Atlantic Literature and Culture, 1918–1939* (Fredericton: Acadiensis Press, 1993). For painting see J. Russell Harper, *Painting in Canada: A History*, 2nd ed. (Toronto: University of Toronto Press, 1977); Dennis Reid, *A Concise History of Canadian Painting*, 2nd ed. (Toronto: Oxford University Press, 1988); and Ann Davis, *The Logic of Ecstasy: Canadian Mystical Painting, 1920–1940* (Toronto: University of Toronto Press, 1992). On music see George A. Proctor, *Canadian Music of the Twentieth Century* (Toronto: University of Toronto Press, 1980). Ezra Schabas, *Sir Ernest MacMillan: The Importance of Being Canadian* (Toronto: University of Toronto Press, 1994), deals with this important Canadian musician. On sports, see William Houston, *Pride and Glory: 100 Years of the Stanley Cup* (Toronto: McGraw-Hill Ryerson, 1992); and Dan Diamond, ed., *The Official National Hockey League 75th Anniversary Commemorative Book* (Toronto: Firefly Books, 1991).

On theatre in Quebec see Elaine F. Nardocchio, *Theatre and Politics in Modern Quebec* (Edmonton: University of Alberta Press, 1986); and Jean Hamelin, *The Theatre in French*

Canada (1936–66) (Quebec: Department of Cultural Affairs, 1968). On working-class theatre see Richard Wright and Robin Endres, eds., *Eight Men Speak and Other Plays from the Canadian Workers' Theatre* (Toronto: New Hogtown Press, 1976); and Toby Gordon Ryan, *Stage Left: Canadian Theatre in the Thirties* (Toronto: CTR Publications, 1981).

Students should also consult the maps and charts in Donald Kerr and Deryck W. Holdsworth, eds., *Historical Atlas of Canada*, vol. 3, *Addressing the Twentieth Century, 1891–1961* (Toronto: University of Toronto Press, 1990).

CHAPTER THIRTEEN

Canada in World War II

During the 1930s, most Canadians were isolationists. They felt that their government should use its newly recognized autonomy in international affairs to avoid being dragged into the conflicts that developed in Europe, Africa, and Asia. Once Britain declared war on Germany in September 1939, however, no doubt existed that Canada would participate. But to what degree? And in what form? Those questions would be answered in the course of often stormy debates. Then, in the final months of the war, Canada assisted in the creation of new institutions that, it was hoped, would preserve peace. The war and its aftermath thus thrust Canada — not always willingly and enthusiastically — into the international arena.

The Canada of 1945 differed greatly from the country that had embarked on war in 1939. The heavy demands of the wartime economy catapulted the nation out of economic depression and into rapid industrial growth. As people crowded into the cities in search of jobs, the state took an increasingly active role in providing social services. Canada thus moved toward the creation of a modern welfare state. The war also had profound, though in part temporary, implications for Canadian women. The government needed them to participate in war-related activities, to alleviate labour shortages in the war industries, and to support men in the armed forces.

The war had enduring effects on federal–provincial relations, too. The pendulum of power swung toward Ottawa, as the central government mobilized the economy and controlled national finances to further the war effort. The defenders of provincial autonomy fought back, but, more often than not, had no choice but to retreat. In international affairs, Canada shifted its focus from Britain to the United States as its major ally and trading partner.

Canada's Liberal government successfully weathered war-related problems, including a new conscription crisis. Canadians might not have loved their pompous and aging prime minister, but they probably recognized Mackenzie King's uncanny skill in sensing change and, in any case, they certainly could not agree on who might do a better job.

NEUTRALITY

In the 1930s, Canada used its newly won autonomy in foreign affairs to avoid entanglements overseas. When, for example, Japan invaded Manchuria in 1931, Canada refused to endorse sanctions at the League of Nations. Indeed, the Canadian delegate made a speech judged so pro-Japanese that Japan's diplomatic representative in Ottawa thanked the Canadian government! Similarly, after Italian dictator Benito Mussolini invaded the independent African kingdom of Abyssinia (Ethiopia) in October 1935, Canada's two major political leaders, R.B. Bennett and Mackenzie King, then in the midst of a federal election campaign, both agreed that Canada should not become involved.

Nevertheless, events soon forced the Canadian government to respond to this major test of the League of Nations' ability to curb aggression. Walter Riddell, Canada's advisory officer at the league's headquarters in Geneva, personally favoured strong economic sanctions against Italy. Before receiving specific orders from Ottawa, he proposed including oil and other strategic materials on the embargo list. Prime Minister King wanted above all to avoid Canadian participation in any armed struggles not directly related to the country's own interest. Now, on the advice of O.D. Skelton, undersecretary of state for external affairs, and of Ernest Lapointe, his minister of justice as well as his Quebec lieutenant, King repudiated the "Canada proposal." In his own words, he gave Riddell "a good spanking." Britain and France saved Riddell from further embarrassment when, in exchange for peace, they offered Mussolini the territory he had already overrun in East Africa. A few weeks later, King claimed in the House of Commons that Canada had saved Europe from war.

THE RISE OF NAZI GERMANY

Adolf Hitler posed the greatest threat to world peace. Systematically, the Nazi leader, who became chancellor of Germany in 1933, set out to consolidate and to increase Germany's power. First, the German military reoccupied the hitherto demilitarized zone of the Rhineland in March 1936, in violation of the Treaty of Versailles and the Locarno agreements. Then, in March 1938, Hitler forced the *Anschluss*, or union, upon Austria. Next, he seized the Sudetenland, the western region of Czechoslovakia, a conquest that Britain and France, in their desire to avoid war, accepted at the Munich conference in the fall of 1938. Hitler annexed what remained of Czechoslovakia in March 1939. Canada supported Britain and France's policy of appeasement, of making concession after concession to Hitler.

Mackenzie King visited Hitler in 1937. Convinced of his divine mission as international peacemaker, the Canadian prime minister described the führer as "a man of deep sincerity and a genuine patriot" — a modern-day Joan of Arc who would deliver his people. Hitler convinced King that he did not want war but was concerned with the spread of communism. In early 1939, King, who still believed that war could be avoided, wrote to the German chancellor to assure him of their mutual friendship. Indeed, King seemed to fear that London would do more to provoke a war than Berlin. At no point did Canada foresee the ultimate implications of the Nazis' anti-Semitism.

REASONS FOR APPEASEMENT

Many supporters of appeasement in Canada saw Hitler and Mussolini as bulwarks against the spread of communism, as defenders of order in an era of chaotic revolution. They viewed General Francisco Franco, the fascist leader who won power in Spain in 1939 after a bitter civil war, in the same light. Rodrigue Cardinal Villeneuve, archbishop of Quebec, reminded his clergy in May 1937 that "dictatorship is better than revolution." To the embarrassment of the Canadian government, however, 1250 Canadian volunteers formed the Mackenzie–Papineau battalion to fight for the Spanish republic against Franco's fascists.

Other explanations exist for Canada's policy of appeasement. King and his foremost advisers, like Skelton, favoured appeasement out of fear that British policies might undermine Canadian autonomy and draw the country into imperial conflicts, as they had in the past. With his sure political instincts King also knew that another war, just like World War I, risked dividing Canadians in a bitter internal conflict that could destroy national unity as well as his government and the Liberal party.

Furthermore, isolationist sentiment ran deep in Canada, as it did in the United States, which had never even joined the League of Nations. Historian Frank Underhill said it more bluntly than most when he asserted at the time that "all these European troubles are not worth the bones of a Toronto grenadier." Many English-speaking Canadian politicians and professional policy advisers wanted Canada to take, at most, a "back seat" in the international "lunatic asylum," as Loring Christie, an external-affairs adviser, described the world. French Canada, in particular, wanted to keep its distance from Europe. Demographically and sentimentally, French Canadians had long been detached from the Old World; most French-Canadian families' Canadian roots went back more than two centuries.

Finally, a policy of appeasement reflected the belief of many Canadians that the country could have no impact upon events. In 1933, Prime Minister R.B. Bennett wrote candidly to a Toronto clergyman: "Canada is not an important member of the League.... Our military prowess in the next war is regarded as of little concern." With respect to his own role, he added: "What can one man do who represents only ten and a half millions of people?"

Little changed over the next five years. On the eve of war, Canada had only seven diplomatic missions abroad. In 1938–39, the country's total budget for the armed forces was just $35 million. Twenty years of neglect had weakened Canada's defences. The nation could not even defend its own coasts, let alone dispatch fully equipped and trained forces to Europe. The navy had fewer than a dozen fighting ships, and the air force, at best, only 50 modern military aircraft. The professional army had just 4000 troops; the navy, 3000; and the air force, only 1000.

CANADA AND THE WAR AGAINST THE AXIS

On September 1, 1939, German troops invaded Poland. On September 3, Britain and France declared war on Germany. Canada followed a week later, a somewhat belated gesture that symbolically demonstrated the nation's newly acquired sovereignty. A small number of Canadians opposed the war on moral grounds. These included pacifists in the Women's International League for Peace and Freedom as well as pacifists and anti-imperialists in the CCF. But there was never any real possibility that Canada would remain neutral, as the United States chose to do until the Japanese attacked Pearl Harbor in December 1941. Canada's emotional ties with Britain still remained strong, well after its colonial ties had ended.

THE BRITISH COMMONWEALTH AIR TRAINING PLAN

The first few months of warfare, described as the "phoney war," made it possible for the Canadian government to postpone making wrenching decisions concerning the nature of Canada's participation in the conflict. Nevertheless, during this period one vitally important part of Canada's contribution to the war got under way: the British Commonwealth Air Training Plan (BCATP), which was conducted in, and heavily funded by, Canada. The BCATP eventually trained 130 000 aviators, nearly half the Commonwealth's air crews.

Negotiations with Britain to establish the terms of Canada's involvement proved arduous, even rancorous. As historian Desmond Morton observes, "King's attachment to England did not always extend to Englishmen."[1] The final plan, agreed upon in 1939, gave control of the schools to the Royal Canadian Air Force (RCAF), which the federal government had organized immediately after World War I. The plan had other virtues. This kind of "at home" Canadian participation would be acceptable to French Canadians (although most Quebeckers were automatically disqualified because they did not speak English). It would also avoid the heavy casualties that Canada had suffered in World War I. Finally, the project gave a tremendous boost to the aeronautics industry and, thanks to the more than $2 billion spent, to the Canadian economy in general.

CANADA'S MILITARY CONTRIBUTION

The Nazis' unexpected invasion of neutral Denmark, Norway, and the Low Countries in the spring of 1940 transformed the war. The rapid German advance led to the near capture of the entire British Expeditionary Force at Dunkirk. After France fell in June, Britain and its dominions stood alone against the German and Italian aggressors. Overnight, Canada had become Britain's chief ally. Until the German invasion of the Soviet Union in June 1941, it remained so. During these dark months, Britain's surrender seemed highly possible.

To assist Britain and combat the Nazis, Canada spared no expense. It built up a much larger army, constructed dozens of warships and hundreds of aircraft, and converted the entire economy to war production. In response to Britain's wartime financial needs, Canada lent, and then gave, huge sums of money — more than $3 billion — through mutual-aid agreements, with no strings attached, although most of the money was spent in Canada.

The Royal Canadian Navy (RCN), which enlisted 100 000 men and 6500 women during the war, took on the responsibility of defending the convoys that transported troops and supplies to Britain. The job was dangerous. Moreover, living conditions on the escorting corvettes were often terrible, as seawater penetrated continually during bad weather. "The smell just got worse and worse," one sailor remembered. "The ship was a floating pigpen of stink. You couldn't get away from it. The butter tasted of it ... The bread smelled of feet and armpits." In the first years of the war, Allied naval losses were staggering; by spring 1943, German U-boats in the North Atlantic had sunk more than 2000 ships, and shipyards were unable to build replacements fast enough. Initially, the Canadian navy had few successes in the anti-submarine war, as a result of inexperience, poor crew training, and deficient

A convoy near Halifax, 1941. During the war the Royal Canadian Navy played a major role in defending Allied convoys that transported troops and supplies to Britain.

....

National Archives of Canada/ DND PA-105344.

technical equipment. But once properly trained and equipped, Canadians played a significant role in the Battle of the Atlantic by sinking, or helping to sink, many German U-boats.

Combat action for Canadian troops came first in the Pacific theatre. In hindsight, the federal government had foolishly agreed to reinforce British troops in Hong Kong. Historians W.A.B. Douglas and Brereton Greenhous judge the Canadian prime minister severely: King's "comprehension of strategy and logistics was not very profound and in this essentially military situation his customary political insight deserted him."[2] The British colony fell to the Japanese on Christmas Day, 1941. More than 550 Canadians perished either in the attack or afterwards in the harsh conditions of Japanese slave labour camps. Later, in the Pacific war, Canada played a relatively minor role. Three RCAF squadrons did see action in southeast Asia, but plans to increase Canada's air and sea participation in the Pacific theatre in summer 1945 were cancelled after the Americans dropped atomic bombs on two Japanese cities.

Canadians in Europe experienced their baptism of fire in August 1942, in the ill-conceived major Allied raid on the French coast at Dieppe. In a few terrible hours, more than 60 percent of the 5000 Canadian participants were killed or captured. The Germans then used their documentary film of the slaughter of Canadians on the beach to boost the morale of their own soldiers.

For long months after the tragedy at Dieppe, Canadian troops continued garrison duty in Britain. They were not completely inactive: indeed, thousands of marriages between Canadian servicemen and British women took place. One Montreal journalist commented that the Canadian army was "the first formation in the history of war" in which the birth rate exceeded the death rate.

From July 1943, however, Canadian soldiers saw sustained combat. In the mistaken hope that casualties would be light, Mackenzie King pressured British Prime Minister Churchill to allow Canadian forces to join in the Allied invasion of Sicily. In British General (later Field-Marshal) Bernard Montgomery's view, the Canadians behaved "magnificently." Nearly 100 000 Canadian troops took part in the lengthy Italian campaign that followed. Some 6000 Canadian soldiers lost their lives, another 20 000 were wounded, and untold numbers became neuropsychiatric

Where Historians Disagree

CANADIAN PARTICIPATION IN THE LAND WAR IN NORTHWESTERN EUROPE

In recent years, the media have extensively marked the fiftieth anniversary of the events of World War II. Canadian historians have also shown new interest in that conflict and, in particular, in the role Canadians played in combat in northwestern Europe.

The tragedy at Dieppe in August 1942 has been the subject of several studies. In *Unauthorized Action: Mountbatten and the Dieppe Raid*, 2nd ed. (Toronto: Oxford University Press, 1994), Brian Loring Villa assigns British Chief of Combined Operations Lord Louis Mountbatten responsibility for having ordered the raid. Villa states that Canadian newspaper magnate Lord Beaverbrook minced no words when he encountered Mountbatten later at a dinner party: "You have murdered thousands of my countrymen.... They have been mown down and their blood is on your hands" (p. 18). But Villa also notes that General A.G.L. McNaughton, commander of Canadian forces in Britain, had delivered numerous bellicose statements. When, at last, an opportunity to use Canadian troops presented itself, McNaughton could scarcely decline the offer. Nor, in spite of his typical caution, could Prime Minister W.L.M. King refuse his authorization. He had to take into account the rising criticism of Canadians who wanted to see their country's troops take a more active part in the struggle.

For J.L. Granatstein, General H.D.G. Crerar, who commanded the 1st Canadian Corps, holds responsibility. Crerar, he says, "had come to England convinced that the army had to see action soon, both for its own morale and for domestic Canadian consumption" (*The Generals: The Canadian Army's Senior Commanders in the Second World War* [Toronto: Stoddart, 1993], p. 102). After Dieppe, Crerar's approach was to rationalize the raid by speaking of lessons learned, an approach that Granatstein says "may even be right." Peter Henshaw also believes that the Canadian commanders were primarily responsible for the Dieppe fiasco: "Their struggle for autonomy, and for a leading Canadian role in raids, interacted with British interservice rivalries in a way that was decisive for the progress of the planned raid" ("The Dieppe Raid: A Product of Misplaced Canadian Nationalism?" *Canadian Historical Review* 77 [1996]: 252).

Denis and Sheilagh Whitaker, the former a captain at Dieppe, blame British Prime Minister Winston Churchill, who needed to prove to Soviet dictator Joseph Stalin that it was impossible in 1942 to open a second front against the Germans. They argue that Churchill's strategy "was successful, no matter how high the costs" (*Dieppe: Tragedy to Triumph* [Toronto: McGraw-Hill Ryerson, 1992], p. 290). Moreover, the Allies gained essential experience at Dieppe in preparation for D-Day. The lessons learned, they say, "saved countless lives as a result of their far-reaching influence on the success of future operations" (p. 304). W.A.B. Douglas and Brereton Greenhous agree. Because of Dieppe, the Allies realized that "objectives must be more realistic, tactics more sophisticated, and training more rigorous. Communications must be more comprehensive, equipment more appropriate, and, most of all, fire support by sea and air must be overwhelming" (*Out of the Shadows: Canada in the Second World War*, rev. ed. [Toronto: Dundurn Press, 1995], p. 128).

Canadians participated actively in the invasion of Normandy in June 1944 and in the lengthy campaign in northwestern Europe that followed. Canadian casualties

(continued)

were high. Indeed, in John A. English's view, "the lives of many soldiers were unnecessarily cast away" Who should be blamed? English responds, "those who left them exposed in open wheatfields to be harvested like so many sheaves.... The responsibility must rest with the high command" (*The Canadian Army and the Normandy Campaign: A Study of Failure in High Command* [New York: Praeger, 1991], p. 256). English argues that, when large-scale training exercises finally began for Canadian soldiers garrisoned in England, senior officers had little idea of how to direct a modern army in field operations. Although many Canadian battalions and armoured regiments were well led and proved successful in battle, at the divisional and brigade levels command was often given to regular army officers of doubtful professional competence.

In autumn 1944, Allied troops advanced into Belgium but halted at Antwerp, failing to secure the Scheldt estuary and giving the Germans precious time to set up defences and regroup. It was "one of the wars most costly blunders," conclude Denis and Sheilagh Whitaker, and it had a direct bearing on extending the war by many months (*Tug of War: The Canadian Victory that Opened Antwerp* [Toronto: Stoddart, 1987], p. 373). Responsibility must lie with the supreme commander of the Allied forces, the American General Dwight Eisenhower. Certainly the Canadians paid a high price. In the bitter five-week battle that ensued, Canadian troops sustained more than 6000 casualties before routing the enemy and clearing the estuary.

WEB
LINKS

The Valour and the Horror, a television series on Canada's role in World War II broadcast by the CBC and Radio-Canada in January 1992, provoked bitter controversy. War veterans and several historians accused the writer-producers, Brian and Terence McKenna, of extreme bias and distortion of history. In particular, they felt that the presentation unduly maligned military commanders. A Senate subcommittee held hearings on the series — a gesture that the media attacked as a threat to freedom of expression.

Historians S.F Wise and David J. Bercuson both reviewed the series in the framework of an evaluation done by CBC ombudsman William Morgan. Both found the series to be "bad history" (*The Valour and the Horror Revisited* [Montreal/Kingston: McGill-Queen's University Press, 1994], p. 10). Wise, for example, took issue with the filmwriters' contention that Canadian atrocities in Normandy were equivalent to those perpetrated by German troops. Wise also refuted the film's portrayal of poor Canadian generalship. Bercuson, while affirming a general belief that "the Canadian Army as a whole did not acquit itself well in the Normandy fighting" (p. 51), decries the "failure" to put events in Normandy into a broader context and asserts that British and American units were not well prepared either. In a report partly based on the reviews done by Wise and Bercuson, the CBC ombudsman concluded that the series failed to "measure up to the CBC's demanding policies and standards" (p. 72). The McKennas responded that the ombudsman's choice of historical advisers was "prejudicial" to them and that his judgments were "almost entirely unsubstantiated in fact" (p. 88).

Other theatres of operation have also attracted the interest of historians. Why, for example, did the Royal Canadian Navy have so little success in the first years of the battle against the German U-boat wolf packs? Why were Canadian losses in Bomber Command operations over Germany so heavy, and what was gained by these massive and destructive raids on the German civilian population? Certainly the recent controversies that have developed concerning Canada's participation in the war illustrate the problems of interpreting history and defining the "truth."

A Historical Portrait
SIR FREDERICK BANTING AND PILOT JOSEPH MACKEY

Sir Frederick Banting is well known as the discoverer, with Charles Best, of insulin, used in the treatment of diabetes. Joseph Mackey was an American pilot, one of several hundred pilots and crew who worked for Ferry Command, an enterprise set up by the British in Montreal and responsible for flying more than 9000 planes across the Atlantic for delivery in Great Britain.

The first flights began in February 1941. Banting, wanting to go to England, sought space on an aircraft as a passenger. He was assigned to the Lockheed Hudson piloted by Mackey. After bad weather finally cleared, five planes, including Mackey's, took off from Gander airport in Newfoundland. Shortly after takeoff, the left engine of Mackey's plane failed. The pilot turned back. Then the right engine lost power and the plane crashed near Musgrave Harbour, Newfoundland. Mackey was injured, but not seriously. The other two crew members were killed. Banting suffered a concussion and internal bleeding. He died a few hours later despite Mackey's efforts to save his life. Three days later, Mackey was finally spotted by a plane and rescued. He later sold his story to a Toronto newspaper and then donated the proceeds to the children of his dead radio officer.

More than 500 airmen lost their lives while working for Ferry Command, often in crashes or large Liberator bombers used to bring the crews home. About 50 passengers were killed, too. Banting was the first.

This story is told in Carl A. Christie, *Ocean Bridge: The History of RAF Ferry Command* (Toronto: University of Toronto Press, 1995), pp. 62–72.

---

casualties. The fierce battle to capture the strategic town of Ortona alone cost the Canadians 700 dead: they fought from doorway to doorway, from courtyard to courtyard, from rooftop to rooftop, sometimes even moving from house to house without going outside, through a technique of breaking through the walls between houses known as "mouse-holing." Although they faced Germans who often were better armed, the Canadians relentlessly pushed north, breaching the imposing German fortifications of the Gothic Line in September 1944. American journalist Martha Gellhorn noted a special sadness in this bloody combat, which she witnessed: "It is awful to die at the end of summer or in the gentle days of the new autumn when you are young and have fought a long time . . . and when you know that the war is won anyhow."

Canadians also played a significant role in the Normandy invasion of June 6, 1944. Assisted by the RCN, Canadian troops took an entire German-held beach. The Canadian division suffered greater casualties than the British formations, but it also advanced further inland than any other Allied division on D-Day. Initial successes were made possible by far superior Allied airpower and by the failure of the Germans to mount an immediate counter-attack.

Over the next few weeks, the Canadian army's progress across Normandy was slowed by several costly failures. In possibly the Canadians' worst reversal, a complete

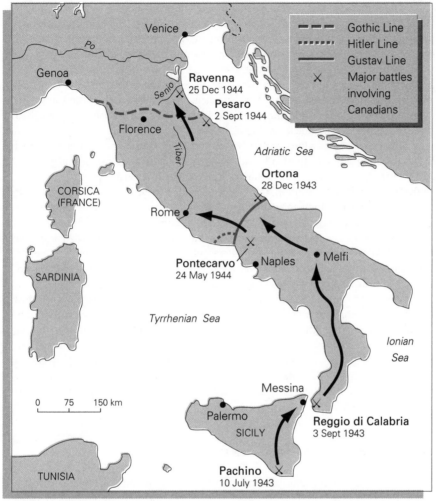

Canadian advances in Italy, indicating the Canadian army's major battles, 1943–1944.

Source: Based on Elizabeth Abbott, ed., *Chronicle of Canada* (Montreal: Chronicle Publications, 1990), p. 711.

battalion, the Canadian Black Watch, was virtually annihilated on July 25 in an unsuccessful attempt to take Verrières Ridge, south of Caen.

Allied bombing errors brought substantial Canadian casualties in the days after the Normandy landings. Moreover, at least 150 Canadian deaths were in reality cold-blooded murders of prisoners of war by German soldiers of the Hitler Youth Division, well behind the lines. In one notorious incident, a group of Canadian prisoners was marched to the Abbaye d'Ardennes, where they were murdered in the garden after interrogation. Kurt Meyer, the German commander held responsible, did serve some time in prison, first in Canada, then in West Germany, before being released to a hero's welcome.

The Canadians also organized the bloody sieges of Boulogne, Calais, and Le Havre. Then, in autumn 1944, in dreadful conditions of cold and mud, Canadian troops played a major role in the fight to secure the approaches to the Belgian port city of Antwerp. One effort involved an attempt to dislodge the Germans on Walcheren Island, at the mouth of the Scheldt delta. This approach by land was over a long, bleak rock-and-earth causeway that became a veritable hell for Canadian attackers raked by intense enemy bombardment. After heavy losses, the Canadians managed to establish a bridgehead on the island; then the British modified their strategy and decided to attack elsewhere.

Finally, in the late winter and early spring of 1945, Canadian troops participated in the liberation of the Netherlands and in the final offensive against Germany. In all, 250 000 troops served in the Canadian army in northwestern Europe; more than 11 000 of them died. In addition, from 1942, Canadian aviators conducted thousands of perilous night-bombing missions that destroyed most of Germany's large cities; Canadians eventually made up about a quarter of Bomber Command's crews. More than 17 000 of the nearly quarter-million Canadians who served in the RCAF lost their lives. All told, more than 1 million Canadians out of a total population of 11.5 million saw military service in Canada and overseas during World War II. About 42 000 were killed, and nearly 55 000 were wounded; many of these would never recover.

Was Canada's role essential to the Allied victory over the Axis powers? Most historians agree that the Allies would have won even without Canada's participation. Canada's military strength certainly paled in comparison with the resources that its huge southern neighbour was able to mobilize and could continue to count on. Yet, for a small country, Canada's contribution was enormous. In the war in Italy and in northwestern Europe, Canadian forces made a decisive contribution. It is safe to say that, without their aid, the war, and the terrible suffering that it wrought, would have dragged on longer.

THE WAR AND NATIONAL UNITY

The war caused innumerable personal tragedies, as thousands of Canadians lost a husband, father, son, brother, or fiancé. Sometimes the sad announcement came brutally. One Canadian girl wrote to her soldier boyfriend in France, and after a few weeks the letter came back stamped "Killed in action." The soldiers' return, in some cases after five years of absence, provoked poignant emotions: time brought change, and lengthy absences had often altered perceptions of relationships. The divorce rate rose substantially.

The government worked to keep support high for the war effort. The National Film Board (NFB), founded in 1939, produced "progressive film propaganda" designed to enhance Canadians' faith in their country. In the same year, Ottawa set up the Bureau of Public Information to promote patriotism and "Canadianism" among all ethnic groups in English-speaking Canada. The need to emphasize Canadian participation was brought home when American newsreels playing in Canadian theatres portrayed the Dieppe raid, in which so many Canadians lost their lives, primarily as an American action. The bureau published hundreds of pamphlets, arranged for news stories, magazine articles, and radio broadcasts, and subsidized "loyal" segments of the foreign-language press.

The town of Leeuwarden, during the liberation of the Netherlands by Canadian troops, April 16, 1945.

Donald I. Grant/National Archives of Canada/ PA-131566.

THE WARTIME TREATMENT OF MINORITY ETHNIC GROUPS

The federal government also established the Nationalities Branch of the Department of National War Services to attempt to combat widespread anti-immigrant attitudes during the war. With its staff of two, the branch was scarcely an adequate response to a very real problem. As the Wartime Information Board reported in 1943, "It is obvious that prejudice against 'foreigners' in general and Jews in particular has grown."

Ironically, while attempting to unite Canadians, the government meted out harsh treatment to members of ethnic groups whose homelands were at war with Canada, believing that they constituted a danger to the state. Under the War Measures Act, the federal government interned hundreds of German Canadians, although the RCMP found no evidence of domestic subversion. Upon Italy's entry into the war, the RCMP began a "mop-up of Italians," as the *Montreal Star* described the operation. It fingerprinted and photographed thousands of Italian Canadians, and arrested some 700, including tailors, miners, shopkeepers, a United Church minister, and almost all doctors. Businessman James Franceschini was one of those interned at Camp Petawawa; he saw his businesses placed in the hands of the Custodian of Alien Property and the equipment sold off at fire-sale prices to his Montreal competitors. Franceschini's lawyer claimed that these business rivals even intervened to hinder his client's release. A few members of the clergy and university professors questioned the arrests. Most Canadians appeared, by their silence, to acquiesce. Indeed, in Cape Breton, coal miners laid down their tools to force their employer to ban Italians from the mines.

More than any other group, Japanese Canadians felt the brunt of Canadians' animosity. After the Japanese surprise raid on Pearl Harbor in December 1941, which brought fears of an invasion of the Pacific coast, the federal government evacuated the more than 20 000 Japanese and Japanese Canadians living in coastal British Columbia. Evacuees were first housed in the exhibition buildings in Hastings Park, Vancouver, where wooden bunks were installed in horse stalls in the livestock barns. Later, most were transported to camps in the interior of the province, but several hundred males deemed "dangerous" were placed under armed guard at a camp in the

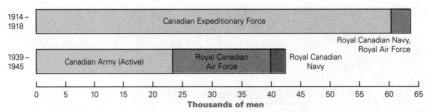

Canadian Fatalities in Two World Wars

Source: Christopher A. Sharpe, "Military Activity in the Second World War," Plate 47 of Donald Kerr and Deryck W. Holdsworth, eds., *Historical Atlas of Canada*, vol. 3 (Toronto: University of Toronto Press, 1990).

Military Fatalities in World War II, Selected Countries

Source: Christopher A. Sharpe, "Military Activity in the Second World War," Plate 47 of Donald Kerr and Deryck W. Holdsworth, eds., *Historical Atlas of Canada*, vol. 3 (Toronto: University of Toronto Press, 1990).

In all, the terrible bloodbath between 1939 and 1945 claimed the lives of nearly 60 million civilians and soldiers.

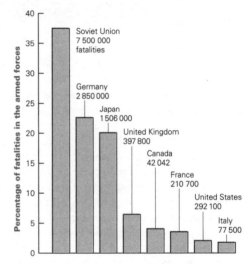

Lake Superior bush country. Those interned saw their property confiscated and auctioned off. Families wishing to stay together had to agree to go to sugar-beet farms in Alberta and Manitoba, where they had to perform the back-breaking labour of sugar-beet topping. After the war, Ottawa resettled the Japanese Canadians across Canada and even attempted to deport thousands — many of whom were Canadian citizens — to Japan. Although the federal government abandoned these plans in 1947, hundreds of Japanese Canadians, embittered by life in Canada, chose to return to Japan.

Most historians view wartime government policy toward the Japanese in Canada as the result of longstanding racial hostility toward this group. "The threat of Japanese subversion was created by the union of traditional racial attitudes and perceptions shaped by the fears and anxieties conjured up by war," writes Peter Ward.[3] A hostile public easily convinced federal politicians to act. Historians Patricia Roy and others, however, have argued that Ottawa carried out the evacuation of the Japanese "as much for their own protection, and, by implication, the protection of Canadians in Japanese hands."[4] Forty years later, the federal government apologized to Japanese Canadians for their wartime treatment and offered financial compensation.

Japanese Canadians being "relocated" to camps in the interior of British Columbia. More than 20 000 Japanese and Japanese Canadians were relocated and their property confiscated and auctioned off after the Japanese attack on Pearl Harbor in December 1941 and throughout the duration of the war.

Tak Toyota/National Archives of Canada/C-46350.

FRENCH CANADA AND THE WAR

French Canada posed a special challenge. Although French Canadians generally accepted participation, as in World War I they remained adamantly opposed to compulsory military service for overseas operations. The stringent Defence of Canada Regulations, which provided for the censorship of anti-war sentiment in the media, attempted to curb opposition to government war policy in Quebec. The CBC also acted as a "propaganda vehicle" in favour of the war effort, but it offered virtually no French-language programs outside Quebec.

As the war dragged on and military leaders demanded reinforcements, an increasing number of English-speaking Canadians called for conscription. For one Toronto Tory member of Parliament, that was the only way to get the "disloyal bloody French" to fight. When King asked Canadians in a plebiscite in April 1942 if they would release the government from its earlier promises not to impose conscription, 80 percent of Canadians outside Quebec responded in the affirmative.

French Canadians held a different view, however. When Ottawa announced the plebiscite on conscription, Quebec nationalists formed the Ligue pour la défense du Canada. It campaigned energetically for a "*non*" vote. Although the Ligue's means were limited and the CBC gave it no air time, the Ligue triumphed: Quebec voted 72 percent against.

Several reasons help to explain French Canada's lack of enthusiasm for the war. During the 1930s many French-Canadian intellectuals showed sympathy for Franco and Mussolini because the fascist leaders portrayed themselves as stalwart opponents of communism. Members of the clergy also complained of the negative effect that military life had on the morals of soldiers who, as a pastoral letter of 1942 warned, all too often tended to pursue "vile pleasures." Traditionalists predicted that the war would cause the break-up of families because it brought women into the factories. For their part, the defenders of provincial autonomy attacked Ottawa's wartime intrusion into the provincial government's jurisdiction. Furthermore, nationalists denounced the danger of linguistic assimilation by a Canadian army in which the French language was often proscribed.

Most French Canadians, however, simply did not feel immediately concerned by a war in Europe. Having been estranged from France politically, culturally, and demographically for nearly two centuries, they had few ties with that country. They certainly felt no strong loyalty to England. Though most would probably have preferred that Canada remain neutral in 1939, as the United States had done, they agreed to Canada's involvement on the condition that enlistment be voluntary.

CONSCRIPTION

King's position on the issue of conscription pleased few. Many English-speaking Canadians interpreted King's delay in implementing conscription as putting political advantage ahead of the war effort. Anti-conscriptionist French Canadians accused the prime minister of betraying his sacred promises.

King did indeed act cautiously. In 1940 his government decreed national registration, but for home service only. (Since it applied just to unmarried men, the regulation had the unintended effect of provoking hundreds of hurried marriages.) After the plebiscite in 1942, King did not immediately introduce conscription for overseas service. Instead, his government amended the National Resources Mobilization Act (NRMA) to permit the dispatch of troops overseas by order in council. This action signified "not necessarily conscription but conscription if necessary." Remembering the disastrous consequences of the conscription crisis of 1917 for national unity and for both major political parties, King hoped that conscription would never be necessary.

During the next two years, Canada relied on voluntary enlistments. Some of the volunteers were NRMA men, "convinced" by moral pressure and even physical abuse to "go active." But in its search for men, the army competed with other government departments in need of workers for war industries. By late 1944, after one year of the Italian campaign and several months of fighting in France, Canadian officers overseas demanded reinforcements, particularly the well-trained home-defence conscripts, or NRMA men. The Conservatives, in opposition, urged that the government stop appeasing Quebec. Within the cabinet, Colonel J.L. Ralston, the minister of national defence, who had just returned from a tour of Canadian forces in Europe, pushed for conscription. King, vexed and still not ready, replaced Ralston with General McNaughton, who promised to continue the voluntary system. As Churchill appealed for fresh troops in the face of the German counteroffensive in late 1944, McNaughton reported that he could not recruit the necessary volunteers. On November 22, just as several of his English-speaking cabinet ministers prepared to resign, King yielded.

Canada would again have conscription, and NRMA men would now be sent to Europe. Few Canadian conscripts ever served overseas, however, and conscription ultimately had no effect on winning the war.

In spite of the criticism from both supporters and opponents of conscription, and perhaps because the criticism came from both ends of the spectrum, King was able to portray himself as a moderate. He and his Liberal party managed to survive the crisis. To their credit, they had limited the ethnic bitterness that occurred in the conscription crisis in 1917.

CANADIAN-AMERICAN WARTIME RELATIONS

Canada did not participate in the basic decisions, taken mainly by the British and the Americans, that determined the direction of the war after 1941. Lester B. Pearson, reflecting on his wartime service at the Canadian embassy in Washington, put it bluntly: "We were not consulted about plans and decisions at high levels unless our agreement was essential, and this was seldom." Pearson worried at first that Canada might be squeezed between the United States and Britain. As time went on, he became convinced that the main problem Canada faced was simply being squeezed out! Even at the two wartime conferences held in Quebec City that brought together the British and the American war leaders, Winston Churchill and Franklin D. Roosevelt, Canada acted merely as host. King's presence was largely confined to the official photos.

War inevitably meant closer relations with the United States. In August 1938, President Roosevelt came to Kingston, Ontario, where he pledged that the United States "would not stand idly by if domination of Canadian soil [was] threatened by any other [than the British] empire." This statement pleased King, although Canadian soil was hardly being threatened at that time.

THE OGDENSBURG AGREEMENT

Two years later, in August 1940, King and Roosevelt signed the Ogdensburg Agreement, which created the Permanent Joint Board on Defence (PJBD), responsible for discussing military questions of mutual interest. As early as 1938, the two countries had begun to exchange military information. In the summer of 1940, King himself pushed for talks on common defence planning. Most Canadians approved of the continental defence tie, as they believed Canada could not rely on its own (then virtually non-existent) defences or on Britain's. Thus, when Roosevelt proposed the PJBD, King was delighted, although he apparently had some doubts about making the board permanent.

Historians differ in their interpretations of this *rapprochement*. Donald Creighton, always alert to the imperial designs of Canada's southern neighbour, saw the Ogdensburg Agreement as a major step toward the Liberals' surrender of Canadian autonomy. He maintained that King "behaved like a puppet which could be animated only by the President of the United States."[5]

In contrast, J.L. Granatstein and Norman Hillmer have argued that King "wanted to protect Canada and to help Great Britain as much as possible, and he understood and accepted that this obliged him to seek even closer relations with Roosevelt's America."[6] Political scientist James Eayrs has denied that King was manipulated by the charming Roosevelt, seeing him instead as a shrewd politician who astutely exploited his friendship with the American president for the good of the Allies.[7]

During the early months of war, Canada enjoyed some influence in the United States, notably through King's use of quiet diplomacy with the president. For example, King won important modifications to the American Neutrality Act, thus enabling Canada and Britain to purchase military supplies while the United States remained neutral. King knew the limits of his influence, however, and also the limits of an American president's powers in the face of a Congress jealous of its prerogatives.

THE HYDE PARK DECLARATION

King and Roosevelt signed a second agreement, the Hyde Park Declaration, at Roosevelt's Hudson River estate on a "grand Sunday" in April 1941. It proved an even more important milestone in Canadian–American relations than the Ogdensburg Agreement.

Canada's wartime economic relations with both Britain and the United States led to this understanding. Since 1939 Britain had ordered ever-increasing amounts of war supplies from Canada and the United States, but it lacked the dollars to pay for them. Meanwhile Canada had accumulated huge deficits in its American trade, largely because of its enormous defence purchases in the United States for equipment destined for Britain. When in 1941 the United States passed the Lend-Lease Act, which exempted Britain from making cash payments on its orders for war materials, Canada worried that it would now lose British business. Britain, for its part, used the threat of shifting orders to the United States to pressure Canada into better terms.

Negotiations with the United States proved arduous. King nevertheless managed to get a reasonably satisfactory agreement: the United States promised to increase its defence purchases in Canada substantially, enabling Canada to make its own purchases of war equipment in the United States. Britain could continue buying Canadian goods and Canada could even get relief, through Lend-Lease, for its American purchases of war supplies to be sent via Canada to Britain. The agreement ended Canada's dollar shortage by 1942. Some scholars see the Hyde Park Declaration as another blow to Canadian independence. In view of Canada's precarious situation, however, the country probably could not have obtained better financial terms.

After Hyde Park, Canada's influence with the United States seriously deteriorated. The American entry into the war in December 1941 substantially changed American perspectives. Relinquishing its isolationism, the United States became more concerned with global rather than hemispheric issues. Canada lost its special status and became a junior partner in the Anglo–American–Russian alliance to defeat the Axis powers from 1942 to 1945.

THE WARTIME ECONOMY

On the eve of war, more than half a million Canadians — one out of five members of the work force — lacked jobs. Barely a year later, full employment was within sight. The wartime emergency led to large-scale federal economic intervention. Soon Canada produced 4000 airplanes a year, as well as ships, tanks, and huge quantities of shells and guns. Investment in industry doubled between 1939 and 1943. War materials had priority over civilian goods, whose production was severely curtailed.

Just as during World War I, the burgeoning economy generated inflationary pressures. In the spring of 1941, prices spiralled upward at an annual rate of more than 12 percent. In response, Ottawa quickly implemented drastic wage and price controls. The government also resorted to so-called voluntary measures. It exhorted homemakers to put their savings into Victory Bonds and urged merchants to offer customers their change in war savings stamps. The government used the revenue from the bonds and stamps to purchase arms and build bombs. And that — as one patriotic poster proclaimed — was how homemaker "Mrs. Morin bombarded Berlin"! Women also established branches of the Consumers Service that, among other activities, denounced merchants who violated the law. Because of such measures, the cost of living went up very little during the remainder of the war.

RATIONING

The relative scarcity of various consumer goods led to rationing. The government issued books of coupons and recruited thousands of female volunteers to distribute them to shoppers. Sugar became the first product to be rationed. Later, Ottawa added tea, coffee, butter, meat, and gasoline to the list. Merchants complained about the paperwork required to administer the coupons. As well, a black market in unused coupons flourished, and some farmers sold produce illegally — for a good price. Some people hoarded scarce goods, in spite of the threat of fines. Occasionally, shortages provoked an outcry. When brewers could not supply enough of their favourite beverage, Ontario workers threatened to boycott the sale of Victory Bonds. "No beer, no bonds!" was their warning.

The lack of automobiles and of the gasoline to make them run explains, together with full employment, an enormous increase in the use of urban public transport. During the war, buses and trams were often severely overcrowded. Mothers shopping for food had to compete with commuters for space. The media urged shoppers to avoid travelling at peak hours. Women frequently faced sexual harassment as men complained about "feminine intrusion into their cultural privacy and social space," particularly "their" smoking section at the rear of the bus.[8]

People in business improved their public image, tarnished during the depression years, by helping the federal government organize the country's war production. Hundreds of them trooped off to Ottawa, often for a symbolic annual salary of one dollar. Many worked for the powerful C.D. Howe, minister of munitions and supply, the department in charge of all war procurement. Howe set up numerous Crown corporations and adopted the techniques of private enterprise. He also avoided the accusations of graft and profiteering that had so plagued Robert Borden's government during World War I. Business leaders admired Howe's no-nonsense efficiency and were proud to be called "Howe's boys."

WEB LINKS

WOMEN AND THE WAR EFFORT

According to traditional Canadian beliefs and practices, married women belonged in the home. War needs, however, forced society to rethink women's roles. While the changes that occurred would by no means be permanent, since pressures for women to return home to their domestic occupations intensified after the war, they did show what might be and what would, eventually, come to be.

Many women, particularly unmarried women, had worked outside the home long before the war, generally in low-paying occupations such as teaching, office work, retail sales, factory labour in textile and clothing mills, and as domestics. Now, in response to the general labour shortage created by the war, many more women entered the civilian work force, mainly in war-related industries. Through the National Selective Service, set up to co-ordinate the mobilization of Canada's labour power, the government encouraged female recruitment. Department of Labour advertisements urged women to "roll up [their] sleeves for victory"; the men overseas needed support and women had to "back them up — to bring them back."

To attract women from other regions of Canada into the industrial centres of Ontario and Quebec, government and industry provided incentives. Employers offered women relatively attractive wages, particularly in war industries; indeed, women's wages increased faster than men's wages during the war years, although they remained substantially lower. Ottawa temporarily amended the income tax laws to make it possible for husbands to continue to enjoy a full married exemption while their wives earned wages.

At first, the government sought only unmarried women and married women without children, but by 1943 a chronic lack of "manpower" made it essential to recruit mothers, at least for part-time, low-paying service jobs. Child care often caused problems for working women. Most left their children in the care of relatives and friends, but a modest number of government-funded nurseries began operating by 1943, on a temporary basis, in Ontario and Quebec.

Patriotic appeals drew thousands of women into volunteer work. They recuperated and recycled such items as paper, metal, fat, bones, rags, rubber, and glass. They also collected clothes for free distribution and prepared parcels to be sent overseas. Together with their unpaid labour in the home, women's voluntary efforts constituted, in the words of historian Ruth Roach Pierson, "far and away the largest contribution made by Canadian women to the war effort."[9]

WOMEN IN THE ARMED SERVICES

For the first time, women served in the armed services. By the end of the war, 50 000 women had enrolled, but these "Jill Canucks" were not "pistol-packing Mommas" and they did not hurl grenades.[10] The armed services assigned them positions considered proper to their sex and always paid them less than males. They remained subordinate to men of the same rank, and they commanded only other women. A special Canadian Women's Army Corps, created in 1941 and incorporated into the Canadian Army (Active) in late winter 1942, supplied female support staff to release men for combat training and other duties. Auxiliary women's units also existed in the air force and the navy. Unilingual French-speaking women were not accepted because training facilities were available in English only.

Women working in a railway yard. Ottawa encouraged women, both married and single, to work outside the home as the labour shortage, especially in war-related industries, became acute.

....

National Film Board of Canada Collection/ National Archives of Canada/C-79525.

Efforts to achieve fairness and equality did not permeate all aspects of life in the services. Male dominance of the military meant a double standard on sexual morality; literature on venereal disease, for example, warned servicemen to beware of "diseased, predatory females," but women received no similar advice regarding "loose men." Pregnancy was cause for an immediate discharge on medical grounds.

In the middle of the war, Ottawa established a special subcommittee to study the role of women in postwar Canada. The members, all women, assumed that many female workers would return to the home. For those who remained employed outside the home, the subcommittee's report recommended expanded employment opportunities, equal pay, better working conditions, and the granting of children's allowances.

These proposals stirred up substantial opposition. Concerned about postwar unemployment, government planners wanted women out of the work force to make room for returning soldiers and workers in shut-down war industries. Unions did not want to see women competing for scarce jobs with their fathers, sons, and future husbands. Polls showed that most Canadians — women as well as men — wanted women back in the home after the war. The war experience was the exception, not the rule. But the House of Commons paid little attention to the report, tabled in early 1944. Other "more pressing" problems had arisen. As historian Gail Cuthbert Brandt writes, the subcommittee's report was "pigeon-holed and forgotten."[11]

Things appeared to return to "normal" at the end of the war. Women in the armed services were demobilized. Many of the formal barriers blocking married women from the work force went back up again. The proportion of women working outside the home plummeted. Although women slowly began to return to the work force after 1945, not until the 1960s would the proportion of female workers return to what it had been in 1944 — 27 percent.

CULTURE AND THE STATE

War also affected cultural life by forging new links between the federal government and the cultural community. The artist Arthur Lismer, the composer Ernest Mac-Millan, and many Canadian writers sought to make their personal contribution to the war effort by choosing subjects and themes related to the conflict. The National Gallery of Canada sent thousands of reproductions of artists' works to Canadian military establishments in the hope that soldiers' morale would be boosted when they contemplated familiar scenes. Artists and writers also organized associations to work for a postwar "cultural reconstruction" in which the state recognized the importance of assisting the arts community. In 1945, however, neither Ottawa nor the provinces were ready to include culture in their postwar plans.

THE EXPANSION OF UNIONS

Organized labour made significant gains in the war years. Thanks to the war, the labour surplus of the 1930s became a shortage in the early 1940s. As employment rose, so, too, did union membership, particularly in the new industrial unions, which combined all workers in a particular industry in a single union. Between 1940 and 1945, union membership doubled to more than 700 000.

Although the war brought jobs and, in general, higher wages, grievances remained. Employers fiercely resisted union attempts to impose collective bargaining, and many bitter strikes resulted from unions' efforts to ensure recognition. In one case, 3000 shipyard workers in Halifax ceased work for one month in 1944 when their employer refused the automatic checkoff of union dues, a right gained by unions in Nova Scotia in 1937. Sometimes militant workers rebelled against their own union leadership, which they judged too conciliatory. When Cape Breton miners struck unsuccessfully for five months in 1941 for better wages and working conditions and more control over the work process, their rallying cry was "down with Hitler and [United Mine Workers officer] Silby Barrett."[12]

The federal government intervened constantly to prevent strikes that could hurt war production. It applied wage controls that labour denounced as inequitable. As historian Laurel Sefton MacDowell's analysis of wartime labour relations has shown, the government felt it necessary, for political reasons, "to conciliate business, its wartime ally in developing the war economy."[13] Business representatives sat on government policy boards; labour did not. Compulsory conciliation often involved interminable delays, a situation that favoured employers. The unions believed that employers alone benefited from this imposed co-operation.

INDUSTRIAL CONFLICTS

Workers' growing resentment contributed to a wave of industrial conflicts that peaked in 1943. That year, one union member in three went out on strike and 1 million working days were lost. A lengthy and very bitter gold-miners' strike in Kirkland Lake, Ontario, in particular, led the archrivals, the Trades and Labor Congress (TLC), an association of skilled craft unions, and the Canadian Congress of Labour (CCL), the leading industrial union, to make joint demands for legislative remedies. Labour's increasing support for the CCF greatly worried Prime Minister King.

The government responded to labour unrest with order in council PC 1003, which recognized the right of workers in industries under federal jurisdiction to join unions and to bargain collectively. It established certification procedures, set out penalties for unfair labour practices by which employers commonly interfered with workers' attempts to set up unions, and established a labour-relations board to administer the law. After the war the federal government adopted new legislation similar to PC 1003, and most provinces passed comparable laws.

A strike at the Ford motor plant in Windsor, Ontario, in 1945 also concerned labour security, among other issues. The union wanted an agreement specifying that all employees had to belong to the union and that the company had to deduct union dues from wage cheques — "union shop and checkoff" was the workers' demand. Ford adamantly refused, although across the river, in Dearborn, Michigan, the company had acquiesced on these issues in 1941. To prevent the company from breaking through the picket line, militant strikers set up a massive automobile blockade in the streets around the plant, imprisoning the vehicles of hundreds of commuters. Federal and provincial authorities as well as the CCL itself intervened, without success.

Finally, both sides agreed to accept binding arbitration. Justice Ivan Rand of the Supreme Court of Canada proposed what became known as the Rand Formula: since all employees benefited from union activities, all should pay union dues, to be collected by the company and remitted to the union. Workers need not join the union, however. Rand also recommended the establishment of a grievance procedure, as well as heavy penalties for unauthorized, or "wildcat," strikes. Although he admitted that a strike was not a "tea party," Rand strongly condemned the workers' motor blockade. He also made a vibrant plea for democratic control of unions and for "enlightened leadership at the top."

The late 1940s saw more dramatic confrontations between labour and management, often in provinces whose governments sided openly with employers. Still, unions felt more secure as the war years ended. The relative labour peace of the 1950s resulted, in part, from these wartime gains.

THE STATE'S NEW ROLE

The war changed Canada in other ways as well. After the depression, Canadians wanted more economic security. Though the war eliminated unemployment and restored a degree of prosperity, it exacted heavy financial sacrifices from the public. By 1943, as war fatigue set in and increasing Allied success pointed the way to the final victory, Canadians reflected on the postwar society they wanted to build. In particular, many wanted governments to introduce measures that would help those in need and establish greater equality within society.

In 1940, with provincial consent and after making a requisite amendment to the British North America Act, the federal government adopted an unemployment-insurance plan whose provisions covered about half the work force. King supported the project because he was "anxious to keep Liberalism in control in Canada [and] not let third parties wrest away from us our rightful place in the matter of social reform." Although the Conservatives tried to project a reformist image with a new leader

WEB

LINKS

(John Bracken), a new name (the "Progressive Conservatives"), and proposals for such reforms as a national health scheme, King felt little threat from them. The left, however, troubled him. By September 1943, chiefly as a result of urban support, the CCF had reached 29 percent in the polls — one percentage point ahead of each of the two major parties.

SOCIAL-WELFARE MEASURES

A report presented in 1943 by Leonard Marsh, research director for the government's Committee on Reconstruction, urged the immediate creation of a full welfare state. It recommended a comprehensive system of social security, including measures to assist the unemployed, a national health-insurance scheme, old-age pensions, and children's allowances. The federal government, fearful of the costs involved, adopted a cautious and piecemeal approach. In 1944, however, it introduced a family-allowance program that initially provided monthly payments of $5–$8 to help Canadian mothers support their children. Certain Conservatives, such as Ontario premier George Drew, denounced the project as a "baby bonus" designed to benefit Quebec with its alleged big families, while nationalists in Quebec condemned the measure as an infringement upon provincial autonomy. Business reacted favourably; it hoped that the allowances would diminish pressure to raise wages.

Housing became a serious problem for increasing numbers of urban Canadians during the war years. As migrants flocked to cities to work in war-related industries, many families lived in garages, empty warehouses, shacks, chicken-coops, "and indeed, in anything that will hold a bed," as one report put it. The influx of military and civilian war workers strained housing facilities in Halifax. By 1943, Montreal claimed it needed 50 000 new dwellings. As the war ended, Canada's rental-controls administrator noted that the country was attempting to solve its shelter problem by "compressing more and more people into the same cubic space." He estimated that at least 200 000 Canadian households were now living "doubled up" or even "tripled up." Ottawa ignored pleas for public intervention to provide low-rental housing; instead, it acted to reduce down payments and to guarantee mortgages in order to stimulate the building of new homes and enable families with moderate incomes to purchase property.

THE 1945 ELECTION

King's cautious, reformist approach to social problems proved politically sound. With the support of four out of every ten voters, he won the election in 1945, a feat the Liberal leader termed "a miracle." In Quebec, internal strife seriously weakened the nationalist Bloc populaire canadien, a situation which favoured the Liberals. The extensive anti-socialist propaganda campaign funded by business helped to undermine the CCF's popularity. Canadians seemed to become more conservative as well. They wanted consumer goods such as refrigerators, automobiles, and houses. Nor did they fear that the war's end would plunge the country back into depression. They thus gave little heed to the CCF's Cassandras who warned of impending economic and social doom.

FEDERAL-PROVINCIAL RELATIONS: TOWARD FEDERAL SUPREMACY

The depression had restricted the autonomy of the provinces, forcing them to rely increasingly on Ottawa for financial assistance. The war created conditions that furthered centralization, as the federal government now took the dominant role in organizing the Canadian economy.

THE ROWELL–SIROIS REPORT

The Rowell–Sirois Commission on Dominion–Provincial Relations, set up by the King government in 1937, made public its report in May 1940. With the objective of stabilizing provincial finances and giving equal services to all Canadians, the commissioners recommended that Ottawa collect all income taxes and succession duties and, in return, make unconditional grants to the provinces. Disadvantaged provinces should receive special subsidies to enable them to offer social and educational services equivalent to those of other Canadian provinces without having to tax more heavily than the Canadian average. The federal government should also assume all provincial debts.

Provincial autonomists condemned the report as a veritable centralizer's "Bible." They argued that its recommendations would place provincial treasuries at Ottawa's mercy and that the federal government would determine provincial activities by what it was willing to pay out. Premier Mitchell Hepburn of Ontario — a province that would not benefit from the special adjustment grants — attacked the report as "the product of the mind of a few college professors and a Winnipeg newspaperman [John Dafoe] who has had his knife in Ontario ever since he was able to write editorial articles."

Most newspapers reacted favourably. Federal ministers and bureaucrats also endorsed the recommendations strongly, particularly those relating to money. Ottawa wanted to ensure control over fiscal policy to pay for the war as well as to diminish inflationary pressures. It thus urged the provinces to "rent" their tax fields to the federal government.

With no illusions about the outcome, King invited the premiers in January 1941 to discuss the proposals. While some provinces insisted on the need for further study, others rejected Ottawa's plans outright. The conference collapsed in deadlock. Ottawa, however, determinedly pressed ahead. It promised, as a "temporary wartime expedient," that the provinces would have to surrender their income taxes only for the duration of the war, and it proposed to compensate the provinces more generously. All the provinces yielded, although some did so reluctantly.

After 1943, the economic planners in Ottawa, many of whom were disciples of British economist John Maynard Keynes, planned for the immediate postwar era. They feared that depression might result from the reconversion of the economy to peacetime conditions, just as had occurred after World War I. Moreover, they wanted to make certain that Ottawa could assume the heavy financial responsibilities and increased debt charges resulting from the war. Ottawa, they urged, should thus act as the "balance wheel" of the economy. If it kept its hand firmly on taxation, it could combat cyclical tendencies, either deflationary busts or inflationary booms; it could maintain high and stable employment; and it could offer costly social-security measures to all citizens, thus supporting consumer buying power. For these civil servants, economic, political, and humanitarian objectives dictated that the federal government continue to take charge. It might, however, consult the provinces in areas of their constitutional jurisdiction, such as social services.

THE DOMINION–PROVINCIAL CONFERENCE ON RECONSTRUCTION

In August 1945, immediately before Japan's surrender, Ottawa convened the Dominion–Provincial Conference on Reconstruction. King assured the provinces that he did not want to weaken or subordinate them but rather wished to ensure their "effective financial independence." He intended to do this by convincing them to continue to allow Ottawa to levy all income taxes in return for increased provincial grants, with no strings attached. The federal government also offered to pay part of the cost of a comprehensive health-insurance plan and of old-age pensions, and to expand the coverage of federal unemployment insurance.

Though most provinces reacted positively, the premiers of Ontario, Quebec, and Alberta objected to what they saw as the concentration of financial and administrative powers in the federal government's hands. Historian Alvin Finkel suggests that King actually hoped that the premiers would oppose his plans so that he would have the "necessary excuse" to abandon plans for costly social programs.[14] Ottawa eventually managed to reach agreement on the tax proposals with all but the two largest provinces. The federalism of the next decade remained highly centralized. As economist R.M. Burns put it, during the 1940s and 1950s "the central authority reached its zenith."[15]

THE PROVINCES IN THE WAR YEARS

The war and the after-effects of the depression fostered the uneven development of regional economies and thus contributed to the growth of regionalism in Canada. The war had diversified Canada's manufacturing capacity, as well as further promoting its resource-based industries. Quebec, British Columbia, and especially Ontario made dramatic advances. In Quebec, industries such as chemical products and aluminum refining expanded rapidly. In Ontario, factory employment increased greatly and the exploitation of the province's huge iron-ore deposits began at Steep Rock Lake north of Lake Superior. On the Pacific coast, the port of Vancouver prospered. Its shipyards and those of Victoria employed 30 000 workers at their peak. Prince Rupert became an important supply centre for American bases in Alaska. The military buildup on the West Coast also stimulated British Columbia's economy. By 1943, British Columbians had the highest per capita income of all Canadians.

THE NORTH

In 1942, the United States Army Corps of Engineers coordinated the construction teams that built, for defence purposes, a 2500 km highway from Dawson Creek in northeastern British Columbia to Fairbanks, Alaska. The next year the Public Roads Administration, an American civilian agency, directed the transformation of the rough

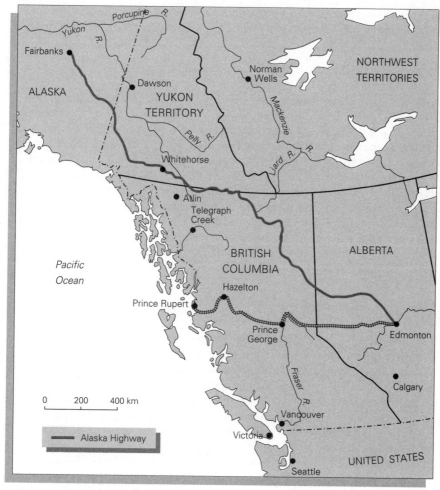

Of the several routes proposed for a road link from western Canada to Alaska, that of the Alaska Highway was selected in 1942.

Source: Based on Kenneth Coates, ed., *The Alaska Highway: Papers of the 40th Anniversary Symposium* (Vancouver: University of British Columbia Press, 1985), p. xix.

military road into a permanent civilian highway, widening it, extending branch roads to the airstrips, and completing a telegraph line along this American highway built on Canadian soil.

The attack on Pearl Harbor also led American defence planners to worry about the threat to energy supplies in the Northwest; oil tankers now appeared vulnerable to Japanese submarine attack. As a result, the Canadian Oil (Canol) project was begun to pipe oil from the Imperial Oil Company's field at Norman Wells, on the Mackenzie River. The Americans made large-scale expenditures to build a pipeline to White-horse, a refinery, and a whole host of subsidiary facilities. This dependable source of oil could then be used in the Pacific war theatre. For three years, thousands of men worked on this second American project on Canadian soil. When the Japanese threat in the Pacific ended, the completed Canol pipeline, now unneeded, was shut down.

CHANGES IN QUEBEC

In Quebec the Godbout government, elected in 1939, initiated important reforms. It formed Hydro-Québec, a publicly owned hydro-electric utility in the Montreal region. To boost educational levels, it made school attendance obligatory until age fourteen. In the Quebec Labour Relations Act, it set out the rules governing collective bargaining. The bill, supported by the unions, was intended to force companies to negotiate with their unionized employees. In 1940, women in Quebec finally obtained the right to vote provincially. Suffragist Idola Saint-Jean argued forcefully for this right: "We vote in federal elections as intelligently as women in neighbouring provinces. Why shouldn't we be concerned with problems debated in the provincial parliament? Don't housing, public health and education concern us much more directly than the problems of federal politics?" The legislative assembly finally agreed, despite the vigorous objections of the church and conservative groups.

ONTARIO: THE RETURN TO CONSERVATISM

In Ontario, the impetuous Mitchell Hepburn appeared mainly interested in pursuing a vendetta against fellow Liberal Mackenzie King. At the same time, the provincial CCF attracted support, largely in urban working-class districts. In the 1943 provincial election, the CCF, with one-third of the popular vote, placed second, just behind George Drew's Conservatives. While Drew denounced the socialists, he energetically pursued reform policies, notably in health, education, and housing. Provincial planning became important in areas such as forest conservation, industrial development, and water use. Profoundly pro-British, Drew also wanted to boost immigration from Britain. He established the War Brides Bureau in London to counsel British wives coming to Canada with their soldier husbands. Drew's enthusiastic salesmanship caused Canadian-born British press magnate Max Aitken, now Lord Beaverbrook, to comment: "Look George, is Ontario a part of Canada or Canada a part of Ontario?"

The CCF proved much less threatening in the Ontario election of 1945. In decline in the cities and lacking a rural base, it became, in addition, the victim of fierce denunciations of "state socialism." Party leader E.B. Jolliffe's sensational "revelations," that Drew was maintaining in Ontario "at this very minute, a secret political police, a paid spy organization, a Gestapo" to keep himself in power, backfired. Drew easily won a majority, and Ontario settled into what would become more than 40 years of Conservative government.

THE MARITIMES AND NEWFOUNDLAND

The war brought fewer economic benefits to Canadians in the three Maritime provinces, although the rise in food prices and the growing demand for minerals and pulp and paper did assist the region. War spending also boosted the regional economy. By 1943, some 75 000 men and women were building and repairing vessels in

After the war an "army" of 40 000 war brides (mainly British) with their 20 000 children, most under the age of three, arrived in Canada.

....

H.B. Jefferson Collection/Nova Scotia Archives and Record Management/N-820.

Maritime shipyards, even at night under floodlights. Halifax became Canada's major port for shipping munitions and other supplies to western Europe.

Historian Ernest Forbes has described the impact of Ottawa's war policies on the Maritimes as "largely negative. While the government did generate economic activity, it created relatively little new industry in the region and even less of a permanent nature."[16] According to Forbes, C.D. Howe believed it was more efficient to develop industry along the St. Lawrence and in the Great Lakes region, a conviction reinforced by the regional prejudices of Howe and his central Canadian political advisers. Nor did provincial governments succeed in obtaining federal funds for necessary infrastructure or private investment in industry. In general, at the war's end, the region appeared ill equipped to undertake any substantial industrial expansion.

Economic weakness meant that governments lacked funds for investment in health and education. In 1945, Prince Edward Island had only half the number of doctors needed to meet the national standard of one doctor per 1000 people. New Brunswick had Canada's highest infant and maternal death rate, and Nova Scotia followed closely. In Prince Edward Island, the great majority of schools had only one room; many needed repair or were beyond repair. Teachers were often poorly qualified, and salaries were low. New Brunswick had Canada's highest illiteracy rate, affecting particularly the province's French-speaking Acadian population. Only after 1940 did the provincial government authorize the use of French-language texts in public schools and recognize the importance of making French the language of instruction in Acadian schools.

Newfoundland's case was somewhat special. At the outbreak of war, low fish prices and uncertain markets left the population of the outports in appalling poverty. The relief rolls overflowed. At first, the war only worsened the situation, resulting in increased taxes and decreased services. Eventually, though, it created a temporary boom in employment through the construction and maintenance of huge American defence projects, especially the bases at Argentia, Gander, and Stephenville. After the British-appointed Commission of Government developed costly plans for postwar reconstruction, Britain came to an understanding with the Canadian government to encourage the island's eventual incorporation into Canada.

THE WEST

The have-not Prairie provinces recovered only slowly, as war spending brought relatively few jobs to the region. But by 1944, farmers increased their incomes substantially thanks to higher prices, caused largely by the much-increased demand for wheat in Europe, and to improved harvests, made possible by better weather conditions. A growing farmers' movement, led by the Canadian Chamber of Agriculture, which had been founded in 1935, set out to defend farmers' interests and improve their lot. Farm incomes had remained much lower than other workers' wages; most rural homes had no indoor plumbing or electricity; and farm villages enjoyed few services.

The war boosted crude-oil production in Alberta, at least until the Turner Valley field near Calgary went into decline after 1942. Coal mines prospered, too, and in Prairie cities the construction industry flourished. But the war did not create the diversified economy that many residents felt the region needed.

Politically, third parties on the Prairies grew stronger, although they tended to moderate their ideology. Social Credit in Alberta, led by William Aberhart until his death in 1943 and then for a quarter-century by his protege Ernest Manning, denounced socialism and centralization, promised able, businesslike administration, and gently laid Social Credit doctrine to rest.

The CCF made inroads in all three Prairie provinces, but scored its first victory in Saskatchewan in 1944. Although it had attenuated the socialism of the Regina Manifesto, its ambitious program promised public ownership of natural resources, security of land tenure for farmers, collective bargaining for workers, educational reform, and social services, including a universal socialized health plan. Baptist preacher and CCF leader Tommy Douglas denounced the economic system that he likened to a cream separator: the farmer pours in the milk, the worker turns the handle, and the capitalist, because he owns the machine, "sits on a little stool with the cream spout fixed firmly in his mouth while the farmer and the worker take turns on the skim milk spout." Once in power, the CCF launched major reforms, particularly during its first two years in office, but financial and other factors soon forced it to make pragmatic policy adjustments.

In British Columbia, the old political order also changed. When the Liberals failed to gain a majority in the 1941 election, party members favouring coalition with the Conservatives ousted their leader, Duff Pattullo, whom they sharply criticized for his feuding with Ottawa, his road-building policy, and his abrasive style. The CCF then formed the opposition to the new Liberal–Conservative alliance.

TOWARD A NEW INTERNATIONALISM

The war in Europe ended when Germany capitulated in May 1945. By September, Japan also surrendered. Peace brought with it new problems and, in particular, the difficult question of how to maintain it. In contrast to its position after World War I, Canada was ready to accept responsibility in world affairs. Like the other Allied countries, it believed in the necessity of establishing an international organization comparable to, but more effective than, the League of Nations. Canada thus participated in the founding conference of the United Nations at San Francisco in April 1945, where it worked to ensure that both the United States and the Soviet Union became members.

*Victory in Europe
(VE) Day, downtown
Calgary, May 8, 1945
— a time of rejoicing.
The war in Europe was
finally over!*

Glenbow Archives, Calgary,
Canada/Herald Collection/
NA-2864-3446.

Canada also pushed for world economic and social co-operation. In late 1945, Lester Pearson chaired the founding meeting of the United Nations Food and Agriculture Organization in Quebec City. As a member of the United Nations Relief and Rehabilitation Administration, Canada became a major supplier of aid to war-torn countries, though it had great difficulty convincing the Americans of its right to participate in determining the operations of the association. Canada also joined the International Monetary Fund, as well as the International Civil Aviation Organization, whose headquarters came to Montreal. As external-affairs officer John Holmes commented later, Canada "moved with the tide," trying to avoid letting the Great Powers control everything.[17] Conscious of its position as a rising middle power, Canada attempted, with some success, to get recognition for states like itself. Willingly it recognized that its influence was less than that of the United States, but it wanted the Great Powers to recognize its middle-power status.

World War II changed Canada profoundly, in the country's relations with the world and at home as well. It effectively ended the isolation of the 1930s. Military technology had advanced to the point where Canada could no longer consider itself geographically isolated.

Involvement in world affairs brought benefits but carried a price. Despite Canada's attempts to develop relationships with multilateral associations of states, such involvement meant closer ties to the United States. For supporters of the *rapprochement*, the closer links brought security and economic prosperity through trade and investment. For critics, the triumphant move toward nationhood in the interwar years appeared to have abruptly ended, with Canada being relegated once more to colonial status — this time, as a colony of the United States.

At home, the war created an economic boom that instilled hopes among Canadians for a better life. Trade-union organizations made notable gains, as governments enacted legislation establishing a new framework for the conduct of industrial relations. The entry of large numbers of women into the work force announced a substantial change in their role. With Canada's new federal social programs, Canadians took a significant step in the direction of the welfare state. In federal–provincial relations, Ottawa reasserted a pre-eminence that endured for two decades. Voters in several provinces elected new governments that stayed in office for lengthy periods. In Ottawa, however, Canadians continued to support King, perhaps because he was, in historian Frank Underhill's words, the leader "who divides us least."[18]

NOTES

1. Desmond Morton, *Canada and War: A Military and Political History* (Toronto: Butterworths, 1981), p. 106.

2. W.A.B Douglas and Brereton Greenhous, *Out of the Shadows: Canada in the Second World War*, rev. ed. (Toronto: Dundurn Press, 1995), p. 111.

3. W. Peter Ward, *White Canada Forever: Popular Attitudes and Public Policy Toward Orientals in British Columbia* (Montreal: McGill-Queen's University Press, 1978), p. 146.

4. Patricia Roy et al., *Mutual Hostages: Canadians and Japanese During the Second World War* (Toronto: University of Toronto Press, 1990), p. 215.

5. Donald Creighton, *The Forked Road: Canada, 1939–1957* (Toronto: McClelland & Stewart, 1976), p. 43.

6. J.L. Granatstein and Norman Hillmer, *For Better or For Worse: Canada and the United States to the 1990s* (Mississauga, ON: Copp Clark Pitman, 1991), p. 144.

7. James Eayrs, *In Defence of Canada*, vol. 2, *Appeasement and Rearmament* (Toronto: University of Toronto Press, 1965), p. 191.

8. Donald F. Davis and Barbara Lorenzkowski, "A Platform for Gender Tensions: Women Working and Riding on Canadian Urban Public Transit in the 1940s," *Canadian Historical Review* 79 (1998): 442–43.

9. Ruth Roach Pierson, *"They're Still Women After All": The Second World War and Canadian Womanhood* (Toronto: McClelland & Stewart, 1986), p. 33.

10. Ruth Roach Pierson, " 'Jill Canuck': CWAC of All Trades, But No 'Pistol Packing Momma,' " *Historical Papers/Communications historiques* (1978): 106–33.

11. Gail Cuthbert Brandt, " 'Pigeon-Holed and Forgotten': The Work of the Subcommittee on the Post-War Problems of Women, 1943," *Histoire sociale/Social History* 15 (1983): 239–59.

12. Michael Earle, " 'Down with Hitler and Silby Barrett': The Cape Breton Miners' Slowdown Strike of 1941," *Acadiensis* 18 (1988): 56–90.

13. Laurel Sefton MacDowell, "The Formation of the Canadian Industrial Relations System During World War Two," *Labour/Le Travailleur* 3 (1978): 186.

14. Alvin Finkel, "Paradise Postponed: A Re-examination of the Green Book Proposals of 1945," *Journal of the Canadian Historical Association* 4 (1993): 128.

15. R.M. Burns, *The Acceptable Mean: The Tax Rental Agreements, 1941–1962* (Toronto: Canadian Tax Foundation, 1980), p. 35.

16. Ernest R. Forbes, *Challenging the Regional Stereotype: Essays on the 20th Century Maritimes* (Fredericton: Acadiensis Press, 1989), p. 195.
17. John W. Holmes, *The Shaping of Peace: Canada and the Search for World Order, 1943–1957*, vol. 1 (Toronto: University of Toronto Press, 1979), pp. 235–36.
18. Frank Underhill, "The End of the King Era," *Canadian Forum* (September 1948); reprinted in F.H. Underhill, *In Search of Canadian Liberalism* (Toronto: Macmillan, 1960), p. 127.

LINKING TO THE PAST

....

The Valour and the Horror

http://www.valourandhorror.com/home.htm

The site of the controversial television series *The Valour and the Horror* features background information on the series itself as well as a wealth of material on Canadian participation in the invasion of Normandy and in World War II in general, including maps, photographs, biographies, personal stories, and much more. This site also features an interesting section on "Women in the War" (http://www.valourandhorror.com/DB/ISSUE/Women/index.htm).

Life on the Homefront

http://www.achq.dnd.ca/htdocs/homefrnt/index.htm

These pages from the Royal Canadian Air Force site provide information about the impact of World War II on Canada; topics include the economy, rationing, the role of women, and wartime innovations.

The National Film Board of Canada

http://www.nfb.ca:80/E/2/3/

A brief history of the National Film Board of Canada. Check out "1940s" for more information about the NFB's activities during that decade.

C.D. Howe

http://www.schoolnet.ca/collections/wayfarers/cdhowe.htm

An illustrated biography of C.D. Howe.

The 1940 Unemployment Insurance Act

http://www.hrdc-drhc.gc.ca/insur/histui/ui_hist/chap04/chap4_e.html

A detailed explanation of the 1940 Unemployment Insurance Act.

RELATED READINGS

....

The following articles from R. Douglas Francis and Donald B. Smith, eds., *Readings in Canadian History: Post-Confederation*, 5th ed. (Toronto: Harcourt Brace, 1998), deal with topics relevant to this chapter: James Eayrs, "'A Low Dishonest Decade': Aspects of Canadian External Policy, 1931–1939," pp. 347–62; J.L. Granatstein, "Staring into the Abyss," pp. 362–76; "The 'Bren Gun Girl' and the Housewife Heroine," pp. 379–97; and W. Peter Ward, "British Columbia and the Japanese Evacuation," pp. 398–414.

BIBLIOGRAPHY

....

Considerable material exists on Canadian foreign policy in the years from 1930 to 1945. The most useful surveys include James Eayrs, *In Defence of Canada*, vol. 2, *Appeasement and Rearmament* (Toronto: University of Toronto Press, 1965); C.P. Stacey, *Canada and the Age of Conflict: A History of Canadian External Policies*, vol. 2, *1921–1948: The Mackenzie King Era* (Toronto: University of Toronto Press, 1981); and John Hilliker, *Canada's Department of External Affairs*, vol. 1, *The Formative Years, 1909–1946* (Montreal/Kingston: McGill-Queen's University Press, 1989). On Canada and the League of Nations' policy toward Mussolini consult Robert Bothwell and John English, " 'Dirty Work at the Crossroads': New Perspectives on the Riddell Incident," *Canadian Historical Association Report* (1972): 263–85. King's illusions concerning Hitler are dealt with in C.P. Stacey, "The Divine Mission: Mackenzie King and Hitler," *Canadian Historical Review* 61 (1980): 502–12. R.D. Cuff and J.L. Granatstein review aspects of Canadian–American relations in *Ties That Bind: Canadian–American Relations in Wartime from the Great War to the Cold War*, 2nd ed. (Toronto: Samuel Stevens Hakkert, 1977). Victor Hoar tells the story of the Canadian volunteers who fought in the Spanish Civil War in *The Mackenzie–Papineau Battalion* (Toronto: Copp Clark, 1969). J.L. Granatstein, *Canada's War: The Politics of the Mackenzie King Government, 1939–1945* (Toronto: University of Toronto Press, 1975), is useful on foreign and domestic policy, as are the relevant chapters in Robert Bothwell, Ian Drummond, and John English, *Canada, 1900–1945* (Toronto: University of Toronto Press, 1987); and in Desmond Morton, *Canada and War: A Military and Political History* (Toronto: Butterworths, 1981). Norman Hillmer et al., eds., present several articles on Canada on the eve of war in *A Country of Limitations: Canada and the World in 1939* (Ottawa: Canadian Committee for the History of the Second World War, 1996).

Excellent syntheses of Canada's participation in the war include W.A.B. Douglas and Brereton Greenhous, *Out of the Shadows: Canada in the Second World War*, rev. ed. (Toronto: Dundurn Press, 1995); David J. Bercuson, *Maple Leaf Against the Axis: Canada's Second World War* (Toronto: Stoddart, 1995); and J.L. Granatstein and Desmond Morton, *A Nation Forged in Fire: Canadians and the Second World War, 1939–1945* (Toronto: Lester & Orpen Dennys, 1989). Other popular accounts are Ted Barris and Alex Barris, *Days of Victory: Canadians Remember, 1939–1945* (Toronto: Macmillan, 1995); and Desmond Morton and J.L. Granatstein, *Victory 1945: Canadians from War to Peace* (Toronto: HarperCollins, 1995). Useful collections of essays include Peter Neary and J.L. Granatstein, eds., *The Good Fight: Canada and the Second World War* (Toronto: Copp Clark Longman, 1994); and Marc Milner, ed., *Canadian Military History: Selected Readings* (Toronto: Copp Clark Pitman, 1993).

For two widely differing analyses of the Dieppe catastrophe consult Brian Loring Villa, *Unauthorized Action: Mountbatten and the Dieppe Raid*, 2nd ed. (Toronto: Oxford University Press, 1994); and Denis Whitaker and Sheilagh Whitaker, *Dieppe: Tragedy to Triumph* (Toronto: McGraw-Hill Ryerson, 1992). Aspects of this ongoing controversy may be found in Peter Henshaw's and Brian Loring Villa's article, "The Dieppe Raid Debate," *Canadian Historical Review* 79 (1998): 304–15. The Hong Kong debacle is described in Brereton Greenhous, *C-Force to Hong Kong: A Canadian Catastrophe, 1941–1945* (Toronto: Dundurn Press, 1996). Daniel G. Dancocks describes the Italian campaign in *The D-Day Dodgers: The Canadians in Italy, 1943–1945* (Toronto: McClelland & Stewart, 1991), while John A. English deals with Canadian participation in the war in northwest Europe in *The Canadian Army and the Normandy Campaign: A Study of Failure in High Command* (New York: Praeger, 1991). For an abundantly illustrated commemorative work on the Normandy campaign see Bill McAndrew, Donald E. Greaves, and Michael Whitby, *Normandy 1944: The Canadian Summer* (Montreal: Art Global, 1994). George G. Blackburn has written two popular accounts of the war in northwest Europe: *The Guns of Normandy: A Soldier's Eye View, France 1944* (Toronto: McClelland & Stewart, 1995), and *The Guns of Victory: A Soldier's Eye View, Belgium, Holland, and Germany, 1944–45* (Toronto: McClelland & Stewart, 1996).

J.L. Granatstein looks at Canada's military leaders in *The Generals: The Canadian Army's Senior Commanders in the Second World War* (Toronto: Stoddart, 1993). On one particular type of battle casualty consult Terry Copp and Bill McAndrew, *Battle Exhaustion: Soldiers and Psychiatrists in the Canadian Army, 1939–1945* (Montreal/Kingston: McGill-Queen's University Press, 1990). Three books study the fate of Canadian prisoners of war: Jonathan Vance, *Objects of Concern: Canadian Prisoners of War through the Twentieth Century* (Vancouver: University of British Columbia Press, 1994); Howard Margolian, *Conduct Unbecoming: The Story of the Murder of Canadian Prisoners of War in Normandy* (Toronto: University of Toronto Press, 1998); and David McIntosh, *Hell on Earth: Aging Faster, Dying Sooner: Canadian Prisoners of the Japanese during World War II* (Toronto: McGraw-Hill Ryerson, 1996). Allan Douglas English studies pilot training in *The Cream of the Crop: Canadian Aircrew, 1939–1945* (Montreal/Kingston: McGill-Queen's University Press, 1996). See also Spencer Dunmore, *Wings for Victory: The Remarkable Story of the British Air Training Plan in Canada* (Toronto: McClelland & Stewart, 1994). Aspects of the controversy surrounding the film series *The Valour and the Horror* are discussed in David J. Bercuson and S.F. Wise, eds., *The Valour and the Horror Revisited* (Montreal/Kingston: McGill-Queen's University Press, 1994).

Carolyn Gossage has written a popular history of women in the armed services, *Greatcoats and Glamour Boots: Canadian Women at War, 1939–1945* (Toronto: Dundurn Press, 1991). See also Sue Ward, *One Gal's Army* (Prince George, BC: Caitlin Press, 1996). The history of the Royal Canadian Navy is told in Marc Milner, *North Atlantic Run: The Royal Canadian Navy and the Battle for the Convoys* (Toronto: University of Toronto Press, 1985); and in Tony German, *The Sea Is at Our Gates: The History of the Canadian Navy* (Toronto: McClelland & Stewart, 1990). Three books recount the RCN's battle against German U-boats: Michael L. Hadley, *U-Boats Against Canada: German Submarines in Canadian Waters* (Montreal/Kingston: McGill-Queen's University Press, 1985); Marc Milner, *The U-Boat Hunters: The Royal Canadian Navy and the Offensive against Germany's Submarines* (Toronto: University of Toronto Press, 1994); and Roger Sarty, *Canada and the Battle of the Atlantic* (Montreal: Art Global, 1998). See also Sarty's *The Maritime Defence of Canada* (Toronto: Canadian Institute for Strategic Studies, 1997). David Zimmerman describes the technical problems encountered by the RCN in developing better-quality radar in *The Great Naval Battle of Ottawa* (Toronto: University of Toronto Press, 1989). For the role of the RCAF the major work is Brereton Greenhous, Stephen J. Harris, William C. Johnston, and William G.P. Rawling, *The Crucible of War, 1939–1945: The Official History of the Royal Canadian Air Force*, vol. III (Toronto: University of Toronto Press, 1994).

John English studies Lester B. Pearson's diplomatic career in *Shadow of Heaven: The Life of Lester Pearson*, vol. 1, *1897–1948* (Toronto: Lester & Orpen Dennys, 1989). On the CCF see Walter Young, *The Anatomy of a Party: The National CCF, 1932–61* (Toronto: University of Toronto Press, 1969); and, on the Conservatives, J.L. Granatstein, *The Politics of Survival: The Conservative Party of Canada* (Toronto: University of Toronto Press, 1967). Robert Bothwell and William Kilbourn study Howe, the "Minister of Everything," in *C.D. Howe: A Biography* (Toronto: McClelland & Stewart, 1979), R.M. Burns, *The Acceptable Mean: The Tax Rental Agreements, 1942–1962* (Toronto: Canadian Tax Foundation, 1980), provides a detailed treatment of federal–provincial fiscal relations.

The best study on conscription remains J.L. Granatstein and J.M. Hitsman, *Broken Promises: A History of Conscription in Canada*, rev. ed. (Toronto: Copp Clark Pitman, 1985). For an explanation of Quebec's reaction see Richard Jones, "Politics and Culture: The French Canadians and the Second World War," in Sidney Aster, ed., *The Second World War as a National Experience* (Ottawa: Canadian Committee for the History of the Second World War, 1981), pp. 82–91. Daniel Byers examines the workings of NRMA camps in

"Mobilising Canada: The National Resources Mobilization Act, the Department of National Defence, and Compulsory Military Service in Canada, 1940–1945," *Journal of the Canadian Historical Association* 7 (1996): 175–203. Wartime censorship is treated in Claude Beauregard's excellent study, *Guerre et censure au Canada, 1939–1945* (Sillery, QC: Septentrion, 1998). On conscientious objectors see Marlene Epp, "Alternative Service and Alternative Gender Roles: Conscientious Objectors in BC during World War II," *BC Studies* 105/106 (1995): 139–58.

Social security is examined in a special issue of the *Journal of Canadian Studies* on "Leonard Marsh and Canadian Social Policy" (vol. 21, 1986). Dennis Guest describes the coming of the welfare state in "World War II and the Welfare State in Canada," in Allan Moscovitch and Jim Albert, eds., *The "Benevolent" State: The Growth of Welfare in Canada* (Toronto: Garamond Press, 1987), pp. 205–22. On the housing crisis in Montreal, consult Jean-Pierre Collin, "Crise du logement et action catholique à Montreal," *Revue d'histoire de l'Amérique française* 41 (1987): 179–203. Doug Owram examines the evolution of ideas concerning the role of the modern state in *The Government Generation: Canadian Intellectuals and the State, 1900–1945* (Toronto: University of Toronto Press, 1986). Carman Miller looks at the effects of war on the Maritimes in "The 1940s: War and Rehabilitation," in E.R. Forbes and D.A. Muise, eds., *The Atlantic Provinces in Confederation* (Toronto: University of Toronto Press, 1993). See also Ernest R. Forbes, "Consolidating Disparity: The Maritimes and the Industrialization of Canada during the Second World War," reprinted in his book *Challenging the Regional Stereotype: Essays on the 20th Century Maritimes* (Fredericton: Acadiensis Press, 1989), pp. 172–99. Material on Newfoundland may be found in Peter Neary, *Newfoundland in the North Atlantic World, 1929–1949* (Montreal/Kingston: McGill-Queen's University Press, 1988).

On women see Ruth Roach Pierson, *"They're Still Women After All": The Second World War and Canadian Womanhood* (Toronto: McClelland & Stewart, 1986); Geneviève Auger and Raymonde Lamothe, *De la poêle à frire à la ligne de feu* (Montréal: Boréal, 1981); and Alison Prentice et al., *Canadian Women: A History*, 2nd ed. (Toronto: Harcourt Brace, 1996), Chapter 12. Ellen Scheinberg shows that the image of the "Bren girl" did not apply to women in traditional manufacturing sectors in "The Tale of Tessie the Textile Worker: Female Textile Workers in Cornwall During World War II," *Labour/Le Travail* 33 (1994): 153–86. Jeff Keshen takes a fresh look at the issue of women in the work force in "Revisiting Canada's Civilian Women During World War II," *Histoire sociale/Social History* 30 (1997): 239–66. Maria Tippett examines culture in wartime in *Making Culture: English-Canadian Institutions and the Arts before the Massey Commission* (Toronto: University of Toronto Press, 1990).

Aspects of union activity are examined in Irving Abella, *Nationalism, Communism, and Canadian Labour: The CIO, the Communist Party and the Canadian Congress of Labour, 1934–1956* (Toronto: University of Toronto Press, 1973); Jacques Rouillard, *Histoire de la CSN, 1921–1981* (Montréal: Boréal, 1981); and Desmond Morton with Terry Copp, *Working People: An Illustrated History of the Canadian Labour Movement*, 3rd ed. (Toronto: Summerhill Press, 1990). On the impact of the war on labour–management relations consult Jeremy Webber, "The Malaise of Compulsory Conciliation: Strike Prevention in Canada During World War II," *Labour/Le Travail* 15 (1985): 57–88; Laurel Sefton MacDowell, *"Remember Kirkland Lake": The History and Effects of the Kirkland Lake Gold Miners' Strike, 1941–42* (Toronto: University of Toronto Press, 1983); and Jay White, "Pulling Teeth: Striking for the Check-Off in the Halifax Shipyards, 1944," *Acadiensis* 19 (1989): 115–41. On the landmark Ford strike see David Moulton, "Ford Windsor 1945," in Irving Abella, ed., *On Strike: Six Key Labour Struggles in Canada, 1919–1949* (Toronto: James, Lewis & Samuel Publishers, 1974).

On the treatment of Japanese Canadians consult Ann Gomer Sunahara, *The Politics of Racism: The Uprooting of Japanese Canadians During the Second World War* (Toronto: James Lorimer, 1981); Peter Ward, *White Canada Forever: Popular Attitudes and Public Policy toward Orientals in British Columbia*, 2nd ed. (Montreal/Kingston: McGill-Queen's University Press, 1990); and Patricia Roy et al., *Mutual Hostages: Canadians and Japanese During the Second World War* (Toronto: University of Toronto Press, 1990). Personal testimonies may be found in Roy Ito, *Stories of My People: A Japanese Canadian Journal* (Hamilton, ON: Nisei Veterans Association, 1994). The wartime experience of various ethnic groups is studied in Norman Hillmer et al., eds., *On Guard for Thee: War, Ethnicity, and the Canadian State, 1939–1945* (Ottawa: Canadian Committee for the History of the Second World War, 1989). Reg Whitaker, "Official Repression of Communism During World War II," *Labour/Le Travail* 17 (1986): 135–66, deals with another group whose civil liberties were repressed under the War Measures Act.

PART FOUR

Modern Canada, 1945–2000

Time Line: 1946–2000

1946 ~ Parliament adopts an act creating a separate Canadian citizenship, distinct from British citizenship

1947 ~ Oil begins to flow from the first well in the Leduc oil field in Alberta

1948 ~ Louis St. Laurent succeeds W.L.M. King, who served 22 years as Canadian prime minister
~ Barbara Ann Scott of Ottawa wins the world figure skating championship for a second consecutive year

1949 ~ Newfoundland joins Confederation
~ The Supreme Court of Canada becomes the country's final court of appeal
~ Canada joins the North Atlantic Treaty Organization (NATO)
~ Asbestos Strike in Quebec
~ The QEW (Queen Elizabeth Way) links Toronto with Buffalo
~ The Royal Commission on National Development in the Arts, Letters and Sciences (the Massey Commission) is established

1950 ~ Outbreak of the Korean War

1951 ~ Thérèse Casgrain chosen as leader of the Quebec CCF party, becoming the first woman to head a political party in Canada
~ The Indian Act of 1876 is revised by the federal government
~ The National Ballet of Canada is established

1952 ~ Canada's first television station begins broadcasting in Montreal
~ The Social Credit party under W.A.C. Bennett wins the provincial election in British Columbia

1953 ~ Opening of the Stratford (Ontario) Shakespearean Festival

1954 ~ Construction begins on the International Seaway and Power Project on the St. Lawrence River; completed in 1959

1955 ~ Distant Early Warning (DEW) Line stations established across the Arctic, from Alaska to Baffin Island

1956 ~ Founding of the Canadian Labour Congress (CLC)

1957 ~ Lester Pearson wins Nobel Peace Prize
~ Federal Progressive Conservatives elected under John G. Diefenbaker
~ Ellen Fairclough becomes the first woman federal cabinet minister
~ Founding of the Canada Council, in support of culture and the arts

~ The North American Air Defence Command (NORAD) comes into being

1958 ~ James Gladstone, a Blood Indian, becomes Canada's first Native senator

~ Seventy-four coal miners die in a mine disaster at Springhill, Nova Scotia

~ The Manitoba Theatre Centre opens in Winnipeg

1959 ~ Diefenbaker terminates the Avro Arrow jet-fighter construction project

~ Woodworkers' strike in Newfoundland

1960 ~ Quebec's new Liberal government undertakes measures later described cumulatively as the "Quiet Revolution"

~ Status Indians (those governed by the federal Indian Act) gain the franchise and can vote in federal elections

~ Louis Robichaud is elected premier of New Brunswick and does much, in his 10 years in office, to advance the rights of francophones in the province

1961 ~ Launching of the New Democratic Party (NDP); Tommy Douglas chosen as leader

1962 ~ Racial discrimination is officially ended in Canada's immigration regulations

~ Medicare is introduced in Saskatchewan

~ Opening of the Trans-Canada Highway from St. John's to Victoria

~ Neptune Theatre founded in Halifax

1963 ~ Federal Liberals elected to office under Lester B. Pearson

1965 ~ Canada's new maple leaf flag replaces the Red Ensign

~ An agreement between Canada and the United States — the Auto Pact — establishes free trade in the automobile industry

1967 ~ Canada celebrates its centennial

~ Expo 67 (Canadian Universal and International Exhibition), held in Montreal, welcomes 50 million visitors

~ The Royal Commission on the Status of Women in Canada is appointed

1968 ~ Federal Liberals elected under Pierre Elliott Trudeau

1969 ~ Federal government introduces White Paper on Indian Affairs

~ Parliament adopts the Official Languages Bill, favouring greater linguistic equality between francophones and anglophones

1970 ~ October Crisis in Quebec; War Measures Act is invoked

1971 ~ The federal government adopts a multiculturalism policy

~ Social Credit rule in Alberta ends with the victory of Peter Lougheed and the Conservatives

1972 ~ Team Canada vanquishes the Soviet hockey team in a series of games that captivates Canadian television audiences

~ Joey Smallwood resigns as Newfoundland's premier

1974 ~ Quebec's National Assembly adopts the Robert Bourassa government's Bill 22, making French the province's official language

1976 ~ Election of the Parti Québécois government in Quebec

~ The Twenty-First Olympic Games held in Montreal

1977 ~ The Berger Commission advises delay in the construction of the Mackenzie Valley Pipeline

~ The Parti Québécois introduces Bill 101, the Charter of the French Language

1979 ~ Election of federal Progressive Conservatives under Joe Clark

~ The James Bay hydro-electric project in Quebec produces its first electricity

1980 ~ Referendum held in Quebec seeking a mandate for the Parti Québécois to negotiate sovereignty-association with the rest of Canada; a majority of Quebeckers vote *non*

1981 ~ Terry Fox dies of cancer after running halfway across Canada

1982 ~ Proclamation of the new Canadian Constitution and Charter of Rights and Freedoms

1984 ~ Federal Progressive Conservatives elected under Brian Mulroney

~ Pope John Paul II visits Canada

1985 ~ Robert Bourassa and the Liberals defeat the Parti Québécois

1986 ~ Expo 86 held in Vancouver

~ Ontario's Lincoln Alexander becomes Canada's first black lieutenant governor

1987 ~ Canada and the United States agree on tougher measures to clean up the Great Lakes

1988 ~ Free Trade Agreement signed between Canada and the United States

1989 ~ Audrey McLaughlin of the NDP becomes the first woman national party leader in Canada

1990 ~ Failure of the Meech Lake Constitutional Accord

~ The NDP, led by Bob Rae, defeats the Liberals and forms Ontario's first NDP government

1991 ~ Canadians begin to pay a Goods and Services Tax (GST) of 7 percent

~ Canada recognizes the independence of the Baltic republics of Estonia, Latvia, and Lithuania

1992 ~ The Charlottetown constitutional accord is defeated in six provinces in a federal referendum

1993 ~ Kim Campbell is chosen as leader of the federal Progressive Conservative party and becomes Canada's first woman prime minister

~ Jean Chrétien and the Liberal party win the federal election; the Bloc Québécois becomes the official Opposition, while the Reform party places a close third; the NDP loses official party status and the Progressive Conservatives elect only two candidates

1994 ~ The North American Free Trade Agreement (NAFTA), linking Canada, the United States, and Mexico, comes into existence

~ The Parti Québécois wins the Quebec provincial election and promises to hold a referendum on sovereignty within a year

1995 ~ The federal government and most provincial governments announce cuts in expenditures in order to diminish and, in some cases, eliminate budgetary deficits

~ The Conservatives return to power in Ontario; new premier Mike Harris announces important cuts in expenditures

~ Referendum is held in Quebec on sovereignty; 49.4 percent vote yes, 50.6 percent vote no

1996 ~ The NDP under new leader Glen Clark is re-elected in British Columbia, though with fewer votes than the Liberals

1997 ~ Jean Chrétien and the federal Liberal party win a second term; the Reform party becomes the official opposition
~ Hibernia offshore oil platform towed into position 315 km off St. John's, Newfoundland
1998 ~ Severe crisis hits Canada's wheat and hog farmers; Ottawa promises help
1999 ~ Department of National Defence sends Canadian forces to support NATO's efforts to resolve the conflict in the Yugoslav province of Kosovo

Introduction

Canada emerged in the last half of the twentieth century as an important industrial nation and a respected secondary world power. Such achievements have brought both benefits and problems. Overall, Canadians have come to enjoy one of the highest standards of living of any country in the world, although certain groups within Canadian society remain seriously disadvantaged and some regions of the country experience greater hardships and fewer advantages than others. How to ensure that all Canadians, regardless of ethnic origin, class, gender, or place of dwelling have equal opportunities has been one of the challenges facing Canadian leaders. Canadians have also had to learn to live in a global economy, where they have less control over their economic destiny than ever before.

Internationally, Canada emerged from World War II prepared to play a much more active role on the world stage. Caught in the middle of the Cold War between the United States and the Soviet Union, the country chose to play the role of middle power, a role well-suited to the country's historic position as the mediator between Britain and the United States. To offset American dominance in the North American defence program, of which Canadians found themselves a part, Canadians have taken an active role in such international organizations as the United Nations, the British Commonwealth of Nations, and the North Atlantic Treaty Organization (NATO). Still, some foreign analysts have criticized Canada for becoming too closely allied to the United States, thus limiting the country's ability to help mediate international disputes.

Politically, one of the two traditional parties has shown incredible resilience at adapting to changes — the Liberal party, having ruled for 40 of the 55 years since the end of World War II. Still, third parties have emerged in what has become at times a multi-party system, as a constant reminder that no party has enjoyed complete support from all regions and all groups within the country. Regional parties have been particularly strong in the West and in Quebec, challenging political leaders to find consensus.

As Canada has modernized, it has become more of a consumer society. Culturally, too, it has taken on the attributes of a mass culture, in which the emphasis is on a popular, mass audience. Both of these trends have moved the country, particularly English-speaking Canada, socially and culturally into the American orbit, making it more difficult to maintain a distinctive Canadian identity. Yet, at the same time, regional and local cultural differences have surfaced to challenge these universal homogenizing trends, enabling Aboriginal, English-speaking, and French-speaking Canada to continue their historic role of offering an alternative North American lifestyle and a counter-culture to that of the United States.

CHAPTER FOURTEEN

An Affluent Society: 1945–1960

After a decade of economic depression and six years of war, Canadians wanted to make up for lost time, forget a bleak past, and look toward the future. Consumers wanted cars, household appliances, adequate housing, and more leisure. Business-people wanted to boost profits. Workers sought stable jobs and better wages. Canadians increasingly looked to governments to provide a variety of health, educational, and social services as a safety net against misfortune. They took pride in Canada's prestigious role in international organizations, and in the welcome their country extended to immigrants from war-torn and economically ravaged Europe.

Attitudes remained basically conservative. Traditional values and beliefs continued to govern the behaviour of a majority of Canadians. Although more women worked outside the home, long-held notions concerning the role of women in society loosened only gradually. By the late 1950s, however, the old mentality was changing. Slower growth with rising unemployment disrupted the postwar boom. Unimaginative politicians who boasted of past successes and talked in platitudinous generalities had few answers to offer. People were ready to welcome new leaders who would put forth new ideas and propose new solutions.

ECONOMIC NIRVANA IN CANADA?

Postwar Canada prospered. *Fortune* magazine called it a "businessman's country." Construction boomed. Total industrial output rose by half in the 1950s, and productivity soared thanks to technological innovation. The lighting of the flame on Leduc no. 1 oil well in a farmer's field near Edmonton on a cold February day in 1947 signalled large-scale job creation and rapid population growth in Alberta. In Ontario, demand for a wide variety of goods stimulated industrial expansion. By 1951, 10 percent of the Canadian labour force had jobs related to motor vehicles, with most of these jobs in southern Ontario. That same year, for instance, the Ford Motor Company announced the construction of a huge plant in the small town of Oakville, just west of Toronto. For a time, Oakville became the richest town in Canada.

The average worker had reason to feel satisfied. Rapid economic growth meant that unemployment rates remained (by contemporary standards) very low: between 2.8 and 5.9 percent. Pay packets for factory workers doubled between 1945 and

1956. Since prices of food and consumer goods increased at barely 2–3 percent annually, workers saw their living standards improve. They also worked less, as the 40-hour week became the norm. In addition, federal transfer payments, like family allowances and old-age pensions, put more money in consumers' pockets.

THE AGE OF THE CONSUMER

The era of the consumer introduced a new lifestyle. In towns, the iceman with his horse-drawn cart lost his remaining customers as Canadians discarded their ice-boxes and equipped their kitchens with electric refrigerators. Coal merchants' sales tumbled as homeowners bought electric ranges and switched to cleaner and more efficient gas and oil heat. Families acquired a variety of new appliances intended to reduce the drudgery of housework. Sales of new automobiles mounted in the 1950s as Canadians bought sleek American Fords and Chevrolets, or slim British Morrises and Austins.

Subdivisions proliferated around major cities. A million new homes were built between 1945 and 1960. Canadians could buy a bungalow for $15 000 and then borrow the money to pay for it at a fixed rate of just over 4 percent for 25 years. Proud new homeowners hurried to vary the colour of the trim or to plant shrubs in order to distinguish their dwelling from the identical constructions on all sides. Roofs acquired an important new use — as supports for forests of television antennas. Shopping centres sprang up, the first appearing in a Toronto suburb in 1946.

THE ENVIRONMENT

More prosperous Canadians posed new threats to the environment as well as having an increased interest in protecting it. In search of new outdoor recreational opportunities, more mobile urban dwellers invaded provincial parks. Existing parks quickly became saturated. Ontario, for example, embarked upon a major program of park expansion: the number of parks grew from only 8 in 1954 to 94 in 1967. By the late 1950s, however, naturalists and conservationists worried that increased outdoor recreation threatened the survival of natural areas, and they called for the establishment of nature preserves. In 1959, Ontario adopted the Wilderness Areas Act, which set aside areas of natural, historic, and scenic importance.

THE LESS ADVANTAGED

Yet Canadians were often unhappy when they compared themselves, as they did obsessively, with first-place Americans. Magazines and newspapers featured articles that delved into the revenues and expenses of "typical" Canadian and American families. In 1950, Canadian per-capita income was still 40 percent below American levels. Canadians complained that refrigerators costing $400 here could be had for only $275 in the United States. Journalist Blair Fraser remarked that, for Europeans still repairing their war-torn economies, second-place Canadians must have seemed like

A Historical Portrait
BETTY, RUBY, AND THE OTHERS

At the conclusion of World War II, most working women left the work force and became homemakers for their breadwinner husbands, and full-time mothers of the two, three, or often more children who quickly made their appearance. The gendered division of labour seemed normal and natural. The happiest women were supposedly those whose husbands were able to purchase a modest bungalow on a small lot in one of the dozens of suburbs that sprang up around Canada's cities in the 1950s.

Do the life stories of these ordinary women confirm the myths of contentment in the home in suburbia? Betty's husband bought a bungalow in Cooksville, Ontario, a west Toronto suburb. Betty, who had a B.A. in music and had worked until her marriage, now settled in as a full-time homemaker; Betty's husband, John, commuted to work in downtown Toronto. He did not have a job, he had a "vocation." The distinction signified that John viewed his work as "socially important" and that he had to devote virtually all his time to it. Betty was thus often home alone with the children because John was away on business. She was convinced that she was doing what was expected of her. "A woman's place is in the home," she repeated. John agreed. He was sure that women working outside the home were an important cause of divorce.

One day Betty decided to begin giving piano lessons at home. Perhaps she merely wanted some extra spending money of her own; perhaps she felt that her musical talents were being wasted; perhaps she was simply bored and lonely. Earnings from the job were modest; indeed, John often belittled his wife's efforts. At the same time he did not hesitate, over Betty's protests, to delve into the piano money box when he needed some spare change.

Ruby was another Ontario homemaker in the 1950s. Her sister, Edna Staebler, has edited the letters that Ruby wrote to members of her family. Ruby worried about her appearance — she constantly complained about being overweight. She talked a lot about her children. She also got a job outside the home. In a touching letter to sister Kay, she expounded upon her decision.

> I'm so thrilled and so nervous I don't know what to do. I won't sleep a wink tonight I'll bet. You know I've been talking about getting a job for so long because (husband) Fred wasn't earning enough and I guess he got sick of hearing about it. . . . I finally got up enough nerve to go down to the employment office to see what they could do for me. . . . I'm to go to Musser's store on Monday afternoon and start selling gloves. I'm so scared. I'll have to make change and fit people and be on my feet all those hours — and what will Fred say when he comes home tonite and I tell him?
>
> Gosh, why did I do it? I could be so comfortable here just watching TV and working on my rug and I wouldn't need many clothes. . . . If I work . . . I'll always be in a rush with my housework and have to make dinner at noon. And I won't be home when the kids get here from school. . . . (But) it would be good training. And I could use the extra money for so many things we need around here. . . . (*Haven't Any News: Ruby's Letters from the Fifties* [Waterloo, ON: Wilfrid Laurier Press, 1995], p. 58.)

(continued)

"Home dreams" did not meet the aspirations of all Canadian women after 1945, as historian Veronica Strong-Boag concludes ("Home Dreams: Women and the Suburban Experiment in Canada, 1945–60," *Canadian Historical Review* 72 [1991]: 504). Yet much work still needs to be done to reconstitute the life experiences of ordinary women in this period and to re-examine traditional interpretations.

the impoverished tycoon who was down to his last million. Nevertheless, many people of talent, especially entertainers, researchers, and engineers migrated south, while those who remained behind bemoaned the "brain drain."

Many Canadians saw no boom at all. University graduates found good jobs easily, but few Canadian men and far fewer women had university degrees. Salaries were often low, especially for non-unionized workers, immigrants, and women, even taking into account the fact that the dollar's purchasing power was at least five times what it is today. Native Canadians on reserves often lived in poverty. In rural Canada before 1950, only a minority of households even had electricity. The 1951 census revealed that half of Canadian families, particularly on farms and in outlying areas, still did not own an electric refrigerator or a vacuum cleaner; 60 percent had no car; 40 percent had no telephone; and 25 percent did not have an electric washing machine. Indeed, one dwelling in three did not have hot and cold running water. Thousands of small farmers, incapable of earning a living, abandoned their land. Incomes of residents of the Atlantic provinces remained nearly 40 percent below the Canadian average. New Brunswick was sharply divided into the impoverished north and east, largely Acadian, and the more favoured south, mostly English-speaking. Thousands of Montrealers with incomes below the poverty line lived in the tenements of St. Henri, which were portrayed poignantly by Gabrielle Roy in her novel *Bonheur d'occasion* (*The Tin Flute* in English). In Quebec, unilingual anglophones enjoyed income levels twice those of unilingual francophones and one-third higher than those of bilingual francophones. In the West, Winnipeg suffered from the decline of old industries, and the relocation of Canadian Pacific Airlines to Vancouver in 1948, which cost the city many jobs.

Disadvantaged provinces offered social services of inferior quality. When Newfoundland entered Confederation in 1949, two-thirds of its schools had only one room and lacked electricity and running water. In Quebec, the wages of primary school teachers, often barely $600 a year, did little to attract talented personnel into the teaching profession. Throughout Canada, the underprivileged, whether unemployed or sick, handicapped or elderly, could not count on the array of social welfare benefits that, in spite of recent cutbacks, still exist today.

Canada had many second-class citizens, too. Women did not enjoy the same employment opportunities as men. Discrimination also afflicted Canada's Aboriginal peoples as well as blacks, Jews, Jehovah's Witnesses in Quebec, Hutterites in Alberta, and recent immigrants. The French suffered a linguistic disadvantage, even within Quebec.

In an era in which society emphasized family and reproductive heterosexuality, gays and lesbians faced social stigma as "perverts" and "sex deviates," as well as job discrimination. Immigration law prevented homosexuals from entering Canada.

In 1953, lesbian practices were criminalized for the first time. Gay men were also often viewed as potential child molesters and, in the climate of the Cold War, as security risks to be purged from government service. By the mid-1960s, RCMP files reportedly contained the names of 7500 homosexuals. Most homosexuals hid their sexual orientation except from a few persons close to them. The war experience itself appears to have led to an expansion of gay and lesbian networks in Canadian cities. Gay men met in bars, baths, parks, and theatres, while lesbians socialized at bars that women could frequent and at house parties. Newspapers in Montreal and Toronto reported frequent arrests of gay men in parks and theatres.

The inequalities suffered by many Canadians engendered increasing discontent. Not clearly articulated in the 1950s, dissatisfaction provoked far-reaching change in the 1960s and 1970s.

PROSPERITY AND TRADE

After demobilization, the federal government worked to convert the Canadian economy back to a free-enterprise system and to avoid a repetition of the severe recession that followed World War I. To achieve this objective, C.D. Howe, Canada's manager of wartime production and now in charge of the country's postwar reconstruction, sold war plants for a fraction of their cost, on condition that they reopen for business. He also wanted to liberalize international trade: only if markets abroad were open, he believed, could a country like Canada, with its economy largely based on exports, prosper. He also wanted the government to use tax policy to promote investment and create jobs.

Canada's trade did expand, albeit unevenly. From the late 1940s, the country had a persistently negative trade balance as imports rose faster than exports. The trade balance would have been even worse had prices for Canada's forest products and minerals not remained high. In real terms, Canada exported less in the mid-1950s than at the end of the war. Most Canadian-made manufactured products could not compete in international markets. Canadian production costs remained high because Canadian companies manufactured a wide variety of products in small quantities, and they often relied heavily on imported American components.

As trade with Britain declined after World War II, Canada moved to establish closer economic ties with the United States. "It could not be faulted for that," concludes historian B.W. Muirhead.[1] In 1947, for example, Canada experienced a severe shortage of American dollars as imports from the United States increased sharply and Canada was unable to convert into dollars the pounds it earned in trade with Britain. One solution was to negotiate a free-trade agreement with the Americans. But King recalled Laurier's stinging defeat in the "Reciprocity Election" of 1911. The prime minister then vetoed the project: "I would no more think of, at my time of life and at this stage of my career, attempting any movement of the kind than I would of flying to the South Pole."

A safer move was to try to convince the Americans to permit European countries receiving American aid through the Marshall Plan to use a portion of it to buy Canadian goods. The Americans agreed, thus resolving the dollar crisis. Ottawa also hoped that the General Agreement on Tariffs and Trade (GATT) would come to its aid. This multilateral trade agreement, signed in Geneva in 1947, aimed at stimulating world trade by reducing tariffs. It included accords between Canada and its two principal trading partners, the United States and Britain.

AN INVESTMENT BOOM

Regardless of Canada's rejection of free trade, continental economic integration proceeded apace. Foreign capital, mostly American, poured into Canada. To get around Canadian tariffs, American multinational corporations established, especially in central Canada, numerous branch plants that manufactured consumer products and industrial goods. Canada represented in itself a stable and wealthy market. The Americans also sought Canada's resources, as production of some important minerals declined in the United States. Moreover, the Korean War in 1950–53 promoted an investment boom in Canada's resource and defence industries.

THE ROYAL COMMISSION ON CANADA'S ECONOMIC PROSPECTS

Most Canadians assumed that, despite closer economic links with the United States, Canada could maintain its political sovereignty. Some provinces, in fact, actively encouraged the entry of foreign capital by keeping taxes and labour costs down. Nevertheless, some observers worried about the "complacency" with which Canadians sold out the country's resources. In particular, the Royal Commission on Canada's Economic Prospects recommended in a preliminary report in 1956 that Canada control foreign investment.

Advocates of North American integration argued that multinationals gave jobs to Canadians and helped the country's balance of payments by reducing imports. Howe protested in a speech in 1956 that "had it not been for the enterprise and capital from the United States . . . our development would have been slower, and some of the spectacular projects of which we are so proud . . . would still be in the future." He called the Royal Commission's preliminary report "manure" — employing, in fact, a more earthy expression.

Investment, both Canadian and foreign, financed several important development projects. Pipelines carried oil and gas from Alberta to markets in Ontario and the United States; a railway nearly 600 km long, from Sept-Îles, Quebec, opened up ore-rich Labrador; and the construction of the St. Lawrence Seaway and the Trans-Canada Highway began.

Then the boom ended. By 1958, slow growth raised unemployment to nearly 10 percent. Automation eliminated some jobs. When railways switched to diesel engines, for example, they needed fewer machinists, blacksmiths, and firemen. The high-valued Canadian dollar, which brought a premium when exchanged for an American dollar, hurt exports.

A GOVERNMENT OF EFFICIENT ADMINISTRATORS

In the late 1940s and early 1950s, voters wanted politicians who would manage the country efficiently and achieve greater prosperity. They also called upon the state to protect them from the risks of unemployment, illness, and poverty. The Liberal government of businessmen and administrators largely fulfilled this need. It was a regime that reflected an era.

When William Lyon Mackenzie King finally retired in 1948, he had led the Liberal party for nearly 30 years and could boast of having been the longest-serving prime minister in the history of the British empire. Jurist Frank Scott, who objected indignantly to King's being given credit for everything but putting the oil under Alberta, attributed King's success to his blandness: "He will be remembered wherever men honour ingenuity, ambiguity, inactivity, and political longevity."

Yet many observers of Canadian politics admired King for his accomplishments, even though they disliked him personally and found him uninspiring. He seemed to follow rather than lead, and to be more concerned with his own and the Liberal party's fortunes than with the country's well-being. Nevertheless, he had — like Macdonald and Laurier before him — held the country together effectively through difficult times. His government had also taken the first steps toward establishing a welfare state in Canada.

THE ST. LAURENT GOVERNMENT

WEB LINKS

Louis St. Laurent, chosen as King's successor in 1948, was a former corporation lawyer from Quebec City and the second French-speaking, though fluently bilingual, prime minister. Denounced in his home province during the war for his approval of military conscription, he was clearly no Quebec nationalist. On constitutional questions he opposed the provincial autonomists in Quebec and elsewhere. In foreign affairs, he appeared more internationalist than most Canadians.

The new prime minister followed his predecessor's "accommodative approach," acting only after consensus had been achieved. While the Progressive Conservatives in opposition suffered from their links with the rabidly Tory "Bay Street interests," and doctrinaire socialists in the CCF vainly preached the need to "share the wealth" so that every family could have "a good kitchen sink and a first-class bathroom," the Liberals continued to occupy the centre of the political spectrum and thus established the consensus so necessary to govern Canada. Prosperity facilitated their task.

Some Liberal strategists worried about St. Laurent's possibilities as a vote-getter, because initially he appeared ill-at-ease with the public. Their fears proved groundless. Before the 1949 election campaign had begun, St. Laurent adopted a new, relaxed platform style, particularly with small groups. One reporter for a Conservative newspaper remarked: "Uncle Louis is going to be hard to beat." The nickname stuck and brought enormous dividends.

NEWFOUNDLAND ENTERS CONFEDERATION

WEB LINKS

In 1949, soon after the St. Laurent government took office, Newfoundland became Canada's tenth province. On April 1, the *St. John's Evening Telegram* observed, "Newfoundland slipped as quietly into Confederation last midnight as the grey mist which settled over the capital early this morning."

A bitter struggle had been waged during the preceding months. Joey Smallwood, leader of the confederate forces, campaigned tirelessly, at times from an old seaplane equipped with loudspeakers, to prove that Newfoundlanders "would be better off in pocket, in stomach, and in health" within Canada. Anti-confederationists

Louis St. Laurent (left) and Prime Minister Mackenzie King (centre), at the national Liberal convention of 1948 at which St. Laurent was chosen to succeed King as Liberal leader and prime minister. In the background is a portrait of former Liberal leader and prime minister Wilfrid Laurier.

William Lyon Mackenzie King Collection/ National Archives of Canada/C-23278.

denounced those who would "lure Newfoundland into the Canadian mousetrap." They called Smallwood a "Judas" who belittled Newfoundland's good name and lamented that at least Iscariot had had the decency to hang himself.

The referendum held in June 1948 allowed Newfoundlanders to choose among three options: Confederation, favoured by both Britain and Canada; responsible government or dominion status, perhaps leading to economic union with the United States; and the unpopular existing system, by which a commission of British-appointed officials governed Newfoundland. Responsible government won; Confederation placed second. Since no clear majority had emerged, a second referendum was held in July in an atmosphere of sectarian bitterness. Most Roman Catholics, fearing loss of their denominational schools, spoke against Confederation, while many Protestants favoured it. In general, the urban commercial classes opposed Confederation, fearing the competition of the big Canadian department stores (such as Eaton's) and the mail-order companies. The confederates won narrowly this time, with a majority of 52 percent. Canadians and Newfoundlanders now set about negotiating the final terms of union.

Historian David Alexander argues that the decline of the fishing economy, which fell victim to tumbling prices and oversupply, "led Newfoundlanders reluctantly into Confederation."[2] Poverty was endemic: in 1949, the island's citizens had incomes only one-third as high as those of Canadians. Death rates for diseases associated with poverty stood two to three times higher than Canadian rates. Canada's "safety net" of social programs looked inviting.

In addition, Britain clearly desired to quit Newfoundland. In the words of historian Peter Neary, Britain arranged its departure "with a hard logic and clinical precision she would not manage in other parts of her far-flung but now crumbling empire."[3] Yet, Canada also wanted Newfoundland. During World War II, federal civil servants and politicians had discovered the island's strategic and economic importance. Canadians also worried that the United States might seek to strengthen its ties with the island.

Newfoundland's integration into Canada proceeded rapidly. Immediately upon confederation, family allowances and other federal social programs were ready to function. Income levels improved. Yet the federal government did little to favour the

A Newfoundland woman votes in the referendum of 1948. Although Newfoundlanders opted for responsible government over union with Canada, the indecisive results forced a second referendum, which the confederationists won. On March 31, 1949, Newfoundland joined Confederation as Canada's tenth province.

C.F. Marshall/Centre for Newfoundland Studies, Queen Elizabeth II Library, Memorial University of Newfoundland.

province's economic development, and the province simply "shifted its dependence from London to Ottawa."[4]

FEDERAL–PROVINCIAL TENSIONS

The Liberal government's preoccupation with maintaining a buoyant economy had serious implications for Canadian federalism. Civil servants and politicians in Ottawa believed that the federal government should maintain and even strengthen the fiscal and legislative pre-eminence that it had acquired during the wartime emergency. Disadvantaged provinces had benefited financially. New Brunswick, for example, reaped substantial increases in its revenues when it ceded to Ottawa its right to collect income taxes. But several provinces objected to Ottawa's aggressive centralization. Nova Scotia premier Angus L. Macdonald complained that federal subsidies destroyed provincial independence and transformed the provinces into "mere annuitants of Ottawa." Ontario insisted on its right to formulate its own economic priorities and programs. In Quebec, the Duplessis government feuded continuously with Ottawa over federal tax and spending policies. The province's Royal Commission of Inquiry on Constitutional Problems (the Tremblay Commission) called in 1954 for an end to federal "imperialism" and a return to "true federalism."

TOWARD A WELFARE STATE

Neither federal–provincial tensions nor the Liberals' moderate conservatism halted Canada's movement toward a welfare state. In 1948, Ottawa enacted the National Health Program, which provided for federal grants to each province in the fields of hygiene and health. In 1952, after all the provinces had agreed to the requisite constitutional amendment, Ottawa began sending old-age-security cheques in the amount of $40 a month to all Canadians over the age of 70 and to needy Canadians over 65. After a national publicity campaign by the Canadian Welfare Council, Parliament enacted the Unemployment Assistance Act of 1956, a shared-cost program designed to assist employable persons on welfare.

Most Canadians who became ill in the 1950s knew the prohibitive cost of health care. One Montreal businessman, after paying the bills occasioned by his wife's serious illness, commented wryly, "There are two things that can send you to the poorhouse: hospital bills and borrowing from loan sharks. And 90 percent of the borrowing from loan sharks is to pay hospital bills!" Many Canadians tried to cover eventual health costs at least partially by participating in Blue Cross or other doctor-sponsored insurance plans, but at least half of Canadians had no direct coverage for medical care.

Calls for a national health plan were heard constantly. Anxious doctors warned that such a plan would rob them of their independence, lower their standards, and interfere with the intimate doctor–patient relationship. Finally, in 1957, after lobbying by several provincial premiers and some of St. Laurent's own ministers, Parliament adopted the Hospital Insurance and Diagnostic Services Act. It provided federal financial assistance to provinces willing to set up a publicly administered hospital-insurance program with universal coverage. Provinces also spent significantly more on welfare as case numbers increased. Yet allowances failed to take into account increased housing and clothing costs. For historian James Struthers, in Ontario "the poor went hungry to pay the rent."[5]

THE GOLDEN AGE OF CANADIAN DIPLOMACY

After 1945, Canada had to adapt to a new world power structure. It could no longer rely on a permanently weakened Britain as a counterweight to American influence. To offset growing American power, Canada worked to build strong multilateral institutions. At the same time, it had little desire to let world organizations interfere in its relations with the United States, which it believed it could conduct better alone.

CANADA IN THE COLD WAR ERA

Disappointments were rife in these years, as the postwar era rapidly gave way to the Cold War. At the Paris Peace Conference of 1946, Canada had hoped to play a role in the European settlement commensurate with its contribution to the war effort. For Canada, however, in historian J.F. Hilliker's words, there was "no bread at the peace table."[6] The country went virtually unnoticed and thus, ironically, played a much less active role in peacemaking than it had in 1918–19.

As relations between the United States and the Soviet Union soured, Canadian foreign-affairs officials feared that the often bellicose attitude of the United States would only make matters worse. In the view of external-affairs official John Holmes, the American position was to refuse to negotiate with the Soviet "devil," while Canadians wanted only to make him behave.[7]

Events soon shook Canadians' faith in the West's capacity to reach some kind of reasonable entente with the Soviet Union. In late 1945 Igor Gouzenko, a cipher clerk at the Soviet embassy in Ottawa, defected. He revealed the existence of a Soviet espionage network in Canada that reached into several government agencies. By the time the press published details in early 1946, the Canadian government had made several arrests. Dana Wilgress, who headed the Canadian mission in Moscow from

In September 1945, Igor Gouzenko, a cipher clerk at the Soviet embassy in Ottawa, defected, and reported on several Soviet spy networks in Canada. To protect his identity, he always wore a mask in public. He appeared on numerous radio and television shows to talk about his novel, The Fall of a Titan, which won the Governor General's Award in 1954.

Montreal Star Collection/National Archives of Canada/PA-129625.

1944 to 1947, showed the evolution of Canadian thinking when he denounced the "irresponsible opportunism" of Soviet policies.

The intensification of the Cold War led Canada into ever-closer relations with the United States. Britain's own decline left Canada little choice. "London's impotence," historian Jack Granatstein argues, compelled Canadian governments to seek "shelter within Uncle Sam's all-encompassing embrace."[8]

THE NORTH ATLANTIC TREATY ORGANIZATION

As people lost hope that the United Nations could assure world peace through collective security, the Canadian government pushed for an Atlantic alliance for mutual self-defence. Escott Reid, an external-affairs officer, first publicly advocated a collective defence system for the West in a speech in the summer of 1947. Then, in September, Louis St. Laurent, secretary of state for external affairs, gave an address in New York in which he described the United Nations Security Council as being regretfully "frozen in futility and divided by dissension." Dissatisfied democratic and peace-loving member states could be well justified, as a last resort, in coming together and accepting more specific international obligations in return for a greater measure of national security.

The Americans and the British showed interest in the proposal. Consultations with the western European powers proceeded in the summer of 1948. By December, work began on a draft treaty to form the North Atlantic Treaty Organization (NATO). The United States envisaged a purely military pact, but Canada sought co-operation in other sectors that might eventually unite the Atlantic nations into a closely knit community. For that reason, Canada fought for the inclusion in the draft treaty of an article indicating general economic and social aims.

Canada's interest was clear. Links with western Europe would strengthen Canada in its relationship with the militarily dominant Americans. The so-called "Canadian article" did get into the treaty, in spite of the adamant opposition of American Secretary of State Dean Acheson to this product of "typical Canadian moralizing." In March 1949 the House of Commons approved the treaty, and on April 4, in an atmosphere of euphoric optimism, NATO came into existence. But the Canadians' hard-won victory soured quickly, for the "Canadian article" was never put into practice. Rising East–West tensions, especially the outbreak of war in Korea in 1950, turned NATO into an almost exclusively military alliance. Even so, as historian David J. Bercuson has shown, Canada did indeed make a significant difference to NATO in the alliance's early years "in both the quantity and the quality of its military contribution."[9] Then, as defence spending fell and Canada's priorities became continental, its influence declined.

THE NEW INTEREST IN THE NORTH

With the development of the Cold War in the late 1940s, the Canadian North again became an area of vital strategic interest to both Canada and the United States. Acting together, the two countries worked to provide a warning system in the event of a Soviet nuclear attack on Canadian and American cities. A chain of more than 40 Distant Early Warning (DEW) Line stations was built in the 1950s across the Arctic, from Alaska to Baffin Island. The DEW Line allowed for four to six hours' warning of a manned Soviet bomber attack across the North Pole. Begun in 1954 and completed in 1957, the system remained in full operation for nearly a decade, until intercontinental ballistic missiles largely replaced the bomber threat. With the warning time now calculated in minutes rather than hours, the DEW Line lost much of its effectiveness. in 1957, Canada and the United States signed the North American Air Defence Agreement (NORAD), which formally co-ordinated the two countries' air forces.

In the 1950s, the Canadian government apparently used a number of Quebec Inuit to affirm Canadian sovereignty. The DEW Line and other American proposals revived fears about Canada's sovereignty in the Arctic. Recognizing that one of the surest grounds for Canada's claim would be "effective occupation," the federal government in 1953 arranged for seven Inuit families in northern Quebec to relocate nearly 2000 km away. The migrants who were established on Cornwallis and Ellesmere islands in the high Arctic lost contact with their relatives and, the government's promises aside, found themselves in a much more inhospitable environment than the one they had left behind.

WEB
LINKS

THE COMMONWEALTH

In keeping with its desire to balance closer links to the United States with an increased international participation, Canada looked with hope to the evolving British Commonwealth of Nations. Mackenzie King, however, strongly opposed the idea of a uniform Commonwealth foreign policy put forth by certain British politicians; to him, such a plan recalled the days of the empire centralizers. Moreover, the Commonwealth was changing, with the addition of new members such as India, Pakistan, and Ceylon. Canada helped move the Commonwealth in directions that made it an acceptable organization for these new states. It also supported and contributed to the Colombo Plan, which was set up at a meeting of Commonwealth foreign ministers in 1950 to promote economic development in Commonwealth countries in Asia.

PEACEKEEPING

Canada's attempts at peacekeeping produced mixed results. In 1950, when communist North Korea invaded South Korea and the United Nations Security Council (which the Soviet Union was boycotting) denounced this act of aggression, Canada contributed a brigade to fight alongside mostly American troops in the name of collective security. As the war moved toward a stalemate, Lester B. Pearson, then Canada's minister of external affairs, helped to restrain the "overzealous" Americans from actions that risked bringing China and the Soviet Union into the war. Then, in 1954, Canada agreed, with considerable apprehension, to join Poland and India in a three-country International Control Commission to supervise the peace in Indochina.

Finally, in 1956, came what many considered to be Canada's greatest contribution internationally. In October, despite strong American opposition, Israel, together with Britain and France, invaded Egypt, in response to Egypt's nationalization of the Suez Canal. Wary of the dangerous split developing in the western alliance, Pearson proposed the creation of a multinational United Nations emergency peacekeeping force in the region. He then lobbied tirelessly to have the plan accepted by the General Assembly. For his efforts, he won the Nobel Peace Prize in 1957. Biographer John English judged Pearson's initiative as having "strengthened the United Nations, moderated the tensions between Washington and London, and helped to maintain both the Commonwealth and NATO."[10]

POLITICAL CHANGE

When Canadians went to the polls in 1957 to select a government, another Liberal victory seemed likely. Most political observers were surprised when the Progressive Conservatives, under their new leader, John Diefenbaker, won a narrow victory. Stunned Liberals, as cabinet minister J.W. Pickersgill later put it, wondered why they had to suffer a Tory government once in every generation. The CCF, which had restated its original aims in less revolutionary fashion in its Winnipeg Declaration of Principles in 1956, felt bitterly disappointed over its failure to arrest its decline in popularity.

Although the Liberals boasted during the election campaign that voters would not "shoot Santa Claus," not all Canadians were prosperous in 1957. Residents of the Prairies and the Maritimes complained of their regions' underdevelopment. Many senior citizens agreed with Conservative assertions that unindexed old-age pensions were scandalously insufficient. Most of all, voters probably wanted a change from what appeared increasingly to be cold, insensitive, uncreative leadership by an aging Liberal gerontocracy.

The electorate also responded to Conservative charges that the Liberals had behaved in an undemocratic, even dictatorial, fashion. The culmination of purported Liberal arrogance was the Trans-Canada Pipe Lines affair in 1956. The government had planned to make an important loan to Trans-Canada Pipe Lines, a private company formed by American and Canadian business interests, to assist in building the western section of a pipeline to carry Alberta gas to central Canadian markets. In a hurry because of a timetable he wanted to respect, Minister of Trade and Commerce C.D.

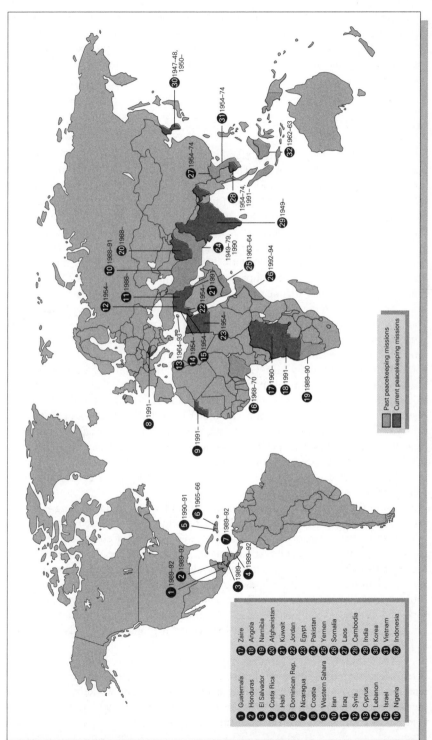

Canada's United Nations peacekeeping missions, from 1947 to the present.

Source: Adapted from *The Integrated Atlas: History and Geography of Canada and the World* (Toronto: Harcourt Brace, 1996), p. 120. Reprinted by permission of Harcourt Brace & Company Canada Ltd.

Howe pushed the bill through the House of Commons, unamended, by imposing closure and cutting off debate at each stage. Diefenbaker denounced the Liberal cabinet, sitting on the front benches, as "arrogant, overbearing, condescending ... sneering at suggestions that they were becoming all-powerful." Many Canadians obviously agreed.

THE "DIEFENBAKER PARTY"

WEB LINKS

John Diefenbaker surely played a significant role in the success of what became known as the "Diefenbaker party." The party's new leader sought to change voters' traditionally negative image of the Tories. He took control of the party from the hands of the Toronto business elite and gave it to "outsiders," many of whom came from western Canada. He used to great effect his oratorical talents, which far outshone anything the Liberals could muster. At Massey Hall in April 1957, the modern-day Jeremiah proclaimed the message to his "fellow Canadians": "This party has a sacred trust. It has an appointment today with destiny, to plan and to build for a greater Canada ... one Canada, with equality of opportunity for every citizen and equality for every province from the Atlantic to the Pacific."

The federal election of 1957 served as a dress rehearsal for that of March 1958. The new government barely had time to adopt a few popular measures designed to assist the unemployed, Prairie farmers, and Maritimers before Diefenbaker, anxious to form a majority government, called a new election. The prime minister then presented his "vision of opportunity" for Canada, a vision based on the development of resources and of the North. Liberal newspapers like the *Toronto Star* mocked Diefenbaker's admittedly vague program as "humbug and flapdoodle served up with an evangelistic flourish." New Liberal leader Lester B. Pearson, whose soporific oratorical style betrayed his diplomatic career, attempted to brush off what he termed the "oracular fervour and circus parades." The result was a Diefenbaker landslide, with the Progressive Conservatives winning what was proportionally the greatest majority in Canadian electoral history: 208 of the 265 seats in the House of Commons, including 50 seats from Quebec.

From the start, the Conservatives had difficulty governing. So long had they sat in the political wilderness that all the new ministers lacked experience. In many cases, they questioned the loyalty of civil servants accustomed to a close working relationship with Liberal politicians. For most Quebec Tory MPs, the triumph of 1958 was their first — and last — electoral victory. Their unilingual Baptist leader from Saskatchewan knew little about Quebec and entrusted no senior cabinet portfolios to Quebeckers. Diefenbaker's vision of northern development, of "opening Canada to its polar reaches," did not capture the imagination of southern Canadians. Liberals mocked what they called a program of "roads from igloo to igloo."

The Conservative government's major problem arose from the country's deteriorating economic situation. It responded to rising unemployment with winter works programs, subsidies, and welfare benefits for seasonal workers. As expenses increased and government receipts declined, budgetary deficits grew and the business community complained of financial mismanagement.

LABOUR RELATIONS IN TIMES OF PROSPERITY

Postwar economic growth gave a powerful boost to the unions. In 1950, union membership passed the 1 million mark, or 30 percent of the work force. "Elite" unions in sectors such as heavy manufacturing enjoyed strong bargaining power and succeeded in negotiating high wages. They had frequent recourse to strikes, particularly in the late 1940s. In 1946, for example, one worker in six went on strike, resulting in a total loss of 4.5 million workdays. These strikes aimed at forcing employers to recognize union rights, improve working conditions, and increase salaries. In retaliation, companies frequently hired strikebreakers, and violent confrontations sometimes ensued. Provincial governments supported employers directly through anti-union legislation and the use of the police and the courts.

INDUSTRIAL UNREST

Although most workers signed contracts without going on strike and although sickness resulted in far more loss of work time than did strike activity, certain sensational confrontations earned a place in the annals of Canadian working-class history. In one dramatic encounter in 1946, Steel Company of Canada (Stelco) management used airplanes and boats to avoid picket lines and to transport food and supplies to strikebreakers inside its plant at Hamilton, Ontario. In the same year, textile workers, many of them women, struck in Valleyfield, Quebec. Led by Madeleine Parent and Kent Rowley, the strikers obtained recognition for their union only after bloody skirmishes with police.

In 1947, Nova Scotia fishermen went on strike against National Sea Products, the monopoly conglomerate, in an attempt to gain union recognition. The company waged a fierce anti-labour campaign and, with assistance from the courts and later from the provincial government, broke the strike. A year later, the Prince Edward Island government seized a Canada Packers plant during a strike, hired non-union labour, and reopened the plant. It then adopted legislation prohibiting labour affiliation with any union organization outside the province. In 1949, 5000 Quebec asbestos workers struck for five months to improve wages and working conditions. Some members of the clergy, including Archbishop Joseph Charbonneau of Montreal, sided openly with the strikers, one of whose supporters was a young Montreal lawyer, Pierre Elliott Trudeau. The Duplessis government sided with the companies, decertified the union, and sent in special police squads. Though the settlement gave workers no significant material gains, the strike itself took on great symbolic value: Quebec sociologist Jean-Charles Falardeau even viewed it as a "quasi-revolution."[11]

Conflict continued into the 1950s, a period that labour historian Bryan D. Palmer sees as one of "consolidation" for labour, now that union recognition was more generally assured.[12] Major strikes occurred among loggers, fishers, government employees, and longshoremen in British Columbia, building-trades workers in Halifax and Vancouver, gold miners in Ontario and Quebec, and automobile workers and employees of the International Nickel Company (Inco) in Ontario. In August 1950, 130 000 employees of Canada's two major railways left their jobs, but the government, declaring that "the country cannot afford a railway strike," ordered the workers

The Stelco strike, Hamilton, summer 1946. The union blockaded roads around the plant, but carefully avoided violence. Management countered by using airplanes and boats to avoid the picket lines while transporting food and supplies to strikebreakers inside the plant.

United Steelworkers of America Collection/
National Archives of Canada/PA-120521.

back. Textile workers at Louiseville, Quebec, went out for ten months in 1952, while copper workers at Murdochville, Quebec, struck for seven months in 1957 in a violent but vain confrontation. In 1959, Newfoundland loggers, members of the International Woodworkers of America (IWA), went on strike. They wanted better wages, a shorter work day, and camp amenities. Violence broke out when the company recruited fishers to replace strikers. In one skirmish, a policeman suffered fatal injuries. In an effort to break the IWA, Premier Joseph Smallwood set up a union and had the legislature outlaw the IWA in the province. The federal government refused to send the RCMP reinforcements that Smallwood demanded, but the strike nonetheless failed.

WORKERS VERSUS WORKERS

Workers not only fought management and governments, they also feuded with one another for political and personal reasons. On the left, communists and democratic socialists battled each other in fratricidal fury. Both clashed with conservative unionists, who viewed all political links as dangerous for the labour movement.

Anti-communists in the Canadian Congress of Labour (CCL) insisted that "we can't fight the communists with one hand and the bosses with the other. To fight the boss we must get rid of the communists." The CCL thus manoeuvred to oust certain affiliate unions whose executives it charged with being "complete vassals of uncle Joe Stalin." The communist-led Canadian Seamen's Union (CSU) was crushed when the Canadian and American governments combined with the shippers and Trades and Labor Congress (TLC) officers to replace the CSU with the rival Seafarers' International Union (SIU). (After a judicial inquiry later found the SIU guilty of racketeering and a host of other improper practices, Ottawa placed the union under a government trusteeship. Its director, Hal Banks, who had boasted of his ambition to control "everything that floats," forfeited bail and fled to the United States.) Some Canadian unionists thought that the battle against communists merely permitted American unions to reinforce their hold in Canada. According to labour historian

Irving Abella, the communist purge did little to strengthen the union movement and, in hindsight, was probably "neither necessary nor wise."[13]

Greater labour unity came in 1956, when the TLC and the CCL formed the Canadian Labour Congress (CLC). This union followed the merger in 1955 of the American labour congresses, the AFL and the CIO. The costly raids by TLC and CCL unions on each other, with no total gain in membership, then ended. Claude Jodoin, a well-known Quebec labour leader and president of the TLC, became president of the new million-member CLC. Many of the CLC unions were affiliated with the American AFL–CIO, and they remained subject to American influence. Most Canadian workers, who were employed by American branch companies, found nothing unusual in belonging to American-dominated unions. This, however, was one of the reasons that the Quebec-based CTCC refused to join the CLC.

Although unions made major gains in the postwar period, much work remained. Collective agreements generally left managers with complete authority over the work process on the shop floor. Union organizers had yet to reach vast numbers of workers, especially in the service sector. Labour legislation in several provinces was unsympathetic to unions. Automation made job security an increasingly serious issue. Worker safety also caused concern: accidents on the job caused nearly 5 million injuries and more than 12 500 deaths between 1945 and 1959. When fire killed five Italian labourers laying a water main in the Hogg's Hollow district of Toronto, the coroner denounced management's "callous attitude" toward worker safety and noted that "almost all the safety regulations ... were violated at one time or another, and many of the regulations were violated continuously."

THE STATUS OF WOMEN

During World War II, many women had entered the work force. Once the war ended, most Canadians, including a majority of women, thought women — especially married women — should leave the paid work force. Cultural stereotypes reinforced the "traditional" role of women: school textbooks depicted men in interesting careers while portraying women as staying at home, cooking meals, and scolding children. Women who continued in paid employment outside the home still had to perform all the domestic and family chores. As one woman journalist wrote: "A man whittles himself down to less of a man by consistently performing women's work." Women's magazines such as *Chatelaine* and the *Canadian Home Journal* contained many articles on sewing, homemaking, gardening, and fashion, but very few on such areas of male hegemony as politics or business. Women were paternalistically excluded from sports judged "unsuitable" for females.

WOMEN IN THE WORK FORCE

Slowly, female participation in the work force increased. In 1951, one paid worker in four was a woman, usually unmarried. During the 1950s the proportion of married women workers also increased, as mothers rejoined the work force after their youngest children enrolled in school. Most worked as secretaries, nurses, sales personnel, and clerks. As late as 1960, only a handful of women were professionals; they

Where Historians Disagree

WOMEN AND UNIONS IN POSTWAR CANADA

By 1964, 30 percent of employed workers were women. However, only 16 percent of union members were women. Most women entered non-unionized sectors of activity, such as clerical and domestic work. Of those who worked in industry, many joined unions. What did they seek to obtain from unions? Did they see themselves primarily as workers who, like the men, simply wanted to improve wages and working conditions? Or did they see themselves primarily as women with objectives that were different from, and at times contradictory to, those of men? And how did men react to the entry of women into "their" workplace?

Labour historians, preoccupied with labour's battles against employers, did not at first ask these questions, particularly as they pertain to the postwar years. Bryan Palmer describes the rise of the Communist-led United Electrical, Radio and Machine Workers' Union (UE), whose expansion was fostered by enormous consumer demand for electrical products. The union waged a number of bitter strikes in 1946. Though Palmer notes that a significant part of the UE's membership was female, he does not imply that their struggle was other than a workers' struggle against the bosses (*Working Class Experience: Rethinking the History of Canadian Labour, 1800–1991*, 2nd ed. [Toronto: McClelland & Stewart, 1992], p. 287). Craig Heron states that industrial unions of these years had difficulty eliminating the segregation of women into low-wage job ghettos, and then comments, revealingly, that "even if the male unionists' pride had allowed more equity, most men still assumed that women should be at home, supported by a male wage" (*The Canadian Labour Movement: A Short History*, 2nd ed. [Toronto: James Lorimer, 1996], p. 78).

In her study of working women in Peterborough, Ontario, Joan Sangster shows how unions and labour disputes have been arenas of both gender conflict and class solidarity (*Earning Respect: The Lives of Working Women in Small-Town Ontario, 1920–1960* [Toronto: University of Toronto Press, 1995], p. 167). Looking at the UE, she notes that union leadership proclaimed its faith in gender equality, partly in order to gain women workers' support for the UE's struggle against a rival union. The UE also tried to focus on grievances that could unite men and women, such as more equal pay rates, because men feared the substitution of female for male labour. On other issues, notably the contentious question of merging male and female seniority lists, the union equivocated. Sangster notes also how difficult it was for women to become involved in union activities. While the union itself gave pre-eminence to class rather than to gender, separate organizations for women within unions eventually provided an innovative means for women to demand better working conditions and wages.

Julie Guard has also studied the experience of women within the UE. ("Fair Play or Fair Pay? Gender Relations, Class Consciousness, and Union Solidarity in the Canadian UE," *Labour/Le Travail* 37 [1996]: 149–77). This union, a quarter of whose members in 1954 were women, endorsed the principle of gender equality. Guard shows, however, that the union was interested in the class struggle, not in women's rights. The union made slow progress in endorsing equal pay for women, in spite of women's attempts to prove that low pay for women put a brake on male

(continued)

wages. Few women participated in union leadership, a fact that men attributed to personal choice rather than to the "inherent gender bias of union structure and culture" (p. 176).

Joy Parr has examined the effect of gender on strike action against a textile company in Paris, Ontario, in 1949. About one-half of the workers were women and, although women were less inclined to join the union than were men, female militancy on the picket line was considerable. Yet, whereas the union itself whipped up male strikers' militancy, female militancy was "forged and sustained in family and neighbourhood relationships" rather than through union organization (*The Gender of Breadwinners: Women, Men, and Change in Two Industrial Towns, 1880–1950* [Toronto: University of Toronto Press, 1990], p. 108).

In her study of the United Auto Workers in Canada (*Labour's Dilemma: The Gender Politics of Auto Workers in Canada, 1937–1979* [Toronto: University of Toronto Press, 1994]), Pam Sugiman shows that the UAW was traditionally viewed as a progressive union that gave vocal support to women's rights in society; yet, at the same time, it showed persistent gender bias and allowed blatant inequalities to persist in the working environment (pp. 4–5). Male union officials were reluctant to view the special concerns of female dues-paying members as legitimate union issues. In the immediate postwar years, women did not generally challenge gender ideologies, separate seniority lists, and large pay differentials. Even in the 1950s, women still did not "openly contest their subordination as a sex" although they did develop "a stronger self-identification as wage earners and as unionists" (p. 99). Thanks to improving economic conditions, women became bolder and made use of grievance procedures to protest inadequate wages and to try to improve working conditions.

Were female unionists as militant as male unionists? Or did they follow the leadership of their husbands at home and their male co-workers? Robert Ventresca has studied the behaviour of women workers, many of them Italian immigrants, in two industrial conflicts in Welland, Ontario ("'Cowering Women, Combative Men?' Femininity, Masculinity and Ethnicity on Strike in Two Southern Ontario Towns, 1964–1966," *Labour/Le Travail* 39 [1997]: 125–58). During the lengthy strike at the Lanark auto parts plant in 1964, some women did cross the picket lines; most did not. Yet most Italian workers demonstrated only weak support for unionization. For Ventresca, the union focused on "class struggle," not gender (p. 141). More research will be necessary to understand the "structural and cultural constraints which have historically conditioned labour militancy" (p. 142).

Ester Reiter sees industrial unions as having functioned traditionally as protectors of male privilege. Yet during the strike against Lanark, a plant whose workers had been recently organized by the UE, the union gave "strong support" to women workers even though it knew that its chances of winning were slight ("First-Class Workers Don't Want Second-Class Wages: The Lanark Strike in Dunnville," in Joy Parr, ed., *A Diversity of Women: Ontario, 1945–1980* [Toronto: University of Toronto Press, 1995], p. 170). Reiter argues that working men's class interests led them in some cases to support women's struggles. In the case of the strike at Lanark, both the UE and the UAW were engaged in a bitter struggle against a rival union that had been ousted from the Lanark plant by the UE. The UE and the UAW supported the Lanark

(continued)

workers, mostly women, because of union interests, not because, or in spite of the fact that, most of the workers were women. Yet, although labour leaders called for solidarity for Lanark workers, they also called on strong men to defend their weaker sisters and daughters. "Their energies in this strike were directed against their unfair treatment as workers, rather than the particular injustices they suffered as women workers" (p. 194).

Research on the situation of women within postwar unions is only beginning. Many other case studies will have to be carried out on different aspects of the question before it will be possible to reach general conclusions.

accounted for just 7 percent of doctors, 3 percent of lawyers, and a mere 1 percent of engineers.

For female workers, inequality abounded. Men generally received higher wages for performing the same tasks. At BC Electric, for example, the wage differential between higher-paid men and lower-paid women in the same job group averaged 17 percent during the 1950s and 1960s. Universities paid female professors less than male professors of the same rank and experience. Nor did women have equal opportunity for promotions, even in female-dominated sectors such as teaching. Across Canada, men had a far greater chance of becoming school principals. Minimum wage rates, fixed by governments, were usually lower for women than for men. Wage parity (equal pay for performing the same task) was only beginning to be an issue when Ontario's Female Employees Fair Remuneration Act was passed in 1951. Though the legislation had obvious political value, historian Shirley Tillotson's research shows that it had little tangible effect; the opposition CCF Status of Women Committee called it "a toothless ghost of a real equal pay bill."[14]

Churches such as the United Church of Canada placed numerous obstacles in the paths of women seeking to become ordained ministers. United Church moderator James Mutchmor gave Lois Wilson, a minister's wife, reasons for objecting to her ordination: who would "wear the pants" in the family? Who would have priority in the use of the car? Wilson succeeded in gaining ordination because prominent men supported her. She later became the United Church's first woman moderator.

Only a few women held positions of influence in business or politics in the 1950s. Between 1930 and 1960, the federal government named only seven women senators, while more than 250 men received the coveted lifetime appointment. Few women ran in elections. Those who did generally ran as their party's sacrificial lambs in impossible races. Only in 1957 did a prime minister, John Diefenbaker, appoint a woman to a federal cabinet post — Ellen Fairclough, from Hamilton, Ontario. Fully aware of widespread discriminatory behaviour against women, Fairclough was determined not to let herself be co-opted as an "honorary man." Many observers saw this nomination as only a modest beginning. Charlotte Whitton, Ottawa's feisty mayor, predicted that women were growing so impatient with "the man-made messes of a man-made world" that they would soon insist on a much larger voice in public affairs.

THE BABY BOOM

With good times, a higher proportion of young adults married. They also married earlier — age 22 for women, a little older for men. As Mary Louise Adams explains, "Marriage was a legitimate avenue of sexual expression for those men and women who felt caught between the incitement to sex in the culture at large and the proscriptions against their own engagement in it. Early marriage was one way to bring changes in sexual behaviour into line with the established moral order."[15]

As Canadian women began, on an impressive scale, to have children, a veritable "baby boom" set in. By 1947, the birth rate had increased to nearly 29 per thousand, and the average family had three or four children. This relatively large contingent of youth, which some demographers have described as the "pig in the python," has had enormous repercussions on Canadian society. The precise nature of the impact would alter with time, as the baby boomers went through childhood, adolescence, young adulthood, and middle age. The baby boom led to a rapid increase in Canada's population. During the 1950s, births exceeded deaths by 3 million. Including immigration, the annual growth rate exceeded 3 percent, equivalent to that experienced by many developing countries today.

HIGHER EDUCATION

Few Canadians attended colleges or universities in the 1950s. In 1951, Canada's institutions of higher learning had only 60 000 students, barely 4 percent of the eligible age group. Only about one university student in four was a woman. Most female students enrolled in programs in education or the liberal arts; few entered the sciences or the professional schools. In Quebec, until 1960, the provincial government denied classical colleges for women the state funds that were made available to all-male colleges. Religious authorities encouraged Quebec women to attend "family institutes," nicknamed "schools of happiness," where they would learn to take up the challenges of life in the home. In Toronto, the elite University of Toronto Schools (whose graduates almost all went on to university) admitted no women, even though it was largely state-supported.

WEB LINKS

In 1951, the Royal Commission on National Development in the Arts, Letters and Sciences, chaired by Vincent Massey, declared that Canadian universities faced "a financial crisis so great as to threaten their future usefulness." It recommended direct federal financial support. Then, as the first of the baby boom generation reached high school in 1956, the National Council of Canadian Universities warned that enrolments would soon dramatically increase. The Soviet launching of *Sputnik*, the first space satellite, in 1957, proved an unforeseen boon to Canadian universities. The fear of Soviet scientific superiority convinced many Canadians that governments should invest much more in higher education. Provincial authorities loosened the purse strings and the federal government instituted a system of grants. Facilities for higher education expanded, as several new universities came into being in the late 1950s.

Zoologist William Rowan lecturing at the University of Alberta, Edmonton, before 1957. Beginning in the 1960s, class sizes would expand to the bursting point with the arrival of the baby boomers at the universities.

University of Alberta Archives/
Acc. 82-29-37.

CULTURE: CANADIAN VERSUS AMERICAN

In the postwar era, Canadian nationalists increasingly felt the dangers of dependence upon American culture. Reduced funding for the Canadian Broadcasting Corporation (CBC) threatened to undermine public broadcasting. Private broadcasters, who wished to offer more American-produced commercial programming, resented the CBC's regulatory role. The federal government also reduced the National Film Board's budget after the war, and private filmmakers sought to obtain its work. Institutions such as the Public Archives of Canada and the National Museum of Canada suffered from lack of co-ordination, while the country still had no national library. After three-quarters of a century, the National Gallery of Canada still remained in borrowed space.

Cultural associations that enjoyed strong cabinet support convinced the government to establish the Massey Commission. As historian Paul Litt has shown, these associations influenced the commission to obtain the recommendations they wanted.[16] The commissioners agreed that the CBC should retain its supervisory powers over broadcasting. In 1959, however, the Conservative government created instead an independent regulatory body for broadcasting, the Board of Broadcast Governors.

WEB LINKS

The Massey Commission in 1951 had recommended the establishment of a national arts-funding body, one free of partisan and bureaucratic control. Finally, six years later, the Liberals founded the Canada Council. It used its endowment to help a multitude of arts organizations, among them ballet companies, theatre troupes (including the Stratford Shakespearean Festival), and orchestras. The council also gave grants to writers and scholarships to graduate students. Critics denounced what they viewed as extravagant expenditures, financed by ordinary folk to support long-hair, highbrow misfits and freeloaders.

POPULAR CULTURE

Prosperity enabled many Canadians to spend lavishly on entertainment. They purchased new long-playing records (LPs), often of poor quality and, in terms of current wages, at high cost. In the late 1940s, they flocked to the movie theatres that had

Television broadcaster René Lévesque interviews Lester Pearson, Canada's minister of external affairs, outside the Canadian embassy in Moscow, in 1955, for his popular current affairs program, Point de mire, *aired on French-language Radio Canada.*

....

Soviet/National Archives of Canada/ PA-117617.

proliferated. The real revolution in the entertainment industry, however, came in the early 1950s with television. Canadians living close to the American border rushed to buy television sets with the standard ten-inch black-and-white screen, at first a status symbol because of the relatively high cost. By 1952, Canada's own television broadcasting began in Toronto and Montreal. It quickly expanded to other cities. The CBC and the French-language Radio Canada aired many news programs, including René Lévesque's current affairs program, "Point de mire." Canadian public broadcasting also presented numerous cultural programs, which had a small, but influential, audience.

The advent of television increased popular interest in sport. Armchair spectators marvelled at the exploits of the Edmonton Eskimos' football dynasty. Watching "La Soirée du hockey," or "Hockey Night in Canada," became a popular pastime on Saturday night. Fans avidly discussed the feats of Syl Apps, Maurice "The Rocket" Richard, and Gordie Howe, and celebrated the Stanley Cup triumphs of the Toronto Maple Leafs in the late 1940s and of the Montreal Canadiens in the late 1950s. From 1942 to 1967, the National Hockey League (NHL) remained a stable six-team league. The NHL made numerous changes to make television viewing easier. It had ice surfaces painted white and lighting improved, and it dressed on-ice officials in striped jerseys.

Canadian performances in international sport brought much less satisfaction. Not only did Canadian players suffer ignominious defeats in world and Olympic hockey, they also attracted attention for boorish behaviour. As one sports writer put it bluntly, Canadians on the ice were "ruthless hooligans" who "hit anything that moved."

English-speaking Canadians enjoyed newspaper supplements like the *Star Weekly* and *Weekend*, while French Canadians read a variety of tabloid newspapers. By the end of the 1950s, however, American mass-circulation magazines, among them *Time*, *Reader's Digest*, and its French edition, *Sélection du Reader's Digest*, accounted for 75 percent of the Canadian general-interest magazine market.

Most movies were American made, though some came from Britain or, in the case of the Quebec market, from France. The Canadian National Exhibition in Toronto always imported American talent, such as Danny Kaye or Jimmy Durante, as the major attractions for its grandstand shows. The Calgary Stampede also invited American celebrities like Bing Crosby, Walt Disney, and Bob Hope to serve as parade marshals.

Although the CBC presented Canadian variety shows such as *Showtime*, which featured dance, song, music, and comedy, it also imported popular American variety shows to boost its ratings and increase its commercial revenues. On Sunday evenings, millions of Canadians loyally watched the most famous and longest-lasting of these, *The Ed Sullivan Show*. Sullivan introduced Elvis Presley and his hip gyrations to Canadians in September 1956. He also boosted the fortunes of Canadian comedians Johnny Wayne and Frank Shuster. Both CBC and private television imported popular American comedies such as *I Love Lucy* and *The Jackie Gleason Show*, and presented contemporary American singers like Perry Como and Dinah Shore. Baby-boom children watched Roy Rogers, Lassie, and Walt Disney programs.

French-language television had more local content. While it beamed a French-speaking *Hopalong Cassidy* and many other programs dubbed in French into Quebec living rooms and kitchens, it also carried original productions, such as the Wednesday-night series adapted from novelist Roger Lemelin's *La famille Plouffe*. The CBC's very successful variety show, *Music Hall*, produced in Montreal, featured French-speaking stars such as Monique Leyrac, Edith Piaf, Maurice Chevalier, and Charles Aznavour. By 1957, television production in Montreal, historian Susan Mann Trofimenkoff writes, was "third in the world to New York and Hollywood and second to none in French."[17]

ENGLISH-CANADIAN LITERATURE

Canadian literature in both languages came into its own in the post–World War II era. In Montreal, Hugh MacLennan published his celebrated novel *Two Solitudes*, with its theme that Canada's two major linguistic communities needed to demonstrate more mutual tolerance. In Vancouver, Earl Birney, a professor of English at the University of British Columbia and part of a new generation of Canadian poets, published his collection of poems, *Now Is Time*. In *The Mountain and the Valley*, Ernest Buckler examined the dilemma faced by a brilliant and ambitious Nova Scotia boy who found his creativity stifled by his deep attachment to rural life. W.O. Mitchell, in *Who Has Seen the Wind*, interpreted the struggles of a small-town Saskatchewan boy at the time of the depression. Throughout the 1950s, Mitchell produced his highly successful "Jake and the Kid" stories for magazine and radio.

Mordecai Richler's *The Apprenticeship of Duddy Kravitz*, a portrait of a young Montreal Jewish entrepreneur, established the Montreal author as a successful novelist. Adele Wiseman's first novel, *The Sacrifice*, was strongly influenced by the experiences of her Russian-Jewish parents. In 1951, Morley Callaghan's highly acclaimed *The Loved and the Lost*, set in Montreal, appeared. Robertson Davies gained early recognition as an essayist and brilliant novelist. Poet Dorothy Livesay won Governor General's awards for *Day and Night*, in 1944, and *Poems for Peace*, in 1947, while the versatile and flamboyant Irving Layton produced numerous volumes of love poems and prose.

FRENCH-CANADIAN LITERATURE

At the same time, an "aesthetic thaw" came slowly to Quebec. In *Refus global*, a manifesto written in 1948, Paul-Émile Borduas condemned Quebec's asphyxiating orthodoxy. The artist's cry for the right to total freedom of expression cost him his teaching job at the École du Meuble in Montreal. He left first for New York, then later settled in Paris. Novelists cast aside traditional themes of religion and rurality. Some, such as Roger Lemelin in *Au pied de la pente douce*, used urban working-class settings. Others, such as Anne Hébert in *Le Torrent* and André Langevin in *Poussière sur la ville*, forcefully portrayed personal dramas. Yves Thériault won international fame with *Agaguk*, a novel about the Inuit. Professional theatre troupes proliferated, with some of their repertories supplied by Quebec playwrights. The play *Tit-Coq*, by Gratien Gélinas, encountered spectacular success. The film that followed attracted 300 000 spectators. Quebec culture seemed to have attained new vibrancy, despite the province's tiny market and few public libraries and bookstores.

Canadians generally continued to cherish conservative values. Books were often censored, particularly when they described sex scenes too explicitly. Censorship in all provinces regulated the movies Canadians saw. The British Columbia Moving Pictures Act, for example, outlawed films "considered injurious to morals or against public welfare, or which may offer evil suggestions to the minds of children." Alberta's censors watched carefully for "any materialistic, undemocratic, un-Christian propaganda disguised as entertainment." Sometimes the cuts produced films probably more objectionable than the original version. One Quebec film featured a scene in which a married man obtained a divorce so that he could pursue a love affair with his girl-friend. The censors in this still very Catholic province cut out the divorce scene — and the couple thus appeared to go on living happily ever after in unwedded bliss!

RELIGION

Religion "stands out as one of the great gulfs" separating the 1950s from today, writes historian Doug Owram.[18] In that period, the majority of Canadians still attended church or the synagogue regularly. Indeed, a higher proportion of Canadian Protestants belonged to churches and enrolled their children in Sunday schools than had done so in the 1930s. Religion was present in most schools across the country, even in so-called public schools. Pious Quebeckers knelt around the radio after supper for the "Family Rosary" and read the *Annales de Sainte-Anne* or other religious material. Nevertheless, the influence of religion often appeared superficial. Possibly, religious practice was linked more to socialization than to faith. The *United Church Observer* frequently bemoaned the limited commitment of many adherents. Presumably church-going Quebeckers bought a million copies each weekend of sex-and-crime tabloids like *Allo Police*, which flourished in spite of — and possibly because of — the opposition of the Roman Catholic church.

The quiet Sundays of English-speaking Canada also came under attack. It was said that in Toronto one could harmlessly fire a cannon ball down Yonge Street on a Sunday, and the local press editorialized in favour of the maintenance of Toronto's "typically Canadian" Sunday. But the citizens of "Toronto the Good" voted in favour of Sunday sports in a plebiscite and, in December 1951, elected as their mayor Allan Lamport, a churchgoer who had pledged to make it possible to watch double-headers on Sundays at Maple Leaf Stadium. Across English-speaking Canada, provincial drinking restrictions that determined who could drink, where they could drink, and under what conditions, were increasingly challenged.

Loggers listening to Mass on the radio at a camp at Lac Long, Quebec, 1948.

Malak/National Archives of Canada/ PA-144679.

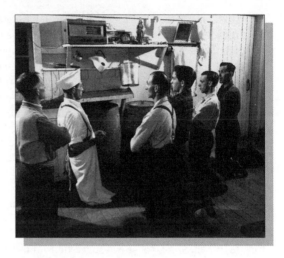

In the late 1940s and the 1950s, Canadian consumers had more money to spend and new products to spend it on. Workers in most regions of the country easily found jobs, and pay scales increased substantially. Governments went about the task of managing economic growth. For a time, Canada's postwar prosperity camouflaged the poverty and inequalities that remained the lot of many Canadians, in spite of the appearance of several new social programs. When, by the late 1950s, the postwar boom appeared to have run its course, new tensions emerged in society. Canadians now seemed to believe that it was time for a change.

NOTES

1. B.W. Muirhead, "Canada, the United States, and the GATT Review Session, 1954–55: A Clash of Perceptions," *Canadian Historical Review* 73 (1992): 506.
2. David G. Alexander, *Atlantic Canada and Confederation: Essays in Canadian Political Economy* (Toronto: University of Toronto Press, 1983), p. 32.
3. Peter Neary, *Newfoundland in the North Atlantic World, 1929–1949* (Montreal/Kingston: McGill-Queen's University Press, 1988), p. 359.
4. Raymond Blake, *Canadians at Last: Canada Integrates Newfoundland as a Province* (Toronto: University of Toronto Press, 1994), p. 6.
5. James Struthers, *The Limits of Affluence: Welfare in Ontario, 1920–1970* (Toronto: University of Toronto Press, 1994), p. 180.
6. J.F. Hilliker, "No Bread at the Peace Table: Canada and the European Settlement, 1943–7," *Canadian Historical Review* 51 (1980): 69–86.
7. John W. Holmes, *The Shaping of Peace: Canada and the Search for World Order, 1943–1957*, vol. 2 (Toronto: University of Toronto Press, 1982), p. 36.
8. J.L. Granatstein, *How Britain's Weakness Forced Canada into the Arms of the United States* (Toronto: University of Toronto Press, 1989), p. 3.
9. David J. Bercuson, "Canada, NATO, and Rearmament, 1950–1954: Why Canada Made a Difference (But Not For Very Long)," in John English and Norman Hillmer, eds., *Making a Difference? Canada's Foreign Policy in a Changing World Order* (Toronto: Lester, 1992), p. 104.

10. John English, *The Worldly Years: The Life of Lester Pearson*, vol. II, *1949–1972* (Toronto: Knopf Canada, 1992), p. 145.

11. J.-C. Falardeau, *Bulletin des Relations industrielles* 4 (1949), quoted in Fraser Isbester, "Asbestos 1949," in Irving Abella, ed., *On Strike: Six Key Labour Struggles in Canada, 1919–1949* (Toronto: James, Lewis & Samuel Publishers, 1974), p. 163.

12. Bryan D. Palmer, *Working-Class Experience: Rethinking the History of Canadian Labour, 1800–1991*, 2nd ed. (Toronto: McClelland & Stewart, 1992), p. 299.

13. Irving Abella, *Nationalism, Communism, and Canadian Labour: The CIO, the Communist Party, and the Canadian Congress of Labour, 1935–1956* (Toronto: University of Toronto Press, 1973), p. 221.

14. Shirley Tillotson, "Human Rights Law as Prism: Women's Organizations, Unions, and Ontario's Female Employees Fair Remuneration Act, 1951," *Canadian Historical Review* 72 (1991): 532–57.

15. Mary Louise Adams, *The Trouble with Normal: Postwar Youth and the Making of Heterosexuality* (Toronto: University of Toronto Press, 1997), pp. 105–106.

16. Paul Litt, *The Muses, the Masses, and the Massey Commission* (Toronto: University of Toronto Press, 1992).

17. Susan Mann Trofimenkoff, *The Dream of Nation: A Social and Intellectual History of Quebec* (Toronto: Gage, 1983), p. 284.

18. Doug Owram, *Born at the Right Time: A History of the Baby-Boom Generation* (Toronto: University of Toronto Press, 1996), p. 103.

LINKING TO THE PAST

WEB LINKS

Louis St. Laurent

http://cnet.unb.ca/achn/pme/lsslcb.htm

A brief biography of Louis Stephen St. Laurent, with details about his background and career. A more descriptive biography can be accessed at the bottom of the page.

The Newfoundland Act, 1949

http://www.geocities.com/Yosemite/Rapids/3330/constitution/1949ntu.htm

The full text of the Newfoundland Act of 1949, which made Newfoundland Canada's tenth province.

The Inuit Resettlement Project, 1953

http://www.carc.org/pubs/v19no1/2.htm

This essay, "A Case of Compounded Error: The Inuit Resettlement Project, 1953, and the Government Response, 1990," by Shelagh D. Grant (published by the Canadian Arctic Resources Committee) evaluates the government's 1953 decision to relocate seven Inuit families and the aftermath of this decision.

John Diefenbaker

http://diefenbaker.ottawa.com

This site about Canada's thirteenth prime minister features a wealth of information on Diefenbaker, including a brief biography, famous quotations, photographs and sound bites, articles and excerpts from books, and much more.

The Massey Commission

http://www.nlc-bnc.ca/massey/emassey.htm

Full text of the report submitted by the Royal Commission on National Development in the Arts, Letters and Sciences (the Massey Commission), courtesy of the National Library of Canada.

The Canada Council
http://canada.justice.gc.ca/STABLE/EN/Laws/Chap/C/C-2.html
The full text of the Canada Council Act, from the Department of Justice. To find out more about what the Canada Council for the Arts does, visit http://www.canadacouncil.ca/about/about.htm.

RELATED READINGS

Two essays in R. Douglas Francis and Donald B. Smith, eds., *Readings in Canadian History: Post-Confederation*, 5th ed. (Toronto: Harcourt Brace, 1998), pertain to topics in this chapter: Veronica Strong-Boag, "Home Dreams: Women and the Suburban Experiment in Canada, 1945–60," pp. 417–42; and John Herd Thompson, "Canada's Quest for Cultural Sovereignty: Protection, Promotion, and Popular Culture," pp. 442–55.

BIBLIOGRAPHY

A good general study of this period is Robert Bothwell, Ian Drummond, and John English, *Canada since 1945: Power, Politics, and Provincialism*, rev. ed. (Toronto: University of Toronto Press, 1989). Social history receives better treatment in Alvin Finkel, *Our Lives: Canada after 1945* (Toronto: James Lorimer, 1997). Doug Owram, *Born at the Right Time: A History of the Baby-Boom Generation* (Toronto: University of Toronto Press, 1996), is a captivating story. Material on economic development may be found in Kenneth Norrie and Douglas Owram, *A History of the Canadian Economy*, 2nd ed. (Toronto: Harcourt Brace, 1996).

Aspects of the welfare state are discussed by James Struthers in a book, *The Limits of Affluence: Welfare in Ontario, 1920–1970* (Toronto: University of Toronto Press, 1994), as well as in two articles, "Shadows from the Thirties: The Federal Government and Unemployment Assistance, 1941–1956," in Jacqueline S. Ismael, ed., *The Canadian Welfare State: Evolution and Transition* (Edmonton: University of Alberta Press, 1987), pp. 3–32; and "Building a Culture of Retirement: Class, Politics and Pensions in Post–World War II Ontario," *Journal of the Canadian Historical Association* 8 (1997): 259–82. Jane Ursel, *Private Lives: 100 Years of State Intervention in the Family* (Toronto: Women's Press, 1992), contains a particularly interesting chapter on the establishment of family allowances. See also Gale Wills, *A Marriage of Convenience: Business and Social Work in Toronto, 1918–1957* (Toronto: University of Toronto Press, 1995); Shirley Tillotson, "Citizen Participation in the Welfare State: An Experiment, 1945–57," *Canadian Historical Review* 75 (1994): 511–42; and Alvin Finkel, "Even the Little Children Cooperated: Family Strategies, Child-care Discourse, and Social Welfare Debates 1945–1975," *Labour/Le Travail* 36 (1995): 91–118. The Quebec experience is discussed in Dominique Marshall, "The Language of Children's Rights, the Formation of the Welfare State, and the Democratic Experience of Poor Families in Quebec, 1940–55," *Canadian Historical Review* 78 (1997): 409–41. Housing is studied in John R. Miron, *Housing in Postwar Canada: Demographic Change, Household Formation, and Housing Demand* (Montreal/Kingston: McGill-Queen's University Press, 1988).

Among the works on prime ministers see Dale C. Thomson, *Louis St. Laurent, Canadian* (Toronto: Macmillan, 1967); Peter Newman's very critical *Renegade in Power: The Diefenbaker Years*, rev. ed. (Toronto: McClelland & Stewart, 1989); and Denis Smith, *Rogue Tory: The Life and Legend of John G. Diefenbaker* (Toronto: Macfarlane Walter & Ross, 1995). On the "Minister of Everything" consult Robert Bothwell and William Kilbourn,

C.D. Howe: A Biography (Toronto: McClelland & Stewart, 1979). J.M. Beck, *Pendulum of Power: Canada's Federal Elections* (Scarborough, ON: Prentice-Hall, 1968), is also useful. Reginald Whitaker looks critically at the Liberals in *The Government Party: Organizing and Financing the Liberal Party of Canada, 1930–58* (Toronto: University of Toronto Press, 1977). Walter D. Young studies the CCF in *The Anatomy of a Party: The National CCF 1932–61* (Toronto: University of Toronto Press, 1969). J.L. Granatstein examines the role of federal bureaucrats in *The Ottawa Men: The Civil Service Mandarins, 1935–57* (Toronto: University of Toronto Press, 1998), while Patrick H. Brennan looks at newspaper editors' support for the Liberals in *Reporting the Nation's Business: Press-Government Relations during the Liberal Years, 1935–1957* (Toronto: University of Toronto Press, 1993).

Three books study Newfoundland's entry into Confederation: David MacKenzie, *Inside the Atlantic Triangle: Canada and the Entrance of Newfoundland into Confederation, 1939–1949* (Toronto: University of Toronto Press, 1986); Peter Neary, *Newfoundland in the North Atlantic World, 1929–1949* (Montreal/Kingston: McGill-Queen's University Press, 1988); and Raymond B. Blake, *Canadians at Last: Canada Integrates Newfoundland as a Province* (Toronto: University of Toronto Press, 1994). On one aspect of Ontario provincial politics see Dan Azoulay, *Keeping the Dream Alive: The Survival of the Ontario CCF/NDP, 1950–1963* (Montreal/Kingston: McGill-Queen's University Press, 1997).

On Canadian foreign policy of the late 1940s and 1950s see James Eayrs, *In Defence of Canada: Growing Up Allied* (Toronto: University of Toronto Press, 1980); Denis Smith, *Diplomacy of Fear: Canada and the Cold War, 1941–1948* (Toronto: University of Toronto Press, 1988); and John Hilliker and Donald Barry, *Canada's Department of External Affairs. II: Coming of Age, 1946–1968* (Montreal/Kingston: McGill-Queen's University Press, 1995). In *Pragmatic Idealism: Canadian Foreign Policy, 1945–1995* (Montreal/Kingston: McGill-Queen's University Press, 1998), Costas Melakopides looks at Canada's involvement in peacekeeping, arms control, and human rights. Contemporary accounts by members of the Canadian foreign service include Escott Reid, *Radical Mandarin: The Memoirs of Escott Reid* (Toronto: University of Toronto Press, 1989); and John W. Holmes, *The Shaping of Peace: Canada and the Search for World Order, 1943–1957*, 2 vols. (Toronto: University of Toronto Press, 1979, 1982). Aspects of the Korean War are covered in Denis Stairs, *The Diplomacy of Constraint: Canada, the Korean War, and the United States* (Toronto: University of Toronto Press, 1974); and Robert S. Prince, "The Limits of Constraint: Canadian–American Relations and the Korean War, 1950–51," *Journal of Canadian Studies* 27 (1992–93): 129–52. Joseph Levitt examines Canada's role as a "junior partner" in arms-control talks in *Pearson and Canada's Role in Nuclear Disarmament and Arms Control Negotiations, 1945–1957* (Montreal/Kingston: McGill-Queen's University Press, 1993). Relations with Israel are studied in Zachariah Kay, *The Diplomacy of Prudence: Canada and Israel, 1848–1958* (Montreal/Kingston: McGill-Queen's University Press, 1996). Postwar Canadian–American relations are discussed in R.D. Cuff and J.L. Granatstein, *Ties That Bind: Canadian–American Relations in Wartime from the Great War to the Cold War* (Toronto: Samuel Stevens Hakkert, 1977), and in their *American Dollars/Canadian Prosperity: Canadian–American Economic Relations, 1945–50* (Toronto: Samuel Stevens Hakkert, 1978). Lawrence Aronsen looks at American investment in Canada in "An Open Door to the North: The Liberal Government and the Expansion of American Foreign Investment, 1945–1953," *American Review of Canadian Studies* 22 (1992): 167–97. Also on trade policy see B.W. Muirhead, *The Development of Postwar Canadian Trade Policy: The Failure of the Anglo-European Option* (Montreal/Kingston: McGill-Queen's University Press, 1992).

For relations in the defence sector see Joseph T. Jockel's study, *No Boundaries Upstairs: Canada, the United States and the Origins of North American Air Defence, 1945–1958* (Vancouver: University of British Columbia Press, 1987); Shelagh D. Grant, *Sovereignty or*

Security: Government Policy in the Canadian North, 1936–1950 (Vancouver: University of British Columbia Press, 1988); and Craig Stewart, *Shutting Down the National Dream: Avro and the Tragedy of the Arrow* (Toronto: McGraw-Hill Ryerson, 1988). Espionage is examined in J.L. Granatstein and David Stafford, *Spy Wars: Espionage in Canada from Gouzenko to Glasnost* (Toronto: Key Porter, 1990). Security vetting is discussed in Larry Hannant, *The Infernal Machine: Investigating the Loyalty of Canada's Citizens* (Toronto: University of Toronto Press, 1995). See also Reg Whitaker and Gary Marcuse, *Cold War Canada: The Making of a National Insecurity State, 1945–1957* (Toronto: University of Toronto Press, 1994).

A general synthesis of union activity in the postwar years is available in Bryan D. Palmer, *Working Class Experience: Rethinking the History of Canadian Labour, 1800–1991*, 2nd ed. (Toronto: McClelland & Stewart, 1992), chapter 6. On particular aspects of union life consult Gad Horowitz, *Canadian Labour in Politics* (Toronto: University of Toronto Press, 1968); Irving Martin Abella, *Nationalism, Communism, and Canadian Labour* (Toronto: University of Toronto Press, 1973); and Irving Abella, ed., *On Strike: Six Key Labour Struggles in Canada, 1919–1949* (Toronto: James, Lewis & Samuel, 1974). William Kaplan chronicles Maritime labour strife in *Everything That Floats: Pat Sullivan, Hal Banks, and the Seamen's Unions of Canada* (Toronto: University of Toronto Press, 1987). Doug Smith presents the biography of a communist union leader in *Cold Warrior: C.S. Jackson and the United Electrical Workers* (St. John's: Canadian Committee on Labour History, 1997). On the history of the Canadian Autoworkers see Charlotte Yates, *From Plant to Politics: The Autoworkers Union in Postwar Canada* (Philadelphia: Temple University Press, 1993). On labour–capital relations, consult Don Wells, "The Impact of the Postwar Compromise on Canadian Unionism: The Formation of an Auto Worker Local in the 1950s," *Labour/Le Travail* 36 (1995): 147–74.

Two excellent general syntheses of women's history exist: Micheline Dumont et al., *Quebec Women: A History* (Toronto: Women's Press, 1987); and Alison Prentice et al., *Canadian Women: A History*, 2nd ed. (Toronto: Harcourt Brace, 1996). Patricia T. Rooke and R.L. Schnell, *No Bleeding Heart: Charlotte Whitton, A Feminist on the Right* (Vancouver: University of British Columbia Press, 1987), examines the career of one famous individual. Dan Azoulay studies women in left-wing politics in an article "Winning Women for Socialism: The Ontario CCF and Women, 1947–1961," *Labour/Le Travail* 36 (1995): 59–90. Gillian Creese looks at the question of equal pay in "Power and Pay: The Union and Equal Pay at B.C. Electric/Hydro," *Labour/Le Travail* 32 (1993): 225–45. On relations between the sexes on public transit, see Donald F. Davis and Barbara Lorenzkowski, "A Platform for Gender Tensions: Women Working and Riding on Canadian Urban Public Transit in the 1940s," *Canadian Historical Review* 79 (1998): 431–65. The issue of female clergy is addressed in Valerie J. Korinek, "No Women Need Apply: The Ordination of Women in the United Church, 1918–65," *Canadian Historical Review* 74 (1993): 473–509. Discrimination against women in unemployment insurance is described in Ann Porter, "Women and Income Security in the Post-War Period: The Case of Unemployment Insurance, 1945–1962," *Labour/Le Travail* 31 (1993): 111–44. Veronica Strong-Boag examines the life of suburban women in "Home Dreams: Women and the Suburban Experiment in Canada, 1945–60," *Canadian Historical Review* 72 (1991): 471–504. See also her article, "Wage-Earning Wives and the Construction of the Middle Class, 1945–60," *Journal of Canadian Studies* 29 (1994): 5–25. Several essays on aspects of women's life in Ontario in this period may be found in Joy Parr, ed., *A Diversity of Women: Ontario, 1945–1980* (Toronto: University of Toronto Press, 1995). Joan Sangster studies working women in Peterborough, Ontario in *Earning Respect: The Lives of Working Women in Small-Town Ontario, 1920–1960* (Toronto: University of Toronto Press, 1995).

On heterosexuality and homosexuality, see Mary Louise Adams, *The Trouble with Normal: Postwar Youth and the Making of Heterosexuality* (Toronto: University of Toronto Press, 1997); and Gary Kinsman, *The Regulation of Desire: Sexuality in Canada* (Montreal: Black Rose Books, 1987). Two articles study the campaign against homosexuals in the civil service: Gary Kinsman, "'Character Weaknesses' and 'Fruit Machines': Towards an Analysis of the Anti-Homosexual Security Campaign in the Canadian Civil Service," *Labour/Le Travail* 35 (1995): 133–61; and Daniel J. Robinson and David Kimmel, "The Queer Career of Homosexual Security Vetting in Cold War Canada," *Canadian Historical Review* 75 (1994): 319–45. William Kaplan recounts the struggle for rights of the Jehovah's Witnesses in *State and Salvation: The Jehovah's Witnesses and Their Fight for Civil Rights* (Toronto: University of Toronto Press, 1989). The role of religion at the University of Toronto is discussed in Catherine Gidney, "Poisoning the Student Mind? The Student Christian Movement at the University of Toronto, 1920–1965," *Journal of the Canadian Historical Association* 8 (1997): 147–63. Paul Litt tells the story of the Massey Commission in *The Muses, the Masses, and the Massey Commission* (Toronto: University of Toronto Press, 1992). Paul Rutherford looks at television fare in *When Television Was Young: Primetime Canada 1952–1967* (Toronto: University of Toronto Press, 1990).

Useful maps and charts on Canada in the World War II and postwar period appear in Donald Kerr and Deryck W. Holdsworth, eds., *Historical Atlas of Canada*, vol. 3, *Addressing the Twentieth Century, 1891–1961* (Toronto: University of Toronto Press, 1990).

CHAPTER FIFTEEN

An Era of Change: The 1960s

Canada experienced profound social and cultural upheavals in the 1960s. Young people, in particular, challenged authority. "A new student class has emerged, aware of its power, ready to act," *Maclean's* proclaimed in November 1967. The universities became centres of protest as demonstrations occurred on campuses. Youth began to reject traditional social and cultural values, and sexual taboos weakened.

Other groups as well wanted to be heard. Women questioned the inequalities of their condition. Labour became more militant in its attacks on the business "establishment." French-speaking Canadians sought linguistic rights that would place them on an equal footing with English-speaking Canadians. An important minority in Quebec believed that only independence could ensure real equality. English-speaking Canadian nationalists denounced the powerful American presence in most aspects of Canadian life. A Native resurgence began in reaction to fears of assimilation and an end to special status. No longer could a small group of middle-aged and elderly men, primarily of British origin, rule Canada politically. New interest groups had entered the political forum. For many observers, diversity had now triumphed over unity within Canada.

The economic stability of the postwar years ended in the 1960s. As the decade opened, Canada faced the highest unemployment levels since the Great Depression. Although prosperity returned, inflation became a new problem in the late 1960s. Economic difficulties led to social problems. Canadians demanded that their governments at all levels intervene more actively to find solutions.

The political stability of the postwar years also disappeared in the 1960s; indeed, minority governments ruled the country for much of the decade. Canadians sought new leaders, but tired of them rapidly when they failed to deliver what was expected of them.

REVOLT AND PROTEST

Canadian society in the 1960s became even more secular. In Quebec, the influence of the Roman Catholic church waned as that institution largely abandoned to the state its historic role in education and in social institutions and as church attendance declined. Many clergy left the orders, and new recruitment fell rapidly.

Elsewhere in Canada, the major Protestant denominations also lost ground. Sunday school attendance in the Protestant churches fell precipitously. In his book *The Comfortable Pew*, author Pierre Berton attacked the churches for their lack of relevance, as they vainly attempted to combat the supporters of beer parlours, Sunday movies, and Sunday sports. Rev. James Mutchmor, the head of the United Church's board of evangelism and social service and later moderator of the church, outspokenly denounced the new trends. The "voice against vice" became the most-quoted cleric in Canada in the mid-1960s. Mutchmor's critics mocked: "Let's have much less of Mutchmor!"

As churches attempted to come to terms with change, their congregations often represented a wide spectrum of opinion. Liberal Roman Catholics applauded the decisions of the Vatican II Council, which modernized certain religious practices; more conservative adherents feared the loss of essentials to the faith. Many Protestants who felt that the traditional denominations had become too liberal joined conservative fundamentalist groups such as the Pentecostals, which grew prodigiously. By the late 1960s, a wide variety of sects and cults attracted Canadians.

Much of the revolt against established social and cultural patterns was superficial. High school boys put away their hair oil and let their hair grow, while their mothers remonstrated with them in vain and barbers lost business. "Flower children" dressed in fringes and beads and displayed psychedelic colours. Blue jeans became the uniform of a generation. Speaking of hair styles and clothing fashions, one Montreal high school principal complained, "These eccentric habits are meant to distract the attention of other students and that's exactly what we don't want." College students and non-students began to sport moustaches, sideburns, and beards. Youth denounced age and experience and promised to stay young. A drug culture flourished, as did sexual experimentation.

Young English-speaking Canadians empathized with the peace-and-love message of American folk singers such as Bob Dylan and Joan Baez. But Canadian folk singers, including Ian and Sylvia Tyson, Gordon Lightfoot, and Joni Mitchell, also achieved an international reputation. Orillia-born Lightfoot began his career in coffee houses and bars; as composer of such pieces as "Early Morning Rain" and "For Lovin' Me," he soon drew crowds to his performances at the Mariposa folk festival and elsewhere. As the decade advanced and interest in folk music waned, Lightfoot enlarged his public by making the transition to pop and country music.

In French Canada, young people flocked to listen to the *chansonniers* who sang, accompanied only by their guitars or the piano, in the *boîtes à chanson* that sprang up across Quebec in the early 1960s. Félix Leclerc and Raymond Lévesque pioneered this form of entertainment. At first, the lyrics dwelt on apolitical themes such as love and nature. Later, as a powerful nationalist current surged through the province, new themes bearing on the historical experience of Quebec's people and their identity dominated singers' repertoires. Gilles Vigneault, who came from a tiny hamlet on the lower north shore of the St. Lawrence River, became one of the most well-known singer-songwriters of the era — and his "Mon pays" became the anthem of a generation. The *chansonniers* soon gave way to popular singers, among whom figured a strong feminine contingent, including Ginette Reno, Renée Claude, Pauline Julien, and Monique Leyrac. Robert Charlebois's audacious creativity, evident in his recording of "Lindberg" in 1968, made him one of the most popular male performers of the era.

Popular English-Canadian folk singers Ian and Sylvia released their first album, Four Strong Winds, *in 1963. The title song of the album could be heard in coffee houses and at folk festivals across the country.*

Photograph: Moving Images and Sound Archives/National Archives of Canada/ 15682. Used by permission of the Canadian Broadcasting Corporation. Music: Copyright © 1963 Warner Bros. Inc. (Renewed). All Rights Reserved.

Many young Canadians listened avidly to rock music during the 1960s. Enthusiastically they fell victim to Beatlemania, and thousands of Canadian rock bands sprang up, usually modelled on British and American groups. But because of the popularity of foreign groups, few Canadian rock-music records appeared. Many Canadian groups that did reach the airwaves made their recordings in the United States. Canadian singers received a substantial boost in 1970, when the Canadian Radio-Television and Telecommunications Commission (CRTC) established Canadian-content rules for broadcasters.

CAMPUS UNREST

For historian Doug Owram, the 1960s constituted "the moment in history that forever defined the baby boom as a distinct generation."[1] The boomers' centres of activity were the university campuses (although the majority of boomers never went to university), which became centres of protest in the 1960s. Infused with the spirit of "peace and love," Canadian students, like American and western youth in general, picketed against the war in Vietnam and for a wide range of reformist causes. Nationalist protest took root and flourished, often tended closely by university professors. Academics in the social sciences, particularly in Toronto, prepared research studies to show the extent to which Canada had become an American colony, and proposed measures for buying or taking it back. In Quebec's universities, equal fervour was applied to proving that Quebec was a Canadian colony and to devising plans for liberating it.

| Mon pays ce n'est pas
    un pays c'est l'hiver
Mon jardin ce n'est pas
    un jardin c'est la
    plaine
Mon chemin ce n'est
    pas un chemin c'est
    la neige
Mon pays ce n'est pas
    un pays c'est l'hiver. | My country is not a
    country, it is winter
My garden is not a
    garden, it is a plain
My road is not a road,
    it is the snow
My country is not a
    country, it is winter. | *The Refrain of "Mon pays"*
....
Source: Gilles Vigneault/Éditions du
Vent qui Vire. |

University protest had political repercussions. In Quebec, where most intellectuals were strong nationalists, it contributed to bringing the language question to the floor of the National Assembly and assisted the rise of the Parti Québécois. In Ottawa, it helped Pierre Trudeau, who appeared to challenge the establishment and who brought new ideas to the fore, to win the Liberal leadership and the federal election of 1968. In addition, by 1970, the nationalist outcry from the universities caused the Liberals to question the continentalism they had espoused in the 1950s.

Students abandoned classes and occupied administrative offices, demanding more active participation in the university community and the recognition of students' rights. Their protests were all the more visible, in part, because students were now far more numerous. University enrolments doubled during the 1950s, then tripled during the 1960s and 1970s. The parents of baby boomers, many of whom had never finished high school, preached the virtues of a university degree as the key to a bright future.

HIGHER EDUCATION

Provincial governments, convinced that higher education would bring enormous economic benefits to society, dramatically increased spending on university education and established a host of new institutions. British Columbia Premier W.A.C. Bennett told the chairman of B.C. Hydro in 1963: "I want you to be the chancellor of a new university. Select a site and build it and get it going. I want it open in September 1965." As a result Simon Fraser University opened in 1965, atop Burnaby Mountain, with 2500 students. University of Alberta campuses in Calgary and Lethbridge became separate universities. Ontario set up such new universities as Laurentian, Trent, Brock, and Lakehead, as well as Erindale and Scarborough colleges, affiliated with the University of Toronto. Quebec established the public Université du Québec in Montreal with several regional affiliates. New Brunswick's francophones obtained their own university at Moncton. Regional and community colleges began operations in several provinces. The federal government, which had been making grants directly to the universities since 1951, began in 1966 to make contributions to provincial governments for the financing of postsecondary education. In all, government spending on universities increased sevenfold during the 1960s.

A Historical Portrait

THE STUDENT RADICALS AT SIR GEORGE WILLIAMS UNIVERSITY

The late 1960s saw frequent protests against virtually all aspects of the established order. The most vigorous protesters were students on college campuses, in France, in the United States, in Canada, and elsewhere. They militated for a wide variety of causes, some of which regarded the universities themselves, while others were concerned with the wider society, such as the ban-the-bomb protests and the demonstrations against the war in Vietnam. Preferred methods were strikes and occupations of buildings.

The great majority of students were not militants but rather passive spectators. Among the militants, some were ready to take extreme measures in defence of causes that appeared increasingly imprecise. The events of February 11, 1969, at Sir George Williams University (today Concordia University) in Montreal appeared to mark a watershed.

"Police rout SGWU militants; $1 million computer centre wrecked." Thus read the *Montreal Star*'s headline that day. The damage figure was revised upward the next day to $2 million, or approximately $10 million in today's dollars.

In December 1968, some students had levelled charges of racism against a biology professor at the university. In early February 1969, they occupied the Faculty Club in the nine-storey Henry Hall Building in support of their cause. At first they succeeded in generating considerable sympathy. Over time, however, the militant group, thanks to new additions, became more radical, and moderates tended to distance themselves. One prominent militant proclaimed that he didn't really care about the charges of racism against the professor. "All we want to do is burn down the university. We want the police to come, we want violence."

Militants then broke into the cafeteria on the seventh floor and hurled chairs and tables down escalators, stairwells, and elevator shafts. As police moved against the crowd, occupants turned on the fire hoses against them, then retreated to the computer centre on the ninth floor. When police attempted to evict them from the centre, militants threw computers, punch cards, tapes, and furniture onto the street, and then set fire to the centre. Outside, other students showed their antagonism to militants by shouting "Burn, burn!"

Police made 90 arrests; those arrested included 42 non-nationals, mainly from the Caribbean and from England. Thirty of those arrested were not students at Sir George Williams.

The events at Sir George Williams provoked a sharp backlash and a demand for a return to order. Although the *Montreal Star* argued that university administrations were frequently guilty of a lack of responsiveness to honest and often reasonable demands, it denounced what it termed "an indefensible act by student anarchists." When the Quebec student union, UGEQ, declared its complete support for the rioters, SGWU students quit its ranks. Acts of intimidation, disruption, and even violence were occurring at the same time on other campuses. But for historian Doug Owram, the SGWU episode, because of the degree of violence and destruction, "foreshadowed the end of the 1960s era" (*Born at the Right Time: A History of the Baby-Boom Generation* [Toronto: University of Toronto Press, 1996], p. 286).

The Montreal campus of the Université du Québec, one of the new universities that sprang up during the 1960s. To build the campus, a church and a convent were torn down. The architects integrated parts of the church's facade into the new structure. Besides this Montreal campus, the Université du Québec has a number of regional affiliates.

Université du Québec à Montréal.

As a result of their rapid growth, universities faced serious shortages of trained staff. English-speaking universities recruited heavily on American campuses. By 1968, fewer than half of the university professors in Canada were Canadians. In that same year, only one of every eight positions filled went to a Canadian. Critics accused universities of ignoring Canadian university graduates in their hiring policies. Celebrated Canadian author Hugh MacLennan, who, years earlier, had been unable to find a teaching position even with degrees from Oxford and Princeton universities, lamented that Canadian universities had embarked on a "program of national suicide." Carleton University professors Robin Mathews and James Steele, after reviewing the statistics on university hiring policies, called for the Canadianization of faculties.

GOVERNMENT INTERVENTION

Although university teachers and students were among the loudest voices calling for change, Canadians in general endorsed increased state intervention, at all levels, as a necessary tool for reform. They pressured municipal governments to improve the quality of life in cities by controlling the heights of buildings, curtailing expressway expansion, promoting urban transit, fighting urban blight, improving parks and libraries, and protecting established neighbourhoods. They demanded that provincial governments expand social services. By the beginning of the 1970s, Canada had a relatively comprehensive national health scheme or, rather, it had ten provincial health plans funded largely by the federal government. Various groups urged provincial governments to legislate to protect consumers, promote the equality of women, and combat discrimination against minority groups. Reformers wanted Ottawa to take measures to protect society's weaker elements, such as the unemployed and citizens of the disadvantaged regions. They also requested financial aid to assist Canadian cultural development.

The Canadian welfare state became entrenched during this period. Patricia Armstrong argues that the welfare state's various programs and services "established rights based on a notion of collective responsibility."[2] (She also asserts that this notion largely disappeared in the 1980s and 1990s.) In the early 1960s, Ottawa improved its social-security programs for the poor. Then, in 1966, it adopted the Canada Assistance Act, which was designed to aid persons who were unable to work or were ineligible for unemployment insurance. In 1967, it established a guaranteed income supplement for low-income pensioners. However, it turned down proposals by reformers to establish a national guaranteed income for all Canadians, not only for financial reasons but also because it feared that such a program would reduce incentives to work. Finally, in 1971, it substantially widened coverage under the Unemployment Insurance Act, partly to benefit regions where little full-time year-round work existed. These programs were expensive: health costs alone nearly doubled from $3.3 billion in 1965 to $6 billion in 1970. Ottawa registered what would be its last budgetary surplus for nearly 30 years in 1969–70.

Governments also intervened modestly to supply disadvantaged Canadians with low-income housing. In the late 1940s, large areas of Cabbagetown, a working-class slum in Toronto, had been cleared and replaced with three-storey brick apartment buildings with open spaces and playgrounds. The 1960s saw the construction of large apartment buildings in the same area, but with much less space, a situation that gave rise to a variety of social problems. Vancouver's Strathcona area, Halifax's Uniacke Square, and Montreal's Jeanne Mance Park saw similar developments.

Most Canadians dreamed of owning a house in the suburbs. Federal government programs made low-cost mortgages available, provincial governments built roads, and local authorities installed services. The Don Mills community of Toronto, built in 1952–62, served as the prototype of a planned corporate suburb. Around a core area containing a shopping centre and a high school at the intersection of two arterial roads, developers built small apartment buildings and townhouses. Beyond them were four low density neighbourhood units. Edmonton had its own planned suburb, Mill Woods. Developers made plans for a population of 100 000, which was to live in 23 neighbourhoods that were focused on a town-centre complex containing the necessary services. All large Canadian cities saw these suburbs mushroom in the 1960s.

THE CULTURAL REVOLUTION

Both English-speaking and French-speaking cultural expression underwent a renaissance in the 1960s. Universal education increased the potential market for cultural products, and higher disposable incomes and more leisure time made it possible for people to enjoy them. Federal and provincial grant agencies gave considerable assistance to cultural endeavours, funding both organizations and individual artists. The Canada Council, for example, helped to finance the activities of the Montreal and

Toronto symphony orchestras, several ballet companies, the Stratford Shakespearean Festival, and the Shaw Festival at Niagara-on-the-Lake. Most provinces also invested substantially in libraries, museums, theatres, and concert halls.

LITERATURE

The 1960s saw the rapid growth of a vibrant and diverse literature in both English and French, due in part to Canada Council grants and other federal and provincial government support programs. By 1970, most universities in English-speaking Canada offered courses in Canadian literature in English, as did Quebec universities on French-Canadian literature. New literary periodicals such as *Canadian Literature* and *Liberté* were established to publish and critique Canadian writing. Several new publishing houses also appeared.

Many of the most popular writers of the decade were women. Margaret Laurence, who spent her early life in Neepawa, Manitoba, and then lived in Africa for many years, settled for a time in England, where she wrote *The Stone Angel* and *A Jest of God*. Both these novels were set in the fictitious town of Manawaka, which bore a close resemblance to Neepawa. In some of her short stories set in Ontario's Huron County, Alice Munro examined the difficulties experienced by an adolescent girl in coming to terms with her family and with life in a small town. Margaret Atwood, hitherto known as a poet, published her first novel, *The Edible Woman*, in 1969, on the theme of women's alienation.

A sense of place and of identity was important for many novelists. Ernest Buckler situated his *Ox Bells and Fireflies* in Nova Scotia. Robert Kroetsch, who grew up in rural Alberta, published an "Out West" series of novels before moving mainly into poetry. Rudy Wiebe, a Mennonite from the prairies, set out to explore his religious roots in *Peace Shall Destroy Many*.

The revolution in poetry brought youth to the fore. Indeed, a volume on Canada's fifteen most outstanding poets in 1970 featured only three who were well known before 1960. Irving Layton, a Romanian Jew whose family settled in an impoverished immigrant district in Montreal, filled his poems with his early impressions and experiences. His provocative views on Israel, anti-Semitism, and other subjects attracted much attention. Al Purdy chronicled the geographical and historical complexities of Canada in such volumes as *The Cariboo Horses*, which he wrote after a trip to Baffin Island. Milton Acorn's populist poetry featured left-wing causes popular in this era. In 1964, Acorn helped found the underground magazine *Georgia Straight* in Vancouver. Leonard Cohen of Montreal was also a popular success, both as a poet and as a singer and songwriter. Raymond Souster continued to influence the direction of Canadian poetry by editing the volumes of many poets and by organizing public readings. A number of Canadian poets, including Souster, gave readings at the Bohemian Embassy, a Toronto coffee house established in 1960 by five CBC television staff members. (Bell Canada, not yet "in," listed this establishment in its yellow pages under the general heading "Embassies and consulates.")

WEB
LINKS

Some Quebec authors found their inspiration in the turbulent nationalism of the Quiet Revolution. Poet Fernand Ouellette dwelt upon the alienation and oppression of the Québécois in *Le Soleil sous la mort*, while Jacques Ferron's short stories dealt with the problems of maintaining Quebec's cultural identity. Hubert Aquin wrote

Prochain épisode while being held in a Montreal psychiatric clinic pending trial on a weapons charge; the novel's narrator, also confined to a psychiatric hospital, awaits trial on charges related to his underground activities as a revolutionary separatist.

Nationalism formed only part of the general theme of liberation being experienced in Quebec during these years. Many novelists examined the emancipation of the person in relation to society. *Une saison dans la vie d'Emmanuel*, which presented a sombre portrait of a tyrannical Quebec family, brought novelist Marie-Claire Blais a wide international audience. Feminist concerns permeated Françoise Loranger's *Encore cinq minutes*, while themes of war, sexual repression, and exploitation of the weak were central to Roch Carrier's highly acclaimed work *La guerre, yes sir!*

A deep concern for Aboriginal rights inspired much of the work of novelist Yves Thériault. In his *Ashini*, the hero, a Montagnais or Innu, commits suicide in the hope that his death will awaken his people from their apathy and bring them to claim their ancestral lands. Playwrights Marcel Dubé and Michel Tremblay made major contributions to French-language theatre; Tremblay's *Les belles-soeurs* violated traditional codes by being the first play to be written entirely in *joual*, or working-class slang.

FILM-MAKING

Canada's film industry in both languages underwent substantial development in the 1960s. Through its diverse activities, the National Film Board made both French- and English-speaking Canadians more conscious of their history and culture. In English, producers worked mainly on documentaries. *Memorandum*, an hour-long documentary on Hitler's "final solution" to the "Jewish question," helped build an enviable reputation for producer Donald Brittain, who had previously directed *Fields of Sacrifice*, a memorial to Canadians killed in action during World War II. Brittain filmed it on battlefields from Hong Kong to Sicily. Canada's centennial year, 1967, saw other noteworthy productions, including *Labyrinth*, which used the Greek myth of Theseus, who entered a labyrinth to find and kill the Minotaur, to symbolize the universality of a person's journey throughout the world. The lavish film, seen by 1.3 million people at Expo 67 in Montreal, attracted much positive press reaction internationally.

French-language filmmakers experimented with subjects linked to French Canada's social ferment. Denys Arcand's *On est au coton* was a film about the textile industry and workers' fears of unemployment because of factory closures. Pierre Perrault's *L'Acadie! L'Acadie!* featured the struggle by Acadian students at the Université de Moncton for the recognition of language rights. Quebec film-makers also set about making what one magazine called "maple leaf porno." Denis Héroux produced *Valérie* in 1969, asserting the need to "undress the Quebec female." One-third of Quebec's population went to the movies in 1970 to see Claude Fournier's *Deux femmes en or*, a similar production.

POPULATION TRENDS

Demographically, the 1960s saw the baby boom of the late 1940s and 1950s turn into a "baby bust." In one decade, the rate of growth of Canada's population dropped by nearly half. Newfoundland's birth rate remained the highest, at 24.3 births per thousand people in 1970; its decline came only in the following decade. Quebec went from having one of the highest birth rates of all the provinces in 1960 to having the lowest rate in 1970, just 16.1 per thousand. The two-child family — the minimum to maintain the current size of the population — briefly became the norm in Canada.

Demographers and sociologists had difficulty explaining the demographic revolution, although other industrialized countries experienced the same phenomenon. Some Quebec analysts attributed the decline in the birth rate to the secularization of Quebec society, but similar trends occurred in all the provinces. Many observers emphasized the availability of better contraceptive methods, particularly the birth-control pill, which became available in Canada in 1966.

Contraception and birth-control methods gained much more exposure and publicity. In 1961, a Toronto couple, Barbara and George Cadbury, founded Planned Parenthood of Canada, an information and referral service. Only in 1969, however, did Parliament amend Canada's Criminal Code to permit the distribution of birth-control information and devices.

Obviously, Canadians wanted fewer children, and they wanted them later in life. A century earlier, large families had been a necessity — on farms, for example, children meant additional workers and, in general, the extended family cared for its elderly members. In Canada's modern social welfare state, the aged relied less on adult children for financial assistance. As well, the ever-increasing costs of raising and educating them made children appear as financial liabilities.

CHANGING FAMILY PATTERNS

A general revolution in family patterns began in the 1960s. Conservative-minded Canadians had long looked askance at the frequency of marriage breakdown in the United States, symbolized by the rapidly moving love-lives of glamorous Hollywood stars. After 1968, when Parliament modified Canadian laws, divorce became frequent in Canada, too. By the 1970s, Canada registered one divorce for every three marriages. The trend was particularly apparent in Quebec, where, as in Newfoundland, divorce procedures had previously been exceedingly complicated and divorces rare.

Traditional sexual taboos gradually became more relaxed. Gay and lesbian relationships became more open after the government, promising to stay out of the nation's bedrooms, legalized homosexual practices between consenting adults in 1969. While the Canadian Bar Association supported the decriminalization of homosexual acts in private, the Canadian Association of Police Chiefs vigorously opposed the legislation, asserting that it would lead to "depravity, robbery, and murder." Gays and lesbians worried that their concerns had now been reduced to narrow issues of criminal-law reform. A coalition of gay and lesbian liberation groups stated that, in spite of the reform, "we are still confronted with discrimination, police harassment, exploitation and pressures to conform which deny our sexuality."

Young people in general began to experiment with different types of living arrangements. For a time, communes were in fashion, although few lasted long. "Living together," or common-law marriage, hitherto frowned upon socially, gained popularity. Some women favoured living together because they opposed marriage in principle as a form of economic servitude — women working without pay — disguised by the myth of romantic love. In most cases, for both women and men, convenience was probably a compelling factor in favour of such unions.

WOMEN: THE LONG ROAD TOWARD EQUALITY

The desire for smaller families symbolized a more general wish by women for a change in their condition. In this age of protest, women's groups began to demand that governments intervene, at both the federal and the provincial levels, to promote equality. Thus began the "second wave" of the women's movement.

Women disagreed strongly over the nature of the "ideal woman." Historian Valerie Korinek describes a contest created by *Chatelaine*, Canada's only mass-market women's magazine, a publication that contained numerous feminist articles and editorials. The goal of the contest was to discover Canada's foremost homemaker, "Mrs. Chatelaine," a stay-at-home wife and mother who also did volunteer work and could serve as a role model for readers of the magazine. Some women, however, proposed other models. One suggested setting up a "Mrs. Slob contest," and named herself as winner. She admitted that she did not always serve nourishing meals, she liked fish and chips, she "entertained" only when her neighbours came in to gab, and she didn't find time to do much volunteer work. She offered her philosophy: "Be happy, don't worry. You do what you can with what you've got when you feel like it."[3]

As the 1960s began, many women felt ready to speak out about the affairs of the country. When *Toronto Star* journalist Lotta Dempsey lamented what appeared to be the increasing danger of nuclear war and wondered where the voice of women was, she hit a raw nerve: hundreds of women turned out for a public meeting at Massey Hall. Thus was born the Voice of Women, whose membership grew to 10 000 in less than a year. Although it was soon racked by internal disputes, the organization, in historian Barbara Roberts's view, had "a 'multiplier effect' on Canadian society out of all proportion to its size and the middle-class character of its membership."[4] Many of its participants later became activists in other women's associations.

Convinced that much more needed to be done, Laura Sabia, president of the Canadian Federation of University Women, called together delegates from 32 women's organizations across Canada who agreed in 1966 to form a new group dedicated to advancing the cause of women. Representatives from this non-partisan Committee for the Equality of Women in Canada then met members of the federal cabinet to press for the creation of a royal commission on the status of women in Canada. Thérèse Casgrain and other members of the Fédération des femmes du Québec also attended in order to demonstrate that francophone women were making the same demands as their anglophone sisters. The federal government finally agreed, the following year, to undertake such a study, but only after the committee threatened to organize a huge march on Ottawa.

The royal commission, chaired by professional broadcaster Florence Bird, held hearings across Canada and received nearly 500 briefs. Issued in September 1970, its report, which one journalist called "a bomb, already primed and ticking," called for a societal change of attitude toward women. It proposed dozens of recommendations concerning women in the workplace, in political life, in education, and in family life.

WOMEN IN THE PAID WORK FORCE

Male-dominated legislatures did adopt some laws that improved the lot of women. They made divorce simpler and maternity benefits more generous, and they granted tax deductions for child-care expenses. However, women's major demands for change

— and, indeed, the changes themselves — occurred in the workplace. In 1961, only one married woman in five was in the labour force, often in part-time employment. Public attitudes still strongly disapproved of married mothers taking paid employment. By 1971, however, as increasing numbers of married women sought jobs outside the home, the proportion had risen to one in three. By 1981, it reached one in two.

Women who worked outside the home needed to find some type of day care for their small children. Until the 1960s, it was expected that they would make their own arrangements. Then feminists began to call for affordable state-supported day care that could enable women to exercise their right to work. It would be necessary to wait until the 1970s, however, before even modest state subsidies for provincial day-care centres were made available.

Sex segregation in the workplace, resulting in "pink-collar ghettos," still remained the norm. As retail stores proliferated in a consumer-oriented society, many women found jobs as salesclerks. The expansion of health care and education also created traditional employment for women. As office clerical work, too, was considered "women's work," expanding governments hired large numbers of women. Indeed, in the late 1960s, the federal government became the largest employer of women in Canada. Eighty percent of its female employees worked in office or administrative-support jobs. Men dominated in the higher-level, better-paying managerial positions.

Ontario innovated in 1963 by establishing a women's bureau within the provincial Department of Labour. Although primarily responsible for research and public relations, the bureau became interested by the late 1960s in policy development and anti-discrimination initiatives. It thus helped bring about the adoption of the Women's Equal Employment Opportunity Act in 1970. In spite of many loopholes, the law provided for legal unpaid maternity leave and banned the firing of women upon marriage. Business complained that maternity leaves would eventually lead to paid leaves, a kind of "reward for pregnancy"; unions with largely male memberships also showed little enthusiasm for measures against discrimination.

Women disagreed over the means to effect necessary changes and, indeed, over the changes that they should seek. Some shared the liberal view that legislative reform would give women more equal opportunities. Other younger, more radical feminists, inspired by theorists such as the American Kate Millett and the Australian Germaine Greer, believed that only a fundamental transformation of the economic and social structures that perpetuated the dominance of men would end female oppression. This group regarded the Bird Report as far too conservative; indeed, some feminists distrusted the political process itself. From the late 1960s, they waged a militant campaign for women's liberation through newsworthy demonstrations and rallies, in innumerable organized discussions, and in newspapers and other printed literature. Feminists were particularly active on university campuses, where they established women's caucuses of Students for a Democratic Union. Some favoured socialism or Marxism; in Quebec, the Front pour la libération des femmes du Québec also sought national independence.

ECONOMIC CHANGE

Canada in the 1960s entered a postindustrial era, in which services, such as those provided by governments, schools, hospitals, the communication industry, retail trade, and financial institutions, constituted the largest sector of employment. Manufacturing placed second. Primary industries, including agriculture, came last — a complete reversal of the Canada of 1867.

Such sectors as transportation and communications developed spectacularly as a result of new technologies. Often they had difficulty finding the highly trained personnel they needed. In several other sectors, workers faced painful adjustments in the wake of job losses. Though employees in traditional "soft" industries such as footwear and textiles, hard hit by lost markets and cheap imports, suffered particularly, other industries also faced problems. Shipbuilders, for example, laid off thousands of workers as the federal government reduced subsidies and Canadian shipyards remained internationally uncompetitive.

Declining prices for their products and fierce competition from abroad led Canada's important natural-resource industries to modernize in order to reduce costs. In addition, an increasingly vocal environmental movement now pointed to pulp and paper companies and smelters as major polluters of the nation's air and water. They urged governments to force such companies to bear some of the huge costs of cleaning up the production process.

Technological change and market forces led to new challenges in agriculture. Large farms, with the equipment necessary to work more land and boost yields, became the norm. Small farmers lacked the means to make the necessary adjustments. In eastern Canada, for example, as dairies forced farmers to switch from cans to expensive bulk-storage equipment, farmers who kept only a few cows were forced out of business. Many abandoned the land that their families had farmed for generations.

Some regions of Canada — southern Ontario, the West Coast, and Alberta — prospered in the climate of change during the 1960s. For others, including the Atlantic provinces, much of Quebec, and parts of the Prairies, change brought unemployment and poverty and provoked widespread discontent.

BUST AND RECOVERY

The great postwar economic boom ended in the late 1950s as Canada entered its most serious recession since the Great Depression of the 1930s. The economy began its decline in 1956, as industry and agriculture encountered more difficulty in selling goods to foreign markets. Worldwide overproduction and declining prices hit farmers particularly hard. A pronounced downturn in the Canadian economy took hold in the spring of 1960, and the winter of 1961 proved especially harsh; 11 percent of Canada's workers found themselves jobless — a very high figure for those years.

John Diefenbaker's Progressive Conservative government, first elected in 1957 and re-elected in 1958 with an overwhelming majority, tried to attack unemployment by means of budget deficits, increased tariffs, and a devalued Canadian dollar. It also increased spending to stimulate the economy. Higher tariffs made it more expensive for consumers to buy American-made products, while a lower dollar supposedly made Canadian exports more attractive. In general, the business and financial community reacted negatively to these economic policies. The Canadian Chamber of Commerce decried the nearly $800 million deficit in 1961 as "staggering" and judged investors to be "as nervous as cats in a dog pound."

In the spring of 1962, shortly after announcing why it was inappropriate to peg the Canadian dollar, the government fixed it at a relatively low (for that era) 92.5 cents (U.S.). This measure provoked both outright condemnation by importers and enthusiastic approval by exporters. The Liberals protested noisily that devaluation would mean higher prices for consumers. They printed thousands of so-called "Diefenbucks" — 92.5-cent dollars adorned with the prime minister's likeness — which they used effectively during the election campaign of June 1962. Diefenbaker lost his majority in Parliament that year. In the next election, in 1963, he lost power to the Liberals.

INFLATION

By 1963, recovery seemed well under way as unemployment dropped to about 5 percent. Even the usually despondent *Globe and Mail* expressed optimism: "Where gloom and doom about the future of Canada has been the governing mood in recent years, there is now buoyancy and optimism." By 1966, however, a new, worrisome trend became evident: prices were moving up more quickly. Angry shoppers boycotted supermarkets, accusing them of price gouging. Prime Minister Lester B. Pearson's Liberal government raised some taxes in an effort to dampen demand. The Conservative opposition denounced the new taxes; the party's financial critic boldly compared the Liberal minibudget to then fashionable miniskirts: "Taxes are getting higher and higher and covering less and less." Most Canadians strongly disagreed with the economists' explanation that inflation was caused by the fact that consumers had too much money to spend.

Canadians battled inflation in various ways. The members of strong unions in key sectors of the economy, such as transportation, won massive pay increases. Seaway workers demanded a 35 percent raise over two years and obtained 30 percent. Railway workers struck and won 24 percent spread over three years. Air Canada's machinists went out in support of their demand for 20 percent in one year. These large increases added to inflationary pressures. In 1967, while inflation showed no signs of abating, the economy slowed down noticeably. Economists coined a new word — *stagflation* — to describe the phenomenon of inflation at a time of slow economic growth. First-year economics textbooks insisted that this combination could not occur — but it did, in Canada and throughout much of the world.

Not all economic news was bad. Canada's foreign-trade balance on goods improved in spite of a growing deficit on finished products. Early in the 1960s, the Diefenbaker government finally found markets — in the People's Republic of China, the Soviet Union, and eastern Europe — for Canada's surplus grain. These new sales improved many western farmers' incomes.

ENVIRONMENTAL CONCERNS

Some Canadians came to realize that economic development was having deleterious effects upon the physical environment. In Ontario, environmentalists focussed their attention on water quality in heavily industrialized areas of the province. The *Hamilton Spectator* complained in 1962: "Sewage, detergents, sludges, chemicals, oil ... they all pour into the harbour." Detergent manufacturers vied with each other to create the longest-lasting suds for washing machines and dishwashers. These suds eventually piled up along the shores of lakes and rivers. Finally, in the face of public outcry, the industry regulated itself and developed more biodegradable detergents.

Later, in the 1960s, algae proliferated in southern Ontario's waters, depleting oxygen levels and killing multitudes of fish. The cause was phosphates, again from detergents. At the University of Toronto, anti-pollution campaigners founded Pollution Probe, staging such events as a mock funeral for Toronto's "dead" Don River. After 1970, governments agreed to take steps to cut phosphate use dramatically in an effort to improve water quality.

ECONOMIC RELATIONS WITH THE UNITED STATES

Throughout the 1960s, Canada registered trade deficits with the United States. Although the Diefenbaker devaluation of the dollar in 1962 did stimulate exports, Canadian subsidiaries sent back dividends to the United States and Canadian visitors spent heavily there.

Various measures further increased trade with the United States. In 1959 Canada and the United States renewed their defence production treaty, thereby stimulating the arms trade between the two countries. Then, in 1965, the Liberals signed the Automotive Products Agreement with the United States. The "Auto Pact" provided for free trade among the manufacturers; Canadian drivers could not, however, bring automobiles back duty-free from the United States. Most economists agree that the pact, accompanied by a lower Canadian dollar, strongly benefited the Canadian economy. In particular, it brought increased prosperity to southern Ontario, where most of Canada's automobile industry is located. Manufacturers now rationalized their production. Canadian plants specialized in producing relatively few models.

Canadians passionately debated the issue of American ownership of Canadian industries in the 1960s. Diefenbaker hoped to diminish the attractiveness of foreign investment in Canada by applying a tax on interest, dividends, and profits sent to non-residents. In practice, the measure had little effect. Ironically, in 1963, U.S. President John F. Kennedy, in an attempt to find a solution to American balance of payments problems, put a 15 percent tax on purchases by Americans of stocks and bonds in foreign countries, including Canada. As the *Globe and Mail* noted, the measure hit Canadian markets "with all the delicacy and force of a wet moccasin across the face." Canada protested and eventually obtained an exemption. Perhaps Canadians were proclaiming a double standard by demanding restrictions on American capital but then condemning similar limits imposed by the Americans. Canadians thought *they* — not Americans — should decide how much foreign capital should come to Canada.

Even when the supposedly pro-American Liberals returned to power in 1963, the problem of foreign investment refused to go away. Walter Gordon, the Liberal finance minister, announced a tax on takeovers of Canadian firms by foreigners, but the ensuing outcry forced him to retract the proposal. Undaunted, Gordon published in 1966 *A Choice for Canada*, in which he argued that the country would have to choose between political and economic independence or colonial status in the

American empire. He also set up a task force on the structure of Canadian industry, chaired by University of Toronto economist Mel Watkins, to study "the significance — both political and economic — of foreign investment."

At this time, however, the Liberal government contained very few economic nationalists. Mitchell Sharp, named minister of finance in 1965, did not even want to publish the task force report, while trade and commerce minister Robert Winters assured a San Francisco audience that "Canada welcomes foreign capital regardless of doubt-provoking remarks to the contrary from time to time." Canadians had not yet reached a consensus on the issue.

BUSINESS AND LABOUR

In the 1960s radicals in the universities, in the churches, and in the media joined economic nationalists in their criticism of the large multinational corporations. They accused these corporations of being the principal villains in society and the prime forces of conservatism. They castigated business in general for its unquenchable thirst for profits and for its failure to display any social conscience. They flayed developers for destroying old urban neighbourhoods to build highrise luxury apartment buildings and office towers. Finally, in this age of rising inflation and of concern for consumers' rights, they denounced companies for "gouging" consumers by endlessly raising prices.

Attacks on business and on "the establishment" also came from reformist political parties such as the Parti Québécois, with its initial pro-worker bias, and the New Democratic Party, the beneficiary of considerable union support. The major organized assault on business, however, came from unions.

UNIONS

Canadian workers became increasingly restive during the 1960s. The labour force grew younger as the first cohorts of baby boomers reached the workplace. Many of these new workers had high expectations, which they hoped to realize quickly. As well, in the late 1960s, rising consumer prices made it imperative for workers to obtain generous wage settlements.

The union rank and file vigorously attacked authority. Militant workers frequently rebelled against their conservative leaders by launching wildcat strikes (illegal work stoppages), some of which paid handsome dividends. A lengthy wildcat strike by Inco workers at Sudbury brought miners the highest wages in North America. Another clash at the Stelco plant in Hamilton, with much violence and destruction of property, permitted steelworkers to obtain very substantial wage increases. During an illegal work stoppage on the railways, one striker explained that the "young guys" were "fearless. They don't give a damn for the company or the government or the union. It's a new generation. . . . We're our own boss now."

Many unionized workers were women. In contrast with the 1950s, when women often hesitated in their resistance to discriminatory practices in the workplace, they now began to wage "a more concerted and organized campaign for gender

WEB
LINKS

equality." In this regard, their actions became part of the emerging women's rights movement in the wider society. Results came slowly. In 1968, women employees of General Motors with six years' seniority were being laid off while the company continued to hire new men. One woman vented her frustration with a poem in the newspaper of the local United Auto Workers to which she belonged:

> I read that whole darn paper and never make the grade;
> Do they just count the females when union dues are paid?
> We wait on recognition and it better show up soon,
> I feel more isolated than the men that walked the Moon.
> So all you fancy journalists, here's one thing to remember:
> I'm classed as just a female, but I'm still a union member.[5]

Workers, often women, in the rapidly growing public sector — teachers, hospital workers, civil servants, municipal employees, and others — also sought to improve salaries and working conditions. They successfully lobbied governments to place them on an equal footing with workers in the private sector, to recognize their right to form unions and, in many cases, to strike. Public sector unions soon became the largest in Canada and among the most militant. Lengthy work stoppages in the post office, for example, beginning with postal workers' illegal walkout in 1965, became notorious.

Unlike the American-controlled "international" unions to which many private-sector workers belonged, public-sector unions were entirely Canadian. Indeed, in the climate of rising nationalism that characterized the 1960s and 1970s, some Canadian sections of international unions withdrew and formed their own Canadian unions.

POLITICS IN THE AGE OF MASS MEDIA

Since Confederation, Canadian politics has focussed increasingly on personalities. Political scientists have attempted to explain this tendency by suggesting that the two major parties have come to differ less and less on questions of basic principle and that "long-standing and well-understood ideological differences do not emerge during campaigns."[6] Parties have offered different leaders, making leadership either a significant asset or a liability for them.

The advent of television undoubtedly increased this focus on the leader. Television has been a rapid and effective means of communicating information. Through the news and televised events such as leadership conventions and election campaign debates, it has brought politicians into the homes of Canadians. At the same time, as political scientist Frederick J. Fletcher has pointed out, television has inhibited the thoughtful exposition of policies and promoted "simple and flashy promises and one-line put-downs of the opposition."[7] The media have stressed conflict and confrontation in their coverage, emphasizing sensational and exciting occurrences. Prime Minister Lester Pearson once complained that "when we do discuss policies seriously ... reporters do not even appear to listen, until we say something controversial or personal, charged with what they regard as news value." In spite of television's particular deficiencies, it began to play a major role in moulding the images — favourable and unfavourable — of politicians.

DIEFENBAKER: A PROPHET OUTCAST

Progressive Conservative leader John Diefenbaker, prime minister from 1957 to 1963, benefited in 1957 and again in 1958 from a remarkably positive image. By 1960, however, he had acquired a very negative one. His electoral triumph in 1958, after nine months of minority government, was parallelled only by his fall from grace in 1962, when he barely managed to retain power with a minority government. Defeated a year later, he returned to the opposition benches. It took only five short years to destroy the boundless confidence that Canadians had placed in "Dief the Chief."

This downfall, in part, arose from his weak basis of support, notably in Quebec, where the Conservatives' organization had long been deficient. Diefenbaker's attempts at speaking French were often the subject of ridicule. In particular, his love of the British monarchy, his ferocious loyalty to the Canadian ensign at the time, with the Union Jack in its corner, during the flag debate of 1964, and his championing of "unhyphenated" Canadianism alienated French-speaking Canadians. Moreover, Diefenbaker understood little of Quebec's awakening in the early 1960s. Indeed, the Conservative party would struggle unsuccessfully for two decades to deal with the complex "Quebec question." The Conservatives also quickly found that they could not easily reconcile the interests of urban and rural voters, or those of central Canadians and Canadians living in other provinces.

The government also seemed disorganized and rife with dissension: Diefenbaker complained that enemies from within were plotting to "deliver up my head on a silver platter." Most to blame, in journalist Peter Newman's opinion, was Diefenbaker himself, a "renegade in power" who had conquered a generation and brought only disillusionment.[8]

To some extent, the controversial prime minister became a victim of circumstances. After 22 years in opposition, the Conservatives had no experience with the art of governing, nor could they count on the support of many Ottawa bureaucrats whose loyalties lay with the Liberal party. The severe recession of 1960–61 was not Diefenbaker's fault any more than the Great Depression had been R.B. Bennett's. Still, the bad times inevitably had deleterious effects on Conservative budgets, and they considerably reduced the government's ability to launch new policies. Instead of bringing forward development proposals, the minister of finance had to resort to austerity measures and to arrange credits with the International Monetary Fund.

Diefenbaker's critics certainly did not hesitate to charge him with economic mismanagement as the Canadian economy weakened after 1960. Although Atlantic and western Canada continued to endorse the Conservatives, Ontario and Quebec, and especially the cities, opposed him. By 1962, even traditionally Conservative newspapers such as the Toronto *Globe and Mail* and the Montreal *Gazette*, evoking the business community's loss of confidence in Diefenbaker, were calling for a Liberal government to "get us out of the abyss."

STRAINED CANADIAN–AMERICAN RELATIONS

Other critics deplored strained Canadian–American relations and what they felt was Canada's deteriorating international image. Diefenbaker had promised to divert more trade to Great Britain, but he failed to recognize Britain's need to join the European

Economic Community and to distance itself from the Commonwealth. He hoped to control American investment in Canada, but in fact took no steps toward doing so. Shortly after the 1957 election, he had, without benefit of cabinet scrutiny, committed Canada to the North American Air Defence Command (NORAD), the continental air-defence alliance headed by a U.S. Air Force general. Then, in 1962–63, in a reversal of his original position, Diefenbaker refused to accept the nuclear warheads that the Americans wanted installed in their anti-aircraft missiles on Canadian soil. Moreover, he intensely disliked President Kennedy, a feeling the American president reciprocated. Lawrence Martin, at the time the *Globe and Mail*'s Washington correspondent, wrote that Canadian–American relations were plunged into what was, up until then, their "worst state of disrepair in the century."[9] In these years of renascent Canadian nationalism, Canadians began to agonize over the kind of relationship they wanted with their southern neighbour. Diefenbaker's attempts to reorient Canadian policy reflected the will of part of the electorate, but they also provoked the disgruntlement of many other Canadians, including several Conservative cabinet ministers.

THIRD PARTIES, RIGHT AND LEFT

The rapid decline of federal Conservative strength in Quebec coincided with the rise of a third party in that province. Since the 1930s, Social Credit had remained a fringe group in Quebec. Then, in the 1962 federal election, to the surprise and even stupefaction of most observers, it won one-quarter of the popular vote and 26 seats — one-third of the province's total. In evaluating the *créditistes*, the *Montreal Star* recalled a comment by the Duke of Wellington, the British general of the Napoleonic era, who welcomed a battalion of new recruits of doubtful quality with the remark, "I don't know how Napoleon will find them but, great God, they frighten me!"

Social Credit's success in the election may be explained partly by Quebeckers' obvious desire for change. A vote for the *créditistes* was a way of striking back against the establishment. Leader Réal Caouette, an automobile salesman from Rouyn who had joined Social Credit in 1939, carried his crusade through rural and small-town Quebec. He promised a national dividend to all citizens to raise consumers' buying power. He pledged help for the aged, the unemployed, and large families. Most of all he assured voters that they had nothing to lose by trying Social Credit. The fiery orator delivered the same message to weekly television audiences.

Political scientists Maurice Pinard and Vincent Lemieux emphasized other dimensions of Social Credit's success. Pinard demonstrated that its strongest support came in regions of traditional Liberal weakness. Lemieux studied the formidable organizational work carried out by party members, often in the kitchens of ordinary citizens, far from the prying eyes of curious journalists.[10]

Social Credit's success had a considerable impact on federal Liberal fortunes. It seriously reduced the party's strength in Quebec, probably costing it the election in 1962 while ensuring that it could form only a minority government in 1963 and again in 1965.

Less spectacular was the reconstitution of the national CCF. After its very poor showing in the federal election of 1958, the CCF decided to co-operate with the Canadian Labour Congress and with left-wing organizations to form a broad-based movement for social reform. In 1961 these groups launched the New Democratic

John Diefenbaker on the campaign trail in Edmonton during the 1965 election campaign. "Dief the Chief" led the Progressive Conservative party to the largest electoral victory in Canadian history in 1958, winning 208 of the 265 seats in Parliament. By 1965, however, he was on the defensive. He lost to the Liberals under Lester Pearson in 1963 and would lose again in the 1965 election.

Duncan Cameron/National Archives of Canada/PA-115755.

Party (NDP), choosing Tommy Douglas, then premier of Saskatchewan, as its leader. The party program called for jobs, health insurance, free education, and, in a break with the CCF's past tendency to favour a powerful central government, a policy of "co-operative federalism." Financial and organizational difficulties quickly put an end to the euphoria of the new party's first moments. As well, electoral results during the 1960s at both the federal and provincial levels proved disappointing. In particular, even most union members failed to support the NDP, which feared becoming too closely identified with unions. Most workers now saw the Liberal party as the party of social welfare and reform.

POLITICS IN DISARRAY

Politics in the early 1960s promoted cynicism among many voters. The country faced grave problems with, at the beginning of the decade, more Canadians out of work than at any time since the Great Depression. Canada also incurred large deficits in foreign trade. The increasing cost of living provoked costly demands from some unions. Relations with the provinces were strained, while growing discord also characterized ties with the United States. Yet neither Progressive Conservative leader

John Diefenbaker nor Liberal leader Lester B. Pearson appeared to have a vision or long-term plan about what could be done.

Four times these two knights in tarnished armour faced each other on the electoral battlefield; only at the first encounter, in 1958, were they greatly mismatched. In 1962, 1963, and again in 1965, neither won enough seats in the House of Commons to form a majority government. Each made numerous — and costly — promises in attempts to rally more voter support. Some of their techniques, borrowed from Madison Avenue, elicited mockery and disdain. The Liberals, for example, published colouring books portraying Diefenbaker riding backwards on a rocking horse. They also formed a "truth squad" to pursue the Conservatives relentlessly across the country to make sure they told the truth. (The squad lasted three days.) Once elected, Canada's parliamentarians devoted themselves to discussing a seemingly endless succession of alleged scandals. In his memoirs, Pearson gave the title "Politics in Disrepute" to a chapter on the years 1964 and 1965.

THE PEARSON YEARS

While in office from 1963 until 1968, Lester B. Pearson attempted to find solutions to Canada's problems. He sought to conciliate the provinces and initiated a series of federal–provincial conferences on the Canadian Constitution. In answer to French Canadians' claims for linguistic equality, he set up the Royal Commission on Bilingualism and Biculturalism to study the issue and make recommendations. His government adopted numerous social measures, such as the Canada Pension Plan and universal medicare. Also, after weeks of debate, the Pearson government gave Canadians a national flag.

PEARSON'S CRITICS

Yet Pearson had numerous critics. Most reproached the Liberal prime minister for his failure to give the country firm and sure leadership (in the direction they wished). Business considered his election promises irresponsibly costly and blamed him for surrendering too easily to the unions. Labour portrayed itself as the victim, not the cause, of inflation. Canadian nationalists accused him of doing little to counter the Americanization of Canada. In cultural matters, for example, legislation designed to assist Canadian magazines contained important exemptions for the two biggest American magazines in Canada, *Time* and *Reader's Digest*. To defend Canada, Pearson revised his earlier position and authorized nuclear warheads for American missiles in the country. Canadians hotly debated the issue of American ownership of the Canadian economy, but the Pearson government did little to control American investments. Although finance minister Walter Gordon did include proposals to limit foreign investment in his budget in 1963, he had to withdraw them.

Quebec nationalists thought that Pearson was resisting their province's legitimate demands, while strong centralists declared that his concessions to Quebec and the other provinces were balkanizing the country and whetting the appetites of separatists. Monarchists censured him for tolerating creeping republicanism, while French Canadians and new Canadians favoured a loosening of Canada's ties with the British crown. Unhappy residents of the Atlantic provinces thought he was doing little to alleviate regional disparities, and westerners judged him ill-attuned to their region's interests. In sum, Pearson endeared himself to virtually none of the regions or major interest groups.

Perhaps Pearson and his Liberal administration should not have been expected to build a consensus on the major questions of the day when Canadians themselves disagreed so strongly on the answers. The 1960s were a time of increasing polarization. In that climate, Pearson manoeuvred with some skill. The policy of "co-operative federalism," by which Ottawa showed greater sensitivity to provincial concerns, was perhaps the best that could be hoped for in a climate of confrontation between Ottawa and the provinces, particularly Quebec. In regard to French–English relations, the establishment of a royal commission, though hardly a solution, appeared a logical step to take. As for the economy and the growing problem of inflation, no obvious long-term solutions existed. Also, even though the Pearson government did have more than its share of scandals, the prime minister's own conduct remained above suspicion.

Finally, concerning American–Canadian economic and cultural relations, Canadians first had to debate options before they could make decisions. American participation in the Vietnam War certainly poisoned relations between the North American neighbours. After Pearson made a speech in Philadelphia in April 1965 urging Americans to stop bombing North Vietnam, President Lyndon B. Johnson invited him to Camp David. There, greatly irritated, he seized Pearson by the shirt and told him in earthy language what he thought of this speech delivered in Johnson's own "backyard." As the war escalated, so did Canadian criticism of American actions in Vietnam. The American government could only express regret for the lack of support from its northern ally.

Many Canadians have viewed the Diefenbaker–Pearson years as the culminating point of a bygone and increasingly repugnant brand of politics. The public longed for a new style, a new type of leadership, an imaginative and refreshing approach to the complex issues of the day. In 1968, many believed that they had found all this in Pierre Elliott Trudeau.

TRUDEAUMANIA

It was not apparent who might succeed Pearson when the Liberal leader announced his resignation in late 1967. Claude Ryan of *Le Devoir* wrote that the Liberal party was in need of as profound a transformation as the American Democratic party had undergone with Kennedy. A number of central Canadian intellectuals, including historian Ramsay Cook, actively promoted Trudeau's candidacy. Trudeau, as justice minister, attracted much attention at the constitutional conference in early 1968, where he jousted with Premier Daniel Johnson of Quebec over the role of the federal government.

TRUDEAU'S BACKGROUND

Trudeau had been elected for the first time in 1965, when Pearson had convinced him, along with labour leader Jean Marchand and journalist Gérard Pelletier, to enter the House of Commons to help renew Quebec's presence in Ottawa. Prior to that

One prime minister and three future prime ministers in April 1967. From left to right: Pierre Trudeau, John Turner, Jean Chrétien, and Lester Pearson.

Duncan Cameron/National Archives of Canada/PA-117107.

period, Trudeau had generally favoured the NDP and its predecessor, the CCF. During the Duplessis years, Trudeau had been a bitter critic of the Union Nationale regime and, with Pelletier, had established a small-circulation magazine called *Cité libre* to give a voice to liberal-minded Quebeckers. He had also studied at Harvard and the London School of Economics, and he had been a globetrotter. But was he the leader the Liberals needed? Quebec nationalists had no liking for this intellectual who incessantly stigmatized separatism. Business did not have confidence in a candidate who lacked experience in the corporate world; indeed, the business community had its own candidate at the 1968 leadership convention — Robert Winters, one of St. Laurent's appointees to the federal cabinet.

Nevertheless, Trudeau's style and background intrigued delegates at the Ottawa leadership convention. His image was of a wealthy bachelor surrounded by beautiful women. He was athletic, drove a Mercedes-Benz sports car, and often dressed flamboyantly. As the *Globe and Mail* put it: "He is the man we all would like to be: charming, rich, talented, successful." This image was certainly at the base of the wave of "Trudeaumania" that broke out during the Liberal leadership race and reached its zenith during the June 1968 federal election, which the Liberals won easily.

TRUDEAU'S PROGRAM

Trudeau's program differed from both Pearson's and Diefenbaker's. In the 1968 election campaign, he made few specific promises designed to buy blocks of voters with their own money. Rather, he expressed a number of general priorities. He attempted to define the "just society" that he wanted Canadians to build: a society whose personal and political liberties were ensured by a charter of rights, a society in which minorities would be sheltered from the caprices of majorities, in which regions and social groups who had not participated fully in the country's material abundance would have greater opportunities. He wanted to discuss with Canadians their country's future. This emphasis on participatory democracy appealed to and attracted many electors. In addition, Trudeau promised a complete revision of Canada's foreign policy in an effort to reorient and reinvigorate Canadian activity abroad.

Trudeau had much to say on the constitutional question as well. When he asked for a strong mandate to oppose the Quebec government's ambitions to play a

Expo 67, Montreal 1967 — an exciting celebration of Canada's centennial year. Canada put forward its very best and invited the world. Some 50 million visitors attended.

Malak/National Archives of Canada/C-18536.

role in international affairs, Toronto newspapers congratulated him for his "firmness." He vigorously attacked new Conservative leader Robert Stanfield's implicit support for the "two nations" doctrine of a more decentralized Canada. For advocates of a strong central government, here was someone who would stand up to the provinces, which they viewed as continually encroaching upon Ottawa's authority. Trudeau could also promise Quebec that he would promote bilingualism in Canada, notably in the federal civil service, and that he would give Quebec and French Canada a major role to play in federal politics. Moreover, like Laurier and St. Laurent before him, he was a French-speaking Canadian. Trudeau's triumphant victory in the 1968 election suggested that he might succeed in building a new consensus among Canadians if he could overcome the Liberals' weakness in the West.

AN ERA OF GREAT CELEBRATIONS

The 1960s were a time of celebration as well as confrontation. In 1967, the year of the Canadian centennial, provinces and municipalities organized various festivities to mark the event. Typically subdued Canadians gave vent to few of the effusions of American-style patriotism, and many wondered whether the country was going to succeed in holding itself together.

One centennial activity was not restrained: Expo 67, staged on an island in the St. Lawrence River at Montreal. The showpiece event brought together more than 60 nations to celebrate the theme "Man and His World." Fifty million visitors passed through the turnstiles, and governments, both federal and provincial, spared no expense, perhaps unfortunately for the taxpayer.

The Canada of 1970 differed greatly from the country that had timidly embarked on an era of change in the late 1950s. Materially, most Canadians were better off than they had been a decade earlier. They were also better educated and certainly more liberal in their views. Minority groups now defended their interests more vigorously and found that society was at least somewhat more attentive to their claims.

Many Canadians, particularly older Canadians, found it difficult to accept the rapid pace of change. They criticized what they saw as a general decline in respect for authority and particularly the many excesses that accompanied social transformation. Others felt that the heightened individualism of the era was incompatible with the need to preserve the nation's unity. For the moment, however, these voices of caution had little impact. Indeed the 1970s would bring more change against a background of increasing economic difficulties and political disunity.

NOTES

1. Doug Owram, *Born at the Right Time: A History of the Baby-Boom Generation* (Toronto: University of Toronto Press, 1996), p. 159.
2. Patricia Armstrong, "The Welfare State as History," in Raymond B. Blake, Penny E. Bryden, and J. Frank Strain, eds., *The Welfare State in Canada: Past, Present and Future* (Concord, ON: Irwin, 1997), p. 61.
3. Valerie J. Korinek, "'Mrs. Chatelaine' vs. 'Mrs. Slob': Contestants, Correspondents and the Chatelaine Community in Action, 1961–1969," *Journal of the Canadian Historical Association/Revue de la Société historique du Canada* 7 (1996): 266.
4. Barbara Roberts, "Women's Peace Activism in Canada," in Linda Kealey and Joan Sangster, eds., *Beyond the Vote: Canadian Women and Politics* (Toronto: University of Toronto Press, 1989), p. 299.
5. Pamela Sugiman, *Labour's Dilemma: The Gender Politics of Auto Workers in Canada, 1937–1979* (Toronto: University of Toronto Press, 1994), p. 136.
6. William P. Irvine, "The Canadian Voter," in Howard R. Penniman, ed., *Canada at the Polls, 1979 and 1980: A Study of the General Elections* (Washington, DC: American Enterprise Institute for Public Policy Research, 1981), p. 67.
7. Frederick J. Fletcher, "Playing the Game: The Mass Media and the 1979 Campaign," in Penniman, *Canada at the Polls*, p. 319.
8. Peter C. Newman, *Renegade in Power: The Diefenbaker Years*, rev. ed. (Toronto: McClelland & Stewart, 1989).
9. Lawrence Martin, *The Presidents and the Prime Ministers: Washington and Ottawa Face to Face: The Myth of Bilateral Bliss, 1867–1982* (Toronto: PaperJacks, 1983), p. 193.
10. Maurice Pinard, *The Rise of a Third Party: A Study in Crisis Politics* (Englewood Cliffs, NJ: Prentice-Hall, 1971), pp. 21–35; Vincent Lemieux, "The Election in Lévis," in John Meisel, ed., *Papers on the 1962 Election* (Toronto: University of Toronto Press, 1964), pp. 33–52.

LINKING TO THE PAST

Leonard Cohen
http://nebula.simplenet.com/cohen/frame.html
A comprehensive introduction to Leonard Cohen's work, including a bibliography, a discography, and lyrics to many of his songs.

The Cradle of Collective Bargaining
http://www.schoolnet.ca/collections/E/
Click on "Labour" and then on "Cradle of Collective Bargaining." This site presents a history of unionization in Hamilton, Ontario. Check out the slide show for an illustrated overview of the labour movement (including strikes at the Stelco plant between the 1940s and the 1970s) and read the essay "Women, Work, and Unions" to learn about women's working conditions.

Lester B. Pearson
http://cnet.unb.ca/achn/pme/lbpcb.htm
A brief biography of Lester B. Pearson, with details about his background and career. A more descriptive biography can be accessed at the bottom of the page.

The Canada Pension Plan
http://canada.justice.gc.ca/STABLE/EN/Laws/Chap/C/C-8.html
The full text of the Canada Pension Plan legislation.

Canada's Flag: A Search for a Country
http://www.schoolnet.ca/collections/flag/
Read all about the history of the Canadian flag and view prototypes of the flag as well as political cartoons related to its development.

Pierre Elliott Trudeau
http://cnet.unb.ca/achn/pme/petcb.htm
A brief biography of Pierre Elliott Trudeau, with details about his background and career. A more descriptive biography can be accessed at the bottom of the page.

BIBLIOGRAPHY

A good synthesis of political and economic history of the 1960s is Robert Bothwell, Ian Drummond, and John English, *Canada since 1945: Power, Politics, and Provincialism*, rev. ed. (Toronto: University of Toronto Press, 1989). Much social history is available in Alvin Finkel, *Our Lives: Canada after 1945* (Toronto: James Lorimer, 1997). J.L. Granatstein, *Canada, 1957–1967: The Years of Uncertainty and Innovation* (Toronto: McClelland & Stewart, 1986) provides a useful overview. Doug Owram proposes an excellent study of the baby boom's effects in *Born at the Right Time: A History of the Baby-Boom Generation* (Toronto: University of Toronto Press, 1996). The *Canadian Annual Review*, published since 1961, contains a wealth of information on a variety of subjects.

David Cameron provides much material on universities in the 1960s in *More Than an Academic Question: Universities, Government, and Public Policy in Canada* (Halifax: institute for Research on Public Policy, 1991). Some aspects of higher education are examined in Paul Axelrod and John G. Reid, eds., *Youth, University and Canadian Society: Essays in the Social History of Higher Education* (Montreal/Kingston: McGill-Queen's University Press, 1989).

The evolution of Canada's welfare state is discussed in Jacqueline S. Ismael, ed., *The Canadian Welfare State: Evolution and Transition* (Edmonton: University of Alberta Press, 1987); Keith Banting, *The Welfare State and Canadian Federalism*, 2nd ed. (Montreal/ Kingston: McGill-Queen's University Press, 1987); and Allan Moscovitch and Jim Albert, eds., *The "Benevolent" State: The Growth of Welfare in Canada* (Toronto: Garamond Press, 1987). On the 1960s in particular see Penny E. Bryden, *Planners and Politicians: The Liberal Party and Social Policy, 1957–1968* (Montreal/Kingston, McGill-Queen's University Press, 1997). On the Ontario experience see James Struthers, *The Limits of Affluence: Welfare in Ontario, 1920–1970* (Toronto: University of Toronto Press, 1994). Alvin Finkel examines the question of day care in "Even the Little Children Cooperated: Family Strategies, Child-care Discourse, and Social Welfare Debates 1945–1975," *Labour/Le Travail* 36 (1995): 91-118. Rodney S. Haddow has studied government policy toward the poor in *Poverty Reform in Canada, 1958–1978: State and Class Influences on Policy Making* (Montreal/ Kingston: McGill-Queen's University Press, 1993). Studies of housing include John R. Miron, *Housing in Postwar Canada: Demographic Change, Household Formation, and Housing Demand* (Montreal/Kingston: McGill-Queen's University Press, 1987); Michael Doucet and John Weaver, *Housing the North American City* (Montreal/Kingston: McGill-Queen's University Press, 1991); John R. Miron, ed., *House, Home, and Community: Progress in Housing Canadians, 1945–1986* (Montreal/Kingston: McGill-Queen's University Press, 1993); and John C. Bacher, *Keeping to the Marketplace: The Evolution of Canadian Housing Policy* (Montreal/Kingston: McGill-Queen's University Press, 1993).

Useful biographical material on writers may be found in *ECW's Biographical Guide to Canadian Novelists* and in *ECW's Biographical Guide to Canadian Poets* (Toronto: ECW Press, 1993). See also Carl F. Klinck, ed., *Literary History of Canada: Canadian Literature in English*, 2nd ed., vol. 3 (Toronto: University of Toronto Press, 1976). All aspects of music are discussed in Helmut Kallmann et al., eds., *Encyclopedia of Music in Canada*, 2nd ed. (Toronto: University of Toronto Press, 1992). Gary Evans, *In the National Interest: A Chronicle of the National Film Board of Canada from 1949 to 1989* (Toronto: University of Toronto Press, 1991), contains a good description of the activity of an important cultural institution. Television is examined in Andrew Stewart and William H.N. Hull, *Canadian Television Policy and the Board of Broadcast Governors, 1958–1968* (Edmonton: University of Alberta Press, 1994). Paul Rutherford offers a lengthy description of television programs of the era in *When Television Was Young: Primetime Canada, 1952–1967* (Toronto: University of Toronto Press, 1990). Ted Magder studies the history of Canadian film-making in *Canada's Hollywood: The Canadian State and Feature Films* (Toronto: University of Toronto Press, 1993). See also Mary Vipond, *The Mass Media in Canada* (Toronto: James Lorimer, 1989).

An excellent study of women in Canada is Alison Prentice et al., *Canadian Women: A History*, 2nd ed. (Toronto: Harcourt Brace, 1996). On women in Quebec, a detailed synthesis by Micheline Dumont et al. has been translated into English: *Quebec Women: A History* (Toronto: Women's Press, 1987). The *Report of the Royal Commission on the Status of Women in Canada* (Ottawa: Information Canada, 1970) remains a good survey of women's questions as posed in the late 1960s.

Books that study the role of women in politics include Sydney Sharpe, *The Gilded Ghetto: Women and Political Power in Canada* (Toronto: HarperCollins, 1994); Sylvia Bashevkin, *Toeing the Lines: Women and Party Politics in English Canada*, 2nd ed. (Toronto: Oxford University Press, 1993); and Linda Kealey and Joan Sangster, eds., *Beyond the Vote: Canadian Women and Politics* (Toronto: University of Toronto Press, 1989). Women in one industrial union are studied in Pamela Sugiman, *Labour's Dilemma: The Gender Politics of Auto Workers in Canada, 1937–1979* (Toronto: University of Toronto Press, 1994). Lucille Marr tells the story of one important contributor to the peace movement in the 1960s in

" 'If You Want Peace, Prepare for Peace': Hanna Newcombe, Peace Researcher and Peace Activist," *Ontario History* 84 (1992): 263–81. Joan Sangster examines the Ontario government's measures against discrimination in "Women Workers, Employment Policy and the State: The Establishment of the Ontario Women's Bureau, 1963-1970," *Labour/Le Travail* 36 (1995): 119–46. On birth control consult Angus McLaren and Arlene Tigar McLaren, *The Bedroom and the State: The Changing Practices and Politics of Contraception and Abortion in Canada, 1880–1980* (Toronto: McClelland & Stewart, 1986). Homosexuality is discussed in Gary Kinsman, *The Regulation of Desire: Sexuality in Canada* (Montreal: Black Rose Books, 1987). See also Donald W. McLeod, *Lesbian and Gay Liberation in Canada: A Selected Annotated Chronology, 1964–1975* (Toronto: ECW Press, 1996).

A detailed survey of the economy may be found in Kenneth Norrie and Douglas Owram, *A History of the Canadian Economy*, 2nd ed. (Toronto: Harcourt Brace, 1996). On government fiscal policy see Robert M. Campbell, *Grand Illusions: The Politics of the Keynesian Experience in Canada, 1945–1975* (Peterborough, ON: Broadview Press, 1987). Canadian–American economic relations in general are examined in Denis Stairs and Gilbert R. Winham, *The Politics of Canada's Economic Relationship with the United States* (Toronto: University of Toronto Press, 1985). Michael A. Hennessy examines government policy toward shipbuilding in "The Fall and Rise of Free Enterprise: State Intervention in Canadian Shipbuilding, 1945–1966," *Journal of the Canadian Historical Association* 2 (1991): 149–75. Environmental problems are discussed in Jennifer Read, " 'Let us heed the voice of youth': Laundry Detergents, Phosphates and the Emergence of the Environmental Movement in Ontario," *Journal of the Canadian Historical Association* 7 (1996): 227–50.

Among syntheses of labour history containing material on the 1960s are Craig Heron, *The Canadian Labour Movement: A Short History*, rev. ed. (Toronto: James Lorimer, 1996); Desmond Morton with Terry Copp, *Working People: An Illustrated History of the Canadian Labour Movement*, 3rd ed. (Toronto: Summerhill Press, 1990); and Bryan D. Palmer, *Working-Class Experience: Rethinking the History of Canadian Labour 1800–1991*, 2nd ed. (Toronto: McClelland & Stewart, 1992). The political links of labour are studied in Keith Archer, *Political Choices and Electoral Consequences: A Study of Organized Labour and the New Democratic Party* (Montreal/Kingston: McGill-Queen's University Press, 1990).

Canadian politicians have been thoroughly studied by political scientists, journalists, and historians, as well as by themselves. Recent works on John Diefenbaker include Garrett Wilson and Kevin Wilson, *Diefenbaker for the Defence* (Toronto: James Lorimer, 1988); and Denis Smith, *Rogue Tory: The Life and Legend of John G. Diefenbaker* (Toronto: Macfarlane Walter & Ross, 1995). Diefenbaker published his autobiography in three volumes: *One Canada: Memoirs of the Right Honourable John G. Diefenbaker* (Toronto: Macmillan, 1973–77). See also Peter C. Newman's contemporary account, *Renegade in Power: The Diefenbaker Years*, rev. ed. (Toronto: McClelland & Stewart, 1989). Newman also offers a "strip-tease contribution" (in Pearson's words) of the Diefenbaker–Pearson rivalry in *The Distemper of Our Times*, rev. ed. (Toronto: McClelland & Stewart, 1990). On Pearson consult the diplomat-politician's *Mike: The Memoirs of the Right Honourable Lester B. Pearson*, 3 vols. (Toronto: University of Toronto Press, 1972–75), as well as John English's biography, *The Worldly Years: The Life of Lester Pearson*, vol. 2: *1949–1972* (Toronto: Knopf Canada, 1992). For material on Pierre Elliott Trudeau's early career see Stephen Clarkson and Christina McCall Newman, *Trudeau and Our Times*, vol. 1, *The Magnificent Obsession* (Toronto: McClelland & Stewart, 1990); and, in translation, Michel Vastel, *The Outsider: The Life of Pierre Elliott Trudeau* (Toronto: Macmillan, 1990).

Maurice Pinard analyzes the Social Credit phenomenon in Quebec in *The Rise of a Third Party: A Study in Crisis Politics* (Montreal/Kingston: McGill-Queen's University Press, 1975). On the NDP see Desmond Morton, *The New Democrats, 1961–1986: The Politics of*

Change (Toronto: Copp Clark Pitman, 1986); and Alan Whitehorn, *Canadian Socialism: Essays on the CCF–NDP* (Toronto: Oxford University Press, 1992). Among other works on political parties consult Joseph Wearing, *The L-Shaped Party: The Liberal Party of Canada, 1958–1980* (Toronto: McGraw-Hill Ryerson, 1981); and William Christian and Colin Campbell, *Political Parties and Ideologies in Canada* (Toronto: McGraw-Hill Ryerson, 1995). A brief summary of election campaigns in the 1960s is available in J. Murray Beck, *Pendulum of Power: Canada's Federal Elections* (Scarborough, ON: Prentice-Hall, 1968). A good study of federal–provincial relations in the 1960s is Richard Simeon, *Federal–Provincial Diplomacy: The Making of Recent Policy in Canada* (Toronto: University of Toronto Press, 1972).

On aspects of Canada's international relations see Paul Painchaud, ed., *De Mackenzie King à Pierre Trudeau: Quarante ans de diplomatie canadienne/From Mackenzie King to Pierre Trudeau: Forty Years of Canadian Diplomacy, 1945–1985* (Québec: Presses de l'Université Laval, 1989); and for the Diefenbaker period, H. Basil Robinson, *Diefenbaker's World: A Populist in Foreign Affairs* (Toronto: University of Toronto Press, 1989). Paul M. Evans and B. Michael Frolic, eds., *Reluctant Adversaries: Canada and the People's Republic of China, 1949–1970* (Toronto: University of Toronto Press, 1991), examines the question of Canada's recognition of China. Canada's policy toward Israel and the Arab states is analyzed in David Taras and David H. Goldberg, eds., *The Domestic Battleground: Canada and the Arab–Israeli Conflict* (Montreal/Kingston: McGill-Queen's University Press, 1989). John English and Norman Hillmer, eds., *Making a Difference? Canada's Foreign Policy in a Changing World Order* (Toronto: Lester, 1992), contains a number of articles concerning the 1960s. Several volumes in the series *Canada in World Affairs* are available for the 1960s.

A good study of Canadian–American relations is J.L. Granatstein and Norman Hillmer, *For Better or For Worse: Canada and the United States to the 1990s* (Toronto: Copp Clark Pitman, 1991). For a journalistic account see Knowlton Nash, *Kennedy and Diefenbaker: Fear and Loathing Across the Undefended Border* (Toronto: McClelland & Stewart, 1990). For a provocative essay on the subject see George Grant, *Lament for a Nation: The Defeat of Canadian Nationalism* (Toronto: McClelland & Stewart, 1965). A good study of Grant, a hero to English-Canadian cultural nationalists in the 1960s and 1970s, is William Christian's *George Grant: A Biography* (Toronto: University of Toronto Press, 1993). Two volumes discuss Canada's involvement in the war in Vietnam: Douglas Ross, *In the Interests of Peace: Canada and Vietnam, 1954–1973* (Toronto: University of Toronto Press, 1984); and Victor Levant, *Quiet Complicity: Canadian Involvement in the Vietnam War* (Toronto: Between the Lines, 1986).

CHAPTER SIXTEEN

Aboriginal Canada: World War II to the Present

WEB LINKS

Over the last half-century the Native peoples have become the fastest-growing group in Canada. The birth rate among the Inuit and status Indians — those registered under the federal Indian Act — is the highest in the country. What a contrast with the situation immediately after Confederation, when the Aboriginal population continued to decline due to tuberculosis and other communicable diseases introduced by Europeans. As late as 1932 Diamond Jenness, the distinguished Canadian anthropologist, wrote in *The Indians of Canada*: "Doubtless all the tribes will disappear. Some will endure only a few years longer, others, like the Eskimos, may last several centuries."[1]

The growing perception after World War II that the Native peoples were not "vanishing" led to the development of new attitudes in the dominant society. Equally important, particularly from the 1930s onward, a new group of politically conscious Aboriginal leaders, with a knowledge of the larger society and an ability to articulate their demands in English or French, made their voices heard. The Indian resistance to the federal government's assimilationist "White Paper" of 1969 led to its withdrawal. Land claims began in the mid-1970s for over half of Canada. Successful political lobbying in the 1970s contributed to the inclusion of the Aboriginal peoples — Amerindians, Inuit, and Métis — in Canada's new Constitution in 1982. Widespread recognition of the concept of Aboriginal rights, including Native self-government, followed in the late 1980s and early 1990s. The federal government pledged to create in 1999 a separate political jurisdiction in the eastern Arctic, Nunavut, which the Inuit would control.

THE YALE-TORONTO CONFERENCE ON THE NORTH AMERICAN INDIAN

The University of Toronto and Yale Conference on the North American Indian that met in Toronto in early September 1939 symbolized the transition from the old to the new Canada on Native issues. Organized by Dr. Tom McIlwraith, the first academic anthropologist employed at a Canadian university (the University of Toronto) and the curator of ethnological collections at the Royal Ontario Museum, the conference was designed "to reveal the conditions today of the white man's Indian wards, and in a scientific, objective and sympathetic spirit, plan with them for their future." Over

70 Canadian and American government officials, missionaries, and academics attended. More importantly, thirteen invited Amerindians participated. It was the first conference ever held to discuss Amerindian welfare and the first scholarly meeting to include First Nations delegates.

For nearly two weeks, the conference delegates discussed North American Native cultures, reserve economics, health, and education. Perhaps the most revealing information about Canada's Native peoples came from federal government officials who pointed out that, beginning in the mid-1930s, Canada's Indian population had reversed its previous decline and was increasing annually by 1 percent, thanks to both an increase in the birth rate and a decline in the death rate. On the last day of the conference, delegates passed resolutions urging greater attention to "the psychological, social, and economic maladjustments of the Indian populations of the United States and Canada." They established a committee to oversee the publication of the conference's papers and the dissemination of information on North America's Native peoples.

Then a dramatic event took place. The Native delegates broke away from the main group and met separately to pass their own resolutions. They objected to government officials, missionaries, and non-Native sympathizers speaking for them. "We hereby go on record as hoping that the need for an All Indian Conference on Indian Affairs will be felt by Indian tribes, the delegates to such a conference be limited to *bona fide* Indian leaders actually living among the Indian people of the reservations and reserves, and further, that such a conference remain free of political, anthropological, missionary, administrative, or other domination." Unfortunately, their appeal went largely unheard by a Canadian public now totally preoccupied by the outbreak of World War II, but in retrospect the conference was a turning point.

THE NATIVE PEOPLES IN WARTIME

In 1936, the federal government demoted the Department of Indian Affairs to a branch of the Department of Mines and Resources. A reformist group within the new Indian Affairs Branch did recognize the need to increase spending for Indian schools, as well as medical care. But, with the outbreak of the war, no additional funds were forthcoming.

During the war, the status Indian population experienced increased oppression. Acting against oral treaty promises in the treaties in western Canada, the federal government initially tried to include status Indians among those eligible for overseas military conscription. Other arbitrary wartime measures included the seizure of reserve lands, the transfer of reserve populations, and the revision of band membership lists. When, for example, the federal government decided in 1942 that it needed a military training facility on Lake Huron, it used the War Measures Act to expropriate Ontario's Stoney Point Reserve, which represented one-third of the Kettle and Stoney Point Band's total reserve lands, despite the fact that the band had previously voted 59 to 13 against the land surrender.

Financial exigency during the war also contributed to First Nations resentment. To save money and promote self-sufficiency, the Indian Affairs Branch unilaterally proposed a centralization plan designed to remove status Mi'kmaq (Micmac) in Nova Scotia from nineteen small reserves to two large inland ones, one at Eskasoni, 50 km southwest of Sydney, and the other at Shubenacadie, 65 km northwest of Halifax. The

The delegates to the Yale–Toronto Conference on the North American Indian, September 1939. This was the first conference held in Canada to discuss Amerindian welfare and the first scholarly conference to include First Nations delegates. The photo was taken on the lawn at the back of the Royal Ontario Museum.

Pringle and Booth/Courtesy of Ken Kidd, a delegate at the conference.

abandoned reserves were to be sold. Only mounting Native opposition led to the cancellation of the project.

In northern Alberta, Malcolm McCrimmon, a zealous Indian Affairs Branch official, created havoc in 1942 when he revised the membership lists in the Lesser Slave Lake agency to trim 700 individuals who he claimed were not "true Indians." McCrimmon argued that anyone added to the lists after 1912 needed to prove that his or her father was a "full blood Indian" to be on the membership list. His action revitalized the already existing First Nations political organization, the Indian Association of Alberta.

These actions undermined the Indian Affairs Branch's credibility among the Indians themselves, as did the fact that in 1944 Native people constituted only two of the branch's 65 members. Moreover, few of the non-Native branch officials had any previous experience in Aboriginal affairs.

The war years were important to the several thousand status Indians who served in Canada's armed forces. After the victory in Europe, the demobilized status First Nations veterans returned home only to resume their lives as "wards of the Crown." But many had gained proficiency in English and a knowledge of the larger society. Equally, the war years contributed to a deeper Native political consciousness.

ABORIGINAL CANADA IMMEDIATELY AFTER WORLD WAR II

First Nations people in lightly populated areas, distant from large non-Native settlements, escaped the full weight of the Indian Act in the interwar years. The federal government paid little attention to groups like the Dene in the Mackenzie River valley and the Cree in the James Bay area. The northern Native peoples — Amerindians,

Private Huron Eldon Brant, member of the Tyendinaga Mohawk community, receiving the Military Medal for bravery at Grammichele, Sicily, 1943, from General Bernard Montgomery.

....

Captain Frank Royal/National Archives of Canada/PA-130065.

Inuit, and Métis — and the dominant society in the south functioned in isolation from each other until World War II.

During the war, however, the isolation ended. Thousands of armed-service personnel and civilians established military airstrips and radio stations in the North. Small communities arose around these posts. Furthermore, in the late 1940s the fur market collapsed and the caribou migration failed, reducing the Inuit to desperate conditions. Throughout the eastern Arctic, isolated Inuit bands starved. Ottawa took emergency action and flew starving families to fur trading posts, where food supplies existed.

The federal government also became more active in the region. It brought in nurses and doctors to look after the Inuit refugees coming off the land. It built hospitals and schools, as well as living quarters. As soon as these non-Native medical personnel, administrators, and teachers arrived, even on a semi-permanent basis, the federal government built permanent installations, such as power plants, water and sewer systems, and roads. The small non-Native bureaucracy that administered the social-assistance programs gained enormous control over the Inuit.

For those Inuit who had tuberculosis or other communicable diseases, the government provided medical assistance. In the case of tuberculosis patients, it X-rayed as many individuals as possible and immunized them with anti-tubercular vaccine. Those patients requiring immediate hospitalization were sent south by plane or boat. By the 1950s, hundreds had been hospitalized and the Department of Health and Welfare had succeeded in lowering substantially the high mortality rate among the Inuit.

Ottawa now saw its task as bringing the Mackenzie valley First Nations to a level comparable to that of the Inuit in the eastern Arctic. In the Mackenzie valley, the Native peoples had not experienced the same economic collapse as the Inuit had after World War II. Moreover, they already lived in semipermanent camps or cabins around Hudson's Bay Company posts and Christian missions. Ottawa replaced the mission schools with public schools and provided the same medical services and administrative help as in the eastern Arctic. The government clashed, however, with local chiefs and elders who resented its intrusion into their communities. Up to this time the First Nations in the Mackenzie valley had run their own affairs.

A NEW POSTWAR ATTITUDE TOWARD THE NATIVE PEOPLES

After World War II, Canadians developed a more positive attitude toward Native peoples. Several reasons account for this. First, social scientists discredited the pseudo-scientific race theory of the late nineteenth and early twentieth centuries that had upheld the belief that certain "races" were inherently inferior to others. Second, many Canadians learned through the press and radio, and, in the 1950s, through television, of the impoverished health and living conditions of the northern First Nations and Inuit. Improvements in water and especially air transportation brought even the most remote regions of the Arctic into the southern Canadian consciousness. Third, the expansion of the natural-resource frontier took southern Canadians into Aboriginal territory where they remained the majority (a situation that brought Aboriginal land claims throughout northern Canada to the public's attention). Fourth, the decoloni-zation movement in Asia and Africa and later the civil-rights movement in the United States in the 1950s and early 1960s contributed to a new consciousness of injustices to minorities, including the Native peoples.

Most importantly, Native leaders, as they had at the Yale–Toronto Conference in 1939, made their demands known. A number of demobilized Indian veterans, for example, demanded freedom from tutelage. Modern technology enabled the new Native leadership to communicate easily in a new common language, English, and, in parts of southern Quebec, French.

After the war, the Indian Association of Alberta campaigned to have Parliament review the Indian Act. Some veterans' organizations and church groups assisted Native political leaders in pressuring Ottawa to lift the restrictions on reserves. Had not the First Nations done enough to merit better treatment? Even though they were not recognized as citizens, they had enlisted in large numbers in the Canadian army in the war.

For the first time, Parliament listened. The Indian Association of Alberta and other provincial Indian organizations participated in the hearings of the Joint Com-mittee of the House of Commons and the Senate on the Indian Act, held from 1946 to 1948. Out of these deliberations came a new revision of the Indian Act in 1951.

The new Indian Act allowed band councils more authority. Women also gained the vote in band council elections. It lifted bans on the potlatch and Sun Dance. Com-pulsory enfranchisement for status Indian males was swept away. In one respect, how-ever, the new act reflected prevailing attitudes. Its underlying goal remained the assimilation of the status Indian.

By the 1970s, Ottawa had phased out most of the residential schools (the last federal residential school closed in 1988) and had integrated Native children into provincially controlled programs. But integrated schooling did not prove entirely successful. Its shortcomings led a number of bands in the early 1970s to call for com-munity control of their schools. Blue Quills, near St. Paul, Alberta, became the first band-controlled school in 1970. Others followed, and in 1973 the federal govern-ment endorsed Native-controlled schools.

Gradually the federal government softened its hard line on local band gov-ernment. In 1960, for example, the Walpole Island band council in southwestern Ontario assumed responsibility for road improvements and other public works on the reserve. Five years later, the same band council gained control over the administra-tion of its own local affairs. By 1966, approximately one-third of all bands in Ontario administered their own welfare services. Other bands created their own police forces, as Walpole Island did in 1967.

During the 1950s and early 1960s, the dominant society showed a greater sensitivity to some Aboriginal issues. In 1960, Ottawa extended the right to vote in federal elections to all status Indians (at that time approximately three out of four status Indians could not vote in federal elections), without requiring First Nations people to give up their Indian status. The federally appointed Hawthorn Commission on the Indian reported in the mid-1960s. It found that the Native people occupied the lowest economic rung on Canada's economic ladder and recommended that they be treated as "citizens plus." The report concluded that "in addition to the normal rights and duties of citizenship, Indians possess certain additional rights as charter members of the Canadian community." After the publication of the report, Prime Minister Lester Pearson committed his government to revising the Indian Act, after prior consultation with First Nations people.

The federal government, now having adopted a more supportive role toward the Native peoples, helped to build a pavilion for the Amerindians of Canada at Montreal's Expo 67. The Native organizers of the pavilion used the building to tell the story of the First Nations. At the entrance, this message greeted visitors: "The Indian people's destiny will be determined by them and our country, Canada, will be better for it." Inside, visitors saw, in bold script, statements such as "Give us the right to manage our own affairs" and "Help us preserve the moral values, the meaningful way of life, the inheritance of our forefathers." The anti-assimilationist messages announced the First Nations' political agenda for the next third of the century.

DEVELOPMENTS SINCE 1969

WEB
LINKS

In 1969 the recently elected Liberal government of Pierre Trudeau inadvertently contributed to the Native resurgence. The Hawthorn Report had recommended that First Nations people be treated as "citizens plus." Trudeau's predecessor, Lester Pearson, had promised that the Indian Act would be revised after prior consultation with Indian people. But, without any meaningful prior consultation, the Trudeau administration now promoted an end to the Indian Act, to the reserves, to "citizens plus." Without any further delay, First Nations people would be brought immediately into the mainstream society. In the "White Paper" on Indian policy, Minister of Indian Affairs Jean Chrétien called for the end — within five years — of the Department of Indian Affairs, the repeal of the Indian Act, the elimination of reserves, and the transfer to the provinces of many of the federal government's responsibilities for Indian affairs. Prime Minister Trudeau also announced his government's refusal to negotiate land settlements for the roughly one-half of the country that was not under treaty. Without delay, young educated Indian leaders joined ranks with Native elders to oppose the government's position paper. Although unsatisfied with the colonial relationship imposed by the Indian Act, the First Nations leaders realized that the legislation did at least recognize their special constitutional status. Without the act, they risked being absorbed into the mainstream of non-Native Canadian society. Together they succeeded in convincing the Liberal government to withdraw the White Paper in March 1971. The provincial and territorial Native political associations representing status Indians in Canada and the National Indian Brotherhood (reorganized in 1981 as the

Jean Chrétien, minister of Indian affairs, meeting with a delegation from the Indian Association of Alberta and other First Nations groups in Ottawa, June 1970. Prime Minister Pierre Trudeau is seated beside Jean Chrétien. The First Nations representatives have just presented the "Red Paper," their response to the government's controversial "White Paper."

Duncan Cameron/National Archives of Canada/PA-170161.

Assembly of First Nations) worked next to secure the constitutional entrenchment of Aboriginal and treaty rights.

Assisting the Native activists in their cause was the decision of the Supreme Court of Canada in the Nisga'a case of 1973, which upheld the legitimacy of Aboriginal rights. Thus the federal government was pressured into accepting comprehensive claims in the areas of Canada where treaties had not been signed, and accepting specific claims elsewhere. More limited than comprehensive land claims, specific claims usually relate to demands for compensation or the restitution of land or money on the basis of the unfulfilled terms of an existing treaty, or formal legal agreement with the government. Ottawa established an Office of Native Claims in 1974 to rule on Aboriginal claims. In the fiscal year 1992–93, the federal government made $7.8 million available in contributions for the research, development, and presentation of specific claims.

Native land claims are currently under way in many parts of the country, particularly in British Columbia. After over a century of opposition to negotiated land claims, British Columbia made a historic change in policy in 1990 and agreed to enter into treaty negotiations with First Nations groups. The first of the modern-day treaties in British Columbia is with the Nisga'a in the Nass valley, in the northwestern corner of the province. Currently 50 First Nations groups are involved in negotiations to

Status of Native Land Claims, 1990. Although the pace of the resolution of Native land claims has picked up in the 1990s, the process remains quite slow.

....

Source Statistics Division and Educational Branch, Department of Indian and Northern Affairs (1990). Reproduced in Richard T. Price, *Legacy: Indian Treaty Relationships* (Edmonton: Plains Publishing, 1991), p. 94.

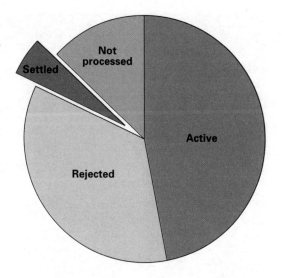

make similar agreements. British Columbia's Aboriginal groups might obtain firm title to about 5 percent of the province's land mass, an amount of land that currently corresponds to the Aboriginal proportion of the province's total population. In contrast, in the Treaty Seven area to the east, the reserves constitute only about 1 percent of the total land area of southern Alberta.

The first comprehensive land claim signed immediately after the enactment of the new federal policy in 1974 was the James Bay and Northern Quebec Agreement in 1975. By this treaty, the Cree and Inuit surrendered their Aboriginal rights to 1 million square kilometres of land, an area the size of British Columbia. In return, they gained control, in and around their communities, of over 14 000 km², an area twice the size of Prince Edward Island, as well as exclusive hunting, fishing, and trapping rights over 150 000 km², an area roughly the size of all three Maritime provinces. They were also awarded $225 million (in 1975 dollars) over a period of 25 years.

The inability of the federal government to settle the complex, two-centuries-old land claim of the Mohawks at Kanesatake (Oka) contributed to the outbreak of violence in the summer of 1990. The Mohawks resisted attempts by the town of Oka, 50 km west of Montreal, to extend a golf course over disputed lands. Only the Canadian army's intervention, after a 78-day armed stand-off, led to a dismantling of the Mohawks' barricades.

A major unsettled land claim in Alberta is that of the Cree of Lubicon Lake in northern Alberta. Geographical remoteness had kept this community out of Treaty Eight, signed in 1899. It has taken its case to the United Nations. But the community's distance from major southern urban centres has denied its claim the same attention as Kanesatake has received. The breakdown in negotiations with Ottawa comes over the nature of the claim. The federal government will recognize the claim only as an unfulfilled treaty entitlement, a specific claim, based on Treaty Eight. The Cree of Lubicon Lake, in contrast, argue that they have unextinguished Aboriginal title and consequently a comprehensive claim. They want a modern-day

Where Historians Disagree

HOW HAVE HISTORIANS INTERPRETED TREATIES ONE TO SEVEN IN WESTERN CANADA?

Over the past quarter-century, a series of Supreme Court of Canada legal decisions have upheld the argument that Aboriginal rights exist under Canadian law. Aboriginal rights include those outlined in treaties, possibly the best known of which are the numbered Treaties One to Seven, signed between 1871 and 1877 in what is now northwestern Ontario and the Prairie provinces. According to Canadian judicial interpretation — before the constitutional reform of 1982 — Aboriginal treaties could be amended or altered by federal statute, without the approval of the First Nations parties to them. The Constitutional Act of 1982, however, entrenches treaty rights. How have the important numbered treaties of the 1870s been interpreted by historians in Canada over the past century?

Duncan Campbell Scott, deputy superintendent of Indian affairs from 1913 to 1932, wrote the first history of federal Indian administration in 1914. The federal civil servant strongly stressed the honourable and just nature of the policy: "As may be surmised from the record of past Indian administration, the government was always anxious to fulfil the obligations which were laid upon it by these treaties. In every point, and adhering closely to the letter of the compact, the government has discharged to the present every promise which was made to the Indians" (Duncan Campbell Scott, "Indian Affairs, 1867–1912," in Adam Shortt and Arthur G. Doughty, eds., *Canada and Its Provinces* [Toronto: Glasgow, Brook and Co., 1914], p. 600). There were no subtleties of interpretation here: the treaties were fair and honourably respected by the Canadian government.

The first university-trained historian to study the western treaties did so in a far more rigorous manner than did Scott. In 1936, George F.G. Stanley, from Calgary, published his D.Phil. thesis for Oxford University as *The Birth of Western Canada* (London: Longmans, Green, 1936; Toronto: University of Toronto Press, 1960). His study, while far more sophisticated than Scott's, reached similar conclusions on the western treaties: "On the whole, Canada has followed the tradition of the Imperial Government in its relations with native tribes, and has endeavoured to deal fairly with her aboriginal wards" (p. 214).

In their brief references to western Canada in the 1870s, most historians for the next 35 or so years accepted the "honourable and just" interpretation of the treaties — or ignored the agreements altogether (just check the indexes in most general Canadian history texts up until the 1980s). There was no real historical debate about the western treaties until the 1970s.

A new look at the numbered treaties followed two decades or so after World War II. The gaining of independence by former European colonies throughout Asia and Africa brought new perspectives into play. Much of the new criticism also came from Aboriginal people themselves, frustrated that their side of the story had not received attention. In 1969, Harold Cardinal, a young Cree politician and author, published *The Unjust Society* (Edmonton: Hurtig, 1969), a fiery indictment of Canadian Indian policy: "The truth of the matter is that Canadian Indians simply got swindled. Our forefathers got taken by slick-talking, fork-tongued cheats" (p. 39). His

(continued)

book sold 100 000 copies. Indian oral traditions of the treaties began to be published, such as the interviews in the timely book edited by Richard Price, *The Spirit of the Alberta Indian Treaties* (Montreal: Institute for Research on Public Policy, 1979). More recently the Treaty Seven Elders and Tribal Council have made available First Nations accounts of Treaty Seven in what is now southern Alberta, *The True Spirit and Original Intent of Treaty 7* (Montreal: McGill-Queen's University Press, 1996).

Historians such as John Leonard Taylor (in his essays, "Canada's Northwest Indian Policy in the 1870s: Traditional Premises and Necessary Innovations" and "Two Views on the Meaning of Treaties Six and Seven," in Richard Price, ed., *The Spirit of the Alberta Indian Treaties*, pp. 3–46); John L. Tobias ("Canada's Subjugation of the Plains Cree, 1879–1885," *Canadian Historical Review* 64[4] [1983]: 519–48); David Hall ("'A Serene Atmosphere'? Treaty 1 Revisited," *Canadian Journal of Native Studies* 4[2] [1984]: 321–58); and Jean Friesen ("Grant Me Wherewith to Make My Living," in Kerry Abel and Jean Friesen, eds., *Aboriginal Resource Use in Canada: Historical and Legal Aspects* [Winnipeg: University of Manitoba Press, 1991], pp. 141–56) added greatly to the richness of the debate. They argued that the First Nations recognized that it was in their interest to secure the best terms possible in the treaty — that schools and a helping hand to adjust to farming would assist them. Problems arose, however, when the federal government did not fulfil the First Nations' oral understandings of the agreements. In Taylor's words, "It appears that government and Indians began from different assumptions, and that there was little attempt on the part of the government either to understand the Indian viewpoint or to convey its own to the Indian people" ("Two Views on the Meaning of Treaties Six and Seven," pp. 44–45).

George Stanley, still actively involved in historical research and debate in the 1980s, revised his thesis of nearly half a century earlier. In 1983, he still dismissed the thought that there were deliberate attempts to deceive the First Nations. Instead he saw the problems as arising from the misunderstandings of treaty terms. As he wrote in his important essay, "As Long as the Sun Shines and Water Flows: An Historical Comment" (in Ian A.L. Getty and Antoine S. Lussier, eds., *As Long as the Sun Shines and Water Flows* [Vancouver: University of British Columbia Press, 1983]): "The probability that promises were made to the Indians, which they remember and the Whites have forgotten, seems strong" (p. 16). In short, a historical question that seemed in the early twentieth century to be well understood is now interpreted by historians in a far fuller and more complex way. A new reading of the old documentary evidence and the availability of Aboriginal oral testimony, as well as a new postcolonial context for discussion, have contributed to new viewpoints.

treaty similar to that of the James Bay Cree, or the Nisga'a and other First Nations in British Columbia.

First Nations groups contend that the whole federal claims-resolution process is unfair. Ottawa sets the rules and controls the agenda. Under the existing system, Aboriginal communities lacking sufficient economic resources must obtain research and legal funds from the same government that will decide whether or not to accept their claim for negotiation.

"IT'S ALL VERY WELL TO ACCUSE THE JUSTICE SYSTEM OF FAILING NATIVES.... BUT WHERE'S YOUR PROOF."

This cartoon captures the reality of the situation facing many Native people in the Canadian judicial system.

Malcolm Mayes, *Edmonton Journal*, March 28, 1991, p. A22.

CONTEMPORARY LIVING CONDITIONS ON RESERVES IN THE SOUTH

The findings of the Royal Commission on Aboriginal Peoples in the mid-1990s confirmed the continuing economic and social inequality of the Native peoples in Canada with the non-Native population. In 1998, a study conducted by the Department of Indian Affairs revealed that the quality of life for on-reserve First Nations people — nearly 400 000 individuals — is on par with Brazil generally and other countries considered to have only a medium level of human development. For the 270 000 registered Indians living off the reserves, the quality of life is somewhat better, but still substantially below that of the average non-Native Canadian. No equivalent information exists on the Métis. (According to the Aboriginal peoples' survey completed in conjunction with the census of 1991, there were about 210 000 Métis in Canada and about 50 000 Inuit. In short, Aboriginal people constitute about 3 percent of Canada's total population.)

Education is one area where there has been great improvement. As late as 1900 only 47 percent of on-reserve students stayed until the end of high school; today 70 percent do. Enrollment in post-secondary education has grown phenomenally. In 1960–61, only 60 status Indians were enrolled at university; today over 27 000 are at postsecondary institutions.

Over the last quarter of a century, there has been an explosion in Native writing in English (and French). In the 1960s, a difficult decade in terms of both physical and ideological survival for Aboriginal people, little was produced. But since the 1970s the number of Native writers has greatly increased. Aboriginal writers such as Basil Johnston, Maria Campbell, and Thomson Highway have achieved prominence. They join a growing number of Native artists, such as Norval Morrisseau, Daphne Odjig, and Bill Reid, who have used art to strengthen and affirm their Aboriginal identity. The musical group Kashtin, and Inuit singer Susan Aglukark, have succeeded in the popular music field. Tom Jackson has achieved a prominent role in both music and acting. Architect Douglas Cardinal has won numerous international awards for his work. The advance has been on other fronts as well. Over the past decade, Aboriginal people have served in many important administrative posts, including the CBC board of directors (Kim Bell), ombudsman of Ontario (Roberta Jamieson), Canadian high commissioner to South Africa (James Barteleman), Canadian ambassador to Costa Rica (Dan Goodleaf), and chancellor of Trent University (Mary Simon).

New and Reactivated Cases of
Tuberculosis in Canada, 1996

Source: Health Canada, *Tuberculosis in Canada 1996*, http://www.hc-sc.gc.ca/hpb/lcdc/publicat/tbcan96/index.html (June 15, 1999), Tables 1A and 6.

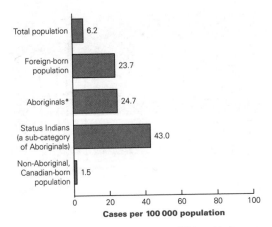

*Includes status Indians, non-status Indians or Métis, and Inuit
Data from Statistics Canada

Admittedly, great challenges remain. As Marianne O. Nielsen observed, Canada's Aboriginal population is "seriously and tragically overrepresented among the inmates incarcerated in federal and provincial correctional institutions."[2] The overall death rate among Aboriginals is still higher than the national rate. In 1981, the life expectancy at birth for status Indians was approximately ten years less than that of the non-Native Canadian population. Although the infant mortality rate among status Indians is one-sixth of what it was in 1960, it remains double that of the general Canadian population. In the 1990s, the rate of tuberculosis was much higher among status Indians than among the non-Aboriginal Canadian-born population.

Many status Indians have left their communities to escape their reserves' depressed economic condition. Generally, the over 2350 reserves (and many rural communities of non-status Indians and Métis) are very small, scattered, and distant from large urban areas. They lack the resources and the infrastructure to sustain their increasing populations.

Before World War II, nearly all Amerindians lived in rural areas. At first only the most adventurous or better educated left for the cities, where they found ready employment. When large numbers went to find industrial jobs, however, the situation changed. Despite the abundance of work, few jobs existed for anyone with only an elementary-school education and little or no vocational training. Racial discrimination also proved a formidable obstacle. It took various forms, from the refusal of accommodation to discrimination in hiring processes: last hired, first fired. To help individuals adjust, Native friendship centres were formed in the late 1960s and 1970s. Although these centres helped Native people feel at home in the city, they could not alter economic conditions.

THE EFFECT OF BILL C-31 ON RESERVE COMMUNITIES

Recently the pressures on reserves to provide housing and other services for their members has increased. Under the Indian Act of 1876, and in its revision of 1951, a

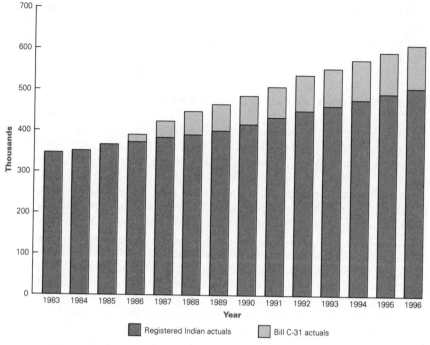

Registered Indian Population Growth Showing Bill C-31 Actuals

Source: Indian and Northern Affairs Canada, *Basic Departmental Data 1993* (Ottawa, 1994), p. 6. Reproduced with permission of the Minister of Supply and Services Canada, 1995; *Basic Departmental Data 1997*, http://www.inac.gc.ca/stats/bdd97/bdd97.html (June 15, 1999), Table 2.

status Indian woman who married a non-status Indian, a Métis, or any other non-Indian automatically lost her Indian status and became a Canadian citizen. In 1985, Parliament passed Bill C-31, which removed this discriminatory clause. Henceforth, status Indian women could retain their status regardless of whom they married, and those who had previously lost their status could apply to have it restored (as well as regaining it for their immediate descendants). Reinstatement as a status Indian entitles the individual to receive free medical care, subsidies for housing and higher education, and exemption from all federal and provincial taxation on monies earned on any reserve. Those gaining membership in a specific Indian band gain a share of the band's assets, the right to reside on the band's reserve, all hunting and fishing rights, eligibility for federal loans and grants to establish reserve businesses, and free schooling on the reserve.

By 1999, Bill C-31 registrants numbered approximately 100 000 individuals, or roughly one-sixth of the total registered Indian population. A number of First Nations leaders have protested that this addition of thousands of newly registered Indians to band membership lists has created chaos in their communities: the already crowded reserves cannot accommodate the influx of reinstated women, their non-Native husbands, and their children. The bands need more land and increased funds. The federal government, they argue, should have left the membership procedure as it was until the Indian Act could be completely overhauled, with full Native consultation, or until Amerindian communities gained self-government — for the Native leaders contend that the First Nations themselves are in the best position to decide the nature of their own membership.

FIRST NATIONS POLITICAL DEMANDS

The definition of Aboriginal rights and the demand for self-government became the major constitutional questions for Native people in the 1980s and early 1990s. Section 35 of Canada's Constitution of 1982 recognized existing treaty and Aboriginal rights, such as those outlined in the Royal Proclamation of 1763. Yet, at a series of four subsequent meetings held between 1983 and 1987, the prime minister, the provincial premiers, and Native representatives failed to reach agreement either on a definition of the meaning of the phrase "Aboriginal rights" or on a definition of Native self-government. These meetings did, however, give Aboriginal issues a very high public profile. The House of Commons Committee on Indian Self-Government in 1983 had endorsed in the Penner Report the concept of full Native control over matters such as education, child welfare, health care, and band membership. For the first time in a federal document, the term "First Nation" was used.

With the end of the constitutional conferences on Aboriginal rights in 1987, the battleground between Native groups and the federal government shifted back to the courts. But the Aboriginal involvement in the campaign against the proposed Meech Lake Accord in June 1990 and the confrontation at Oka, Quebec, from July to September 1990 moved the debate into the political arena, where progress has been made. Native involvement in the failed Charlottetown Accord (1992) was very strong. Four Native leaders joined the federal and provincial prime ministers and territorial leaders in the preliminary talks before the national referendum.

WEB LINKS

In the early 1990s, action on Native grievances moved at the fastest rate in Canada's history. Ontario, the province with the largest status Indian population in Canada, recognized the Aboriginal people's inherent right to self-government. After more than a century of opposition, British Columbia began land-claims discussions with Aboriginal groups. The federal government established a Royal Commission on Aboriginal Peoples; four of its seven commissioners were Aboriginal people. Established in April 1991 "to examine the economic, social and cultural situation of the aboriginal peoples of this country," the commission continued for five and a half years. In late 1996, the commissioners tabled their five-volume final report (roughly 3500 pages) in the House of Commons. Their 440 recommendations covered a wide range of Aboriginal issues, but essentially all focussed on four major concerns: the need for a new relationship in Canada between Aboriginal and non-Aboriginal peoples; Aboriginal self-determination through self-government; economic self-sufficiency; and healing for Aboriginal peoples and communities. The report and its accompanying research papers constitute the most in-depth analysis ever undertaken on Aboriginal people in Canada.

The federal government waited 14 months before issuing its reply. Finally, on January 7, 1998, it issued its response in a document entitled *Gathering Strength: Canada's Aboriginal Action Plan*. Although the statement committed the federal government to a new approach to Aboriginal policy in Canada, it replied directly to only a few of the commission's 440 recommendations. In general terms, Ottawa accepted the treaty relationship as the basis for Canada's relationships with First Nations. Second, it promised a more stable, long-term fiscal relationship with Aboriginal groups. Third, in future, it would increase efforts to prepare First Nations for self-government. Fourth, increased access would be given to land and resources. Several months later, the federal government also set aside $350 million to support community-based healing initiatives for Native people affected by the legacy of Indian residential schools. Georges Erasmus, former co-chair of the royal commission, became the first chair of the Aboriginal-run, not-for-profit Aboriginal Healing Foundation, established to oversee the management of the fund.

THE MÉTIS, THE INUIT, AND THE FEDERAL GOVERNMENT

The Métis position differs from that of status Indians. The federal government has maintained that Canada's obligations to the Métis ended once it had dealt with the Métis land claim under the Manitoba Act and issued land allowances (or the money equivalent) to the Métis in the North-West Territories in 1885 and in 1899–1900. The federal government contends that the provinces have responsibility for the Métis. The high point of the Métis's political struggle for recognition came when they succeeded in achieving identification in the Constitution Act of 1982 as an Aboriginal people. One of the difficulties, however, of describing the Métis lies in the lack of an easy definition of Métis ethnicity. According to historian Jennifer Brown, "Métis as a term has become a net cast over a growing variety of people of mixed European–Indian ancestry. It still refers to the first group widely known as Métis (people of Cree-Ojibwa, French-Canadian descent, largely Roman Catholic, and based on the Canadian prairies), but it now also commonly subsumes others of mixed heritage who have been known as 'halfbreeds,' non-status Indians, or by other labels depending on their historical contexts, occupational classes, and other factors."[3]

Of the three Native groups, the Inuit have the best chance of retaining control of their lands, because they constitute the majority of the population in the eastern Arctic. Due to the remoteness of the area and, from a southerner's perspective, the severity of its climate, the Inuit will probably always be the majority on the treeless northern tundra. The Inuit Tapirisat of Canada, a national Inuit organization, in 1976 proposed the creation of Nunavut (meaning "our land" in Inuktitut), a new territory in the central and eastern area of the Northwest Territories where the Inuit are the majority of the population. The new jurisdiction would administer justice, education, housing, land-use planning, and wildlife management.

ABORIGINAL DEVELOPMENTS IN THE YUKON AND THE NORTHWEST TERRITORIES FROM THE 1970S TO THE 1990S

The northern First Nations and Inuit have contributed greatly to the placing of Aboriginal issues on the public-policy agenda. Until recently, the Yukon Native peoples were assigned a peripheral role, both economically and politically. Native political awareness arose in the Yukon in the late 1960s. Elijah Smith, the late chief of the Champagne Aishihik First Nations, urged his people to start looking for guarantees of their rights to their homeland. In the Yukon, and indeed throughout Canada, a new generation of bilingual Native leaders, men and women in their twenties, came forward to fight for Aboriginal land claims and an end to the federal government's assimilationist policies. In 1973, the Yukon Native Brotherhood (which became the Council of Yukon Indians later that year) began formal talks with the federal government about unsurrendered Aboriginal rights in the Yukon.

Native demands for political control in the neighbouring Northwest Territories also date back a quarter-century. As part of Canada's centennial activities in 1967, the federal government brought communities in the Mackenzie valley together to celebrate the event. In effect, these gatherings helped to bring about a new political awareness and Native pride. Discussions began in 1968 to form the first territorial Aboriginal organization, and in the following year sixteen chiefs from sixteen villages founded the Indian Brotherhood of the Northwest Territories, now called the Dene Nation. In 1970, the Committee for the Original Peoples' Entitlement (COPE) was formed in Inuvik to protect the interests of the Inuit in the Mackenzie Delta — or the Inuvialuit, as the Inuit of the western Arctic refer to themselves. Later, in 1973, the Métis formed their own association, the Métis Association of the Northwest Territories, which eventually joined with the Dene Nation to submit a joint land claim.

In 1971 an Inuit organizing committee formed the Inuit Tapirisat of Canada (originally called the Eskimo Brotherhood), a pan-Inuit organization with a mandate to address questions of northern development and to work to preserve Inuit culture. The Committee for the Original Peoples' Entitlement (COPE) became one of the regional associations affiliated with the Inuit Tapirisat of Canada. Later, the Inuit of the eastern and central Arctic established the Tungavik Federation of Nunavut to represent their specific regional concerns.

THE MACKENZIE VALLEY PIPELINE PROPOSAL

The Berger Inquiry in the mid-1970s did a great deal to obtain a national audience for First Nations and Inuit concerns. In 1972, the building of a Canadian pipeline to carry American oil and gas from the vast Prudhoe Bay field on the northeastern coast of Alaska south through the Mackenzie valley seemed a certainty — until a royal commission was set up to investigate its feasibility. In March 1974, Prime Minister Trudeau selected Thomas Berger, a justice of the British Columbia Supreme Court and a legal expert on Native and civil rights questions, to head the commission.

No one expected Berger to undertake the massive study he then began. The federal government had hoped that the royal commission, like so many before it, would bury the issue by holding hearings in Yellowknife, far from the national media. Instead, Berger undertook a free-ranging and comprehensive environmental, social, and cultural impact study. When pressed, he refused to be rushed, and despite initial resistance, he obtained $2 million in federal funds to help special-interest groups prepare their submissions to the commission. Berger encouraged wide media coverage of the proceedings. His staff contacted radio stations, television networks, newspapers, and even the National Film Board to ensure their presence at the hearings. The coverage swung public opinion in favour of the Native peoples' and environmentalists' concerns. Berger himself held the community hearings, not just in Yellowknife but in 34 other settlements potentially affected by the pipeline. A thousand people participated, with sessions lasting at times from early afternoon until after midnight. The commissioner also held hearings in the major southern cities from Halifax to Vancouver.

Berger's final report in 1977 called for the prior settlement of Native land claims and a ten-year delay on the development of the Mackenzie valley pipeline. The report eloquently reported the Native peoples' conviction that the North was their own distinct homeland, and not simply a resource frontier for southern Canada. The National Energy Board, the national regulatory body, also rejected the proposed development in the Mackenzie valley. The Native peoples' concerns contributed to the decision to postpone the pipeline. Only in the early 1980s was a pipeline built, and then only half-way up the valley, to Norman Wells.

NUNAVUT AND DENENDEH

In 1979, the Aboriginal majority in the legislative assembly of the Northwest Territories endorsed the proposed division of the territories. The government of the Northwest Territories held a plebiscite on the issue in 1982, in which 56 percent of the votes cast favoured division. Later that year, the federal government accepted the proposal in principle. An Inuit constitutional forum representing Nunavut and a second forum representing the western district, or Denendeh, a northern Athapaskan word meaning "land of the people," were formed to discuss how the territorial division might be accomplished. A major stumbling block became the proposed border between the two jurisdictions. To whom would the Inuvialuit, the Inuit of the western Arctic, adhere?

Despite blood ties with their fellow Inuit in the east, the Inuvialuit decided to keep their economic links with the west. The adherence of the western Arctic, rich in newly discovered oil and gas potential, to Denendeh greatly pleased the Dene and the Métis. The addition of the 2500 Inuvialuit would help raise the Native population of Denendeh to near-equality (15 000) with that of the non-Native population (17 000). On January 15, 1987, leaders of the two constitutional forums confirmed in Iqaluit the decision to divide the Northwest Territories. Subsequently the Northwest Territories legislative assembly and the federal government approved the division of the Northwest Territories, which occurred on April 1, 1999.

Native control of government is much more natural in the Northwest Territories than in the Yukon, since a clear Aboriginal majority exists there. The population of the Northwest Territories consists of approximately 50 000 people, split almost equally into three groups: Inuit and Inuvialuit, First Nations and Métis, and non-Natives. What is extraordinary about the Northwest Territories is the speed with which the Aboriginal people have taken control of the political structures. In 1991, the commissioner of the Northwest Territories was a Métis; his deputy commissioner, an Inuk (Inuk is the singular of Inuit); and the government leader, a non-Native. The previous two government leaders were a Métis and an Amerindian. Many Aboriginal people now fill senior administrative posts. Native self-government, the goal of the southern Aboriginal people, is at least partially a reality in the Northwest Territories.

Nunavut might well strengthen Canada's sovereignty in the Arctic, as its claims to the Northwest Passage are based largely on the Inuit's use and occupancy of the area. The voyages through the waters of the Canadian Arctic Archipelago by the *Manhattan*, an American oil tanker, in 1969, and by the *Polar Sea*, an American icebreaker, in 1985, awakened Canadians to the uncertain status of their northern waters. Yet, as Gordon Robertson, formerly commissioner of the Northwest Territories

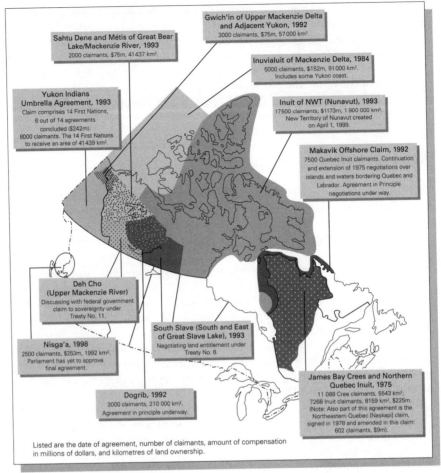

Gwich'in of Upper Mackenzie Delta
and Adjacent Yukon, 1992
3000 claimants, $75m, 57 000 km².

Sahtu Dene and Métis of Great Bear
Lake/Mackenzie River, 1993
2000 claimants, $75m, 41 437 km².

Inuvialuit of Mackenzie Delta, 1984
5000 claimants, $152m, 91 000 km².
Includes some Yukon coast.

Yukon Indians
Umbrella Agreement, 1993
Claim comprises 14 First Nations,
6 out of 14 agreements
concluded ($242m).
8000 claimants. The 14 First Nations
to receive an area of 41 439 km².

Inuit of NWT (Nunavut), 1993
17 500 claimants, $1173m, 1 900 000 km².
New Territory of Nunavut created
on April 1, 1999.

Makavik Offshore Claim, 1992
7500 Quebec Inuit claimants. Continuation
and extension of 1975 negotiations over
islands and waters bordering Quebec and
Labrador. Agreement in Principle
negotiations under way.

Deh Cho
(Upper Mackenzie River)
Discussing with federal government
claim to sovereignty under
Treaty No. 11.

South Slave (South and East
of Great Slave Lake), 1993
Negotiating land entitlement under
Treaty No. 8.

Nisga'a, 1998
2500 claimants, $253m, 1992 km².
Parliament has yet to approve
final agreement.

Dogrib, 1992
3000 claimants, 210 000 km².
Agreement in principle underway.

James Bay Crees and Northern
Quebec Inuit, 1975
11 088 Cree claimants, 5543 km²;
7268 Inuit claimants, 8159 km², $225m.
(Note: Also part of this agreement is the
Northeastern Quebec [Naskapi] claim,
signed in 1978 and amended in this claim:
602 claimants, $9m).

Listed are the date of agreement, number of claimants, amount of compensation
in millions of dollars, and kilometres of land ownership.

Status of several northern land claims, 1999.

Source: Based on *Compass* (November/December 1994): 16. Data from *Arctic Circle* (November/December 1990): 20–21; Department of Indian and Northern Affairs, *Information Sheet*, no. 59 (March 1994). Indian and Northern Affairs Canada, http://www.inac.gc.ca/subject/claims/comp/briem.html (June 15, 1999) and http://www.inac.gc.ca/news/may99/99106bkl.html (June 15, 1999); Northern News Service Online, http://www.nnsl.com/ops/claims.html; Nunavut Planning Commission, http://npc.nunavut.ca/eng/nunavut/general.html.

and deputy minister of northern affairs and national resources, has written, "The application of the laws of a Canadian Inuit government to an ice and water region used by them would be a valid and genuine form of occupation."[4]

In the western Arctic in 1984, COPE, the political organization of the 2500 Inuvialuit, signed the first comprehensive settlement with the federal government in the Yukon and the Northwest Territories. In return for surrendering their claim to the title of approximately 345 000 km² of land, the Inuvialuit obtained title to about 90 000 km² (an area larger than New Brunswick), including subsurface mineral rights for 13 000 km² of this area. They also received $152 million (in 1984 dollars) in financial compensation.

By the terms of a tentative agreement between the federal government and the Council of Yukon Indians that was reached in 1994 after 21 years of negotiations, the Yukon's fourteen Indian bands would retain nearly 9 percent of the territory's land mass. In the land-claim settlement, they would also receive approximately $250 million (in 1989 dollars) in cash over a fifteen-year period.

In 1990, the Amerindians and Métis of the Mackenzie valley area signed a tentative land-claim agreement. Had both Native groups ratified the agreement, they would have received surface title to an area one-third the size of Alberta and $500 million in cash. Later in the year, however, some individuals rejected what is known as the extinguishment clause in the "agreement-in-principle." Three of the five regional groups believed that the clause required them to give up all treaty and Aboriginal rights, and they consequently refused to ratify the agreement. In late 1990, the federal government announced that it would negotiate new claims with each of the regions in the Native territory separately. Parliament accepted the Gwich'in comprehensive land-claim agreement in late 1992 and the Sahtu Dene and Métis land-claim agreement in 1993, thus settling two of the five regions' land claims.

In the eastern and central Arctic, the Tungavik Federation of Nunavut and the federal government reached an agreement-in-principle in 1990. Three years later, they signed a land-claim settlement that will give the Inuit absolute ownership of parcels of land totalling approximately 350 000 km^2, a territory roughly one-half the size of the province of Saskatchewan. They will also receive $580 million for relinquishing their Aboriginal claim to 2 million square kilometres, an area twice the size of the province of Ontario. In June 1993, Parliament passed the Nunavut Land Claims Agreement, which in conjunction with the act to create the territory of Nunavut redrew the map of Canada in April 1999.

NOTES

1. Diamond Jenness, *The Indians of Canada* (Ottawa: King's Printer, 1932), p. 264.
2. Marianne O. Nielsen, "Introduction," in Robert A. Silverman and Marianne O. Nielsen, eds., *Aboriginal Peoples and Canadian Criminal Justice* (Toronto: Harcourt Brace, 1994), p. 3.
3. Jennifer S.H. Brown, "Review of *Structural Considerations of Métis Ethnicity: An Archaeological, Architectural and Historical Study* by David V. Burley, Gayel A. Horsfall, and John D. Brandon," *Ethnohistory* 41(4) (Fall 1994): 680.
4. Gordon Robertson, "Nunavut and the International Arctic," *Northern Perspectives* 15 (May–June 1987): 9.

LINKING TO THE PAST

Aboriginal Links for Canada and the United States
http://www.bloorstreet.com/300block/aborcan.htm
This comprehensive site features hundreds of links to and resources about or by Aboriginal peoples.

The Indian Act
http://canada.justice.gc.ca/STABLE/EN/Laws/Chap/I/I-5.html
The full text of the current Indian Act from the Department of Justice. Scan through the text to find some of the major revisions made in 1951.

Trudeau's Remarks on Treaty Rights
http://www.yukoncollege.yk.ca/~agraham/nost202/trud1.htm
"Prime Minister Trudeau: Remarks on Indian Aboriginal and treaty rights, part of a speech given August 8, 1969 in Vancouver, British Columbia." This excerpt provides Trudeau's rationale behind the "White Paper" proposed in 1969.

Royal Commission on Aboriginal Peoples
http://www.inac.gc.ca/rcap/index.html
This site includes the full report submitted by the commission. See also "Forging a New Relationship: Proceedings of the Conference on the Report of the Royal Commission on Aboriginal People, McGill University, January 31–February 2, 1997" at http://www.arts.mcgill.ca/programs/misc/rcappub.htm.

The Nunavut Planning Commission
http://npc.nunavut.ca/
The Nunavut Planning Commission site offers information on the history of land claims in this area, as well as an overview of Nunavut's government, economic policy, and land use.

Native Land Claims
The full text of several Native land claims acts, from the Department of Justice.
• Nunavut Land Claims Agreement Act:
  http://canada.justice.gc.ca/STABLE/EN/Laws/Chap/N/N-28.7.html
• Gwich'in Land Claim Settlement Act
  http://canada.justice.gc.ca/STABLE/EN/Laws/Chap/G/G-11.8.html
• Sahtu Dene and Métis Land Claim Settlement Act
  http://canada.justice.gc.ca/STABLE/EN/Laws/Chap/S/S-1.5.html

RELATED READINGS

R. Douglas Francis and Donald B. Smith, eds., *Readings in Canadian History: Post-Confederation*, 5th ed. (Toronto: Harcourt Brace, 1998), contains the following article relevant to this chapter: Michael Asch, "To Negotiate into Confederation: Canadian Aboriginal Views on Their Political Rights," pp. 492–507.

BIBLIOGRAPHY

Recent surveys of the history of Aboriginal Canada include Olive Patricia Dickason, *Canada's First Nations: A History of Founding Peoples from Earliest Times*, 2nd ed. (Toronto: Oxford University Press, 1997); and Arthur J. Ray, *I Have Lived Here Since the World Began: An Illustrated History of Canada's Native People* (Toronto: Key Porter, 1996). Edward S. Rogers and Donald B. Smith, eds., *Aboriginal Ontario* (Toronto: Dundurn Press, 1994), looks at the history of the First Nations in Ontario.

For a review of Canadian Indian policy in the early twentieth century see E. Brian Titley, *A Narrow Vision: Duncan Campbell Scott and the Administration of Indian Affairs in Canada* (Vancouver: University of British Columbia Press, 1986). Two important summaries of federal Indian policy are included in Ian A.L. Getty and Antoine S. Lussier, eds., *As Long as the Sun Shines and Water Flows* (Vancouver: University of British Columbia Press, 1983): George F.G. Stanley, "As Long as the Sun Shines and Water Flows: An Historical Comment," pp. 1–26; and John L. Tobias, "Protection, Civilization, Assimilation: An Outline History of Canada's Indian Policy," pp. 39–55. J.R. Miller provides a complete account in *Skyscrapers Hide the Heavens: A History of Indian–White Relations in Canada*, rev. ed.

(Toronto: University of Toronto Press, 1991); see also Noel Dyck, *What Is the Indian "Problem." Tutelage and Resistance in Canadian Indian Administration* (St. John's: Institute of Social and Economic Research, Memorial University of Newfoundland, 1991). Unfortunately, there are few historical studies of provincial policies toward Native people, but a recent contribution by F. Laurie Barron, *Walking in Indian Moccasins: The Native Policies of Tommy Douglas and the CCF* (Vancouver: University of British Columbia Press, 1997), covers Saskatchewan's Aboriginal policies from 1944 to 1961 very well.

Other valuable introductory studies of the Canadian Indian in the mid-twentieth century include Hugh Dempsey, *The Gentle Persuader: A Biography of James Gladstone, Indian Senator* (Saskatoon: Western Producer Prairie Books, 1986); Harold Cardinal, *The Unjust Society: The Tragedy of Canada's Indians* (Edmonton: Hurtig, 1969) — a Cree's indictment of Canadian Indian policy; Donald Purich, *Our Land: Native Rights in Canada* (Toronto: James Lorimer, 1986); and Edgar Dosman, *Indians: The Urban Dilemma* (Toronto: McClelland & Stewart, 1972).

For an overview of health among the Native population see G. Graham-Cumming, "Health of the Original Canadians, 1867–1967," *Medical Services Journal of Canada* 23 (1967): 115–66. A regional study is T. Kue Young's *Health Care and Cultural Change. The Indian Experience in the Central Arctic* (Toronto: University of Toronto Press, 1988). George Jasper Wherrett, "Tuberculosis in Native Races," in his *The Miracle of the Empty Beds: A History of Tuberculosis in Canada* (Toronto: University of Toronto Press, 1977), pp. 98–120, is also useful. For a history of the tuberculosis epidemic among the Inuit in the mid-twentieth century see Pat Sandiford Grygier, *A Long Way From Home* (Montreal/Kingston: McGill-Queen's University Press, 1994).

For an understanding of the Indian residential schools see J.R. Miller, *Shingwauk's Vision* (Toronto: University of Toronto Press, 1996), an encyclopaedic look at the topic — the essential starting point. John Milroy examines the schools over a shorter time period in his new study based on his research for the Royal Commission on Aboriginal Peoples, *'A National Crime': The Canadian Government and the Residential School System, 1879 to 1986* (Winnipeg: University of Manitoba Press, 1999). A look at the experience of residential schooling in one particular area, in this case Prince Albert, Saskatchewan, is provided by Noel Dyck in *Differing Visions: Administering Indian Residential Schooling in Prince Albert 1867–1995* (Halifax: Fernwood, 1997). Scott Trevithick's "Native Residential Schooling in Canada: A Review of Literature," *The Canadian Journal of Native Studies* 18(1) (1998): 49–86 provides a welcome overview of a number of the major studies on this important topic.

Three collections of articles on Aboriginal history include: Ian A.L. Getty and Antoine S. Lussier, eds., *As Long as the Sun Shines and Water Flows* (Vancouver: University of British Columbia Press, 1983); Robin Fisher and Kenneth Coates, eds., *Out of the Background: Readings on Canadian Native History* (Toronto: Copp Clark Pitman, 1988); and J.R. Miller, ed., *Sweet Promises: A Reader in Indian–White Relations in Canada* (Toronto: University of Toronto Press, 1991). Two recent studies provide the best overviews of contemporary conditions for Native people in Canada: James S. Frideres, *Aboriginal Peoples in Canada: Contemporary Conflicts*, 5th ed. (Scarborough, ON: Prentice-Hall, 1998), and J. Rick Ponting, ed., *First Nations in Canada: Perspectives on Opportunity, Development, and Self-Determination* (Toronto: McGraw-Hill Ryerson, 1997).

Aboriginal literature is reviewed by Penny Petrone in *Native Literature in Canada: From the Oral Tradition to the Present* (Toronto: Oxford University Press, 1990). Students should also consult her two edited collections: *First People, First Voices* (Toronto: University of Toronto Press, 1983), and *Northern Voices: Inuit Writing in English* (Toronto: University of Toronto Press, 1988); and Helmut Lutz, *Contemporary Challenges, Conversations with Canadian Native Authors* (Saskatoon: Fifth House, 1991).

A great deal of work remains to be done on the history of the Métis in the twentieth century. D. Bruce Sealey and Antoine S. Lussier provide one of the few historical overviews in the final chapters of their study, *The Métis: Canada's Forgotten People* (Winnipeg: Manitoba Métis Federation Press, 1975), pp. 143–94. Murray Dobbin reviews the Métis's political struggle in western Canada in *One-and-a-Half Men: The Story of Jim Brady and Malcolm Norris, Métis Patriots of the 20th Century* (Vancouver: New Star Books, 1981). Donald Purich provides a survey in *The Métis* (Toronto: James Lorimer, 1988).

The literature of the Native peoples of the Yukon and the Northwest Territories is extensive. Ethnographic background is provided in the following volumes of the *Handbook of North American Indians*: vol. 5, *The Arctic*, edited by David Damas (Washington: Smithsonian Institute, 1984) introduces the Inuit, and vol. 6, *The Subarctic*, edited by June Helm (Washington: Smithsonian Institute, 1984) introduces the Dene of the Northwest Territories. René Fumoleau's *As Long as This Land Shall Last: A History of Treaty 8 and Treaty 11, 1870–1939* (Toronto: McClelland & Stewart, 1973) reviews Native land claims. For a survey of the history of the Yukon First Nations, see Catharine McClellan's *Part of the Land, Part of the Water* (Vancouver: Douglas & McIntyre, 1987). An overview of the Inuit in the early twentieth century is supplied by Diamond Jenness in *Eskimo Administration*, vol. 2, *Canada* (Montreal: Arctic Institute for North America, 1964). William R. Morrison's *A Survey of the History and Claims of the Native Peoples of Northern Canada* (Ottawa: Indian and Northern Affairs Canada, 1983) reviews that important topic. For a discussion of federal Indian policy in the Yukon see Ken Coates, *Best Left as Indians: Native–White Relations in the Yukon Territory, 1840–1973* (Montreal/Kingston: McGill-Queen's University Press, 1991). An interesting Amerindian's view of the Dene's history in the Mackenzie Valley is George Blondin's *When the World Was New: Stories of the Sahtu Dene* (Yellowknife: Outcrop, 1990). Federal policy toward the Inuit is reviewed in Frank J. Tester and Peter Kulchyski, *Tammarniit (Mistakes): Inuit Relocation in the Eastern Arctic, 1939–63* (Vancouver: University of British Columbia Press, 1994). For discussions of Nunavut see Donald Purich, *The Inuit and Their Land: The Story of Nunavut* (Toronto: James Lorimer, 1992); R. Quinn Duffy, *The Road to Nunavut* (Montreal/Kingston: McGill-Queen's University Press, 1988); and John Merritt et al., *Nunavut: Political Choices and Manifest Destiny* (Ottawa: Canadian Arctic Resources Committee, 1989).

Historical studies of the North include two volumes by Morris Zaslow: *The Opening of the Canadian North, 1870–1914* (Toronto: McClelland & Stewart, 1971), and *The Northward Expansion of Canada, 1914–1967* (Toronto: McClelland & Stewart, 1988). Gurston Dacks emphasizes political developments in *A Choice of Futures: Politics in the Canadian North* (Toronto: Methuen, 1981). Gordon Robertson has written *Northern Provinces: A Mistaken Goal* (Montreal: Institute for Research on Public Policy, 1985). A good overview is William R. Morrison's *True North: The Yukon and Northwest Territories* (Toronto: Oxford University Press, 1998). Kenneth Coates and William R. Morrison have completed a survey of the Yukon's history, *Land of the Midnight Sun* (Edmonton: Hurtig, 1988). Mark Dickerson looks at political developments in the Northwest Territories in *Whose North?: Political Change, Political Development and Self-Government in the Northwest Territories* (Vancouver: University of British Columbia Press, 1992).

Post–World War II developments in the North are reviewed in Shelagh D. Grant, *Sovereignty or Security: Government Policy in the Canadian North, 1936–1950* (Vancouver: University of British Columbia Press, 1988); Robert Page, *Northern Development: The Canadian Dilemma* (Toronto: McClelland & Stewart, 1986); and John David Hamilton, *Arctic Revolution: Social Change in the Northwest Territories, 1935–1994* (Toronto: Dundurn Press, 1994).

Useful collections of articles include Morris Zaslow, ed., *A Century of Canada's Arctic Islands, 1880–1980* (Ottawa: Royal Society of Canada, 1981); Kenneth S. Coates and William R. Morrison, eds., *For Purposes of Dominion: Essays in Honour of Morris Zaslow*

(North York, ON: Captus Press, 1989); Kenneth S. Coates and William R. Morrison, eds., *Interpreting Canada's North: Selected Readings* (Toronto: Copp Clark Pitman, 1989). For an overview of the most recent studies of the Arctic consult Shelagh D. Grant, "Point-Counterpoint. Arctic Historiography: Current Status and Blueprint for the Future," *Journal of Canadian Studies* 33(1) (Spring 1998): 145–53.

Students interested in Aboriginal politics in the last 30 years are encouraged to consult, as a starting point, Sally M. Weaver, *Making Canadian Indian Policy: The Hidden Agenda, 1968–1970* (Toronto: University of Toronto Press, 1981); and Rick J. Ponting, ed., *Arduous Journey: Canadian Indians and Decolonization* (Toronto: McClelland & Stewart, 1986). Studies of important First Nations leaders include: Peter McFarlane's *Brotherhood to Nationhood: George Manuel and the Making of the Modern Indian Movement* (Toronto: Between the Lines, 1993); Roy MacGregor, *Chief: The Fearless Vision of Billy Diamond* (Toronto: Penguin, 1989); and Pauline Comeau's *Elijah: No Ordinary Hero* (Vancouver: Douglas & McIntyre, 1993).

On Aboriginal self-government see Frank Cassidy and Robert L. Bish, *Indian Government: Its Meaning in Practice* (Lantzville, BC: Oolichan Books, 1989); and Dan Smith, *The Seventh Fire: The Struggle for Aboriginal Government* (Toronto: Key Porter, 1993). An excellent sourcebook on Aboriginal rights is Bradford W. Morse, ed., *Aboriginal Peoples and the Law: Indian, Métis and Inuit Rights in Canada*, rev. 1st ed. (Ottawa: Carleton University Press, 1989). Important studies of this question include Michael Asch, *Home and Native Land; Aboriginal Rights and the Canadian Constitution* (Toronto: Methuen, 1984); and his edited work, *Aboriginal and Treaty Rights in Canada* (Vancouver: University of British Columbia Press, 1997); Menno Boldt and J. Anthony Long, eds., *The Quest for Justice: Aboriginal Peoples and Aboriginal Rights* (Toronto: University of Toronto Press, 1985); Leroy Little Bear, Menno Boldt, and J. Anthony Long, eds., *Pathways to Self-Determination: Canadian Indians and the Canadian State* (Toronto: University of Toronto Press, 1984); J. Anthony Long and Menno Boldt, eds., *Governments in Conflict? Provinces and Indian Nations in Canada* (Toronto: University of Toronto Press, 1988); Menno Boldt, *Surviving as Indians: The Challenge of Self-Government* (Toronto: University of Toronto Press, 1993); and Ken Coates, ed., *Aboriginal Land Claims in Canada: A Regional Perspective* (Toronto: Copp Clark Pitman, 1992). Boyce Richardson's edited collection *Drumbeat: Anger and Renewal in Indian Country* (Toronto: Summerhill Press, 1989) contains valuable essays on current Aboriginal issues.

Historical accounts of Oka, where the troubles of the summer of 1990 occurred, include Serge Laurin's review of the history of the Amerindians at Lac-des-Deux-Montagnes in his second chapter "L'occupation amérindienne" in *Histoire des Laurentides* (Quebec: Institut québécois de recherche sur la culture, 1989), pp. 49–75 and 799–80. The most complete account currently available is that written by journalists Geoffrey York and Loreen Pindera, *People of the Pines: The Warriors and the Legacy of Oka* (Toronto: Little, Brown, 1992). Les Pal and Robert Campbell, both political scientists, have produced a detailed academic treatment of the Oka crisis, "Feather and Gun: Confrontation at Oka/Kanesatake," in their book *The Real Worlds of Canadian Politics: Cases in Process and Policy* (Peterborough, ON: Broadview Press, 1991), pp. 267–345. An excellent collection of articles on the historical background to the crisis at Oka appears in the special issue of *Recherches amérindiennes au Québec* (printemps 1991): 21, 1–2.

Two interesting reviews of non-Native Canadians' images of Amerindians are Daniel Francis, *The Imaginary Indian: The Image of the Indian in Canadian Culture* (Vancouver: Arsenal Pulp Press, 1992); and Bruce G. Trigger's chapter, "The Indian Image in Canadian History," in his *Natives and Newcomers* (Montreal/Kingston: McGill-Queen's University Press, 1985), pp. 3–49.

CHAPTER SEVENTEEN

The Making of Modern Quebec

Quebec underwent an era of rapid change at all levels in the years after 1960, as the province evolved into a modern, dynamic, secular society. In many ways, Quebec seemed to become more like other regions of North America. Yet, at the same time, most French-speaking Quebeckers (or Québécois, as many French-speaking Quebeckers began to style themselves in the late 1960s) thought it important that their society reinforce its unique linguistic and cultural character.

Most historians argue that the processes of modernization and secularization began well before 1960, during World War II and even earlier. What changed in 1960 was that a new government showed a readiness to make important reforms. An increasingly interventionist Quebec state became a catalyst for change in nearly all sectors of activity, from the economy and education to health and culture. At the same time, just as was the case elsewhere in the western world, many Quebeckers demanded and welcomed change.

What really attracted outside attention to Quebec was the powerful resurgence of nationalism in the province and the profound implications it had for the rest of Canada. When the Québécois complained of being second-class citizens and demanded increased recognition for the French language within the federal government and for the French-speaking minorities outside Quebec, English-speaking Canadians had to respond. When various political movements and parties vied with one another in claiming greater political autonomy for Quebec — and even sought outright independence — Canada's future appeared to be in doubt. In this regard, the aspirations of many Quebeckers appeared threatening.

QUEBEC AFTER WORLD WAR II

Maurice Duplessis and his conservative Union Nationale party first took power in Quebec in 1936, during the Great Depression. Rejected in 1939 by an electorate that believed that the Liberals could best prevent military conscription, Duplessis made a surprising comeback in 1944. Although the Quebec Liberal government of Premier Adélard Godbout adopted a number of important measures while in office, it lost support over issues linked to the war and to the federal Liberals, such as conscription and provincial autonomy. With Duplessis's return, the Union Nationale began an unbroken sixteen-year reign.

During the period 1945–60, Quebec changed in many respects. The province's population, like Canada's, increased rapidly, by more than 25 percent in the 1950s. Although 400 000 immigrants settled in the province in the years 1946–60, most of the rise in population stemmed from a sharply increased birth rate. In addition, large numbers of rural inhabitants moved to the cities, in search of work.

Quebec also underwent rapid economic growth as investment — much of it foreign — accelerated. The United States not only provided a market, it supplied development capital for resource industries such as mining. Employment in the principal manufacturing industries also rose significantly, but the major gains in jobs came in the service industries. Thanks to the booming economy, Quebeckers who, like other Canadians, had endured the sacrifices of depression and war now began to enjoy greater prosperity.

Traditional ideas and values began to give way. Religious practice began to decline, particularly in Montreal. Radio and, especially, television introduced new ideas, new norms. As historian Susan Mann Trofimenkoff puts it, "Television brought the world, no longer filtered by press, priest, or politician, into Quebec's kitchens and living rooms."[1] It was incontestably a subversive influence.

Amid these changes, the very conservative Duplessis, supported by traditional elites, emphasized the importance of religious values and of respect for the established order. His government favoured private enterprise, encouraged the entry of foreign (largely American) capital, and kept taxes low. It built roads and bridges, especially in election years, and aided small-scale farmers, from whom it derived its firmest electoral support.

LABOUR UNREST

Duplessis's policies alienated Quebeckers who were committed to social change. The premier opposed militant union activity because he believed it deterred investment and economic development. He also saw it as a source of social disorder. As a result, his government designed labour legislation to limit strikes, and provincial labour boards generally showed a pro-employer bias. The government even occasionally used the provincial police to protect strikebreakers or break up demonstrations. Non-unionized workers faced working conditions that were generally less favourable than those enjoyed by unionized employees. The government set a low minimum wage, which affected large numbers of working women and immigrants. Other glaring inequalities, which the government did little to alleviate, also cast a pall over the general atmosphere of prosperity. Average wages of French Canadians as a group were lower than those of most other ethnic groups in the province.

OPPOSITION TO DUPLESSIS

In the 1950s, Duplessis's opponents became increasingly vocal. They included political foes, union leaders, a few members of the clergy, and the newspaper *Le Devoir*, as well as intellectuals such as Pierre Trudeau, who, with Gérard Pelletier, published *Cité libre*, a moderately reformist magazine uncompromisingly hostile to the Union

In 1955, the graduating class of the Collège des Trois-Rivières met Premier Maurice Duplessis. Immediately behind the premier, to the right, is student Jean Chrétien, a future prime minister of Canada.

....

Office of the Prime Minister of Canada.

Nationale. Several university professors, among them Dominican priest Georges-Henri Lévesque, dean of the Faculty of Social Sciences at Université Laval, also risked criticizing the government. Although all wanted a more liberal, more modern Quebec, these critics differed considerably in their views on nationalism. Some, like Trudeau, believed that nationalism, by definition conservative and reactionary, could only result in ethnic bitterness and conflict. Others, among them journalist André Laurendeau, who later was co-chair of the Royal Commission on Bilingualism and Biculturalism, saw nationalism as a potentially progressive force.

Duplessis's adversaries also attacked the Union Nationale's corrupt political and electoral behaviour. They showed how the party machine shamelessly extorted money from commercial establishments and entrepreneurs throughout the province, and then used it to buy political support so as to ensure re-election. Election day witnessed such abuses as stuffed ballot boxes, police intervention in favour of government candidates, and "telegraphs," whereby electors voted under false identities. These practices demonstrated clearly, as journalist Pierre Laporte pointed out in a series of articles after the election of 1956, that Duplessis did not win his elections "by prayers alone."

Progressive elements inside and outside the Roman Catholic church grew restive as the church hierarchy uncritically supported Duplessis in return for subsidies for church schools, hospitals, and social agencies. As well, critics censured the government for "reactionary" attitudes in labour relations, education, and health. They castigated incompetent civil servants chosen primarily for their political loyalty. Some critics claimed that the government's economic-development policies resulted in a virtual giveaway of the province's natural resources to foreigners. Others blamed Duplessis for his obstinate refusal to accept federal money to finance necessary social and educational programs. They decried the Union Nationale's neglect of urban Quebec, a failure made possible by an outdated electoral map that blatantly favoured rural areas and that the government refused to revise. By 1956, some urban ridings had more than 100 000 voters, while many rural ridings, which tended to elect Union Nationale candidates, counted fewer than 10 000.

Anti-Duplessis forces also deplored *le chef*'s vendetta against opposition groups. Duplessis had sought to discredit opponents by linking them with communism at a time when anti-Soviet sentiment in the West remained strong. His government went farther by applying the notorious "padlock law" of 1937 that authorized police to lock premises from which alleged communist activities were conducted. In other attacks on civil liberties, the government brought hundreds of Jehovah's Witnesses before the courts for distributing brochures on the streets and had them fined and imprisoned. Moreover, Duplessis often ran the legislative assembly as a personal fiefdom, with total disregard for parliamentary procedure.

THE RE-EVALUATION OF THE DUPLESSIS ERA

In their harsh assessment of the Duplessis record, critics often ignored certain important factors. Patronage, although rife in the Duplessis regime, had been endemic in Canadian political life from the country's birth. The premier's refusal of federal funds for roads, universities, and other programs appeared negative, but how else could he fight Ottawa's intrusions into areas of provincial jurisdiction? Even Pierre Trudeau supported Duplessis's refusal to accept federal funds for higher education. Duplessis did welcome foreign capital, just as premiers Lomer Gouin and Louis-Alexandre Taschereau had done before him. Such investment provided jobs and opened up new areas of the province for development. The government's spending policies were admittedly conservative, but they made it possible to keep taxes low. At the same time, the government did substantially boost spending on social services and education.

Even more telling is the fact that the Union Nationale enjoyed very substantial public support, winning four consecutive elections between 1944 and 1956. Fifty percent of all Quebeckers and more than 60 percent of French-speaking electors voted for the party. Although the over-represented rural counties formed its base of support, the Union Nationale carried most urban districts as well, with the exception of the English-speaking areas of the island of Montreal. Even in 1960, a tiny shift of votes would have assured the Union Nationale's re-election. Yet by this time Duplessis, who died in 1959, and Paul Sauvé, his popular, reform-minded successor, who died after scarcely three months in office, were gone, and the once-powerful party appeared a spent force compared with the Liberals, who offered a capable new leader, a dynamic team, and a revitalized program. Perhaps many of those who, in the midst of the Quiet Revolution, viewed the Duplessis era as Quebec's *grande noirceur*, or "Dark Ages," were actually comparing the sombre realities of the Union Nationale years with their own heady visions and ambitious aspirations. Not surprisingly, they found the Union Nationale regime wanting.

WEB LINKS

THE QUIET REVOLUTION

The term "Quiet Revolution" was coined by a journalist to describe the years 1960–66, during which Liberal Premier Jean Lesage and his *équipe du tonnerre* brought rapid but non-violent change to Quebec. In fact, the major changes occurred before 1964. Nevertheless, some observers with a mind to historical continuity point out that the Union Nationale, when it returned to power in 1966, continued the reforms, as did the Liberals under Robert Bourassa after 1970. The Parti Québécois also had an agenda of reform that it implemented in 1976–80. Thus, it might be said that the Quiet Revolution, in spite of pauses, lasted for two decades.

Although the Liberals came to power with numerous plans for reform in 1960, they had little idea of how much they would be able to accomplish. Lesage's cabinet contained a few progressive individuals, such as René Lévesque and Paul Gérin-Lajoie. It also harboured many solid conservatives who, while they accepted the need for change, did not want to revolutionize Quebec society. When, for example, the Union Nationale attempted in 1960 to discredit its opponents by pointing out that the Liberals threatened the Roman Catholic church's role in Quebec life, the Liberals countered by publishing biographical sketches of their own candidates that emphasized the number of priests, nuns, and brothers among their relatives. Jean Lesage, for example, was presented as having fought for Roman Catholic schools for the "Eskimos" and as having had an audience with Pope Pius XII.

LIBERAL REFORMS

Once in power, the Liberals ended electoral corruption. They also cleaned up much of the petty patronage practised by the Union Nationale, though in so doing they alienated many supporters who wanted a share in the spoils now that their party had at last taken power. Early in its mandate, the government also set up a royal commission, chaired by Monseigneur Alphonse-Marie Parent, of Université Laval, to examine Quebec's educational system. Then it established a provincial ministry of education, thus asserting state control over a sector in which the church had hitherto played such a powerful role. Paul Gérin-Lajoie, the minister, reorganized the province's hundreds of school commissions into 55 regional districts. The government built large, "polyvalent" (comprehensive) secondary schools, improved teacher training, revised curricula, and broadened access to educational facilities. The church retreated. In fact, it had little choice, since it simply did not possess the huge financial and human resources that had to be devoted to schooling in the wake of Quebec's postwar population explosion. Even more serious, the recruitment of new clergy, both male and female, declined noticeably during the 1950s.

Although educational reforms constituted a very important part of the Quiet Revolution, change pervaded all sectors of Quebec society. In 1962, after heated cabinet debate, René Lévesque convinced Lesage to nationalize the province's private electrical power companies and to merge them with the Crown corporation Hydro-Québec. That giant corporation contributed enormously to the province's development over the next two decades. The government also set up the Société générale de financement to serve as a holding company that would acquire small companies in difficulty. This was but one of a series of initiatives taken to promote a more dynamic francophone presence in an economy dominated by capital from outside the province.

The government improved the financial situation of Quebec's municipalities and established a ministry of cultural affairs with a modest budget. In the important sector of labour relations, the government revised the labour code and, significantly, granted most employees in the public sector, with the exception of police officers and firefighters, the right to strike. Progressive but costly measures in the field of health care included the establishment of a provincial hospitalization insurance plan, one of the Liberals' major electoral promises in 1960. Their campaign literature presented a cartoon in two segments comparing hospital care in the Union Nationale era with what the Liberals pledged. On the left, the bad old days: the patient is pictured arriving at the hospital, bounced around on his stretcher by two uncaring orderlies, as a hand is thrust forth from the admissions window. Beneath is the caption: "How much do you earn?" To the right, the Liberal future: the patient is reclining comfortably in bed, a celestial smile on his face, while a nurse standing beside him inquires gently: "What can we do to help you?"

QUEBEC–OTTAWA RELATIONS

In his dealings with Ottawa, Lesage adopted an aggressive autonomist stance. He created the Department of Federal–Provincial Affairs and named himself minister. Shortly after coming to power, he promised to put an end to conditional subsidies, by which the federal government paid for part of the cost of a program in return for setting its conditions. Lesage now demanded financial compensation for those federal programs in which Quebec did not participate. He also insisted that Ottawa turn more tax money over to Quebec in view of the province's "prior needs." Ottawa, he asserted, took in more money than it needed, leaving the provinces financially starved. After the Pearson government in Ottawa unveiled its proposals for the Canada Pension Plan in 1963, Lesage successfully responded with a separate pension plan for Quebec — one that allowed the province to invest the enormous sums of money generated by such a plan as it saw fit. The Caisse de dépôt et placement du Québec would administer funds from Quebec's own pension plan. Particularly in the late 1970s, the Caisse sponsored the expansion of a number of francophone-controlled firms in Quebec and purchased shares in Canadian corporations. It used its ownership role to advance the promotion of French Canadians to the boards of directors of these corporations, thus increasing francophone involvement. By 1999, the Caisse, Canada's largest investment fund, had a portfolio of $64 billion.

The Quiet Revolution altered the face of Quebec dramatically. Sociologist Guy Rocher sees these years as a "cultural mutation," signifying that, beyond the structural reforms, Quebeckers' basic attitudes and values changed.[2] The transformations announced the end of what remained of traditional clerical society as the influence of the Roman Catholic church rapidly waned. Talented authors, musicians, and other artists captured the new spirit in their works (see Chapter Fifteen).

The Québécois also acquired a new confidence in themselves that encouraged them to challenge the inequalities they faced as French-speaking Canadians. They strongly criticized a Canada in which the federal bureaucracy spoke only English, in which French enjoyed no official recognition in nine provinces, and in which the economy functioned — even within Quebec — largely in English. Here indeed were the makings of a new nationalism.

REVOLUTION AND REACTION

Perceptions of the Quiet Revolution have varied considerably. Many in the urban middle class have viewed it as the birth of a modern Quebec or, as sociologist Marcel

Rioux expressed it poetically, "the reappearance of a spirit of independence that had frozen in the course of the long winter that had endured for more than a century."[3] For this group, the Quiet Revolution signified needed reforms in the important sectors of education, political life, the social services, the civil service, and the economy. A more modern Quebec offered obvious advantages to both them and their children.

The breathless pace of change upset many more conservative Quebeckers. Rural Quebec felt ignored and grew nostalgic for the Duplessis era. Disadvantaged citizens in French-speaking districts of Montreal also felt bypassed by the major thrust of the Quiet Revolution, as large-scale spending on education and the rapid growth of the civil service did little for them. For some Quebeckers, state interference in the school system meant that religion was being ruthlessly driven out. "Give Jean Lesage breeches and a beard and he'll be a Castro," Union Nationale opposition leader Daniel Johnson warned. In rural Quebec, where hundreds of small schools had been closed and children were being transported long distances by bus to large, impersonal institutions, discontent was rife. After his defeat in 1966, Lesage complained that "education beat us." His biographer, Dale C. Thomson, confirmed that change in this sector "generated more discontent than satisfaction."[4]

The Quiet Revolution engendered big government and bureaucracy, coldly technocratic and often insensitive to the needs of the individual. Higher spending and increased taxes won Lesage the politically disadvantageous nickname of "Ti-jean La Taxe." Aggressive public-sector labour unions made use of their newly acquired right to strike. The press increasingly criticized Lesage for his "arrogance," a characteristic that came to the fore during the election of 1966, when he campaigned virtually alone. Conservatives felt that the government should pause in the implementation of change.

A small but vocal minority on the left also attacked Lesage. Some urban Quebeckers doubted the government's continuing commitment to reform, especially after 1964. The Marxists and socialists writing in such magazines as *Socialisme* and *Parti pris* went farther and called for the overthrow of capitalism. Militant left-wing nationalists viewed Lesage's objective of greater autonomy for the province as insufficient. They favoured separation, with the creation of an independent French-speaking state, as outlined in the program of Pierre Bourgault's Rassemblement pour l'indépendance nationale (RIN). The RIN and a right-wing separatist group, the Ralliement national, managed to win nearly 9 percent of the votes in the election of 1966. The fact that the RIN took votes mostly from the Liberals enabled the Union Nationale to win in several close races.

RETURN OF THE UNION NATIONALE TO POWER

Led by Daniel Johnson, the Union Nationale regained power in 1966, thanks to strong support in rural Quebec and to Lesage's failure to redraw the electoral map. Indeed, although it won the largest number of seats, the UN received 7 percent fewer votes than the losing Liberals. Many wondered what would become of the Quiet Revolution, and whether Johnson would attempt to undo the Liberals' reforms. Surprisingly, however, the Union Nationale under Johnson, and then under Jean-Jacques Bertrand, who became premier after Johnson's sudden death in September 1968, did not attempt to turn back the clock. In the field of education, Johnson applied the recommendations of the Parent commission and established the Collèges d'enseignement général et professionnel (called CEGEPs), the junior colleges that allowed Quebec students to enrol in occupational programs or to prepare for entrance into the universities. It also established a fourth French-language university, the public Université du Quebec, which opened campuses in regional centres throughout Quebec.

During the late 1960s, the polarization of Quebec society between left and right over issues such as labour–management relations increased. Strike activity, notably in the public sector, grew dramatically, and, as elsewhere in the western world at this time, protests shook colleges and universities.

The protest movements in Quebec took on a distinct national and cultural hue. Before winning power, Johnson had published a manifesto, *Egalité ou indépendance*, in which he warned that if French Canada could not achieve equality within Canada, it must seek independence. He set out his demands for equality for French Canadians during the Confederation of Tomorrow Conference, organized by Ontario Premier John Robarts in Toronto in November 1967.

Johnson wanted more than linguistic equality for French Canadians. In keeping with Quebec's time-honoured political tradition, he also sought greater autonomy for the province. Quebec, the home of more than 80 percent of French-speaking Canadians, represented one of Canada's two major ethnic communities or "nations." Johnson argued that a new Constitution should recognize this fact through an appropriate division of powers.

Ottawa and most of the other provinces appeared willing to discuss the constitutional issue, but Pierre Trudeau, Canada's prime minister after 1968, warned that he would not allow any reduction of federal authority. To Trudeau, the federal government represented all Canadians — not just English-speaking Canadians — and he believed Ottawa could, and should, act to further linguistic equality across the country. Some English-speaking Canadians, however, opposed Quebec's demands from the outset; they had vigorously denounced Trudeau's predecessor, Lester B. Pearson, for appeasing "greedy" provinces and thus helping to "balkanize" the country.

THE DEBATE OVER LANGUAGE

WEB LINKS

Conflict over language was inevitable in Quebec after the Quiet Revolution. Many Québécois felt that their language did not occupy the position it deserved in the province. While elsewhere in Canada most francophones learned English, the language of the majority, most English-speaking Quebeckers knew little French. By necessity, communication between French- and English-speaking Canadians within Quebec was carried on in the language of the minority. The powerful Montreal business establishment included few French Canadians. Many stores in downtown Montreal failed to offer service to customers in French. Commercial signs in Montreal were often only in English. Yet the provincial government had rarely intervened in matters of language in the past. Indeed, when Duplessis tried in 1937 to give priority to French in interpreting certain laws, anglophone opposition was strong enough to force him to rescind the legislation.

Quebec's English-speaking community possessed its own institutions, including Protestant and Catholic schools, universities, newspapers, hospitals, churches, and municipal councils. This was the only province where the linguistic minority — in this case, English-speaking — could function entirely in its own language. No French-speaking minority in the English-speaking provinces came close to occupying such a position. Moreover, census statistics confirmed that French Canadians outside Quebec were, except in eastern Ontario and northern New Brunswick, losing their battle against assimilation: in 1971, approximately three out of ten Canadians whose mother tongue was French had shifted to English as the main language of the home. Only in certain areas could French-speakers be assured of getting at least part of their education in French. In addition, the language of the workplace was almost always English.

Since Confederation, Quebec residents had enjoyed the right or privilege of choosing whether their children would be educated in French or English. In practice, however, the great majority of immigrants to Quebec since World War II saw little reason to learn French, and they had enrolled their children in English-language schools to assure their integration into the English-speaking community. Demographers warned that if current trends continued, Montreal would have an English-speaking majority by the year 2000. For those Québécois concerned about the survival of their language, "free choice" of the language of education represented a serious threat.

CONFLICT OVER ENGLISH-LANGUAGE SCHOOLS

Conflict over the language of education first erupted in the Montreal Island community of St. Leonard, when the Roman Catholic school board's French-speaking majority voted in 1967 to convert an English-language school, attended mainly by children of Italian origin, into a French-language school. The crisis symbolized the determination of many French-speaking Quebeckers to ensure that children of non-English origin enrolled in French schools. It also demonstrated to the English-speaking community that the traditional free choice of the language of education was threatened. Each group pressured the government to support its position. The Union Nationale government ruled against obligatory French-language schools. While Bill 63, which recognized the right of any Quebecker to enrol his or her child in an English-language school, pleased the non-French population, it unleashed storms of protest among French-speaking Quebeckers. Language thus became a full-fledged political issue.

A POLARIZED QUEBEC

The 1970s constituted a difficult period for Quebeckers. Issues such as language, Quebec's future political status, inflation and other economic problems, union unrest, and generational conflict divided the province. In 1970, in the midst of an economic downturn, the Liberals, led by youthful economist Robert Bourassa, won power.

WEB LINKS

The new government soon found itself stumbling from crisis to crisis. Shortly after assuming power, it was confronted with the "October Crisis." Since 1963, a revolutionary fringe group, the Front de libération du Québec (FLQ), dedicated to the establishment of an independent, socialist Quebec, had been involved in numerous bank robberies, thefts of dynamite, and bombings. The climax of the FLQ's terrorism occurred in October 1970, when members of the group kidnapped James Richard

Cross, a British trade representative in Montreal, and, five days later, Pierre Laporte, a Quebec cabinet minister. (Laporte was subsequently found murdered.) When Bourassa hesitated and seemed to favour negotiations with the terrorists, the federal government intervened: for the first time in peacetime, it invoked the War Measures Act, which enabled police to arrest more than 500 "suspects" on the mere suspicion of their being sympathetic to the revolutionaries. Nearly all those arrested were eventually released, with no charges being laid against them.

Bourassa appeared equally hesitant in 1971 when, after lengthy discussions on the Constitution, he finally said no to the Victoria Charter, a package of constitutional proposals assembled by the federal government, which included an amending formula and a bill of rights. Hopes for a renewed federalism then dissipated. At the same time, Quebec Liberals faced growing animosity from public-sector unions, whose leaders spoke ominously of their desire to overthrow the government and to replace the capitalist system with socialism. Contract negotiations with the unions led to unruly public-service strikes and even, in 1973, to the arrest and imprisonment of the three major union leaders.

BILL 22

Nor could Bourassa avoid dealing with the complex language question. His solution, Bill 22, aimed at increasing the use of French in the workplace mainly through persuasive measures. With regard to the language of education, the bill gave access to English-language schools only to children whose mother tongue was English and to those of non-French origin who could pass a language test. It also created enrollment quotas for English-language schools in each school district. In the end, Bill 22 pleased no one. Nationalists complained that the law would do little to bring immigrants into French-language schools and feared that Protestant school boards would interpret it with the greatest possible latitude in order to boost enrollment in English schools. The English-language community and ethnic groups bitterly denounced the law as arbitrary and even totalitarian. The issue cost Bourassa support in the election of 1976, which he lost to the Parti Québécois.

Perhaps historians will judge the first Bourassa regime (1970–76) more kindly than did contemporary observers. Defenders of the multibillion-dollar James Bay hydro-electric project have argued that its economic advantages have outweighed damage caused to the northern environment and that a substantial financial award compensated for the loss of livelihood sustained by the Cree communities of northern Quebec. Others point to the provincial medicare program, financed in part by federal monies, or the Quebec Charter of Rights and Freedoms, one of whose articles made Quebec the first Canadian province to protect gays and lesbians from discrimination.

THE GROWTH OF NATIONALISM

Quebec nationalism had been intensifying since the late 1960s, with calls for constitutional reform, stricter language legislation in Quebec, more bilingualism in the federal government, and an increased francophone presence in Quebec's economy.

"Vive la France! Vive le Québec!
Vive le Québec libre!" The
crowd roared with approval
when French President Charles
de Gaulle made his famous
remark at Montreal's City Hall,
July 24, 1967, in support of an
independent Quebec.

CP Picture Archive.

Some English-language journalists blamed a few individuals for this heightened nationalism, accusing Jean Lesage and Daniel Johnson of undermining Quebeckers' loyalty through their aggressive stance in relations with Ottawa. They also censured French President Charles de Gaulle for the support he appeared to give the cause of independence in his celebrated cry of "Vive le Québec libre!" during a brief speech from the balcony of Montreal's city hall during the Expo 67 celebrations.

While politicians may have adopted nationalist slogans to gain votes in elections, the real roots of protest went much deeper. Nationalism has been a force in Quebec since at least the early nineteenth century; although its themes had varied over time, it was not a new phenomenon in the 1960s.

Contemporary nationalists, however, tended to be members of the new middle class, including teachers, civil servants, and journalists; some even came from the business and professional communities. Critics have pointed out that these groups had a vested interest in nationalist causes. A bilingual civil service in Ottawa, for example, would create job openings for francophones. But these nationalists also resented the inferior position that French-speakers occupied in Canada and, to a certain extent, in Quebec itself. Events elsewhere in the world influenced them. The movements of national liberation in Africa and Asia, and the struggle of American blacks for civil rights, reminded many French Canadians of what they perceived to be their own condition. In one poignant autobiographical account, *Nègres blancs d'Amérique* (*White Niggers of America* in English translation), journalist and FLQ theorist Pierre Vallières portrayed French-Canadian workers as cheap labour, as exploited second-class citizens who had no control over their own society and economy.

THE RISE OF THE PARTI QUÉBÉCOIS

Nationalism escalated in the late 1960s. In 1967, René Lévesque, dissatisfied with the Liberals' constitutional policies, quit the party; the following year, he founded the Parti Québécois (PQ). Bringing together groups as disparate as the right-wing Ralliement National and the left-of-centre Rassemblement pour l'indépendance nationale proved easier than expected. Lévesque had the prestige and stature needed to rally the great majority of nationalists.

René Lévesque at the Paul Sauvé Arena, Montreal, on the night of the Quebec election, October 29, 1973. His recently created Parti Québécois won 33 percent of the popular vote in that election, but only six seats. By 1976, the party would be in power.

....

Duncan Cameron/National Archives of Canada/PA-115039.

The rise of the PQ was striking. Quickly realizing that only a small minority of Quebeckers considered themselves unconditional independentists, party leaders set out to convince more moderate nationalists that independence would greatly improve their lot. While in opposition, the PQ successfully linked nationalism to a variety of social causes, thus enabling it to build a relatively broad coalition of supporters.

The *péquistes*'s electoral gains confirmed the success of this strategy. The party won one-quarter of the vote in the first election it contested in 1970. In that election, economic problems, particularly a high unemployment rate, caused Quebeckers to favour the Liberal party, whose leader, Robert Bourassa, promised to create 100 000 jobs. Three years later, although the Liberals took virtually all the seats in the National Assembly, PQ support rose to one-third. Then, in 1976, with slightly more than 40 percent of the vote, the PQ won an election contested by three major parties.

Many *péquistes* saw their victory as a vote for independence, the first step in the march toward national liberation. Certainly, the "happening" in the Paul Sauvé Arena in Montreal on the night of November 15, as party militants savoured victory, showed vividly that hopes were high. Other observers, however, saw the PQ success simply as a vote for good government and against the scandal-ridden Bourassa regime. The PQ had, after all, promised that it would not try to separate Quebec from Canada until the decision was approved in a referendum. Most voters therefore believed that they had voted only for a change in government.

QUEBEC UNDER THE PARTI QUÉBÉCOIS

The new PQ government pursued reforms that continued the Quiet Revolution of the 1960s. In order to democratize Quebec politics and prevent powerful interests from "buying" favourable legislation, it overhauled the electoral law to prohibit large — mainly corporate — contributions to political parties. The government also introduced a no-fault system of automobile insurance, covering all personal injuries sustained; private companies continued to insure drivers for damage to vehicles. It brought in agricultural zoning legislation designed to protect increasingly scarce good farm land, much of which had disappeared due to urban sprawl since World War II. It set up a dental care plan for children, adopted new legislation to protect consumers, and froze tuition fees for university students at the lowest levels in Canada. It also supported unions through an anti-strikebreaking law, a move that management bitterly opposed.

In contrast to Bourassa's vacillation on the language question, the Parti Québécois appeared uncompromising. Nonetheless, on many occasions since 1968, that issue had threatened party unity. Party leader René Lévesque frequently intervened against militant hard-liners who favoured the elimination of publicly financed English-language schools. Then, in 1977, the government adopted Bill 101, a charter of the French language, which was intended to make Quebec as overwhelmingly French as Ontario was English. This controversial legislation opened English-language schools only to children who had at least one parent educated in English in Quebec. That "objective" criterion was used because of the impossibility of verifying a child's mother tongue, one of the conditions used by Bourassa's Bill 22, to determine admission. French, with a few exceptions, was to become the language of the workplace. Professionals were required to have a knowledge of the French language. Most signs were to be posted in French only. In short, the Parti Québécois hoped to obtain by law for French in Quebec what the "free market" and "free choice" assured English elsewhere in Canada.

The new minority status of Quebec anglophones necessitated often-painful adjustments. Although the federal commissioner of official languages commented in 1978, after the adoption of Bill 101, that "Quebec's anglophones are much better off than their francophone counterparts in other provinces," many Anglo-Quebeckers concluded that they could have a better future elsewhere. Between 1976 and 1981, about one-seventh of their number, including a large proportion of young adults, left the province. At the same time, a large number of corporate head offices in Montreal, complaining of the language legislation, high taxes, the dangers of separatism, and poor relations with unions, decided to move westward, mainly to Toronto.

Among the English-speakers who chose to stay in Quebec, however, bilingualism increased significantly; by 1996, 62 percent of this group were bilingual. Even so, Quebec's anglophones remained Canada's least bilingual "official language minority" (84 percent of francophones outside Quebec reported that they could also speak English). At the same time, Quebec's unilingual "Frenchness" was attenuated by the fact that fully 34 percent of the majority French-language group reported that they could also speak English. The pressures of the labour market help explain this phenomenon. (Bilingualism outside Quebec, among English-speakers, grew slowly but remained largely an elitist phenomenon; in 1996, about 7 percent of anglophones also spoke French.)

With considerable federal support, some anglophones in Quebec responded to Bill 101 by launching or supporting legal challenges to several of its clauses. Court rulings, as well as amendments to the law introduced by both the Parti Québécois and, after 1985, the new Quebec Liberal government under Robert Bourassa, moderated the legislation. While many anglophones judged the amendments insufficient and indeed wanted an end to all language legislation, francophones continued to worry over the fragility of the status of French.

THE REFERENDUM DEBATE, 1980

Of greater interest to Canadians than the language question, which was basically an internal Quebec issue, was Quebec's referendum on political sovereignty, which

Where Social Scientists Disagree

THE ORIGINS AND EFFECTS OF QUEBEC'S LANGUAGE LEGISLATION

In 1969, the Quebec government began to adopt laws intended to augment the use of French in the province. These laws, the most important aspects of which have affected education, the workplace, and public signage, have provoked passionate debate and intense conflict.

Most social scientists have viewed the linguistic revolution as the result of a *prise de conscience* (realization) by the French-speaking majority of its economic inferiority in Quebec. In his article "State, Language and Society: The Vicissitudes of French in Quebec and Canada," in Alan C. Cairns and Cynthia Williams, eds., *The Politics of Gender, Ethnicity, and Language in Canada* (Toronto: University of Toronto Press, 1986), geographer Eric Waddell points out that, traditionally, those Québécois who wished to function in the world of industry and commerce had to achieve fluency in English, even though French-speakers were a large numerical majority in the province. In this environment, most anglophones remained unilingual. "Transported to a country-wide level in which francophones were an effective *minorité*," Waddell argues, "such inequalities could only be reinforced" (p. 88). Quebec's language laws should thus be seen as attempts to come to terms with the "asymmetrical" nature of French–English relations in Canada. The Canadian and North American context places the French language at a heavy disadvantage in regard to English. Even in Quebec, the English language enjoys a visibility that French does not possess outside Quebec. In marked contrast to Waddell's reasoning, the federal Official Languages Act places all minorities on a theoretically equal footing.

Political scientist Richard Handler, in his book *Nationalism and the Politics of Culture in Quebec* (Madison: University of Wisconsin Press, 1988), also asserts that language laws were "aimed at redressing the economic balance of power within Quebec" (p. 170). Marc V. Levine reaches similar conclusions in his analysis of Quebec's efforts to promote the visibility of French in "Language, Policy, and Quebec's *Visage Français*: New Directions in *La Question Linguistique*" (Quebec Studies 8 [1989]). In a study covering a portion of the 1980s, Levine noted the extent of the francophone reconquest of Montreal's economy by that time and concluded that Quebec's language legislation had indeed made an important contribution to this dramatic change (Marc V. Levine, *The Reconquest of Montreal: Language Policy and Social Change in a Bilingual City* [Philadelphia: Temple University Press, 1990]).

While agreeing with the fundamental importance of the economic roots of Quebec's linguistic upheaval, some analysts have delved more deeply into the class composition of Québécois society in search of the forces underlying the measures taken to strengthen the role of the French language. Political scientist William Coleman, for instance, stresses the class nature of language reform: university-educated Québécois working in the public sector, the main component of a "petite bourgeoisie," successfully "francized" schools and public signs, but their advances in the private sector were largely blocked in the 1970s by powerful anglophone and conservative francophone capital ("The Class Basis of Language Policy in Quebec, 1949–1975," in *Studies in Political Economy* [Spring 1980]: 93–117).

(continued)

The new and obviously less powerful status of Quebec's anglophones has been the subject of several studies. Many anglophones left Quebec in the 1970s, presumably motivated at least in part by political and linguistic fears. In a controversial study, however, Uli Locher concludes that, even after the adoption of Bill 101 in 1977, anglophones were leaving Quebec primarily because of the lure of greater prosperity in Toronto and the West (*Les anglophones de Montréal: emigration et évolution des attitudes, 1978–1983* [Québec: Conseil de la langue française, 1988]). Most observers judge that anglophones remaining in Quebec still enjoy far greater rights and privileges than most francophones do elsewhere in Canada. But political scientist Garth Stevenson, in his book *Unfulfilled Union: Canadian Federalism and National Unity*, 3rd ed. (Toronto: Gage, 1989), cautions that Quebec's more generous treatment of its minority cannot be explained solely by the goodwill of the majority. Rather, it is a logical consequence of the demographic balance in Canada and in North America as well as of the vast economic power that anglophones wielded in Quebec until recent times.

Philosopher Charles Taylor attempts to define the basis for the divergent views of anglophones and francophones on the language question. He sees most anglophones, like Americans, putting forth a liberal view of society in which individual rights must take precedence over collective goals. Provisions for bilingualism in federal law can be justified in terms of individual rights: francophones across Canada, at least theoretically, can obtain federal government services in French. Francophones espouse a collective goal: to ensure that there will still be francophones in the next generation. Taylor believes that Quebeckers also share liberal values but that, in order to retain their identity, they distinguish between fundamental liberties, which should never be infringed, and privileges, which are only important (Charles Taylor, "Shared and Divergent Values," in Ronald L. Watts and Douglas M. Brown, eds., *Options for a New Canada* [Toronto: University of Toronto Press, 1991]).

The issue of language continues to be debated within Quebec. Many English-speakers continue to decry the very existence of language legislation, while francophones will always feel culturally insecure because of the enormous pressures of the continent's English environment. Because of the emotional nature of the question, it will remain an important challenge for Canadian society and a subject of discussion for social scientists.

would decide Quebec's — and Canada's — future. In a shrewdly worded question, the Parti Québécois government asked voters for a mandate to negotiate political sovereignty within an economic association with the rest of Canada. In the hope of obtaining majority support, the government appealed both to Quebeckers' desire for change and, by asking voters to give it only the right to *negotiate*, to their more conservative instincts. No unilateral declaration of independence would follow a positive vote. The campaign debate was fierce, dividing families and friends, but it was not violent. Claude Ryan, Robert Bourassa's successor as the Quebec Liberal leader, led the *non* forces. Prime Minister Trudeau intervened late in the campaign, promising unspecified constitutional change if Quebeckers voted *non*.

On May 20, 1980, Quebeckers defeated the referendum proposal by a 60–40 margin. While almost all non-French-speaking Quebeckers voted no, the French-

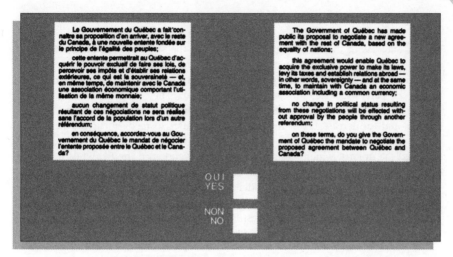

Le Gouvernement du Québec a fait con-
naître sa proposition d'en arriver, avec le reste
du Canada, à une nouvelle entente fondée sur
le principe de l'égalité des peuples;

cette entente permettrait au Québec d'ac-
quérir le pouvoir exclusif de faire ses lois, de
percevoir ses impôts et d'établir ses relations
extérieures, ce qui est la souveraineté — et,
en même temps, de maintenir avec le Canada
une association économique comportant l'uti-
lisation de la même monnaie;

aucun changement de statut politique
résultant de ces négociations ne sera réalisé
sans l'accord de la population lors d'un autre
référendum;

en conséquence, accordez-vous au Gouvernement du Québec le mandat de négocier
l'entente proposée entre le Québec et le Canada?

The Government of Québec has made
public its proposal to negotiate a new agreement with the rest of Canada, based on the
equality of nations;

this agreement would enable Québec to
acquire the exclusive power to make its laws,
levy its taxes and establish relations abroad —
in other words, sovereignty — and at the same
time, to maintain with Canada an economic
association including a common currency;

no change in political status resulting
from these negotiations will be effected without approval by the people through another
referendum;

on these terms, do you give the Government of Québec the mandate to negotiate the
proposed agreement between Québec and
Canada?

OUI / YES

NON / NO

The Quebec referendum ballot, May 20, 1980. The Parti Québécois asked only for the right to negotiate political sovereignty within an economic association with the rest of Canada, not for immediate independence.

Le Directeur Général des Élections du Québec.

speaking population split virtually down the middle. Analyses of the vote showed that the older age groups, the economically disadvantaged, and those with relatively little education tended to vote *non*. Those in the younger age groups and people with more education and higher incomes more often answered *oui*.

THE 1980S: THE WHEEL TURNS

The mood of the early 1980s in Quebec was pessimistic. The 1981–82 recession dramatically cut employment in the resource and manufacturing industries. Unions suffered membership losses as well as rising unpopularity among a public weary of strikes and agitation. Quebeckers complained about the declining quality of education and, as in other provinces, the universities bitterly condemned the government's stringent cutbacks in financing.

Nor did the outcome of the constitutional debate cause much rejoicing in Quebec. The federal government's proposals gave Quebec none of the powers that its provincial governments had consistently claimed since 1960, powers that even a discussion paper issued by Claude Ryan's provincial Liberal party had urged during the referendum campaign. Moreover, Ottawa managed to isolate Quebec by playing it off against the other nine provinces. In slightly amended form, the constitutional proposals became law despite Quebec's objections. Neither Premier René Lévesque nor opposition leader Claude Ryan attended the celebrations on April 17, 1982, when Queen Elizabeth II proclaimed the new Constitution. Quebec was legally bound by the terms of the new Constitution, but the document lacked moral legitimacy in the province.

Perhaps Quebeckers looked for a balance when they re-elected the Parti Québécois in 1981. They had said no to the separatist government's constitutional proposition in May 1980; the next year they said no to the strongly federalist provincial Liberal party. Regretting their victory, some *péquistes* warned that the PQ needed a spell in opposition to rethink its positions and that the economic downturn did not favour the party's chances for the immediate future. They proved to be right. The harsh recession as well as a severe budget crisis forced the government to reduce services and to increase taxes. Its draconian measures to recover part of the salary increases that had been granted to civil servants, hospital personnel, and teachers alienated the unions, which had so enthusiastically endorsed the PQ while it was in opposition before 1976. Moreover, the era of large-scale spending and government interventionism had passed as budget deficits increased and a new conservative mood gained strength throughout the western world, including Quebec. Individualism was celebrated as the new cult, and business leaders became its high priests.

NATIONALISM IN DECLINE

Nationalist sentiment weakened after the defeat in the referendum of 1980. The now middle-aged champions of yesterday's nationalist causes became disillusioned, and younger Quebeckers worried more about finding jobs than about championing political causes. The growing unpopularity of the PQ led some observers to predict nationalism's demise. Sensing the waning of nationalist fervour in the face of the stinging defeats of 1980 and 1982, René Lévesque decided to put aside, at least for the foreseeable future, the issue of sovereignty-association. This decision provoked a dramatic revolt within the party in late 1984 and early 1985; several veteran cabinet members, including Camille Laurin, the father of Bill 101, and Jacques Parizeau, minister of finance, resigned. As the party's popularity continued to sink, pressures forced Lévesque to quit. The new leader, Pierre-Marc Johnson, son of former Union Nationale premier Daniel Johnson, prevented an electoral debacle, but, in the elections held in December 1985, the party lost power to the Liberals under their resurrected leader, Robert Bourassa. Disapproval within the party of Johnson's moderate nationalist stance forced the new leader's rapid resignation. Jacques Parizeau, Johnson's reputedly more orthodox successor in 1988, soon promised that a Parti Québécois government would not act to decide Quebec's future without first seeking popular approval by means of a referendum.

In the years following the recession of the early 1980s, Quebec's economic growth placed it at, or near, the lead of the recovery among Canada's provinces. Reassured by the new political stability and by the reduced level of government interference, investment accelerated and business flourished. The provincial government held spending in check and reduced certain taxes. Since taxes were increasing in other provinces, Quebec's competitive position improved.

While the Bourassa government prided itself on offering competent administration, it failed to exercise leadership with regard to environmental issues. Paper mills, aluminum manufacturing plants, and other industries continued to foul the water and the air with chemical pollutants, often in flagrant violation of existing regulations. Agricultural wastes, fertilizers, and pesticides also polluted the province's rivers. Critics worried that the huge new hydro-electric megaprojects planned for

Quebec's north would go forward without adequate study of the potential threats to the environment. Several incidents involving fires deliberately set in toxic waste and tire dumps dramatized both the dangers of pollution and the government's ecological neglect. While it was no worse than that of several other provinces, Quebec's environmental record gave Quebeckers, reputed by polls to be among the most environmentally conscious of Canada's citizens, little cause for satisfaction.

THE REVIVAL OF NATIONALISM

Those who had proclaimed nationalism's demise in the early 1980s proved poor prophets. By the end of the decade, both the language issue and Quebec's future links with Canada again became important public topics. The language issue emerged with renewed force in late 1988 over the relatively minor issue of public signs. When the Supreme Court of Canada found Quebec's sign law (which required French-only signs) to be in violation of the freedom of expression provisions of both the federal and the Quebec charters of rights, Bourassa had to act. The Supreme Court had admitted that signs solely in English could be prohibited and that the government could require "the predominant display of the French language, even its marked predominance." Bourassa's solution was to invoke the Constitution's "notwithstanding clause," which enables a province to suspend certain rights for five-year periods, and to introduce Bill 178, requiring French-only signs outdoors, while authorizing bilingual signs within certain stores. Quebec's, and Canada's, anglophones protested vehemently, and three English-speaking ministers resigned from Bourassa's cabinet. In the 1989 election, many English-language voters abandoned the Liberals and rallied to the Equality party, a new political formation committed to anglophone rights.

Supporters of French-only signs argued fervently that Quebec needed a French "face" in order to persuade new immigrants to integrate into the francophone community. They added that the enormous weight of English in the North American context could be counterbalanced only by legislation protecting the French majority. The debate became rancorous; even historians (reputed to be coldly analytical) entered aggressively into the fray. One historian quoted in the *Toronto Star* suggested that an army of sign painters be sent to Quebec; a counterpart in Quebec City told readers of *Le Soleil* that the painters should stop off at Cornwall, Ontario, near the Quebec border, where they would find ample work to do painting signs in French. Both obviously preached to a converted audience. Passions cooled over time and, when the five-year period ran out in 1993, the Bourassa government adopted more liberal legislation. The language issue undoubtedly contributed to the failure of the Meech Lake constitutional accord in 1990. Many Anglo-Canadians, ignoring the often unenviable fate of francophone minorities throughout Canada, said they wanted no part of a "distinct society" that would be free to "oppress" its anglophone minority. In turn, francophones within Quebec showed little enthusiasm for an agreement that might not give Quebec sufficient power to act to protect the French language.

Assessing the overall impact of Quebec's controversial language legislation since the early 1970s is a difficult task. In spite of the progressive weakening of Bill 101's clause on the language of signs, Montreal in the mid-1990s "looked" much more French than it had in 1970. By 1990, almost all immigrant children were enrolled in French schools, but, in many of these, they constituted an overwhelming majority and had little contact with Quebeckers whose mother tongue was French. Thanks in part to the exodus of many anglophones, more francophones now held upper-level positions in business. More workers earned their living in French, but language legislation did not cover small enterprises, and many employers insisted that their French-speaking personnel be able to serve anglophones in English. Adversaries of Bill 101, however, warned that the legislation would hurt economic development in the province. They also suspected that it would tarnish Quebec's reputation, since English-language media would give far more publicity to anglophone complaints than to the problems of francophones outside Quebec's borders, or even within the province. At the same time, perhaps no other solution existed to the language problem. It would have been impossible to promote the use of French aggressively without to some degree undermining the important, even dominant, role of English in Quebec, particularly in the province's economy.

MEECH LAKE

The constitutional issue followed the linguistic debate. Meeting in Edmonton in August 1986, the provincial premiers agreed to undertake a "Quebec round" of negotiations, "to bring about Quebec's full and active participation in the Canadian federation" before moving on to other concerns. Quebec put forth five conditions, which, it stipulated, were "minimal." They included the recognition of the province as a "distinct society" and greater powers with regard to immigration.

In June 1987, Prime Minister Brian Mulroney and the ten provincial premiers met in Ottawa and, after arduous all-night negotiations, gave unanimous assent to an accord amending the Constitution. Robert Bourassa proclaimed that Quebec could now adhere to the Canadian Constitution "with dignity and honour." Brian Mulroney euphorically expressed his conviction that "the bonds of Confederation" would be strengthened and the "unity of our people" enhanced.

In the months that followed, the federal government and eight provinces, beginning with Quebec, ratified the proposals. Then the accord began to unravel as newly elected premiers in the two remaining provinces, New Brunswick and Manitoba, argued that they were not bound by their predecessors' signatures. They demanded substantial modifications to the accord. Subsequently, a third premier, Clyde Wells of Newfoundland, had his province rescind its approval. Groups representing women, Native peoples, ethnic associations, and northerners objected that their own concerns had not been addressed. Other critics, including former prime minister Pierre Trudeau, argued that the Meech Lake Accord would seriously weaken federal authority and promote linguistic ghettos within Canada. In addition, while the agreement's opponents in English-speaking Canada feared that the accord would confer unwarranted additional powers on Quebec, some Quebeckers were convinced that their province would in fact obtain too little by virtue of the agreement. Opinion research showed, however, that the great majority of Quebeckers thought that the agreement was a good thing for Canada.

As the three-year period for approval of the accord drew to a close in June 1990, protracted negotiations among the premiers produced an add-on agreement that included promises to work for a revamped Senate that would represent regional interests more effectively. Then, under intense pressure, the premiers of Manitoba and

Newfoundland promised to submit the accord to their respective legislative assemblies. Developments in the final moments were unexpected. With the support of Native leaders from across Canada, Elijah Harper, a Cree NDP member of the Manitoba legislature, denounced the Meech Lake Accord for ignoring the rights of Canada's Aboriginal people and signalled his intention to use the rules of parliamentary procedure to kill it. On June 23, 1990, as the deadline for approval expired, the Meech Lake Accord died.

Most Canadians outside Quebec felt relief at the failure of the accord; polls showed that a growing majority had opposed it. In English-speaking Canada, economic problems seemed more pressing than constitutional issues. In Quebec, however, the failure of this new episode of constitutional reform had dramatic repercussions. Nationalists, including many federalists, perceived the death of the agreement as signifying English Canada's refusal to accommodate even the province's minimal concerns. Independence now seemed the only possible choice for those who could not accept the status quo. Several federal members of Parliament from Quebec quit their parties to join a new group, the Bloc Québécois, headed by former Conservative cabinet minister Lucien Bouchard. To deflect criticism of his government, Robert Bourassa set up a nonpartisan commission to study Quebec's constitutional future, and promised to hold a referendum. Political scientist Vincent Lemieux believes that Bourassa wished to use the "threat of independence" to bring forth new propositions for a reform of Canadian federalism, and thus make it possible to "avoid independence."[5]

ECONOMY, SOCIETY, AND CONSTITUTION IN THE 1990S

The federal government decided to reopen the constitutional issue but, in deference to critics of so-called "executive federalism" by which the federal prime minister and provincial premiers, sitting around a table, decided the country's fate, it began by holding consultations across Canada. This time the Native peoples played a far more important role in the discussions. Quebec, however, which had decided after the failure of the Meech Lake Accord to boycott future talks, was virtually absent until the final round of negotiations, held in Charlottetown. Quebeckers reacted without enthusiasm to the ensuing agreement. Premier Bourassa claimed that it was the best he could do, while his political adversaries asserted that he had accepted much less than the Meech Lake Accord had offered. In a referendum held in October 1992, voters in six provinces, including Quebec, rejected the Charlottetown agreement and constitutional negotiations ceased. Sociologist Maurice Pinard points out that polls showed a strong majority of Quebeckers felt that the accord offered too little to Quebec; in English Canada, nearly 60 percent of voters felt it gave Quebec too much.[6] This time, however, Quebeckers did not view the failure of the agreement as a rejection by English Canada, since they themselves had voted against it.

RECESSION

Economic recession after 1991 provoked a substantial rise in unemployment. By late 1994, Quebec had still not succeeded to the same extent as Ontario and the western provinces in recovering the jobs lost, though the weaker Canadian dollar did boost

About 200 000 people marched in Montreal's St. Jean Baptiste Day parade, June 24, 1994. The lead banner proclaims, "Next year — My country."

CP Picture Archive (Ryan Remiorz).

export markets for the province's resources. Many jobs in inefficient, formerly tariff-protected industries such as textiles and furniture, which came under considerable competition from imports, simply disappeared. Montreal remained afflicted with the highest unemployment rate of any major Canadian city, though in 1990 the Population Crisis Committee in Washington, D.C., did rank the city among the world's most liveable large metropolitan centres, along with Melbourne, Australia, and Seattle, Washington.

Quebec faced other problems that almost all provinces confronted. Provincial budget deficits burgeoned through the early 1990s and, in response, the government increased taxes and attempted to reduce costs, notably in sectors such as health and welfare. Yet deficits remained unacceptably high. In the field of education, the government continued to revise school curricula, but rising numbers of high school dropouts, especially boys, presaged serious social problems for the future.

THE REFERENDUM OF 1995

The seeming impossibility of reaching any constitutional agreement helped set the stage for an increase in nationalist sentiment in Quebec. More importantly, Jean Chrétien, who became Canada's prime minister in 1993 after the Liberal electoral victory, was perceived by even moderate nationalists as rigidly opposed to Quebec's claims for greater autonomy. In that same election, the nationalist Bloc Québécois proved far more popular than Chrétien's Liberals within the province. The return to power of the Parti Québécois in 1994 — although with barely more votes than the provincial Liberals attracted — made a new referendum certain.

In this referendum, held on October 30, 1995, the provincial government asked electors if they wished Quebec to become "sovereign," after having formally offered Canada a new economic and political partnership. The federalist *non* won a razor-thin victory, with only 50.6 percent of the valid votes cast, in a vote in which more than 93 percent of eligible voters participated. Maurice Pinard felt that, had the referendum been held immediately after the failure of the Meech Lake Accord, "the 'yes' vote would have won."[7] For some observers, Lucien Bouchard's increasingly prominent role in the campaign explained the strong showing of the *oui*, favoured by well over 60 percent of French-speaking voters. Yet Vincent Lemieux cautioned that, for many electors, a vote for "sovereignty" did not signify a vote for "independence" and a break with Canada.

Anglophones, allophones, and members of First Nations communities supported the *non* option with near unanimity; their behaviour was not surprising, since these groups shared none of the discontent or the aspirations of the francophones. Strongly attached to Canada, they felt that they had everything to lose and nothing to gain in supporting Quebec sovereignty.

Many English Canadians reacted with bitterness to the outcome of the referendum, feeling it was time to prepare for separation and to prepare to drive a hard bargain with a seceding Quebec that would deprive the province of important parts of its territory. Reflecting public opinion in English Canada, the Chrétien government adopted a hard line and sought legal means to block any effort for Quebec to leave Canada. In an opinion suffused with Solomon-like wisdom, the Supreme Court of Canada affirmed unanimously in 1998 that, indeed, Quebec had no legal right to secede unilaterally. However, if a clear majority of Quebeckers responded "yes" to a clear question on the independence of Quebec, the federal government would be obligated to negotiate in good faith with the province.

Antagonism cooled, however, and the PQ's relatively weak showing in the provincial election of 1998 — it won a strong majority of seats but received fewer votes than the opposition Liberals — made it unlikely that a new referendum would be held in the foreseeable future. Still, relations between Ottawa and Quebec remained testy, as Ottawa undertook new initiatives in such fields of provincial jurisdiction as education and health. While nine provinces agreed to a plan that would in some cases permit provinces to opt out of federal programs, Quebec held that restrictions on federal spending power in areas of provincial jurisdiction were insufficient, and refused to sign.

QUEBEC ON THE EVE OF 2000

Polls have continually shown that constitutional issues have not been Quebeckers' primary concern. People have been more preoccupied with economic and social questions. After 1995, economic growth finally picked up and investments increased strongly. Although many new jobs were created, the unemployment rate remained close to 10 percent. The disastrous ice storm of January 1998, which deprived

A Historical Portrait
LUC PLAMONDON, CÉLINE DION, AND THE GLOBAL VILLAGE

In the 1950s, several Quebec artists, among them poet and singer Félix Leclerc, first achieved fame abroad, particularly in Paris, before continuing their career in Quebec. In the 1960s and the 1970s, stars such as Gilles Vigneault, Jean-Pierre Ferland, and Pauline Julien, many of them ardent nationalists, rose to fame in Quebec, although on occasion they performed abroad. Since the 1980s, however, many of Quebec's most talented artists have quite literally gone global, working in Montreal, Toronto, Los Angeles, Paris, London, and elsewhere. Luc Plamondon and Céline Dion are probably the two best-known examples of the 1980s and 1990s.

Luc Plamondon grew up in modest circumstances in a small town in Quebec's Eastern Townships. He first built a career in Quebec, then extended his activities to France, notably as a songwriter for singer Diane Dufresne. France offered possibilities that Quebec, with its small population, could not. As Plamondon put it, "the Paris region contains 12 million potential spectators, twice the entire population of Quebec." And yet Plamondon has built his major shows, the rock opera *Starmania* and more recently the musical production *Notre-Dame de Paris*, based on Victor Hugo's celebrated novel, largely with Quebec talent. *Starmania* began playing in Paris in 1979; by 1999 it was also scheduled to be performed in Spain, Germany, and Japan. The show's major songs, such as "Le Blues du businessman" and "Les uns contre les autres," have been played on French radio from morning to night. *Notre-Dame de Paris*, which opened in Paris in 1998, attracted tremendous success, with performances always sold out well in advance. Its dazzling choreography, its seductive and romantic music, and its songs, such as the enormously successful "Belle" and "Les temps des cathédrales," sung by Quebecker Bruno Pelletier, captivated audiences. In 1999, the show took to the road to perform in Belgium and Quebec, with plans for an English-language version to be performed in Toronto and London. Plamondon, who promised himself in 1960 that he would create for the French-speaking world a musical comedy that would be what *Hair* was to the English-speaking world, could boast of his contribution to a living French language, as his contemporary hits even managed to push American successes off the airwaves in France.

Céline Dion, another planetary superstar with unpretentious roots, first became a child star in Quebec in the 1980s. In 1984, she sang for Pope John Paul II at Olympic Stadium in Montreal; for some she was reaffirming her traditional Roman Catholic roots, while for others she was simply being tacky. In 1988, she won first place at the annual Eurovision competition, Europe's Olympics of song contest, held at Dublin and apparently viewed by 600 million telespectators. The year 1992 saw her win awards for her album containing songs written by Luc Plamondon, an album that was hugely successful in Quebec and France. Then, in 1993, she won Juno awards in Toronto, singing in recently learned English and, in the words of gushing critics, bridging the cultural gap between Canada's "two solitudes." In 1997, she performed two songs for the Academy Awards to an audience that reportedly numbered one billion people. She also picked up two Grammy Awards in New York City. In her acceptance speech, she addressed Quebeckers in French, a gesture that one *Globe and Mail* columnist thought worth more than "a trillion distinct society clauses." By that

(continued)

time Dion, whom *Time* magazine proclaimed a "global diva," had sold more than 60 million albums, including 25 million copies of her "Falling into You." Her album *Let's Talk About Love* was equally successful, and more Juno and Grammy nominations came her way in 1999. Biographer Barry Grills now saw Dion as building cultural bridges from Quebec to the rest of the planet; she occupied "a huge international territory, while still maintaining a direct connection to the culture where, for her, it all began" (*Falling into You: The Story of Céline Dion* [Kingston, ON: Quarry Press, 1997], pp. 9–10). Yet Dion asserted, in an interview, "I am very much Americanized." In this regard, she simply voiced the attraction to America and the American dream that many Québécois have felt throughout their history.

3 million Quebeckers of electricity, some for lengthy periods of time, triggered a period of particularly rapid growth in the months that followed.

Reductions in government spending and the maintenance of high levels of taxation enabled Quebec to eliminate its budgetary deficit in 1999. At the same time, these cuts brought mounting protests from the sectors most concerned. Considerable dissatisfaction centred on health services, as waiting lists for operations lengthened and emergency wards were overburdened. Educational services were also severely cut back, notably in universities, where declining provincial subsidies combined with low tuition costs to produce a crisis.

Quebec artists, among them singers Céline Dion and Kevin Parent, lyricist Luc Plamondon, and stage director and playwright Robert Lepage, continued to enjoy substantial success (see Chapter 20). At the same time, American cultural products, such as the film *Titanic*, attracted Quebeckers quite as much as they fascinated other Canadians.

The environment became a less popular concern than it had been in the 1980s; reflecting this decreased interest, the provincial government accorded less attention to the question. Agricultural pollution, caused largely by phosphorus from animal manure fouling rivers, remained a serious problem. In the spirit of the times, the provincial government also sought to loosen environmental controls and to rely increasingly on polluters to police themselves. Environmentalists warned that the province's forests were being cut down at a rate substantially in excess of their capacity to regenerate. Well-known pop singer Richard Desjardins even produced a film, *L'Erreur boréale*, denouncing what he saw as the collusion between forest companies and the government. Acid rain continued to destroy the province's lakes, half of it coming from the United States and a quarter from neighbouring Ontario. The World Wildlife Fund gave Quebec an "F" for having created no new terrestrial parks in the 1990s.

Also potentially dangerous for Quebec's future are demographic trends. A low birth rate, similar to that in most other provinces, could cause Quebec's total population to begin to fall early in the next century. Partly in order to offset the decline in births, the province increased the number of immigrants it admitted. Yet retaining them in Quebec, with its relatively high unemployment rate, and integrating them into French-speaking society, remain difficult problems. In addition, Quebec's declining share of Canada's total population portends diminishing political influence for the province.

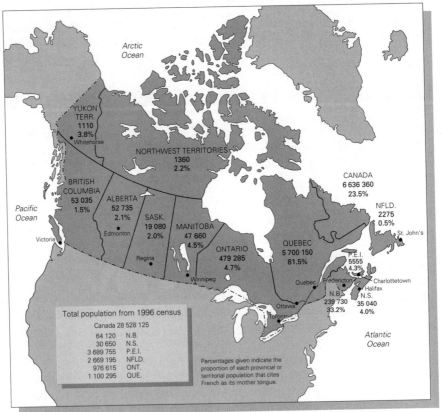

Canada's francophone population, 1996. Note the French-speaking community's strong majority position in Quebec, but minority status (less than 5 percent of the total population) in all other provinces and territories, with the exception of New Brunswick.

Source: Based on data from Statistics Canada, cat. nos. 93F0024XDB96001 in the "Nation Series."

Although Quebec will remain predominantly French-speaking in the foreseeable future, the French language will continue to be spoken by a declining minority outside the province, and by an infinitely smaller minority elsewhere in North America. Canada's commitment to bilingualism and to equal status for its francophone citizens also risks being called into question, notably by groups such as the Reform party. Inevitably, the threat of assimilation will continue to weigh heavily upon francophones, and the French-speaking community will have to devote increasing effort to revitalizing its language and culture.

Regardless of the province's constitutional and linguistic evolution, Quebeckers, like other Canadians, will have to create a society that affords women the same opportunities it offers men, and to find solutions to the problems posed by living in an increasingly pluralistic society As the dramatic confrontation with the Mohawks at Oka in the summer of 1990 acutely demonstrated, Quebeckers, again like other Canadians, must reach an accommodation with the Native peoples in the province to settle long-standing grievances. Much energy will have to be directed to combating such social problems as poverty, youth crime, violence, and a painfully high suicide rate among young males. In addition, all Quebeckers, regardless of language or origin, will have to meet the challenges and pay the high price of creating an environment that can sustain human life of the highest quality.

NOTES

1. Susan Mann Trofimenkoff, *The Dream of Nation: A Social and Intellectual History of Quebec* (Toronto: Gage, 1982), p. 284.
2. Guy Rocher, *Le Québec en mutation* (Montreal: Hurtubise, 1973), p. 18.
3. Marcel Rioux, *La question du Québec* (Paris: Seghers, 1969), p. 104.
4. Dale C. Thomson, *Jean Lesage and the Quiet Revolution* (Toronto: Macmillan, 1984), p. 309.
5. Vincent Lemieux, "Les partis et l'idée de souveraineté," in Maurice Pinard, Robert Bernier, and Vincent Lemieux, *Un combat inachevé* (Ste-Foy, QC: Presses de l'Université du Québec, 1997), p. 18.
6. Maurice Pinard, "Les fluctuations du mouvement indépendantiste depuis 1980," in Maurice Pinard et al., *Un combat inachevé* (Ste-Foy, QC: Presses de l'Université du Québec, 1997), p. 97.
7. Pinard, "Les fluctuations," p. 99.

LINKING TO THE PAST

The Origins of Quebec Separatism
http://www.uni.ca/sep_origins.html
A brief overview of the history of Quebec separatism from The Unity Link web site.

Living in French in Canada
http://www.pch.gc.ca/offlangoff/english/EJ01.htm
This site, from Canadian Heritage's Official Languages Support Program, provides an overview of the use of the French language in Canada. Included are brief descriptions and statistics by province.

The October Crisis
http://24.72.7.107/canada/october.htm
Notes from Trudeau's national broadcast of his October Crisis speech.

The Meech Lake Accord
http://insight.mcmaster.ca/org/efc/pages/law/cons/Constitutions/Canada/English/Proposals/MeechLake.html
The full text of the 1987 Constitutional Accord, also known as the Meech Lake Accord.

Lucien Bouchard and the Parti Québécois
http://www.premier.gouv.qc.ca/personne/indexa.htm
Check out Lucien Bouchard's "Biography" or read up on the Parti Québécois's history of Quebec's sovereignty movement, under "Our Project: Sovereignty."

The Charlottetown Accord
gopher://wiretap.spies.com:70/00/Gov/Canada/charlott.acc
The final draft of the failed Charlottetown agreement.

RELATED READINGS

The following articles in R. Douglas Francis and Donald B. Smith, eds., *Readings in Canadian History: Post-Confederation*, 5th ed. (Toronto: Harcourt Brace, 1998), deal with topics relevant to this chapter in greater depth: Richard Jones, "Politics and the Reinforcement of the French Language in Canada and Quebec, 1960–1986," pp. 460–77; and Kenneth McRoberts, "Separate Agendas: English Canada and Quebec," pp. 477–88.

BIBLIOGRAPHY

Although considerable scholarly material on Quebec exists in English, students wishing exposure to a full range of often controversial viewpoints need a reading knowledge of French. Chapters 17 to 20 of Susan Mann Trofimenkoff's *The Dream of Nation: A Social and Intellectual History of Quebec* (Toronto: Gage, 1983) review this period. Recent research on modern Quebec is summarized in an English translation of a study completed in 1986, Paul-André Linteau et al., *Quebec since 1930* (Toronto: James Lorimer, 1991). A new revised edition is available only in French, *Le Québec depuis 1930* (Montréal: Boréal Express, 1989). A good general interpretation in English is Kenneth McRoberts, *Quebec: Social Change and Political Crisis*, 3rd ed. (Toronto: McClelland & Stewart, 1988). Yves-Henri Nouailhat offers a comprehensive overview of modern Quebec history in *Le Québec de 1944 à nos jours* (Paris: Imprimerie nationale, 1992). Ramsay Cook presents his interpretations in *Canada, Québec, and the Uses of Nationalism*, 2nd ed. (Toronto: McClelland & Stewart, 1995). See also Ronald Rudin's provocative analysis of Quebec historiography, *Making History in Twentieth-Century Quebec* (Toronto: University of Toronto Press, 1997).

On the Duplessis years see Conrad Black, *Render Unto Caesar: The Life and Legacy of Maurice Duplessis* (Toronto: Key Porter, 1998); Herbert F. Quinn, *The Union Nationale: Quebec Nationalism from Duplessis to Lévesque*, 2nd ed. (Toronto: University of Toronto Press, 1979); and, for a brief sketch, Richard Jones's booklet *Duplessis and the Union Nationale Administration* (Ottawa: Canadian Historical Association, 1983). Michael Behiels, *Prelude to Quebec's Quiet Revolution: Liberalism versus Neo-Nationalism, 1945–1960* (Montreal/Kingston: McGill-Queen's University Press, 1985), examines the ideological conflicts among Duplessis's opponents. Recent research on the Duplessis years is available in Gilles Bourque, Jules Duchastel, and Jacques Beauchemin, *La société libérale duplessiste, 1944–1960* (Montreal: Presses de l'Université de Montréal, 1994); and in Alain-G. Gagnon and Michel Sarra-Bournet, *Duplessis: Entre la Grande Noirceur et la société libérale* (Montreal: Québec Amérique, 1997).

Dale C. Thomson studies the early 1960s in *Jean Lesage and the Quiet Revolution* (Toronto: Macmillan, 1984). A summary of Marcel Martel's study of the relations between Quebec and French-speaking minorities is available in English in *French Canada: An Account of Its Creation and Break-up, 1850–1967* (Ottawa: Canada's Historical Association, 1998). John Bosher holds that France plotted to support Quebec separatism in *The Gaullist Attack on Canada, 1967–1977* (Montreal/Kingston: McGill-Queen's University Press, 1998). For a journalistic account of the Bourassa years see Michel Vastel and Herbert Bauch, *Bourassa* (Toronto: Macmillan, 1991). On the independentist movement in general consult William D. Coleman, *The Independence Movement in Quebec, 1945–1980* (Toronto: University of Toronto Press, 1984). Studies of the Parti Québécois include Graham Fraser, *PQ: René Lévesque and the Parti Québécois in Power* (Toronto: Macmillan, 1984); and René Lévesque, *Memoirs* (Toronto: McClelland & Stewart, 1986). Philosopher Charles Taylor proposes an original analysis of French–English relations in Guy Laforest, ed., *Reconciling the Solitudes: Essays on Canadian Federalism and Nationalism* (Montreal/Kingston: McGill-Queen's University Press, 1993).

The constitutional question is examined extensively by Edward McWhinney in *Quebec and the Constitution, 1960–1978* (Toronto: University of Toronto Press, 1979), and in his *Canada and the Constitution, 1979–1982: Patriation and the Charter of Rights* (Toronto: University of Toronto Press, 1982). For Quebec viewpoints see Christian Dufour, *A Canadian Challenge: Le défi québécois* (Lantzville, BC: Oolichan Books, 1990); Louis Balthazar, Guy Laforest, and Vincent Lemieux, *Le Québec et la restructuration du Canada, 1980–1992: enjeux et perspectives* (Sillery, QC: Septentrion, 1991); Alain-G. Gagnon, *Québec: État et société* (Montreal: Québec Amérique, 1994); Gilles Bourque, Jacques Duchastel and Victory Armory, *L'identité fragmentée: nation et citoyenneté dans les débats constitutionnels canadiens, 1941–1992* (Montreal: Fides, 1996); and Robert A. Young, *The Secession of Quebec and the Future of Canada*, 2nd ed. (Montreal/Kingston: McGill-Queen's University Press, 1997). Alan Cairns, *Charter versus Federalism: The Dilemmas of Constitutional Reform* (Montreal/Kingston: McGill-Queen's University Press, 1992), is a thoughtful essay. Other useful articles by Cairns have been collected in Douglas E. Williams, ed., *Disruptions: Constitutional Struggles from the Charter to Meech Lake* (Toronto: McClelland & Stewart, 1991). Among the many publications bearing on the Meech Lake Accord see Michael D. Behiels, ed., *The Meech Lake Primer: Conflicting Views of the 1987 Constitutional Accord* (Ottawa: University of Ottawa Press, 1989); Andrew Cohen, *A Deal Undone: The Making and Breaking of the Meech Lake Accord* (Vancouver: Douglas & McIntyre, 1990); Jean-François Lisée, *The Trickster: Robert Bourassa and the Quebeckers, 1990–1992* (Toronto: James Lorimer, 1994); Guy Laforest, *Trudeau et la fin d'un rêve canadien* (Sillery, QC: Septentrion, 1992); and Patrick J. Monahan, *After Meech Lake: An Insider's View* (Kingston: Institute of Intergovernmental Relations, Queen's University, 1990). A fine overview of English-Canadian reaction to Quebec's post-Meech crisis is provided by Kenneth McRoberts, *English Canada and Quebec: Avoiding the Issue* (North York, ON: Robarts Centre for Canadian Studies, 1991). Later constitutional developments are examined in Kenneth McRoberts and Patrick Monahan, *The Charlottetown Accord: The Referendum, and the Future of Canada* (Toronto: University of Toronto Press, 1993). Maurice Pinard, Robert Bernier, and Vincent Lemieux, *Un combat inachevé* (Ste-Foy, QC: Presses de l'Université du Québec, 1997); and Kenneth McRoberts, *Misconceiving Canada: The Struggle for National Unity* (Toronto: Oxford University Press, 1997) are excellent recent studies. The latter expresses many doubts regarding the efficacy of Pierre Trudeau's policies.

Analyses of the language question include Eric Waddell, "State, Language and Society: The Vicissitudes of French in Quebec and Canada," in Alan C. Cairns and Cynthia Williams, eds., *The Politics of Gender, Ethnicity, and Language in Canada* (Toronto: University of Toronto Press, 1986), pp. 67–110; articles by Richard Jones and William D. Coleman in Michael D. Behiels, ed., *Quebec since 1945: Selected Readings* (Toronto: Copp Clark Pitman, 1987), pp. 223–62; Michel Plourde, *La politique linguistique du Québec, 1977–1987* (Québec: Institut québécois de recherche sur la culture, 1988); Pierre Godin, *La poudrière linguistique: La revolution tranquille, 1967–1970* (Montréal: Boréal Express, 1990); and Marc V. Levine, *The Reconquest of Montreal: Language Policy and Social Change in a Bilingual City* (Philadelphia: Temple University Press, 1990). Ronald Rudin provides an excellent introduction to Quebec's anglophone community in *The Forgotten Quebecers: A History of English-Speaking Quebec, 1759–1980* (Québec: Institut québécois de recherche sur la culture, 1985). See also Josée Legault, *L'invention d'une minorité: Les Anglos-Québécois* (Montréal: Boréal Express, 1992); and Sheila McLeod Arnopoulos and Dominique Clift, *The English Fact in Quebec*, 2nd ed. (Montreal/Kingston: McGill-Queen's University Press, 1984).

Cultural development is examined in Richard Handler, *Nationalism and the Politics of Culture in Quebec* (Madison: University of Wisconsin Press, 1988). A summary in English of Martin Pâquet's important study of immigration is available in a brochure, *Toward a Quebec Ministry of Immigration* (Ottawa: Canadian Historical Association, 1997). Pierre Dubois proposes a study of one important environmental question in *Les vrais maîtres de la forêt québécoise* (Montréal: Editions Ecosociété, 1995). Jean Hamelin chronicles the recent evolution of the Roman Catholic Church in *Histoire du catholicisme québécois: le XXe siècle: II — De 1940 à nos jours* (Montreal: Boréal, 1984). A study of the postwar generation in Quebec is François Ricard, *The Lyric Generation: The Life and Times of Baby Boomers* (Don Mills, ON: Stoddart, 1994). The experience of women in Quebec is covered in Micheline Dumont et al., *Quebec Women: A History* (Toronto: Women's Press, 1987). A revised version of this study is available in French only: *L'histoire des femmes au Québec depuis quatre siècles*, rev. ed. (Montréal: Le Jour, 1992). For a history of one important women's organization, see Yolande Cohen, *Femmes de parole: l'histoire des cercles de fermières du Québec 1915–1990* (Montreal: Le Jour, 1990). Danielle Lacasse examines a social problem in *La prostitution féminine à Montréal, 1945–1970* (Montréal: Boréal, 1994). Pierre Hurteau studies anti-homosexual discourse in "L'homosexualité masculine et les discours sur le sexe en contexte montréalais de la fin du XIXe siècle à la Révolution tranquille," *Histoire sociale/Social History* 26 (1993): 41–66.

Denis Monière's *Ideologies in Quebec* (Toronto: University of Toronto Press, 1981) is a useful intellectual history. On labour history, see Jacques Rouillard, *Histoire de la CSN, 1921–1981* (Montreal: Boréal, 1981) and his *Histoire du syndicalisme au Québec* (Montreal: Boréal, 1989). Three important studies of Quebec society are Fernand Dumont, ed., *La société québécoise après 30 ans de changements* (Québec: Institut québécois de recherche sur la culture, 1990); the same author's *Genèse de la société québécoise* (Montreal: Boréal, 1993); and Simon Langlois et al., *Recent Social Trends in Quebec, 1960–1990* (Montreal/Kingston: McGill-Queen's University Press, 1992).

Several books have been written on the first James Bay hydro-electric project. Roger Lacasse celebrates the $15 billion development in his *Baie James. Une épopée. L'extraordinaire aventure des derniers des pionniers* (Montréal: Libre expression, 1983). Sylvie Vincent and Garry Bowers have edited a collection of essays on the project, *Baie James et nord québécois: dix ans après/James Bay and Northern Quebec: Ten Years After* (Montréal: Recherches amérindiennes au Québec, 1988). Richard F. Salisbury's *A Homeland for the Cree: Regional Development in James Bay, 1971–1981* (Montreal/Kingston: McGill-Queen's University Press, 1986) is another important analysis of the project's impact on the Cree. Studies of Quebec-based businesses include Maurice Chartrand and René Pronovost, *Provigo: An Outstanding Entrepreneurial Success* (Scarborough, ON: Prentice-Hall, 1989); and Peter Hadekel and Ann Gibbon, *Steinberg: The Breakup of a Family Empire* (Toronto: Macmillan, 1990).

CHAPTER EIGHTEEN

The English-Speaking Provinces since 1960

The discussion of Quebec's constitutional future and of the issue of language after 1960 tended to obscure two important realities. First, English-speaking Canada was not a monolith; in fact, the bonds of interregional and interprovincial unity within English Canada were not really as cohesive as proponents of a "dual Canada" seemed to believe. Second, in spite of the substantial coverage that the media devoted to the dramatic events in Quebec, important changes transformed the other provinces as well.

A history textbook published in the mid-1960s, *Canada: Unity in Diversity*, acknowledged the importance of the regions and devoted separate chapters to their study.[1] Not surprisingly, provincial politicians have strongly affirmed the distinctive character and interests of their own provinces. Local media have also argued for greater recognition of their region's particular problems. Culture also reflects these differences, and certainly since 1960 all the regions of Canada have seen literature and other forms of art flourish, reflecting a diversity of local experiences.

Regionalism has been a powerful theme throughout Canadian history, and no less so in recent decades. Geographer Cole Harris has observed that regionalism is "anchored in the country's geographical spine."[2] Certainly geography helps explain the substantial economic differences, with their political, social, and cultural ramifications, that exist among the provinces. Such differences mould regional identities; they also contribute to interregional friction.

THE ATLANTIC PROVINCES

Canada's four easternmost provinces — Newfoundland, Nova Scotia, New Brunswick, and Prince Edward Island — are often considered as one unit. Their combined population is barely 8 percent of Canada's total. The region attracts few immigrants; indeed, out-migration has often been substantial. During the period 1951–71, for example, 15 percent of Atlantic Canada's inhabitants left the region. Newfoundland saw about 1 percent of its residents leave the island each year during the 1990s. Its relative demographic decline portended diminishing political influence in Ottawa.

As early as 1949, Premier Joseph R. Smallwood of Newfoundland proposed a union of the four eastern provinces to enable them to increase their bargaining power with the federal government. In 1970, the Deutsch Commission on Maritime Union recommended "full political union as a definite goal." But grassroots support for such a step was lacking, and the politicians themselves, with their priorities reflecting different ambitions and concerns, had a vested interest in maintaining the status quo. Only four years later, Nova Scotia Premier Gerald Regan pronounced Maritime union "as dead as a door nail." In 1996, newly elected Prince Edward Island Premier Pat Binns said as much: "Maritime union as a project would be very expensive, so why would we do it?" Yet various programs and bodies have, over the years, assured greater regional co-operation. The Atlantic Economic Council, for its part, recommended that provincial governments and other organizations work to favour increased economic integration.

PROBLEMS OF THE ATLANTIC ECONOMY

The major problems of the Atlantic region have been economic. The provinces' economies remain relatively undiversified and rely heavily on agriculture, forestry, mining, and, although less than in the recent past because of the decline of fish stocks, fishing. Export prices for primary products often fluctuate wildly in international markets. Few manufacturing industries locate in this area, since distances from major markets are substantial and local markets are small. Consequently, unemployment remains high, afflicting 10–20 percent of each province's work force in recent years.

Not surprisingly, inhabitants of the Atlantic provinces have ceaselessly decried the country's regional disparities, of which they are the major victims. Before World War II, central Canadians largely ignored Maritime discontent and tended to blame the region's problems on its inhabitants' alleged unprogressiveness. More recently, as historian David Alexander put it, many residents of Canada's more-favoured heartland continued to dismiss Atlantic protest as "an illogical and petty resentment of the inexorable march of industry into southern Ontario."[3]

Since the 1960s Ottawa has recognized the legitimacy of Atlantic complaints, although its numerous policy changes, as well as the criticism they have provoked, indicate that long-term solutions are elusive. The Atlantic Development Board, set up in 1962, funded projects and improved the region's infrastructure. (Political and patronage considerations often determined its choices.) Such initiatives, together with equalization grants and other subsidies, facilitated the creation of jobs, albeit often temporary ones, and ensured that the area could offer its citizens services reasonably similar to those provided by wealthier provinces. In 1969, the newly established federal Department of Regional Economic Expansion (DREE) began to offer incentives to encourage companies to locate in less-favoured areas of the country, such as the Atlantic provinces, in the hope of redressing regional economic disparities. The department spent money on highway construction, schools, and municipal services, and also attracted some new industry. R. Harley McGee, a student of regional development, concluded that DREE represented "the best approach to both regional development policy and its implementation."[4]

In the early 1980s, the Trudeau government dismantled DREE, feeling that the economic environment was improving and that Ottawa was receiving insufficient credit for its efforts. Eventually the Mulroney government gave responsibility for regional development to a new body, the Atlantic Canada Opportunities Agency, a measure which critics derided as "just another shuffle of the ancient cards of regional inequality." Ottawa's growing deficit soon forced it to reduce the new agency's funding. All told, federal grants to businesses in Atlantic Canada, totalling more than $5 billion since 1970, have produced "no appreciable closing of the gap between have and have-not provinces as measured by per capita income or unemployment rates."[5] Direct money transfers from Ottawa to individuals, in the form of unemployment insurance, welfare, and other payments, however, have helped to boost household incomes.

FEDERAL–ATLANTIC RELATIONS

The 1997 federal election saw the Atlantic region elect several NDP candidates to Parliament. It was the region's first significant experiment with third parties to convey dissatisfaction with the federal government, in this case the Liberals, who had reduced transfer payments and restricted admissibility to unemployment benefits for seasonal workers. Previously, Maritime MPs sought to promote regional interests either within governing parties or by voting for the main opposition party. At the provincial level, Atlantic Canadians first elected Liberals who strongly defended provincial interests, such as Joey Smallwood in Newfoundland, Louis Robichaud in New Brunswick, and "All's Well with Angus L." Macdonald (an electoral slogan that served Macdonald well) in Nova Scotia; then hedged their bets and chose Conservatives during the long years of Liberal rule under Pierre Trudeau, and Liberals as discontent with the Mulroney Conservatives grew.

Historian George Rawlyk has defined Atlantic Canada's attitudes toward the federal government as "ambivalent."[6] Although Confederation has yielded obvious benefits for the Atlantic provinces, most easterners believe that Ottawa's policies have brought far more prosperity to central Canada. Despite perennial manifestations of economic discontent, Atlantic Canadians have generally defended the principle of a strong federal government, even in the 1960s and 1970s, when many Canadians elsewhere sought to weaken federal authority. Atlantic Canadian discontent — as strong as it has been and still is — has not, since the turn of the century, attempted to find a voice in local separatist movements, mainly because few Atlantic Canadians could argue convincingly that the region would be better off without Canada.

NEW BRUNSWICK

Speaking of Atlantic Canada as a whole belies the very real differences among the four provinces it comprises. New Brunswick's major difference from the other three provinces lies in the ethnic and linguistic mix of its population, one-third of which is French-speaking. Long at a disadvantage both economically and linguistically, the French-speaking Acadians have sought and, to a considerable extent, achieved greater equality. In the early 1970s, Acadians confronted Moncton's mayor, Leonard Jones, an adamant opponent of bilingual municipal services. Jones's obstinacy — which students from the Université de Moncton underlined by depositing a severed pig's head on the mayor's doorstep — probably served as a catalyst for the Acadians' struggle. The Parti Acadien was formed in 1972 to promote Acadian interests, but it never succeeded in drawing Acadians' loyalty from the established parties.

In 1968, New Brunswick adopted an Official Languages Act that gave official recognition to linguistic rights. Then, through the 1970s, the provincial government cautiously proclaimed and applied the various clauses of the legislation. Attitudes changed slowly. One survey in 1986 showed that more than half of New Brunswick's francophones saw themselves as victims of discrimination, while three-quarters of the province's anglophones denied the existence of such discrimination.

Since World War II, New Brunswick's governments have sought in various ways to stimulate economic development. In the 1950s, provincial planners hoped that cheap electric power would attract heavy industry to the province. After 1960, the Liberal government led by Louis Robichaud intervened actively in the development of provincial resources. When pulp and paper companies failed to use Crown lands they held under long-term lease, the government cancelled their licences and awarded them to other companies. When an American mining company reduced operations in its lead and zinc mine near Bathurst, Robichaud engineered a buyout by Canadian investors, including native son K.C. Irving, who set about building a huge smelter complex.

The Irving family's business interests included 3000 gas stations, trucking and bus lines, shipbuilding, huge forest reserves, paper and saw mills, radio and television stations, and the province's English-language newspapers; these companies employed roughly 25 000 people in New Brunswick. Irving's biographer claimed that "surely no individual in any single Canadian province ... ever held so much raw economic power."[7]

Irving's local roots and power gave him considerable bargaining clout with the provincial government, which he exploited to win concessions. Historian James Kenny concludes that New Brunswick may have escaped dependence on foreign capital, but it entered into a "new and perhaps more dependent relationship" with Irving.[8] Irving hired his own companies to perform the construction work on the smelter complex, but delays and ballooning costs finally brought the provincial government to allow a takeover by Noranda. Although the value of the mineral industry increased spectacularly in the 1960s, the industry did not have the desired transforming effects on provincial and local economies.

Social change came rapidly to New Brunswick in the 1960s under Louis Robichaud, the province's second Acadian premier. Robichaud's Equal Opportunity program aimed at improving the lot of the province's poorer citizens, often Acadians who lived in rural areas in the north and east; in particular, the government greatly expanded health, social, and educational services. These measures generated fierce opposition among anglophones in the south, who regarded them as proof of a costly Liberal plot to "rob Peter to pay Pierre."

K.C. Irving vigorously opposed Robichaud's Equal Opportunity plan. A cartoon in one of the Irving newspapers pictured a despotic Robichaud as a modern Louis XIV, with wild eyes, crown askew, and hand clutching a sword threatening his foes. Significantly, in the 1967 election, Robichaud's Liberals lost almost all the predominantly English seats.

In the 1970s, Progressive Conservative Premier Richard Hatfield attempted several experiments designed to stimulate New Brunswick's economy and to compensate for the decline of the agricultural sector. Forest and mining industries did expand, and the federal government made substantial grants to the province. But one notable industrial venture in which the provincial government invested heavily, the

New Brunswick Premier Louis Robichaud, the province's second Acadian premier. His administration in the 1960s built many hospitals, schools, and public buildings.

Provincial Archives of New Brunswick/ P57-15.

Bricklin automobile project, failed totally. Premier Hatfield came under increasing attack in the 1980s for government measures to extend bilingualism, for his flamboyant lifestyle (Liberal critics nicknamed him "Disco Dick"), and for some of his ministers' personal use of public funds. According to biographer Richard Starr, what expanded during the premier's tenure was not the economy, as he had promised, but the government deficit, unemployment, the premier's waistline, and his cabinet. Finally, in October 1987, New Brunswick's voters displayed their discontent in no uncertain terms: they elected Liberals, led by Frank McKenna, in every district in the province.

Job creation and a balanced budget were the new government's priorities. In the early 1990s, expansion in the food-processing industry, new power plants, and more service-related jobs in sectors such as telecommunications helped compensate for employment losses in the forest industry. McKenna also froze public servants' wages; cut spending in health, education, and social services; and increased taxes. In addition, he attempted to redesign welfare in order to bring recipients back into the work force.

In 1998, McKenna's successor, Camille Thériault, was forced to deal with the difficult issue of Native logging rights on Crown land. He also had to face growing dissatisfaction due in part to spending cuts on welfare and health, and to plans to levy tolls on portions of the Trans-Canada Highway. Unemployment remained high, particularly in the Acadian peninsula. Promising to cut taxes and to avoid deficits while, at the same time, increasing spending on health and education, the Conservatives, under their youthful new leader, Bernard Lord, put an end to twelve years of political misfortunes by winning a strong victory at the polls in June 1999.

NOVA SCOTIA

Nova Scotia, the most populous and prosperous of the four Atlantic provinces, has the most diversified economy. Primary industries have been a mainstay of the province's economy, and Nova Scotia's service sector is more developed than that of the other three provinces. Secondary industry is frequently linked to the processing of primary products. Some areas of the province, mainly Cape Breton Island, have suffered chronically high unemployment as local industries such as coal and steel have declined. Ottawa committed hundreds of millions of dollars in investments in attempts to create employment. Moreover, during a period of 30 years after 1968, Ottawa remitted subsidies totalling $1.7 billion to publicly owned mines that produced high-polluting sulphurous coal. Then, in 1999, Ottawa announced the closure of one coal mine and put the other up for sale, offering compensation for workers who would lose their jobs. Frustrated miners demanded that the provincial premier defend them: "You're not going to destroy our lives and the lives of our children.... We just want to survive."

Coal-mining in particular was dirty, difficult, and especially dangerous work. At the mines in Springhill, on the Chignecto isthmus, more than 400 persons lost their lives between 1881 and 1969. In October 1958, the collapse of a tunnel in a mine nearly 4 km deep caused the deaths of 74 miners. Then, in May 1992, a devastating explosion at the Westray mine in Pictou County killed 26 miners. Shaun Comish later recalled his fellow workers' constant fears but explained that the men needed a job, any job, to support their families. He also spoke of their hesitancy to unionize in the face of strong company opposition, and of the frequent violations of basic safety regulations, usually with management's knowledge if not at its insistence.

Tourism provides an important source of income in Nova Scotia, and the province has had enormous success in marketing a traditional, rather folkloric image of itself. Historian Ian MacKay shows how folksong collector Helen Creighton and handicrafts revivalist Mary Black presented and packaged folk expression. Through the efforts of Black and others, new handicraft traditions became part of the provincial identity. The Nova Scotian tartan, in particular, became "a fully accepted symbol of the province's imagined Scottish essence and its thriving handicraft tradition."[9] The tourist industry enthusiastically promoted this traditional image of the province and invented a host of cultural "traditions." An official tourist brochure proclaimed in 1986, "Nova Scotia is a province that becomes more itself every decade." It was the land of the Folk, of handicrafts, of the simple life. Sophisticated urban Haligonians expressed fondness for this image of an earlier era, slower and more authentic.

Economic issues have generally dominated provincial politics in Nova Scotia. By the mid-1950s, the province's relative economic stagnation helped bring the Progressive Conservatives, under Robert Stanfield, to power. They improved education and paved roads, but Stanfield's priority was economic development. He created Industrial Estates Limited, with well-known businessman Frank Sobey as its first president, to invest in local enterprises; serious losses, however, notably in stereo equipment and heavy water, followed the investment company's initial successes.

In the 1970s, Gerald Regan's Liberal government also planned many development projects, including an oil refinery complex on the Strait of Canso intended to strengthen Nova Scotia's industrial base. But the harsh economic realities of the late 1970s, including substantial increases in hydro-electric power rates, brought the Conservatives, led by John Buchanan, back to power. The new government's anti-union legislation, while embittering relations with labour, helped to create jobs by convincing Michelin Tire to expand production in the province. In addition, the discovery of gas and oil off the Atlantic coast, followed in 1982 by an agreement with the federal government regarding the sharing of revenues from offshore oil development, raised hopes for economic recovery. Buchanan proclaimed optimistically that exploitation of these offshore oil resources would end "going down the road" in search of jobs. But the federal government's decision to reduce funding for drilling, together with a dramatic plunge in oil prices in the mid-1980s, left these hopes unfulfilled.

In Nova Scotia, efforts to balance the budget in the 1990s gave rise, as was the case elsewhere, to considerable dissatisfaction and even to the election of a strong NDP contingent to the provincial legislature. As the decade ended, hopes for economic improvement ran high. Plans moved ahead for the construction of the $2 billion Sable Island offshore natural-gas pipeline project. Halifax, the Atlantic seaboard's deepest natural harbour, aspired to be chosen for the site of a superport capable of handling the huge new container ships that now ply the sea lanes.

PRINCE EDWARD ISLAND

Prince Edward Island has undergone substantial change since World War II. The face of farming was transformed as many small farmers, unable to compete because of low potato prices, left the land. More than two-thirds of the island's farms have disappeared since 1951, though total hectarage in potatoes has increased. High energy costs and transportation difficulties also hindered the growth of industry.

Governments responded to changing attitudes. In 1970, the province's Liberal government launched with considerable fanfare a Comprehensive Development Plan for social and economic change and industrial development, which was to be financed largely by Ottawa. A decade later, one journalist wrote of the program: "It's still a big, fat flop." Little economic diversification had taken place and unemployment increased. In turn, the Liberal government's enthusiasm for rapid and unrestricted growth lessened. In 1989, as land speculation and the proportion of island land in the hands of non-residents increased, Premier Joe Ghiz appointed a royal commission to study land ownership and land use. The government also signed agreements with two food-processing giants to build plants on the island and increase the percentage of potatoes being processed in the province.

Many islanders have long feared that pressures from the mainland would destroy Prince Edward Island's way of life. A patriotic society established in 1972, the Brothers and Sisters of Cornelius Howatt (named for an anti-confederate leader of the 1870s), campaigned vigorously against the acquisition of land by non-residents. In the late 1980s, fears of too-rapid development, coupled with environmental considerations, led many islanders to criticize federal plans to build a "fixed link" across Northumberland Strait to New Brunswick. Another group, "Islanders for a Better Tomorrow," brought together spokespersons for agriculture, who sought cheaper transportation, and for tourism, in support of the project. Ottawa, which had made such promises since 1959, decided, this time, to move ahead after 60 percent of islanders voted "yes" to the project in a referendum in 1989. The Confederation Bridge, 13 km long, was opened in 1997. That year, tourism increased by 60 percent over the preceding year. Some critics feared, however, that Maritime day-trippers would transform the gulf province into a Canadian Coney Island and that new development would destroy the island's rural charm.

Other economic and social questions also preoccupied Prince Edward Islanders. When Ottawa announced the closure of the military base at Summerside, discontent brought Ottawa to install the administrative headquarters for the new Goods and Services Tax on the island. In addition, decisions made by the provincial government in its efforts to balance the budget provoked dissatisfaction, as civil servants saw their wages cut and country schools and hospitals were threatened with closure. Ottawa's decision to reduce benefits for the seasonally unemployed also provoked ire. The provincial Conservative party benefited from this discontent and gained power under their leader, Pat Binns, in 1996.

NEWFOUNDLAND

On May 9, 1997, politicians and business people gathered at Bull Arm, northwest of St. John's, to christen the new Hibernia off-shore oil production platform, which had been built with government and private money at a cost of $6 billion. The festive occasion was marred by a demonstration by hundreds of unemployed fishery workers, protesting against Ottawa's compensation program for the collapsed cod fishery. For some, that event dramatized the contrast between the Newfoundland of yesterday, a province of low incomes and a slowly dying fishing industry, and the Newfoundland of tomorrow, richer and more developed.

The fishing industry was already in difficulty in the 1950s. After Newfoundland entered Confederation in 1949, the federal government failed to take the necessary steps to restructure the industry, especially the inshore fishery. What Ottawa did do, in the relatively prosperous 1950s, was to extend unemployment insurance coverage to seasonal fishers, a measure that helped increase the number of fishers at a time when the continued health of the industry necessitated significant downsizing.

The liberalization of unemployment insurance access rules in the early 1970s gave the fishing industry a vested interest in creating a maximum number of short-term jobs that would give unemployment insurance to everyone in the off-season. The provincial government subsidized the building of numerous fish-processing plants, which hired for 10-week periods so that very large numbers of workers would qualify for benefits. By 1984, such payments constituted about a quarter of the total income of the average full-time fisher. The root cause of the dependence on government aid, however, was the industry's "chronic underdevelopment," brought about by a lack of capital investment and by resistance to technological innovation.[10]

WEB
LINKS

Employment in the fishing industry attained a peak in 1988: 90 000 jobs, although many were part-time and made possible only by subsidies. Then employment plummeted in the early 1990s as cod and other ground-feeding fish stocks, hitherto thought to be inexhaustible, declined precipitously as a result of overfishing, both domestic and foreign, and possibly, too, because of environmental factors. Ottawa imposed a moratorium on catches and then, in 1994, announced a five-year, $1.9 billion compensation plan that was to eliminate 15 000 jobs in the Atlantic fishery.

Although 12 000 workers ostensibly left the fishery, thanks to the program, 80 percent remained on some sort of government assistance. Many workers had low levels of formal education; they were familiar only with fishing and fish-processing; they lived in outports that had no other employment opportunities; and they owned houses that could not be sold. In 1998, Ottawa injected another $730 million into a program to buy back fishing licences and provide some assistance.

ECONOMIC DIVERSIFICATION

Since Confederation, Newfoundland's governments have sought with limited success to favour a more diversified economy. Joey Smallwood, Newfoundland's premier for more than two decades after 1949, hoped to carry out an industrial revolution to create thousands of new jobs, stem emigration, and drag the province "kicking and screaming into the twentieth century." He encouraged foreign investment and sponsored projects to develop the province's natural resources, such as iron and pulpwood, as well as Labrador's vast hydro-electric potential at Churchill Falls. There were some successes, but many costly failures.

Conservative Premier Brian Peckford's stewardship after 1979 was marked by acrimonious confrontations with the federal government over offshore oil rights and fisheries, with Quebec over electric power sales regulated by a contract that brought immense windfall profits to Hydro-Québec, and with the province's labour unions, particularly those in the public sector. Newfoundland's deteriorating economy and rising discontent with the federal Conservatives aided the Liberals in their return to power in 1989 under Clyde Wells, an implacable opponent of the Meech Lake Accord. His successor, Brian Tobin, elected in 1996 and re-elected in 1999, promised to act so that Newfoundland would cease being the poor relation of Canada.

The start of the Hibernia project proved disastrous. In 1982, the *Ocean Ranger* exploratory drilling rig capsized in the Hibernia field, killing all 84 crew members. Work was again halted in the late 1980s because of falling oil prices. Doubts about the financial feasibility of the project grew in the early 1990s. But the Hibernia field, in the Atlantic Ocean some 315 km from St. John's, began producing in late 1997. Two other offshore fields were scheduled to be in production around the year 2002. It was estimated that Newfoundland could furnish about a fifth of total Canadian oil production and that the provincial government would eventually derive important revenues from the project. Plans moved forward slowly to begin exploiting a huge nickel deposit at Voisey's Bay, in Labrador, but falling nickel prices, Premier Tobin's demand that a smelter be built within the province, and opposition by the Innu of Labrador have delayed the project. Other projects concerned non-resource-based manufacturing.

BRITISH COLUMBIA

British Columbia's rapidly growing population (nearly 4 million in 1998), its high per-capita incomes, and its rich resource base have made it one of Canada's "have" regions; enthusiastic newcomers, younger people as well as retirees from elsewhere in Canada, have called it a "lotus land." The province's location on the Pacific Ocean gives it a unique orientation. For historian Jean Barman, "The more British Columbians looked toward the Pacific Rim, the more the rest of Canada receded into irrelevance."[11] In 1990, with more than 40 percent of the province's exports already going to Pacific Rim nations, Vancouver mayor Gordon Campbell affirmed: "Over the next decade or two, we will be independent of the Canadian economy." Trade with Asia continued to increase in the years 1990–96. Massive inflows of investment as well as large numbers of new immigrants helped maintain an economic boom while the rest of Canada slid into recession. In the late 1990s, however, Asia's faltering economy had a strongly negative impact on British Columbia, precipitating it into recession.

A Historical Portrait

NEWFOUNDLAND FISHERS THROUGH ART AND SONG

Culture transmits, through its diverse forms, the experiences that mark human life. In a plan to fight the poverty rife in the Newfoundland outports, the Smallwood government, mainly during the 1960s, had 250 smaller communities totally evacuated in household resettlement programs involving nearly 30 000 people. Many inhabitants were moved against their will

Newfoundland artist David Blackwood memorialized the experience in his paintings. One work, titled *Resettlement*, showed an outport family in a boat piled high with their belongings, heading out to sea toward an unknown destination. The painting captured the profound despair of people who had lost all control over their own destiny. Artist Gerry Squires also did several works on the same theme. He commented on one of them, *The House Where Nobody Lives*, which showed one of the thousands of abandoned dwellings: "I still see the fear and the tears when people realized they could never come back."

The experience of relocation was also transmitted through songs that revealed the deep sadness of people at being separated from traditional livelihoods and familiar surroundings:

> No more we'll watch the caplin as they wash upon the sand,
> The little fish they used for bait, to fertilize their land;
> No more they'll watch their gardens grow or their meadows full of hay,
> Or walk the roads in their working clothes in the good old-fashioned way.*

The new communities into which outport residents were transplanted did not offer what had been promised. Songs such as this one revealed the bitterness and frustration of those who had been uprooted and transplanted:

> To a place called Placentia, some of them went
> And in finding their new homes their allowances spent
> So for jobs they went looking, but they looked all in vain
> For the roof had caved in on the Government Game.
> It's surely a sad sight, their moving around
> Wishing they still lived near the cod-fishing ground
> But there's no going back now, there's nothing to gain
> Now that they've played in the Government Game.†

* Reproduced with permission of Ernie Wilson. © Ernie Wilson.
† Reproduced with permission of Pat Byrne and Al Pittman. © Pat Byrne and Al Pittman.

Since the 1980s, environmentalists and partisans of economic growth in British Columbia have waged a bitter struggle. Traditional development policy emphasized rapid timber harvesting and economic development. As late as 1980, most logged land was not reforested. The provincial government generally accommodated the industry's wishes. In 1989, for example, Premier Bill Vander Zalm vetoed a cabinet proposal to reduce pulp and paper industry pollutants such as dioxins, declaring: "While I love the environment … I also love those … pulp mill workers and someone has to stand up for their jobs." (The succeeding NDP government adopted tough pulp-mill pollution laws.)

The new sensitivity to the protection of wilderness areas and the maintenance of ecosystems to ensure biodiversity provoked increasing criticism of clear-cut logging and, in particular, of forestry companies' plans to cut important stands of old-growth timber. Preservationists charged that forestry policies made the province "the Brazil of the North." At the same time, workers and particularly residents of rural communities dependent on logging worried about eventual job losses. In 1993, the forestry giant MacMillan Bloedel obtained permission to clear-cut up to 70 percent of the temperate rain forest of Clayoquot Sound, an area comprising some 350 000 ha on the west coast of Vancouver Island. Environmentalists waged a veritable "war in the woods," a campaign of civil disobedience, to protest against the government's action and attract international attention. They also targeted industrial consumers of British Columbia forest products in Europe and threatened boycotts of their products if they did not cease their purchases. The government had 800 protestors arrested, charged, and jailed or fined. It did, however, set up a panel to examine forest practices (and then adopted stringent new regulations), and it also agreed on co-management of the area with Native peoples. Government attempts to develop a more comprehensive approach gave rise to substantial opposition from industry and labour. Plans for protecting areas of Vancouver Island, for example, led to massive demonstrations by loggers and their supporters.

LEFT AND RIGHT IN BRITISH COLUMBIA

From 1952, when Social Credit won its first electoral victory, until the 1990s, British Columbia had a unique political history, with Social Credit and the CCF–NDP as the two major parties. W.A.C. Bennett, the new Social Credit leader, succeeded in rallying traditional Liberal and Tory supporters by emphasizing the party's role as the new standard-bearer of free enterprise. Bennett governed for the next 20 years, keeping the "socialist hordes" at bay and, as Bennett himself once said, "making policies for the hour."

During the Bennett years, British Columbia's economy developed rapidly. The state played a considerable role despite Social Credit's much-vaunted dedication to private enterprise. It improved highway, maritime, and rail transportation. It extended, at heavy cost, the Pacific Great Eastern Railway, linking the northern interior to the rest of the province. It nationalized the giant B.C. Electric Company and undertook hydro-electric projects. One of these, the gigantic Peace River Dam, built across the Rocky Mountain Trench, created Williston Lake, the province's largest body of water. Bennett also battled with the federal government over the terms of the Columbia River Treaty signed between Canada and the United States in 1961. The premier wanted to sell British Columbia's power allotment from the Columbia dam to the United States, while Ottawa opposed the sale.

Having succeeded in becoming a respectable alternative party, and benefiting from the disenchantment with Bennett's policies on education, health care, and welfare, the NDP finally won power in 1972. Under combative leader Dave Barrett, it initiated many controversial reforms — its opponents accused it of "legislating by thunderbolt" — including public automobile insurance, a new innovative labour code, and an attempt to preserve agricultural land. Barrett's reforms, high spending, and new taxes led conservative forces to unite in reaction. An economic downturn assisted this new coalition in bringing the populist Social Credit party back to power in 1975, under W.R. "Bill" Bennett, W.A.C. Bennett's son. Critics mocked Bennett's broad coalition of supporters by calling it the "united vegetable party."

In the early 1980s, the fall in world market prices for British Columbia's major exports, notably forest products and minerals, pushed the province into a prolonged recession. In 1984, 15 percent of the work force lacked jobs. The government's attempts to curtail spending on education and social services, in the face of a sharp drop in provincial revenues, provoked a fierce confrontation with the public-sector unions, mobilized within "Operation Solidarity," and Social Credit's popularity sank to new lows. But the climate of optimism brought on by Expo 86, which attracted large numbers of visitors, and the "sunshine offensive" of William Vander Zalm, Social Credit's charismatic new leader, enabled the party to win re-election easily. The Vander Zalm government pushed through new legislation to curb union power and privatized certain governmental services.

In the spring of 1991, serious conflict-of-interest allegations forced Vander Zalm to resign. Rita Johnston took over the premiership, becoming the first woman in Canada to head a provincial government. In the elections that soon followed, the NDP, led by former Vancouver Mayor Mike Harcourt, took power, promising it would favour moderate, "sustainable development" policies. (In that election, 25 percent of the victorious candidates were women, the highest percentage of any Canadian legislative body.) The province's economy remained strong; its diversification continued, as new service-sector jobs, many related to tourism, more than compensated for the loss of employment in the primary sector. Harcourt's consensual approach in regard to questions such as the environment, social issues, and labour satisfied few British Columbians and indeed made the premier appear weak and indecisive. Higher taxes as well as other measures taken to control the budget deficit also proved unpopular.

Prosperity brought its share of problems. New jobs went principally to the Lower Mainland; resource-based communities in the interior, such as Kimberley, lost jobs and feared for their future. But burgeoning Vancouver showed another face, as less prosperous citizens struggled to find scarce affordable accommodation, and homelessness increased. East Hastings Street remained one of the poorest areas of Canada. In addition, problems of traffic congestion and air pollution threatened to overwhelm the city.

The late 1990s were harsh times for many British Columbians. Lost Asian markets, American trade policies, and low prices brought sawmill closures and job losses. Some critics also blamed environmental regulations which increased industry costs. The forestry workers' union denounced "Greenpeace and other radical preservationist groups," while companies demanded that environmental standards be relaxed for logging operations on public lands. The decline of forest-industry taxes also proved a hard blow for provincial finances, and deficits increased.

Other problems, such as the massive cost overruns of a project to build three of the world's largest aluminum catamaran ferry boats, made the NDP government look incompetent. In addition, the signing of a treaty in 1998, which gave the Nisga'a First Nation $300 million and title to 1900 km^2 of land in northwest British Columbia, as well as unprecedented self-government powers, generated substantial opposition and demands that a referendum be held on the treaty.

British Columbia Premier W.A.C. Bennett (on the right) presenting an award to Major J.S. Matthews, first city archivist of Vancouver, April 27, 1968. Bennett's Social Credit party first came to power in 1952, and he remained premier for the next twenty years. He was succeeded by his son, Bill Bennett, who became premier in 1975.

Roma Photo/City of Vancouver Archives/Port. P1779, N1120.

THE WEST

The term "the West" is a more appropriate designation than "the Prairies" for the region that consists of Manitoba, Saskatchewan, and Alberta. The latter term evokes an image of immense fields of golden wheat with grain elevators on the horizon rising into the azure-blue sky. This stereotypical image no longer reflects the reality of the region.

The wheat economy has contributed greatly to the region's historically embittered relations with central Canada. Farmers railed against protective tariffs and denounced greedy grain traders, as well as the villainous banks and profit-hungry railways headquartered in Montreal and Toronto. Over time, grievances have changed, but they have become no less intense. Westerners have complained bitterly of what might be called their "hinterland status," which applies to culture as much as it does to politics and economics and which means an absence of control over decisions that affect the West.

Since World War II, the West has undergone immense change. Although the majority of westerners now work in the rapidly expanding service sector, the economies of the three provinces have lost much of their former similarity. Oil and gas have replaced agriculture as by far the leading components of the Alberta economy. Agriculture occupies a much greater position in Saskatchewan, while Manitoba boasts a more diversified economy. In the period after 1960, the West's sense of powerlessness remained: the region saw itself as a victim of federal policies on energy and other resources, on railway transportation, on the marketing of Prairie wheat, and on assistance to farmers suffering from crushing debt or failed crops.

WESTERN ALIENATION

During the prosperous 1970s, western dissatisfaction grew as the federal government in general, and Prime Minister Pierre Trudeau in particular, seemed to give little heed to the region's aspirations. Westerners felt they had little influence on national politics, since federal parties depended on Ontario and Quebec for most of their votes. Anger peaked in 1980, when the unpopular Trudeau announced the National Energy Program. The suddenly respectable separatist parties urged westerners "to take to the lifeboat of independence before it's too late." All of these movements denounced what they perceived as the federal government's subservience to Quebec. They also shared a common enmity for Pierre Trudeau, whom Elmer Knutson, an elderly millionaire from Calgary and founder of a movement called West-Fed, described as "this little yahoo down there on the left ... who says we have to be bilingual."

Wracked by internal wrangling and splits, western separatism failed to become more than a fringe phenomenon, primarily centred in Alberta and having no real impact on electoral politics. The recession of 1981–82 undermined the heady confidence that many westerners had felt during the prosperous 1970s. Then the departure of Pierre Trudeau removed the principal target of western anger. When the federal Conservatives won power in 1984 with a strong Prairie contingent, westerners were at first reassured. But soon falling prices for agricultural commodities, oil, and other resources, as well as Ottawa's perceived preoccupation with Quebec, provoked new frustrations. Many westerners sought increased political power for the region through a revised "Triple-E" Senate, which would be *equal* (with the same number of senators from each province, regardless of population), *elected*, and *effective*; hopes for such institutional change died with the defeat of the Charlottetown Accord in 1992.

WEB LINKS

The meteoric rise of the Reform party after 1987, under the leadership of Preston Manning, son of former Alberta Premier Ernest Manning, again showed the West's dissatisfaction with the mainstream parties. Proclaiming that "the West wants in," the party condemned the federal government's financial mismanagement, its "welfare-state approach" to meeting social needs, and its commitment to official bilingualism and multiculturalism as well as its immigration policy. For journalists Sydney Sharpe and Don Braid, "a hostile reaction to Quebec" in particular contributed strongly to the rise of Reform.[12] Although the party soon toned down its western rhetoric in an effort to win support in Ontario and Atlantic Canada, Reform's major successes occurred in Alberta and British Columbia in the federal elections of 1993 and 1997.

ALBERTA

The three western provinces have developed along separate paths, particularly in the last half-century. By the late 1950s, revenues from the sale of oil and gas in the United States and eastern Canada enabled the Alberta government to spend more money per capita, notably on health and education, than any other province. In 1961 the Diefenbaker government acted to prevent Montreal refineries, using less expensive crude oil from Venezuela, from entering the Ontario market. This policy forced Ontario to buy slightly more costly oil from the West, and Alberta production increased. Many Albertans felt, however, that imported crude should also have been excluded from Montreal and that Ottawa gave too much consideration to pressures from Quebec and the multinational petroleum companies.

The sharp increase in international oil prices in the mid-1970s brought wealth to Alberta as well as a new sense of independence and self-confidence. A bitter crisis in Edmonton–Ottawa relations followed. Strongly influenced by Ontario's pressures to have oil and gas considered "national commodities, belonging to all Canadians," the federal government imposed a "made-in-Canada" oil price that allowed central Canadian consumers to pay prices lower than the world price. The producing provinces resented federal price controls, which deprived them of billions of dollars. They argued that they deserved the best deal possible before the depletion of their reserves. At one point, the Alberta government reduced the flow of crude oil to the East, and some Alberta automobile bumpers sported stickers belligerently inviting easterners to "freeze in the dark." Alberta also vigorously opposed the Trudeau government's policy of Canadianization of the oil industry, blaming it for the decline in investment in the oil fields.

The expanding oil industry promoted rapid population growth in Alberta in the 1970s as easterners migrated in search of high-paying jobs. Construction boomed. Dozens of new office towers sprang up in Calgary and Edmonton. The residential home market saw prices skyrocket. Other regions of the province also prospered. Fort McMurray, for example, had only 1200 residents in 1964, when work began on a huge project to extract synthetic crude oil from the Athabasca tar sands. By 1978, when the Syncrude plant opened, the town had a population of 35 000. In enviable financial health, the Alberta government placed substantial sums from oil royalties in a Heritage Fund — money, in Premier Peter Lougheed's words, "for our children and for our grandchildren." The province's financial health allowed Albertans to enjoy high-quality social services while paying the country's lowest provincial income taxes, no provincial sales tax, and, until 1987, no tax on gasoline.

The decline in demand for oil during the 1982 recession, followed by sharply lower oil prices in 1986, checked Alberta's growth and clearly showed the basic fragility of its resource-based economy. Construction on the huge synthetic-oil production and heavy-oil upgrading projects ceased. The jobless rate matched eastern Canadian levels; indeed, many unemployed workers returned to eastern and central Canada. Real estate values fell sharply. Two major Albertan bank ventures collapsed resoundingly, though the federal government agreed to finance a costly bailout. The oil industry called upon both Edmonton and Ottawa for assistance; in particular, it urged Ottawa to apply a floor price to provide some stability to the industry. At the same time, agriculture faced serious difficulties, as drought afflicted farmers in the province's southern region and declining world prices and increased costs wiped out profit margins.

Politically, Albertans have long favoured one-party dominance. For 36 years, until 1971, they supported the Social Credit party. From the late 1940s, the once-reformist party led by Ernest Manning provided conservative government in a climate of general prosperity fuelled by rising oil revenues. Tensions developed beneath the surface: unions resented labour-relations laws with strong anti-strike provisions, and many Albertans, particularly the Native peoples, failed to benefit from the new riches. In the late 1960s, Calgary lawyer Peter Lougheed revived the provincial Progressive Conservative party, infusing it with the promise both of change and of continuity with

Prime Minister Pierre Trudeau and Alberta Premier Peter Lougheed, 1973, at the Western Economic Opportunities Conference in Calgary. Appearances can be deceiving — despite the cordiality evident in this photograph, animosity existed between the two leaders over the federal government's pricing of Alberta oil and gas.

Herald Collection/Glenbow Archives, Calgary, Canada/NA-2864-23502.

conservative traditions. Strongly supported by urban Alberta, the Conservatives won power in 1971 and established a new political dynasty. The immense amounts of oil money flowing into the Alberta treasury greatly assisted the Lougheed government, although it did have to face a resurgence of union militancy during the recession of the early 1980s.

Don Getty, a former player with the Edmonton Eskimos football team and Lougheed's successor as Conservative leader, won a comfortable majority in the provincial election of 1986. The election of 1989 reduced Getty's majority, and the premier, beaten in his own riding in Edmonton, was compelled to seek a safe rural seat. The onset of a new recession in Canada struck Alberta relatively mildly. The cattle industry prospered thanks to lower grain prices, while huge federal subsidies helped cushion the blow for wheat farmers. Government investment in the oil and gas industry, diversification into petrochemicals, and especially a buoyant small-business sector also provided economic stimulus. In addition, Edmonton announced huge new job-creating investments, mainly Japanese, in pulp and paper plants and sawmills in the north.

Far higher government expenditures on education and health and welfare services soon led to massive budgetary deficits. Several enterprises in which the Getty government invested money from the Heritage Fund went into bankruptcy. After Getty's resignation in 1992, new leader Ralph Klein, a former mayor of Calgary, successfully warded off Conservative collapse in an election campaign based largely on personality, and then instituted a policy of radical budget cuts to social spending designed to eliminate the deficit. Some critics claimed, however, that it was unfair to blame public programs for the financial troubles of 1986–93. Rather, they should be attributed to massive private-sector subsidies and to falling resource revenues. In the lead-up to the election of 1997, however, which he won easily, Klein did announce some reinvestment, and increased royalties from gas and oil brought the province large budgetary surpluses.

The rapid demographic growth of the city of Calgary symbolized Alberta's prosperity in the late 1990s, as newcomers poured in. Characterized by a more diversified economy, it now became the financial capital of western Canada and advanced technology sectors such as telecommunications and information services thrived. Artistic enterprise also flourished in this sophisticated city, once called Cowtown, and French-immersion enrollment rivalled Toronto's.

Economic growth, however, carried a price. The provincial government showed scant interest in studying the potentially negative effects of development projects on the environment. In 1995, the World Wildlife Fund (WWF) awarded the province an "F" for its failure to move forward on its commitment to protect wilderness. Although the province had elaborated a Special Places 2000 policy, the WWF insisted that it was actually an industrial development strategy rather than one to protect the environment. Increased logging, together with industrial activity and mining, threatened the last portions of wilderness in the province's northern forests.

SASKATCHEWAN

Neighbouring Saskatchewan's political development differed substantially from Alberta's. In 1944, the moderately socialist CCF gained office under Baptist preacher Tommy Douglas and began implementing a series of social and economic reforms, including a pioneering hospital-services plan that offered hospital care at public expense. Saskatchewan became the first province to enact medicare in 1962. In 1964, the Liberals, under Ross Thatcher, who saw himself as "chosen by God to get rid of these socialists," defeated the CCF (now the NDP). The Liberals did not, however, dismantle the political reforms. The Thatcher government had notorious disagreements with the federal Liberals over natural-resources development and federal fiscal measures. The NDP, which regained power in 1971, moved to make the provincial government a major player in economic development. After nationalizing a large American-owned potash company, it set up the Potash Corporation of Saskatchewan. Later it pursued a vigorous exploration and development program in uranium. In addition, it established Crown Investments Corporation, an enterprise that served as a holding company for the province's state-owned companies such as Sask Tel, Sask Power, and Saskoil, and that also bought large blocks of shares in private companies. Relations between the NDP government of Allan Blakeney and the Trudeau government in Ottawa were frequently strained as both governments struggled over the control of resources and the pricing and taxing of oil, gas, and potash.

Saskatchewan's booming economy in the 1970s generated increasing revenues, which enabled the Blakeney government to expand health care. Blakeney considered the gap between living standards of whites and the Native peoples to be the province's most serious social problem. Although his government acted to improve living conditions in Aboriginal communities in the north, it failed to address the serious social problems of Natives living in the cities.

Agriculture, the province's largest industry, remained subject to violent swings, depending on world wheat prices, export markets, and weather conditions. Low prices for grain and the high costs of technological innovation forced smaller and less efficient farmers to sell their land to larger operators and to migrate elsewhere in search of work. In an attempt to stem the decline of the family farm, the Blakeney government set up the Land Bank to provide small farmers with low-cost leased land from the government. Opponents immediately attacked the plan as a plot by "Big Brother" to turn the province's farmers into serfs. Though the Land Bank did enjoy some success, serious administrative problems and wildly fluctuating land prices eventually undermined it.

In 1982, the Progressive Conservatives, led by Grant Devine, scored a resounding victory, assuring electors, "There's so much more we can be," and promising measures to increase the ordinary person's disposable income and particularly to abolish the provincial gasoline tax. By the late 1980s, however, an alarming rise in the province's budget deficit forced the Devine government to make substantial cuts in social services. It also cancelled the Home Improvement Program and re-imposed a provincial gasoline tax. The Conservatives also pursued an aggressive privatization strategy, but rising opposition forced them to retreat from a plan to sell off Sask Energy, the province's natural-gas distributor. Although the Conservatives did take some steps to protect wildlife habitat and foster soil conservation, environmentalists faulted it for refusing to submit major projects, such as the construction of the Rafferty-Alameda dams, to full environmental-impact assessments. In 1991, popular discontent, particularly rife in urban areas, brought the NDP, now led by Roy Romanow, back to power. The province's dire financial problems forced the new government to increase sales and income taxes and make large spending cuts, provoking the discontent of public-sector unions, who wanted a better contract with the government. By 1994, however, a year before being re-elected, the Romanow government succeeded in recording its first budgetary surplus. But cuts in funding precipitated a health-care crisis, as dozens of small hospitals were closed. The province's outstanding writers, visual artists, and musicians also suffered as the Saskatchewan Arts Board, set up by the CCF government of Tommy Douglas, saw its already modest means frozen.

MANITOBA

Manitoba's diversified farming industry occupies a relatively small area in the southwestern portion of the province. Manufacturing is important, while mining and hydro-electricity have undergone considerable development in the north since the mid-1950s. Exploitation of the West's non-agricultural resources at first generated new markets for Winnipeg manufacturers, but the rise of Calgary and Edmonton meant new competition. Winnipeg suffered, too, from the decline of traditional industries such as meat-packing and from the loss, in the 1960s, of Air Canada's repair facilities. Agriculture has been a victim of global forces such as intense international competition and subsidy wars, and farm closures and bankruptcies have been numerous. Since the mid-1970s, plant closures and the restructuring of industries such as clothing have resulted in substantial job losses.

Politically, since the 1950s, the Conservatives and the NDP, the latter particularly strong in the poorer northern parts of the province and in northern and central districts of metropolitan Winnipeg, have dominated Manitoba politics. Duff Roblin's Progressive Conservative government of the 1960s proved more progressive than conservative, spending heavily on health, welfare, and education. The Roblin government also invested heavily in northern development, where it favoured hydro-electric projects, such as the huge installations on the Nelson River, and it attempted to attract private capital through loans and other concessions. Some projects such as the rich Inco mine at Thompson proved successful. Others failed: for instance, the Churchill Forest Industries complex at The Pas, which involved a government loan of $100 million, was halted when the owners disappeared with most of the money. Higher taxes also weakened support for the Conservative government.

In 1969, after building a broad electoral base, popular NDP leader Ed Schreyer succeeded in defeating Roblin's Conservative successor, Walter Weir. In these years of relative prosperity, the Schreyer government, promising to "open a new way to those who have previously known only disparity and discrimination," spent heavily on public housing and adopted major tax and social reforms. It also launched a second huge hydro-electric development project in the north. Conservative critics denounced the NDP's public automobile-insurance plan, its higher taxes, its investment of public monies in firms of doubtful financial health and, in general, state intervention, warning that Manitoba was moving toward socialism. When the Conservatives took power in 1977, new premier Sterling Lyon proceeded with a program of restraint and lower taxes, but in 1981 cutbacks and the province's dismal economic performance contributed to a return to power of the NDP, led by Howard Pawley.

In the 1980s, the Pawley government stimulated the province's economy and employment levels by beginning work on still another hydro megaproject and by participating in huge reconstruction projects such as the Core Area Initiative in downtown Winnipeg. By 1987, however, massive tax increases gave rise to much discontent. Moreover, the question of the linguistic rights of the weakening Franco-Manitoban community generated fierce debate. In 1971, the Schreyer government had authorized the use of French as a language of instruction in schools, thus restoring a right taken away in the nationalist frenzy of World War I. Then, in the late 1980s, another NDP government proposed to extend French-language services. This time, however, the adamant opposition of the Conservatives to new "concessions" forced the government to retreat. When, however, the Conservatives formed a minority government after the 1988 election, they bitterly attacked Quebec's Bill 178, which restricted the use of English on commercial signs. In a new election in 1990, Premier Gary Filmon won a majority, in part because of his strong criticism of the unpopular Meech Lake Accord. A policy of holding the line on taxes helped Filmon win a third mandate in 1995.

Free trade with the United States boosted Manitoba's exports to that country in the 1990s. Industrial products also saw new markets open. By early 1999, the province enjoyed Canada's lowest unemployment rate. Provincial finances were healthy as a buoyant economy brought in increased revenues and, together with spending cuts, made it possible to eliminate budget deficits and even begin to pay off accumulated debt. Some Manitobans, however, thought it was time for tax cuts or for increased spending on health, education, and physical infrastructure. Others worried about pressing social issues such as youth crime, gang violence, and the huge social and economic challenges linked to the province's burgeoning Aboriginal population.

ONTARIO

In a country marked by profound economic imbalances, Ontario has traditionally been Canada's major "have" region. About 40 percent of Canadians live there, assuring the province a major role in determining national policy. Half of Canada's new immigrants choose Ontario, and the province also generally attracts substantial in-migration from other less-favoured provinces. Immigration has made Toronto Canada's largest city and transformed it into one of the world's most culturally diverse cities. Benefiting from the postwar decline of Montreal, Toronto has become Canada's financial capital. It also has nearly half the country's head offices and three-quarters of the members of journalist Peter Newman's list of "Canadian national business establishments." In the 1980s, unemployment rates in the province were usually the lowest in Canada. Manufacturing, including 95 percent of the huge automobile and parts industry, whose health is responsible for the province's prosperity to a considerable degree, is concentrated here. Southern Ontario has also prospered because of a favourable geographical location.

Ontario's material success and political power have coloured other Canadians' views of the province and its citizens. Westerners and Maritimers have suspected central Canada of using Confederation to cement its economic mastery over the rest of the country, especially through protective tariffs. They were also convinced that the economic nationalism of the 1970s, fostered by the *Toronto Star* and Ontario university professors, among others, contained little promise for them. They judged that regions afflicted with relatively high unemployment could not enjoy the luxury of picking and choosing among investors. Joey Smallwood had affirmed in his typically colourful manner that he would not hesitate to deal with the devil if he had money to invest. Westerners furiously denounced Ottawa for an oil policy that favoured Ontario. Quebeckers pointed to the striking difference between the two provinces' jobless rates as proof that the power of central Canada really meant the power of Toronto.

Ontarians held the outsiders' views as largely unjustified, the product of envy, resentment, and frustration. The province has prospered, but there have been periods of adversity. Ontarians point out that their taxes pay a large portion of the cost of the equalization grants, unemployment insurance, farm subsidies, and industrial-development projects that the federal government gives poorer regions. The province, they insist, has done its share to shoulder the "burden of unity."

ONTARIO'S ECONOMIC DEVELOPMENT

The 1950s and 1960s were prosperous years for Ontario. Demand for a wide variety of goods stimulated industrial expansion, especially in the south. Services — banking, merchandising, education, health, government — multiplied. The province budgeted large sums for improving and expanding higher education; between 1950 and 1975, the number of publicly supported universities increased from three to fifteen. The construction industry prospered thanks to strong demand for housing. Governments at all levels invested heavily in the construction of highways and urban expressways. They also built watermains and sewers, promoted urban transit, sponsored electric-power projects, including nuclear-power plants, and completed work on the St. Lawrence Seaway. This intense activity explains why the unemployment rate generally stayed below 4 percent from 1945 until 1970. It rose slightly after the mid-1970s but remained below the national average. Economist Kenneth Rea calls these the "prosperous years."[13] Rea adds that while the Ontario government might take credit for permitting growth to occur and even, on occasion, stimulating it, the motor pushing Ontario's growth was in fact the private sector.

Ontario found the 1970s more difficult as jobs, capital, and people moved west and energy prices skyrocketed. In response, the provincial government tried to control public spending. In the field of higher education, increasingly the subject of

On the 56th floor of the Toronto-Dominion Centre, Toronto, April 1966. Constructed from 1963 to 1969, this building was designed by the German-American architect Mies van der Rohe, and reflected the International Style of architecture. Skyscrapers like this one came to dominate cityscapes from the 1960s onward.

Globe and Mail/66104-38.

intense public criticism, Queen's Park moved to get, in the words of historian Paul Axelrod, "more scholar for the dollar."[14] The severe recession in the dominant automobile industry in the early 1980s also hit Ontario hard. After 1984, however, rapid recovery followed, once again giving Ontario Canada's lowest unemployment rate and its citizens the country's highest income levels. By 1989, Ontario's share of the national gross domestic product reached 42 percent. In a magazine that it produced, the provincial government reminded the world that, if opulent Ontario were a sovereign state, it would rank as the eleventh-strongest economy in the world. Then, in 1990, recession descended on the province and unemployment increased dramatically, especially in manufacturing industries, construction, and retail sales. Economists blamed high interest rates, high wage rates, and high prices for commercial real estate. It would take until 1994 for Ontario to recover the jobs lost during the severe downturn. Yet even at the height of the recession, the proportion of Ontarians with jobs remained higher than in all but two provinces, and average family income was the highest in Canada.

The rapid expansion of the 1980s and the late 1990s proved a mixed blessing. Development for residential and commercial use meant the progressive destruction of prime agricultural land; since 1931, more than a quarter of southern Ontario's farmland has been lost to suburban sprawl. Historic buildings were demolished thanks to what the Architectural Conservancy of Ontario described as "the worst heritage laws in the Western world." Toronto's living costs, among the highest in the Americas, imposed severe burdens on its poorer citizens. Homelessness and other social problems became more acute. Highway congestion worsened as millions of residents of relatively low-density communities beyond Toronto's core relied mainly on their automobiles for travel.

POLITICS IN ONTARIO

Politically, the Progressive Conservatives dominated Ontario throughout the period, until the Liberal victory of 1985. Three premiers in particular made their mark: Leslie Frost, "Old Man Ontario," who co-operated with the federal Liberals in many development projects; John Robarts, a self-described "management man," who oversaw the expansion of the education system and adopted a conciliatory attitude to Quebec's calls for constitutional reform in the 1960s; and William Davis, a pragmatic politician who was Trudeau's strongest ally in the patriation of the Canadian Constitution.

Davis's unpopular successor, Frank Miller, portrayed by his more liberal competitors as a "Ronald Reagan of the North," lost the provincial election of 1985. New Liberal Premier David Peterson saw his popularity boosted by the province's economic health. Peterson's government frequently found itself in conflict with Ottawa, especially over free trade with the United States and over the content of federal proposals to bring Quebec into the Constitution.

In the election of 1990, called by the overconfident Liberals after only three years in office, the NDP won a stunning upset victory. During the campaign, the NDP had promised to "fight the Free Trade Agreement every step of the way," to make corporations pay their fair share of taxes, to increase the minimum wage, and to stiffen pollution controls. In a significant move toward gender equality, Premier Bob Rae named eleven women to his cabinet. He also imposed a moratorium on the construction of nuclear-power plants. But he cautioned against high expectations of radical change: "We can't just let 'er rip and hope that it'll work." Yet, when it brought down its first provincial budget in April 1991, the NDP government opted for a massive deficit of nearly $10 billion in an effort to counteract the deleterious effects of the recession on Ontario's economy and its poorer citizens. Rapidly rising welfare and interest payments on the debt contributed to successive large budget deficits, as did Ottawa's refusal to share the cost of higher welfare payments. Such financial problems, together with substantially higher taxes and severe spending cuts, helped ensure the Rae government's defeat in 1995 at the hands of the Progressive Conservative party led by Mike Harris, who promised to implement a "Common Sense Revolution."

Harris cut provincial income taxes by 30 percent and promised a balanced budget by 2000. Government finances were assisted by a booming economy, thanks to low interest rates, a dynamic U.S. economy, and a low Canadian dollar. Harris also cut spending by decreasing the number of public servants, hospital workers, and teachers. These cuts provoked "Days of Action" protests led by organized labour against "Mean Mike" and his policies. Then the province announced it would take control of education funding, removing financing from municipally levied, residential property taxes. In return, new responsibilities were to be devolved upon municipalities, including welfare, child care, care for the elderly, social housing, health programs, and public transit. It introduced a new market-value property tax assessment system, and it ordered the merger of Metro Toronto's six municipalities. These measures provoked some of the most acrimonious debates in the province's history among prospective winners and losers.

Certain decisions of the Harris government worried environmentalists. In 1997, for example, the province's environmental commissioner issued a scathing report condemning the provincial government for its "alarming lack of environmental vision." Yet in 1999, the government concluded its "Lands for Life" study of Crown lands by announcing that huge new tracts of land in northern Ontario would be set aside as wilderness.

Since Confederation, Canada has been an often uneasy association of regions and sub-regions. Differences in geography, culture, language, and population reinforce regionalism, but within English-speaking Canada, economic issues have probably been most significant. The nature of the Canadian economy has been such that the nation's wealth has been concentrated in relatively small areas of the country. Such profound imbalances, though inevitable, create tension.

In the course of debates over the distribution of national wealth and the determination of national policy, the federal government has often played the role of arbiter. The party in power typically seeks to mitigate regional conflict, since dissatisfaction risks alienating voters; no federal budget, however, can be sufficient to satisfy all the demands upon it. Each major federal decision provokes the anger of regions that, rightly or wrongly, blame Ottawa for being overly attuned to the needs and interests of other regions.

Canada's history, both early and recent, demonstrates the strength of regionalism within the country, the power of regional interest groups, and the intensity of regional problems. In this regard, the future will likely resemble the past, and regionalism will thus remain a major challenge to Canadian unity.

NOTES

1. Paul Cornell, Jean Hamelin, Fernand Ouellet, and Marcel Trudel, *Canada: Unity in Diversity* (Toronto: Holt, Rinehart and Winston, 1967).
2. Cole Harris, "Within the Fantastic Frontier: A Geographer's Thoughts on Canadian Unity," *Canadian Geographer* 23 (1979): 197.
3. David G. Alexander, *Atlantic Canada and Confederation: Essays on Canadian Political Economy* (Toronto: University of Toronto Press, 1983), p. 45.
4. R. Harley McGee, *Getting It Right: Regional Development in Canada* (Montreal/Kingston: McGill-Queen's University Press, 1992), p. xxiv.
5. Robert Finbow, "Atlantic Canada: Forgotten Periphery in an Endangered Confederation?" in Kenneth McRoberts, ed., *Beyond Quebec: Taking Stock of Canada* (Montreal/Kingston: McGill-Queen's University Press, 1995), p. 67.
6. G.A. Rawlyk, "The Maritimes and the Problem of the Secession of Quebec, 1967 to 1969," in R.M. Burns, ed., *One Country or Two?* (Montreal/Kingston: McGill-Queen's University Press, 1971), p. 212.
7. J.E. Belliveau, *Little Louis and the Giant K.C.*, quoted in Rand Dyck, *Provincial Politics in Canada* (Scarborough, ON: Prentice-Hall, 1986), p. 171.

8. James L. Kenny, "A New Dependency: State, Local Capital, and the Development of New Brunswick's Base Metal Industry, 1960–1970," *Canadian Historical Review* 78 (1977): 38.

9. Ian McKay, *The Quest of the Folk: Antimodernism and Cultural Selection in Twentieth-Century Nova Scotia* (Montreal/Kingston: McGill-Queen's University Press, 1994), p. 212.

10. L. Richard Lund, "'Fishing for Stamps': The Origins and Development of Unemployment Insurance for Canada's Commercial Fisheries, 1941–71," *Journal of the Canadian Historical Association* (1995): 205.

11. Jean Barman, *The West Beyond the West: A History of British Columbia*, new ed. (Toronto: University of Toronto Press, 1996), p. 351.

12. Sydney Sharpe and Don Braid, *Storming Babylon: Preston Manning and the Rise Of the Reform Party* (Toronto: Key Porter, 1992), p. 154.

13. K.J. Rea, *The Prosperous Years: The Economic History of Ontario, 1939–75* (Toronto: University of Toronto Press, 1985).

14. Paul Axelrod, *Scholars and Dollars: Politics, Economics, and the Universities of Ontario, 1945–1980* (Toronto: University of Toronto Press, 1982), pp. 141–78.

LINKING TO THE PAST

WEB LINKS

Statistics Canada's People Page
http://www.statcan.ca/english/Pgdb/people.htm
Check out recent statistics on each province's population and growth, education, employment, housing, and much more.

The Council of Maritime Premiers
http://www.cmp.ca/
This site features the history of the council, descriptions of its agencies, the full text of annual reports, and links to sites for the individual Maritime provinces.

A History of the Northern Cod Fishery
http://www.schoolnet.ca/collections/cod/home1.htm
An extensive, illustrated history of the cod fishery in Atlantic Canada. Of special interest for this chapter are the last six sections, which provide information on the destruction of this natural resource and on attempts to rebuild the Atlantic fish stocks.

W.A.C. Bennett
http://sunnyokanagan.com/wacbennett/index.html
A page devoted to W.A.C. Bennett that features an informal biography and numerous photographs, including a reproduction of the Canada Post stamp that bears his likeness.

Friends of Clayoquot Sound
http://www.island.net/~focs/index.htm
This site includes background information on the logging dispute in Clayoquot Sound as well as a detailed, illustrated report.

Preston Manning
http://www.reform.ca/manning/bio.html
Preston Manning's biography, from the office of the leader of the opposition, which includes his recent speeches.

BIBLIOGRAPHY

Studies of regionalism include Janine Brodie, *The Political Economy of Canadian Regionalism* (Toronto: Harcourt Brace Jovanovich, 1990); and Stephen G. Tomblin, *Ottawa and the Outer Provinces: The Challenge of Regional Integration in Canada* (Toronto: James Lorimer, 1995). On economic inequalities see R. Harley McGee, *Getting It Right: Regional Development in Canada* (Montreal/Kingston: McGill-Queen's University Press, 1992). Among the numerous studies available on provincial politics, Rand Dyck, *Provincial Politics in Canada: Towards the Turn of the Century* (Toronto: Prentice-Hall, 1999), offers a substantial bibliography. See also Chris Dunn, *Provinces: An Introduction to Canadian Provincial Politics* (Peterborough, ON: Broadview Press, 1996).

David G. Alexander, *The Decay of Trade: An Economic History of the Newfoundland Saltfish Trade, 1933–1965* (St. John's: Institute of Social and Economic Research, Memorial University of Newfoundland, 1977), is an excellent study of a major economic issue; his *Atlantic Canada and Confederation: Essays in Canadian Political Economy* (Toronto: University of Toronto Press, 1983) contains several articles bearing on underdevelopment and dependence. See also L. Richard Lund, "'Fishing for Stamps': The Origins and Development of Unemployment Insurance for Canada's Commercial Fisheries, 1941–71," *Journal of the Canadian Historical Association* (1995): 179–208. For a biography of Joseph Smallwood see Harold Horwood, *Joey: The Life and Political Times of Joey Smallwood* (Toronto: Stoddart, 1989). A biography of a more recent premier is Claire Hoy, *Clyde Wells: A Political Biography* (Toronto: Stoddart, 1992).

The best overview of the four Atlantic provinces is E.R. Forbes and D.A. Muise, eds., *The Atlantic Provinces in Confederation* (Toronto: University of Toronto Press, 1993). Another useful survey is George Peabody, Carolyn MacGregor, and Richard Thorne, eds., *The Maritimes: Tradition, Challenge and Change* (Halifax: Formac, 1987). The best study of the Acadian community is Richard Wilbur, *The Rise of French New Brunswick* (Halifax: Formac, 1989). On the language issue see also Donald A. Desserud, "The Exercise of Community Rights in the Liberal-Federal State: Language Rights and New Brunswick's Bill 88," *International Journal of Canadian Studies* 14 (Fall 1996): 215–38. Economic development in New Brunswick in the 1960s is examined in James L. Kenny, "A New Dependency: State, Local Capital, and the Development of New Brunswick's Base Metal Industry, 1960–1970," *Canadian Historical Review* 78 (1997): 1–39. Biographies of New Brunswick premiers include Della M.M. Stanley, *Louis Robichaud: A Decade of Power* (Halifax: Nimbus, 1984); Richard Starr, *Richard Hatfield: The Seventeen Year Saga* (Halifax: Formac, 1987); and Michel Cormier and Achille Michaud, *Richard Hatfield: Power and Disobedience* (Fredericton: Goose Lane Editions, 1992). The fascinating story of New Brunswick's major business magnate is told in Douglas How and Ralph Costello, *K.C.: The Biography of K.C. Irving* (Toronto: Key Porter, 1993).

Several useful articles on the Maritimes are available in Ernest Forbes, *Challenging the Regional Stereotype: Essays on the 20th Century Maritimes* (Fredericton: Acadiensis Press, 1989). An excellent study of federal government intervention in Nova Scotia's economy is James P. Bickerton, *Nova Scotia, Ottawa, and the Politics of Regional Development* (Toronto: University of Toronto Press, 1990). Some aspects of culture are examined in Ian McKay, *The Quest of the Folk: Antimodernism and Cultural Selection in Twentieth-Century Nova Scotia* (Montreal/Kingston: McGill-Queen's University Press, 1994). Peter Kavanagh, *Nova Scotia Politics: The Buchanan Years* (Halifax: Formac, 1988), examines a recent Progressive Conservative government. Douglas Baldwin discusses the history of Canada's smallest province in *Land of the Red Soil: A Popular History of Prince Edward Island* (Charlottetown: Ragweed Press, 1990). Two studies of Atlantic economic issues are Gary Burrill and Ian MacKay, eds., *People, Resources, and Power: Critical Perspectives on Underdevelopment and Primary Industries in the Atlantic Region* (Fredericton: Acadiensis Press, 1987); and Bryant Fairley, Colin Leys, and James Sacouman, eds., *Restructuring and Resistance from Atlantic Canada* (Toronto: Garamond Press, 1990).

Two general surveys of Ontario are Robert Bothwell, *A Short History of Ontario* (Edmonton: Hurtig, 1986); and Randall White, *Ontario, 1610–1985: A Political and Economic History* (Toronto: Dundurn Press, 1985). White has prepared a sequel to his study, *Ontario since 1985: A Contemporary History* (Toronto: General, 1998). For an excellent study of Ontario's economy see K.J. Rea, *The Prosperous Years: The Economic History of Ontario, 1939–75* (Toronto: University of Toronto Press, 1985). A good study of a major enterprise is Neil B. Freeman, *The Politics of Power: Ontario Hydro and Its Government, 1906–1995* (Toronto: University of Toronto Press, 1996). The evolution of Ontario's parks system is described in Gerald Killan, *Protected Places: A History of Ontario's Provincial Parks System* (Toronto: Dundurn Press, 1993). On higher education in Ontario consult Paul Axelrod, *Scholars and Dollars: Politics, Economics, and the Universities of Ontario, 1945–1980* (Toronto: University of Toronto Press, 1982). Biographical material on Ontario politics includes Allan K. McDougall, *John P. Robarts: His Life and Government* (Toronto: University of Toronto Press, 1986); Georgette Gagnon and Dan Rath, *Not Without Cause: David Peterson's Fall from Grace* (Toronto: HarperCollins, 1991); Patrick Monahan, *Storming the Pink Palace: The NDP in Power, a Cautionary Tale* (Toronto: Lester Publishing, 1995); Thomas Walkom, *Rae Days: The Rise and Follies of the NDP* (Toronto: Key Porter, 1994); John Ibbotson, *Promised Land: Inside the Mike Harris Revolution* (Scarborough, ON: Prentice-Hall, 1997); and Diana Ralph et al., eds., *Open for Business, Closed to People: Mike Harris's Ontario* (Halifax: Fernwood, 1997). Other useful books on Ontario politics include J.T. Morley, *Secular Socialists: The CCF/NDP in Ontario: A Biography* (Montreal/Kingston: McGill-Queen's University Press, 1984); Rosemary Speirs, *Out of the Blue: The Fall of the Tory Dynasty in Ontario* (Toronto: Macmillan, 1986); and Graham White, *The Ontario Legislature: A Political Analysis* (Toronto: University of Toronto Press, 1989).

Western Canada has been widely studied, but only a few titles can be mentioned here. Gerald Friesen, *The Canadian Prairies: A History* (Toronto: University of Toronto Press, 1984), provides a highly original synthesis that emphasizes social and economic history. See also the same author's *River Road: Essays on Manitoba and Prairie History* (Winnipeg: University of Manitoba Press, 1996). An excellent collection of essays focussing on the West is A.W. Rasporich, ed., *The Making of the Modern West: Western Canada since 1945* (Calgary: University of Calgary Press, 1984). Roger Gibbins, *Prairie Politics and Society: Regionalism in Decline* (Toronto: Butterworths, 1980), offers an overview. R. Douglas Francis shows how views of the west have evolved in *Images of the West: Changing Perceptions of the Prairies, 1660–1960* (Saskatoon: Western Producer Prairie Books, 1989). Western Canadian attitudes on Meech Lake are discussed in Roger Gibbins et al., *Meech Lake and Canada: Perspectives from the West* (Edmonton: Academic Printing, 1988). Saskatchewan's Liberal government of the 1960s is studied in Dale Eisler, *Rumours of Glory: Saskatchewan and the Thatcher Years* (Edmonton: Hurtig, 1987). On the Blakeney years see Dennis Gruending, *Promises to Keep: A Political Biography of Allan Blakeney* (Saskatoon: Western Producer Prairie Books, 1990); and Jim Harding, ed., *Social Policy and Social Justice: The NDP Government in Saskatchewan during the Blakeney Years* (Waterloo, ON: Wilfrid Laurier University Press, 1994). Unflattering portraits of the Devine government may be found in James Pitsula and Ken A. Rasmussen, *Privatizing a Province: The New Right in Saskatchewan* (Vancouver: New Star Books, 1990); and Leslie Biggs and Mark Stobbe, eds., *Devine Rule in Saskatchewan: A Decade of Hope and Hardship* (Saskatoon: Fifth House, 1991).

On Alberta, Howard and Tamara Palmer's *Alberta: A New History* (Edmonton: Hurtig, 1990) is an excellent survey. For material on the province's political history consult Alvin Finkel, *The Social Credit Phenomenon in Alberta* (Toronto: University of Toronto Press, 1989); David G. Wood, *The Lougheed Legacy* (Toronto: Key Porter, 1985); Mark Lisac, *The Klein Revolution* (Edmonton: NeWest Publishers, 1995); Barry Cooper, *The Klein Achievement* (Toronto: Centre for Public Management, University of Toronto, 1996); the very critical Kevin Taft, *Shredding the Public Interest: Ralph Klein and 25 Years of One-Party Government* (Edmonton: University of Alberta Press, 1997); and Allan Tupper and Roger Gibbins, eds., *Government and Politics in Alberta* (Edmonton: University of Alberta Press, 1992). Environmental issues are studied in David H. Breen, *Alberta's Petroleum Industry and the Conservation Board* (Edmonton: University of Alberta Press, 1993); and in Larry Pratt and Ian Urquhart, *The Last Great Forest: Japanese Multinationals and Alberta's Northern Forests* (Edmonton: NeWest Publishers, 1994). Robert A. Stebbins studies Calgary's small francophone community in *The Franco-Calgarians: French Language, Leisure, and Linguistic Life-style in an Anglophone City* (Toronto: University of Toronto Press, 1994). For a review of the left's activity in Manitoba see Nelson Wiseman, *Social Democracy in Manitoba: A History of the CCF–NDP* (Winnipeg: University of Manitoba Press, 1983); and James Mc-Allister, *The Government of Edward Schreyer: Democratic Socialism in Manitoba* (Montreal/Kingston: McGill-Queen's University Press, 1984). Jim Silver and Jeremy Hull, eds., *The Political Economy of Manitoba* (Regina: Canadian Plains Research Centre, University of Regina, 1990), contains articles on many aspects of the provinces economy. James B. Waldram's *"As Long as the Rivers Run"* (Winnipeg: University of Manitoba Press, 1988) examines the negotiations between Manitoba and Saskatchewan with Native people over hydro-electric development in the 1960s and 1970s.

Western discontent is examined in numerous works including David Kilgour, *Uneasy Patriots: Western Canadians in Confederation* (Edmonton: Lone Pine, 1988); Don Braid and Sydney Sharpe, *Breakup: Why the West Feels Left Out of Canada* (Toronto: Key Porter, 1990); the more scholarly Larry Pratt and Garth Stevenson, *Western Separatism: The Myths, Realities and Dangers* (Edmonton: Hurtig, 1981); and in two books respectively edited and authored by George Melnyk: *Riel to Reform: A History of Protest in Western Canada* (Saskatoon: Fifth House, 1992), and *Beyond Alienation: Political Essays on the West* (Calgary: Detselig Enterprises, 1993). See also Roger Gibbins and Sonia Arrison, *Western Visions: Perspectives on the West in Canada* (Peterborough, ON: Broadview Press, 1995). Studies of the Reform party include Sydney Sharpe and Don Braid, *Storming Babylon: Preston Manning and the Rise of the Reform Party* (Toronto: Key Porter, 1992); and Trevor Harrison, *Of Passionate Intensity: Right-Wing Populism and the Reform Party of Canada* (Toronto: University of Toronto Press, 1995).

Jean Barman, *The West Beyond the West: A History of British Columbia*, rev. ed. (Toronto: University of Toronto Press, 1996); and Hugh Johnson et al., eds., *The Pacific Province: A History of British Columbia* (Vancouver: Douglas & McIntyre, 1996) are general surveys of the province's history. R.K. Carty, ed., *Politics, Policy, and Government in British Columbia* (Vancouver: University of British Columbia Press, 1996), contains many informative articles, notably on the environment. Also on the environment see Jeremy Wilson, *Talk and Log: Wilderness Politics in British Columbia* (Vancouver: University of British Columbia Press, 1998). Among other works on the recent history of British Columbia, the following provide strongly contrasting views: David J. Mitchell, *W.A.C. Bennett and the Rise of British Columbia* (Vancouver: Douglas & McIntyre, 1983); and Martin Robin, *Pillars of Profit: The Company Province, 1934–1972* (Toronto: McClelland & Stewart, 1973). Books that study government policies in British Columbia in the 1980s include Warren Magnusson et al., *The New Reality: The Politics of Restraint in British Columbia* (Vancouver: New Star Books, 1984); Warren Magnusson et al., *After Bennett: A New Politics for British Columbia* (Vancouver: New Star Books, 1986); David J. Mitchell, *Succession: The Political Reshaping of British Columbia* (Vancouver: Douglas & McIntyre, 1987); Stan Persky, *Fantasy Government: Bill Vander Zalm and the Future of Social Credit* (Vancouver: New Star Books, 1989); and Daniel Gawthrop, *Highwire Act: Power, Pragmatism, and the Harcourt Legacy* (Vancouver: New Star Books, 1996). Terry Morley interprets provincial politics in "Politics as Theatre: Paradox and Complexity in British Columbia," *Journal of Canadian Studies* 25 (1990): 19–37. Two articles study provincial social policy: Chris R. McNiven, "Social Policy and Some Aspects of the Neoconservative Ideology in British Columbia," in Jacqueline S. Ismael, ed., *The Canadian Welfare State: Evolution and Transition* (Edmonton: University of Alberta Press, 1987), pp. 300–26, and Bryan Palmer, "The Rise and Fall of British Columbia's Solidarity," in his *The Character of Class Struggle* (Toronto: McClelland & Stewart, 1986), pp. 176–200. Aboriginal issues are reviewed in Paul Tennant, *Aboriginal Peoples and Politics: The Indian Land Question in British Columbia, 1849–1989* (Vancouver: University of British Columbia Press, 1990).

Several journals specialize in regional history: *BC Studies*, *Alberta History*, *The Beaver*, *Saskatchewan History*, *Manitoba History*, *Ontario History*, *Nova Scotia Historical Review*, *Acadiensis*, and *Newfoundland Studies*.

CHAPTER NINETEEN

Immigration and Ethnicity

In the 1960s, members of Canada's non-French, non-British ethnic minorities began to question their place in Canadian society. They naturally expressed serious reservations about the then popular concept of two nations, or two founding peoples, which, while it ignored the existence of the Native peoples, appeared to give special status to Canadians of French and British origins. The federal government's multiculturalism policy, announced in 1971, accorded minority ethnic groups an official status they had not enjoyed in the past. It served as recognition of how Canada, in one century, had become a multi-ethnic and multicultural society, one in which those of backgrounds other than English or French made up nearly one-third of the total population.

The history of immigration since 1945 involves three closely intertwined elements: the Canadian government's immigration policy; Canadians' response to recent newcomers who have made Canada their new home; and the experience of the immigrants themselves. This final topic gives rise to several more specific questions: Where have the immigrants come from, and why? How have they reacted and adapted to their new environment? How have immigrant communities been transformed, and what impact have they had on Canadian society?

POSTWAR EUROPEAN IMMIGRATION, 1945–1947

In 1946, millions of destitute refugees from war-torn areas of Europe remained crowded in camps, awaiting a permanent haven. Canada felt little responsibility for them. The country had received virtually no immigration during the preceding 15 years. Most Canadians, tired of being told to "do their part," probably agreed that the country had other, more urgent, priorities to attend to. Canada had its own children, as well as its injured soldiers and veterans, to look after. Furthermore, economists worried that the war's end would bring on another depression, as it had immediately after World War I. A wave of new arrivals risked swelling the ranks of the unemployed.

EUROPEAN REFUGEES

Sensing the nation's mood, Prime Minister William Lyon Mackenzie King understood Canadians' hesitancy about immigration. He saw little electoral advantage to be gained by opening the country's doors to Europe's homeless. Pressure, however, continued to mount. In the House of Commons, a few, mainly CCF, MPs denounced the government's "shameful" vacillation and insisted on Canada's "moral and Christian duty" toward the unfortunates of Europe. Certain religious groups and ethnic associations also spoke in favour of the refugees. Finally, after hearings in the spring of 1946, the Senate Committee on Immigration and Labour recommended that immigration offices be opened in Europe to process as many displaced persons and refugees as the country could absorb.

The Canadian government moved cautiously. The first refugees to arrive in 1946 were some 4000 Polish veterans who had fought with British military units in the war. Hugh Keenleyside, deputy minister of mines and resources (the department that had responsibility for immigration), believed Canada must act quickly to select the best immigrants. By admitting a few thousand displaced persons immediately, he argued, Canada could obtain good candidates, improve the country's international image, and encourage other nations to follow suit. John Holmes, an external-affairs officer, claimed that Canada selected refugees "like good beef cattle, with a preference for strong young men who could do manual labour and would not be encumbered by aging relatives."[1] By the fall of 1948, 40 000 refugees had reached Canadian shores. Although the numbers then began to decrease, about 165 000 refugees had come to Canada by 1953. Many of them, after arrival, applied to bring in their close relatives.

Canada also admitted 15 000 *Volksdeutsche*, ethnic Germans expelled from territories formerly belonging to Hitler's Reich whom the Canadian Christian Council for the Resettlement of Refugees defended as a strong bulwark against communism. Other refugees came from the now-communist countries of eastern Europe. At the end of the war, the Red Army had forcibly repatriated thousands of eastern Europeans behind the "iron curtain," often condemning them to prison, persecution, and even death. Some of those who escaped this fate eventually reached Canadian shores with barely a suitcase containing their meagre belongings. A number were well-educated professionals or highly skilled workers. Often, they concealed their training in order to better their chances with Canadian officials, who sought manual labourers. Industries in need of unskilled labour sponsored many of the refugee immigrants, who readily accepted almost any job, salary, and working conditions. Once in Canada, they fulfilled their contractual obligations on farms, in lumber camps, in mines, and often, in the case of women, in domestic service, before moving on to more suitable occupations.

IMMIGRANT LABOUR

Employers frequently exploited new immigrants. One notorious scheme involved Ludger Dionne, an MP and owner of the Dionne Spinning Mill Company at Saint-Georges-de-Beauce, south of Quebec City. In 1947, Dionne obtained government authorization to recruit 100 Polish women for his mill. *Time* reported that he paid them 20 cents an hour; after deductions of $6 a week for board, they were left with $3.60 weekly. Dionne assured parliamentarians that young women from Quebec City did not want to work in the small towns and that his working conditions were better than those in Toronto. For good measure, he also accused his detractors of being propagandists for communism.

Economically, many immigrants progressed rapidly. By 1971, Latvians and Estonians, for example, had incomes that were 25 percent higher than the Canadian average. Political scientist Karl Aun explains this evolution in part by the fact that such groups included unusually large numbers of educational, community, cultural, and political leaders.[2] Yet stories abound like the one about the poor Estonian fisherman who, after settling in southern Ontario, saved as much as possible from the earnings of all family members. Then, with the help of a loan from the Estonian Credit Union, he bought a house with several apartments, continued saving and purchased a second apartment house, moved into the best unit, and eventually sent his children to university.

Historian Franca Iacovetta has described the lives of many poor peasant farmers and rural artisans from southern Italy who settled in Toronto; they faced considerable hardships before they were able to secure a stable life for themselves and their families.[3] Jobs were often dirty, disagreeable, and risky.

Each story was unique. Iacovetta tells of one immigrant, 18-year-old Elena Krotz, recruited by Canadian officials in a displaced-persons camp in West Germany. Krotz had fled her native Czechoslovakia when communist authorities sought to arrest her after she participated in a student protest. After staying for a few weeks at a government hostel in Canada, Krotz was sent to the home of a farm couple in southwestern Ontario, to work as a servant. She arrived with all her worldly belongings in two tiny bags: a blanket and one change of clothes. A drive to succeed, the encouragement and mutual support of the community, and the relative youth of the newcomers combined to help these immigrants adjust to their new environment.

FEDERAL IMMIGRATION POLICY

WEB LINKS

Since most prospective immigrants to Canada, even in the early postwar years, were not refugees, the country needed a general immigration policy. In a much-discussed speech to the House of Commons on May 1, 1947, Prime Minister King attempted to satisfy both supporters and opponents of immigration. He said that Canada would benefit by boosting its population and that immigration would make the country more prosperous and more secure. At the same time he put forth the nebulous notion of Canada's "absorptive capacity," promising that the government would "ensure the careful selection and permanent settlement" of only as many as could "advantageously be absorbed in our national economy." The number admitted could vary from year to year, in an alternating open-door/closed-door approach.

King's comments also reveal Canadian racial attitudes of the era. Responding to those who denounced racial distinctions in immigration policy, the prime minister asserted Canada's right to choose its future citizens. The government did repeal the blatantly discriminatory Chinese exclusion law of July 1, 1923. Nevertheless, it continued to apply severe restrictions on Asian immigration since, in King's words, the "massive immigration of Orientals would alter the fundamental composition of the Canadian population" and "give rise to social and economic problems."

CANADIAN RESPONSES TO POSTWAR IMMIGRATION

Canadians could not agree on how many immigrants the country needed and who should be admitted. Business and financial leaders lobbied for substantial immigration. They argued that a larger population would benefit the economy and yield per-capita savings in areas such as transportation and administration. Ethnic associations and several religious groups also favoured increased immigration.

Many Canadians, however, were reluctant to receive a sizable influx of immigrants. By 1954, only 45 percent of Canadians favoured increased immigration, down from 51 percent in 1947. Many Canadians of British origin feared that immigration would weaken the British element in Canada. Workers often viewed immigrants as competitors willing to work for lower wages. The unions wanted immigrants to be carefully selected and preferably to occupy unattractive jobs in remote regions that Canadians did not want. As the economy began to slow in the late 1950s, a majority of Canadians felt the country was accepting too many immigrants. Senator David Croll, an enthusiastic advocate of higher immigration a decade before, now joked: "If you put pants on a penguin, it could be admitted to this country." After 1957, the new Progressive Conservative government substantially reduced immigration levels.

FRENCH IMMIGRATION

Many French Canadians worried that a flood of new immigrants would undermine their position in Canada. As late as 1947, it appeared that if the birth rate of French Canadians remained high and if immigration were restricted, French Canadians might one day constitute the largest part of Canada's population. Francophone Quebeckers feared in particular that the immigrants' tendency to integrate into the English-speaking community would ultimately make French-speakers a minority in Montreal, the province's largest city.

In the fall of 1948 the federal government, in hopes of satisfying French-speaking members of the Liberal caucus as well as French-Canadian public opinion, put French nationals on an equal legal footing with British subjects and American citizens for purposes of entry into Canada. Civil servants, however, immediately slowed down the new policy for "security" reasons, arguing that a large proportion of would-be French immigrants might be either communists or former Nazi collaborators.[4]

All told, Ottawa's new policy on French immigration had only a slight effect: between 1946 and 1950, fewer than 5000 French immigrants came to Canada. Although the French authorities did not encourage emigration, prospective immigrants literally besieged Canadian consular offices in Paris. While the Canadian consul in Paris made urgent requests for more staff and more office space, Hugh Keenleyside advised the deputy minister of labour to channel "all efforts in the same direction, that is to say, the encouragement of British immigration to Canada."

French immigration did increase in the 1950s and 1960s, before declining again. In the years 1945–80, between one-half and two-thirds of immigrants to Canada were English-speaking, whereas French-speakers numbered about 3 percent, and bilinguals 4 percent. The remainder, speaking other languages, soon learned English. Immigration, then, reinforced the numerical strength of English-speaking Canada linguistically, although diversifying it ethnically and culturally.

BRITISH IMMIGRATION

Of all groups, the Canadian government preferred British immigrants. J.W. Pickers-gill, minister of citizenship and immigration, stated in 1955: "We put forth much more effort in the United Kingdom than in any other country." It was only natural, he asserted, that Canada favour British immigration since it was easier to transplant individuals into "similar soil." Although he viewed the massive influx of new arrivals in 1956–57, 40 percent of whom were British, as "too big for Canada to digest," he added candidly that any attempt to stem the tide of British immigration "would be the finish of the Liberal party in many Anglo-Saxon constituencies."

AN EVALUATION OF POSTWAR IMMIGRATION POLICY

This first wave of immigration, which brought 1.7 million immigrants to Canada, ended in the late 1950s, when rising unemployment led the Canadian government to reconsider its policy. The year 1957, however, proved a sort of boom before the bust, with 282 000 arrivals — a figure that still pales in comparison with the 400 000 immigrants who came in 1913. Some 37 000 of these new arrivals were mainly young and often highly skilled Hungarians who fled their homeland in 1956 as Soviet armies crushed the Hungarian revolution. Among them came the entire student body and faculty of a Hungarian school of forestry. Transported across Canada on a "freedom train," they were relocated at the University of British Columbia. In general, the re-settlement of the Hungarian refugees proceeded smoothly.

Such major movements of people gave rise to myths and half truths. In theory, humanitarian ideals and a sense of international responsibility guided Canadian immigration policy. Canadians believed themselves to be generously offering liberty and opportunity to victims of persecution. In practice, however, economics usually dictated which, and how many, immigrants came to Canada. Ottawa sought immigrants possessing certain skills, and initiated bulk labour schemes. Federal authorities directed many immigrants, once in Canada, to farms and to unattractive jobs in remote resource regions. Once they fulfilled their contracts, however, many immigrants soon left for the cities.

Racial bias explains why few immigrants gained entrance from outside Europe and the United States. In 1958, the director of the Immigration Branch explained why "coloured British subjects" from the Caribbean were excluded from Canada: "They do not assimilate rapidly and pretty much vegetate to a low standard of living." The introduction of tiny quotas, which remained in effect until 1967, limited immigration from the Indian subcontinent. The location of immigration offices also ensured that the great majority of immigrants came from Britain and the European continent, as well as from the United States. The government thus confined its promotional activities to these areas.

EMIGRATION

During the economic downturn of the late 1950s and early 1960s, the unwelcome obverse side of immigration came to the fore. Disappointed with the lack of opportunities

Jack Pickersgill (right), the federal minister responsible for immigration in the St. Laurent government, greets the dean of the faculty of forestry engineering at the University of Sopron, Hungary, in Montreal, 1957. Some 37 000 young and highly skilled Hungarians, including the entire faculty and student body of this faculty, arrived in Canada during and immediately after the Hungarian uprising of 1956.

Champlain Marcil/National Archives of Canada/PA-147725.

in Canada and embittered by what they considered false promises on Canada's part, thousands of immigrants, particularly British, returned home. There they contributed to tarnishing Canada's image, if only temporarily. From the early 1950s to the early 1970s, one in every three or four immigrants either returned home or moved to the United States.

Even more worrisome to many Canadians was the movement southward of 800 000 native-born Canadians in the period 1952–71. Perhaps one-tenth of this group consisted of professionals or managers — the much-publicized "brain drain." *Maclean's* estimated in 1963 that 8000 graduates of the University of Toronto lived in the United States and that 800 of these taught in American colleges. Historian Arthur Lower conjectured that this loss of talent helped keep Canada "in that state of low water which has always been the object of the Yankee's good-natured scorn."[5] After a temporary reversal of the brain drain in the 1960s and early 1970s, at the time of the Vietnam War and race riots in the United States, the movement to the South resumed in the late 1970s and 1980s. In the mid-1980s, 50 000 Canadians departed annually, attracted largely by the dynamism of the American economy and, perhaps, by southern sunshine.

The problem worsened in the 1990s. In 1993–94 alone, 1100 nurses emigrated to the United States, a figure representing about 40 percent of the number of graduates from Canada's nursing schools. The number of physicians leaving in 1996 and 1997 was the equivalent of half the number who earned diplomas from Canadian medical schools. In addition, many engineers, scientists, and other professionals joined the trek south, "pushed" out of Canada, as a report stated, by a lack of suitable work, and "pulled" to the United States by the prospect of better working conditions, higher salaries, and lower taxes. The cost to Canada was substantial, as emigrants took with them skills they had developed in largely publicly financed post-secondary schooling.

THE IMMIGRANT EXPERIENCE SINCE THE 1960S

Due to an economic slowdown, the Diefenbaker years (1957–63) witnessed a slump in immigration. Fewer agents staffed Canadian immigration offices abroad. Unions exerted pressure to decrease immigration, and most MPs were at best indifferent. Even Diefenbaker, despite favourable public pronouncements in speeches aimed at ethnic groups, appeared to have little interest in the question.

Sometimes immigration made sensational headlines. For example, the press reported numerous cases of foreign seamen who jumped ship in Canadian waters and then hurriedly married Canadian women in order to remain in Canada. Large-scale illegal Chinese immigration, promoted by a Hong Kong–based group that bought and sold false identities, also appeared to overwhelm the government. Ottawa promised to grant amnesty to most illegals who would come forth and declare themselves (many thousands did), but the program did not eliminate the illegal immigration rings.

The Conservatives introduced new regulations in 1962 that ended the use of race and national origin as reasons for exclusion from Canada. The old discriminatory provisions appeared unacceptable in an era that discredited racism. In 1960, Diefenbaker had proudly presented the Canadian Bill of Rights, which rejected discrimination by reason of race, national origin, colour, religion, or sex. Economic factors also contributed to the reversal of the former policy: Canada could no longer obtain the labour it needed from the "old countries." For a time, southern Europe supplanted Britain and northern Europe as the area of origin of most immigrants to Canada. Then, immigration diminished from these countries, too, and Canada turned its attention toward Asia and the Caribbean.

WEB

LINKS

A NEW WAVE OF IMMIGRANTS

The return of economic prosperity in the early 1960s heralded a steep rise in immigration. The Pearson government (1963–68) also instituted structural changes. In 1966, it established the Department of Manpower and Immigration, a move that showed the government's intention to relate immigration to the needs of the labour market. The Department of the Secretary of State obtained responsibility for the integration of immigrants into Canadian society.

New immigration regulations effective in October 1967 completely eliminated the old discriminatory provisions and made it more difficult for sponsored dependants and, particularly, for non-dependent relatives to gain admittance. Independent applicants were to be selected with the aid of a point system based on such criteria as education and training, personal qualities, occupational demand, and age and linguistic capacity. In addition, the government set up the independent Immigration Appeal Board, which was almost immediately overwhelmed with appeals from alleged "visitors" who had applied to stay but had been refused and ordered deported.

The gradual elimination of racial discrimination from Canada's immigration policy, the decline of European sources of immigrants, and the expansion of the network of immigration offices around the world transformed the ethnic mix of Canadian immigration. In 1966, for example, 87 percent of immigrants were of European

The Haim Abenhaim family, Sephardic Jewish immigrants from Morocco, arriving in Montreal, 1960. In the early 1970s, immigrants from developing countries began to come to Canada in significant numbers.

Canadian Jewish Congress National Archives/PC 2/1/7 A.4.

origin; only four years later, 50 percent came from other regions. The West Indies, Haiti, Guyana, India, Hong Kong, the Philippines, and Indochina all figured among the major suppliers of immigrants in the 1970s and 1980s. By the 1990s, Sri Lanka and Taiwan had replaced the Caribbean nations among the most important source countries. Visible ethnic and racial minorities thus became part of Canada's social fabric. Such minorities already made up over 11 percent of the country's population, and over 30 percent of the populations of Vancouver and Toronto. While only 12 000 West Indians lived in Canada in 1961, the figure climbed to 225 000 in 1986. The number of Canadians of Chinese origin increased from 60 000 to nearly 350 000 in the same period, and then to 860 000 by 1996. South Asians numbered 670 000.

IMMIGRANT SETTLEMENT

The new immigrants, like those of the 1950s and 1960s, did not spread out evenly across the country. They came mainly to metropolitan areas such as Toronto, Montreal, and Vancouver and, particularly in the oil-boom years of the late 1970s, to Calgary and Edmonton. Big-city Canada thus became much more cosmopolitan. Newcomers to major urban areas usually settled in ethnically segregated neighbourhoods.

The major pole of attraction since 1945 has been Ontario, especially southern Ontario, where more than half of all immigrants to Canada have chosen to settle. Good employment opportunities and the region's prosperous image attracted immigrants, as did well-established ethnic communities with religious centres, clubs, welfare organizations, newspapers, and professional and other services. Quebec, with

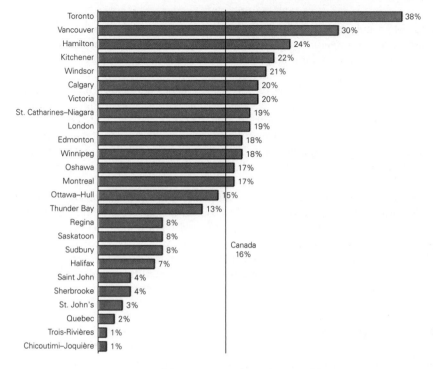

Immigrants as a Percentage of Census Metropolitan Areas, 1991

....

Source: Adapted from Statistics Canada, 1991 Census of Canada, *Canadian Social Trends* (Summer 1993): 10, cat. no. 11-008. Reproduced by authority of the Minister of Industry, 1999.

one-quarter of Canada's population, has received fewer than 15 percent of new arrivals — about the same proportion as British Columbia. Winnipeg and the major cities of Alberta have also attracted many immigrants. The Atlantic provinces and Saskatchewan have, by comparison, experienced little immigration.

ADAPTATION

....

Most immigrants from developing countries found their new life in Canada a considerable material improvement over the past. Furthermore, political conditions prevented many immigrants from returning home, even if they so desired. They did, however, face a much greater cultural shock than did earlier British and European immigrants. Provincial governments and community associations have, to an extent, attempted to assist the new arrivals. Mutual aid and support among families have also been important. Still, it has often been difficult to find jobs to match past occupational experience, especially in times of economic slowdown.

Immigrants have also faced the upsetting necessity of coming to terms with Canadian customs. Anthropologist Norman Buchignani has shown in his study of South Asians (people from India, Pakistan, Bangladesh, and Sri Lanka) that "only a small proportion" of homeland cultural practices survive the settlement process.[6] Eating habits and cultural celebrations tend to be maintained in those cities where immigrant groups are sufficiently numerous, but it is more difficult to retain religious practices: Hindu parents, for example, often find that children know far more about Christianity than they do about Hinduism.

Furthermore, the clash between Canadian values and mores and accepted values and attitudes in the country of origin has frequently caused painful problems for immigrants. For example, the close interaction of the extended family, common in many cultures and providing an extensive support system, has gradually disappeared in North America, where the functional unit is now the nuclear family. The role of women in the family, particularly in southern European and South Asian cultures, has generally been defined very rigidly; male authority generally goes unchallenged, and male financial supremacy backs up that authority. Contact with Canadian mores in this regard has often provoked conflict within the immigrant family. Parental authority has also weakened in the context of Canada's much more permissive society. In South Asia, for example, parents tend to choose marriage partners for their children, and dating is a "foreign" practice. In Canada, the generation gap between immigrant parents and their children has often deepened into a gulf as children become Canadianized through the schools, television, and contacts with friends.

DISCRIMINATION

Many immigrants, especially members of visible minorities, have suffered discrimination in Canada. The media gave wide publicity to certain cases, such as one in which white and South Asian members of a railway crew in Daysland, Alberta, clashed with bottles and axes. In numerous instances in the late 1970s, Sikhs were attacked and had their turbans forcibly removed. Blacks were frequently harassed or physically assaulted. In Montreal, a taxi company fired its Haitian drivers, claiming that it was losing business to companies that employed only white drivers. (Haitians responded in 1990 by buying the city's second-largest taxi company.) Incidents of police shootings of young black people in Montreal and Toronto sparked widespread demands for inquiries into racism in police forces.

Historian Stanley Barrett's research on a suburban Toronto community in the early 1990s showed the existence of widespread racism against visible minorities. He suggested that South Asians saw racism as inevitable, and sought to defend themselves by fostering strong links with their own ethnic communities. African Canadians, more in contact with the white community, often felt bitterness and anger in the face of what they perceived as rejection by their neighbours. Barrett also found strong negative attitudes toward French Canadians, who were seen as "intent on taking over and ruining the country."[7]

Most complaints about discrimination have concerned employment and housing. A study done in Toronto in 1985 found that when South Asians or Caribbean blacks with the same qualifications as white applicants applied for job openings, they learned, in two cases out of five, that the opening no longer existed. In some instances, the same employer on the same day then interviewed white candidates for the same position. One survey showed that three-quarters of West Indians judged employment discrimination in Toronto to be "very serious." Surveys in eleven other

A Historical Portrait
THE IMMIGRANT EXPERIENCE

For many immigrants who have come to Canada, material betterment has been accompanied by a painful sense of cultural loss. In *The Four Quarters of the Night: The Life Journey of an Emigrant Sikh* (Montreal/Kingston: McGill-Queen's University Press, 1995), historian Hugh Johnson has recorded the story of Tara Singh Bains, a Punjabi who arrived in Vancouver in 1953 and has since made many journeys back to the land of his origin. Thousands of Sikhs have immigrated to Canada since the late 1960s, many settling in British Columbia Lower Mainland communities such as Surrey. The now-elderly Bains, a man of strong religious convictions, told Johnson he deplored what he saw as the erosion of spiritual values among members of his community. Bains testifies, "Materialism has created so many doorways to attract human thinking towards luxury, enjoyment, and selfishness, and in Western society … the guidance of the family, the school and the church has fallen away" (p. 227).

Serious generational conflicts among members of ethnic communities, as among Canadians in general, have been frequent. In her book, *Inside Ethnic Families: Three Generations of Portuguese-Canadians* (Montreal/Kingston: McGill-Queen's University Press, 1997), sociologist Edite Noivo studied the life histories of members of three generations of Portuguese Canadians living in Montreal. These stories reveal sharp tensions.

Noivo found, for example, that many first-generation parents objected to a son's wish to marry because his departure represented a serious financial loss. One father reported that he told his son that "we couldn't afford it now and that he had to wait a couple of years more." Although the son at first agreed to abide by his father's will, he later, in the father's words, "got impatient and started to make a big fuss … so I allowed him to get married" (pp. 67–68). Sons, not surprisingly, saw marriage as an advantage because it would bring financial independence. One son explained, "I had been handing over my weekly pay since the age of fourteen.… By the time I was 22, I still didn't have a penny for myself.… So I figured that I had to get married.… If I got married I'd keep my paycheque" (p. 68).

A young third-generation Portuguese Canadian adapted in a different fashion to parents' constraints in matters concerning relations with the opposite sex. He reported, "None of the Portuguese girls I know are allowed to go to parties.… I can go, but my sister and cousins never do.… I can't take them along, my parents and their parents don't trust me.… Of course, none of my girlfriends are Portuguese, but they're just for fun. Like my mother says, a girl who is not a virgin at marriage is no good; I mean, she can't be trusted.… Sure I'll want to get married … to someone Portuguese like myself" (p. 119).

Noivo herself had to face her respondents' disapproval of her own lifestyle. One first-generation male told her that she was only "half a woman.… One cannot be a full woman unless one is married and a mother" (p. 39). A second-generation female made the same comment "in a more acrid and distasteful tone."

LEADING SOURCE COUNTRIES OF IMMIGRANTS, SELECTED YEARS

1960	1968	1976	1984	1991–96
Italy	Britain	Britain	Vietnam	Hong Kong
Britain	United States	United States	Hong Kong	China
United States	Italy	Hong Kong	United States	India
Germany	Germany	Jamaica	India	Philippines
Netherlands	Hong Kong	Lebanon	Britain	Sri Lanka
Portugal	France	India	Poland	Poland
Greece	Austria	Philippines	Philippines	Taiwan
France	Greece	Portugal	El Salvador	Vietnam
Poland	Portugal	Italy	Jamaica	United States
Austria	Yugoslavia	Guyana	China	Britain

Source: Employment and Immigration Canada, *Immigration Statistics*, various years.

Canadian cities repeated the same finding. Provincial human-rights commissions have received numerous complaints of discrimination; sociologists have argued that most victims fail to report incidents, believing that nothing will be done or, worse, fearing retaliation. Human-rights defence groups have criticized the courts for their slowness and their leniency, and have denounced existing laws for their lack of severity.

The Employment Equity Act of 1986 helped bring about a striking increase in the representation of visible minorities in private companies regulated by federal statute, such as banks and transport companies. But Ottawa has been much less successful in improving its own poor hiring record: only 3.6 percent of its employees were members of visible minorities in 1991.

"Established" Canadians have had mixed reactions to the new arrivals of the 1970s and 1980s. Religious and civic groups have strongly urged the admission of refugees, such as the Indochinese "boat people" in the late 1970s, though the general population has shown substantial opposition to increased immigration in general, and to immigration from developing countries in particular. Various studies have shown that many Canadians dislike immigrants' speaking their home languages in public or wearing traditional dress. They tend to see immigrants as ignorant of Canadian cultural practices and unwilling to "act like Canadians," and they have expressed discomfort with the changes in Canadian society that have been brought about by immigration. For example, in 1975, Vancouver Mayor Arthur Phillips urged the government to cut down on the pace of immigration, since "a community can only assimilate immigrants from a drastically different culture at a particular rate." One federal MP, in a controversial statement, urged the "planned assimilation of other races, people who are foreign to our ideologies and way of life."

The arrival in Canada, particularly in Vancouver, of a relatively large number of wealthy Chinese immigrants from Hong Kong in the late 1980s provoked considerable reaction. Government and business leaders appreciated the large financial investments a number of newcomers made. But some Canadian residents spoke with derision of the "yacht people," criticizing what they perceived as ostentatious displays of wealth, such as the construction of "monster homes." Reacting to a number of unpleasant incidents, Vancouver's first Chinese-Canadian alderman complained,

"The Chinese are damned if they're poor and damned if they're rich." British Columbia's lieutenant governor, Chinese-Canadian David Lam, attempted to calm tensions, recommending that newcomers become more involved in the community and that older residents turn a blind eye to pretentious houses.

IMMIGRATION IN THE 1980S AND 1990S

The deep recession of the early 1980s again caused immigration to decline. Moreover, economic problems contributed to an anti-immigrant backlash, as many Canadians saw immigrants as competitors for scarce jobs or believed they were crowding the welfare rolls.

Yet most studies on the relationship between immigration and employment tend to demonstrate that immigrants do not increase unemployment among indigenous workers but rather help to create a larger, more flexible, and more adaptable labour force. Immigrants often work at jobs that Canadians cannot or will not do. For some time after arrival, they may require more social services; yet a report produced by the Economic Council of Canada in 1992 concluded that the proportion of welfare recipients among recent immigrants is not significantly different from that of the native-born. Moreover, through their need for housing, food, clothing, and other consumer goods, immigrants increase the size of the domestic market and thereby assist in boosting growth. Additional research carried out by two York University sociologists indicated that "the objective evidence does not support the view that the relation between immigration and unemployment is a major problem."[8] Other studies have shown that most immigrants have been able to obtain suitable jobs soon after arrival, although Third World immigrants in the independent immigrant category, despite high education levels, usually earn less than other immigrants.

The image of immigrants lined up outside employment offices in times of recession has surely influenced public opinion far more than sociological studies have. Thus, in 1982, the government felt it necessary, in view of Canada's economic problems, to enact new restrictions. As the government revised each year's quotas downward, according to its vague predictions of what the economy could bear, immigration declined to its lowest levels in more than two decades. The government did, however, facilitate entry into Canada, after 1986, for several thousand "business-class" immigrants — wealthy entrepreneurs, especially from Hong Kong. These individuals declared that they were prepared to invest their capital in Canada, set up businesses, and thus create jobs for Canadians. Most immigrant investors chose to settle in British Columbia.

Although a large number of Canadians believed that the country was accepting too many immigrants, other observers of Canadian immigration policy expressed concern about the downward trends and urged the government to put long-term goals ahead of short-term considerations. Immigration Canada warned in 1985 that, if current low fertility rates and low immigration rates continued, the country's population would begin to decline after 2025. Some middle-aged Canadians began to worry about who would pay for their old-age pensions and future health care, and suggested the government bring in more young immigrants.

In the late 1980s, Ottawa gradually raised the ceiling on immigration from 100 000 to 200 000. But taking into account annual emigration of at least 50 000, the net immigration figure was substantially lower. Then, in late 1990, the federal government announced further increases to more than 250 000 per year — a politically risky decision at a time when recession was again settling in on the country and certain groups, such as the Reform party, vehemently criticized immigration and multiculturalism policies. In fact, an average of 210 000 immigrants were admitted to Canada each year during the period 1992–98. Most immigrants came from Asia, but after the cession to China of the British colony of Hong Kong in 1997, immigration from that state declined precipitously.

In 1991, out of a total of more than 200 000 immigrants, fewer than 40 percent belonged to the so-called "economic class" in which one family member, the principal applicant, was assessed for skills deemed in demand in Canada or for a potential investment in the Canadian economy. Fully 75 percent of immigrants had belonged to this class in 1968. By far the great majority of immigrants admitted to Canada now belong to the other two categories of "family class" (that is, close relatives of Canadian residents) and refugees. Most immigrants now spoke neither English nor French, and Ottawa promised to invest more money in language training to assist newcomers in adapting more quickly to Canadian society. Women immigrants in particular, as "dependents," had been previously unable to gain access to language courses.

REFUGEES

Much of the criticism directed at federal immigration policy since the 1980s has concerned refugees. Across the world, millions of human beings became refugees, fleeing war and persecution in their own lands. Canada could not be immune to such mass movements. Humanitarian and refugee-advocacy groups as well as ethnic communities favouring more immigration from their home countries judged Canada's refugee quotas to be unreasonably low. They also denounced the government's cumbersome procedures for studying the cases of refugee-status claimants; indeed, by 1987, more than 50 000 claimants were waiting to have their cases heard, and the backlog was growing larger each year.

Public opinion, however, seemed to become less sympathetic to the cause of refugees: surveys showed that nearly half of all Canadians thought Canada had no moral obligation to open its doors to persons fleeing persecution in other lands. Many critics were undoubtedly influenced by the large numbers of would-be immigrants who entered Canada illegally — so-called "queue jumpers" — and who claimed refugee status, but whose reasons for emigrating from their countries of origin seemed to be primarily economic. Indeed, the hearing that virtually all refugee-status claimants now requested — an unforeseen consequence of earlier legislation — became "a routine channel for evading the normal admission requirements and getting easy access to Canada."[9] In 1986, the dramatic arrival on the shores of Newfoundland of a large group of Tamil immigrants from Sri Lanka and, on the coast of Nova Scotia the following year, of a group of Sikhs from India, was sufficient proof for many Canadians that Ottawa had lost control over entry into the country.

Public pressure led the Mulroney government to act against illegal immigration in 1988, at which time government efforts to clear the huge backlog of some 125 000 refugee-status claimants had become hopelessly bogged down. In addition, immigration officials now had to study the applications of new refugees who arrived at

Canada's borders and airports. The number of new claimants did decline, and the government declared that it had succeeded in driving off manifestly unfounded claims. Religious and ethnic groups were convinced, however, that true political refugees were also being discouraged. As the acceptance rate of refugee claimants declined from about 75 percent in 1989 to about 50 percent in 1993, refugee lawyers blamed "compassion fatigue": panel members, they said, were becoming hardened to stories of abuse and persecution. Government spokespersons countered that the lower acceptance rate of those claiming refugee status merely reflected improved circumstances in countries such as Poland.

New legislation that came into effect in 1993 sought to diminish the exploding administrative costs of immigration programs. The new law limited the right of rejected applicants to appeal and resulted in a substantial drop in the number of claimants arriving in Canada. Yet Canada remained far more open to refugees than did other countries of the western world, most of which had toughened their own entry rules and accepted only between 5 and 25 percent of applicants.

MULTICULTURALISM

WEB LINKS

Canadians have often taken pride in the image of their country as a "cultural mosaic" (or a "tossed salad," in one writer's words), rather than as an American-style "melting pot." Official policy no longer favours rapid assimilation, and social scientists prefer to speak of integration or of acculturation. In his first speech in the Senate in 1964, Senator Paul Yuzyk, born in Manitoba of Ukrainian origin, discussed the emergence of what he termed a "third force," consisting of Canadians of neither French nor British descent. The Royal Commission on Bilingualism and Biculturalism also widened its scope to include a study of the cultural contributions of other ethnic groups.

In October 1971, Prime Minister Trudeau told the House of Commons that the government "accepts the contention of other cultural communities that they, too, are essential elements in Canada and deserve government assistance in order to contribute to regional and national life in ways that derive from their heritages." Multiculturalism — but not multilingualism — was to be encouraged. The 1982 Constitution gave additional, though somewhat vague, protection to multiculturalism by declaring that the Canadian Charter of Rights and Freedoms "shall be interpreted in a manner consistent with the preservation and enhancement of the multicultural heritage of Canada." Yet the Canadian Ethnocultural Council, a lobby composed of numerous ethnic associations, denounced what it termed the unacceptable primacy that the Charter accorded English and French in Canada. Then, in 1988, a revised Multiculturalism Act provided new funds for promoting cultures and reducing discrimination. Contrary to what many ethnic groups had sought, however, it did not take the highly symbolic step of establishing a separate ministry of multiculturalism.

Politicians understood the potential electoral benefits of recognizing the contributions of ethnic groups. Journalist Richard Gwyn perceived the program as "a slush fund to buy ethnic votes." Also, the Trudeau government hoped that recognition of multiculturalism would attenuate existing hostility toward bilingualism and biculturalism and that it would appeal to English-Canadian nationalists who wanted a distinct

Hockey legend Willie O'Ree, the first black player in the NHL, chats with children at the Harmony Brunch in East Preston, Nova Scotia, held to commemorate the International Day for the Elimination of Racial Discrimination.

Nova Scotia Human Rights Commission.

Canadian identity. These rather ambitious objectives were certainly not fulfilled. The great majority of Canadians, including the British, the French, and the "lukewarm white ethnics" from northern and western Europe, found multiculturalism meaningless. As time went on, impatience with the whole concept grew, especially when governments agreed to provide funding.

By the mid-1980s, the federal government was investing modestly in multiculturalism, funding ethnic day-care centres, heritage-language classes, cultural festivals, and conferences and providing grants for the preparation of histories of the major Canadian ethnic groups. Money was made available to complete the revitalization of Vancouver's Chinatown and to transform this ethnic neighbourhood into a shining symbol of Canada's new multicultural nature and, at the same time, a valuable tourist attraction. (By 2000, however, Vancouver's Chinatown was in decline and ravaged by crime; in addition, it had lost its exclusiveness as new Chinatowns grew up in suburbs such as Richmond.) Several provincial governments also contributed financially to support multicultural policy. The Ontario government, for example, used its Wintario lottery funding program to create a research institute, the Multicultural History Society of Ontario. Many school boards set up courses in non-official languages. In Edmonton, public schools began offering immersion schooling in Arabic, Chinese, Hebrew, Ukrainian, and German. Such policies have practical relevance: already by the late 1980s, English was *not* the mother tongue of 50 percent of the children enrolled in Toronto public schools and of 40 percent of those enrolled in Vancouver schools.

Where Social Scientists Disagree
EVALUATING CANADA'S MULTICULTURAL POLICY

The arrival in Canada of large numbers of immigrants, first from Europe and, since the late 1960s, from the Caribbean, Latin America, Asia, and Africa, has immensely diversified Canada's population. Until the 1950s, the federal and the provincial governments espoused a policy of rapid assimilation of newcomers into the "Canadian mainstream." But many immigrants and their descendants attempted to conserve at least part of their ethnic heritage. As interest in the rights of minorities grew throughout the western world during the 1960s, these groups sought government intervention to help them attain their goals. In response, the federal government elaborated, in 1971, a somewhat vague multicultural policy. Since then, governments and public agencies at all levels have launched programs favouring the retention of national cultures.

Official federal policy views multiculturalism as "a powerful bonding agent" that "helps unite us and identify us, while at the same time allowing every element of our society to retain its own characteristics and cultural heritage" (*Multiculturalism ... Being Canadian* [Ottawa: Secretary of State for Multiculturalism, 1987], p. 9). Historians and other social scientists have generally been somewhat suspicious of these stated intentions. In *"Coming Canadians": An Introduction to a History of Canada's Peoples* (Toronto: McClelland & Stewart, 1988), Howard Palmer described federal policy as an attempt to win the ethnic vote in urban Ontario and to temper western Canada's rising opposition to the policy of bilingualism. Jean Burnet has criticized the "ambiguous conceptualization" of multiculturalism but believes that its basic aims are an inevitable response to the Canadian situation ("Multiculturalism Ten Years Later," in Jean Leonard Elliott, ed., *Two Nations, Many Cultures* [Scarborough, ON: Prentice-Hall, 1983], p. 241).

Regardless of the inevitable political considerations underlying the policy, has multiculturalism been worth pursuing? Yes, thinks Norman Buchignani, who feels that federal policy has helped groups such as the South Asians feel "comfortable about being South Asian and Canadian at the same time" (*Continuous Journey: A Social History of South Asians in Canada* [Toronto: McClelland & Stewart, 1985], p. 227). He also views multicultural policy as heightening awareness among native-born Canadians of the new communities that have recently established themselves in their midst. Elliot L. Tepper agrees; in his view, multiculturalism "fosters acceptance of the reality that Canada is a nation of immigrants" ("Immigration Policy and Multiculturalism," in J.W. Berry and J.A. Laponce, eds., *Ethnicity and Culture in Canada: The Research Landscape* [Toronto: University of Toronto Press, 1994], p. 95). Lance W. Roberts and Rodney A. Clifton argue in "Multiculturalism in Canada: A Sociological Perspective," in Peter S. Li, ed., *Race and Ethnic Relations in Canada* (Toronto: Oxford University Press, 1990) that the policy at least has symbolic value, permitting members of ethnic groups to "participate and benefit as members of a complex industrial society while retaining the sense that they belong to a smaller, more intimate community" (p. 133).

Other observers are more critical of multiculturalism. C. Michael Lanphier and Anthony H. Richmond doubt that it is possible to reconcile equality of opportunity

(continued)

and integration with "the maintenance of separate identities and cultural pluralism" ("Multiculturalism and Identity in 'Canada outside Quebec,'" in Kenneth McRoberts, ed., *Beyond Quebec: Taking Stock of Canada* [Montreal/Kingston, McGill-Queen's University Press, 1995], p. 314). Gilles Paquet agrees. He sees multiculturalism as having heightened the belief among "other" Canadians that they do not have to adapt their mores while, at the same time, the "dominant cultures" have remained dominant. "The gap between expectations and realities has generated much … frustration" ("Political Philosophy of Multiculturalism," in J.W. Berry and J.A. Laponce, eds., *Ethnicity and Culture in Canada: The Research Landscape* [Toronto: University of Toronto Press, 1994], p. 63). Peter S. Li and B. Singh Bolaria hold a similar opinion. For them, multiculturalism is "the failure of an illusion, not of a policy" (*Racial Minorities in Multicultural Canada* [Toronto: Garamond Press, 1983]). The illusion is that a cultural solution, such as multiculturalism, could solve problems such as ethnic inequality and racial discrimination, whose roots are political and economic. Novelist Neil Bissoondath argues in his controversial book *Selling Illusions: The Cult of Multiculturalism in Canada* (Toronto: Penguin Books, 1994) that the policy of multiculturalism actually highlights the differences that divide Canadians rather than the similarities that unite them by encouraging immigrants to focus on "There," the ancestral homeland, rather than on "Here," the new homeland.

Robert A. Harney, a student of the Italian community in particular, sees in the policy neither great success nor abysmal failure. For him, multiculturalism is part of Canada's eternal search to define itself. "Survival," he wrote in his article "'So Great a Heritage as Ours': Immigration and the Survival of Canadian Policy," in *Daedelus* 117 (Fall 1988), "lies in traveling toward an identity, and we will all be better served if that traveling itself remains our identity" (p. 93).

The federal government's support of ethnic diversity has given rise to the question of who really speaks for the ethnic communities and, thus, of which associations the government ought to support. Twenty organizations, for example, now represent 8000 Edmontonians of various Asian origins. In Vancouver, the well-established Chinese Benevolent Association has on occasion feuded with newer, more activist, organizations, such as the Chinese Cultural Centre, over various local issues, in particular a plan to build a freeway through Chinatown. West Indians have a multitude of often-competing organizations whose membership is determined by island of origin.

Indeed, the ethnic communities themselves have questioned whether the federal and provincial governments fund the right programs, or whether they have preferred short-term, highly visible manifestations of what has been labelled "ethnic exotica." Perhaps rather than keeping immigrants "singing and dancing and talking their own language," as journalist Caitlin Kelly put it, the federal government should address "real" problems such as ethnic inequality in the Canadian labour market. Certain groups such as the Ukrainians have vigorously proposed the recognition of minority-language rights. Other students of multiculturalism doubt that English–French dualism and ethnocultural pluralism can really be reconciled, or that the vastly diverse multicultural third force has the power to assure changes in

Note the "skill-testing question" at the bottom of this cover page of The University of Calgary Alumni Magazine: "Which of these students is international?" The answer is given inside: only the woman on the right, an exchange student from Sweden, is not a Canadian. Today, Canada's multicultural society makes it impossible to distinguish Canadians on the basis of race, colour, religion, or family name.

David Brown/*The University of Calgary Alumni Magazine*, Spring 1994.

the traditional bases of Canadian society. Further attempts to foster ethnic and linguistic heterogeneity might facilitate national unity or, conversely, might make unity more difficult to attain. Agreement on such issues currently appears impossible.

NON-OFFICIAL LANGUAGES

Heritage-language programs emphasize retention of the mother tongue and are seen to have moral and psychological value. However, immigrants and their offspring, in order to integrate into Canadian society, have had to learn English or, in Quebec, to a lesser degree, French. And although such groups as the Portuguese, the Greeks, and the Chinese have had considerable success in retaining the language of the country of origin, assimilative trends generally become more pronounced over time and the retention of non-official languages diminishes sharply. As ethnolinguist Joshua Fishman put it, "for 95 percent of the third generation, the language of the cradle is the language of the streets."[10]

Barely 15 percent of Ukrainian Canadians, for example, speak Ukrainian as a home language, and intermarriage has hastened the pace of assimilation. Historian Varpu Lindstrom-Best views second- and third-generation Finns as having become an "indistinguishable part" of Canadian society, although they will still glue a Finnish flag to their bumper or, after relaxing in the sauna, "demonstrate their legendary 'sisu' (tenacity) by jumping for a refreshing dip in an icehole"![11] Dutch Canadians have also become "invisible ethnics."[12] In a study of Poles in Canada, Henry Radecki concludes that ethnic identification will have to depend on knowledge of Poland's culture and

TOP TEN COUNTRIES OF BIRTH FOR RECENT IMMIGRANTS AND ALL IMMIGRANTS, 1996

Recent immigrants[1]	Number	%	All immigrants	Number	%
1. Hong Kong	108 915	10.5	1. United Kingdom	655 540	13.2
2. P.R. of China	87 875	8.5	2. Italy	332 110	6.7
3. India	71 335	6.9	3. United States	244 695	4.9
4. Philippines	71 325	6.9	4. Hong Kong	241 095	4.8
5. Sri Lanka	44 235	4.3	5. India	235 930	4.7
6. Poland	36 965	3.6	6. P.R. of China	231 055	4.6
7. Taiwan	32 140	3.1	7. Poland	193 375	3.9
8. Vietnam	32 060	3.1	8. Philippines	184 550	3.7
9. United States	29 020	2.8	9. Germany	181 650	3.7
10. United Kingdom	25 425	2.4	10. Portugal	158 820	3.2
Total	539 295	100.0	Total	2 658 820	100.0

[1]IMMIGRANTS WHO CAME TO CANADA BETWEEN 1991 AND 1996

Source: Adapted from Statistics Canada, cat. no. 93F0023XDB96003 in the "Nation Series." Reproduced by authority of the Minister of Industry, 1999.

history rather than on "rapidly declining" mastery and use of the language in Canada.[13] Of Toronto's half-million-strong Italian community, historian Robert Harney estimated in 1984 that fewer than 150 000 (belonging generally to the original immigrant generation) were "active in Italian institutions."[14] In his opinion, large numbers of Italians have deliberately broken their ethnic links and taken refuge in "Anglo conformity" because of the prejudice they have faced. Studies carried out by sociologist Jeffrey Reitz suggest strongly that linguistic assimilation leads to destruction of the cohesive ethnic community.[15] While the prognosis for linguistic survival appears bleak for older ethnic communities from Europe, the number of Canadians speaking such languages as Chinese, Spanish, Punjabi, and Arabic is increasing rapidly as immigration rejuvenates these groups.

THE IMPACT OF IMMIGRATION

WEB LINKS

Immigrants have had an immeasurable impact on Canada's economic, political, social, and cultural life. The contributions of entrepreneurs such as the Reichmann brothers (born in Austria and Hungary), Thomas Bata and Stephen Roman (both born in the former Czechoslovakia), and David Lam (from Hong Kong), of journalist Peter Newman (born in Austria), Montreal publisher Alain Stanké (born in Lithuania), and politician David Lewis (born in Poland) are well known.

Since the late 1970s the number of non-British, non-French writers in Canada has grown substantially and Canadian literature has become more and more diversified. Joy Kogawa's novel *Obasan* and Denise Chong's memoir *The Concubine's Children: Portrait of a Family Divided*, notably, have gained wide acclaim. Increasingly, Canada became part of the literary global village as many novels written by new Canadians featured settings that often had little to do with Canada. Indian-born Rohinton

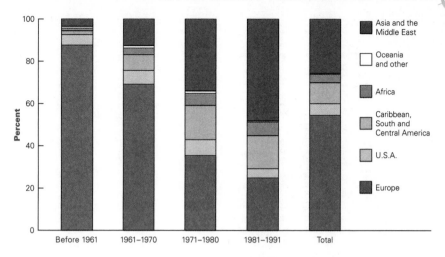

Immigrant Population by Place of Birth and Period of Immigration, 1991

....

Source: Adapted from Statistics Canada, 1991 Census of Canada, *Canadian Social Trends* (Summer 1993): 11, cat. no. 11-008. Reproduced by authority of the Minister of Industry, 1999.

Mistry used Bombay as his setting for *Such a Long Journey*, while American-born Carol Shields, in *The Stone Diaries*, chronicled a woman's life in Canada, the United States, and the Orkney Islands. Both novels won Governor General's awards. Thus, in virtually all spheres of activity, the Canada of 2000 reflects increasingly the presence of the Asians, Latin Americans, West Indians, Europeans, and other immigrants who settled in the country in the 1970s, 1980s, and 1990s.

The presence of immigrants has brought new political questions, not least of which is immigration policy, to the fore, and the ethnic vote is significant in many constituencies. Though immigrants traditionally favoured the Liberal party, to whose immigration policies they owed their arrival in Canada, their descendants' political loyalties have been much more volatile. Immigration has also enabled Canada to acquire a much more diverse and vibrant cultural life. Demographically, immigration has boosted Canada's population significantly: from 1981 to 1986, net immigration represented 21 percent of the country's population growth; from 1991 to 1996, fully 51 per cent. With immigration, the importance of both the British and the French elements has declined, while, from a linguistic point of view, the fact that the great majority of immigrants have adopted English as their new language has contributed to weakening the relative position of Canada's francophone population and increasing that community's fears for survival.

Immigration brought much of the blue-collar labour that the country needed for large-scale industrial and resource development in the 1950s. By 1961, 12 percent of the country's work force, and fully one-fifth of Ontario's, was composed of post-war immigrants. Immigration also provided many of the skilled workers and professionals that the country needed. In the 1960s, for example, hundreds of American university professors entered the country, permitting the rapid expansion of the Canadian university system but also setting the stage for the nationalist outcry against

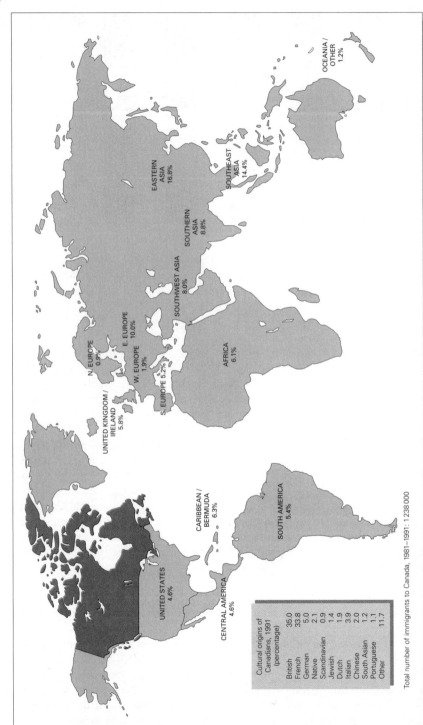

Sources of immigration to Canada, 1981–1991, by percentage.

Source: Adapted from data from *The Integrated Atlas: History and Geography of Canada and the World* (Toronto: Harcourt Brace, 1996), p. 121. Reprinted by permission of Harcourt Brace & Company Ltd.

American domination in the early 1970s. Bringing in educated immigrants at that time helped ease the pressure on an already overburdened educational system in Canada, a country with a much higher proportion of young people than the United States and most European nations. Ironically, for a country that has often complained of suffering a brain drain to the United States, Canada has been criticized by some developing countries for attracting the highly qualified people that those developing nations so desperately need to keep at home.

Immigration will surely remain a much-discussed issue. There is little prospect that Canadians can ever agree on how many immigrants the country needs, how many refugees it should welcome, where immigrants should come from, and what role they should play in Canadian society. Nevertheless, there can be no doubt that, partly because of immigration, the Canada of the year 2000 differs greatly from the country that emerged from World War II.

NOTES

1. John W. Holmes, *The Shaping of Peace: Canada and the Search for World Order 1943–1957*, vol. 1 (Toronto: University of Toronto Press, 1979), p. 101.
2. Karl Aun, *The Political Refugees: A History of the Estonians in Canada* (Toronto: McClelland & Stewart, 1985).
3. Franca Iacovetta, *Such Hardworking People: Italian Immigrants in Postwar Toronto* (Montreal/Kingston: McGill-Queen's University Press, 1992).
4. The subject of postwar French immigration is examined in Richard Jones, "Spécificités de l'immigration française au Canada au lendemain de la deuxième guerre mondiale," *Revue européenne des migrations internationales* 2 (1986): 127–43.
5. Quoted in Christina McCall Newman, "The Canadian Americans," *Maclean's*, July 27, 1963, p. 10.
6. Norman Buchignani and Doreen M. Indra with Ram Srivastiva, *Continuous Journey: A Social History of South Asians in Canada* (Toronto: McClelland & Stewart, 1985), p. 163.
7. Stanley R. Barrett, *Paradise: Class, Commuters, and Ethnicity in Rural Ontario* (Toronto: University of Toronto Press, 1994), p. 235.
8. Quoted in Henry Aubin, "Do Immigrants Steal Jobs or Create New Ones?" *The Gazette* (Montreal), January 10, 1985.
9. Gerald E. Dirks, *Controversy and Complexity: Canadian Immigration Policy During the 1980s* (Montreal/Kingston: McGill-Queen's University Press, 1995), pp. 79–80.
10. Quoted in Robert Harney, "'So Great a Heritage as Ours': Immigration and the Survival of the Canadian Policy," *Daedelus* 117 (Fall 1988): 83.
11. Varpu Lindstrom-Best, *The Finns in Canada* (Ottawa: Canadian Historical Association, 1985), p. 18.
12. Herman Ganzevoort, *A Bittersweet Land: The Dutch Experience in Canada, 1890–1980* (Toronto: McClelland & Stewart, 1988), p. 127.
13. Henry Radecki with Benedykt Heydenkorn, *A Member of a Distinguished Family: The Polish Group in Canada* (Toronto: McClelland & Stewart, 1976), p. 106.
14. Quoted in Margot Gibb-Clark, "'Italian Community's a Myth,' Historian Says," *Globe and Mail*, October 20, 1984, p. 14.
15. Jeffrey G. Reitz, "Language and Ethnic Community Survival," in Jay E. Goldstein and Rita M. Bienvenue, eds., *Ethnicity and Ethnic Relations in Canada* (Toronto: Butterworths, 1980), p. 122.

LINKING TO THE PAST

WEB

LINKS

Population Statistics

http://www.statcan.ca/english/Pgdb/People/popula.htm

A detailed look at population statistics from Statistics Canada. The statistics under "Origins and visible minorities," "Languages," and "Immigrant population" are of particular relevance to this chapter.

The Canadian Bill of Rights

http://canada.justice.gc.ca/STABLE/EN/Laws/Chap/C/C-12.3.html

The full text of the Canadian Bill of Rights from the Department of Justice.

The Employment Equity Act

http://canada.justice.gc.ca/STABLE/EN/Laws/Chap/E/E-5.4.html

The full text of the Employment Equity Act from the Department of Justice.

Multiculturalism in Canada

http://canada.gc.ca/canadiana/faitc/fa26_e.html

A brief history and outline of the federal government's initiatives related to multiculturalism. Other relevant sites related to multiculturalism in Canada include:

- The full text of the Canadian Multiculturalism Act:
  http://canada.justice.gc.ca/STABLE/EN/Laws/Chap/C/C-18.7.html.
- Annual reports from the Canadian Heritage and Multiculturalism branch of government, on the operation of the Canadian Multiculturalism Act:
  http://www.pch.gc.ca/multi/html/reports.htm.
  Each report includes detailed analysis of economic, legal, health, and cultural issues in light of the government's multiculturalism policy.

Coming to Canada

http://cicnet.ci.gc.ca/english/coming/index.html

Information from Citizenship and Immigration Canada about regulations and application procedures.

Immigration Research in Canada

http://canada.metropolis.globalx.net/research-policy/wienfeld/index_e.html

This site offers a thorough overview of immigration research in the areas of demography, urban studies, criminology, economics, sociology, and social psychology.

BIBLIOGRAPHY

A good recent overview of Canada's immigration policy is Donald H. Avery, *Reluctant Host: Canada's Response to Immigrant Workers, 1896–1994* (Toronto: McClelland & Stewart, 1995). The 1980s in particular are examined in Gerald E. Dirks, *Controversy and Complexity: Canadian Immigration Policy during the 1980s* (Montreal/Kingston: McGill-Queen's University Press, 1995). Another major study of immigration policy is Freda Hawkins, *Canada and Immigration: Public Policy and Public Concern*, 2nd ed. (Montreal/Kingston: McGill-Queen's University Press, 1988). A brief account of Canada's immigration history may be found in Valerie Knowles, *Strangers at Our Gates: Canadian Immigration and Immigration Policy, 1540–1995*, rev. ed. (Toronto: Dundurn Press, 1997). On refugees see Gerald E. Dirks, *Canada's Refugee Policy: Indifference or Opportunism?* (Montreal/Kingston: McGill-Queen's University Press, 1977); for a solid monograph on one group of refugees see Milda Danys, *DP: Lithuanian Immigration to Canada After the Second World War* (Toronto: Multicultural History Society of Ontario, 1986). An analysis of the costs and gains of immigration is available in Don J. DeVoretz, ed., *Diminishing Returns: The Economics of Canada's Recent Immigration Policy* (Toronto: C.D. Howe Institute, 1995). Critical studies of Canadian immigration policy include Victor Malarek, *Haven's Gate: Canada's Immigration Fiasco* (Toronto: Macmillan, 1987); Reg Whitaker, *Double Standard: The Secret History of Canadian Immigration* (Toronto: Lester & Orpen Dennys, 1987); and David Matas and Ilana Simon, *Closing the Doors* (Toronto: Summerhill Press, 1989). Policy pertaining to two specific groups of immigrants is analyzed in Vic Satzewich, *Racism and the Incorporation of Foreign Labour: Farm Labour Migration to Canada since 1945* (London: Routledge, 1991); and in Angelika E. Sauer, "A Matter of Domestic Policy? Canadian Immigration Policy and the Admission of Germans, 1945–1950," *Canadian Historical Review* 74 (1993): 226–63.

Among the many publications on ethnicity see Peter S. Li, ed., *Race and Ethnic Relations in Canada* (Toronto: Oxford University Press, 1990); Leo Driedger, ed., *Ethnic Canada: Identities and Inequalities* (Toronto: Copp Clark Pitman, 1987); Jean Leonard Elliott and Augie Fleras, *Unequal Relations: An Introduction to Race and Ethnic Dynamics in Canada* (Scarborough, ON: Prentice-Hall, 1992); Jay E. Goldstein and Rita M. Bienvenue, eds., *Ethnicity and Ethnic Relations in Canada* (Toronto: Butterworths, 1985); Raymond Breton et al., *Ethnic Identity and Equality: Varieties of Experience in a Canadian City* (Toronto: University of Toronto Press, 1990); Barry R. Chiswick, ed., *Immigration, Language, and Ethnicity: Canada and the United States* (Washington, DC: AEI Press, 1992); and Raymond Breton and Jeffrey Reitz, *The Illusion of Difference: Realities of Ethnicity in Canada and the United States* (Toronto: C.D. Howe Institute, 1994). Two useful articles are Raymond Breton, "Multiculturalism and Canadian Nation-Building," in Alan C. Cairns and Cynthia Williams, eds., *The Politics of Gender, Ethnicity, and Language in Canada* (Toronto: University of Toronto Press, 1986); and Robert A. Harney, "'So Great a Heritage as Ours': Immigration and the Survival of the Canadian Policy," *Daedelus* 117 (Fall 1988): 51–98. For an examination of Quebec's experience, see Jacques Langlais et al., eds., *Le Québec de demain et les communautés culturelles* (Montréal: Editions de Méridien, 1990).

Howard Palmer and Tamara Palmer, eds., *Peoples of Alberta: Portraits of Cultural Diversity* (Saskatoon: Western Producer Prairie Books, 1985) is a good study of one province's ethnocultural groups. Dutch immigration and assimilation are described in Herman Ganzevoort, *A Bittersweet Land: The Dutch Experience in Canada, 1890–1980* (Toronto: McClelland & Stewart, 1988); the very different Chinese experience is examined in Peter S. Li, *The Chinese in Canada* (Toronto: Oxford University Press, 1988). On Asians see Norman Buchignani et al., *Continuous Journey: A Social History of South Asians in Canada* (Toronto: McClelland & Stewart, 1985). A very readable book on the Italians is Kenneth Bagnell, *Canadese: A Portrait of Italian Canadians* (Toronto: Macmillan, 1989). Franca Iacovetta studies one Italian community in *Such Hardworking People: Italian Immigrants in Postwar Toronto* (Montreal/Kingston: McGill-Queen's University Press, 1992). Scholarly works on the Jewish community include Robert J. Brym, William Shaffir, and Morton Weinfeld, eds., *The Jews in Canada* (Toronto: Oxford University Press, 1993); and Alan T. Davies, *Antisemitism in Canada: History and Interpretation* (Waterloo, ON: Wilfrid Laurier University Press, 1992). Irving Abella has produced a well-illustrated history of Jews in Canada: *A Coat of Many Colours: Two Centuries of Jewish Life in Canada* (Toronto: Lester & Orpen Dennys, 1990). Harold Troper and Morton Weinfeld examine the painful problem of intergroup relations in *Old Wounds: Jews, Ukrainians and the Hunt for Nazi War Criminals in Canada* (Markham, ON: Viking, 1989). For vigorous critiques of multiculturalism see Reginald Bibby, *Mosaic Madness: The Poverty and Potential of Life in Canada* (Toronto:

Stoddart, 1990); and Neil Bissoondath, *Selling Illusions: The Cult of Multiculturalism in Canada* (Toronto: Penguin, 1994). An important historiographical work is J.W. Berry and J.A. Laponce, eds., *Ethnicity and Culture in Canada: The Research Landscape* (Toronto: University of Toronto Press, 1994).

Language retention is discussed in J.G. Reitz, *The Survival of Ethnic Groups* (Toronto: McGraw-Hill Ryerson, 1980); Ronald Wardhaugh, *Language and Nationhood: The Canadian Experience* (Vancouver: New Star Books, 1983); and Edward N. Herberg, *Ethnic Groups in Canada: Adaptations and Transitions* (Scarborough, ON: Nelson, 1989). Ethnic groups in politics is the subject of a study prepared for the Royal Commission on Electoral Reform: Kathy Megyery, ed., *Ethnocultural Groups and Visible Minorities in Canadian Politics: The Question of Access* (Toronto: Dundurn Press, 1992). The political activities of the Canadian Ethnocultural Council are examined in Leslie A. Pal, *Interests of State: The Politics of Language, Multiculturalism, and Feminism in Canada* (Montreal/Kingston: McGill-Queen's University Press, 1993). Beverly Rasporich and Tamara P. Seiler discuss the cultural contribution of new Canadians and their descendants in "Multiculturalism and the Arts," in David Taras and Beverly Rasporich, eds., *A Passion for Identity: An Introduction to Canadian Studies*, 3rd ed. (Toronto: Nelson, 1997).

Barry Broadfoot, *The Immigrant Years: From Europe to Canada, 1945–1967* (Vancouver: Douglas & McIntyre, 1986) presents interviews bearing on the immigrant experience. Racial discrimination is studied in B. Singh Bolaria and Peter S. Li, *Racial Oppression in Canada*, 2nd ed. (Toronto: Garamond Press, 1988); Evelyn Kallen, *Label Me Human: Minority Rights of Stigmatized Canadians* (Toronto: University of Toronto Press, 1989); Frances Henry *The Caribbean Diaspora in Toronto: Learning to Live with Racism* (Toronto: University of Toronto Press, 1994); and Frances Henry et al., *The Colour of Democracy: Racism in Canadian Society*, 2nd ed. (Toronto: Harcourt Brace, 1999).

The scholarly review *Canadian Ethnic Studies*, published at the University of Calgary since 1968, contains a wealth of material on the various facets of the immigrant experience. An ongoing series published by the Canadian Historical Association, with the support of the Canadian government's multiculturalism program, provides useful syntheses of the experiences of several ethnic groups. For book-length studies of various ethnic groups see the "Generations: A History of Canada's Peoples" series, published by McClelland and Stewart in conjunction with the Multiculturalism Directorate; it includes histories of the Portuguese, the Poles, the Japanese, the Scots, the Dutch, the Norwegians, the Greeks, the Arabs, the Hungarians, the Estonians, the Ukrainians, the Croatians, the Chinese, and the South Asians. Appearing only after all of these were published was an introductory volume to the series: Jean R. Burnet with Howard Palmer, *"Coming Canadians": An Introduction to a History of Canada's Peoples* (Toronto: McClelland & Stewart, 1988). Up-to-date statistical information on immigration is available at the following Internet address: www.statcan.ca.

CHAPTER TWENTY

Contemporary Canada

The era of rapid transformation and experimentation, begun in the 1960s and continuing into the 1970s, appeared by 1980 to have run its course. Economic difficulties, including a severe bout of inflation and deep recessions, contributed to fostering more individualistic preoccupations, and more conservative attitudes now asserted themselves. The transition proved painful. Increased state intervention in most aspects of life after 1960 had made citizens more dependent on governments and thus more demanding of them, even when overstrained public finances dictated cuts in expenditures and rising taxes. Governments were urged not only to maintain social services but to address new challenges, among them the aging of the nation's population, increasing homelessness, and widespread poverty among groups such as single mothers with children. Prime Ministers Pierre Trudeau and Brian Mulroney succeeded in convincing Canadians to give them solid mandates, but both found it increasingly difficult to maintain a workable political consensus in the face of rising discontent. Voters showed more volatility, as old political loyalties broke down. For some observers, Canada was becoming a fragmented society, in which the agendas of groups took priority over the common welfare.

The 1990s provided a certain respite. Economic expansion after 1993 made Canadians more optimistic. Unemployment rates dropped slowly. Budget deficits turned into surpluses for the federal government and for most of the provinces, and beleaguered taxpayers called for tax relief. Ordinary Canadians also demanded that governments reinvest in services, particularly health care.

INFLATION IN THE 1970S

For most of the contemporary period, Canadians' major concern has been the economy. From the early 1970s until the mid-1980s, rising prices in particular worried them. In 1973, the cost of living increased by 9 percent. Food and housing costs went up much more steeply. That year shoppers paid 30 percent more for meat, 40 percent more for poultry, and 40 percent more for eggs. House prices that jumped upward by as much as 20 percent in cities such as Vancouver, Toronto, and Ottawa pushed younger Canadians out of the housing market. Prices rose even higher in 1974 as the country endured double-digit inflation. Low-income families, who had to spend three-quarters of their income on food and housing, were hardest hit because the prices of these two components of the cost of living index increased the fastest.

Politicians blamed outside forces for these substantial price increases. After all, inflation plagued most other countries, particularly the United States, where it was fed by the war in Vietnam. Moreover, world food prices, in the face of insufficient production, moved sharply upward. The Organization of Petroleum Exporting Countries (OPEC) increased oil prices substantially too, in 1973 and again in 1979.

Nevertheless, domestic causes of inflation also existed. Unions were accused of making unrealistically high wage demands that forced companies to raise their prices. In turn, labour blamed rising prices on excessive corporate profits. Inflation conditioned individuals to expect more inflation and to demand bigger wage increases. This behaviour, though understandable, ensured that the problem persisted.

THE TRUDEAU GOVERNMENT

The failure to curb inflation only partially explains rising popular discontent. The wave of Trudeaumania on which Pierre Elliott Trudeau had ridden to power in 1968 had, by 1972, been transformed into a swelling tide of Trudeauphobia, as the seemingly modest Trudeau of 1968, who had said that he wanted to "dialogue" with Canadians, became an arrogant, remote, temperamental personality. The election of 1972 brought near defeat. Questions of policy influenced electors as well. In a few districts, the backlash against bilingualism and French power cost the Liberals dearly. The government's apparent inability to handle economic questions — not only inflation, but also unemployment, welfare, strikes, and high taxes — also helped to explain voter disaffection. NDP leader David Lewis's aggressive campaign against the "corporate welfare bums" who had unjustifiably benefited from government subsidies and tax privileges accounted for that party's relatively strong performance.

MINORITY RULE

During the two-year minority government that followed the election of 1972, the Trudeau government worked to win back voter approval. It greatly increased public spending on social programs and indexed income-tax brackets and exemptions to the cost of living in order to protect taxpayers from inflation. (These measures had catastrophic effects on government finances.) To win support in populous central Canada, the government promised to keep oil prices (then increasing rapidly) at levels substantially below world levels — a policy that naturally infuriated the oil-producing western provinces. When opposition leader Robert Stanfield promised a wage and price freeze in 1974, labour hesitated, then gave its support to Trudeau, who declared his opposition to such a freeze. "Zap! You're frozen!" he mocked in one notorious repartee. Voters gave Trudeau a majority in 1974. The next year the Liberals reversed themselves and adopted a wage and price freeze. These controls, which affected the public sector and large private companies, lasted three years. The rate of increase in prices did slow, but it took more than controls and guidelines to defeat inflation.

THE RISE AND FALL OF ECONOMIC NATIONALISM

By 1970, many Canadians, particularly in industrialized southern Ontario, expressed concern for the high degree of foreign (especially American) ownership of the Canadian economy. Nationalist authors published books with provocative titles: *Silent Surrender*; *The Precarious Homestead*; *Partner to Behemoth*; and *The Elephant and the Mouse*. These works portrayed Canada as a satellite of the American metropolis. Journalist Peter Newman warned that "the end of the Canadian dream" was imminent.

Some critics did offer solutions to the dilemma of foreign ownership. The militant socialist and nationalist Waffle group within the New Democratic Party (NDP) urged large-scale nationalization of foreign-owned businesses and resources. More moderate nationalists called for a gradual buying back only of large enterprises. Still others believed that actual ownership mattered little if Ottawa exercised stronger control over giant foreign-owned corporations operating in the country.

In an effort to appease nationalist discontent, the Trudeau government in 1971 set up the Foreign Investment Review Agency (FIRA) to screen takeovers and determine whether they were of "significant benefit" to Canada. Yet, by 1980, according to political scientist Stephen Clarkson, FIRA had shown itself to be a "paper tiger" that had not noticeably prevented American investment in Canada.[1] American ambassador Thomas Enders himself expressed satisfaction with the agency's 90 percent approval rate.

RISING DISCONTENT

Between 1974 and 1979, the polls showed support for the Liberals fluctuating wildly. By 1979, with Canada again in a severe inflationary crisis, the business community in particular worried about the foundering economy and the rapidly rising federal deficit, which the government financed by borrowing heavily, even at historically high interest rates. (Rather than tax more or cut expenditures, the government had adopted the painless, though admittedly short-term, remedy of borrowing more.)

Regional discontent increased, too. The West, in particular, complained that Trudeau paid little heed to its concerns. Frustrated wheat farmers, for example, hurt by mounting world surpluses of wheat and sagging prices, exhorted the federal government to act, while a frustrated Prime Minister Trudeau asked rhetorically: "Why should I sell your wheat?" With the notable exception of Quebec, the Trudeau consensus largely broke apart, with the result that the Progressive Conservatives, under their new leader, Joe Clark, a federal MP from Alberta, won a fragile mandate in the May 1979 election.

JOE CLARK'S GOVERNMENT

WEB
LINKS

Joe Clark's unfavourable image, though largely undeserved and based on a superficial appreciation of the individual, proved a heavy yoke for the Conservatives to bear. The morning after his victory in the 1976 Conservative leadership race, a *Toronto Star* headline read "Joe Who?" The gibe remained to haunt Clark even after

A cartoon depicting Pierre Trudeau's return to the prime minister's official residence at 24 Sussex Drive, after the election of 1980. Joe Clark is opening the door.

....

Aislin/*The Gazette*, Montreal.

he became prime minister. Journalist Jeffrey Simpson concluded that the Tories won the election of 1979 not because of Clark but in spite of him. Although Clark was not afflicted with Trudeau's arrogance, he lacked the Liberal leader's enviable international reputation.

The energy question resulted in the collapse of Clark's brief government and a return to power of the Liberals in the February 1980 election. Promoting a policy of "short-term pain for long-term gain," Clark's finance minister announced a 4-cent-per-litre excise tax on gasoline designed to bring billions of dollars into the federal treasury in order to attack the rising deficit. Defeated in the House of Commons, the government resigned. During the ensuing election campaign, Trudeau promised to revoke the immensely unpopular tax, while Clark continued to suffer from his decidedly negative image as a weak and indecisive prime minister.

THE END OF THE TRUDEAU ERA

....

Trudeau's final mandate proved difficult. He immediately launched the National Energy Program (NEP) to Canadianize the petroleum industry by reducing the role of American oil companies in Canada. Alberta's Premier Peter Lougheed, galled by the federal government's intention to appropriate a greater share of huge oil revenues for itself, likened the plan to "having strangers take over the living room." Ottawa responded that too great a transfer of wealth to one province would upset the equilibrium of Confederation. The western Canadian business community denounced Ottawa's intervention, while American trade representative William Brock threatened: "We have a quiver full of arrows and we are prepared to shoot them in self-defense if we must."

The federal government's initiative proved ill-timed. Just as it spent billions of dollars purchasing foreign oil companies and assisting exploration by Canadian companies, oil prices crashed dramatically. Canada's biggest corporate liability became Dome Petroleum, a creation of Liberal energy policies that had accumulated a debt of more than $6 billion by the mid-1980s. Ironically, it was then sold to an American oil company.

The signing of the Canadian Constitution by Her Majesty Queen Elizabeth II, April 1982. Prime Minister Trudeau looks on. The agreement ended the British Parliament's power to amend the British North America (BNA) Act, and also established, for the first time, a Canadian Charter of Rights and Freedoms.

Bob Cooper/National Archives of Canada/PA-140705.

THE CONSTITUTION OF 1982

Trudeau also went forward with a plan to "patriate" the Constitution and particularly to insert within it a Canadian Charter of Rights and Freedoms and an amending formula by which the United Kingdom's consent would no longer be necessary for constitutional changes. Although most Canadians outside Quebec approved of Trudeau's initiative, Quebec refused to sign the agreement, which had been negotiated in its absence during what that province's delegates termed "the night of the long knives." Thus, the province that since 1960 had been most insistent on the need for constitutional change was not a party to the reformed Constitution.

Women's groups won the inclusion in the Charter of an article affirming the equality of male and female persons. For their part, the Native peoples' associations succeeded in their efforts to entrench Aboriginal and treaty rights. The Métis also achieved constitutional recognition as an Aboriginal people. The Charter recognized only existing rights, and left these undefined.

Most Canadians were, however, primarily interested in bread-and-butter issues. When a recession hit Canada in 1981–82, they blamed Ottawa for mismanagement of the economy. The recession resulted in part from government monetary policy, particularly high interest rates, designed to dampen inflationary pressures. (Indeed, there appeared to be no solution that would enable governments to combat inflation and unemployment simultaneously.) Recession also stemmed from worldwide over-production in the resource industries, in agriculture, and in secondary manufacturing. The daily press offered a sombre litany of factory closings, layoffs, and cutbacks. Magazine articles frequently evoked the Great Depression of the 1930s. Finally, the constantly unfavourable polls and the selection by the Conservatives of businessman Brian Mulroney to replace Joe Clark as party leader convinced Trudeau that he should resign.

TRUDEAU'S RECORD

The Trudeau years were replete with paradoxes. Trudeau championed the trusty Liberal theme of national unity at each election. Yet, during his term in office, the country faced the most serious threats to its existence that it had ever confronted, especially from Quebec and the western provinces. Trudeau had also pushed for the inclusion of the Canadian Charter of Rights and Freedoms in the Constitution, insisting on the need to defend Canadians' political liberties. Yet, during the FLQ crisis of October 1970, his government invoked the War Measures Act and thereby effectively suspended civil liberties, enabling the police to arrest hundreds of individuals and to hold them incommunicado for several days, without ever laying charges against most of them.

Trudeau frequently denounced the dangers of nationalism, but his legislation controlling foreign investment, as well as his National Energy Program of 1980, convinced Americans that he was a strident nationalist. Furthermore, his government adopted the Official Languages Act in 1969 in an effort to ensure greater equality for French-speaking Canadians by making government services more widely available in French. While many French Canadians despaired of ever attaining genuine equality, many English-speaking Canadians complained that they were now the victims of unfair treatment. Finally, Trudeau had promised to battle regional imbalances. Although measures such as increased equalization payments and other transfers helped reduce disparities, they had "little effect," as economist Paul Phillips has pointed out, "on their root causes."[2]

Trudeau had long spoken of the need to build a "just society," but what role were women to play in bringing such a society about? During the first Trudeau mandate (1968–72), the House of Commons had only one female member. A *Chatelaine* article commented: "There are 56 whooping cranes in Canada, and one female federal politician." Politically active feminists complained that parties showed no interest in working to recruit promising female candidates. Although society's changing attitudes brought a slow improvement, by 1980 only 15 women representing three parties won seats in the House. A decade later, although more women were involved in the various phases of party activity, most continued, in political scientist Sylvia Bashevkin's words, to "toe the lines" and to fill "conventional maintenance roles."[3]

In foreign affairs, Trudeau rejected Canada's traditional role as a "helpful fixer" in favour of a policy based on national self-interest. Certainly the sale of arms to military dictatorships during his tenure showed the precedence commercial interests took over human rights. Nonetheless, Canada did increase its developmental assistance to Third World nations significantly. In the early 1970s Trudeau cut defence spending, thereby incurring the wrath of Canada's NATO allies. But Canada ultimately retained all of its alliance commitments, and defence spending steadily increased thereafter.

THE PROGRESSIVE CONSERVATIVES IN POWER

Trudeau left John Turner, his successor as Liberal party leader and prime minister, to justify his failures. Canadians reacted by voting for what appeared to be real change: they gave Brian Mulroney and his Conservative party a resounding victory, with 211 of the 282 seats in the House of Commons, including a majority of Quebec's ridings. Though women still held fewer than 10 percent of the seats in the House, they made up 21 percent of Mulroney's first cabinet.

The Canada of the mid-1980s differed greatly from that of the 1970s. As in the United States, a conservative mood prevailed. For many Canadians, Liberal support of state intervention and of the federal government's strategic role in the economy now signified unacceptably high levels of government spending, rising taxes, and government interference. The Conservatives' praise for free enterprise and their vision of a more decentralized Canada, a "community of communities," appeared more appropriate.

CORPORATE HEROES

As a sign of the times, a new group of entrepreneurs kindled popular interest. Among them were the Bronfmans, whose corporate empire included 152 companies, with assets of $120 billion in 1988; Albert and Paul Reichmann, who built a vast real-estate and resource empire, much of which crashed down with the collapse of property values after 1990; Conrad Black, of the Toronto-based Argus Corporation, whom journalist Peter Newman presented rather heroically as the new prince of the Canadian establishment; developer Robert Campeau, whose purchases of American department-store chains with borrowed money brought admiration for his gall, then perhaps amazement at his almost immediate fall in the fourth-largest bankruptcy in American history; and Pierre Péladeau, of Quebecor in Montreal, whose holdings grew from a tiny periodical, bought in 1950 with a loan of $1500, to a $450 million newspaper and printing empire. Canadians also watched in alarmed fascination as big businesses became even bigger through mergers frequently worth billions of dollars.

THE FIRST MULRONEY GOVERNMENT

WEB

LINKS

Although business welcomed the new Conservative government, Mulroney's appeal was much wider. He had promised an "era of national reconciliation," notably in federal–provincial relations. In 1984–85, regional dissensions seemed indeed to diminish: Mulroney appeased the West by dismantling the National Energy Program; he satisfied Nova Scotia and Newfoundland by yielding them control of offshore mineral resources; and he pleased the Quebec government by promising to negotiate Quebec's acceptance of the Constitution of 1982.

The Conservatives had also blamed the Liberals for Canada's poor relations with the United States. Announcing that Canada was again "open for business," the Mulroney government defanged what it called "the FIRA tiger," transforming it into a new agency, Investment Canada, with a mandate to encourage foreign investment. In the course of Mulroney's two mandates, Canada–U.S. relations were to undergo, as historian John Thompson put it, "a revolutionary shift toward ideological and political convergence and a remarkable accommodation on a wide range of divisive issues."[4]

Other Conservative foreign-policy initiatives gained approval from specific interest groups. Human-rights advocates praised Mulroney for his condemnation of racial discrimination in South Africa and vigorous support of sanctions against that country. French Canada approved of Mulroney's efforts to forge closer links with *la francophonie*, a loose association of the world's French-speaking states. Most Canadians took pride in Canada's commitment to international peacekeeping and to developmental assistance. Peace, women's, labour, and religious groups did, however, criticize

Prime Minister Brian Mulroney greets American President Ronald Reagan on his arrival for the "Shamrock Summit" at Quebec City, 1985, during which both leaders made much of their Irish origins. Mulroney hailed the summit as the inauguration of a new positive era in Canadian–American relations.

CP Picture Archive (Paul Chiasson).

the government's decision to commit modest Canadian forces to the Persian Gulf War against Iraq in 1991; they favoured giving sanctions more time to work.

The strong economic recovery also aided the Conservatives. Unemployment fell, although young people still found it difficult to find jobs. The decline in the inflation rate, from 12.5 percent in 1981 to only 4 percent in 1985, brought interest rates down, making it possible again for businesses and consumers to borrow. The omens appeared favourable for the construction of a new political consensus among Canadians.

The Conservative honeymoon proved brief. The Mulroney government's frequent bouts with scandal soon hurt its public image. Regionalism rose phoenix-like out of the country's flagrantly unequal economic recovery. While metropolitan Toronto and southern Ontario basked in virtually full employment, Quebec, the West, and the Atlantic provinces faced continued high jobless rates. The decline of oil and resource prices, coinciding with a severe farm crisis, hurt the economies of the western provinces.

THE FEDERAL DEFICIT

Mulroney also found it difficult to reduce his government's budgetary deficit. In 1985, the government had a record shortfall of more than $38 billion. A newspaper item depicted a wailing infant above the caption: "Already $8000 in debt." That was each Canadian's share of the $200 billion-and-growing national debt. By 1996, the baby owed nearly $27 000 when rising provincial and municipal indebtedness was taken into account, and Ottawa devoted about one-quarter of its revenues simply to paying the interest on its borrowings. Most economists and business leaders saw the deficit as a "time bomb, ticking away." In 1986, Brian Mulroney promised Canadians: "Our determination to reduce it or eradicate it is, and will be, unyielding and successful."

Such valiant stands had been made earlier, and they would be made again. The political necessity of maintaining federal expenditures hampered plans to control spending. Beleaguered farmers pleaded for cash compensation to shield them from depressed world grain prices. After two western banks crashed resoundingly in 1985, investors successfully sought a multibillion-dollar bailout. When refineries closed in impoverished east-end Montreal, pressures mounted for Ottawa to intervene. In areas of high unemployment, local potentates sought an array of subsidies and low-cost loans for business to help create new jobs or save threatened ones. The defence lobby demanded money to overhaul and improve the country's defence capability.

When Ottawa reduced grants to the provinces, provincial governments accused it of pushing its deficit on them. Ordinary Canadians, especially the worried middle classes, prevailed upon the government to reaffirm its somewhat wavering faith in the universality of social programs such as old-age pensions. Indeed, when the Mulroney government expressed its intention to index old-age pensions only partially to cost-of-living increases, seniors mobilized and forced the government into a hasty retreat. After a study of unemployment insurance in 1987 recommended substantial changes to reduce costs, labour and the poorer provinces rallied to the defence of the much-maligned program. Ottawa clearly understood the political risks of effecting drastic cuts. "Rattlesnakes get warmer welcomes," said the Montreal *Gazette* of the government's own reaction to the report.

Rather than cutting expenses, the government found it easier to raise income and sales taxes substantially, and to continue to borrow. By 1991, the federal deficit still hovered at around $30 billion. Ottawa now needed 35 cents of each tax dollar to pay interest on its previous borrowings, which now approached a total of $400 billion. In fact, Ottawa now spent more on interest payments than it did on health and welfare.

THE GREAT FREE-TRADE DEBATE

The conclusion of a comprehensive trade agreement with the United States became the Mulroney government's most passionately debated initiative during its first mandate.

Canada has always sought wide access to foreign markets for its exports, while simultaneously attempting to reduce imports to protect Canadian jobs in industries that were unable to withstand competition from abroad. Throughout the 1970s, the government kept tariffs, especially on manufactured products, among the highest in the industrialized world. When multilateral trade negotiations in the framework of GATT discredited protective tariffs, Canada, like many other countries, erected a host of non-tariff barriers such as quotas in an effort to impede the entry of cheap imports of goods such as clothing and footwear. The downward slide of the Canadian dollar after 1976 — the year it reached a high of $1.04 U.S. — helped less productive Canadians compete in foreign markets. It also meant that imports cost more.

TRADE RELATIONS WITH THE UNITED STATES

As trade increased with the United States, Canada insistently proclaimed its belief in diversification. It seemed risky to rely on a single country for almost all of its imports and exports. Rejecting both the status quo and continental integration, the government proposed, in 1972, a "Third Option," which implied less dependence on the United States and stronger links with Europe and other countries.

The new policy failed. Canadian trade with Britain, for example, continued to decline, particularly after that country entered the European Common Market in 1974.

By 1985, fully 80 percent of Canada's exports went to the United States, and 70 percent of its imports originated there.

Prime Minister Brian Mulroney now told Canadians that a free-trade agreement with the United States would help lower the unemployment rate. Increased sales of goods in that market would also diminish Canada's burgeoning balance of payments deficit in relation to the flow of investment income, tourism, services, and interest payments to foreign lenders to finance the growing mountain of federal debt.

Support for free trade came from many sources. The Royal Commission on the Economic Union and Development Prospects for Canada strongly endorsed it in 1985. Many sectors of the business community had long favoured it. Polls showed that, in the early stages of the debate, a solid majority of Canadians backed it, too. Consumers were generally convinced that free trade would bring lower prices.

OPPOSITION TO FREE TRADE

As the debate heated up, public support for free trade cooled. American protectionist measures weakened Canadian enthusiasm, though at the same time they seemed to make some form of agreement even more urgent. Labour unions, farmers, the churches, the federal NDP and Liberal parties, some provinces (especially Ontario), and several businesses asserted that free trade would cost thousands of jobs. They argued that American companies might close their higher cost branch plants in Canada and serve the Canadian market from their more cost-efficient American bases. Canada might lose control over the pricing of resources and be forced to abandon transport subsidies. Anti-free traders further warned that a deal could endanger Canada's social programs. Worst of all — here were shades of the 1911 election and the reciprocity debate — free trade could jeopardize Canada's political sovereignty.

THE CANADA–U.S. FREE-TRADE AGREEMENT

Arduous negotiations culminated in an accord in 1987. By its terms, tariffs would end gradually, and Canada would gain enhanced access to most sectors of the American market. Canada did not succeed in obtaining the much-sought-after "binding mechanism for dispute resolution"; instead the agreement created a less satisfactory binational review panel that would ensure that each country's trade agencies made their decisions on the basis of existing law. In future, Canada could no longer bar most American takeovers of Canadian industries. Moreover, although Canada gained unrestricted access for energy exports to the United States, the deal also secured American access to Canadian supplies even in times of shortages. But Canada did obtain exemptions for its agricultural products sold through marketing boards and its threatened cultural enterprises. Negotiators left the delicate issue of trade-distorting subsidies, given by governments to favour certain industries, to later discussion.

By refusing to accept the accord, the Liberal-dominated Senate forced an election in late 1988. Discussion of free trade became the major issue. During a televised

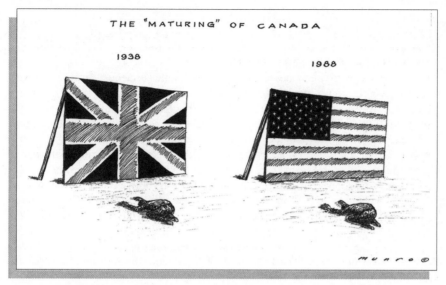

By the late 1980s, it seemed to some Canadians that Canada had simply passed from British colonial status to American. The free-trade agreement that went into effect in early 1989 certainly increased Canada's close economic ties with the United States.

Cartoon by Ken Munro.

debate, Liberal leader John Turner accused Prime Minister Mulroney: "I happen to believe you have sold us out.... You will reduce us ... to a colony of the United States." The Conservative victory, though with a substantially reduced majority, ensured ratification of the agreement in early 1989. As plant closures brought steep job losses in 1989 and 1990, the labour movement blamed free trade. Other observers placed the responsibility on high interest rates, a rising Canadian dollar, a relative decline in productivity, increased taxes, and a deteriorating international economic situation. The Conservative government pushed on. Shortly after the election, it agreed to sign a new treaty with the United States and Mexico forming a North American free trade zone.

THE COLLAPSE OF CONSENSUS

The re-election of the Conservative government soon brought about leadership changes in the two opposition parties. The NDP chose Audrey McLaughlin to succeed Ed Broadbent; she thus became the first woman in Canadian history to lead a national political party. Jean Chrétien, who had occupied several cabinet posts under Trudeau, easily won the Liberal leadership, though his support in Quebec was weak due in part to his perceived insensitivity to Quebec's exclusion from the constitutional agreement of 1982.

Where Social Scientists Disagree

THE DEBATE OVER FREE TRADE

In the years 1985–88, historians, economists, and political scientists waded into the fray to debate the issue of free trade with the United States. Economist Fred Lazar, in "The Trade Agreement: A Dissenting Opinion," in Marc Gold and David Leyton-Brown, eds., *Trade-Offs on Free Trade: The Canada–U.S. Free Trade Agreement* (Toronto: Carswell, 1988), judged that the agreement "curtailed Canada's sovereignty to an unwarranted degree" (p. 435) and virtually gave the American government the right to determine acceptable Canadian government policies. Political scientist Garth Stevenson also examined the likely political implications of free trade in "The Agreement and Dynamics of Canadian Federalism," in *Trade-offs on Free Trade*. For him, free trade risked undermining the central government's raison d'être since Ottawa could exercise "only minimal powers over the economy" (p. 140).

Political scientist Daniel P. Drache expressed strong opposition as well in "The Mulroney–Reagan Accord: The Economics of Continental Power," in *Trade-Offs on Free Trade*. In his view, Canada, "with its weak industrial sector, sharp regional divisions and stark social inequalities," would now be subject to market forces alone; governments would have to give up their time-honoured right and ability to intervene to come to the aid of the disadvantaged (p. 87). As for economist James Laxer, free trade was a "leap of faith" into the unknown that Canada would do well to avoid (*Leap of Faith: Free Trade and the Future of Canada* [Edmonton: Hurtig, 1986]).

Other observers judged the project more favourably. For economist Richard Lipsey, in *Trade-Offs on Free Trade*, Canadians had "little to lose but [their] fears." Access to the American market represented an enormous advantage. Economist John Crispo, in his *Free Trade: The Real Story* (Toronto: Gage, 1988), agreed, challenging his opponents to note that an economically more dynamic Canada could also provide more support for culture, social security, and regional development (p. 204).

Many critics feared that Canada would ultimately be obliged to harmonize its policies with American policies. In the opinion of political scientist Peter Cumming ("Impact of the Free Trade Agreement on Public Policy," in *Trade-Offs on Free Trade*), it would be in Canada's own best interest if it forced the country to "revamp outdated policies" (p. 433). According to political scientist David Leyton-Brown, the real question was whether free trade would bring about a greater degree of "harmonization" than would have occurred without free trade. His modest reply: "That question is of course unanswerable" ("The Canada–U.S. Free Trade Agreement," in Andrew B. Gollner and Daniel Salée, eds., *Canada Under Mulroney: An End-of-Term Report* [Montreal: Véhicule Press, 1988], p. 117).

In the field of culture, negotiators contended that Canada's sovereignty was protected. For historian John Herd Thompson, however, Canada appeared to admit the American definition of culture, that cultural industries were a business like any other. Thompson sees this convergence of understandings of culture as holding "greater peril for Canada's cultural sovereignty than any threatened U.S. retaliation to specific Canadian policies of cultural protection and promotion" ("Canada's Quest for Cultural Sovereignty: Protection, Promotion, and Popular Culture," in Stephen J. Randall and Herman W. Konrad, eds., *NAFTA in Transition* [Calgary: University of Calgary Press, 1995], p. 410).

(continued)

By the late 1990s, Canada's exports to the United States had increased massively, but Canada's unemployment rate remained much higher than the American rate. For critics, the low Canadian dollar was the real cause of the rise in trade. Moreover, they pointed out, the United States continued to use protectionist measures to limit imports from Canada in such sectors as lumber and agricultural products. Had Canadians become more like Americans? There could be no doubt, answered historian Jack Granatstein. Canadians "are American in all but name" (*Yankee Go Home? Canadians and Anti-Americanism* [Toronto: HarperCollins, 1996], p. 9). Certainly not, replied Michael Adams, of the polling firm Environics Research. Americans "have become a nation of God-fearing Darwinists, we have become a collection of tolerant social democrats" (*Sex in the Snow: Canadian Social Values at the End of the Millennium* [Toronto: Penguin Books, 1998], p. 194). Consensus is apparently still far off.

OPPOSITION TO MULRONEY

After the election, the Conservatives soon plummeted to third place in the polls. One journalist described the sour public mood: "The Mulroney government is ... loathed and despised in most parts of the country." Those who had fought free trade now reviled Mulroney. Better-off Canadians complained when the government "clawed back" their family allowances and old-age pensions. The harsh budget of 1989, with its new tax increases, and, even more, the government's decision to replace the hidden manufacturers' sales tax with a fully visible goods and services tax (GST) of 7 percent, from January 1991, provoked vehement opposition. Other measures, such as cuts in subsidies to Via Rail and to the Canadian Broadcasting Corporation (CBC) as well as the privatizing of Crown corporations, also generated strong disapproval: critics accused Mulroney of dismantling national institutions. The deepening crisis in public finances limited the government's ability to respond to the demands placed on it. High interest rates and much increased unemployment brought on by the harsh recession of 1990–91, particularly in the central provinces, only compounded the prevailing discontent.

Many Canadians outside Quebec blamed Mulroney for the constitutional fiasco of the Meech Lake Accord, designed to bring Quebec to give its assent to the Constitution of 1982 (see Chapter Seventeen). Within Quebec, support for sovereignty bounded upward. For their part, western Canadians saw the Mulroney government as overly attuned to the interests of central Canada; the meteoric rise in popularity of the Reform party provided evidence of a powerful wave of discontent.

The Conservatives tried again to achieve an agreement on constitutional reforms in 1991–92. This time, wide consultations took place before the federal, provincial, and territorial first ministers, and the heads of Native organizations met at Charlottetown in 1992 and agreed on proposals that attempted to respond to a host of agendas for change, including Senate reform and Aboriginal self-government. A referendum held in October 1992 saw the voters of six provinces, including Quebec, reject the agreement. A Decima poll showed that "Quebec got too much" was the most favoured reason for voting "no" outside that province; Quebeckers in turn said that

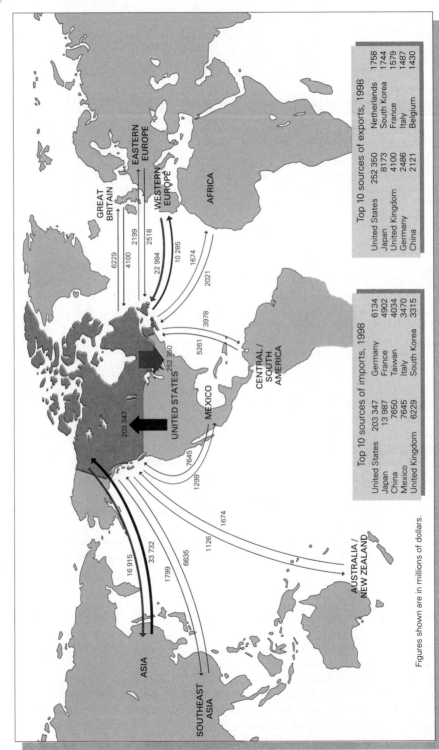

Top 10 sources of exports, 1998			
United States	252 350	Netherlands	1758
Japan	8173	South Korea	1744
United Kingdom	4100	France	1579
Germany	2486	Italy	1487
China	2121	Belgium	1430

Top 10 sources of imports, 1998			
United States	203 347	Germany	6134
Japan	13 987	France	4902
China	7650	Taiwan	4034
Mexico	7645	Italy	3470
United Kingdom	6229	South Korea	3315

Figures shown are in millions of dollars.

Canada's trade patterns, 1998. Note the importance of our trade links with the United States.

they believed Quebec had obtained too little, noting in particular the gutted distinct-society clause. Constitutional change appeared dead.

THE 1993 ELECTION

The federal election of 1993 revealed the importance of Canada's regional divisions. The Progressive Conservatives, now led by Kim Campbell, met with a defeat of prece-dent-setting proportions: only two of their candidates were elected. The Liberals won a majority, thanks in large part to Ontario. Their leader, Jean Chrétien, was the first French-speaking "old party" leader since Confederation to fail to take a majority of Quebec's seats. Quebec voters preferred to give their support to a party committed to Quebec's independence, the Bloc Québécois; indeed, that party elected the second-largest number of candidates, thus becoming the official opposition in Ottawa. Close behind came the West-based Reform party. Studies showed that Reform supporters tended to reject the welfare state, multiculturalism, distinct-society status for Quebec, full gender equality, and civil rights for homosexuals. Finally, the New Democratic Party's dismal performance cost it official-party status in the House of Commons. The unpopularity of provincial NDP governments in Ontario and British Columbia contributed heavily to its poor showing.

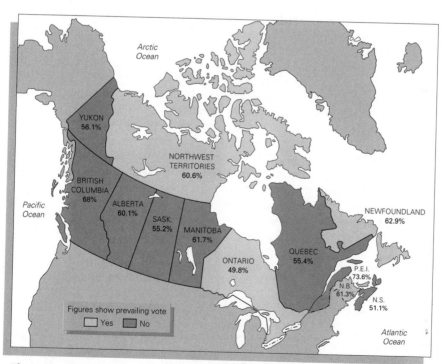

The results of the referendum on the Charlottetown Accord, 1992.

Source: Based on data from Elections Canada.

The virtual destruction of the Conservatives seemed to confirm that another attempt to build a new harmony, with a solid mandate, a new style, and an updated message, had come to nought. Again, the positive image of a party and its leader had been transformed virtually overnight. Diefenbaker, Pearson, Trudeau, Clark, Mulroney — Canadians relentlessly criticized all of them, and often judged them failures. The complexity of Canada's problems and the widely divergent expectations of its citizens appeared to have made any durable political consensus impossible.

THE LIBERAL GOVERNMENT

WEB LINKS

Once in power, the new Liberal government behaved much like the Conservative government it displaced. After severely criticizing free trade during the election campaign, it adopted the North American Free Trade Agreement (NAFTA) with the United States and Mexico. It gave no indication that it was ready to let inflation rise, although during the campaign it had denounced the Conservative "obsession" with fighting inflation.

In spite of a federal budget deficit that had climbed to $42 billion, the Chrétien government did find money to launch a $6 billion infrastructure program, as it had promised during the election campaign. To control spending, it froze civil servants' wages. It continued to cut unemployment benefits and tighten eligibility rules, provoking strong reaction among groups of workers concerned. At the same time, it transferred into its general revenue fund most of the surplus that the unemployment insurance fund now accumulated because of high premiums levied on employees. The government also made substantial cuts in grants to the provinces for health, education, and social welfare.

By 1998, thanks to spending cuts and especially to increased revenues from high taxation rates and increased economic activity, Ottawa registered a surplus. In 1999, a second surplus enabled it to reduce income taxes slightly, and to begin to pay down accumulated debt, which had reached $580 billion. The interest payable annually on this debt remained Ottawa's major expenditure.

Improved finances also enabled governments, both federal and provincial, to reinvest modestly in health care and other services. It was clear, however, that the universal welfare state of the 1970s was now dead. Critics such as Maude Barlow denounced the Liberal government for having become "the political agent of big business interests." Some deplored the death of a widespread consensus on collective responsibility and shared risk. They blamed former deficits not on social spending but rather on the decreases in corporate taxation instituted by the Conservatives and maintained by the Liberals. Others urged governments to target benefits increasingly to specific groups of needy and vulnerable individuals.

An improved economic climate in the late 1990s helped explain high levels of popular satisfaction with the Chrétien government; a divided and regionalized opposition assured the government's re-election in 1997, with less than 40 percent of the popular vote. Twenty-one percent of the new parliamentarians were women, a new milestone. In Quebec, the Bloc Québécois weakened somewhat. The Reform party replaced it as the official opposition. Wishing to expand its influence beyond the West, that party now sought to regroup right-wing support within a new organization, the United Alternative. For its part, the Progressive Conservative party, under new and former leader Joe Clark, attempted to regain lost popularity. The NDP, led by Alexa McDonough, searched for new credibility; now strongly supported in Atlantic

Canada, its pessimistic warnings and its promises to spend more freely appealed less to voters living in more favoured regions.

DEMOGRAPHY

Urban Canada continued to grow after 1970, though more slowly than in the 1950s and 1960s. By 1996, some 62 percent of Canadians lived in 25 metropolitan areas covering less than 1 percent of Canada's land mass. More than one-third of Canada's population inhabited just four large metropolitan areas: Toronto, Montreal, Vancouver, and Ottawa–Hull. More Canadians now lived in condominiums and high-rise apartment buildings that altered the landscape of the inner suburbs or formed part of huge redevelopment projects in derelict port and industrial districts such as Vancouver's False Creek and Toronto's Harbourfront.

THE BIRTH RATE

After 1970, Canada's birth rate fell slightly and then stabilized. Recourse to new birth-control methods became more frequent. For example, thousands of men and women in their thirties underwent voluntary sterilization. The number of abortions also

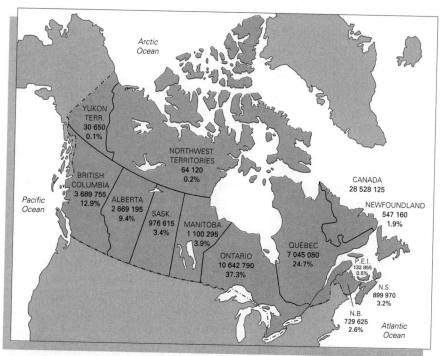

Distribution of Canada's population by province and territory, 1996.

Source: Based on data from Statistics Canada, cat. no. 93F0024XDB96001 in the "Nation Series."

increased, to approximately one for each five births. In 1988, according to Statistics Canada, there were 17 abortions for every 100 live births in Canada (these figures did not take into account probable significant underreporting); the highest rate — 25 for every 100 — was in British Columbia.

The issue of abortion began to provoke passionate debate in Canada in the 1960s. Under a law adopted by Parliament in 1969, abortions remained illegal except when continued pregnancy threatened a woman's life or health. Discontented with the arbitrariness of the law, women's groups mobilized to demand the decriminalization of abortion. Finally, in 1988, the Supreme Court of Canada found the abortion law to be unconstitutional. Although the Mulroney government attempted to recriminalize abortion in a new bill in 1990, the Senate defeated the measure.

By the mid-1980s, though babies were not yet on the endangered species list, the average Canadian family had shrunk to include a mere 1.6 children. Sociologists noted an increase in "yuppie-style" marriages they called "dinks" — dual-income, no kids — as many couples found it difficult to juggle children and careers. Slow population growth was the norm across much of Canada. Provinces whose population continued to expand rapidly, such as Alberta in the 1970s and 1990s, Ontario in the 1980s and late 1990s, and British Columbia in the early 1990s, were those whose vigorous economies attracted newcomers both from abroad and from other Canadian provinces. By 1998, Canada's population surpassed 30 million and was increasing, thanks to immigration, at a rate of more than 1 percent a year. Canada was growing slightly faster than the United States, and much more rapidly than most European countries or Japan.

AN AGING POPULATION

WEB LINKS

As birth rates plummeted and advances in medicine enabled people to live longer, Canadian society began to age. The over-65s numbered more than 12 percent of the population by 1996 — a figure well above the 8 percent criterion used by the United Nations to signify an aging population. As the baby boomers embarked on a collective mid-life crisis and the relative size of the younger age groups diminished, "flower power" began to yield to "grey power," forcing politicians to heed the concerns of seniors. Education, emphasized so strongly in the 1960s and 1970s as the baby boomers passed through the system, had to share some of the attention (and the funding) with health care, pension reform, and other issues of particular interest to older Canadians. The cost of health care in particular became a grave problem: Canada, with its still relatively young population, spent more per capita on health care than any other industrialized country except the United States, which lacked a universal health-care system.

CHANGING FAMILY PATTERNS

The revolution in family patterns, begun in the late 1960s, continued into the 1980s and 1990s. Divorces became even more frequent, particularly after 1985, when new legislation made "marital breakdown," evidenced by a year or more of separation or by adultery or cruelty, the only grounds for divorce. Revised laws granting each spouse half of the property accumulated during the life of the marriage also contributed to making a divorce a viable financial option for the spouse who owned no property independently — most often, the wife. Common-law marriages gained in popularity, especially among younger Canadians. By 1996, one couple in seven in Canada (one in four in Quebec) were living common-law, and governments moved to adapt legislation to this trend.

Marital breakdown, together with the trend to reject the institution of marriage, resulted in large numbers of single-parent families, most of them headed by women. Statistics Canada estimated that, in 1992, half the families headed by single women, many of whom were poorly educated, had incomes below what it defined as the poverty line. In comparison, only one in ten of Canada's two-parent families was classed as poor.

Canada's gays and lesbians demanded that governments act to protect them from violence. They also sought the removal of discrimination from laws and, in particular, legal recognition for same-sex couples. British Columbia and Ontario were the first provinces to move in that direction. Gays also became increasingly visible. For example, 750 000 people attended a Gay Pride parade in Toronto in 1996, more than in any other North American city. Some universities, such as Ryerson Polytechnic in Toronto, introduced lesbian–gay studies into curricula. There were moving moments. After a class discussion on stereotypes relating to lesbians, one teacher commented, "We can test the stereotypes by looking at a real live lesbian. I am a lesbian ... and I don't think you would have identified me from those stereotypes." She then explained, "Coming out to my classes as a lesbian is my own personal choice. I judged that I had little to lose ... Many women cannot make that choice for fear of losing their jobs, alienating workmates, losing custody of their children."

THE CHANGING ROLE OF WOMEN

After 1970, relations between the sexes underwent a fundamental transformation. By 2000, though the goal of full equality was still far from being achieved, the male-dominated society of a generation earlier had been substantially eroded. Women worked within a multitude of organizations, and promoted a variety of visions, to bring about these changes.

INSTITUTIONALIZED FEMINISM

When the government failed to act quickly on the recommendations of the Royal Commission on the Status of Women, women established, in 1972, the National Action Committee on the Status of Women, an umbrella organization now embracing 600 widely disparate associations representing 5 million members. Women formed similar groups across Canada to lobby provincial governments. Growing pressure brought Prime Minister Pierre Trudeau to appoint a minister responsible for the status of women and to establish, in 1973, the Canadian Advisory Council on the Status of Women. Most provinces appointed similar advisory councils. Quebec's Conseil du statut de la femme, equipped with funds for research,

FAMILY PORTRAITS

Where have all the children gone?
Proportion of the population aged 14 and under, 1851 to 2036

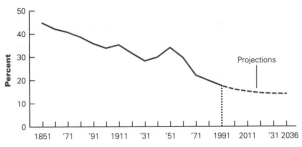

Source: Statistics Canada and Roderic Beaujot at the University of Western Ontario

As the chart shows, nearly half Canada's population was under fifteen a century and a half ago. By 1961, as the baby boom ended, that percentage had dropped to about a third. Today it's about 20 percent, and by 2036 it is projected to be less than 15 percent.

Much of this dramatic shift is the result of medical advances. People live much longer now, and birth control is readily available.

The flip side of the decline in children in the population is the growth in senior citizens: in 1851, just 2.7 percent were seniors; by 2036, it will be about 25 percent.

What does this mean?
While there is still much discussion about the quality of education (that's the gourmet-baby phenomenon — there aren't that many, so we want them to be well educated), it's small wonder that concerns about RRSPs, pensions and assisted suicide are taking up a greater portion of the social agenda.

Derived from *Profiling Canada's Families*, Vanier Institute of the Family

Source: Alanna Mitchell, *Globe and Mail*, November 2, 1994.
Reprinted with permission of the *Globe and Mail*.

produced a detailed plan for change, *Égalité et indépendance*. Women's groups organized a multitude of conferences and workshops during 1975, the year the United Nations decreed to be International Women's Year.

THE HOME

In part, the home became the battleground for equality of the sexes. Change came slowly, and child care continued to be mainly women's work. Polls suggested that Canadians in general wanted men to take responsibility for a greater share of the housework; men themselves were not so sure. A federal government poster published during International Women's Year extolled the homemaker's virtues by linking "women's" jobs in the home to prestigious occupations: nurse, teacher, accountant, plumber, chef. Women criticized the publicity for failing to mention a homemaker's less-prestigious occupations: janitor, launderer, dishwasher, waitress, taxi driver, and maid.

The 1980s brought to the fore one very sombre element, hitherto seldom discussed openly: violence against women. In 1982, a House of Commons report on violence in the family showed that as many as 10 percent of wives suffered beatings and noted that the numbers appeared to be increasing. Five years later, in response to another bleak report, *Battered But Not Beaten*, Ottawa announced major funding initiatives. Local women's groups opened shelters to assist homeless and battered women. They also set up rape-crisis centres, fought for laws restricting pornography, and organized assistance for Native women, immigrant and refugee women, and women on welfare.

WOMEN IN THE WORK FORCE

Unionization improved working conditions and pay in some traditional female occupations, particularly in health care, education, and the public-service sector. In the 1970s, union membership grew four times more quickly among females than it did among males, although among workers women were still less likely than men to belong to unions. Many of the unprotected majority worked in difficult-to-organize sectors such as banks, restaurants, offices, and retail stores. They often worked part-time as well. As part-time work and teleworking increased in the 1990s, Judy Rebick, former president of the National Action Committee on the Status of Women, denounced "all the vanguard destructive forces of the right" that are "hitting women first."

Unions themselves started to pay greater heed to women's needs. In 1979, women backed by the United Steel Workers filed a complaint for discrimination with the Ontario Human Rights Commission, to force Stelco to hire women for production jobs at its plant in Hamilton. Over the preceding two decades, Stelco had received 300 000 job applications, including those of 30 000 women; it had hired 33 000 men, but no women. The commission's verdict was favourable, and Stelco began hiring women for these well-paid jobs. (Ironically, massive layoffs in the late 1980s eliminated almost all the women employed in production.) In Quebec, women's committees succeeded in convincing their unions to adopt policies on child care, maternity benefits, equal pay for work of equal value, job safety, sexual harassment, and discrimination. The myth of female docility evaporated rapidly as women-dominated organizations such as nurses' unions waged bitter, sometimes illegal, strikes against what they judged to be unsatisfactory working conditions. Although women remained underrepresented in union executives, particularly in international unions, they began to play a greater role, as symbolized by the election in 1975 of Grace Hartman as president of the Canadian Union of Public Employees (CUPE), Canada's largest union, and in 1986 of Shirley Carr as head of the Canadian Labour Congress. Yet Judy Darcy, elected president of CUPE in 1991, complained of the double standards that made many active women unionists feel guilty: guilty because their union work made them poor mothers, and guilty because their family responsibilities meant that they devoted less time to union duties.

Working outside the home necessitated better day-care facilities, and governments moved to make such care more affordable and available. Opposition to the trend did make itself felt. Newfoundland's minister of social services told lobbying

GENDER FILE

	Male	Female	Women as % of total
Population of Canada			
1921	4 529 643	4 258 306	48.5
1956	8 151 879	7 928 912	49.3
1991	13 454 580	13 842 280	50.7
Canadian life expectancy			
1966	68.80	75.20	
1989	73.66	80.35	
1990	73.97	80.60	
Number of physicians and surgeons			
1871	2 791	1*	1.7
1921	8 554	152	1.7
1971	25 515	3 070	10.7
1991	38 690	10 616	22.0
Medical degrees awarded by Canadian universities			
1940	584	25	4.1
1960	805	66	7.6
1970	945	129	12.0
1980	1 180	562	32.3
1990	957	751	44.0
1992	983	765	43.8
Enrolment in Canadian faculties of medicine			
1962–63	3 199	371	10.4
1982–83	4 553	2 939	39.2
1992–93	3 817	3 224	45.8
Women as a percentage of full-time medical school faculty, 1990			
Canada			14.0
United States			19.0

*DR. EMILY STOWE

Source: Alanna Mitchell, *Globe and Mail*, April 24, 1993.
Reprinted with permission of the *Globe and Mail*.

women that the province needed "more conscientious mothers to sacrifice their careers and stay home to take care of their children."

By the 1970s, the principle of equal pay for men and women performing the same task had gained wide recognition. Yet, in the 1980s, the average woman's wage remained at only about 65 percent of the average man's. Although women's lesser work experience and the generally lower educational levels of older women explained part of this difference, the continued concentration of women in low-paying occupations appeared to be the principal factor.

EMPLOYMENT EQUITY

In 1984, the federal Commission on Equality in Employment recommended mandatory employment-equity programs, to be implemented through affirmative action. Ottawa responded by requiring employers under federal jurisdiction, such as banks and national transportation companies, to give women and minorities better job opportunities. It also made affirmative-action plans mandatory for all firms doing business with the government.

The notion of equal pay for work of equal value, or pay equity, became the battleground of the 1990s, as women argued that they were generally paid less than men for jobs requiring similar skills, effort, responsibility, and educational levels, and entailing similar working conditions. Ottawa and some provinces instituted pay-equity laws, but the Ontario government went much farther by forcing employers to compare the value of the work being done in their male- and female-dominated work categories and then to increase the wages of any women who, according to the results of the comparisons, were being underpaid. Reactions were predictable: the male-dominated business community expressed considerable hostility, while the 1-million-member Equal Pay Coalition was disappointed that the measure did not cover casual workers and women working in small enterprises or in all-female establishments.

DIFFICULT TIMES FOR LABOUR

While the claims of women moved forward rapidly after 1970, those of labour encountered serious obstacles. The numerous strikes in the public sector during the 1970s alienated public opinion. Taxpayers quickly realized that they would have to foot the bill for what many viewed as excessive government generosity. Moreover, two of every three Canadian workers did not belong to unions. They, as well as many workers affiliated to small organizations, resented the attempts of the most powerful unions to secure a greater share of the national wealth for their members. Canada acquired a negative image for the frequency of its strike activity — only Italy had a worse record. Yet, although 11 million workdays were lost to strikes in 1975 (a particularly bad year), that figure represented barely 1.5 percent of total working time. Accidents, illness, and general absenteeism affected productivity to a far greater extent.

Union militancy in the 1970s usually aimed at obtaining higher salaries and better working conditions. In some cases, however, unions attacked the capitalist system itself, seeking to replace it with a socialist regime. In Quebec, union militants published manifestoes urging a socialist and independent Quebec. Here, indeed, was the high point of labour's confrontation with employers.

The 1980s brought new challenges. A more conservative public approved governments that moved to restrain wages and limit strikes. Manufacturing industries and resource-sector companies laid off workers. Strong unions fought — sometimes quite successfully, as in the case of the autoworkers and the steelworkers — for job security and better pensions, and for wage protection against inflation and new taxes. Canadian autoworkers, favouring a less bureaucratic and more militant and democratic union, broke away from the American union in 1985 and then negotiated a made-in-Canada agreement with their employers. To reverse the decline in their numbers, unions signed up workers from outside their original jurisdictions. The steelworkers' union, for example, enrolled security workers, restaurant workers, and employees of fish-processing plants, promising that, "if it moves or eats with a knife and a fork, we'll organize it." By 1986, such efforts had brought union strength back up to where it had been in 1975: 37 percent of the non-farm work force.

CUTBACKS

The early 1990s proved even more difficult. Cutbacks by governments at all levels led to layoffs, wage freezes, and wage cuts. In Ontario, for example, the NDP government imposed a "social contract" on public-sector unions, with forced holidays without pay, popularly called "Rae days" after Bob Rae, Ontario's premier. In Alberta, the Conservative government of Ralph Klein went further: it introduced drastic wage reductions sufficient to eliminate the province's annual deficit within four years.

Private-sector unions fared no better. Many high-paying manufacturing jobs disappeared as companies "rationalized" their operations, and union membership again declined. New contracts often imposed wage rollbacks, or pegged wages to profitability, or imposed a reduced pay scale for new employees. The recession undermined the bargaining power of unions and thus severely limited the number of work stoppages. Unions themselves were often torn by internal strife.

Observers differed in their explanations of the origins of union problems. For some, the unions themselves, through high wages and labour market inflexibility, were bringing about their own demise. Others blamed globalization and the world capitalist economy for having substantially diminished the power of labour.

CULTURAL CONCERNS

During the 1970s, provincial governments took steps to slow university expansion. Student enrolments increased only modestly, although women were far more numerous. Then, during the 1980s and early 1990s, deficit-ridden provinces forced universities to accept real cuts in spending per student. As provincial grants declined, most provinces imposed higher tuition fees and turned enthusiastically to corporate benefactors for additional financing. Significantly, not one new university opened its doors in Canada between 1980 and 1994, when the University of Northern British Columbia, at Prince George, began operations. The outlook for public reinvestment in universities remained bleak in the late 1990s as a health-care crisis mobilized popular attention.

CONTEMPORARY RELIGION

Immigration from Asia diversified Canada's religious face, as sizable communities of Muslims, Buddhists, and Hindus became established. For most Canadians, however, the emphasis on individuality meant that religion became largely a personal matter. Canadians moved away from religions based on theology and denominational identification, and toward a view of religion as an inspiration for moral and ethical behaviour. The great majority said they still expected to turn to organized religion for

New religious groups in Canada. A photo taken on Ste. Catherine Street, Montreal, May 1, 1993. Religion has become both more personal and highly diversified. Sociologist Reginald Bibby claims that Canadians now want "religion à la carte," preferring to pick and choose beliefs, practices, programs, and professional services from a religious smorgasbord.

Photograph by Michel Brunelle.

rites such as baptisms, weddings, and funerals but, with the notable exception of members of smaller Protestant conservative and evangelical churches, they attached diminishing importance to regular attendance at worship services. Boomers, in a collective existential crisis, turned in the 1990s to spiritual books and seminars. Sociologist Reginald Bibby, a long-time observer of Canadian religious behaviour, judged that Canadians now wanted "religion 'à la carte,' preferring to pick and choose beliefs, practices, programs, and professional services from increasingly diversified religious smorgasbords."[5] At the same time, he viewed most churches as simply unable to "sell their product effectively."

LEISURE

In the health-conscious 1970s and 1980s, many Canadians devoted long hours to exercise: they walked, they cycled, they swam, they jogged, they did aerobics, and they gardened, sometimes relentlessly. When they tired of strenuous activity, they played Trivial Pursuit, invented by two Montrealers; it became the most popular board game of the 1980s. Or they learned to cook using the microwave ovens that entered a large majority of their homes in the course of the decade. They also watched more television, with more channels (for which they paid more money), or played interactive games such as Nintendo on their home computers. In the 1990s, they also became increasingly addicted to buying lottery tickets or to gambling in the casinos that cash-starved provincial governments now approved.

SPORTS

Spectator sports dominated popular culture. Athletes basked in glory as long as they scored goals, hit runs, or won races on the slopes in the winter and on the speedways in the summer, and as long as they avoided the steroids that proved to be widely used in certain field sports. Hockey enjoyed immense interest, but it now had to share the spotlight with football, baseball, and, increasingly, basketball. Big-league baseball came to Montreal in 1969, when the Expos began to play. Toronto had to wait until 1977 for its team, the Blue Jays, which became the most financially successful enterprise in any sport and went on to win the World Series in 1992 and in 1993. The Ontario government invested huge sums in the building of an immense closed stadium in Toronto, the SkyDome, where the Jays entertained their local fans after its opening in 1989.

Hockey underwent an important expansion in the 1970s as the National Hockey League took in several franchises from the failed World Hockey Association. Although most players were Canadian, most new teams were American. American directors also made the important decisions, leading sports critic Bruce Kidd to decry the takeover of Canadian hockey by U.S. business interests. Wayne Gretzky, undoubtedly the sport's major revelation of this era, attained the crowning glory of being pictured on the cover of *Time*. Shortly afterward the Edmonton Oilers relinquished their superstar to the Los Angeles Kings — an act akin to high treason in the eyes of many angry fans.

In the late 1960s, Ottawa discovered the importance of sport as an instrument for promoting national unity and yielding political capital. It then began investing heavily in high-performance sports in order to produce more medal-winners in international competitions. The Canada–Soviet hockey series in 1972 showed that the return on such investments could be considerable. Watched by the largest Canadian television audience on record, Team Canada won the series in the last seconds of the dramatic final encounter. One ecstatic Canadian university president suggested that the series probably did more to create a Canadian identity than ten years of Canada Council fellowships. Politicians saw a triumph for "Canadian virtues" and for capitalist liberal democracy.

Montreal hosted the summer Olympic Games in 1976, the first time that this prestigious international gathering took place in Canada. (In 1988, Calgary was the site of the winter Olympics.) Provincial and municipal taxpayers were uneasy at the prospect of new budget deficits, but Montreal mayor Jean Drapeau assured them there was no more possibility of incurring a deficit than there was of his becoming pregnant. After the Olympic lottery, Olympic coins, Olympic stamps, and other promotional paraphernalia failed to prevent a massive deficit, delighted cartoonists drew sketches of a pregnant mayor. The games themselves provided much excitement, though Canadian prowess would be much greater at the Los Angeles Olympics in 1984.

THE AMERICANIZATION OF CULTURE

In the nationalist climate of the 1970s, cultural development came to be inextricably linked to the affirmation of national identity. For many Canadians, the danger to survival came increasingly from the United States, mainly because many other Canadians avidly consumed that country's cultural products.

FAMILY PORTRAITS

Religious faith and Canadians, then and now

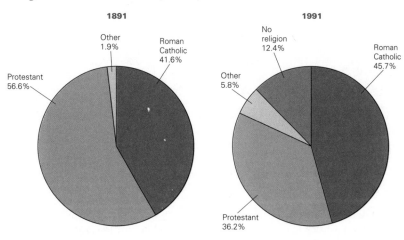

1891

Other 1.9%

Roman Catholic 41.6%

Protestant 56.6%

1991

No religion 12.4%

Roman Catholic 45.7%

Other 5.8%

Protestant 36.2%

Source: Statistics Canada

The vast majority of Canadians — more than eight in ten — consider themselves Christian. The number has fallen off somewhat over the past two decades largely because those expressing no religious affiliation have jumped from just half of 1 percent in 1961 to 12.4 percent in the 1991 census.

The proportion of Canadians who belong to the "other" category, including Eastern Orthodox, Jewish and Eastern non-Christian religions, has remained roughly the same since the early years of this century. In 1921, for example, it was 5.2 percent, compared with 5.8 percent in 1991.

What does this mean?

There is much debate these days about what part Christian traditions ought to play in state decisions, whether in relation to store openings or school holidays. In part, this is being portrayed as the fruit of an increasingly multicultural society. But more than anything, the trend toward secularism is prompting this fundamental rethinking of how religion and state interact.

Derived from *Profiling Canada's Families,* Vanier Institute of the Family

Source: Alanna Mitchell, *Globe and Mail,* October 12, 1994. Reprinted with permission of the *Globe and Mail.*

After 1970, the Americanization of Canadian broadcasting in English continued apace. Thanks to cable television, almost all Canadians now had access to the major U.S. networks. Other statistics showed the extent of foreign domination of Canada's cultural industries. In 1990, for example, foreign-owned publishers held 80 percent of Canada's book market. Nearly 85 percent of record sales were foreign, as were 80 percent of magazines sold in Canada. When Canada moved to protect Canadian

---

FAMILY PORTRAITS

....

Big people toys

	Number of families	% of families
Colour TV	7 026 600	98.7
Microwave oven	5 909 341	83.0
VCR	5 848 094	82.2
Cable TV	5 170 762	72.6
Gas barbecue	4 385 823	61.6
Dishwasher	3 752 288	52.7

Source: Centre for International Statistics, using Statistics Canada data, 1990

Canadian families are great consumers of modern conveniences. Almost all of them — more than 7 million — own a colour television, while 83 percent can nuke their veggies in a microwave oven and about 80 percent have a vehicle of some sort.

At least 22 percent now have call waiting on their telephones while 8 percent can cool off in a swimming pool.

What does this mean?

There is a downside to the fact that Canadians at all income levels are relatively rich in material goods. Consumer debt has been growing in recent years, as have personal bankruptcies. One study showed that most of those who go bankrupt are married men with families and jobs. The straw that often breaks the financial camel's back? Car loan payments.

Derived from *Profiling Canada's Families*, Vanier Institute of the Family

....

Source: Alanna Mitchell, *Globe and Mail*, May 6, 1994.
Reprinted with permission of the *Globe and Mail*.

---

magazine publishers in 1998, the United States immediately threatened economic reprisals. In movie theatres, Canadian films had less than 5 percent of screen time, although a growing number of American producers filmed in Vancouver and Toronto, together considered a "Hollywood North." Attempts on the part of the Canadian and Quebec governments to ensure a greater distribution in movie theatres of Canadian films provoked conflict with the major American distributors, forcing a Canadian retreat. Yet some critics insisted that while Canadians consumed and borrowed American cultural products, they also reconstituted them and imprinted them with Canadian values. Sometimes they even sold them back to the Americans. One success story: Loverboy, the Vancouver rock group, which sold more than 3 million copies of its album *Get Lucky* in the United States. In this way, cultural anthropologist Frank Manning maintained, "the beaver can, and does, bite back," although Manning was uncertain whether the bite was serious or only a playful nip.[6]

Canadian cultural industries enjoyed some protection through regulatory barriers. These determined, for example, how much non-Canadian programming could be broadcast on Canadian television stations. Ottawa also provided subsidies for artists of all sorts and funded cultural infrastructures. The CBC continued to affirm its objective of preserving and enriching Canadianism. Yet, in the 1980s, as new

The 1988 winter Olympics opening at McMahon Stadium, Calgary — a proud moment in the city's and the country's history. In 1976, Montreal became the first Canadian city to host the Olympic Games; twelve years later, Calgary was the first Canadian city to hold the winter Olympics.

Dave Chidley, *Calgary Sun.*

demands were made for public broadcasting to meet specific needs such as those of women, ethnic groups, Native peoples, and regions, the federal government reduced its financing. By the late 1980s, one former president of the CBC was describing government policy as "Americanization by importation, by privatization, and by fiscal deprivation." The National Film Board (NFB), another important publicly supported institution, produced numerous high quality documentaries, a field in which it excelled. Producer Claude Jutra's *Mon oncle Antoine*, a touching story of a boy's coming of age and loss of innocence, achieved the second-highest network ratings both on Radio-Canada and, in English translation, on CBC in 1973–74. Later, Bonnie Sherr Klein's documentary on pornography ran into problems with censors but proved a box-office success. The Canadian Film Development Corporation, later Telefilm Canada, gave financial backing to several critical successes, among them Peter Carter's *The Rowdyman* and Gilles Carle's *La vraie nature de Bernadette*. After the mid-1980s, it shifted its emphasis toward television production.

The late 1980s and 1990s saw several notable Canadian feature films. Denis Arcand portrayed decadent history teachers in his *Decline of the American Empire*.

David Cronenberg's *Dead Ringers* proved a financial success, while several films by Atom Egoyan, among them *Speaking Parts* and *Exotica*, earned him an international reputation. François Girard's film *The Red Violin*, capturing the odyssey of a violin across four centuries and three continents, won wide public praise, while Don Mc-Kellar's first feature-length film, *Last Night*, in which he mocks presumably Canadian virtues such as politeness and the welfare state, won a prize at the Cannes Festival. Radio-Canada produced the television series *Lance et compte*, centred on the professional and love lives of a few hockey players; it proved an astounding success, attracting nearly half of the total French-language viewing public. In the late 1990s, the comedy series *La petite vie* also drew most Quebeckers to their television sets on Monday evenings.

In music, such groups as the Philosopher Kings, Tragically Hip, and Barenaked Ladies carried off numerous awards, while Alanis Morissette enjoyed enormous success with "Supposed Former Infatuation Junkie," "Uninvited," and other songs. Singer Céline Dion and songwriter Luc Plamondon gained international reputations (see "A Historical Portrait," Chapter Seventeen). Gaspé native Kevin Parent's folk-tinged rock was a huge hit with Quebeckers. His "Fréquenter l'oubli" was chosen song of the year in 1998 by the Quebec public. Still, francophone Quebec artists had barely a quarter of the provincial market; the government promised to inject more money into the industry.

CANADIAN LITERATURE

After 1970, there were more Canadian writers and they wrote more. The development of institutions like the universities, as well as increased government funding and a larger population, explain this significant growth.

Literature mirrored Canadians' preoccupations, attitudes, and aspirations. Nationalist themes, for example, recurred frequently in novels in both English and French Canada, particularly during the 1970s. The works that secured Margaret Atwood's international reputation, including *Surfacing* and, later, *The Handmaid's Tale*, contained trenchant nationalist critiques. They were also feminist, and indeed much fiction of the contemporary period portrayed the everyday lives of women.

Many literary works explored the experience of minority groups such as Native peoples and immigrants. In his novel *The Temptations of Big Bear*, for example, Alberta writer Rudy Wiebe dwelt upon the conflict between European and Native cultures provoked by the arrival of European settlers. Joy Kogawa, in her novel *Obasan*, poignantly evoked the fate of Japanese Canadians during World War II. Acadian author Antonine Maillet painted a new image of Acadia and its people in her works. In her play *La Sagouine*, an old Acadian woman reminisces about the material and spiritual suffering she has known. In *Pélagie-la-Charrette*, winner of the prestigious Prix Goncourt, Maillet tells the story of returning Acadian exiles. Other novels, such as those of Jane Rule and Gail Scott, and *The Wars* by Timothy Findley, which describes the growing madness of a young Canadian army officer, explore lesbian or gay themes.

Historical settings were also common. Al Purdy, the poet of a dozen styles, evoked Canada's past in such works as *In Search of Owen Roblin* and *A Splinter in the Heart*, the latter portraying a Trenton, Ontario, youth in 1918, whom events turn rapidly into a man. *Les filles de Caleb*, Arlette Cousture's novel about the life of a family in the Mauricie region of Quebec a century ago, inspired a long-lasting television series that regularly attracted more than 3 million viewers.

Internationally acclaimed novelists Marie-Claire Blais and Réjean Ducharme were among those Quebec authors whose works sought to reveal the asphyxiating nature of traditional family relationships and religion. When Denise Boucher attacked the stereotypes of orthodox Roman Catholicism in *Les fées ont soif*, religious groups obtained an injunction forbidding public presentations of her play. The Supreme Court eventually decided in favour of the author.

Some writers set their works in small towns with closed societies. An example was Deptford, the scene of a powerful trilogy of novels by Robertson Davies featuring vivid central characters. Others dwelt upon the realities of urban living. Quebec play-wright Michel Tremblay's works, performed around the world, have featured a wide variety of Montrealers, including elegant upper-class ladies, drag queens, country singers, and very ordinary mortals from the working-class neighbourhoods he knew as a boy. Montreal served also as the setting of Yves Beauchemin's *Le Matou*, a fast-moving thriller that sold 1 million copies worldwide.

Canadian literature also underlines the important role that regions have played in Canadian life. Atlantic writer David Adams Richards wrote of poverty and pride in northeastern New Brunswick in *The Coming of Winter* and *Blood Ties*, while W.O. Mitchell's *Roses Are Difficult Here* chronicled a year in the life of an Alberta foothills town called Shelby. Prairie geography inspired Robert Kroetsch's poetry. Small local publishers helped to foster a regional consciousness. One Winnipeg house, Turnstone Press, promoted poetry from all regions of the country. During the 1970s, regional theatres sprang up across the country; Theatre Calgary, for example, featured western Canadian playwrights.

More recently, an increasing number of Canadian authors have been writing for international audiences; Anne Michaels's novel *Fugitive Pieces* was, for example, a huge success in Germany. The themes chosen by some novelists have few or no links with Canada. Italian-born Nino Ricci, in *Lives of the Saints*, focused on a village in the Italian Apennines whose inhabitants he portrayed, while Sri Lankan–born Michael Ondaatje set his third novel, *The English Patient*, in Tuscany in the closing moments of World War II. Both won Governor General's awards. Margaret Atwood's novel *Alias Grace* saw phenomenal sales, while Alice Munro's book of short stories *The Love of a Good Woman* boosted that talented writer's international reputation. Large foreign-owned companies did much of the publishing, leaving small presses to take their chances with first novels. Quebec theatre directors Robert Lepage and Denis Marleau won accolades in Paris and New York, while Calgary's One Yellow Rabbit theatre was a regular visitor to Edinburgh. In the words of one critic, foreign attention proved a wonderful reinforcement for "neurotically insecure Canadians." Here, perhaps, was the globalization of Canadian culture.

NEW CONCERNS

The 1970s and 1980s defined new challenges. Canadians became more conscious of the need to take preventive measures to ensure personal good health. The warnings were unpleasant: the Canadian Cancer Society estimated that one Canadian male in four and one female in five would die of cancer. Other studies highlighted the risks and causes of heart disease. Canadians began to heed appeals to eat less salt, sugar, and fat, and to consume more fibre. In addition, all age groups, with the tragic exception of young women, smoked less. Non-smokers brought pressure to bear, legislative and otherwise, to force smokers to respect their air space. The rapid spread of the deadly AIDS (Acquired Immune Deficiency Syndrome) virus, which by 1997 had killed more than 10 000 Canadians, finally brought health authorities to launch campaigns promoting "safe sex" or abstinence. Automobile associations and victims of drunk drivers lobbied governments to take measures to reduce carnage on the highways.

POVERTY AND CRIME

Throughout the 1980s and 1990s, poverty remained a serious problem despite what was, generally, a growing economy. Governments revamped social programs such as aid to families and pensions to seniors, taking away payments from higher-income Canadians but increasing assistance to the poorest. At the same time, spending cuts pushed Canadians on social assistance below low-income cutoff lines. The poor failed to come any closer to the rich in terms of income. Moreover, the middle class itself had shrunk since 1967. More workers had highly skilled, well-paid, stable jobs, but there were also additional workers in the lower-income category, often employed in part-time or temporary jobs in the traditional service sector.

As unemployment grew during the recession of 1990, rising demand over-whelmed food banks in urban areas. Canadian cities also saw the emergence of a homeless class that included refugees, people with mental and physical disabilities, Native people, single mothers with children, youth, and substance abusers. In some cases, the new homeless had been evicted by developers who then renovated and upgraded dwellings before selling them to more affluent individuals. Increasingly, however, provincial spending cuts to welfare and social housing were seen as primary causes. In 1998, in a highly political move, the city of Toronto declared homelessness a national disaster and sought disaster-relief funds.

Rising crime rates became a serious social concern in the 1970s and 1980s. Many offences were drug-related. Although violent crime nearly doubled in the 1982–92 decade, rates for murder and armed robbery remained far lower than in the United States. (Those least at risk from crime were teetotalling homebodies living in rural areas of eastern Canada. Those most at risk were urban males aged 18 to 29 who were members of gangs or engaged in the drug trade.) Crime rates in Canada varied from one province to another, but they tended to increase steadily from east to west. Per-plexed criminologists blamed a "frontier mentality" and higher alcohol consumption in the West, but some westerners blamed imported easterners. In October 1990, when one big-city newspaper swathed its front page with the headline "Our Violent City: Anyone, Anywhere, Can Be Hit," it highlighted, and undoubtedly contributed to, the fact that the fear of crime had become a more present reality than crime itself. Canadians wanted the courts to hand down more severe sentences, and even favoured the return of capital punishment. After 1991, crime rates dropped steadily, as the cohort of young Canadians decreased in size, although rates still remained more than double what they had been in 1969.

THE ENVIRONMENT

Environmental issues gained increasing visibility after 1970 as Canadians discovered the negative aftermath of the unbridled, almost unregulated, development of past decades. They also learned that environmental issues were global in nature: the "greenhouse effect," the depletion of the ozone layer, the pollution of air and water, and the destruction of tropical rain forests all involved worldwide responsibility, and solutions required international co-operation. During the 1980s, Canada signed several multilateral agreements on the environment, notably those concerning climate change and ozone depletion. Then, in 1992, Canada played a key role at the Earth Summit at Rio de Janeiro, where it signed a convention on biological diversity by which it agreed to take measures to protect threatened species. Legislation introduced in 1996, denounced by environmentalists for its insufficiencies, was never passed. Canada also signed an international pact in Kyoto, Japan, in 1997 to reduce greenhouse gases. By 1999 the country was well behind its target.

More importantly, many Canadians came to see themselves as part of the problem. An expanding and wealthier population oriented toward consumption produced increasing quantities of wastes. The burning of fossil fuels to heat homes, to run automobiles, and to drive industries fouled the air. In particular, as thousands of the lakes and streams of the Canadian Shield became lifeless and as the surrounding vegetation showed increasing evidence of damage, Canadians realized the devastating effects of acid rain. Many industries also spewed chemical effluents into both air and water. For example, in 1999, Ontario Hydro's five coal-burning plants accounted for 16 percent of the province's emissions of sulphur dioxide and a significant part of smog-producing nitrogen dioxides. Agricultural methods contributed to the erosion of topsoil and, through the use of pesticides and herbicides, to the pollution of water. Good agricultural land surrounding cities disappeared beneath low-density suburbs. Ecologically sensitive wetlands were drained for agricultural purposes, logging companies prepared to harvest the country's last old-growth stands of timber, and untouched wilderness receded still further north.

No easy solutions existed. Concerned citizens set up associations to act as watchdogs, publicizing environmental dangers. Some had international ramifications, such as Greenpeace; others were Canadian creations, such as Pollution Probe in Toronto and SVP (Société pour Vaincre la Pollution) in Montreal. Public pressure brought governments to take an interest in the environment. In 1971, the federal government established the Department of the Environment, and most provinces soon followed suit. Governments established standards for clean air and clean water, and set up agencies to monitor compliance. They also provided for environmental assessments of important projects such as the construction of dams, but these proved difficult to carry out when powerful economic interests as well as provincial governments supported the project, as was the case with the building of the Old Man River dam in southern Alberta. In 1994, Ontario became the first province to adopt an Environmental Bill of Rights enabling individuals to force the government to investigate suspected polluters. Lower budgets for departments of the environment in the late 1990s meant that governments failed to apply their own laws, notably the Canadian Environmental Protection Act, which regulates toxic chemicals, and the Fisheries Act, which prohibits polluting oceans, rivers, and lakes.

Disposal of the millions of tonnes of wastes that Canadians produced annually proved increasingly onerous. In the early 1970s, landfill sites replaced open garbage dumps, but rural residents strenuously resisted having these sites in their "back yards." Some wastes could be incinerated, a costly process that produced dangerous gases. With the aid of provincial subsidies, municipal governments gradually instituted recycling programs for glass, metals, paper, and plastics. Tire dumps constituted a special problem, demonstrated in devastating fashion when a massive fire at a Hagersville, Ontario, site raged out of control for weeks in 1990. Even worse was the problem of storing or eliminating toxic wastes. A fire at a storage site for PCBs near Montreal necessitated the evacuation of an entire suburb.

The battle for clean air and water involved tradeoffs. Pulp and paper mills polluted rivers and smelters fouled the air, but they also provided jobs. When provincial governments attempted to impose pollution controls on Noranda's copper smelter at Rouyn, Quebec, and Kimberly-Clark's pulp-mill plant at Terrace Bay, Ontario, both companies resisted and threatened to shut down. To save jobs, federal and provincial governments gave grants to pulp mills to enable them to install expensive equipment that would limit environmental damage.

Controlling pollution also meant difficult and prolonged negotiations with the United States, whose industries were major polluters of Canada's water and air. In 1987, Canada and the United States signed a tougher version of the Great Lakes Water Quality Agreement of 1978. Although the Americans were more reluctant to force coal-burning thermal energy plants to reduce emissions of the sulphur dioxide responsible for acidifying Canadian lakes, the U.S. Congress finally adopted, in 1990, the Clean Air Act. (A Canadian lobby group played a significant role in the bill's passage by bringing constant pressure to bear on American legislators.)

Preserving what remained of Canada's wilderness became another environmental objective, particularly after the United Nations urged member states to set aside 12 percent of their territory for this purpose. The Canadian government took one important step in this direction in 1986, when it created Ellesmere Island National Park Reserve, Canada's thirty-second national park, thus protecting a biologically unique ecosystem situated close to the North Pole. In answer to the World Wildlife Fund's effort to assure preservation of representative parts of Canada's nearly 500 natural regions, Canada's governments pledged to establish reserves to protect the habitat of the country's approximately 300 000 plant and animal species. By 1999, however, about half of the natural regions had little or no protected areas. Moreover, forestry, mining, and agriculture in natural areas adjacent to parks caused increased ecological stress on the parks themselves.

Provinces also created new parks. Ontario, for example, doubled its parks system in the 1980s, although debate raged on over the issue of allowing logging, mineral exploration, sport hunting, and commercial tourism in the parks. British Columbia, where tensions between preservationists and companies desirous of exploiting forest and mineral resources ran high, attempted unsuccessfully to achieve a consensus on land use among interested parties. The government still proceeded with a plan to double the province's wilderness areas to 12 percent by 2000. One important step toward the realization of that goal was the creation of Tatshenshini-Alsek Wilderness Park in northwestern British Columbia.

Since 1867, Canada has evolved into an increasingly complex society. The nation's population diversified ethnically and culturally in the nineteenth and, more rapidly, in the twentieth century. Material progress and improved living conditions, though by no means continuous, were generally apparent; their attendant costs, both human and environmental, were less apparent, except to their immediate victims. The role of the state increased greatly, especially after 1930, when governments came to play a role in virtually every aspect of human existence. Associations of all types proliferated as Canadians sought to counter the powerlessness of the individual acting alone.

Although Canada has undergone immense change, in many respects the basic themes of the country's early history remain operative today. In 1867, four major groups made up Canada's population — the Native peoples, French-speaking Canadians, English-speaking Canadians, and immigrants; today, the same four groups are evident, although not in the same proportion as in 1867. Canada in 1867 was a nation of regions; despite modern transportation and the communications revolution, it remains so today — indeed, to such an extent that doubts have often abounded about the survival of existing political arrangements. By the 1880s, federal–provincial affairs had become acrimonious; more than a century later, conflict continues to pervade intergovernmental contacts. French–English relations were the source of bitter controversy in the nineteenth century; intercultural relations have continued to generate passionate debate in the twentieth. Relations with the Native peoples were an important preoccupation in the nineteenth century as European settlement expanded westward; during the second half of the twentieth century, Aboriginal rights have become a complex but very present public-policy question.

In 1867, British and American influences weighed heavily on the new nation; today, the impact of the United States on Canada — culturally, politically, and economically — is in many ways even more weighty. Finally, despite the coming of the welfare state, flagrant social inequalities distinguish Canadians from one another, much as they did in the past. Reductions in government spending for social services may well increase these inequalities. Constant change, but equally apparent continuity — these are the two themes that reflect the past as the inhabitants of the northern half of North America enter the twenty-first century.

NOTES

1. Stephen Clarkson, *Canada and the Reagan Challenge: Crisis in the Canadian–American Relationship*, rev. ed. (Toronto: James Lorimer, 1985), p. 90.
2. Paul Phillips, *Regional Disparities* (Toronto: James Lorimer, 1982), pp. 118–19.
3. Sylvia Bashevkin, *Toeing the Lines: Women and Party Politics in English Canada*, 2nd ed. (Toronto: Oxford University Press, 1993), p. vi.
4. John Herd Thompson and Stephen J. Randall, *Canada and the United States: Ambivalent Allies* (Montreal/Kingston: McGill-Queen's University Press, 1994), p. 274.
5. Reginald Bibby, *Mosaic Madness: The Poverty and Potential of Life in Canada* (Toronto: Stoddart, 1990), p. 84.
6. David H. Flaherty and Frank E. Manning, eds., *The Beaver Bites Back? American Popular Culture in Canada* (Montreal/Kingston: McGill-Queen's University Press, 1993), p. 4.

LINKING TO THE PAST

WEB

LINKS

Biographies of Prime Ministers since 1980
- Joe Clark: http://cnet.unb.ca/achn/pme/cjccb.htm
- Brian Mulroney: http://cnet.unb.ca/achn/pme/mbmcb.htm
- Kim Campbell: http://cnet.unb.ca/achn/pme/akccb.htm
- Jean Chrétien: http://cnet.unb.ca/achn/pme/jjjccb.htm

The Constitution Act, 1982
http://www.solon.org/Constitutions/Canada/English/ca_1982.html

The North American Free Trade Agreement
http://www.sice.oas.org/trade/nafta/naftatce.stm
The full text of the North American Free Trade Agreement.

Canada's Seniors at a Glance
http://www.hc-sc.gc.ca/seniors-aines/seniors/pubs/poster/seniors/page1e.htm
This Health Canada web site provides quick facts (with graphs) about Canada's aging population, such as life expectancy, income, expenditures, living arrangements, and health.

The Great Lakes Water Quality Agreement
http://www.ijc.org/agree/quality.html
The full text of the Great Lakes Water Quality Agreement of 1978, with 1987 amendments.

RELATED READINGS

The following article in R. Douglas Francis and Donald B. Smith, eds., *Readings in Canadian History: Post-Confederation*, 5th ed. (Toronto: Harcourt Brace, 1998), is of relevance to this chapter: Robert MacNeil, "Looking for My Country," pp. 511–19.

BIBLIOGRAPHY

Robert Bothwell, Ian Drummond, and John English, *Canada since 1945: Power, Politics, and Provincialism*, rev. ed. (Toronto: University of Toronto Press, 1989); and Alvin Finkel, *Our Lives: Canada after 1945* (Toronto: James Lorimer, 1997), provide useful syntheses. *The Canadian Encyclopedia* on CD-ROM (Toronto: McClelland & Stewart, 1999) contains useful articles on many subjects examined in this chapter.

For material on the contemporary economy consult Kenneth Norrie and Doug Owram, *A History of the Canadian Economy*, 2nd ed. (Toronto: Harcourt Brace, 1996); and Wallace Clement, ed., *Understanding Canada: Building on the New Canadian Political Economy* (Montreal/Kingston, McGill-Queen's University Press, 1996). Links between demography and the economy are discussed in David K. Foot and Daniel Stoffman, *Boom, Bust and Echo 2000: Profiting from the Demographic Shift in the New Millennium* (Toronto: Stoddart, 1998). Economist William Watson proposes a provocative critique of Canadian identity in *Globalization and the Meaning of Canadian Life* (Toronto: University of Toronto Press, 1998).

Foreign ownership of the Canadian economy is examined in Gordon Laxer, *Open for Business: The Roots of Foreign Ownership in Canada* (Toronto: Oxford University Press, 1989). Two studies of Canadian–American economic relations are Stephen Clarkson, *Canada and the Reagan Challenge*, 2nd ed. (Toronto: James Lorimer, 1985); and Lawrence

Martin, *Pledge of Allegiance: The Americanization of Canada in the Mulroney Years* (Toronto: McClelland & Stewart, 1993).

Concerning the free-trade debate see the titles quoted in this chapter's "Where Social Scientists Disagree." Other thoroughly negative appreciations are Duncan Cameron and Mel Watkins, eds., *Canada Under Free Trade* (Toronto: James Lorimer, 1993); and Mel Hurtig, *The Betrayal of Canada*, 2nd ed. (Toronto: Stoddart, 1992). Also see Mel Hurtig's memoirs, *At Twilight in the Country: Memoirs of a Canadian Nationalist* (Toronto: Stoddart, 1996).

The spate of studies on business history bears witness to a high level of public interest. Recent monographs include Patricia Best and Ann Shortell, *The Brass Ring: Power, Influence and the Brascan Empire* (Toronto: Random House, 1988); Robert Bothwell, *Nucleus: The History of Atomic Energy of Canada Limited* (Toronto: University of Toronto Press, 1988); Peter Haddow and Ann Gibbon, *Steinberg: The Breakup of a Family Empire* (Toronto: Macmillan, 1990); Peter Foster, *Towers of Debt: The Rise and Fall of the Reichmanns* (Toronto: Key Porter, 1993); Walter Stewart, *Too Big To Fail: Olympia and York: The Story Behind the Headlines* (Toronto: McClelland & Stewart, 1993); Richard Siklos, *Shades of Black: Conrad Black and the World's Fastest Growing Press Empire* (Toronto: Reed Books, 1995); and Paul Waldie, *A House Divided: The Untold Story of the McCain Family* (Toronto: Penguin Books, 1997). Peter C. Newman offers a provocative examination of the influence of these magnates in *Titans: How the New Canadian Establishment Seized Power* (Toronto: Penguin Books, 1998).

The energy question is discussed in G. Bruce Doern and Glen Toner, *The Politics of Energy* (Toronto: Methuen, 1985); and John Erik Fossum, *Oil, the State, and Federalism: The Rise and Demise of Petro-Canada as a Statist Impulse* (Toronto: University of Toronto Press, 1997). Two studies of western agriculture are Grace Skogstad, *The Politics of Agricultural Policy-Making in Canada* (Toronto: University of Toronto Press, 1987); and Barry Wilson, *Farming the System: How Politicians and Producers Shape Canadian Agricultural Policy* (Saskatoon: Western Producer Prairie Books, 1990).

Among writings on the environment see G. Bruce and Thomas Conway, *The Greening of Canada: Federal Institutions and Decisions* (Toronto: University of Toronto Press, 1994); Chad Gaffield and Pam Gaffield, eds., *Consuming Canada: Readings in Environmental History* (Toronto: Copp Clark, 1995); Kathryn Harrison, *Passing the Buck: Federalism and Canadian Environmental Policy* (Vancouver: University of British Columbia Press, 1996); and Melody Hessing and Michael Howlett, *Canadian Natural Resource and Environmental Policy: Political Economy and Public Policy* (Vancouver: University of British Columbia Press, 1997).

A general study of political parties is William Christian and Colin Campbell, *Parties, Leaders and Ideologies in Canada* (Toronto: McGraw-Hill Ryerson, 1995). Excellent journalistic accounts of the Trudeau years are Christina McCall Newman, *Grits: An Intimate Portrait of the Liberal Party* (Toronto: Macmillan, 1982); and Stephen Clarkson and Christina McCall, *Trudeau and Our Times*, vol. 1, *The Magnificent Obsession*; vol. 2, *The Heroic Delusion* (Toronto: McClelland & Stewart, 1990, 1994). A variety of opinions, generally highly favourable, may be found in Andrew Cohen and J.L. Granatstein, eds., *Trudeau's Shadow: The Life and Legacy of Pierre Elliott Trudeau* (Toronto: Random House, 1998). See also Guy Laforest, *Trudeau and the End of a Canadian Dream* (Montreal/Kingston: McGill-Queen's University Press, 1995). On Joe Clark's brief government see Jeffrey Simpson's well-documented study, *Discipline of Power: The Conservative Interlude and the Liberal Restoration* (Toronto: University of Toronto Press, 1996). John Turner's short period of leadership is presented in Greg Weston, *Reign of Error: The Inside Story of John Turner's Troubled Leadership* (Toronto: McGraw-Hill Ryerson, 1988). Two books offer a critical dissection of the Mulroney government: Brooke Jeffrey, *Breaking Faith: The Mulroney Legacy of Deceit,*

Destruction and Disunity (Toronto: Key Porter, 1992); and Linda McQuaig, *The Quick and the Dead: Brian Mulroney, Big Business and the Seduction of Canada* (Toronto: Viking, 1991). See also John Sawatsky, *Mulroney: The Politics of Ambition* (Toronto: Macfarlane Walter & Ross, 1991). Corruption and patronage are studied in Jeffrey Simpson, *Spoils of Power: The Politics of Patronage* (Toronto: W. Collins & Sons, 1988); and Stevie Cameron, *On the Take: Crime, Corruption and Greed in the Mulroney Years* (Toronto: Macfarlane Walter & Ross, 1994). Kim Campbell has written her memoirs, *Time and Chance: The Political Memoirs of Canada's First Woman Prime Minister* (Toronto: Doubleday Canada, 1996). Peter C. Newman defends an interesting thesis in *The Canadian Revolution, 1985–1995: From Deference to Defiance* (Toronto: Penguin Books, 1995). For an analysis of recent developments see Jeffrey Simpson, *The Anxious Years: Politics in the Age of Mulroney and Chrétien* (Toronto: Lester, 1996). On the Reform party consult Trevor Harrison, *Of Passionate Intensity: Right-Wing Populism and the Reform Party of Canada* (Toronto: University of Toronto Press, 1995).

Recent works on the Canadian left include John Richards, Robert Cairns, and Larry Pratt, eds., *Social Democracy without Illusions: Renewal of the Canadian Left* (Toronto: McClelland & Stewart, 1991); Alan Whitehorn, *Canadian Socialism: Essays on the CCF–NDP* (Toronto: Oxford University Press, 1992); and Ian McLeod, *Under Siege: The Federal NDP in the Nineties* (Toronto: James Lorimer, 1994). Judy Steed proves a sympathetic biographer in *Ed Broadbent: The Pursuit of Power* (Markham, ON: Viking, 1988).

For syntheses of labour history of this period see Bryan D. Palmer, *Working-Class Experience: Rethinking the History of Canadian Labour, 1800–1991*, 2nd ed. (Toronto: McClelland & Stewart, 1992); and Craig Heron, *The Canadian Labour Movement: A Short History*, rev. ed. (Toronto: James Lorimer, 1996). Charlotte Yates studies one union in *From Plant to Politics: The Autoworkers Union in Postwar Canada* (Philadelphia: Temple University Press, 1993). On labour in the steel industry see June Corman et al., *Recasting Steel Labour: The Stelco Story* (Halifax: Fernwood, 1993). Keith Archer examines the political links of labour in *Political Choices and Electoral Consequences: A Study of Organized Labour and the New Democratic Party* (Montreal/Kingston: McGill-Queen's University Press, 1990).

Electoral histories abound. The elections of 1974, 1979, and 1980 are covered in two books edited by Howard R. Penniman: *Canada at the Polls: The General Election of 1974* and *Canada at the Polls, 1979 and 1980: A Study of the General Elections* (Washington, DC: American Enterprise Institute for Public Policy Research, 1975 and 1981, respectively). Alan Frizzell et al. have also published election histories: *The Canadian General Election of [1984, 1988, or 1993]: Politicians, Parties, Press and Polls* (Ottawa: Carleton University Press, 1985, 1990, and 1994); and Alan Frizzell and Jon H. Pammett, eds., *The Canadian General Election of 1997* (Toronto: Dundurn Press, 1997). On the 1988 free-trade election see also Graham Fraser's journalistic account, *Playing for Keeps: The Making of the Prime Minister, 1988* (Toronto: McClelland & Stewart, 1989). Kim Campbell's disastrous campaign in 1993 is recounted in David McLaughlin, *Poisoned Chalice: The Last Campaign of the Progressive Conservative Party?* (Toronto: Dundurn Press, 1994).

Useful works on federal–provincial relations include David Milne, *Tug of War: Ottawa and the Provinces under Trudeau and Mulroney* (Toronto: James Lorimer, 1986); Garth Stevenson, *Unfulfilled Union: Canadian Federalism and National Unity*, 3rd ed. (Toronto: Gage, 1989); and Richard Simeon and Ian Robinson, *State, Society, and the Development of Canadian Federalism* (Toronto: University of Toronto Press, 1990). Keith Banting and Richard Simeon, eds., *And No One Cheered: Federalism, Democracy and the Constitution Act* (Toronto: Methuen, 1983) presents a highly critical analysis of patriation. See also David Milne, *The Canadian Constitution: From Patriation to Meech Lake*, new ed. (Toronto: James Lorimer, 1989). On the referendum of 1992 see Richard Johnston et al., *The Challenge of Direct Democracy: The 1992 Canadian Referendum* (Montreal/Kingston: McGill-Queen's

University Press, 1996). Susan Delacourt has written a good journalistic account: *United We Fall: The Crisis of Democracy in Canada* (Toronto: Viking, 1993). For other studies on constitutional issues consult the bibliography in Chapter Seventeen. For titles on Aboriginal issues see the bibliography in Chapter Sixteen.

John English and Norman Hillmer, *Making a Difference? Canada's Foreign Policy in a Changing World Order* (Toronto: Lester, 1992), contains useful essays on Canada's international relations since 1970. Costas Melakopides examines different strands composing Canada's foreign relations in *Pragmatic Idealism: Canadian Foreign Policy, 1945–1995* (Montreal/Kingston: McGill-Queen's University Press, 1998). J.L. Granatstein and Robert Bothwell, *Pirouette: Pierre Trudeau and Canadian Foreign Policy* (Toronto: University of Toronto Press, 1990), is a good study of international affairs during Trudeau's tenure. A brief synthesis of Canada–U.S. relations may be found in Robert Bothwell, *Canada and the United States: The Politics of Partnership* (Toronto: Macmillan, 1992). John Herd Thompson and Stephen J. Randall offer a thorough study in *Canada and the United States: Ambivalent Allies* (Montreal/Kingston: McGill-Queen's University Press, 1994). Canada's defence policy is examined in D.W. Middlemiss and J.J. Sokolsky, *Canadian Defence: Decisions and Determinants* (Toronto: Harcourt Brace Jovanovich, 1989); and Joel J. Sokolsky and Joseph T. Jockel, eds., *Fifty Years of Canada–United States Defense Cooperation: The Road from Ogdensburg* (Lewiston, NY: E. Mellen, 1992). Aspects of the arms trade are examined in Ernie Regehr and Simon Rosenblum, eds., *The Road to Peace: Nuclear Weapons, Canada's Military Policies* (Toronto: James Lorimer, 1988). Canada's role in disarmament is the subject of Albert Legault and Michel Fortmann, *Diplomacy of Hope: Canada and Disarmament, 1945–1988* (Montreal/Kingston: McGill-Queen's University Press, 1992). On the Gulf War see Richard Gimblett and Jean Morin, *Operation Friction: Canadian Forces in the Gulf War* (Toronto: Dundurn Press, 1996).

On higher education see David Cameron, *More than an Academic Question: Universities, Government, and Public Policy in Canada* (Halifax: Ashgate, 1991); and the very critical David J. Bercuson et al., *Petrified Campus: The Crisis in Canada's Universities* (Toronto: Random House, 1997). David H. Flaherty and Frank E. Manning, eds., in *The Beaver Bites Back? American Popular Culture in Canada* (Montreal/Kingston: McGill-Queen's University Press, 1993), look for originality in Canadian culture. On institutions designed to favour the development of Canadian culture see Marc Raboy, *Missed Opportunities: The Story of Canada's Broadcasting Policy* (Montreal/Kingston: McGill-Queen's University Press, 1990); Gary Evans, *In the National Interest: A Chronicle of the National Film Board of Canada from 1949 to 1989* (Toronto: University of Toronto Press, 1991); and Ted Magder, *Canada's Hollywood: The Canadian State and Feature Films* (Toronto: University of Toronto Press, 1993). Richard Collins, *Culture, Communications, and National Identity: The Case of Canadian Television* (Toronto: University of Toronto Press, 1990), is a useful study. For a panorama of the burgeoning writing of Canadians during the years 1970–85, W.H. New, ed., *Literary History of Canada: Canadian Literature in English*, 2nd ed., vol. 4 (Toronto: University of Toronto Press, 1990) is the standard authority. See also Elspeth Cameron, *Canadian Culture: An Introductory Reader* (Toronto: Canadian Scholars' Press, 1997).

Ian Angus, *A Border Within: National Identity, Cultural Plurality, and Wilderness* (Montreal/Kingston, McGill-Queen's University Press, 1997), suggests reasons why the existence of Canada has significance. Daniel Francis explodes myths in his very readable *National Dreams: Myth, Memory, and Canadian History* (Vancouver: Arsenal Pulp Press, 1997). Informative studies of sports history include Donald Macintosh and David Whitson, *The Game Planners: Transforming Canada's Sport System* (Montreal/Kingston: McGill-Queen's University Press, 1990); Richard Gruneau and David Whitson, *Hockey Night in Canada: Sport, Identities, and Cultural Politics* (Toronto: Garamond, 1993); and Donald

Macintosh and Michael Hawes, *Sport and Canadian Diplomacy* (Montreal/Kingston: McGill-Queen's University Press, 1994). Reginald Bibby proposes a provocative analysis of contemporary religion in *Unknown Gods: The Ongoing Story of Religion in Canada* (Toronto: Stoddart, 1993). On the Roman Catholic church see Tony Clarke, *Behind the Mitre: The Moral Leadership Crisis in the Canadian Catholic Church* (Toronto: HarperCollins, 1995). On gays and lesbians see Becki Ross, *The House that Jill Built: A Lesbian Nation in Formation* (Toronto: University of Toronto Press, 1995); and Gary Kinsman, *The Regulation of Desire: Sexuality in Canada* (Montreal: Black Rose Books, 1987).

An excellent synthesis on the history of women in Canada is Alison Prentice et al., *Canadian Women: A History*, 2nd ed. (Toronto: Harcourt Brace, 1996). The best treatment of women in unions is Julie White, *Sisters and Solidarity: Women and Unions in Canada* (Toronto: Thompson Educational Publishing, 1993). Numerous studies of contemporary Canadian feminism are available: see Nancy Adamson, Linda Briskin, and Margaret McPhail, *Feminist Organizing for Change: The Contemporary Women's Movement in Canada* (Toronto: Oxford University Press, 1988); Sandra Burt, Lorraine Code, and Lindsay Dorney, eds., *Changing Patterns: Women in Canada* (Toronto: McClelland & Stewart, 1988); Constance Backhouse and David H. Flaherty, eds., *Challenging Times: The Women's Movement in Canada and the United States* (Montreal/Kingston: McGill-Queen's University Press, 1992); Ruth Roach Pierson et al., *Canadian Women's Issues*, vol. 1, *Strong Voices*; vol. 2, *Bold Visions* (Toronto: James Lorimer, 1993, 1995); and Caroline Andrew and Sandra Rogers, eds., *Women and the Canadian State/Les femmes et l'État canadien* (Montreal/Kingston, McGill-Queen's University Press, 1997). Pauline Greenhill and Diane Tye, eds., explore a variety of women's experiences in *Undisciplined Women: Tradition and Culture in Canada* (Montreal/Kingston: McGill-Queen's University Press, 1997). On the women's movement's major lobby see Jill Vickers, Pauline Rankin, and Christine Appelle, *Politics As If Women Mattered: A Political Analysis of the National Action Committee on the Status of Women* (Toronto: University of Toronto Press, 1993). Other books are listed in Chapter Fifteen.

In addition to the works indicated in Chapter Fifteen, the evolution of Canada's welfare state is discussed in Raymond Blake and Jeff Keshen, eds., *Social Welfare Policy in Canada: Historical Readings* (Toronto: Copp Clark, 1995); Raymond B. Blake, Penny E. Bryden, and J. Frank Strain, eds., *The Welfare State in Canada: Past, Present and Future* (Concord, ON: Irwin Publishing, 1997); and Patricia M. Evans and Gerda R. Wekerle, eds., *Women and the Canadian Welfare State: Challenges and Change* (Toronto: University of Toronto Press, 1997). Maude Barlow and Bruce Campbell, *Straight Through the Heart: How the Liberals Abandoned the Just Society* (Toronto: HarperCollins, 1995), strongly criticize government policies on welfare. On poverty see Patrick Burman, *Poverty's Bonds: Power and Agency in the Social Relations of Welfare* (Toronto: Thompson Educational Publishing, 1996). The role of government in health care is the subject of C. David Naylor, ed., *Canadian Health Care and the State: A Century of Evolution* (Montreal/Kingston: McGill-Queen's University Press, 1992). On housing, consult John R. Miron, ed., *House, Home, and Community: Progress in Housing Canadians* (Montreal/Kingston: McGill-Queen's University Press, 1993). Crime is addressed in D. Owen Carrigan, *Crime and Punishment in Canada: A History* (Toronto: McClelland & Stewart, 1991). A critical study of the evolution of government is Walter Stewart, *Dismantling the State: Downsizing to Disaster* (Toronto: Stoddart, 1998).

Canadian Prime Ministers since Confederation

Sir John Alexander Macdonald
Conservative, 1867–73, 1878–91

Alexander Mackenzie
Liberal, 1873–78

Sir John Joseph Caldwell Abbott
Conservative, 1891–92

Sir John Sparrow David Thompson
Conservative, 1892–94

Sir Mackenzie Bowell
Conservative, 1894–96

Sir Charles Tupper
Conservative, 1896

Sir Wilfrid Laurier
Liberal, 1896–1911

Sir Robert Laird Borden
Conservative and Unionist, 1911–20

Arthur Meighen
Conservative and Unionist, 1920–21, 1926

William Lyon Mackenzie King
Liberal, 1921–26, 1926–30, 1935–48

Richard Bedford Bennett
Conservative, 1930–35

Louis Stephen St. Laurent
Liberal, 1948–57

John George Diefenbaker
Progressive Conservative, 1957–63

Lester Bowles Pearson
Liberal, 1963–68

Pierre Elliott Trudeau
Liberal, 1968–79, 1980–84

Charles Joseph Clark
Progressive Conservative, 1979–80

John Napier Turner
Liberal, 1984

Martin Brian Mulroney
Progressive Conservative, 1984–93

Kim Campbell
Progressive Conservative, 1993

Jean Chrétien
Liberal, 1993–

Index

Abella, Irving, 249, 375
Aberhart, William, 295, 305, 342
Abitibi Paper Co., 268
Aboriginal populations, *see* First Nations; Inuit;
    Métis
Abortion, 163–64, 174, 301, 541–42
Acadians
  at Confederation, 1, 4
  education, 98–99, 341
  language, 341, 473
  poverty, 361
Acheson, Dean, 368
Acorn, Milton, 397
Action catholique, L', 177
Action française, 245
Action libérale nationale, 298
Adams, Mary Louise, 379
Adams, Michael, 537
African-Canadians
  at Confederation, 2–3
  Black immigration discouraged, 70, 503
  hostility toward, 3, 75, 503, 508
  in World War I, 228
Agriculture
  agrarian protest, 259–64
  agrarian reform, 246
  as cornerstone of society, 273
  at Confederation, 10–11
  Bennett's measures, 293
  crisis in 1980s, 487–88, 532
  impact of mechanization, 155–56
  in British Columbia, 143
  in Ontario, 10–11, 14
  in Prince Edward Island, 477
  in Quebec, 10
  in West, 66–67, 69, 301–302, 483, 485–88,
    532
  land lost to development, 491
  problems after World War II, 361, 402
  Progressive movement, 259–64
  Union catholique des cultivateurs, 277
  wheat, 10–11, 69, 143–44, 155, 232–33,
    259, 267–68, 288, 290–91, 293, 302,
    342, 403, 483, 527
  zoning legislation, 453, 477, 482
AIDS, 556
Air transport, 269, 302
Aitken, Max (Lord Beaverbrook), 138–39,
    320, 340
Alabama, the, 107–108
Alaska Boundary Dispute, 120–22
Alaska Highway, 299, 338–39
Albani, Emma, 197
Alberta, *see also* Elections; Federal–provincial
    relations; West
  economy, 144, 342, 358, 363, 483–87
  enters Confederation, 102
  environment, 487, 557
  Great Depression, 295
  immigration to, 68, 73
  migration to, 485, 542
  politics, 260, 295, 342, 485–86
  unions, 485–86
  urbanization, 144
Alcoholism, 187, *see also* Prohibition
Alexander, David, 365, 472
Algoma Steel Co., 139
Algonquin Park, 180
Allan, Hugh, 49, 55
All-Canadian Congress of Labour, 277,
    299–300
Allen, Richard, 263, 305
Amalgamated Mine Workers of Nova Scotia,
    275